KING
Came
PREACHING

THE PULPIT POWER OF
DR. MARTIN LUTHER KING JR.

DR. MERVYN
A. WARREN

InterVarsity Press
Downers Grove, Illinois

InterVarsity Press
P.O. Box 1400, Downers Grove, IL 60515-1426
World Wide Web: www.ivpress.com
E-mail: mail@ivpress.com

InterVarsity Press® is the book-publishing division of InterVarsity Christian Fellowship/USA®, a student movement active on campus at hundreds of universities, colleges and schools of nursing in the United States of America, and a member movement of the International Fellowship of Evangelical Students. For information about local and regional activities, write Public Relations Dept., InterVarsity Christian Fellowship/USA, 6400 Schroeder Rd., P.O. Box 7895, Madison, WI 53707-7895, or visit the IVCF website at <www.ivcf.org>.

All Scripture quotations, unless otherwise indicated, are taken from the Holy Bible, New International Version®. NIV®. *Copyright ©1973, 1978, 1984 by International Bible Society. Used by permission of Zondervan Publishing House. All rights reserved.*

Appendixes one through four are transcripts of speeches and sermons by Dr. Martin Luther King Jr., and are reprinted by arrangement with the heirs to the estate of Martin Luther King Jr., c/o Writers House, Inc., as agent for the proprietor.

Cover photograph: © Flip Schulke. All rights reserved.
Interior photographs (as indicated): © Michael Hubbard, Flip Schulke or McCann L. Reid.

ISBN 0-8308-2658-0

Printed in the United States of America ∞

Library of Congress Cataloging-in-Publication Data
Warren, Mervyn A.
King came preaching : the pulpit power of Dr. Martin Luther King Jr. / Mervyn A.
Warren ; foreword by Gardner Taylor.
p. cm.
Includes bibliographical references and index.
ISBN 0-8308-2658-0 (alk. paper)
1. King, Martin Luther, Jr., 1929-1968. 2. Preaching—United States—History—20th
century. 3. Progressive National Baptist Convention—Sermons. 4. Sermons,
American—African American authors. 5. Sermons, American—20th century. I. Title.
BV4208.U6 W36 2001
251'.0092—dc21

2001039356

23 22 21 20 19 18 17 16 15 14 13 12 11 10 9 8 7 6 5 4 3 2 1

21 20 19 18 17 16 15 14 13 12 11 10 09 08 07 06 05 04 03 02 01

To my wife, Barbara,
our sons, daughters and grands,
and all who, in the spirit of MLK Jr.,
perpetuate the love ethic in tender and tough ways.

CONTENTS

Foreword

A prominent New York lawyer, a descendant of the abolitionist William Lloyd Garrison, once said in my hearing that Martin Luther King was not only a preacher. This was true, but anyone who knew Dr. King will know that his highest purpose was to be a preacher of the gospel of Jesus Christ.

Martin King would feel greatly gratified by Mervyn Warren's book *King Came Preaching*. It is a thoroughly examined analysis of the preaching of the man who gave to America "a new birth of freedom." One will not be far into this book without seeing that the rare pulpit gifts of America's only true spiritual genius, Martin King, have been carefully and faithfully dissected. Dr. Warren has made all students of King and of preaching his debtors.

Dr. Gardner C. Taylor

Exordium

Surely another book on preaching should not expect to stir up the band or cause flags to unfurl—unless of course it plays the right music or at least whispers a gentle breeze. If time means anything, this book has certainly had sufficient to simmer and season, for it really began back during the latter years of Martin Luther King Jr., with his personal permission and cooperation. My doctoral research at Michigan State University caught the attention of a professor there, Dr. Robert Green of the education department, who happened to have just marched earlier with Dr. King in Selma, Alabama. Dr. Green made an initial contact with Ms. Dora McDonald, personal secretary to King, eventually winning me a letter of approval and a green light for further extensive research, including interviews with Dr. King himself and a number of his mentors, professors and colleagues. Although King's requested copy of the completed dissertation was not delivered to him before his assassination, it was presented posthumously to his widow, Mrs. Coretta Scott King, during the 1988 King Week Celebration in Atlanta; this copy is housed in the special collection at the Martin Luther King Jr. Center for Social Change.

That was then, this is now. The dissertation was prepared for academicians while this present book is recast for "general consumption"—especially for persons interested in taking a look, whether for the first time or for a refreshing review, at some of the fundamentals of sermon preparation and delivery practiced by one of the most effective and celebrated preachers in Western history.

This book attempts to avoid two extremes: a mere biographing of a preacher with only incidental references to his hands-on process of bringing a sermon to readiness and presentation, and a flooding of readers and practitioners with homiletical assumptions whose vagueness and impalpability would be mere shadows for chasing around discussion tables in ivory towers. Somewhere between these extremes lies a blend of relevant biography with practical, understandable, doable homiletical theory, offering clear and tried alternatives without claiming to exhaust the subject or parading as the last word. Experienced preachers as well as those just beginning their journey of proclaiming the gospel of Jesus Christ should find this book helpful and rewarding. And there is much here also for those who find value in meaningful intellectualizing about sermons without sapping pulpit proclamation of its lifeblood.

How blessed and privileged you and I are to have lived in an age that produced an exemplary and effectual preaching model like Martin Luther King Jr.! If you love "good preaching" as a practitioner, learner or listener, if you appreciate clues that help bring it about and cues that might enhance your own proclamation, I believe you have come to the right pages. Enjoy the journey.

Mervyn A. Warren
Huntsville, Alabama

Acknowledgments

Teachers in abundance: C. T. Richards, Frank W. Hale Jr., Winton H. Beaven, John Cannon, Charles Weniger, Kenneth G. Hance and Martin Luther King Jr., the latter through a kind of "distance learning" as I observed and was deeply moved by his proclamation of the Word. The former six are those in whose homiletic and speech classrooms I sat, whose wisdom I absorbed and who ever since I have striven to emulate.

Students galore: Often exceeding what classroom credit allows, pupil scholars enduring my lectures and spiel are often the real informers who teach me more than I offer them. To all who so privileged me over the years, especially at Oakwood College, Seminary of Andrews University and Vanderbilt Divinity School, I am indebted beyond expression.

Supporters aplenty: Within and outside the home. Principally my wife, Barb, whose love tenders the fuel. Office secretaries, Shirley Bailey and Gretchen Brown, who readily respond to shrill cries for help when this computer novice needs rescuing. Central United Methodist Church (Detroit) and their historian, Will Rutt, who graciously assisted in trying to locate any additional MLK sermon tapes extant in the church's collection. Flip Schulke, who made available his wonderful wealth of King photos. Johnny Mack, former student and present friend, whose timely tips led to invaluable sources and resources. And Cynthia Bunch of IVP, editorial adviser par excellence.

God above all: There are times when a Presence seems to inspire and encourage the pen along, and I can only be grateful.

1
A HOMILETICAL BIOGRAPHY

And the child grew and became strong in spirit.
LUKE 1:80

I am . . . the son of a Baptist preacher, the grandson of a Baptist preacher and the great grandson of a Baptist preacher. The Church is my life and I have given my life to the Church."[1]

With this succinct autobiographical statement Martin Luther King Jr. summarized the professional stock from which he sprang—one in which preaching loomed large and all-consuming. Yet he is telling us more. King first entered our world through the womb of the black church tradition which, as several biographers like Lewis Baldwin, James Cone, Taylor Branch and others attest, remained his conscious ancestral home, continually feeding and flavoring his religious and educational development as well as his clerical activities.[2] Later influences on King are understood to have provided form, nomenclature, and refinement to lifelong concepts derived initially from the black church.

The preacher heritage to which he refers consisted of Rev. Martin Luther King Sr., father; Rev. A. D. Williams, grandfather; and another Rev. Mr. Williams, great-grandfather. The Baptist preacher of whom Dr. King was a great-grandson ministered during the early days of the family's history in Georgia. Because this was his maternal great-grandfather, Dr. King directed me to his mother, Mrs. Alberta King, for biographical information.[3] Mrs. King said of her son's great-grandfather, "Many times I heard my father talk about him, an Old Country preacher, not widely known. I never knew him, as he died long before I was born when my father was very young."[4] She continued, "All I can remember is he was an Old Country preacher, Rev. Williams, Greene County, Ga."

King's maternal grandfather, Adam Daniel Williams, the second preacher in his heritage, began his Atlanta pastorate in 1894, one year after the death of Frederick Douglass and one year before the celebrated "Atlanta Speech" of Booker T. Washington.[5] Pastoring the Ebenezer Baptist Church until his death in 1931, Rev. Williams's ministry functioned under the shadow of four significant molders of thought regarding the place of the emancipated Negro in American society. These four—Frederick Douglass, Booker T. Washington, W. E. B. Du Bois and Marcus Garvey—represented up to that time what is generally regarded as the most talented leadership in the history of Negro resistance to racial segregation and discrimination.

☐ Douglass the protester (the first great national Negro leader and the boyhood idol of Martin Luther King Jr.) would seek full citizenship of the Negro by sustained contention and political and legal maneuvers within the system.

☐ Washington the conciliator would operate through compromise with, and acceptance of, the system, advocating the proving of self and race via head, hand and heart education.

☐ Du Bois the revolutionary would work (sometimes on the edges of and sometimes outside of the system) by marshaling white liberal and Negro militant forces mainly through the "mightier pen." It was Du Bois who, in June 1905, summoned the first assembly of the Niagara Movement, the civil and human rights organization that developed into the National Association for the Advancement of Colored People (NAACP).

☐ Garvey the black nationalist would call for separation from the system through the abandonment of the United States and the creation of a Negro state in Africa.[6] A later heir of Garvey's approach was Elijah Muhammad, leader of the Black Muslims of the Nation of Islam, with whom the human rights approach of King Jr. would later clash.

It is quite probable that Williams was not unconscious of these divergent voices and may have been influenced by all. By virtue of his heading the large Ebenezer Baptist Church in Atlanta, not only the city of Washington's famous address and the headquarters (for a while) of Du Bois's activities but also the center of Negro militancy, Williams moved to the forefront as one of the early leaders of Atlanta's NAACP.

Martin Luther King Sr. succeeded his father-in-law, A. D. Williams, as pastor of Ebenezer in 1931. Continuing the tradition of his predecessor, King Sr. found a place among the leading spirits of the modern Negro resistance cause in

Atlanta. The context of his leadership and his method of action were perhaps prevalent among Negro clergymen of his day:

> Negro preachers, men made in the image of King the elder and his father-in-law, were pivotally successful in molding the leadership tradition of this movement, a tradition that stressed lyrical and somewhat effulgent oratory and a cautious "realistic" approach to the problems of a racial minority which lacked absolute initiative vis-à-vis their oppressors and had to attack therefore with tact and with caution. The limitations of this tradition, its inarticulation with the great masses of Negroes and its reliance on the goodwill and generosity of the oppressors, were, in part, a reflection of the Negro situation, a situation defined by powerlessness.[7]

The NAACP, dominated in the beginning by white liberals, awakened the Negro to a whole new vista of respectable social protest—litigation, lobbying, propaganda of enlightenment. During the 1920s branches of the organization sprang up in all sections of the United States, not excluding Atlanta, a hub for the spokes of the "new protest." While frightening some Negroes of that day, the "new protest" seemed tame enough to others, including Asa Philip Randolph,[8] then a young labor leader deriding sterile protest and calling for a breakthrough to the masses.

Birth, family and environment. In such an arena of activity Martin the younger was born on January 15, 1929, in Atlanta, Georgia. Ten months later, November 13, the nation would experience the death of the "big bull market," the dying of Coolidge-Hoover prosperity, the crash of the American economy.[9] Atlanta, like other cities, struggled for survival.

During this time of economic turmoil King Sr., who served as associate pastor to his father-in-law two years before the latter's death, was also sharing the twelve-room house of his in-laws, thus rendering himself sufficiently secure to provide for his family. He eventually assumed full responsibility for both the parish and the household.

This period of American history witnessed a rural population decrease and an increase in urban residence. Negroes were migrating from the South and its segregationist and discriminatory policies in quest of better times in the North. By 1930, 20 percent of African Americans were living in cities of the North.[10]

A significant segment of Protestantism, meanwhile, was going through a transition from hard-core fundamentalism to a searching liberalism. Many Protestant clergymen abandoned traditional Christian doctrines such as the infallibility of Scripture, the bodily resurrection of Jesus and miracles and embraced what William Hordern calls "a reconstruction of orthodox Christianity."[11]

> Although the fundamentalist saw the liberals as subversives of the faith, liberals
> saw themselves as the saviors of the essence of Christianity. For the liberal, it was
> the fundamentalist who was destroying Christianity by forcing it into the molds of
> the past and making it impossible for any intelligent man to hold it. Typical of the
> attitude of liberals was the oft-quoted statement of Fosdick that, for him, it was not
> a question of new theology or old but a question of new theology or no theology.[12]

Liberalism, which would later have a significant effect on Martin Jr., was an
attempt to modernize Christianity, to reframe it in thought forms believed to be
more comprehensible to the modern world. Seeking to reconcile Christianity
with modern science and scholarship, liberalism refused to accept religious
beliefs on the basis of authority alone; instead it demanded that all theology pass
the bar of reason and experience, using higher criticism as one of its basic tools.[13]
One of the important elements of liberalism, as well as later neo-orthodoxy, especially in relation to the ministry of Martin Luther King Jr., was the "social gospel," a school of theology that could claim as its champions men like Reinhold
Niebuhr. (An explanatory discussion of the social gospel can be found in chapter
six under "Themes.")

Martin Jr. would later encounter liberal theology during his senior year at
Crozer Theological Seminary. In his book *Strength to Love* King graphically
describes his intellectual journey from a strict fundamentalist tradition to what he
calls a more satisfying liberalism. Certain aspects of liberal theology held lasting
appeal for young Martin:

☐ devotion to the search for truth
☐ insistence on an open and analytical mind
☐ refusal to abandon the best lights of reason[14]

Eventually, however, he became disenchanted with liberalism's theological
anthropology, which taught essentially the natural goodness of human beings and
the natural power of human reason. The tragedies of history and humanity's consistent inclination to war, bloodshed, graft, corruption and injustice caused King
to see the depths and strength of sin. He then charged liberalism with having a
"superficial optimism concerning human nature" and with overlooking human
beings' inability to rid themselves of sinfulness.

Although King Jr. abandoned liberal theology's doctrine of humanity, he did
not return to fundamentalism; rather, he began to consider neo-orthodoxy (or
what L. Harold DeWolf would prefer calling neo-Reformation theology) as

championed by such renowned theological thinkers as Karl Barth, Emil Brunner, Reinhold Niebuhr and Paul Tillich.[15] Here is King's own assessment of his consideration of neo-orthodoxy:

> Although I rejected some aspects of liberalism, I never came to an all-out acceptance of neo-orthodoxy. While I saw neo-orthodoxy as a helpful corrective for a sentimental liberalism, I felt that it did not provide an adequate answer to basic questions. If liberalism was too optimistic concerning human nature, neo-orthodoxy was too pessimistic. Not only on the question of man, but also on other vital issues, the revolt of neo-orthodoxy went too far. In its attempt to preserve the transcendence of God, which had been neglected by an overstress of his immanence in liberalism, neo-orthodoxy went to the extreme of stressing a God who was hidden, unknown, and "wholly other." In its revolt against overemphasis on the power of reason in liberalism, neo-orthodoxy fell into a mood of anti-rationalism and semi-fundamentalism, stressing a narrow uncritical biblicism. This approach, I felt, was inadequate both for the church and for personal life.
>
> So although liberalism left me unsatisfied on the question of the nature of man, I found no refuge in neo-orthodoxy, I am now convinced that the truth about man is found neither in liberalism nor in neo-orthodoxy. Each represents a partial truth. A large segment of Protestant liberalism defined man only in terms of his essential nature, his capacity for good; neo-orthodoxy tended to define man only in terms of his existential nature, his capacity to evil. An adequate understanding of man is found neither in the thesis of liberalism nor in the antithesis of neo-orthodoxy, but in a synthesis which reconciles the truths of both.[16]

DeWolf places King Jr. with "moderate" liberals such as John C. Bennett, then president of Union Theological Seminary (New York), and Walter G. Muelder, at the time dean of the School of Theology, Boston University. "Moderate liberalism," according to DeWolf, continues the theological stress of applying "Christian principles not only to personal life but also to the solution of the great social problems of our time" but differs from pure liberalism in that it is not visionary concerning the nature of humankind.[17] Moderate liberal theologians are deeply aware of the desperate sinfulness "embedded and perpetuated in social relations and institutions." Confident that "the power and love of God can outmatch all other powers, moderate liberals have sought to give appropriate and healing expression to this faith in social policy," concerned especially with selfish and materialistic structures as seen in (1) much economic policy, (2) the sensual indulgence of conspicuous consumption, (3) the denial of brotherhood between races and classes, and (4) the warring hostilities between nations, which threaten world catastrophe.

This discussion of religious liberalism is called for here given the condition of flux and change in the theological world during the 1930s, the years when Rev. King Sr., a Baptist preacher of the fundamentalist order, was guiding young Martin Jr., the whole King family and his church along traditional paths of evangelical religion.

Under the leadership of King the elder, Ebenezer grew from a membership of six hundred to four thousand.[18] Such phenomenal growth likely indicates good leadership and effective communication—qualities that King Jr. inherited. Not only were young Martin, his sister Willie Christine (one year older) and his brother Alfred Daniel (one year younger) reared in an atmosphere that promoted public speaking, but public address seemed destined to become the salient source of the family's income.

During most of the time that King Jr. led the civil rights movement, Willie Christine taught in a Baptist college for girls, Martin Jr. ministered as associate pastor with their father in Atlanta, and Alfred Daniel also pastored in Atlanta. That the daughter should follow the occupation of the mother, Alberta King, and the sons that of the father suggests a strong influence exerted by the parents. In any event, children of the King household were taught "to love and respect . . . parents and elders. The old-fashioned verities of hard work, honesty, thrift, order and courtesy were adhered to faithfully. Education was looked upon as the path to competence and culture. The church was the path to morality and immortality."[19]

King's Personality

Physical aspects. Martin Jr. could have easily been taken for an athlete—five feet seven inches tall, broad shoulders, muscular neck, tipping the scales at "a heavy-chested 173 lbs."[20] Though his physique may have struck the eye as being that of a lightweight pugilist, his slender hands suggested a less rough profession. Loudon Wainwright observed that King's hands were "tapered and slim, delicate adjuncts of his compelling voice."[21]

The first detailed biographical sketch of King said that "Dr. King is a rather soft spoken man with a learning and maturity far beyond his twenty-seven years. His clothes are in conservative good taste and he has a small trim mustache."[22] Perhaps the most descriptive observation of the physical King came from his first biographer, L. D. Reddick:

> King's face is boyish. His features are soft and rounded, except for his eyes, which
> have a slight Oriental slant. His lips and nose are full and well formed; his forehead
> is rather high with a receding hairline. His clear brown eyes sparkle. He wears a
> small mustache. . . . . King keeps his crinkly black hair close cut and well trimmed.
> . . . In a word, Martin Luther King is an attractive, healthy, physical type, easy
> going, with good motor control and all of his senses active. His robust health is per-
> haps part of the basis for his energy and poise.[23]

In short, the man was quite gifted physically. His paper for a class at Crozer
Seminary admitted as much: "From the very beginning I was an extraordinar-
ily healthy child. It is said that at my birth the doctors pronounced me a one
hundred percent perfect child, from a physical point of view. Even today this
physical harmony still abides, in that I hardly know how an ill moment
feels."[24]

Emotional aspects. King was a man of even temperament, amazing calm and
an almost imperturbable equilibrium. He offered the following cryptic self-analysis: "I am an ambivert—half introvert and half extrovert."[25] Although biographers
invariably relate instances of his early "nonviolent" tendencies, they also point
out the element of tension between his introversion and extroversion.

Young Martin twice attempted suicide before his thirteenth birthday. The
first attempt came after his brother A. D. slid down a banister and accidentally
knocked their grandmother unconscious. Thinking his grandmother mortally
injured, Martin dashed to a second-floor window and jumped. Lying motionless
on the ground, oblivious to hysterical screams, he seemed dead. But "then, as
though nothing had happened, he got up and walked away."[26] A second leap
from the second-floor window occurred in 1941 on the death of his grandmother. Again he survived, sustaining mere minor bruises. These responses,
against the backdrop of his customary shunning of schoolboy spats and fights,
suggest that with King we are dealing with "a man of considerable complexity."[27]

Further insight into the emotional makeup of the man comes from observing
his parents. Father King has been characterized by such terms as "volatile,"
"emotional," "trigger-tempered"; Alberta King has been called "calm," "cool,"
"slow to anger," "deliberate in speech and action."[28] The pendulum of King's
emotional makeup seems to have swung in the direction of his mother. King Jr.
exuded an easygoing, unaffected friendliness.

According to Reddick, "King's naturalness is felt by everyone who comes face to face with him. To meet him is to enter an atmosphere of simplicity, free of pretense or posing. He smiles and shakes hands easily. He is unhurried. He never seems to respond impulsively or impatiently."[29] Sometimes depicted as possessing a limited sense of humor, as laughing only "politely, a split second too late,"[30] he was also known to be at times the "life of the party." Again Reddick comments: "Never given to clowning in public, King will regale his friends at private parties with his imitations of religious entertainers and fellow preachers."[31]

King explained his more general lack of humor in reference to certain encounters he had after the movement began in Montgomery. He admitted: "I'm sure I've become more serious. I don't think I've lost my sense of humor, but I know I've let many opportunities go by without using it. I seldom joke in speeches any more. I forget to."[32]

In an interview with Wainwright, King confessed to being too tolerant: "It is one of my weaknesses as a leader. I'm too courteous and I'm not candid enough. However, I feel that my softness has helped in one respect: People have found it easy to become reconciled around me."[33]

Wainwright warns, however, against misinterpreting such attitudes in King: "The impression of otherworldliness, or passivity, does not last. However gentle King's voice, however soft his mien, these attitudes cannot completely mask the mind behind them. It is brilliant, one-track and tough, constantly on the move toward its single goal."[34]

Wainwright also made the following observation:

> When he is not on a platform, King does not at first convey any overpowering strength of personality. A deferential conversationalist, he replies to questions with as much courtesy as conviction. He often seems curiously at rest, even somnolent. He appears beyond surprise, beyond disappointment, beyond jubilation, a man who has seen it all before and knew it would all happen.[35]

Spiritual aspects. If any one word could express King's spiritual motivation, it would be *love.* He never ceased to emphasize that at the heart of the nonviolent movement was the principle of love. "The nonviolent resister," he contended, "not only refuses to shoot his opponent but he also refuses to hate him."[36]

This love to which King would have all humanity subject is described as "understanding," "redeeming good will for all men," "purely spontaneous," "unmotivated," "groundless," "creative." Averred King, "It is not set in motion by any quality or function of its object. It is the love of God operating in the human heart."[37] The importance and significance of King's ethic of love were explored by Carl T. Rowan, successor to Edward R. Murrow and former director of the U.S. Information Agency, who sketched a contrast between King, an apostle of love, and W. E. B. Du Bois, an apostle of its counterpart:

> [Du Bois and King] personify the colored man's quandary: whether to fight hate with hate or with love. Du Bois is an old man whose cup of racial bitterness runneth over—a nonagenarian brooding out his last days in a desperate admiration of things Russian and an irreconcilable hatred of things white American. King, a mere thirty [thirty-seven in 1966], is a bright new intellectual general in America's racial wars, unique in that he offers the refuge of love to those who might follow Du Bois down that forlorn trail of bitterness.
>
> The contrast between these two leaders goes to the very heart of the Negro's dilemma—and perhaps to that of a Western world trying to establish rapport with the emerging masses of Asia and Africa. . . .
> Martin Luther King brings to his mission a belief in the power of religion to move men; Du Bois brought an open contempt for organized religion. The Montgomery pastor seems to know the difference between being courageous and being pugnacious; Du Bois never did. . . .
>
> Because the stakes are so great today for all mankind, one puts down the Du Bois biography with a passionate hope that the strife will be neither so grim nor so daily as Will Du Bois expects. And one cannot escape the concomitant hope that love can—indeed, will—be the powerful, saving force that the young man from Montgomery thinks it is.[38]

King the elder, King the younger. It is only natural that one would attempt to compare the two Kings who copastored the same congregation, Ebenezer Baptist Church in Atlanta. Actually the men probably lend themselves more easily to contrast. Physically, King Sr. was a much larger man, weighing over two hundred pounds. The father exuded a forwardness and confidence that bordered on arrogance. He was equally outspoken. One day when King Jr. was about eight years old, the father took him downtown to a shoe store and sat in its front area awaiting service. A white clerk approached and said, "I'll be happy to wait on you if you'll just move back there to those seats in the rear."

"Nothing wrong with these seats," the elder King retorted.

"Sorry," said the clerk, "but you'll have to go back there."

"We'll either buy shoes sitting here," the father shot back, flaring up, "or we won't buy any shoes at all." Then taking the hand of his son, he stomped, fuming, from the store.[39]

King the elder generally demanded courteous treatment from whites and expressed readiness to demonstrate that his actions could speak as loudly as his words. Well within his rights as dictated by self-respect, he often made on-the-spot protest against the system of segregation. The son tended more toward observing, contemplating, marshaling a strategy and a philosophy with which to strike at the root of the disgraceful system. King Jr.'s presence was quiet and unassuming, while the father made it known that he did not necessarily adhere to "nonviolence," the term that became a watchword of the younger. The father smiled freely, laughed heartily and got angry quickly; the son presented a directly opposite tendency. King the elder was strongly opinionated; the younger offered a more willing ear to the opinions of others. While expressing all due respect for his firstborn son and colleague in ministry, King Sr. sometimes informed an audience that had come expecting to hear the son preach that he too was a preacher of no mean magnitude. Yet the son was not known to let slip the slightest suggestion of self-laudation.

A former Morehouse professor who had the rare privilege of teaching both father King and son King revealed that in academic performance King the younger had the edge over his father. He hastened to add, however, that it is to be considered that the elder King entered college as a much older man.[40]

There were, of course, points of similarity. Both were staunch supporters of human rights; both affirmed that the pulpit holds not only a spiritual but also a social responsibility for the sheep of God's flock. Both were Baptist preachers, the father of the fundamentalist tradition, the son in a more liberal strain.

This excursion over the landscape of the heritage of Martin Luther King Jr. brings to view a soil fertile with discipline, rich with religion, pregnant with possibilities for Christian preaching.

The Seed: King's Education

When his sister, Christine, started attending the Yonge Street Elementary School in 1934, five-year-old Martin, precocious and talkative, tagged along and enrolled also by pushing his age up a year. The secret became known to the teacher when Martin gave himself away by artlessly talking about his last birthday party. He was dismissed and made to wait another year.

Elementary and high school days. From the very outset, Martin liked going to school. "He was a good pupil, and during the course of his elementary and secondary education skipped about three grades."[40] For two years, 1935-1937, he attended Yonge Street Elementary; then he transferred to David T. Howard Elementary School (later Howard became a high school). From Howard he went to the Laboratory High of Atlanta University, a private school, where he was a B+ student. After two years, the private school closed; Martin then returned to public school, one which his grandfather, A. D. Williams, had been influential in persuading the city of Atlanta to build, Booker T. Washington High. Here he skipped both the ninth and the twelfth grades.

The first fifteen years of Martin's life seem to have been stable and relatively privileged: "Physically, he was healthy. Intellectually, he was slightly ahead of his agegroup. Socially, he was enjoying the threshold years of self-discovery and the companionship of the opposite sex. He wore good clothes, had a little money in the bank—and was willing to work for more."[42]

For precocious Martin, high school activities included membership in several clubs and participation in a number of public speaking events. In his senior year, 1944, he won both the local and regional Elks oratorical contest. He considered the accomplishment the "summit of his youthful achievements"; some twenty years later he remembered the subject of the oration as "something about the Negro and the Constitution."[43] It was destined to be a recurring theme in his career addresses.

Morehouse College. At only fifteen, King matriculated in Morehouse College in Atlanta, of which the famed Benjamin Mays was president. Mays, minister-teacher who had received his Ph.D. from the University of Chicago, had set into operation a plan for early admissions at Morehouse. The plan essentially provided for admitting pre-eighteen-year-olds upon evidence (through a series of qualifying examinations) of high intelligence and emotional maturity.

Lloyd O. Lewis, professor emeritus at Morehouse and King's first public speaking teacher, remembers him as "attentive," "serious minded," "open minded (though having a mind of his own)" and a "thinker at fifteen."[44] Mays similarly recollected a "serious minded" lad who "listened more intently than most other students when anyone spoke in chapel."[45]

According to Lewis, while there was no Department of Speech at Morehouse in the early 1940s, effective oral expression was salient among the curriculum requirements. Every student had to take at least one course in the fundamentals of public speaking. Concerning King's performance in the speech class, Lewis remembered little "outstanding" for which to single him out except that the young man possessed unusual "poise" and "self-reliance."[46]

The intense interest in public address young King had discovered in high school continued throughout his time at Morehouse. The environment was unusually favorable, with varied outlets for speech activities. Lewis enumerated such things as weekly assemblies and chapels, student body meetings (when students could set forth and defend their propositions and opinions) and classes themselves. Recalling the meaningful informality surrounding a student's address, the professor told of one day when he interrupted a student assembly speaker who mispronounced a word. "Nipping it in the bud"—correcting the speech violation then and there rather than awaiting a later time—not only reinforced the correct pronunciation in the mind of the embarrassed speaker but also made an indelible impression on the auditors, among whom were other students of public speaking. Another opportunity at Morehouse for encouraging the development of good speech was the annual J. L. Webb Oratorical Contest, in which Mays believes King was a winner for at least two years.[47]

King's Morehouse days were marked by three especially significant developments:

1. He acquired a keen awareness of, and began an intellectual and pragmatic quest for, causes and remedies of the plight of the masses.

2. He decided to become a minister.

3. He preached his first sermon.

Quest for causes. During his early years in college, in addition to wanting at one time to be a physician and later a lawyer, King was a sociology major. He accumulated a commendable classroom record. Yet as a student of sociology, he recognized the need for more than mere textbook knowledge; thus between semesters he sought jobs that would expose him to conditions of the masses. Being the son of a prominent Negro clergyman and civic leader, he could easily have landed a job in any of the numerous black-owned businesses. Instead he chose the work of a common laborer, toiling often at menial, backbreaking jobs with blue-collar people to "learn their plight and feel their feelings."[48] One summer was spent unloading trains and trucks at the Railway Express Company and another helping in the stockroom at the Southern Spring Bed Mattress Company. Observing that African American males received drastically less pay than white males for identical jobs, he confirmed a theory expounded in Professor Walter Chiver's sociology classes that the love of money is the root not only of evil but indeed of race.[49]

But these were not the only experiences that broadened King's sociological understanding. When he was a member of Atlanta's integrated Intercollegiate Council, he associated with whites on a basis of substantial equality for the first time and thus developed a more varied view on race. He later remarked concerning this interracial experience, "The wholesome relations we had in this group convinced me that we have many white persons as allies, particularly among the younger generation. I had been ready to resent the whole white race, but as I got to see more white people my resentment was softened and a spirit of cooperation took its place."[50]

As a nineteen-year-old, King also expressed himself via the written word. In an 1948 article, "The Purpose of Education," for the Morehouse campus paper, *Maroon Tiger,* he argued persuasively concerning the kind of relationship one's education should sustain to the masses. After noting that "most" of his fellow students thought education served to provide a "proper instrument of exploitation" so they could perpetuate the plight of the masses, young King asserted that on the contrary, education should equip persons with "noble ends rather than means to an end." He continued:

> At this point, I often wonder whether or not education is fulfilling its purpose. A great majority of the so-called educated people do not think logically and scientifically. Even the press, the classroom, the platform, and the pulpit in many instances do not give us objective and unbiased truths. To save man from the morass of propaganda, in my opinion, is one of the chief aims of education. Education must enable one to sift and weigh evidence, to discern the true from the false, the real from the unreal, and the facts from fiction.
>
> The function of education, therefore, is to teach one to think intensively and to think critically. But education which stops with efficiency may prove the greatest menace to society. The most dangerous criminal may be the man gifted with reason, but with no morals.
>
> The late Eugene Talmadge, in my opinion, possessed one of the better minds of Georgia, or even America. Moreover, he wore the Phi Beta Kappa key. By all measuring rods, Mr. Talmadge could think critically and intensively; yet he contends that I am an inferior being. . . .
>
> We must remember that intelligence is not enough. Intelligence plus character— that is the goal of true education. The complete education gives one not only power of concentration, but worthy objectives upon which to concentrate. The broad education will, therefore, transmit to one not only the accumulated knowledge of the race but also the accumulated experience of social living.[51]

For King the pattern was set, the formula clear: education + character + a concern for the masses. Even when he was still a teenager, his sky shone with such noble lodestars.

Deciding to become a minister. A decision in favor of gospel ministry as a profession was preceded by a staunch revolt against the religious tradition of African Americans. In spite of a very deep urge in favor of becoming a preacher, King Jr. was repulsed by the emotionalism, hand-clapping, "amening," "shouting" and widely untrained clergy that generally characterized the black church; these things, he felt, were inharmonious with respectable intellectuality and relevant sociology.

Historian Carter G. Woodson's *The History of the Negro Church* examines the probable roots of uneducated Negro ministry. During pre-Civil War days (1830-1860), African American ministers were generally deemed incapable of the mental development of whites. Barred from most theological seminaries in the North, few were given opportunity to complete a formal discipline preparatory to the parish; consequently, many Negro preachers began capitalizing on and taking questionable pride in their predicament. "Preaching to his congregation, the ignorant minister would often boast of having not rubbed his head against the college walls, whereupon the congregation would respond: 'Amen.' Sometimes one would say: 'I did not write out my sermon.' With equal fervor the audience would cry out: 'Praise ye the Lord.' "[52]

King admitted his trepidation and apprehension regarding the ministry: "I had doubts that religion was intellectually respectable, I revolted against the emotionalism of Negro religion, the shouting and the stamping. I didn't understand it and it embarrassed me."[53]

His initial biographer, Reddick, describes Ebenezer Baptist as once containing many of these elements, for it "was essentially a congregation of working class people . . . thoroughly familiar with the high charge of emotion—the shouting and the beautiful but full-throated singing—and the general direct behavior of the evangelical denominations to which the majority of Negroes of America belong."[54] A person very familiar with Ebenezer and its leadership confided that once it indeed was predominantly the typical, emotionally charged "happy" congregation, but the arrival of King Jr., as associate pastor brought a more well-rounded appeal, a greater balance of emotionalism and intellectualism, fundamentalism and liberalism, working-class people and professionals.[55]

King's revulsion against the ministry had been evoked, however, not merely by the extrinsic forms of black worship. He was convinced that emotionally charged worship simply had little, if any, relevance to the real problems and needs of the Negro masses.

Morehouse College, however, had on its faculty several intelligent, seminary-trained clergymen, among whom were Benjamin E. Mays (the president) and George D. Kelsey (then chairman of the Religion Department and later professor of ethics at Drew University). And foremost among full-time pastor-preacher models who mirrored the ideal was Gardner C. Taylor of Brooklyn's Concord Baptist Church. King caught the brilliant reflection and concluded that what he conceived as a respectable ministry was indeed possible. In Mays and Kelsey he saw that "religion could be intellectually acceptable as well as emotionally satisfying."[56]

Eventually, while still at Morehouse, King concluded that ministry provided the only framework in which he could properly position his growing concept of responsibility to his social milieu. Thus in his senior year, in 1947, King answered the sacred summons and decided to enter the ministerial profession. When I asked Mays why he thought King decided to ascend the podium of preaching, he replied that he believes King received "a 'call,' that inner urge which compels one to do this rather than that."[57] Years after accepting the inner challenge to ministerial service, King gave the following statement regarding this "call":

> My call to the ministry was neither dramatic nor spectacular. It came neither by some miraculous vision nor by some blinding light experience on the road of life. Moreover, it was a response to an inner urge that gradually came upon me. This urge expressed itself in a desire to serve God and humanity, and the feeling that my talent and my commitment could best be expressed through the ministry. At first I planned to be a physician; then I turned my attention in the direction of law. But as I passed through the preparation stages of these two professions, I still felt within that undying urge to serve God and humanity through the ministry. During my senior year in college I finally decided to accept the challenge to enter the ministry. I came to see that God had placed a responsibility upon my shoulders and the more I tried to escape it the more frustrated I would become. A few months after preaching my first sermon I entered theological seminary.[58]

The first sermon. Upon informing his pleased parents of the decision to enter the ministerial ranks, young Martin was permitted, perhaps even directed, by his pastor-father to preach a trial sermon. Years later his father remarked that "he started giving the sermon—I don't remember the subject—in the first unit of the church

and the crowds kept coming, and we had to move to the main auditorium."[59] Satisfied not only with Martin's decision but also with the evidence of ability conveyed by the sermon, the father returned home that night and thanked God. Later
in the same year, the son was ordained to the gospel ministry and appointed assistant to his father at Ebenezer Baptist Church.

Crozer Theological Seminary. In June 1948, Martin Luther King Jr., nineteen
years old, graduated from Morehouse with a bachelor of arts degree. The fall of
the same year found the young Atlantan in the North—Chester, Pennsylvania—
matriculating at Crozer Theological Seminary, to which, because of promise as
both a student and minister, he had been given a scholarship. Crozer at that time
was among the top ten theological schools in the United States.

The change from college to seminary scene rather paralleled in time a change
in the spirit and trend of the world. World War II, concluded two years prior, did
not leave the world unchanged; it discharged forces that began disrupting racial
strata. In Asia, Africa and America, people of color were now expressing concern
about world conditions and making significant overtures toward more racially
integrated societies.

During this era of flux and change, King, mature and intelligent beyond his
years, sensed more and more the emerging spirit of assertiveness among the
world's colored peoples. Asa Philip Randolph (an African-American labor leader,
president of the Brotherhood of Sleeping Car Porters and the foremost mass protest organizer at that time) threatened in 1947-1948 to get under way a civil disobedience movement protesting segregation in the U.S. Army.[60] The threat stirred
thousands of Negro collegians. *Newsweek* magazine reported that of 2,200 Negro
college youth polled on twenty-six campuses by the National Association for the
Advancement of Colored People (NAACP), 1,619, or 71 percent, indicated that
they favored Randolph's proposal for resisting the draft under the segregation
policy of the time.[61] At the very time King was registering at Crozer, a conflagra-
tion of contention swept over the United States with regard to an uphill battle for
"strong" civil rights legislation being waged by President Harry S. Truman and
the Progressive Party.[62]

These developments did not go unnoticed by the young seminary student, who
found permissible pride in the expanding ethos of the Negro. What he would later
term the zeitgeist stirring in the womb of time was even then, perhaps, preparing
him to stand at the crossroads of outdated traditionalism and a new outlook
regarding the Negro's place in the modern world.[63]

In the meantime King pursued his studies. Three years of professional discipline at Crozer consisted of history and criticism of the Bible, church history, the
lives and works of the major prophets, psychology of religion, ethics, social philosophy, church administration and homiletics. Morton S. Enslin, a New Testament professor for whom King had the greatest respect, later said the following
about King as an aspiring student of theology:

> When I first met and observed Martin both in my classroom and in my home (he
> dined in my house several times), I saw that he was always a perfect gentleman and
> knew that he was marked for the sword belt [he was destined to succeed]; he was
> going to be someone, not a private but an officer in the rank. He was a smooth boy
> and knew the world was round.[64]

King's homiletics and preaching teacher, Professor Robert E. Keighton,
described the curriculum as covering four areas: (1) sermon preparation, (2) practice preaching (before classmates), (3) preaching problems and (4) preaching in
public (for seniors).[65] According to Keighton, no textbook was used in the course.
He well remembered King but hastened to add in my interview with him that he
recalled nothing especially outstanding about King as a young preacher and had
no particularly high esteem for his preaching during his leadership in the civil
rights movement. Keeping his comments on his former student rather terse, the
former professor labeled King a "product of his environment," a possible "oppor-
tunist." Keighton would not elaborate except to say that he felt King preached
only to those who agree with him. I was not permitted to probe the uncomplimen-
tary comments; nevertheless, I did notice that in all of the published works on
Martin Luther King Jr., lists of eminent and influential teachers of his seminary
and graduate school days do not include his homiletics professor.

Because King very well knew that serious social problems existed in the world
generally and in the United States particularly, he began reading furiously at
Crozer in "a serious intellectual quest for a method to eliminate social evil."[66] The
reading list took him on excursions with philosophers Plato, Aristotle, Jean-
Jacques Rousseau and John Locke; existentialists Søren Kierkegaard, Friedrich
Nietzsche, Jean-Paul Sartre, Paul Tillich, Karl Jaspers and Martin Heidegger;
social theorists Reinhold Niebuhr, Karl Marx, G. W. F. Hegel, Walter Rauschenbusch and Mohandas Gandhi. He reread Henry David Thoreau. Theological concepts exerting the most relevant influence on King will be reviewed in chapter
six.

While King's academic performance at Morehouse (1944-1948) had been commendable, his three years (1948-1951) at the racially integrated Crozer Seminary were nothing short of fantastic. So popular was he that he was elected president of the student government. According to Stephen Oates, his activities included also an experience of interracial dating that was sufficiently serious to speak of love and possible marriage.[67] He received the Plafker Award for most outstanding student and was also senior class president. Graduating as valedictorian with an A average, he received his bachelor of divinity (B.D., the professional seminary degree now known as M.Div. or master of divinity, as changed by the Association of Theological Schools) degree in June 1951. He was awarded the Lewis Crozer Fellowship ($1,200) to register at the graduate school of his choice for doctoral studies. Sankey L. Blanton, president of Crozer, would write to King upon his graduation, "I regard you as one of the most promising students I have met."[68]

Boston University. Impervious to arguments that he would end up "overeducated" for pastoring a lower- or middle-class congregation, King had applied to at least two graduate schools of theology: Edinburgh University (Scotland) and Boston University. Edinburgh responded that his transcripts were of "sufficiently high quality" to admit him to the postgraduate school in 1951.[69] He headed instead for Boston University, a center for "personalism," a philosophical concept emphasizing the value of the human personality. Personalism, treated in more detail in chapter six, would later be expressed in many of King's sermons. His intellectual pursuit begun at Morehouse and accelerated at Crozer gained momentum at Boston. Unstinted credit goes particularly to Edgar S. Brightman and L. Harold DeWolf, two foremost exponents of personalism, or personal idealism, for stimulating his thinking at Boston.

DeWolf, at one time chairman of the systematics department, informed me that of all the doctoral students he had served as major adviser at Boston University (some fifty), he rated King among the top half-dozen; he proudly noted that King was one of only two of his students who completed the Ph.D. requirements within three years. The former Boston professor described his former pupil as "a very good student, all business, a scholar's scholar, one digging deeply to work out and think through his philosophy of religion and life."[70]

King's academic ability did not come to the notice only of those who taught him. While Walter G. Muelder, then dean of the school of theology, did not have him in any classes, he recalled vividly the "serious, mature, brilliant student in philosophical theology."[71]

Interested mainly in King as a pulpit spokesman, I posed this question to his Boston University tutors: "Is it not possible for a pupil to establish himself as an intelligent student by mastering content materials and accurately answering exam questions in a course without necessarily executing efficient oral communication?" Both S. Paul Schilling (professor of systematic theology and the second reader of King's doctoral dissertation) and DeWolf answered yes. However, commenting on King's facility in self-expression, Schilling remarked enthusiastically that he was "direct, very effective, not superfluous."[72] Emphasizing further the clarity with which King communicated, even during the defense of his dissertation, Schilling said that when he was talking, a listener never had to interrupt him to ask, "Now what did you mean back there when you said .. thus and so . . . ?"[73] The student of theology did not use jargon or circumlocutions but was always clear. DeWolf added that not only was he "always clear and precise but meticulously systematic and resourceful. His arrangement of ideas, even in ordinary conversation, was superbly organized."[74]

Only one regret, and that to his student's credit, did DeWolf mention concerning his relationship with King: "Mr. King manifested such initiative and self-disciplined organization of his work that he was rendered more independent than the average doctoral student and, accordingly, sought little time for the guidance and counsel of his major professor."[75]

On the subject of organization, it is noteworthy that when King left Boston and took up the pastorate of Dexter Avenue Baptist Church (Montgomery), he sent plans of his church organization to two friends for criticism. Both recipients, Major J. Jones (who later became dean of the chapel at Fisk University) and Melvin Watson (faculty at Morehouse College) complimented him on the well-thought-through plans but mildly warned him that his "details" might tend toward "over-organization."[76]

Similar to an arrangement he had while at Crozer (taking supplemental courses in philosophy at the University of Pennsylvania), King took classes in philosophy at Harvard while enrolled at Boston. An influence on his speaking, particularly in group discussion, was the philosophical club he organized with Philip Lenud, a divinity student at Tufts University. Having started out as a weekly get-together of a dozen or so students in King's apartment soon grew to larger and encouraging proportions.[77] It apparently was a periodic practice to invite a seminary professor to address the group or lead them in a discussion of a theological subject, for King wrote a letter to DeWolf on May 15, 1954, thanking him for the interesting lecture he had given to "our Theology Club on last Monday evening." As a result of DeWolf's lecture, he said, the club members understood more clearly the "meaning of the Kingdom" and "just how it is to come."[78]

Even in the midst of a very intensive academic program at Boston University, King took time to practice his public address by preaching on weekends. Cities in which he delivered sermons during his B.U. days included Atlanta, Baltimore, Boston, Chattanooga, Washington,, Lansing (Michigan), Methuen (Massachusetts), Montgomery, Philadelphia and Roxbury (Massachusetts).[79]

Successfully passing the oral examination on his dissertation, "A Comparison of the Conceptions of God in the Thinking of Paul Tillich and Henry Nelson Wieman," King was awarded a Ph.D. in systematic theology in June 1955. The same month his major professor, DeWolf, wrote his prize student a personal letter in which he said, "I shall be deeply interested in following both your professional and your personal career. . . . I expect splendid achievements from you and shall always regard you with high appreciation and pride."[80] The teacher's expectation proved prophetic.

Characterized by a brilliant intellect, broad education, powerful capacity for hard work, enormous willpower and large ambition, King set out to face the world. The seed was indeed germinable; it fell not on stony ground.

The Fruition: King's Career

Milieu. In May 1954 the U.S. Supreme Court issued its epochal decision to abolish segregation in public schools.[81] The same month and year marked the genesis of the first church pastorate of Martin Luther King Jr.

For more than half a century segregation had been legalized under the *Plessy* v. *Ferguson* case, affirming the Southern premise that the purpose of the Fourteenth Amendment was not to "enforce social, as distinguished from political equality, or a commingling of the two races."[82] The Negro had argued that social prejudices could be fought by legislative measures; but the Supreme Court, in the 1896 *Plessy* decision, declared that "if one race be inferior to the other socially, the Constitution of the United States cannot put them upon the same plane." Justice John Marshall Harland voiced the lone dissent: "There is no caste here. Our Constitution is color-blind, and neither knows nor tolerates classes among citizens. In respect of civil rights, all citizens are equal before the law."[83]

On May 17, 1954, the Supreme Court (in a 9-0 vote) dissolved the 1896 decision by accepting the weighty, well-documented arguments of Thurgood Marshall and colleagues that racially segregated and discriminatory education did have negative effects on the Negro pupil. Justice Harlan's "color-blind note" resounded once more, and the Court ruled: "We cannot turn the clock back to 1868 when the [Fourteenth] Amendment was adopted, or even to 1896 when *Plessy* vs. *Ferguson* was written. . . . We conclude that in the field of public education the doctrine of 'separate but equal' has no place. Separate educational facilities are inherently unequal."[84]

Marriage. In 1953, while still a resident student at Boston University, King had married the beautiful and talented Coretta Scott, at that time a student at the New England Conservatory of Music. Born and reared in Heiberger, Alabama, Coretta was the second of three children in the household of Obadiah and Bernie McMurry Scott. Her ancestors had owned land in the area since the Civil War. To the union of Martin and Coretta would be born four children: Yolanda, Martin III, Dexter Scott and Bernice. The summer of 1954 witnessed two milestones in the young couple's lives: Coretta graduated from the New England Conservatory of Music, and her husband passed his preliminary examinations at Boston.

Dexter Avenue Baptist Church. Off to the South they went to take up duties at the Dexter Avenue Baptist Church in Montgomery, Alabama. The pastorate had been officially accepted the preceding spring predicated on three considerations: (1) that the parsonage be completely furnished, (2) that King be granted an allowance of time to complete his work at Boston University, coming to Dexter as full pastor not later than September 1, 1954 (in the meantime he would fill the pulpit at least once or twice per month, expecting Dexter to defray expenses in his commuting from Boston to Montgomery), and (3) that the proposed salary ($4,200 per year) be increased as the church progressed.[85]

Why did Martin and Coretta King go to the deep South to pastor a church? What led to the decision? Whatever Martin lacked upon completion of his residence requirements at B.U., it was certainly not opportunities for employment. In addition to at least two from Northern churches and the same number from the South, he had been offered a teaching position, a deanship and an administrative appointment in three colleges.[86] He was ambitious for a minister-teacher career—inspired by the course of his longtime idol, Benjamin E. Mays, then president of Morehouse College. But good judgment suggested that he spend time pastoring before accepting a teaching post in the academic world. Coretta agreed but favored the Northern pulpits. Wouldn't moving to the South curtail her musical career and stifle opportunities for further study and cultural outlets? The South, with its race problems, held no enchantment. Nevertheless, King argued passionately for the hard and narrow path of duty.[87] To the Southland they decided to go.

Dexter was King's preference by virtue of certain advantages. Besides including upper-income parishioners, many of them professionals from Alabama State College (the state-sponsored institution for African Americans), Dexter Avenue Baptist Church was rather "intellectual" and discountenanced "emotionalism" and excessive "amening"—thus promising a more ideal milieu for a young, sensitive and disciplined preacher. King had already "taken the temperature and checked the pulse of Dexter" when, in January 1954, he delivered his trial sermon.[88] He was satisfied; so was the congregation.

Five years later, during a farewell "This Is Your Life" program honoring King as he prepared to take up his new pastorate in Atlanta, the narrator of the program described the attitudes surrounding the initial reception of their pastor:

> He was received kindly by Dexter members but not without mixed emotions. Some were impressed by the pending Ph.D. degree, others were dismayed by his youth [then twenty-five years old]. In spite of some skepticism and mixed emotions, Dexter's members were committed to give their new pastor their best in the spiritual hope that this would elicit from him his best and that in due time he would obtain the stature of greatness. In one respect we were in error, for long before he was "due" as we had envisioned the time table, he had exceeded the greatness much beyond the anticipation of his most devoted admirers.[89]

The narrator then paid implicit tribute to King's facility in pulpit oratory when he referred to how a certain member of the pulpit committee of Dexter, during the process of selecting the new minister, had been strongly advised to delay any recommendation until the church had "heard the young M. L. King."[90]

It has been reported that one woman felt that the twenty-five-year-old cleric looked kind of lost on the platform without his mother. His first sermon at Dexter was entitled "The Three Dimensions of a Complete Life"—love of self, love of neighbors and love of God—auguring well the overall scope of his future. Little did the Dexter church members suspect that this sermon would be later adapted for world audiences.

Very soon, to be sure, word got around, and the Dexter pastor quickly gained the reputation of being an extraordinary preacher. Invitations to preach on special days in other churches became common. Just after one such engagement, the elder Martin Luther King wrote the following fatherly commendation and advice to the up-and-coming clergyman:

> Alexander called me yesterday just to tell me about how you swept them at Friend-
> ship Sunday. Every way I turn people are congratulating me for you. You see, young
> man, you are becoming popular. As I told you, you must be much in prayer. Persons
> like yourself are the ones the devil turns all of his forces aloose to destroy.[91]

What plans would the young pastor outline for his first parish? What nuances of
thought stirred his vision? King later reflected on those early days:

> The first few weeks in the autumn of 1954 were spent formulating a program that
> would be meaningful to this particular congregation. I was anxious to change the
> impression in the community that Dexter was a sort of silk-stocking catering only
> to a certain class. Often it was referred to as the "big folks' church." Revolting
> against this idea, I was convinced that worship at its best is a social experience with
> people of all levels of life coming together to realize their oneness and unity under
> God. Whenever the church, consciously or unconsciously, caters to one class it
> loses the spiritual force of the "whosoever will, let him come" doctrine, and is in
> danger of becoming little more than a social club with a thin veneer of religiosity.[92]

There was time, moreover, for manifest interest in the larger community of the
city. Locked in racial segregation's iron grasp, Montgomery was marked by a
typical sociopoliticoeconomic gulf between its seventy thousand Caucasians
(median income $1,730) and fifty thousand African Americans (median income
$970). While 94 percent of the white families had flush toilets inside their homes,
only 31 percent of Negroes enjoyed such facilities. In the early pages of *Stride
Toward Freedom* King provides quite a graphic picture of the status of the Montgomery environment: racially segregated schools, segregated public transportation, segregated professional organizations (physicians, lawyers, teachers and the
like), segregated ministerial alliance, segregated school of higher learning (Alabama State College, the largest college in the city). Of the thirty thousand
Negroes of voting age in Montgomery, he bemoaned that only about two thousand were registered.

King's concern for these kinds of problems in Montgomery revealed itself in
his organizing his church's Social and Political Action Committee, which worked
to keep the congregation intelligently informed of social, political and economic
issues and to keep before them the importance of the NAACP and the necessity
of being registered voters. Before state and national elections it sponsored forums
and mass meetings to discuss the major issues. King himself became a very

active member of the local branch of the NAACP, raised money in his church and delivered several speeches for the organization.

The pulpit at Dexter will be long remembered for its having been occupied by one who led Montgomery's monumental bus boycott, the episode that Louis Lomax views as the "first major battle" of the Negro revolt.[93] Ironically, Dexter is less than one hundred yards from the Alabama State Capitol, near which in 1861 Jefferson Davis, the Confederacy's new president, was introduced with these words: "The man and the hour have met." In mid-1952, Montgomery and the world would witness the converging of a new man and a new hour.

The career of Martin Luther King Jr. was catapulted into national and international attention when he led a bus boycott prompted on December 1, 1955, when an African American woman, Rosa Parks, refused to move back on a crowded city bus to let a white passenger have her seat. The bus driver had her arrested, the Negro community reacted, the boycott began and lasted for one year until the Supreme Court affirmed the decision of a special three-judge U.S. district court, ruling unconstitutional the Alabama state and local segregation laws on buses.

Fifty thousand African American citizens of Montgomery—ministers, physicians, professors, porters, maids, laborers, housewives and others—shed all claims of rank, class or creed to rally under the leadership and direction of the Montgomery Improvement Association. The MIA elected as its president the youthful preacher Martin Luther King Jr. Among other leaders were E. D. Dixon, treasurer; Fred D. Gray, attorney; and the Rev. Ralph D. Abernathy, minister of the First Baptist Church, Montgomery, who continued throughout the ensuing King-led national civil rights movement to serve as King's "righthand man," counselor and friend. King often seriocomically referred to Abernathy as "my dearest friend and cell mate."[94]

Providing some three hundred automobiles for regular transportation from forty-six pickup stations, the MIA leased space in buildings to receive additional complaints and requests from citizens and kept the community informed on developments and strategy. For mass meetings it used the facilities of various churches on a rotation plan; in these gatherings the people could communicate and express themselves. Montgomery African Americans exemplified the crystallization of a racial self and proved effective opponents of the white city bureaucracy. The *Nation* described the massive front as having "the nature of a miracle, something that has never happened before in the history of the South."[95]

In putting together his first address as president of the MIA, on December 5,

1955, King noted a problem that would perpetually challenge his public speaking on civil rights: how could he make a presentation that would be militant enough to arouse African Americans to positive action yet moderate enough to keep this fervor within controllable and Christian bounds?[96] He decided to face the challenge head on by attempting to combine two apparent irreconcilables: the militant and the moderate forces.

His message that evening at MIA's first mass meeting did not contain any explicit references to the works of Hegel, Rauschenbusch or even Gandhi. He did, however, quote Jesus Christ and Booker T. Washington:

> Our method will be that of persuasion, not coercion. We will only say to the people, "Let your conscience be your guide." . . . Love must be our regulating ideal. Once again we must hear the words of Jesus echoing across the centuries: "Love your enemies, bless them that curse you, and pray for them that despitefully use you." If we fail to do this our protest will end up as a meaningless drama on the stage of history, and its memory will be shrouded with the ugly garments of shame. In spite of the treatment that we have confronted we must not become bitter, and end up hating our white brothers. As Booker T. Washington said, "Let no man pull you so low as to make you hate him." . . . If you will protest courageously, and yet with dignity and Christian love, when the history books are written in future generations, the historians will have to pause and say, "There lived a great people—a black people— who injected new meaning and dignity into the veins of civilization." This is our challenge and our overwhelming responsibility.[97]

Since love and forgiveness, Siamese twins of passive resistance, were conspicuous themes of King's actions during the Montgomery movement, it is quite easy to assume that Gandhism was always at the fore. Not exactly. Note King's reaction to the first bombing of his home, January 30, 1956, which threatened the lives of his wife and baby. Although he had spoken forcefully and persuasively on love and forgiveness at a mass meeting that same evening, the demands of husbandhood and fatherhood brought him to feel a need for self-defense. The next day found him in the sheriff's office applying for a gun permit. He was ultimately denied the permit but by then had come to the conviction that that means of self-defense was not the way.[98] Although his home was bombed three times in all, his self-defense would forever be "the weapon of nonviolence."[99]

In his first major interviews—one with editor Robert E. Johnson of *Jet*, the other with reporter Tom Johnson of the *Montgomery Advertiser*—King made no mention of Mahatma Gandhi. To Tom Johnson, he pinpointed the "social gospel" as his chief motivation:

> Besides the religious philosophers, King was particularly interested in the German
> philosophers Kant and Hegel. The latter, his favorite, fathered the "dialectical pro-
> cess" which holds that change is the cardinal principle of life and that in every stage
> of things there is a contradiction which only the "strife of opposites" can resolve.[100]

Gandhism's avenue into the protest movement apparently came from a Southern white librarian named Juliette Morgan, who noted in a letter to the *Montgomery Advertiser* that similarities existed between the Montgomery protest and Gandhi's passive resistance. MIA leaders, already headed in this direction, capitalized on the idea and thereafter frequently referred to Gandhi as an authority, particularly in their appeals for restraint. Northern and European reporters further emphasized the connection.[101]

This is not to say, though, that King was unfamiliar with the philosophy of Gandhi. As a student at Crozer he had read and reread several books on the Indian protest leader. Nevertheless, Gandhi's thought occupied no overtly conscious position in MIA's initial strategy. (A closer look into the first formal contact of King with the techniques of Mahatma Gandhi will be found in chapter six under "Thematic Sources.")

King was a man of deep inner strength. If any one point marked the moment of conversion from a mere pastor to a minister with illimitable inner resources, it was probably one night in 1956. Pressured by the claims of leadership, engulfed by the omnipresent possibility of sudden violent death, forced to shoulder immense responsibility, King sat dejectedly in his kitchen and told God he could go no further alone. His heart overflowed: "I am here taking a stand for what I believe is right, but now I am afraid. The people are looking to me for leadership, and if I stand before them without strength and courage, they too will falter. I am at the end of my powers. I have nothing left. I've come to the point where I can't face it alone."[102]

What resulted from that prayer of relinquishment? Did God answer the petitioning pastor? "At that moment I experienced the presence of the Divine as I had never experienced Him before. It seemed as though I could hear the quiet assurance of an inner voice saying: 'Stand up for righteousness, stand up for truth; and God will be at your side forever.' Almost at once my fears began to go. My uncertainty disappeared. I was ready to face anything."[103]

And face almost anything he did, including twenty-three arrests between January 26, 1956, and June 11, 1964, and a near-fatal stabbing by a deranged woman in Harlem on September 20, 1958, while he was autographing his first published book, *Stride Toward Freedom*.

By 1957 King was "one of America's most sought after speakers and his name was known in almost every corner of America."[104] In that one year he delivered 208 addresses and traveled some 780,000 miles. James L. Hicks of New York City's *Amsterdam News* singled out the Prayer Pilgrimage to the Lincoln Memorial, May 17, 1957, as moving King beyond being a nationally and internationally known preacher to being the number-one spokesman for the Negro.[105] Bellowing "Give us the ballot" as his theme, he electrified a crowd of twenty-five thousand: "Give us the ballot, and we will transform the salient misdeeds of bloodthirsty mobs into the abiding good deeds of orderly citizens. Give us the ballot . . ."[106] According to Hicks, King "emerged from the Prayer Pilgrimage to Washington as the No. 1 leader of 16 million Negroes. . . . . At this point in his career, they will follow him anywhere."[107] He had been first quoted in *Time*, the leading newsmagazine, on March 5, 1956; by February 18, 1957, *Time* ran a cover story on the Baptist preacher. It would not be the last.

Perhaps for half a century, since the time of Booker T. Washington, African Americans had been looking for a leader. Some now began to mark the beginning of a new era with the emergence of Dr. King.[108] As King's image loomed on the horizon, Negroes en masse were confronting him with the hopeful query: Art thou he who should come or should we look for another?

From Montgomery to Ebenezer and the SCLC. Willing to serve in any honorable way available, in addition to pastoring Dexter Avenue Baptist Church and chairing MIA, King accepted the presidency of the Southern Christian Leadership Conference (SCLC; formerly the Southern Conference on Transportation and Non-violent Integration). The organization was founded January 10-11, 1957, and upon accepting the presidency, King himself became an institution.

On Sunday, November 29, 1959, congregants at Dexter Avenue Baptist Church would hear a saddening announcement. Because of mounting and broadening responsibilities, which King named as his pastorate, presidency of the MIA, presidency of the SCLC, extensive speaking appointments, daily office chores and "the general strain of being known," he made known a "painful decision": "I would like to submit my resignation as pastor of Dexter Avenue Baptist Church to become effective on the fourth Sunday in January."[109]

An associate pastorate with his father, the Rev. M. L. King Sr. of Ebenezer Baptist Church in Atlanta, would not require nearly as many pastoral responsibilities as the pastorate at Dexter. Consequently, he would have more time for the broader universe of the SCLC and the myriad speaking engagements. By 1963 he bore the reputation of being "the most powerful Negro leader in America."[110] Salaried at one dollar a year from SCLC and $6,000 from Ebenezer Baptist Church, King received most of his income from speaking fees, gifts, books and magazine articles. In 1958 he reported a total income of $25,348, over twice as much as the $10,000 later published by *Time*.

The SCLC was able to boast a growth from a nucleus of five workers and a budget of $63,000 in 1960 to a staff of forty and a budget of $800,000 in 1963. As the generally proclaimed number-one African American leader in America, King brought prestige to the SCLC, thus rendering the organization a strong rival of, and cooperator with, the other major civil rights groups, the National Association for the Advancement of Colored People (NAACP), the National Urban League, the Congress of Racial Equality (CORE) and the Student Non-violent Coordinating Committee (SNCC). A spread in *Time* (June 28, 1963, p. 16) presented the basic dogma and emphasis of each of these "mainline" civil rights organizations along with a photograph of each leader: Roy Wilkins (NAACP), Whitney M. Young Jr. (NUL), Floyd B. McKissick (CORE) and Stokely Carmichael (SNCC).

It should be noted that by spring 1966 two of these organizations (CORE and SNCC) had changed leaders, revised their attitudes on nonviolence and taken up a new rallying cry of "black power," the precise definition of which was somewhat elusive. Because of its connotations, the "black power" slogan was rejected by both the SCLC and the NAACP. An updated one-page spread on civil rights movements by *U.S. News & World Report* (July 28, 1966, p. 33) included three additional groups: the "Black Muslims" led by Elijah Muhammad, the Revolutionary Action Movement (RAM) led by Robert Franklin Williams and the Deacons for Defense and Justice led by Charlie Sims.

With the dynamic thrust of Wyatt Tee Walker, assistant to King and executive director of SCLC, the organization moved into the very fore of the civil rights struggle. Others joining the SCLC team included Ralph D. Abernathy (who also moved from Montgomery and took a church in Atlanta), Andrew J. Young (who in 1964 succeeded Walker as executive director), James Bevel, Dorothy Cotton, James Lawson, Fred Shuttlesworth and later, through the Operation Breadbasket arm, Jesse Jackson. With major civil rights campaigns in cities such as Albany, Georgia; Selma and Birmingham, Alabama; and Chicago, and the March on Washington, King spent a great amount of time in airplanes and hotels, at banquets and receptions, on lecture platforms and behind pulpits. Weekly he traveled three to four thousand miles, and each twenty-four-hour period in a major city may well have included two to three formal addresses, a press conference, and several interviews with reporters from radio, television and print media.[111]

Reese Cleghorn wrote of this private citizen during the much-publicized Birmingham civil rights campaign in 1963:

> King's position in the rights movement unquestionably is enhanced by the fact that he has the ear of the President and, for that matter, of figures around the world. . . . Not only is he on speaking terms with African leaders; to an extent few white Americans appreciate, his name is known and revered throughout much of the world.[112]

During the Dwight D. Eisenhower administration, King conferred with the president and with vice president Richard Nixon; later he apparently had an even closer relationship with President John F. Kennedy. He was one of the twelve hundred invited VIPs who attended the Kennedy funeral in St. Matthew's Cathedral, Washington, D.C. Lyndon Baines Johnson, successor to Kennedy, "summoned him almost immediately to the White House to confer on the change of administration."[113] The M. L. King Jr. Collection of Papers at the Boston University Library and Martin Luther King Jr., Center for Social Change contains letters regarding the civil rights movement to King from President Harry S. Truman, President Eisenhower, Vice President Nixon, Senator John F. Kennedy (then a declared candidate for the U.S. presidency), Attorney General Robert Kennedy and President Johnson. Dr. and Mrs. King were invited guests of President Kwame Nkrumah of Ghana, Jomo Kenyatta of Kenya (they did not go to Kenya, however, because of the transition following President Kennedy's assassination which necessitated King's remaining in the United States) and of Prime Minister Jawaharlal Nehru of India.

How did King compare in popularity and effectiveness with other Negro leaders? *Newsweek* conducted a poll among "rank and file" African Americans in twenty-five cities and among one hundred selected Negro "leaders" to gain a reading on how African Americans would rank their own people in the civil rights endeavor. Of the fourteen Negroes receiving significant ratings, King ranked number one with an 80 percent "favorable" rating from the "rank and file" and 95 percent "favorable" from leaders.[114]

Although there have been many influential African American leaders, only King received the distinctive honor of being named Man of the Year by *Time*

(January 3, 1964) and later had a national holiday established in his name by Congress. Regarding Man of the Year, not only was King the first African American so honored but also only the third religious leader (Mohandas K. Gandhi in 1932 and Pope John XXIII in 1962 were the first). The award that unequivocally made him a truly worldwide figure and international preacher was the Nobel Peace Prize of 1964. The thirty-five-year-old King was "the twelfth American, and the youngest person ever, to be so honored."[115]

At thirty-nine, however, he became the unfortunate victim of an assassin's bullet in Memphis, Tennessee, on April 4, 1968, a day of infamy on the American sociopolitical scene—a glaringly heinous trend of murdering its young, powerful leaders, including the likes of President John F. Kennedy at forty-six years of age (1963) and Senator Robert F. Kennedy at forty-three in June of 1968, just two months after the Nobel Prize winning preacher's death.

Martin Luther King Jr. was "a man who . . . earned fame with speeches."[116] The flower of his pulpit ministry blossomed luxuriantly and, in myriad ways because of his enduring influence on modern pulpits and platforms, continues to bloom.

2
KING AS
BLACK PREACHER
& THE LIBERATING WORD

The whole city was stirred and asked, "Who is this?"
MATTHEW 21:10

The Spirit of the Lord is on me . . .
to preach good news to the poor . . .
to proclaim freedom for the prisoners
and recovery of sight for the blind,
to release the oppressed,
to proclaim the year of the Lord's favor.
LUKE 4:18-19

*S*ome decades ago a bold and distinctive kind of gospel proclamation captured academic attention. "Black preaching" then began to receive serious consideration by scholars of homiletics, and over the ensuing years it has gained currency.

After one or two other recognized U.S. schools initiated formal classes on the subject during the 1970s, John Killinger at Vanderbilt Divinity School invited me to offer its first course on this phenomenon together with a seminar on Martin Luther King Jr. Though separate offerings, Black Preaching and the seminar on Dr. King seemed quite appropriate corresponding studies adding fresh relevance to the already strong seminary venue for Christian preaching and homiletic thought.

After working up a syllabus, I contacted Gardner C. Taylor, who at the time was teaching black preaching at Colgate-Rochester Divinity School and at

Crozer. We exchanged syllabi, and I was on my way. Both courses at Vanderbilt piqued interest and proceeded normally enough, yet given the predisposition of graduate students to intellectualize I should have anticipated that especially the black preaching course would evoke questions of definition, criteria and qualification. What did we mean by "black preaching"? Whence did it come, and whither was it tending? Could white Christian ministers and other nonblacks do black preaching and fulfill its function? Must race be the sole determinant? Are there not African American clergy who, through lack of crucial criteria, disqualify themselves? Was Martin Luther King Jr. himself really a black preacher?

Black preaching embodies at once an anomaly and a reality, the former because in the absolute sense the genre of biblical preaching possesses a Christian universality without regard to ethnicity and the latter because historical forces in Western civilization warrant acknowledgement of an emphasis in preaching born legitimately within the church and demanding recognition as a valid reality. But challenges abounded. How well I remember how President Joseph H. Jackson of the National Baptist Convention refused to participate in our black preaching class project, retorting in a stern letter to me, "I believe in 'gospel' preaching not 'black' preaching." On the one hand, his point was well taken. On the other hand, I attempted to explain that the subject was not manufactured or finagled or fancied into existence as some racial ploy but had arisen from authentic circumstances be they ever so embarrassing to the Christian church.

What set of circumstances moved black preachers beyond merely promising bread of eternal life in the hereafter to grasp the need of feeding liberation from religious and civil injustices of the day? We landed some answers that assisted our process of definition and consideration of Martin Luther King Jr. as one who may or may not have practiced authentic black preaching. We found that black preaching has deep roots in the history of the Christian church in America. In the seventeenth century there was the "invisible institution"[1] of worship by slaves in America. Organized institutional black churches began with the break of Richard Allen and Absalom Jones from Methodism in 1876 (followed by the secession of blacks from other denominations).[2] Despite current evidences of progress, we must acknowledge racist-ecclesiastical oppression of African Americans throughout centuries of U.S. history. When any organization persistently approves and practices distinction and privilege based on race or any other unjust criterion, the oppressed will find it necessary to seek redress and survival by creating their own zone of existence free of contrary and frustrating forces.[3]

History has a plethora of precedents. Take the Pilgrims in 1620, fleeing from European oppression in the ardent hope of founding a nation without a king and a church without a pope. All such remedial movements, of course, find their proto-type and draw strength from an enduring scriptural paradigm, the Hebrew exodus from Egyptian bondage. Later in faith history, hunger and thirst for a spiritual relationship that is both theocentric and anthropocentric (Godward as well as per-sonal, existential and contemporary) was a prime reason for Jesus Christ's seced-ing from Judaism and establishing Christianity.

Thus traditional black preaching evolved from authentic spiritual necessity and justifiably assumes validity. Given the extent to which the dominant white Christian church in America had endorsed dehumanization and violation of blacks through intrinsic and systemic racism in spite of the "one blood" ethic of Scripture (Acts 17:26), a need for correctives became critically urgent for return-ing to genuine godliness and meaningful human relations. In this spirit black preaching has served as a gentle yet stern conscience among Christians, remind-ing the sacred community of its past wilderness wanderings and better paths that today deserve our travel.

During those early dialogues dissecting the black preaching idiom in homilet-ics classes, precise definitions eluded easy statements and dogmatic answers (today the discussions are not so difficult, after almost three decades of dialogu-ing and regular seminary courses). Drawing from my own parish ministry back-ground of a few years at the time and several more years teaching homiletics, I shepherded the discussions along practical yet provocative and fruitful lines and suggested a wrap-up of our range of opinions by using the metaphor of three win-dows through which to view black preaching (I recall referring also to a "triumvi-rate of outlooks" and "dimensions"): genetic, generic and geometric.[4]

The genetic dimension of black preaching is built on the singular rock of race, claiming a communicative event peculiar to the African American by virtue of human inheritance and indigenous cultural background. Accordingly, this notion excludes the unlike and limits its practice to a special race-culture group at a par-ticular time in history. Quite obviously here the key word in definition is race, for it is not what you preach or how but who's doing the preaching.

Less provincial is the generic window, endorsing the witness of a pulpit spokesperson of any race who existentially identifies with and commits to the day-to-day experiences of African Americans and their longing need for libera-tion from injustice. From this existential commonality, the preacher actively and persistently seeks through ministry and the best moral means available to destroy racism while promoting spiritual salvation and human liberation through sermon content, ministerial labor and personal living. Here it's not who's preaching or how but what you preach and practice.

Definition and onus for the third outlook, geometric, rest primarily on technique and issues of style and delivery, elusive and virtually inexplicable qualities referenced finally as "soul" or "a certain something." Although certain identifiable nuances of style and delivery may be thought indigenous and unique to the nominal black pulpit, geometric foci deduce the possibility and even probability that also a person not of the African American race can do authentic black preaching simply through his or her distinct stylistic mode. So the geometric dimension considers not who's preaching or what you preach but how.

Needless to say, attempts to paint black preaching into a neat little corner confined to any one of these dimensions fell far short of even a hint of unanimous understanding during classroom dialogue, because African Americanship notwithstanding, black preaching unfolded and unraveled itself increasingly as a verb with intentions, motives and objectives as much as (and sometimes more than) a noun with personal identification. Such an understanding brought the daring notion that some African American pulpit speakers failed the litmus-test criteria (several names of preachers came to mind) while some non-African American ministers do actually make the grade.

By all standards of measurement, however, Martin Luther King Jr. passed our tests with blazing colors. And not only so, but indeed the yardstick and King became largely synonymous: his work rose to epitomize a pulpit communication that held the three window-perspectives in healthy tension, fusion and workable relation.[5] We can now look back and bear witness that neither in the second half of the twentieth century nor in the new millennium would we dare consider the preaching scene without putting King's name prominently among those atop the list. For generations and centuries to come, if the world he endeavored to warn should last, the King who came preaching will remain a consummate standard of proclaiming the good news of salvation in relevance to human needs and summoning "justice [to] roll on like a river, [and] righteousness like a never-failing stream!" (Amos 5:24)

Theological Grounding for King's Liberation Preaching

It was a hot Chicago day in more ways than one. August 31, 1966. The 90-degree windless day in the "windy city" had been preceded that year by a number of searing challenges to the King-led civil rights struggle.[6] In January, Julian Bond was elected to the Georgia legislature but denied his seat on grounds of disloyalty because he opposed the war in Vietnam. In February, King and his family moved into a Chicago tenement apartment to initiate a Chicago project. In June, James Meredith was shot on the first day of his 220-mile "March Against Fear" from Memphis, Tennessee, to Jackson, Mississippi. In July, King's designation of "Freedom Sunday" to spearhead a drive toward making Chicago an "open city" was followed immediately by a riot on the West Side and the killing of two black youths. In early August, King met an assault of stones while leading marchers through Chicago's southwest side.

Such threatening events would singe the spirit of any rights movement and allow scant mood for academic conversation with an unknown inquirer, but divine fortune took up my cause. Toward the end of the month I received a positive response to my request for formal study of the most publicized spokesperson and activist of the twentieth century. Notice arrived that Dora McDonald, personal secretary to King, had secured his permission for me to conduct a face-to-face interview with him for my Michigan State University doctoral research.

The moment arrived. I waited nervously at the announced gate of air-conditioned O'Hare Airport steaming with all manner of expectant persons—FBI agents, media journalists, bystanders, passersby, hoi polloi. Never having been introduced to Dr. King before (although he had spoken at my alma mater, Oakwood College, in Huntsville, Alabama, while I was there in 1962), I wondered how he would identify or recognize me. Had Ms. McDonald given him any special cues? I certainly remembered none shared with me. Only a flight name and number, an arrival time and assurance that King had approved the interview and was expecting me. Watching through all the rush and push and clicking of cameras surrounding this nationally and internationally acclaimed civil rights champion, I shuffled back and forth on the outer fringe, trying to figure out my best move and when to make it if I were to have any chance of contact at all. No quick solution came.

On the verge of despair, I finally heard a voice next to me inquiring just above a whisper, "Are you Mr. Warren?"

"Yes, I am."

"Stay close to me," he said. Right away I recognized the person as Andrew Young, associate to King, and I then knew that the interview plans were intact.

Not much longer than half an hour later, the three of us—King, Young and I—
were strolling down an O'Hare corridor together from where, after a brief pause
by a rent-a-car counter, Young chauffeured us to their motel residence.

All along the way and during the interview, I noticed that King held in hand a
book on the parables of Jesus that he apparently had been reading while in flight
to Chicago that day. Somehow I failed to verify the book's author, but later I
thought it might have been Joachim Jeremias. King did preach a series of sermons on the parables of Jesus Christ at Ebenezer Baptist Church during the latter
half of that year, 1966.

From the motel residence, it was off to a mass meeting and a King speech for
the evening. More than from any article or book about King, I learned from listening to him that day that here was a man who spoke and served from principles
hammered out primarily from family, the Bible and theological underpinnings.[7]
All of his responses to my questions bore indelible marks of a conscious fulfillment of his understanding of God's law of love incumbent on his life—love of
God and love of his fellow human beings—and he could do none other, come
what might. When the divine imperative knocks at your door, you either answer
in the affirmative or pretend you are not home. In his personal conviction, King
answered the call much in the spirit of the principle expressed by the religious
and prophetic interpreter Ellen G. White:

> Different periods in the history of the church have been marked by the development
> of some special truth, adapted by the necessities of God's people at that time. . . .
> The Lord gives a special truth for the people in an emergency. Who dare refuse to
> publish it? . . . They cannot remain silent, except at the peril of their souls. Christ's
> ambassadors have nothing to do with the consequences. They must perform their
> duty and leave results with God.[8]

When applied to a church movement, the divine imperative through the principle
of love might stir up sparks of denominationalism and debates on which is the
best church to fulfill the call. On the level of individual response, though, one
answers out of one's own existential situation. As for King himself, his was not a
church movement but a personal response to move the church. So doing, he led
the way by precept and example from a self-concept that he expressed thus: "As a
minister of the Gospel, I have a priestly function and a prophetic function."[9]

Teachers of King with whom I have talked (and who doubtless had occasion
during his days in their classes to discuss this dual kind of ministry) would elaborate. Walter G. Muelder, dean of the school of theology at Boston University

while King was doing doctoral studies there, saw "many uses of the pulpit" but mainly "mediator" and "prophet leader." The former, he explained, is conciliating and interceding for and among the people, whereas the latter involves leading the people into new and appropriate spheres of witness in their cultural environment. Muelder affirmed that "King is a prophet leader whereas most other ministers are mediators. Yet King is versatile and mediates too. . . . King took the gospel from behind stained-glass windows and placed it on courthouse steps."[10]

Benjamin E. Mays, former teacher of King at Morehouse College and president at the time of our conversation, avowed, "I see no conflict here [between the pulpit and social-political action]. Take the prophets of Israel: they entered the area of social justice and cried out again and again. There are no areas a minister may not enter from ethical and moral conviction and Christian insight."[11] Further discerning the dual ministry of King, S. Paul Schilling, professor of theology at Boston University, asserted that "there is the 'dogmatic' function of the pulpit, and there is the 'kerygmatic' function,"[12] the former being an effort to explore, discover and authenticate biblical truth, the latter entailing the proclamation of that truth.

Harold DeWolf, former Boston University professor and later dean of Wesley Theological Seminary in the District of Columbia, saw no need for King's ministry to remain within narrow bounds: "I see this [the sociopolitical-economic application of the gospel] as a natural and proper outgrowth of [King's] pulpit ministry. The central core of his actions is that whatever he does he always wants to make sure he is doing it as a Christian minister." DeWolf proceeded to touch on the Vietnam War issue; he said that criticisms of King's views on that war were no worry to the human rights advocate, because "he is not interested in building himself up; on the contrary, he is interested in the reconciliation of the peoples of the world."[13]

Beyond a simple statement of his "priestly function and . . . prophetic function," King treated the dual-dimensional ministry concept intellectually in his doctoral dissertation, contrasting the two renowned Christian theologians Paul Tillich and Karl Barth:

> All theology as he (Tillich) sees it, has a dual function: to state the basic truth of the Christian faith and to interpret this truth in the existing cultural situation. In other words, theology has both a "kerygmatic" and an "apologetic" function. Barth's theology performs the first of these tasks admirably. By lifting the message above any frozen formula from the past, and above the very words of Scripture, Barth has been

able to recover the great recurrent refrain that runs through all Scripture and Christian teaching. But he refuses, with the most persistent pertinacity, to undertake the apologetic task of interpreting the message in the contemporary situation. "The message must be thrown at those in the situation—thrown like a stone." Tillich is convinced, on the contrary, that it is the unavoidable duty of the theologian to interpret the message in the cultural situation of his day. Barth persists in avoiding this function.[14]

King the prophet and King the apologist presuppose a biblical grounding for being one who both speaks and acts for God in our time. Richard Lischer says it well:

> What God expects of the prophet is not flowery ritual but a kind of divine madness that shatters the complacency of religious people. . . . Once the prophet sees the true nature of the evil around him, he names it.
>
> In his prophetic ministry, King gave names to what he saw: sin, racism, genocide, doom, cowardice, expediency, idolatry of nation, militarism, religious hypocrisy. In his 1966 sermon on Julian Bond he cries, "And there is a time when prophecy must speak out. Your hands are full of blood, says Isaiah. Get out of my face. Don't pray your long prayers to me, don't come to me with your eloquent speeches. Don't talk to me about your patriotism. Your hands are full of blood. Somebody must tell the nation this."[15]

And the King who came preaching did tell the nation. By so doing and by the way the nation and the world listened, he "legitimized the hearing of African-American preachers" as never before.[16]

So it was not only happenstance that preaching by African Americans began receiving serious and sustained formal hearing in homiletic hallways only in the early or middle 1970s, as we settled to live with King's absence and realize the eternal effect of his preaching ministry on all facets of our lives. In fact the increased visibility and respectability of black preaching in America can be split into two distinct eras, B.K. and A.K.—Before King and After King.

It was remarkable that the culture that shaped King's spirituality and sense of mission comprised a people bereft of Bible reading privileges as slaves, yet amid that very enslavement spawned a preaching genre so decidedly biblical. Leaning more on experience than on explanation, black preaching functions like that of Old Testament prophets, whose preaching during preexilic times (before the synagogue) transcended the proverbial "paralysis of analysis" and settled for simply "a recital of God's dealings with his people in times past, as well as a recollection of the covenant which made Israel the chosen people."[17] In the best of black preaching, biblical content is treated as more than a historical occurrence from which to trace modern applications; it involves an "identification . . . that collapses history, replacing chronological time with a form of sacred time that allows biblical characters to become peers and contemporaries."[18]

In other words, this biblical preaching approach involves a typology of continuation rather than mere interpretation or application. Moses and the Israelites and Jesus and the apostles who fostered liberation are seen as reincarnated through the contemporary experience of liberation struggle. Preaching of this kind demythologizes irrelevant theology, and thus its emphasis on relevant experience weds itself to the earliest prophetic tradition and divorces from the medieval Christian Scholasticism that canonized speculation, analysis and logic.

This experiential emphasis or movement is acknowledged in Henry Mitchell's paralleling of black preaching with the new hermeneutic of European theologians Gerhard Ebeling, Ernst Fuchs and Martin Heidegger: "If the chief task of hermeneutics is to convey the revelation in its contemporary context" through the centrality of language, then by its contemporary and rapport-directed word-symbols black preaching becomes "more understandable to ordinary people than the abstruse German formulation of the new hermeneutics."[19] Ebeling himself declared that "theology and preaching should be free to make a translation into whatever language is required at the moment."[20] Continuing the line of thought, Carl Braaten offers a further assessment of Ebeling, Fuchs and Heidegger: "we are living in a time of counterfeit language, of inauthentic speech, when the language of the Western tradition has degenerated into the corruptible, objectifying language of a technological society that turns man into an object to be controlled and manipulated like other things."[21] While Mitchell seems to link the once newly discovered theological meanings and implications of language only to the literal word-symbols chosen by the black preacher (vernaculars, colloquialisms, codes, regionalisms and idioms), I see the so-called new hermeneutic embodying more than that. Preaching provides a linguistic occasion beyond mere word-symbol boundaries and facilitates the divine purpose's becoming event over and over again through the language understanding of preacher and hearer. Promoting cognizance alone falls far short until the preaching pierces beneath and beyond intellectual comprehension and reaches the realities of experiential life.

The fact that explanation per se failed to attain dominance in traditional and contemporary Negro preaching is not to suppose that the African American pulpit skirted scholarship. Scholarship, however, must always be servant, not master.

Scholarship waits upon preaching as its handmaid. Preaching is a vital and indispensable activity of the church, and scholarship must assist it, not dominate it. Most of the
apparatus of scholarship should never appear in the pulpit at all. Literary criticism, for
example, is a useful thing in its way, but it is not preaching, and preachers are not
called upon to amuse their hearers with tales of the hypothetical Q and the rest of the
critical alphabet. It is the church's business to preach, and it is the scholar's business
not to get in the way of this preaching, but rather to assist it as far as he can.[22]

This tension between scholarship (or "learning") and declaration of the gospel
was acknowledged by W. E. Sangster, who sounded his own note of warning to
appeal for judicious preaching:

Some men parade their scholarship. . . . Having become more interested in books
than in life, they grow less and less able to clothe their ideas for preaching in the
experiences of common men, and need to turn more and more to tombs for the stuff
of their sermons. Consequently, much of it is secondhand and has a musty smell
which normal persons dislike. . . .

    Yet scholarship is important. . . . No man who preaches can ignore an opportu-
nity for learning. . . . But no man in the pulpit ought to parade his learning. Carry it
lightly! . . . Yet be as learned as you can.[23]

The delicate balance negotiated by the best of the black pulpit attempts to assim-
ilate scholarship without becoming henpecked by it.

Born into a typical Southern Christian family of the Baptist persuasion
and nurtured in its ways of religious faith and fervor—including oftimes
what W. E. B. Du Bois called "the frenzy"—Martin King at first shied away from
the ministry because of what he considered uncomely practices and lack of learning among preachers: "I had doubts that religion was intellectually respectable. I
revolted against the emotionalism of Negro religion, the shouting and the stamping. I didn't understand it and it embarrassed me."[24] His ministerial horizon
broadened with his exposure to the likes of Benjamin E. Mays and George D.
Kelsey at Morehouse College. Perhaps thereafter he began understanding himself
as the product of a blend of Baptist experience and formal education, which gave
his preaching a rare balance that reached and touched persons from all walks and
ways of life.[25] Whether addressing the poor or the prosperous, those of low estate
or highbrows, the uninformed or the intellectual, friends or foes, against the
backdrop of the black experience in America, King preached sermons that bore
unmistakable marks of the best Christian preaching—relevance, theological consciousness and biblical grounding.

3
THE AUDIENCE
Those Who Heard &
Those Who Listened

As he was scattering his seed, some fell along the path. . . . Some fell on rocky places. . . .
Other seed fell among thorns. . . . Still other seed fell on good soil.
MATTHEW 13:3-8

*I*t was from Dexter Avenue Baptist Church in Montgomery, Alabama, a traditional yet slightly upscale Southern congregation, that Martin Luther King Jr. catapulted to a speaking circuit before audiences as varied as occasions demanded.
Surprisingly, however, and perhaps at times inadvertently, many observers and
researchers tend to lump together all his formal speeches and sermons, apparently assuming that if the speaker is a gospel minister who integrates biblical
principles into his presentation then he is preaching, irrespective of the dominant
message content or purpose of the assembly.[1] King himself would readily disagree. (Examples of a King "speech" and three King "sermons" which serve as
prototypical contrasts appear in the appendices.)

Homogenizing all audience types might be traceable to unclear distinctions
between public speaking and preaching. General considerations of speech communication tend to round up all oral address into a single corral, while preaching
(or homiletics) claims its own distinctives, mainly because of its principal body
of material, the Bible, as well as its focus on the centrality of the spiritual.

Classical codification of different audience types based on models like Aristotle's from the fourth century B.C. continues to influence our present-day understanding that audience character (or pathos) corresponds to purposes the speaker
brings to the setting rather than merely who is speaking or what professional
position he or she holds or what style of delivery is used. Classical models set

forth three kinds of audiences: deliberative, forensic and epideictic.[2] The deliberative assembly was originally a political or legislative body before which speakers orated the expedient and the inexpedient through exhortation and dissuasion with reference to the future. Lawyers and judges necessitated the forensic audience, or *gemot,* whose interests, concluded Aristotle, lay inevitably in the past: courts of law were concerned with justice and injustice by way of accusation and defense. Epideictic listeners were a levee-group type of confab gathering for the occasional address such as the after-dinner speech, the eulogy, the commencement or the holiday oration. Aristotle observed that epideictic get-togethers were concerned with the present and that its speakers sought to honor or dishonor through praise and blame.

It was left for Christianity to develop and advance what we know today as the church congregation, the *ekklesia,* before which preachers concern themselves with the meaning of life in the light of sacred history, contemporary reality and the untried future as interpreted and influenced principally by divine revelation, especially the Bible. Salvation and liberation through an experiential knowledge of God the Father, Jesus Christ and the Holy Spirit constitute the major goal of the church audience.

I submit then that King's sermons addressed principally religious worship congregations while his civil rights speeches addressed mainly mass rallies and other more sociopolitical gatherings. Below I explore two dimensions of his worship audience: the local black congregation that produced Martin King as a young committed Christian and effective preacher and the broader multiracial congregation that represented the nation and the world. Looking at qualities of these two subsets of the church as well as at their emotional and emotive proofs evoked by King places us at the heart of his speaker-listener relations and opens up a major source of the pulpit power that moved people to respond positively to his preaching.

The Traditional Black Church Audience

Carter G. Woodson, renowned historian of the black experience in America, said during the 1920s that he regarded the black pulpiteer as having "surpassed all ministers of this time in expounding the very principles of Jesus" which "the large majority of the 'chosen people of God' [U.S. non-blacks particularly] have long since repudiated."[3] Doubtless such an assertion is controversial. Yet black religion traditionally transcended limitations imposed by the trichotomy of classical Aristotelian audience types; it functioned not merely as a church audience in the restricted sense but as a body whose particular needs for civil as well as divine justice demand a broadening of definitions and of preachers' topics.

We should keep in mind, moreover, that the traditional marginality and isolation of African Americans from mainstream American society have forced their sociopoliticoreligioeconomic necessities to become relevant pulpit topics in congregations' quest for life and liberation. Consequently, issues that nonblacks ordinarily might reserve for sociopolitical, judicial or ceremonial occasions are common fare for African American church audiences. It has been their historical practice to use the church facility for various functions sacred and secular—a fact crucial for understanding the nature of the black audience and its propensity to look at all reality from a religious point of view.

By essentially concentrating deliberative, forensic and epideictic considerations within the same worship hour, the black church congregation has eluded Aristotle's compartmentalization. Thus most of King's speeches—apart from his sermons—were delivered within the walls of church sanctuaries or were sponsored by churches when a larger facility was needed. And King consistently distinguished between a sermon for worship and a speech for a civil rights mass meeting. This is not to say that his sermons did not address civil rights or his speeches contained no theological information. Purpose of the assembly dictated his form of address, and when he did preach a sermon to an African American congregation, historic racial isolationism (de jure or de facto) rendered it natural to integrate so-called nonreligious concerns into religious presentations.

The use of sermons to address "nonreligious" issues and thus to develop a conscience for everything that affects human beings would further support Woodson's pronouncement that African American preaching has been of surpassing quality. But not without challenges. One of them has been a growing mix of different outlooks and philosophies within the black church, with more educated and less educated persons being members in the same congregations. Arthur W. Smith notes that "the less educated listeners have difficulty adjusting the strange outlook of Black revolutionists to their Christian world view," whereas "the more educated Blacks find the traditional Black preachers less revealing of contemporary realities than are the Black revolutionists."[4]

Centrality. Nothing, absolutely nothing, has occupied center stage in African American life more than the Bible. How black culture came to focus on the Christian's God more seriously than most of the so-called legitimate expositors of the Bible in America is a mystery that boggles the best theological minds. Ironically, the same Bible used by the established church to justify the degradation and dehumanization of blacks, doctrinally underwriting slavery through a wild hermeneutics making Negroes victims of the "curse of Canaan" (Gen 9:25), was taken by blacks as a means to see in apparent hopelessness and sure despair a reason for keeping on, moving reconcilingly toward their oppressor and believingly toward their oppressor's God. Amazing miracle! How baffling the mystery!

Attitudes in favor of justice are decidedly changing today in the white church, but past practices to influence residuals of a racist history to follow a dualism that impedes obedience to biblical love and brother-sisterhood. For example, when faced with the challenge of accepting African Americans into their neighborhoods, churches, private clubs, professions and families (through marriage), many whites are still known, even expected, to reply, "What will my friends or neighbors say?" Such convenient and ready appeal to figures of authority to which whites have felt they must give account must have posed no small enigma to white preachers, knowing that in spite of their own appeal to biblical authority their parishioners inevitably would appeal to other sources for approval—consulting other "gods," a kind of polytheism. Here again, blacks had been inclined to accept "thus saith the Lord" as ultimate authority—more genuine monotheism. The apparent dichotomy in the white churchgoing community in America has been linked to the stiff competition from political, economic and social commitments. African Americans have been without any significant political, economic or social commitments until recently and thus have been less tied to them. If black mass culture has not had freedom internalize materialistic priorities, its Bible has met with little competition in its culture psyche. So far, African Americans as a culture seem not to have yet succumbed to serious polytheistic pressures.

Understandably then, many black Christians are shocked to discover that the majority of Christians in America do not take Christianity and the Bible quite as seriously as they do. Perhaps their traditional centrality of Bible and religious authority is another contribution black Christians are making to contemporary Christianity—a challenge to return to primitive "radical monotheism" (Richard Niebuhr) that elevates no concern of neighbor, employer, friend, whoever or whatever, above the God of gods.

Evidence suggests the Bible was the first book by which black slaves usually became literate, notwithstanding laws prohibiting their learning to read. Certainly a knowledge of Scripture was the foremost requisite for the slave preacher; "however imperfect or distorted his knowledge of the Bible might be, the fact that he was acquainted with the source of sacred knowledge, which was in a sense the exclusive possession of his white masters, gave him prestige in matters concerning the supernatural and religious among his fellow slaves."[5] Indeed, the Bible was the very first literary document so recognized and "canonized" among slaves.

The praxis endures. I never cease to marvel at the depth to which the African American lifestyle has been saturated with Scripture. While selling religious books one summer to raise funds for college tuition, I had occasion to visit home after home of blacks in rural North Carolina and was astonished at how those simple and humble folk kind enough to listen would chime in and complete whatever Bible verse my sales talk rehearsed.

More and more, however, contemporary African Americans are said to be ready to debate the question of authoritative centrality. The question arises: what shall be the contemporary guide to essential, genuine religious experience amid the emerging black consciousness? What shall consitute their *textus receptus,* their Scripture, their inspired Word? Not a few thinkers see the poetry and essays of leading African American writers (such as W. E. B. Du Bois, Langston Hughes, LeRoi Jones, Sonia Sanchez, Don Lee, James Baldwin, Nikki Giovanni, Eldridge Cleaver, Maya Angelou, Bill Cosby and a galaxy of others) as more prophetically relevant to black liberation than the writings of Moses or Amos or Judeo-Christian prophets like Matthew, Mark, Luke, John and Paul. The trend indicates a liberal hermeneutic that considers the Bible deistically indifferent to social, economic and political conditions of human beings—at least the conditions of blacks. Challengers claim that when the sermon speaks "justice" for African Americans, the word from the Lord sounds more like gibberish about pie in the sky in the sweet by and by. There appears no "balm in Gilead," only some impotent quackish elixir that promises but heals not.

I pray for a resurgence of biblical understanding and faith that sees in the incarnation of Jesus Christ a salvation act freeing humankind from spiritual slavery and all other kinds of slavery. The Bible never forsook African Americans. Rather, the Bible has simply had timid and often misinformed spokespersons in pulpits. Should blacks forsake the centrality of the Bible now, mark it! They will capsize in a swirling vortex of destiny that forfeits more, infinitely more, than could ever be thought, desired or deserved.

Dynamics. Time and time again I have heard a preacher, usually nonblack, remark after first delivering a sermon to a black congregation: "My, what an experience! These people really make you wanna preach. Their spontaneity, their warmth, their encouragement, their appreciation—they're something else!" Maybe the typical black audience does provide more audience-speaker interchange than normally experienced in other groups. The hermeneutics of African American preaching and worship liturgy would comprehend the experience as consonant with what Ernst Fuchs and Gerhard Ebeling call an "acoustical event," taking into full account that human beings by nature are linguistic beings and therefore approach existential reality most meaningfully through the impact of word occurrence: preacher and hearer (through sermon, song and prayer) experience the Word of God becoming event again and again and again.[6]

Martin Luther King Jr. recognized and used to his advantage the preacher-audience relation and made direct appeals to the power of African-Americans to continue on with life despite all adversity, for the working dynamics were infinitely more than mere transitory flights of compensation or sublimation: they brought genuine gains, thrusts into the fray of living by blacks in spite of designs for their nonbeing.

Emotion, a very important element in the preaching of King, involves facility to feel and respond to an event. Emotional freedom has been an important quality of the black congregation and as such has never been seriously debated among blacks themselves as some possible bane of the intellectual process. African Americans who frequent church pride themselves on their ready capacity for demonstrative feeling and will look askance, rather pityingly, at anyone who claims to have something superior to genuine emotion.

Black audiences desire and expect emotional proof as an energizer and expediter of behavior. In her study of black churches in Orangeburg County, South Carolina, and Boston, Massachusetts, Ruby F. Johnston equates "emotionalism" with the "psychodramatic" and "cathartic" and "compensatory" and "psychic states" answering the need for the release of submerged feelings unexpressed in sociopoliticoeconomic circumstances.[7] Her understanding of *emotionalism,* however, must be distinguished from *emotion,* for the latter is an indispensable factor in communication, "a component of a complex reaction that an individual undergoes in a given situation. This emotion is characterized by: (1) a marked change in the internal state of the organism, (2) awareness of the change, and (3) behavior resulting from an attempt to adjust to the given situation."[8] Eisenson suggests the impossibility of significant communication without emotional appeal and stresses, as do Lester Thonssen and A. Craig Baird, the dependent balance of emotion and logic: "While we believe that decisions based upon the consideration of evidence and argument are likely to be better than those made under the spell of overwhelming emotion, we also believe that emotional appeals properly may be—and inevitably are—used to reinforce evidence and argument."[9]

In his monumental work on preaching, David Buttrick pushes the case for pulpit emotion even further:

> Many preachers today are scared to death of emotion from the pulpit. Perhaps, we fear the labored histrionics, overblown affective tirades, which, in waves of emotion, swept over pews in days gone by. As a result, many preachers pursue a cult of naturalness, and come across in casual chatter as if they were slightly laid-back talk-show hosts. Of course, the understatement of feeling is itself a form of pretense. In normal conversation we are seldom so modulated. Listen to two animated baseball fans rehearsing a game, and you will overhear emotions that are varied, and often explosive. . . . Therefore, ministers who subdue emotion in the name of naturalness are emphatically unnatural; they border on the bizarre. Because we rightly fear phony affect, we may end up as casual chatterers. . . . There is a deeper issue: the gospel. The speaking of the gospel is an unnatural activity. . . . If the gospel is news of liberation, if it brings to us Jesus Christ the Savior, then it is inevitably urgent. A casual style will contradict the essential character of the gospel. Moreover, casual chatter is scarcely appropriate if, indeed, we stand in the presence of God. . . . No wonder the prophets were urgent . . . apostles strained with emotion. . . . Yes, we must reject all false, put-on emotion, but we must not turn from emotion per se.[10]

John Stapleton likewise argues for "the compelling necessity for the evocation of feelings and emotions, that is, of the passion to which the gospel lays claim" and considers emotion in preacher-pew relationship a part of "the rhetoric of the Spirit."[11] As two sharp blades are needed to scissor cloth, passion and reason are both essential to meet the worship needs of people. Perhaps no one has couched it so succinctly as George Vandeman, speaker emeritus of the *It Is Written* telecast: he says that emotion without reason is reckless; reason without emotion is restless.

Historically black preachers have been in most cases more than alert to the demands of communication psychology, taught by God through intuition and experience; for the overwhelming majority of them never crossed the threshold of a homiletics classroom or cracked open a book formally addressing the subject.[12]

More and more over the years, homileticians are recognizing a nonidentical twin of emotion: *motivation.* Like most African American preachers, Martin Luther King always knew the practical value of delivering his sermons into the beating hearts of his hearers so that they might not only appropriately feel the gospel but be moved by it as well. These two dynamics closely relate to each other, and both play parts in the communication process, but they are not to confused as the same. Emotion is a state of *feeling* (love, hate, joy, sadness and so on) while motivation is an *incentive* or *drive* that prompts action (such as security, self-preservation, sex, altruism and so forth). For example, if the goal of the preacher is that the hearer believe in God, then connecting God to the hearer's motive or drive for self-preservation (or power or pride or anything else that can be ethically channeled) is not only feasible but necessary.[13]

The goal, of course, should conceivably answer the needs of the drive. Jesus himself correlates the kingdom of God with desired fulfillments of his hearers in his famous Sermon on the Mount (Mt 5—7). Centuries later a much-respected work by George Campbell, *Philosophy of Rhetoric* (1776), argued eloquently for the preacher's appealing to the drives and desires of his congregation. Nevertheless, emotion and motivation must be clearly distinguished from emotionalism, an exploitation of emotion but not its exposition.

The emotional readiness of the black congregation complements preaching and Christian theology while keeping alive in the communion of saints a warmth of responsiveness that some nonblack churches have longed to recapture. Perhaps it will be at just this juncture that east and west, black and white, can meet and "ecumenize" the emotional and the perceptual in meaningful history and ritual. J. Archie Hargraves, formerly of the Chicago Divinity School, notes that the African American worshiper has contrasting virtues: "soul" and "cool." "He has learned to blend both, which may provide a useful example to white Christians needing to balance the passionate and the rational in their lives."[14]

Another audience dynamic of which King was aware in the black assembly is *polarization,* which allows the audience members the illusion of thinking as one instead of remaining splintered, which makes positive audience response more difficult. Any ideological tension in an audience of, say, two hundred should be addressed in a manner to influence the whole assembly to polarize itself on some common point. In this way congregation members become one; and it is easier for a preacher to influence one mind than two hundred. An instant point of commonality among African American audiences is mutual suffering under unjust laws and practices in the United States; this makes the traditional church greeting "brother" or "sister" take on a deeper yet broader aspect of relatedness when used by one black to another—they are not only brothers and sisters in Christ but brothers and sisters in oppression. As a matter of fact, the brother-sister greeting has filtered through church confines and spilled over into everyday life, providing an extension of the sense of belonging.

Probably more pronounced in the African American congregation is the dynamic of *social facilitation,* a term employed by F. H. Allport to denote the effect of the response of one or more individuals on the behavior of others in the same audience.[15] Even a few moments in a black worship service give a sense of the "reinforcement effect" of freedom of facial, bodily and verbal expressions by fellow worshipers. Through such overt responses the sermon receives fervent endorsement that is virtually impossible to escape. Long before communication psychologists were discussing audience facilitation as such, the black preaching service rarely convened without its "amen corner," composed usually of a small nucleus of worshipers sitting strategically to one side near the pulpit and providing "atmosphere" by initiating responses to the sermon. Although "amen corners" are on the wane nowadays, and some middle-class African American congregations have moved toward passivity in their liturgy and away from open response of any kind, it finds essential perpetuation through the spontaneous correspondence of sentiment by individuals within any black audience. Social facilitation among these worshipers is customarily sparked by expletive statements, laughter and shouting.

When African Americans hear Bible truth preached within their cognitive grasp and to their contemporary needs, it is virtually impossible not to make a response of assent or action. Following are typical kinds of audibles with which persons in the audience rhythmically and metrically punctuate the sermon in a mysteriously satisfying spiritual happening: "all right," "all right now," "amen," "go 'head now," "ha-ha-ha-ha," "help him, Lord," "fix it," "help yourself," "Lord, Lord," "my Lord," "preach," "say that," "tell it," "tell it like it is," "thank God," "that's right," "huh," "uh, uh, uh," "well," "yeah," "yes suh," "yes, yes," "you're preaching now," "you sho-nuf preaching now." For sure these are acknowledgments of agreement with what the preacher is saying, but they are more: they represent an urging, a coaxing, an encouragement to the preacher who is braving the devil while "speaking a word for the Lord" and doing warfare against the kingdom of evil.

More inhibited worshipers argue that such verbal responses, along with laughter and shouting, are at best conditioned reflex and at worst plays on emotion. Certainly there are members in any assembly who would thoughtlessly call out "amen" even if the preacher did nothing more than recite the alphabet: "A, B, C *(tell it!)*, D, E *(that's right)*, F, G, H *(preach)*," and so on. I remember attending a church service in Dallas, Texas, whose well-liked pastor was preparing to leave, having accepted an invitation to another charge. As the district leader was praising the work and progress of the departing parson before the congregation, the sorrowing church responded amid sobs with fervent "amens." Then when the district leader added, "And now he is leaving us," the mere momentum of a string of previous responses brought one more hearty "amen." To say the least, the speaker had to scramble about to recapture the sense of appropriate solemnity. As for the audience, sensing what it had inadvertently done, it smiled an apology.

We must be aware also, to be sure, of the pulpit charlatan who baits and angles for audience verbal confirmation and brags about being able to "kill 'em dead" or "turn it on and off" at will like a faucet. Away with such insincere nonsense, but don't throw the baby out with the bath water!

Two ineffective extremes in congregational response must be non grata and off limits to sacred worship. These two King himself depicted quite graphically:

> One is a church that burns up with emotionalism and the other is a church that freezes up with classism. The former is a church that reduces worship to entertainment, and places more emphasis on volume than on content. It confuses spirituality with muscleality. The danger of this church is that its members will end up with more religion in their hands and feet than in their hearts and souls. . . .
>
> The other type of Negro church that leaves men unfed . . . is a church that develops a class system within. It boasts of the fact that it is dignified, and most of its members are professional people. It takes pride in its exclusiveness. In this church the worship service is cold and meaningless. The music is dull and uninspiring. The sermon is little more than a nice little essay on current events. If the pastor says too much about Jesus Christ, the members begin to feel that he is taking the dignity out of the pulpit. If the choir sings a Negro spiritual, the members bow their head in shame feeling that this is an affront to their class status.[16]

The Bible says so much about joyfulness, yet some people expend so much energy to disparage it. If there is anything that can transcend the world's darkness and bring deliverance from its slough of despond, it is joy—the joy that God brings. Increasingly people are coming to desire the therapeutic treasures that can make us laugh at the worst of times. But joyfulness in reply to negative forces is only one side of the page, for it can also be a response to positive stimuli from consciousness of the nearness of God. Could anything evoke greater joy? Black worship hermeneutic brings rejoicing into church through laughter, celebration and reverent humor. We do not need clownish, mawkish grinning or irreverent entertainment. On the contrary, we claim the laughter that Reinhold Niebuhr affirmed is next to prayer and ought to be heard in the sanctuary.

Making a case for the presence and prevalence of humor in the teaching and preaching by Jesus Christ, Elton Trueblood declares:

> Perhaps our greatest failure in creating a false picture of Christ has been a failure or logic. We assume that an assertion of sadness entails a denial of humor, but there is no good reason to suppose that such is the case. There is abundant evidence to show that contrasting elements of character, far from being mutually incompatible, are often complementary. The fact that Christ laughed does not, and need not, mean that He did not also weep. . . .
>
> Possibly Christ's humor was one mark of His universality. . . . Rigidity and pretension are what ordinary humans tend to eye with suspicion. This is why the common people apparently rejoiced in Christ's humorous attacks on the Pharisaic party. "A flexible vice," said Bergson, "may not be so easy to ridicule as a rigid virtue." Aristophanes found it easy to make people laugh at the Sophists, partly because people were delighted to see something wrong in a class which claimed so much for itself. The Sophists were vain about their skill in teaching, as the Jerusalem scribes were vain about their legal learning. If it were not for the medicine of created laughter, there would be no adequate antidote to pride and vanity among men. God has created us with a self-consciousness which makes conceit possible, but He has also made us able to laugh and thus to provide a balance to our danger.[17]

Still another dynamic of the traditional African American congregation is the disposition to "get happy" or, as it is also commonly termed, "shouting." Associated with the black folk church, the worship style of shouting is not unknown in the "mixed type" church and has occurred, though rarely, in class congregations. When a person is struck with the consciousness that the preached Word has afforded a much-needed answer to the meaning of life, when the inner being is charged with an inexplicable but real force to express itself through shouting, let no one precipitately judge that experience to be a symptom of mass hysteria or emotional catharsis or psychological reinforcement. Can you justify expressing more enthusiasm and happiness over your favorite team's touchdown, home run, basket or goal than over the powerful realization that God loves you and cares?

We have looked at three dominant factors of black audience dynamic (emotion, polarization, social facilitation). We now come to a fourth: *circular response*. Call it feedback or dialogue, this dynamic describes the interacting effect on the preacher by the visible-audible pathos of his or her congregation, the consequent reinforcement or modification of the preacher's behavior, and its recapitulative influence on the congregation as experienced through smiles, frowns, nods, movements and oral expressions. Being alert to these signals, the preacher can adapt the sermon so that the congregation continues to a crescendo of heightened reverence, adoration and praise. I sometimes refer to this phenomenon as the "antiphonal sermon," because it actually involves two preachers-the person in the pulpit and the people in the pews, both alternately communicating the sermon in unrehearsed dialogue.

King and General Church Audiences

When I asked Dr. King to enumerate characteristics of an excellent and highly effective sermon, his answer spoke volumes about his respect for and perception of preacher-audience relations. "A good, solid sermon has to have three elements which I call 'three p's': it proves an appeal to the intellect, it paints an appeal to the imagination, and it persuades an appeal to the heart."[18] As his answer reveals, he gave due consideration to audience-response values of all his assemblies; and no doubt this is what Ernest Dunbar had in mind when he said King "combines intellect with intensity" and that "his sermons have an electric effect on the congregation."[19] Where logical proof informs (another important element in King's preaching which we shall consider later), emotional proof prompts the listener to *conform,* giving acceptance and action to the preacher's information. "A purely intellectual argument," maintains Robert T. Oliver, "may make the audience say, 'yes, that is true'; but the addition of an emotional plea is needed to make the listeners add, 'And let's do something about it'!"[20]

Earlier "emotion" and "motivation" were distinguished by describing the former as including such emotional states as love, hatred. envy, jealousy, fear and disgust and the latter denoting drives or desires that may give rise to emotions. Arthur E. Phillips was perhaps the first to use the expression "impelling motives" for drives and to provide us with a classification that has served as a basis for subsequent groupings: (1) self-preservation, (2) property, (3) power, (4) reputation, (5) affections, (6) sentiments and (7) tastes.[21] Oliver summarizes a later classification of emotional drives by Frederic Wickert: (1) freedom for themselves (from restraints, routine duties and external domination), (2) helpfulness (working for the welfare of others), (3) new experience (finding novelty and variety in life), (4) power and influence (controlling others), (5) recognition (social acceptance, admiration, fame), (6) response (enjoying friendship, fellowship and intimate personal contacts), (7) security and stability (doing what is sage and conservative), (8) submission (following the crowd), (9) workmanship (doing things well and making them right the first time).[22] General practice, at least up to the King era, seems to bear out a 1939 study by Irving J. Lee finding that the trend in the twentieth century is to obliterate the distinction between "emotion" and "motivation."[23] Nevertheless, practical reality in public address recognizes more and more the distinction and find there a valuable and enduring purpose.

Reviewing these lists of basic emotions and drives, one becomes readily aware that some of them can be selfish and questionable by Christian criteria, and this inevitably raises questions of ethics in appealing to human states and urges. The minister of the gospel of Jesus Christ would be expected to appeal only to those that are consonant with or would ultimately fulfill the high standards and purposes of the Christian pulpit. John A. Broadus expresses the case very directly though briefly: "A preacher must of course appeal to none but worthy motives that are harmonious with Christian moral ideals."[24]

A study of King's sermons reveals that his dominant object was to persuade human beings to live together as brothers and sisters and thereby fulfill a prerequisite to experiencing effectually the spiritual relationship with God as their Father and establishing the kingdom of God both on earth and in human hearts. To reach this objective, what emotions or impelling motives did King elicit? Although several of the motives and drives listed by Phillips and Wickert had a place in King's preaching, he appealed mainly to the three principal emotions mentioned by Broadus: happiness, holiness, love.[25]

When King connects his call to the motive of "self-preservation," this impelling motive should be understood in the general context of happiness (accomplishing genuine personal ends and ambitions), of love (developing a wholesome concern for one's fellow humans) and of holiness (achieving an effectual relationship to God). His appeals generally can be said to stem from a high level of motives. The following sermon excerpts reveal patterns of basic drives to which the preaching of King appealed.

1. *Freedom*

Under Communism man has no inalienable rights. His only rights are those derived from and conferred by the state. Under such a system the fountain of freedom runs dry. Man's liberties of press and assembly, his freedom to vote, his freedom to listen to what news he likes or to choose his books to read are all restricted. Art, religion, education, music and science are all under the gripping yoke of governmental control. Man has to be a dutiful servant to the omnipotent state.

Now there can be no doubt that all of this is contrary not only to the Christian doctrine of God, but also to the Christian estimate of man. Christianity as its best has always insisted that man is an end because he is a child of God, and because he is made in God's image. Man is more than a producing animal guided by economic forces; he is a being of spirit. He is crowned with glory and honor, endowed with the gift of freedom. The ultimate weakness of Communism is that it robs man of that quality which makes him man. Man, says Paul Tillich, is man because he is free. ("How Should a Christian View Communism?")

2. *Response*

The greatest challenge facing the church today is to keep the bread fresh (the bread of faith, hope, love, social justice, and peace) and remain a Friend to men at midnight. ("A Knock at Midnight")

3. *Helpfulness and affections*

True altruism is more than the capacity to pity; it is the capacity to sympathize. Pity may represent little more than the impersonal concern which prompts the mailing of a check, but true sympathy is the personal concern which demands the giving of one's soul. Pity may arise from interest in an abstraction called humanity, but sympathy grows out of a concern for a particular needy human being who lies at life's roadside. Sympathy is fellow feeling for the person in need—his pain, agony, and burdens. Our missionary efforts fail when they are based on pity, rather than true compassion. Instead of seeking to do something with the African and Asian peoples, we have too often sought only to do something for them. An expression of pity, devoid of genuine sympathy, leads to a new form of paternalism which no self-respecting person can accept. ("On Being a Good Neighbor")

4. *Power and influence*

Ever since that time [c. fourth century A.D., when the Christian church began compromising with Rome], the church has been like a weak and ineffectual trumpet making uncertain sounds, rather than a strong trumpet sounding a clarion call for truth and righteousness. If the church of Jesus Christ is to regain its power, and its message its authentic ring, it must go out with a new determination not to conform to this world. ("Transformed Nonconformist")

5. *Reputation*

America is a great nation—but. Behind that but stands two hundred and forty years of chattel slavery. Behind that but stands twenty million Negro men and women being deprived of life, liberty and the pursuit of happiness. Behind that but stands a practical materialism that is often more interested in things than values. So almost every affirmation of greatness is followed not by a period symbolizing completeness, but by a comma punctuating it into nagging partialness. ("The Three Dimensions of a Complete Life")

6. *Security and stability*

Once a helpless child, the Negro has now grown politically, culturally, and economically. Many white men fear retaliation. The Negro must show them that they have nothing to fear, for the Negro forgives and is willing to forget the past. The Negro must convince the white man that he seeks justice for both himself and the white man. A mass movement exercising love and nonviolence and demonstrating power under discipline should convince the white community that were such a movement to attain strength its power would be used creatively and not vengefully. ("Antidotes for Fear")

7. *New experience*

For years we have genuflected before the god of science, only to find that it has given us the atomic bomb, producing fears and anxieties that science can never mitigate. We have worshipped the god of pleasure only to find that thrills play out and sensations are short-lived. We have bowed before the god of money only to find that there are things that money can't buy—love and friendship—and that in a world of possible depressions, stock market crashes, and bad business investments, money is a rather uncertain deity. No, these transitory gods are not able to save us or bring happiness to the human heart. Only God is able. It is faith in Him that we must rediscover in this modern world. ("Our God Is Able")

8. *Self-preservation*

We must decide whether we will allow the winds to overwhelm us or whether we will journey across life's mighty Atlantic with our inner spiritual engines equipped to go on in spite of the winds. This refusal to be stopped, this "courage to be," this determination to go on living "in spite of," is the God in man. He who has made this discovery knows that no burden can overwhelm him and no wind of adversity can blow his hope away. He can stand anything that can happen to him. ("Shattered Dreams")

9. *Property*

Only an irrelevant religion fails to be concerned about man's economic well-being. Religion at its best realizes that the soul is crushed as long as the body is tortured with hunger pangs and harrowed with the need for shelter. Jesus realized that we need food, clothing, shelter, and economic security. He said in clear and concise terms: "Your Father knoweth what things ye have need of." ("The Man Who Was a Fool")

10. *Workmanship*

All labor that uplifts humanity has dignity and significance. It should be carried out with painstaking excellence. If a man discovers that he is called to be a street sweeper, he should seek to sweep streets like Michelangelo painted pictures, like Beethoven composed music, and like Shakespeare wrote poetry. He should sweep streets so well that all the host of heaven and earth will have to pause and say "here lived a great street sweeper who swept his job well." ("Three Dimensions of a Complete Life")

These, then, are some of the salient motives to which King's sermons directed their appeal within the larger framework of holiness, happiness and love. Another emotion King did not ignore is anger, particularly with African American hearers. Although he rarely made a direct, overt appeal to this emotion, his ongoing program of nonviolent demonstrations and marches furnished an avenue for psychological release of pent-up hostilities due to racial injustices.

Also worth noting is his use of such psychological elements as identification, suggestion and attention. On several occasions when I heard him preach, he established common ground with the listeners. For example, at the Central Methodist Church in Detroit, when King stood to preach he identified with the congregation by unaffectedly expressing commendation of its revered former pastor, the Rev. Henry Hitt Crane. In all of his sermons he made plenteous use of the collective pronouns *we, ours* and *us*. When calling his hearers to turn from mindless conformity, he tactfully declared,

Even we preachers have often joined the enticing cult of conformity. We, too, have often yielded to the success symbols of the world, feeling that the size of our ministry must be measured by the size of our automobiles. So often we turn into showmen, distorting the real meaning of the gospel, in an attempt to appeal to the whims and caprices of the crowd. We preach soothing sermons that bypass the weightier matters of Christianity. We dare not say anything in our sermons that will question the respectable views of the comfortable members of our congregations. If you want to get ahead in ministry, conform! Stay within the secure walls of the Sanctuary. ("Transformed Nonconformist")

America's industrial progress is "our" nation's progress ("Transformed Nonconformist), and Jesus' imperative to love challenges "us" with a new urgency ("Loving Your Enemies").

One observer found King's image itself suggestive, especially to African Americans:

Every Negro woman who sees Martin Luther King on a platform, looking, for all his youthfulness and unimpressive stature, so dignified and in command of himself, so well-dressed and graceful, feels that there, somehow, is a son; and more than one Negro, plus some assorted psychiatrists, have said that, for the very young Negro whose own father had probably been powerless or apathetic before the white world, this man who could successfully challenge the white world would become the model, the image of the father-that-might-have-been. In this model, too, there would, presumably, be another element. The young Negro is bound to feel, in some reach of his being, that success in the white world is the real success; and Martin Luther King had not only challenged the white world, he had made a large segment of the white world like it. He was respected by the far-off white world, he was admired, he was an idol, he was on the cover of *Time*.

It was a new kind of success. It combined the best of Joe Louis and Ralph Bunch. It was mass and elite in one package. It was power, black power, but black power revered by the white power that it confounded. So the image was a double one, not only offering a model of aggressive assertion, but a model for public acceptance. The image was, in fact, the answer to the question which Izell Blair had put to himself: "Well, what am I?" It was the image that gave identity. No longer, to use Izell Blair's words again, need you "feel you're rubbed out, as if you never existed." The image gave you a place, a profile, program, and a promise.

But there is one more element in the image which Martin Luther King afforded the young. It converted the inferior outsider—the Negro stranded in the shallows beyond the mainstream of American life—into the superior insider; for the Negro, by appealing to the fundamental premises of American society, to the Declaration of Independence and the subsequent muniments, puts the white community in the position of the betrayers of the dream. The Negro becomes the defender of the faith for the salvation of all. He not only affirms his right to join society; he affirms his mission to redeem society by affirming the premises of society. He is not only an "old American" in the cultural sense; he becomes, as Stokely Carmichael has said of Negroes, "more American than the Americans." He also becomes, if he chooses

to play it that way, more Christian than the Christians, and there are enough pro-
fessing white Christians left in the country to make this line embarrassing—especially in Mississippi, which is a praying country. So, in either social or theological
terms, the Negro can enjoy the superiority of being "the conscience of the community and [can] act out for it the work the community is reluctant to do."[26]

In the King sermons themselves, suggestion is usually direct and positive,
although indirect and negative suggestion may also be made through emotional
proof. The advantage of his using direct over indirect suggestion, however, is that
his audiences are customarily "selected" (that is, a group assembled with a common interest—racial segregation versus racial integration) and therefore have a
relatively high degree of polarization or receptivity.

Scholar H. L. Hollingworth classifies audiences based on their polarization
degree: (1) the Pedestrian Audience (casual and accidental listeners, as on a street
corner), (2) the Passive Audience (listeners assembled for a debate or another performance that demands little or no response to the speakers), (3) the Selected
Audience (listeners assembled for a common core of interest, such as a church or
a club, although they may possess differing points of view), (4) the Concerted
Audience (hearers bent on accomplishing the same end—for example, raising
money for a charitable organization or for purchasing a gift) and (5) the Organized Audience (listeners congregated for a specific project and already loyally
attached to the leader and persuaded of his or her authority).[27] Robert T. Oliver
adds another type of group to this continuum of polarization: the Discussion
Audience, composed of speakers as well as listeners, in a forum, round table or
parliamentary session; he places this group between numbers 2 and 3 of Hollingworth's original list.[28]

Oliver posits that direct suggestion is most effective when the audience is
polarized, when it feels itself intellectually inferior to the speaker and is conscious of the speaker's high prestige, when it consists mostly of youthful auditors, and when it is required to respond with some immediate, defined form of
action.

Hollingworth maintains that getting the attention of an audience is not ordinarily required when a speaker is to address a "Selected" congregation, the type
of audience to which King generally preached. In the following illustration of
Hollingworth's construct, under each kind of audience is shown at which point of
motivation the speaker's task commonly begins and what processes still must be
accomplished for the typical tasks to be carried to completion:[29]

Pedestrian Audience	Passive Audience	Selected Audience	Concerted Audience	Organized Audience
Attention	....	....	....	....
Interest	Interest	....	....	....
Impression	Impression	Impression	....	....
Conviction	Conviction	Conviction	Conviction	....
Direction	Direction	Direction	Direction	Direction

In King's typical preaching situation, beginning with his national prominence (namely, that of a preacher whose theme was predictably and inevitably human rights), the "Selected" nature of his audience rendered it unnecessary for him to "get" attention: his national and international prominence as the leading spiritual spokesman regarding America's number-one problem meant that his very presence arrested attention. There were no conspicuous attention-getting devices in his pulpit setting. And public announcements and placards that sponsoring organizations used to advertise his addresses were usually unadorned, simply indicating his name and the occasion, place and time of his preaching appointment.

Perhaps no other name of a contemporary clergyman commanded more public attention than that of Martin Luther King Jr. As a matter of fact, King Sr. informed me that absolutely no advertising was done for the first Sunday (and sometimes third Sunday) when the younger King occupied the pulpit at Ebenezer. The elder King added that these dates were generally known to "belong" to Dr. King and that larger crowds filled the church on those Sundays.[30]

His sermons themselves contained elements that draw attention such as *concreteness* (through illustrations, stories, examples), *conflict* (the war between segregationists and integrationists), the *familiar-unusual* combination (although King preached a gospel whose essentials were very familiar to both fundamentalists and liberals, he combined it with unusually practical applications), *humor* (employed effectively though sparingly) and the *vital* (his controlling theme, Christian brother-sisterhood, is presented as a matter no human being can escape confronting; it is personal and important for everyone).

The "vital" element can be seen also in a headline over an Associated Press article: "Hurry! Rev. King Tells Northern Cities: Work Fast to Prevent Violence, He Says" (*News-Palladium*, Benton Harbor, Michigan, March 19, 1966). The exclamatory warning was meant to influence city leaders to act quickly to alleviate the economic and social conditions prevalent in black ghettos to forestall an outbreak of violence and rioting akin to the one that wreaked havoc in the Watts area of Los Angeles (*Time,* August 20, 1965, pp. 11-19).

Four months after King's warning, racial violence and rioting did erupt in Chicago, New York, Omaha, Cleveland, Lansing (Michigan), Milwaukee, Baltimore, Waukegan (Illinois), Columbus and Benton Harbor. Clearly King's counsel, in or out of the pulpit, was vitally and strikingly relevant to his contemporary cultural scene, like that of the Old Testament prophet. Indeed his preachments are still practical and applicable and worthy to be heeded decades later.

Many of King's sermon titles served well to rivet attention: "A Tough Mind and a Tender Heart," "Transformed Nonconformist," "A Knock at Midnight," "The Man Who Was a Fool," "The Death of Evil upon the Seashore," "Shattered Dreams," "The Answer to a Perplexing Question," "Paul's Letter to American Christians." Note that though these titles should successfully create interest and capture attention, they avoid the sensational and the gimmicky.

Lloyd O. Lewis, King's first public speaking teacher at Morehouse College, reports that the class's basic textbook was by Alan Monroe. In his teaching he "stressed no one element of public address more than another but rather a combination of elements" based mainly on "the building up of a speech according to the aims of the audience, that is, what the speaker wants the audience to do."[31] Interestingly, another ingredient of King's emotional proof corresponds with Monroe's "motivated sequence," a design for stimulating a sense of need and showing how it can be satisfied.[32] For example, "Our God Is Able" includes the five sequential steps in the following manner:

1. *Attention*

> The center of the Christian faith, the conviction that God is a Power able to do exceedingly abundant things in nature and history, is being seriously threatened by those who would convince us that only man is able.

2. *Need*

> The fact that man has been plagued by such evils as personal trials [diseases and the like], colonialism, racial segregation, and nuclear weapons capable of destroying the world, points to his need for a power able both to cure his personal and social ills and also to sustain the physical universe.

3. *Satisfaction*

> God is able. Christianity must affirm that He is Power.

4. *Visualization*

For years we have genuflected before the god of science only to receive the atomic bomb. We have done likewise with the god of pleasure, the god of money only to discover that thrills and sensations are short-lived and that love and happiness are not guaranteed by materialism. A rediscovered faith in God is the answer.

5. *Action*

Yes, God is able. . . . Go out this morning, and let this affirmation be our ringing cry. It will give us courage to face the uncertainties of the future. . . . This is our hope for becoming better men. This is our mandate for seeking to make a better world.

There was never a time in King's professional life that he was not pastoring a church—and that he pastored only African American congregations, although they shared him with other audiences. Most if not all of his sermons were first delivered to his own parishioners before he adapted them to meet the needs of a broader audience across the nation and around the world.

Such an ethical appeal to a wide range of audiences for godly and humanitarian purposes need not remain as a mere subject of study of a past great preacher; it can serve as a model in all times and climes for persons who would proclaim salvation's good news. For sure, some may give only a casual and cavalier ear to the gospel seed as wayside, stony-ground and thorny-path hearers. Nevertheless, the King preaching model encourages message bearers to take heart, because relevant proclamation that keeps in touch with practical issues of people's lives will make a difference locally, nationally and internationally by opening hearts to become good soil to the saving Word.

4

THE CONTENT
OF THE KING SERMONS,
PART ONE

Reflected in the Person

He taught as one who had authority.
MATTHEW 7:29

*T*he words of the second century B.C. Roman orator Cicero may seem obvious but remain relevant: a speaker "ought first to find out what he should say."[1] More recently the content of a message has been described as the "development of a subject—after it has been selected, narrowed, analyzed, and organized."[2]

Two of the most influential works on preaching during the mid-twentieth century, when Martin Luther King Jr. received his training, were by T. Harwood Pattison and John A. Broadus, who challenged preachers with the responsibility of delivering solid content. The former declared that "in every sermon there should be an element of argument . . . and . . . reason. The power of clear statement is the great power in the pulpit as at the bar."[3] And according to Broadus, "of basic importance in preaching is the ability to lay hold of appropriate materials by use of which the subject may be amplified into a full sermon,—the power to discern new relations of ideas and to join them together in effective discourse."[4] Such an emphasis on what we commonly call "having something to say" is reminiscent of the words of Walter G. Muelder, then dean of the School of Theology at Boston University: "Dr. King possesses not only analytical but also constructive [creative] power. You might call it 'constructive conceptualization.' His artistic homiletical power matches his analytical power, an efficiency and combination very rare in human beings indeed."[5]

Let us review the basic content ingredients of King's preaching as reflected in his *person* (ethos). Subsequent chapters will take up components of his sermon *materials* themselves.

Ethos (Ethical Substance)

Usually a discussion of sermon content focuses primarily on biblical and other supporting information within the discourse itself. While that is certainly important and will be examined later, I propose that *the preacher as person* constitutes the strongest content of any preaching situation. Today this idea goes virtually unchallenged, given the bad press occasioned by televangelists and other pulpiteers whose lifestyles blatantly contradict the gospel they so boldly claim to espouse. Unless the preacher walks the walk, attempting to talk the talk loses effectiveness, and the sermon remains little more than sounding brass and tinkling cymbal. The old adage is apropos: "What you do speaks so loudly I cannot hear what you say."

King himself saw the inescapable interrelation between substance and person and expressed it eloquently on August 28, 1963, in his immemorial March on Washington speech: he had a dream that someday his four little children would be "judged not by the color of their skin but by the content of their character." The perception of character played a particularly important role in King's preaching because he inevitably registered himself in the public eye as a minister of the gospel of Jesus Christ, which generated high expectations and even credibility beyond that afforded to social activists, politicians or community motivators. African Americans give special honor to clergy, for the church has been for decades the center of their life socially and politically as well as religiously. One writer has observed that the black Protestant minister plays most of the leadership roles among African Americans.[6] It was natural, then, that King, as a spokesperson from the church, would have high credibility. And King was a minister in the largest Negro religious denomination in the United States, the National Baptist Convention, USA, which had a membership at that time of over five million persons.[7] This in itself gave abundant opportunity for one who would lead.

Time noted that beyond King's position as a pastor, "he has an indescribable capacity for empathy that is the touchstone of leadership."[8] Measuring favorably by Quintilian's "good man" concept, King himself esteemed the ethical dimension of preaching: "One must not only preach a sermon with his voice, he must preach it with his life." Ernest Dunbar, senior editor of *Look,* added, "King does just that."[9]

A sincere man, King was not a "zeal without knowledge" fanatic; he suffered no illusions about the constant dangers threatening his life but recognized full well that to which he committed himself. Victim of beatings, jailings (approximately twenty times), stabbings, bombings (of his home) and various other kinds of attacks, he consistently took the high road and "turned the other cheek." He often said that every person should have something for which he or she would die, otherwise he or she has nothing worthy for which to live. His willingness to suffer violence, even martyrdom, came from a thoroughgoing religious conviction rooted in the Christian tradition. His sermon "Paul's Letter to American Christians" states convincingly the ground of such a conviction:

> Do not despair if you are condemned and persecuted for righteousness' sake. When you testify for truth and justice, you are liable to scorn. Often you will be called a Communist merely because you believe in the brotherhood of man. Sometimes you may be put in jail. . . . It may mean losing a job or social standing with your group. Even if physical death is the price that some must pay to free their children from psychological death, then nothing could be more Christian. Do not worry about persecution, American Christians; you must accept this when you stand up for a great principle. . . . "Blessed are ye, when men shall revile you, and persecute you, and shall say all manner of evil against you falsely, for my sake. Rejoice, and be exceeding glad, for great is your reward in heaven: for so persecuted they the prophets which were before you."

King was never known to compromise his convictions. At a Southern Christian Leadership Conference (SCLC) convention in Birmingham, Alabama, a visibly disturbed white youth leaped onto the speaker's rostrum and began pummeling King; but King made no effort to defend himself. He even refused to file charges against the youth, who admitted he made the attack because of the preacher's integrationist views. Clearly King was a man of love. He was also a man of humility. Again, Dunbar crystallizes the opinion of many: "Adulation might make some men pompous, but Martin Luther King remains a warm, friendly, human being."[10]

Another element of King's ethos was competence. He was perceived as possessing essential qualifications and abilities to deliver what his preaching promised and attain what was expected of him. That he reached a high level of competence is attested by a statement from a leading theologian who had been his teacher, L. Harold DeWolf: "Martin Luther King Jr. is an able religious thinker, as well as a man of action."[11] As a scholar, the young minister from Atlanta appealed also to both African Americans and Caucasians of the middle and upper classes. The fact that he was not a "jack-leg" preacher but one who had undergone academic study (B.D. [now M.Div.] and Ph.D. degrees) tended to enhance people's confidence in King's competence to carry out the responsibilities and expectations of the ministerial office. His competence resulted from no happenstance. Even as a youth, he wanted to possess rather than merely simulate proficiency; and while his Christian parents taught him to believe that the "church was the path to morality and immortality," he was also taught that "education was . . . the path to competence."[12]

A further element of King's ethos was his reputation as a persuasive preacher. Introductions of this capable speaker consistently called attention to certain indicators of his reputation for competence: (1) his being chosen Man of the Year by *Time* (January 3, 1964), (2) his Nobel Peace Prize (1964) and (3) his being awarded over fifty honorary degrees. Titles of magazine articles on King suggest his high leadership ability: "Render Unto King" (*Time*, March 25, 1966), "King Acts for Peace" (*Christian Century*, September 29, 1965), "Big Man Is Martin Luther King" (*Newsweek*, July 29, 1963), "Martin Luther King Jr., Apostle of Crisis" (*Saturday Evening Post*, June 15, 1963), "Nobleman King" (*Newsweek*, October 26, 1964), "Top Man of the Negro Revolution" (*U.S. News and World Report*, June 19, 1963), "Tribute to Martin Luther King Jr." (*Ebony*, December 1964), "Long Live the King" (*Newsweek*, April 2. 1956), "Dr. King, Symbol of the Segregation Struggle" (*New York Times Magazine*, January 22, 1961).

The fifth dimension of ethos is goodwill, a personal quality of friendliness, congeniality, likableness, rapport, concern, interest, a desire to reach out and help others. Though in some ways the King mystique was almost inexplicable, he remained a clear, living, practical helping hand for humanity albeit a disturbing reality to some. "By deed and by preachment," a *Time* writer lauded, "he has stirred in his people a Christian forbearance that nourishes hope and smothers injustice."[13]

His close friend and fellow minister Ralph D. Abernathy is quoted as saying: "He is a humble man, down to earth, honest. He has proved his commitment to Judaeo-Christian ideals. He seeks to save the nation and its soul, not just the Negro." I agree with one of King's early biographers, Lerone Bennett, that King was a great preacher not just because of his oral sermonic material or his technique but because of his greatness as a man.

Challenges to King's Ethos

There was, however, another side of the coin. As the leading spokesman of a cause that challenged shortcomings of the world's leading established socioeconomic-political system, the United States of America, King was not without critics. A number of the most persistent criticisms leveled at the man will be examined here, since they have a bearing on his ethos. My purpose here is not to deprecate or tear down the charges but rather to acknowledge their existence in all fairness and offer replies. Perhaps the most serious and widely publicized charges before his assassination were that (1) King's civil rights activities were communist inspired and controlled, (2) he was a prevaricator, (3) his doctrine of nonviolence offended other African Americans, (4) his socioeconomic-political activities were a misuse of the pulpit and (5) his employment of nonbiblical sources to support Bible concepts was unchristian. Posthumous charges include (6) plagiarism and (7) adultery.

Charged with having been both initiated and controlled by adherents to *communism,* the civil rights movement led by King was defended by its popular spokesperson. The charge was made, for example, in the spring of 1960 by former U.S. president Harry S. Truman; King answered, in part:

> For many years I have admired you. Like many other Negroes I have deeply appreciated your civil rights record. But I must confess that some of your recent statements have completely baffled me, and served as an affront and disappointment to millions of Negroes of America. Your statement that appeared in the morning paper affirming that the "sit-ins" were Communist inspired is an unfortunate misrepresentation of facts. The more you talk about the sit-ins the more you reveal a limited grasp and an abysmal lack of understanding of what is taking place. It is a sad day for our country when men come to feel that oppressed people cannot desire freedom and human dignity unless they are motivated by Communism. Of course, we in the South constantly hear these McCarthy-like accusations and pay little attention to them; but when the accusations come from a man who was once chosen by the American people to serve as the chief custodian of the nation's destiny then they rise to shocking and dangerous proportions. We are sorry that you have not been able to project yourself in our place long enough to understand the inner longing for freedom and self respect that motivate our action. We also regret that you have not been able to see that the present movement on the part of the students is not for themselves alone, but a struggle that will help save the soul of America. As long as segregation exists, whether at lunch counters or in public schools, America is in danger of not only losing her prestige as a world leader, but also of losing her soul.

I have worked very closely with the students in this struggle and the one thing I am convinced of is that no outside agency (Communist or otherwise) initiated this movement, and to my knowledge no Communist force has come in since it started, or will dominate it in the future. The fact that this is a spiritual movement rooted in the deepest tradition of nonviolence is enough to refute the argument that this movement was inspired by Communism which has a materialistic and anti-spiritualistic world view. No, the sit-ins were not inspired by Communism. They were inspired by the passionate yearning and the timeless longing for freedom and human dignity on the part of a people who have for years been trampled over by the iron feet of oppression. They grew out of the accumulated indignities of days gone by, and the boundless aspirations of generations yet unborn. We are very sorry that you have missed this point, and that you have misled either by your analysis of the struggle or by misinformation that has come to you.

If you feel that this movement is Communist inspired we feel that you should give the public some proof of such a strong indictment. If you cannot render such proof we feel that you owe the nation and the Negro people a public apology. Believing in your sense of good will and humanitarian concern, we are confident that you would want to make such an apology.[14]

On another occasion, after delivering an address at the Ford Hall Forum in Boston, King entertained questions from the audience; there, according to DeWolf, a listener inquired regarding alleged connections between the Communist Party and the civil rights protest movement. King responded that "the Negroes were glad for help from any quarter, but as far as cooperation was concerned, there were certain difficulties."[15] Then he proceeded to delineate the difficulties in the following manner:

1. The civil rights cause is based on belief in God, while communism is based on an atheistic philosophy rejecting religion.

2. The civil rights protest is based on nonviolent methods, seeking always reconciliation of conflicting forces in the community, whereas the communists seek to sharpen the class struggle and to bring it into open conflict and so precipitate a violent revolution.

3. The civil rights movement (as led by King) is pervaded by a spirit of love, whereas the communist cause is pervaded by a spirit of anger and deepening hatred toward the people regarded as unjust.

The two movements, then, according to King, were founded on opposite philosophies, opposite objectives and an opposite spirit.

His most complete and formal argument against communism is found in his sermon "How Should a Christian View Communism?" Here he directs four main points against the Marxist ideology: it is founded on (1) an ethical relativism, (2) a metaphysical materialism, (3) a crippling totalitarianism and (4) a withdrawal of fundamental freedom. King affirmed that neither he or any other Christian could accept such an ideology.[16]

Charges of being a *prevaricator* came to a head following several murders of both African American and Caucasian civil rights workers in the South; since the murderers were not arrested or convicted, King remarked that he questioned the FBI's effectiveness in solving racial matters in Southern communities. On November 18, 1964, J. Edgar Hoover, director of the Federal Bureau of Investigation, commented acidly on King's criticism and said that he considered him "to be the most notorious liar in the country."[17]

Vacationing in the Bahamas and preparing his Nobel Peace Prize acceptance speech at the time, King made the following reply to Hoover's accusation: "I cannot conceive of Mr. Hoover making a statement like this without [his] being under extreme pressure. He has apparently faltered under the awesome burdens, complexities, and responsibilities of his office. Therefore, I cannot engage in a public debate with him. I have nothing but sympathy for this man who has served his country so well."[18]

Newsweek noted that general public "puzzlement persisted over Hoover's decision to speak out when he did, and it posed the query about the seventy-year-old Hoover's readiness for retirement." The article then quoted an editorial of *The New York Herald Tribune* ("The Strange World of J. Edgar Hoover") as saying that the FBI director had shown "a cavalier recklessness with fact and fancy" and a *New York Times* editorial that "it would be wise to let the mandatory provisions of the Federal retirement law take effect on Mr. Hoover's 70th birthday."[19]

Consonant with his ethical spirit of seeking the high ground, in December 1964 King initiated a move toward reconciliation with Hoover and met with him in Washington. (David Garrow credits minister A. Carey and attorney N. Katzenbach for arranging the meeting.) No formal apology was reported; but King described the meeting as a "quite amicable discussion."[20]

I would surmise that King felt not merely taunted but wounded by the criticism that his doctrine of love and nonviolence was an affront to African Americans. True, the black race has been an object of racial hatred and humiliation in America, even since the Emancipation Proclamation. And the normal reaction to such treatment is a desire to retaliate. Given these realities, King's teachings vied for African Americans' allegiance against the teachings of the Black Muslims, led by Elijah Muhammad, and other militant groups like the SNCC and CORE, when the former was led by James Forman and Stokely Carmichael and the latter by Floyd McKissick and James Farmer.

The Muslim doctrine, simply stated, elevated separatism into a religious ethic and proclaimed that African Americans should abandon all notions of racial integration (since the white American majority would never give them a fair deal). Blacks had to face the fact that whites were *incapable* of treating them fairly, because the white man was a devil doomed to destruction.[21] Elijah Muhammad is quoted by Charles Silberman as proclaiming, "The white devil's day is over. He was given six thousand years to rule. His time was up in 1917. These are his years of grace—seventy of them. He's already used up most of those years trapping and murdering the black nations by the hundreds of thousands. Now he's worried, worried about the black man getting his revenge."[22]

Muhammad went on to assert that Allah (God) had postponed the battle of Armageddon to give brainwashed African Americans the opportunity to separate themselves, but "the time of God's coming is upon us." If white America did not repent and grant Muslim demands for separate geographical territory, Muhammad predicted that "all of you, . . . your government, and your entire race will be destroyed and removed from this earth by Almighty God. And those black men who are still trying to integrate will inevitably be destroyed along with the whites; only the faithful will be saved."

The Black Muslims gained an immense audience because they articulated the innermost feelings of anger, hatred and revenge shared by most African Americans—feelings that are seldom voiced publicly.

The specific criticism aimed at Martin Luther King Jr. was that his movement asked not only that African Americans exercise *nonviolence* in the face of injustice but that they actually *love* the oppressor. According to Silberman, some psychologists say few persons can fulfill such a call. And such a response to oppression is tantamount to surrender.

King, whose approach was rooted in the teachings of Jesus Christ (a personality deeply rooted in the culture psyche of black America) and Gandhi, preached with boldness the doctrine of "nonviolence" and "love" yet maintained that his approach involved neither surrender nor passivity. "I believe," he affirmed, "in a militant, nonviolent approach in which the individual stands up against an unjust system, using sit-ins, legal actions, boycotts, votes and everything else—except violence or hate."[23] King's philosophy of nonviolent direct action included five basic tenets:

1. Nonviolence is not a method for cowards; it does resist, creatively so.

2. Nonviolence does not seek to defeat or humiliate the opponent but to win his or her friendship and understanding. The nonviolent resister realizes that non-cooperation with injustice is not an end in itself but a means by which to awaken in the opponent a sense of moral shame; the ultimate end is reconciliation and redemption.

3. It is directed against forces of evil rather than against persons who happen to be doing the evil.

4. It involves willingness to accept suffering without retaliation, to accept blows from the opponent without striking back. It may also violate existing unjust laws, but it willingly accepts the penalty.[24] Nonviolence accepts violence but does not inflict it.

5. Nonviolence avoids not only external physical violence but also internal violence of the spirit. The nonviolent person not only refuses to shoot his or her opponent but also refuses to hate the opponent. At the core of nonviolence stands the ethic of love, the queen of the divine graces. King could have expected to find almost automatic acceptance for love's elevation among a people whose tradition had fervently possessed, preached and practiced Christian love in other settings.[25]

That King as a minister should devote significant time to socioeconomic-polit-ical activities and do so on a tremendously large scale was a point of attack because, so the argument generally ran, the preacher's place is in the church (as the physician's place is in the hospital, or the teacher's in the classroom); hence *his activities were a misuse of the pulpit*. It would probably be superfluous here to enumerate the legion of "secular" matters engaged in by King that brought him under a barrage of criticism from all quarters, including fellow clergy.

One such critic was Senator Thomas J. Dodd, Democrat from Connecticut, who charged that King "has taken advantage of his pulpit and his leadership in the civil rights movement to meddle in U.S. foreign policy." Senator Dodd warned that the Nobel Peace Prize winner "would endanger the respect in which he is held by government leaders including the Senate Foreign Relations Com-mittee" if he were to continue. King had submitted to United Nations Ambassa-dor Arthur Goldberg a four-point program for a peaceful settlement in Vietnam: (1) seating the People's Republic of China at the United Nations, (2) issuing a statement of willingness to negotiate unconditionally with the Vietcong, (3) reevaluating U.S. foreign policy and (4) stopping the bombing of North Vietnamese targets.[26]

Was there a contradiction between King's ecclesiastical function and his immense involvement in social, economic and political arenas? When this momentous question was put to four theological leaders who had contributed to King's training (Benjamin E. Mays, Walter G. Muelder, S. Paul Schilling and L. Harold DeWolf), they all affirmed King's prophetic emphasis on all areas of authentic human need. (See their specific comments in chapter two.)

Another accusation averred that as a Christian preacher, King transgressed his gospel boundaries by *utilizing non-Christian and philosophical sources to establish Christian themes.* Both the origin of this criticism leveled against King and possible answers in support of his practice are discussed in chapter five in reference to his use of the "appeal to authority."

Only after the assassination of King did charges of *plagiarism* and *adultery* gain a public forum. The question of whether he borrowed and plundered others' materials, using them as his own, I also discuss later regarding the similarities between his sermon "Three Dimensions of a Complete Life" and Phillips Brooks's "Symmetry of Life" (see chapter six, p. 134).

When it comes to the issue of sexual misbehavior, it is easy to cross the boundary between intellectual inquiry into King's influence and legacy and probing a juicy bit of postmortem scuttlebutt. Would knowing all and telling all give us valuable insight into King's humanity and enhance our appreciation and rapport?[27] To the contrary, improving our appreciation of King by exposing his private life apparently has not convinced King's surviving critics to hasten along our appreciation of their humanity by disclosing their own small peccadilloes or grievous iniquities.

Unless there is irrefutable evidence that King himself confessed to sexual immorality, or hard evidence such as photographs or tapes, the account would do well to be considered simply a rumor. We are not well served when people endlessly massage the rumor in an attempt to give it muscled reality; it then gains unmerited space and attention and may even be emulated.

For now the most compelling material on the question of King's alleged adulteries has come from his closest confidant, Abernathy, who at the time of his public disclosure was reportedly in the midst of various physical and mental health concerns. Could he accurately recall events from twenty years earlier? Had he been a firsthand witness, or was he merely repeating rumors of the time? Was his disclosure made voluntarily—or was it encouraged or even coerced? A human-rights participant in King circles has noted that when the original manuscript of Abernathy's autobiography, *And the Walls Came Tumbling Down,* was circulated for reading and review, mention of sexual misconduct did not appear in its pages. If that was so, where did the later interpolations come from, and why?

At any rate, truth is always its own defense and will win out ultimately. In the meantime, the opposite of full disclosure is not necessarily full cover-up. If we step outside of motivations of morbid curiosity, popularity, wider readership, marketability, jealousy and revenge, we might be in a better position to make appropriate, objective decisions on what, if anything, should be broadcast of the private lives of fellow citizens and respected leaders.

5
THE CONTENT
OF THE KING SERMONS,
PART TWO
Logos & Pathos

Everyone who heard him was amazed at his understanding and his answers.
LUKE 2:47

Whether King was handling biblical or nonbiblical materials in his sermons, preaching sources came in the form of examples, narratives or stories, statistics and quotations (appeals to authority) which undergirded his process of inferring conclusions from these bodies of evidence. A preacher's *logos* reveals his or her ability to "make sense" of the sermon's evidence; this is usually done by reasoning from example (or generalization), analogy, causal relation or sign. The logical persuasion of King was balanced, incorporating the full spectrum of the reasoning process.

King's Logos (Rational Substance)
With reasoning from *example* or *generalization*, the sermon "Transformed Nonconformist" seeks to discourage social trends toward apathy and the status quo. In one part of the sermon King highlights some people's desire to become "adjusted" and says he believes in a certain kind of "maladjustment." "The world is in dire need of a society of the creative maladjusted," declares King. "It may well be," he continues, "that the salvation of our world lies in the hands of such a creative minority." King then presents examples of persons who were appropriately "maladjusted":

We need men today as maladjusted as the PROPHET AMOS, who in the midst of the injustices of his day could cry out in words that echo across the centuries: "Let justice roll down like waters and righteousness like a mighty stream."

. . . as maladjusted as SHADRACH, MESHACK, and ABEDNEGO who, in the midst of an order from King Nebuchadnezzar to bow down and worship the golden image, said in unequivocal terms: "If it be so, our God whom we serve is able to deliver us, but if not we will not bow."

. .. as maladjusted as ABRAHAM LINCOLN who had the vision to see that this nation could not survive half slave and half free.

. . . as maladjusted as THOMAS JEFFERSON, who in the midst of an age amazingly adjusted to slavery could scratch across the pages of history these profound and eloquent words: "We hold these truths to be self-evident: that all men are created equal; that they are endowed by their Creator with certain unalienable rights; that among these are life, liberty, and the pursuit of happiness."

. . . as maladjusted even as our LORD who, in the midst of the intricate and fascinating military machinery of the Roman Empire, reminded his disciples that "they that take the sword shall perish with the sword."

"Our God Is Able" affirms divine omnipotence and the inevitability of the triumph of God's will by generalizing from the following examples:

> The Hitlers and the Mussolinis may have their day, and for a period they may wield great power, spreading themselves like a green bay tree, but soon they are cut down like the grass and wither as the green herb. . . .
>
> We saw an evil system known as colonialism soar high. Like a plague, it swept across Africa and Asia. . . . But then the quiet invisible law began to operate. . . . The powerful colonial empires began to disintegrate. . . .
>
> In our nation we have seen an evil system known as segregation rise to the throne. . . . But as on the world scale, so in our nation, the wind of change began to blow. Since May 17, 1954, when the Supreme Court rendered its historic decision, one event has followed another to bring a gradual end to the system of segregation.
>
> Yes, God is able to conquer the evils of history.

In "The Death of Evil upon the Seashore" King reasons from *analogy,* comparing the enslavement and liberation of the American Negro to the enslavement and liberation of the Israelites from Egyptian bondage:

> The Emancipation Proclamation did not, however, bring full freedom to the Negro, for although he enjoyed certain political and social opportunities during the Reconstruction, the Negro soon discovered that the pharaohs of the South were determined to keep him in slavery. Certainly the Emancipation Proclamation brought

him nearer to the Red Sea, but it did not guarantee his passage through parted waters. Racial segregation, backed by a decision of the United States Supreme Court in 1896, was a new form of slavery disguised by certain niceties of complexity. In the great struggle of the last half century between the forces of justice attempting to end the evil system of segregation and the forces of injustice attempting to maintain it, the pharaohs have employed legal maneuvers, economic reprisals, and even physical violence to hold the Negro in the Egypt of segregation. Despite the patient cry of many a Moses, they refused to let the Negro people go.

Today we are witnessing a massive change. A world-shaking decree by the nine justices of the United States Supreme Court opened the Red Sea and the forces of justice are moving to the other side. The Court decreed an end to the old *Plessy* decision of 1896 and affirmed that separate facilities are inherently unequal and that to segregate a child on the basis of race is to deny the child an equal legal protection. This decision is a great beacon light of hope to millions of disinherited people. Looking back, we see the forces of segregation gradually dying on the seashore. The problem is far from solved and gigantic mountains of opposition lie ahead, but at least we have left Egypt, and with patient yet firm determination we shall reach the promised land. Evil in the form of injustice and exploitation shall not survive forever. A Red Sea passage in history ultimately brings the forces of goodness to victory, and the closing of the same waters marks the doom and destruction of the forces of evil.

Another sermon, "Antidotes for Fear," addressing the fear of war, proposes a panacea; it then suggests that fear of integration can be eradicated by the same solution:

What method has the sophisticated ingenuity of modern man employed to deal with the fear of war? We have armed ourselves to the nth degree. The West and the East have engaged in a fever-pitched arms race. Expenditures for defense have risen to mountainous proportions, and weapons of destruction have been assigned priority over all other human endeavors. The nations have believed that greater armaments will cast out fear. But alas! they have produced greater fear. In these turbulent, panic-stricken days we are once more reminded of the judicious words of old, "Perfect love casteth out fear." Not arms, but love, understanding, and organized goodwill can cast out fear. Only disarmament, based on good faith, will make mutual trust a living reality.

Our own problem of racial injustice must be solved by the same formula. Racial segregation is buttressed by such irrational fears as loss of preferred privileges, altered social status, intermarriage, and adjustment to new situations. Through sleepless nights and haggard days numerous white people attempt to combat these

corroding fears by diverse methods. By following the path of escape, some seek to
ignore the question of race relations and to close their mind to the issues involved.
Others, placing their faith in such legal maneuvers as interposition and nullification,
counsel massive resistance. Still others hope to drown their fear by engaging in acts
of violence and meanness toward their Negro brethren. But how futile are all these
remedies! Instead of eliminating fear, they instill deeper and more pathological
fears that leave the victim inflicted with strange psychoses and peculiar cases of
paranoia. Neither repression, massive resistance, nor aggressive violence will cast
out the fear of integration; only love and goodwill can do that.

Reasoning from the logical mode of persuasion known as *causal relation* (cause
to effect, effect to cause) in the sermon "On Being a Good Neighbor," King holds
that measures of legislation (in spite of admitted limitations) can produce vital
changes in the process of remedying the race problem:

> Let us never succumb to the temptation of believing that legislation and judicial
> decrees play only minor roles in solving this problem. Morality cannot be legis-
> lated, but behavior can be regulated. Judicial decrees may not change the heart, but
> they can restrain the heartless. The law cannot make an employer love an employee,
> but it can prevent him from refusing to hire me because of the color of my skin. The
> habits, if not the hearts, of people have been and are being altered every day by leg-
> islative acts, judicial decisions, and executive orders. Let us not be misled by those
> who argue that segregation cannot be ended by the force of law.
>
>   But acknowledging this, we must admit that the ultimate solution to the race
> problem lies in the willingness of men to obey the unenforceable.

Clearly King reasoned in ways that would make sense to both the simplest and
the most complex listening minds through a balanced variety of logical means. A
fourth type of logical process, "sign reasoning"—inferring associations between
two phenomena that are not causally related—does not seem to be prominent in
his preaching. The structure of the reasoning of King seems consistently composed of both the inductive and deductive methods.

King's Pathos (Emotional Substance)

As mentioned in chapter three (see "King and General Church Audiences" for
more extensive discussion of emotional and emotive appeal), I asked Dr. King if
he would delineate the characteristics of an excellent and most effective sermon.
He replied, "A good, solid sermon has to have three elements which I call 'three

p's': it proves an appeal to the intellect, it paints an appeal to the imagination, and it persuades an appeal to the heart."[1] A sermon's heart appeal or emotional substance may be summarized as "the affective or 'feeling' response we make to any situation."[2] Purely logical persuasion is an impractical expectation; King was wise to develop a balanced tripartite appeal that invariably gave due consideration to the emotional and emotive values of his listeners.

Materials Within the Sermons

As if savoring a delicious meal and carrying away from the table fond memories of food that nurtured as well as gratified, maturing people who listen to a sermon expect that the preacher will "really say something" that is solid food and not just pabulum or pulpit baby fare. King's listeners recognized readily that they were getting a *message* and not mere "feel-good gibberish."

What are some of the prominent materials or ingredients that contributed to his sermons' substantive content? These materials are those that Aristotle called "proofs . . . such as are not supplied by our own efforts, but existed beforehand,"[3] such as examples, narratives, statistics, quotations.[4] King's use of such elements is exemplary for all who would not be pleased merely to "preach something" but want to "have something to preach," buttressing biblical exegesis, interpretation and application with solid, life-nourishing information.

Examples

Examples abound in King's sermons, both instances and illustrations.[5] Most of his examples are instances, and they occur most often in the first half of the sermon. This may indicate his desire for clarity in developing his subject. The sources of the examples are usually either persons or nations. For example, in "Three Dimensions of a Complete Life" King exemplifies the poetic and philosophical insights of Greece by referring to Aeschylus, Euripides, Sophocles, Plato and Aristotle. Emphasizing the musical contribution of Western civilization, he lists Handel, Beethoven and Bach; then he supports his assertion "We already have inspiring examples of Negroes who have plunged against cloud-filled nights of oppression new and blazing stars of achievement" by mentioning Booker T. Washington, Marian Anderson, George Washington Carver and Ralph Bunche.

Following are additional illustrations of King's use of examples.

Assertion: Regarding racial segregation and discrimination in America, "the wind of change began to blow." *Example:* "May 17, 1954, . . . the Supreme Court rendered its historic decision" ("Our God Is Able").

Assertion: "Abnormal fears are emotionally ruinous and psychologically destructive." *Example:* Differentiating between normal and abnormal fears, "Sigmund Freud spoke of a person who was quite properly afraid of snakes in the heart of an African jungle and of another person who neurotically feared that snakes were under the carpet in his city apartment" ("Antidotes for Fear").

Assertion: Using the Good Samaritan parable (Lk 10) as his foundation, King says, "One of the great tragedies of man's long trek along the highway has been the limiting of neighborly concern to tribe, race, class, or nation." *Examples:*

1. The God of early Old Testament days was a tribal god and the ethic was tribal. "Thou shalt not kill" meant "Thou shalt not kill a fellow Israelite, but for God's sake, kill a Philistine." . . .

2. Greek democracy embraced a certain aristocracy, but not the hordes of Greek slaves whose labors built the city-states. . . .

3. The universalism at the center of the Declaration of Independence has been shamefully negated by America's appalling tendency to substitute "some" for "all." Numerous people in the North and South still believe that the affirmation, "All men are created equal," means "All white men are created equal." . . .

4. Our unswerving devotion to monopolistic capitalism makes us more concerned about the economic security of the captains of industry than for the laboring men whose sweat and skills keep industry functioning. ("On Being a Good Neighbor")

"On Being a Good Neighbor" continues the theme of provincialism and poses the question "What are the devastating consequences of this narrow, group-centered attitude?" The answer is advanced: "It means that one does not really mind what happens to the people outside his group." Disjunctive examples include the following:

1. If an American is concerned only about his nation, he will not be concerned about the peoples of Asia, Africa, or South America. Is this not why nations engage in the madness of war without the slightest sense of penitence? Is this not why the murder of a citizen of your own nation is a crime, but the murder of the citizens of another nation in war is an act of heroic virtue? . . .

2. If manufacturers are concerned only in their personal interests, they will pass by on the other side while thousands of working people are stripped of their jobs and left displaced on some Jericho road as a result of automation, and they will judge every move toward a better distribution of wealth and a better life for the

working man to be socialistic. . . .

3. If a white man is concerned only about his race, he will casually pass by the Negro who has been robbed of his personhood, stripped of his sense of dignity, and left dying on some wayside road.

A final model of King's use of example is the following.

Assertion: "One of the great glories of the gospel is that Christ has transformed so many men, and made sons of nameless prodigals." *Examples:* "He transformed a Simon of Sand into a Peter of Rock. He changed a persecuting Saul into an Apostle Paul. He changed a lust-infested Augustine into a Saint Augustine. Tolstoi's beautiful confession in 'My Religion' is the experience of men in every nation and every tribe: 'Five years ago I came to believe in Christ's teaching, and my life suddenly became changed: I ceased desiring what I had wished before, and began to desire what I had not wished before. What formerly had seemed good to me appeared bad, and what had seemed bad appeared good. . . . The direction of my life, my desires became different: what was good and bad changed places" ("The Answer to a Perplexing Question").

A survey of a large body of King's sermons reveals that the use of examples is the strongest and most prevalent element of content in his preaching.

Narratives and Stories

In contrast to the incidence of examples in King's sermons, narratives and stories appear rather infrequently. While stories would probably have given his sermons a very beneficial means to help sustain interest, further clarify salient points, and create variety and change of pace, King did not make use of stories as often as one might expect. Perhaps this was because he had such a variety of civil rights experiences from which to draw and so many points to make within each sermon's time constraints that he chose to rely on shorter instances and illustrations. In this way he could include more real-life situations to support and clarify more points.

When he does utilize narratives, there is no doubt of the intended purpose, for he consistently follows with a clinching thematic statement. Following are cases in point.

The value of inner spiritual strength

"As I come to the conclusion of my message I would like for you to indulge me as I mention a personal experience." King here told of being utterly discouraged and despondent at one point during the civil rights movement in Montgomery. After another in a series of threatening telephone calls one night, he could not sleep. King then prayed about the situation and "experienced the presence of the Divine as . . . never . . . before." "My experience with God," King said in concluding the narrative, "had given me the strength to face it."

His thematic statement and application: "Yes, God is able to give us the interior resources to face the storms and problems of life" ("Our God Is Able").

Optimism in the face of life's problems
"I recall a very meaningful experience during the bus boycott in Montgomery, Alabama." Here King tells how the successful eleven-month-old car pool was threatened when the mayor instructed the city's legal department to "file such proceedings as it may deem proper to stop the operation of car pool or transportation system growing out of the bus boycott." As chief defendant, King was summoned to court. During a critical moment of the court session, when things were looking rather bleak for the boycotters, a reporter handed King a newspaper that announced, "'The United States Supreme Court today unanimously ruled bus segregation unconstitutional in Montgomery, Alabama.' The night before we were in a confusing midnight, but now daybreak had come."

His thematic statement and application: "Yes, the dawn will come. Disappointment, sorrow and despair are all born in Midnight, but we may be consoled by the fact that morning will come. 'Weeping may tarry for a night,' says the Psalmist, 'but joy cometh in the morning'" ("A Knock at Midnight").

Why we should include God in our plans

The story goes that a wise old preacher went to a distant college to deliver a baccalaureate sermon. After finishing his message he lingered around the campus to talk with some of the members of the graduating class. He soon found himself talking with a brilliant young graduate named Robert. His first question to Robert was: "What are your plans for the future?" "I plan to go immediately to law school," said Robert. "What then, Robert?" inquired the preacher. "Well," responded Robert, "I plan to get married and start a family and then get myself securely established in my law practice." "What then, Robert?" continued the preacher. Robert retorted, "I must frankly say that I plan to make lots of money from my law practice, and thereby I hope to retire rather early and spend a great of time traveling to various parts of the world—something that I have always wanted to do." "What then, Robert?" continued the preacher with almost annoying inquisitiveness. "Well," said

Robert, "these are all of my plans." The preacher, looking at Robert with a countenance expressing pity and fatherly concern, said: "Young man, your plans are far too small. They can extend only seventy-five or a hundred years at the most. You must make your plans big enough to include God and large enough to include eternity."

His thematic statement and application: "This is wise advice. I suspect that all too many of us are still dabbling with plans that are big in quantity, but small in quality—plans that move on the horizontal plane of time rather than the vertical plane of eternity" ("Three Dimensions of a Complete Life").

Determination and fortitude to withstand opposition

When I first flew from New York to London, it was in the days of the propeller type aircraft. The flight took over 9½ hours. (The jets can make the flight in 6 hours.) On returning to the States from London I discovered that the flying time would be twelve hours and a half. This confused me for the moment. I knew that the distance returning to New York was the same as the distance from New York to London. Why this difference of three hours, I asked myself. Soon the pilot walked through the plane to greet the passengers. As soon as he got to me I raised the question of the difference in flight time. His answer was simple and to the point. "You must understand something about the wind," he said. "When we leave New York," he continued, "the winds are in our favor; we have a strong tail wind. When we return to New York from London, the winds are against us; we have a strong head wind." And then he said, "Don't worry though, these four engines are fully capable of battling the winds, and even though it takes three hours longer we will get to New York."

His thematic statement and application:

Well, life is like this. There are times when the winds are in our favor—moments of joy, moments of great triumph, moments of fulfillment. But there are times when the winds are against us, times when strong head winds of disappointment and sorrow beat unrelentingly upon our lives. We must decide whether we will allow the winds to overwhelm us or whether we will journey across life's mighty Atlantic with our inner spiritual engines equipped to go on in spite of the winds. This refusal to be stopped, this "courage to be," this determination to go on living "in spite of," is the God in man. He who has made this discovery knows that no burden can overwhelm him and no wind of adversity can blow his hope away. He can stand anything that can happen to him. ("Shattered Dreams")

Statistics

Of the many sermons by King that I have heard or read, only four contain significant statistical data. By "significant" I mean figures employed not just in passing reference but for the obvious purpose of buttressing a specific point. Typical of the statistics in his sermons are those he presented when I heard him in person at the Central United Methodist Church of Detroit, March 3, 1966. He stated that in Chicago 97.7 percent of Negro people lived in the ghetto, 41 percent of Negro families lived in dilapidated, deteriorated rented housing, 90 percent of Negro students attended schools that had more than 92 percent Negro enrollment—which meant, he continued, that more than 90 percent of Chicago schools were segregated. He also said that three Chicago Negroes to every one white were without work—which meant that some 100,000 Negroes out of a population of one million found themselves chronically unemployed.

King did not use statistics regularly, although he sometimes repeated the same set of figures in different sermons. His statistics are of a high order principally because of relevance and meaningfulness and almost always pertain to the nation's number-one domestic problem—racial inequality. Yet a listener might be inclined to wonder about the validity of king's statistics inasmuch as he seemed never to cite documented sources.

Quotations (or Appeal to Authority)

The fourth type of content material King used was quotes, paraphrases and appeals to authoritative references, usually originating either from literary materials such as the Bible, the U.S. Constitution, the Declaration of Independence and the Emancipation Proclamation or from fact or opinion expressed in the writings of experts in theology, philosophy, sociology and even anthropology.

Appendix five, "King's Use of Quotations," shows that the surveyed sermons contain a total of 178 quotations. Seventy, or 39.3 percent, of these come from the Bible; twenty-one, or 12 percent, from other literary sources; and eighty-seven, or 49 percent, from persons. Thus the Bible is quoted more than all other literary sources combined, while citations from nonbiblical historical and contemporary persons exceed in number all other quoted sources.

Precisely because of King's liberal utilization of nonbiblical and philosophical sources to support biblical themes, he has been attacked and called an eclectic rather than a real Christian preacher.[6] According to L. Harold DeWolf, King's answer to the attack is the fact that historically great theologians have been glad to use as many elements in philosophy and non-Christian sources as would help the cause of Christian religion.

It might be noted further that one of the greatest of Christian preachers, the apostle Paul, when standing at the podium of Mars Hill, quoted non-Christian Athenian poets: "As some of your own poets have said, 'We are his offspring'" (Acts 17:28). Ellen G. White comments that Paul "stood undaunted, meeting his opposers on their own ground, matching logic with logic, philosophy with philosophy, eloquence with eloquence."[7] It would appear, then, that in bringing nonbiblical and philosophical materials into his sermons King was following a legitimate tradition and practice of the ethical employment of "all the available means of persuasion."[8] Relevant and applicable to King's concept of preaching is the definition of the pulpit art provided by Charles E. Weniger: preaching is "that branch of speech which, employing all available means and taking to itself the *whole realm of human knowledge* with emphasis on the Bible, seeks by persuasion to draw men to a better life and a more abundant entrance into the Kingdom of God."[9]

The number of Bible references reached a high of twelve in one discourse and a low of one in another; hence none of King's sermons was devoid of biblical quotation. A grand total of seventy such references in sixteen sermons yields a mean (average) of 4.6 per sermon, a relatively generous serving of Bible texts, particularly in view of what many perceived to be King's liberal theology. His plenteous use stirs little more than gentle surprise, however, when one takes into account King's early roots and strict discipline in fundamentalist theology, as the son of a Southern Baptist clergyman.

The New Testament, with a total of fifty-three quotations, is cited 3.2 times more often than the Old Testament, with a total of only seventeen. Further, of the sixty-six books constituting the Old Testament, the nine from which King quotes represent only 13.6 percent. The thirteen quoted New Testament books are a plentiful 48 percent of that portion of Holy Writ. For the specific biblical references of King's quotes, see the table in appendix five.[10]

Dr. Mervyn A. Warren presenting his Ph.D. dissertation on Dr. King to Mrs. Coretta Scott King, 1988
"King Week Celebration" in Atlanta

Dr. Mervyn A. Warren, Mrs. Coretta Scott King and Dr. Danny Blanchard, 1988

Rev. Andrew Young and Dr. Mervyn A. Warren, 1988

Rev. Martin Luther King Sr., introducing his son to give the Sunday sermon

Mrs. Alberta Williams King and Rev. M. L. King Sr.

The empty pulpit of Dexter Avenue Baptist Church, Dr. King's first pastorate in Montgomery, Alabama

Dr. King preaching at Ebenezer Baptist Church

Greeting worshipers outside Ebenezer Baptist Church

Dr. King giving the Sunday sermon in Ebenezer Baptist Church, Atlanta

Student protest outside Montgomery High School. Various hate groups such as the Ku Klux Klan and White Citizens Council were present.

The King family having Sunday dinner

King giving the "I Have a Dream" speech

On the steps of the Lincoln Memorial

Dr. Martin Luther King and the national guard in Montgomery, Alabama, following the March from Selma, 1968

Dr. King speaking to the protesters waiting to march from Selma to Montgomery

Dr. King with other civil rights leaders in Montgomery. Rev. Andrew Young (far left) and Rev. Hosea Williams (sitting).

6

THE THEMES
OF KING'S
SERMONS

*And beginning with Moses and all the Prophets, he explained to them
what was said in all the Scriptures concerning himself.*
LUKE 24:27

*T*he previous few chapters have explored the process by which King
preached the gospel by bringing together persuasive elements of his person with
sermon materials, components mirroring his black church culture described in
chapter one. From his formative days of boyhood to his mature ministry calling a
nation and world to love and justice, black church traditions provided shape,
identification and framework to King's sermon preparation and his delivery of
themes that flowed like crimson ribbons through the pattern of a beautiful garment. It cannot be overstated that King possessed what Walter G. Muelder of
Boston University termed a "thoroughly thought-out intellectual and theological
position."[1] Let us now take a look at salient *sources* of his theological concepts
and at *example statements* of these concepts in his sermons.

Thematic Sources
Henry David Thoreau. King's first introduction to the notion of nonviolent social
resistance came through his reading, when a student at Morehouse College, of
Thoreau's *Essay on Civil Disobedience.* Although Thoreau addressed himself to
the immediate issue of slavery and the Mexican War, his appeal soared beyond
those concerns; for he "spoke to the issue of the moral law in conflict with government law."[2] He contended that "it is not so desirable to cultivate a respect for

the *law*, so much as for the right. The only obligation which I have a right to assume is to do at any time what I think is right."[3] This duty of "right" above the law would become a fundamental principle of King's social reform movement.

On the relation of unjust laws to moral human beings, Thoreau declared:

> Unjust laws exist: shall we be content to obey them, or shall we endeavor to amend them, and obey them until we have succeeded, or shall we transgress them at once? . . . If it [the government] is to such a nature that it requires you to be the agent of injustice to another, then, I say, *break the law.* . . . What I have to do is to see . . . that I do not lend myself to the wrong which I condemn.[4]

Specifically on the question of slavery, he averred the following:

> I know this well, that if one thousand, if one hundred, if ten men whom I could name—if ten honest men only—ay, if one honest man, in this State of Massachusetts, ceasing to hold slaves, were actually to withdraw from copartnership, and be *locked up in the country jail therefor*, it would be the abolition of slavery in America. For it matters not how small the beginning may seem to be: what is once well done is done forever.[5]

Reportedly when Thoreau was incarcerated for having broken what he considered an unjust law, a friend from the outside recognized him in the jail and remarked, "Why, Thoreau, what are *you* doing in *there?*"

Replied Thoreau, with typically pregnant overtones, "My friend, what are *you* doing *out there?*"

"Under a government which imprisons any unjustly," he later wrote, "the true place for a just man is also a prison."[6]

So profoundly moved was King by this concept of "noncooperation with evil" that he reread Thoreau time and time again.[7] King later said, "This was my first intellectual contact with the theory of nonviolent resistance."[8] At the same time—the middle and late 1940s—while King was being introduced to Thoreau's *Essay on Civil Disobedience,* one Mohandas K. Gandhi was already implementing the philosophy of passive resistance to free India from British rule. Gandhi's renowned movement is said to have been inspired also by Thoreau's concept.[9]

Walter Rauschenbusch. Not until 1948, when he matriculated at Crozer Theological Seminary, did King enter into a "serious intellectual quest for a method to eliminate social evil."[10] Among the varied concepts encountered, the "social gospel," particularly as propounded by Walter Rauschenbusch, gained ascendancy in his thinking. King later wrote of this development:

Although my major interest was in the fields of theology and philosophy, I spent a great deal of time reading the works of the great social philosophers. I came early to Walter Rauschenbusch's *Christianity and the Social Crisis*, which left an indelible imprint on my thinking by giving me a theological basis for the social concern which had already grown up in me as a result of my early experiences.[11]

Yet King did not altogether agree with Rauchenbusch's philosophy. Though finding complete compatibility with the dynamics of a social gospel that demanded that one's religion go beyond oneself to a positive influence on society, he detected in Rauschenbusch's brand at least two unacceptable elements: (1) "the nineteenth century 'cult of inevitable progress' which led Rauschenbusch to a superficial optimism concerning man's nature," and (2) the danger of "identifying the Kingdom of God with a particular social and economic system—a tendency which should never befall the Church."[12]

Two points on which King could find considerable agreement with Rauschenbusch are expressed in these words of the social philosopher:

There are two great entities in human life,—the human soul and the human race,— and religion is to save both.

Christianity must offer every man a full salvation. The individualistic gospel never did this. Its evangelism never recognized more than a fractional part of the saving forces at work in God's world. Salvation was often whittled down to a mere doctrinal proposition; assent to that, and you were saved. Social Christianity holds to all the real values in the old methods, but rounds them out to meet all the needs of human life.[13]

If the pulpit is willing to lend its immense power of proclamation and teaching, it will immeasurably speed the spread of the new conceptions. "With the assistance of the clergy everything in matters of social reforms is easy; without such help, or in spite of it, all is difficult and at times impossible."

None can deny that the pulpit has the teaching function, and that its obligation runs wherever a moral question can be raised. Those who think the institutional Church a departure from the spiritual mission of the Church, must concede all the more that the Church should teach plainly on the moral causes and remedies of social misery. If the Church is not to deal with mass poverty by its organized work, its obligation is all the greater to deal with it by the sword of the word. Preaching on social questions is not an innovation in the history of the pulpit. The Fathers, the great medieval preachers, the leaders of the Reformation—all dealt more boldly with public questions than the classical sermonizers of the generations just preceding ours. In all the history of preaching the pulpit has perhaps never been so silent in this direction as in the nineteenth century before the social movement began to affect Christian thought.[14]

If a minister uses the great teaching powers of the pulpit sanely and wisely to open the minds of the people to the moral importance of the social questions, he may be of the utmost usefulness.[15]

These significant points of agreement may be summarized thus: (1) Religion must concern itself with not only the *future* but also the *present* life, ministering not merely to the individual person but also to the person's environment. (2) The pulpit must be used for the effective dissemination of such a concept if social evils are to be eliminated.

After lauding Rauschenbusch for his insistence that the gospel deal with both individuals and society, King specifies the nature of the social philosopher's influence on his thinking:

It has been my conviction ever since reading Rauschenbusch that any religion which professes to be concerned about the souls of men and is not concerned with the social and economic conditions that scar the soul is a spiritually moribund religion only waiting for the day to be buried. It well has been said: "A religion that ends with the individual, ends."[16]

After reading Rauschenbusch, King no doubt knew that his own pulpit would be a platform for emphasizing a balance between the proverbial "here and now" and the "sweet by and by."

Mohandas K. Gandhi. It was also at Crozer Seminary that young King first read Gandhi. Having just heard Mordecai Johnson (then president of Howard University) give a lecture about his visit to India at the Fellowship House of Philadelphia, the youthful seminarian was so moved and so impressed by the applicability of Gandhi's nonviolent movement to African Americans' struggle that he purchased about six books on the life and work of Gandhi, the renowned man who led in India's passive resistance against British rule.

Later, writing of his study of Gandhi, King said:

As I read his works I became deeply fascinated by his campaigns of nonviolent resistance. The whole Gandhian concept of *satyagraha* (*satya* is truth which equals love and *graha* is force; *satyagraha* thus means truth-force or love-force) was profoundly significant to me. As I delved deeper into the philosophy of Gandhi, my skepticism concerning the power of love gradually diminished, and I came to see for the first time that the Christian doctrine of love, operating through the Gandhian method of nonviolence, is one of the most potent weapons available to an oppressed people in their struggle for freedom.[17]

King hastened to add, however, that at that time he acquired only an intellectual understanding and appreciation of Gandhi's position and possessed "no firm determination to organize it in a socially effective situation."[18] Before reading Gandhi, King had believed that the ethics of Jesus were effective merely in "individual" relationship. Jesus' imperatives to "turn the other cheek" and "love your enemies" were pertinent only, thought King, when an individual was in conflict with another individual. Gandhi, however, altered King's thinking by broadening his perspective to apply the Jesus ethics to racial groups versus racial groups or nations versus nations

Gandhi deeply respected Jesus of Nazareth and accepted his pronouncements in the Sermon on the Mount (Mt 5—7) as furnishing significant bases for Gandhi's own creed of nonviolence.[19] And it was by studying Gandhi that King's thinking on the power of love vis-à-vis social problems began to crystallize. King maintains:

> Gandhi was probably the first person in history to lift the love ethic of Jesus above mere interaction between individuals to a powerful and effective social force on a large scale. For Gandhi love was a potent instrument for social and collective transformation. It was in this Gandhian emphasis on love and nonviolence that I discovered the method for social reform that I had been seeking for so many months. The intellectual and moral satisfaction that I failed to gain from the utilitarianism of Bentham and Mill, the revolutionary methods of Marx and Lenin, the social-contracts theory of Hobbes, the "back to nature" optimism of Rousseau, and the superman philosophy of Nietzsche I found in the nonviolent resistance philosophy of Gandhi. I came to feel that this was the only morally and practically sound method open to oppressed people in their struggle for freedom.[20]

King was quoted in *Time* (January 3, 1963, p. 14) as saying that from his background he gained his regulating Christian ideals, while from Gandhi he learned his operational technique.

Reinhold Niebuhr. In his senior year at Crozer, King came into contact with the writings of Niebuhr, who according to William Hordern was "the most important living American theologian" during King's lifetime.[21] Niebuhr's theology, an effort to apply Christianity to sociopoliticoeconomic spheres, always "begins with the human, the material, the social."[22]

Niebuhr seems to have been open to violent resistance to totalitarianism. At least he interpreted Gandhi's nonviolent resistance as being dependent on circumstances when he wrote that "violence could be used as the instrument of moral goodwill, if there was a possibility of a triumph quick enough to obviate the dangers of incessant wars," which means, he continued, "that nonviolence is a particularly strategic instrument for an oppressed group which is hopelessly in the minority and has no possibility of developing sufficient power to set against its oppressors."[23]

Yet in 1932, when Martin Luther King Jr. was only three years old, Niebuhr presaged that "the emancipation of the Negro race in America probably waits upon the adequate development of this kind of social and political strategy [nonviolent resistance]."[24] He recognized, moreover, that "the white race in America will not admit the Negro to equal rights if it is not forced to do so. Upon that point one may speak with a dogmatism which all history justifies."[25] One premise for such a conclusion might be Niebuhr's belief that power and pride are closely allied and that the ego, when threatened by insecurity, grasps for more power rather than relinquishing or liberally sharing it.[26]

Whereas King agreed that power concedes nothing without demand (à la Frederick Douglass), he disagreed with Niebuhr's charge that "pacifism" is a kind of passive nonresistance to evil asserting naive trust in the power of love. Niebuhr apparently viewed pacifism as an unrealistic submission to evil power. But King contends that true pacifism is

> a courageous confrontation of evil by the power of love, in the faith that it is better to be the recipient of violence than the inflicter of it, since the latter only multiplies the existence of violence and bitterness in the universe, while the former may develop a sense of shame in the opponent, and thereby bring about a transformation and change of heart.[27]

Still, there remained much in Niebuhr's thinking that King found palatable: (1) Niebuhr refuted the false optimism characteristic of a large segment of Protestant liberalism, without falling into the antirationalism of Karl Barth or the semifundamentalism of other dialectical theologians, and (2) he exercised unusual insight into human nature and the behavior of nations and social groups, the complexity of human motives and the relation between morality and power, and kept in view the reality of sin. Writing with prophetic accuracy, the noted theologian seemed to have envisioned the eventual emergence of a nonviolent protest movement by African Americans:

> One waits for such a campaign with all the more reason and hope because the peculiar spiritual gifts of the Negro endow him with the capacity to conduct it success-

fully. He would need only to fuse the aggressiveness of the new and young Negro with the patience and forbearance of the old Negro, to rob the former of its vindictiveness and the latter of its lethargy.[28]

Personalism. It is altogether relevant to devote attention to the concept of personalism, for King considered it his basic philosophical position. While a student at Boston University, under the direction of Edgar S. Brightman (one of America's leading advocates of this concept) and L. Harold DeWolf, King delved deeply into personal idealism, or personalism, which maintains that personality is the clue to the meaning of ultimate reality and insists on the dignity of human personality.[29]

Borden Parker Bowne, predecessor of Brightman and also a leading exponent of personalism, provides a rather explicit brand of the philosophy:

> Personalism conceives reality as a self or belonging to a self. By self is meant a unitary, self-identifying conscious agent. A self capable of the realization of values may be called a person. . . . Synopsis is the ultimate form of intelligibility. All parts can be understood only when interpreted through their membership in the whole person to which they belong. . . .
>
> Reality is rational and hence in some way an organic whole. . . . In the final synopsis of thought all reality must be viewed as conscious experience . . . [signifying] that concrete reality is a self or person.[30]

Giving a further definition of personalism and reflecting on its moral implications and King's relation thereto, DeWolf said:

> Briefly, personalists believe that the basic reality is personal. The supreme Person, God, is the source of all that process which we call the physical universe and the creator of all other persons. Since human personality is in the likeness of God and the object of God's own love, every human person, however humble or wicked, must be treated as of inestimable dignity and worth. In metaphysics the personalists believe that the physical universe exists only by the energizing of God in the experience of persons, including himself. I do not know whether Dr. King subscribes to this account of the physical universe or not. However, he has been, as he confesses, deeply influenced by other ontological and ethical ideas of personalism.[31]

Because personalism assumes a religious and ethical view of life, King could identify with it and inculcate it into his theological presuppositions. The demand of personalism that only personality (finite and infinite) is ultimate reality afforded King two convictions: (1) a metaphysical and philosophical foundation for the idea of a personal God, and (2) a metaphysical footing for the dignity and worth of all human personality.

G. W. F. Hegel. Just prior to the death of Edgar S. Brightman, King had been studying under him at Boston University in an analysis of that monumental work of Hegel, *Phenomenology of Mind.* He read also, in his spare time, Hegel's *Philosophy of History and Philosophy of Right.* One of the prominent concepts of this philosopher was "absolute idealism," which has been described as follows:

> Idealism is based on the belief that, if man is to have any faith in his knowledge, he must presuppose a rational structure to the world apart from his mind. Man's reasoning powers, his logic and his a priori assumptions can only understand the world if the world acts in accordance with them. In other words, we can only trust our minds if the world is ultimately based on mind or reason. Idealism thus came to interpret all reality as the manifestation of a divine mind. Idealism seemed very appealing to many Christians because it attacked all philosophies of materialism.
>
> Idealists like Royce and Hegel had made Christian terminology an inherent part of their systems. But to these men the Christian doctrines were only symbols of rational truths known to man's reason. Thus the divinity of Jesus was a symbolic statement for the fact that all men have a divine aspect to their natures. The basic concept of the Bible, which is that God has revealed himself in certain events of history, was considered by the idealists as naive and pre-philosophical.[32]

King strongly disagreed with the Hegelian philosophy of absolute idealism, considering it "rationally unsound" as "it tended to swallow up the many in the one."[33] Other aspects of Hegel's thinking, however, King found stimulating, and some he concurred with. For example, Hegel's contention that "truth is the whole" led King to what he later termed "a philosophical method of rational coherence."[34] King admitted further that Hegel's analysis of the dialectical process aided him in realizing that growth comes through struggle.

In a laconic tribute to King's facility in translating his complex formal learning into appropriately simple symbols and thought forms for sermon situations, Ernest Dunbar, senior editor of *Look,* wrote: "In the pulpit, King summons up masterful oratory that blends Hegel with Hallelujahs."[35]

Agape versus *philia* and *eros.* That the love ethic provides the basic framework within which King functioned as both preacher and human rights leader is a given and needs little if any substantiation. He often underscored the particular emphasis of love that motivated his activities by referring to the three most popular Greek words for love—*eros, philia* and *agape.*

King stated that in the philosophy of Plato *eros* denoted the yearning of the soul for the divine.[36] He further noted that *eros* had later come to depict a rather aesthetic or romantic sort of love. The semanticist would probably direct us to the current denotation and connotation of the English *erotic* (a derivative) to remind us of the general present-day interpretation of *eros*. In antiquity, the Greeks viewed *eros* as a "daemon" driving man beyond himself to fulfillment which, in Plato's opinion, could be achieved only in the soul's final vision of truth, beauty and goodness in eternity.[37] King understood *philia* to mean an "intimate affection between personal friends," a kind of "reciprocal love; the person loves because he is loved."[38]

King emphasized that when he preached about *loving* those who oppose you, he meant neither *eros* nor *philia* but *agape,* an understanding, redeeming good-will for all humankind, an overflowing love that is altogether spontaneous, unmotivated, groundless, and creative and is set in operation by no quality or function of its object.[39]

In a sermon King would almost always introduce the terms for love by saying, "In the Greek New Testament are three words for love." (An example is his sermon on "Loving Your Enemies.") When I called his attention in conversation to the fact that only two of the words actually occur in the New Testament itself (though the Greek language does contain them all), he expressed interest in hearing more and was kindly receptive to my observation.

King gave some further descriptions of *agape:* (1) It is disinterested love—that is, the person exercising it seeks not his or her own good but the good of his or her neighbor. (2) It springs from the need of the other person. (3) It is not weak and passive but "love in action." (4) It denotes a recognition of the fact that all life is interrelated.[40] In the New Testament *agape* reaches its most exalted function in God's love revealed through the giving of Jesus Christ for a sinful world.[41] King firmly believed that only *agape* love would heal a community beset by racial ills and that he was called of God to preach and practice this caliber of love in order to "restore" the community, resist injustices and meet the needs of humanity.

The social gospel. A product of liberal theology, social gospel stresses "the need to apply Christian principles, not only to personal life, but also to the solution of the great social problems of our time."[42] As an effort to Christianize society, the social gospel is not really new in history. Medieval Catholicism, Calvinism and the Protestant Reformation movements certainly bore a message for society; nevertheless, "there was a modern twist . . . as it appeared among liberal Christians of the late nineteenth and early twentieth centuries."[43] Social gospelers insisted that it is not sufficient to preach a fire-insurance gospel to save a person from hell. It is useless, they contended, to save people *one by one* while a corrupt social system is "damning them by the thousands."[44] As human beings live in and are largely molded by society, the social gospel argued, a corrupt society inevitably corrupts them.

Many social gospelers supplanted the hope of life after death with a hope for a utopian earthly community. Quite frequently the "kingdom of God" to which Jesus Christ summoned men and women was interpreted to mean not life after death or an earthly society established with the second advent of Christ but rather a society where humans live in brother-sisterhood, love and justice. Not God but humankind with the help of God was to construct such a society. Extreme social gospel purports to save the world without any divine aid but through education, technology, scientific genius, medical skills and politicosocioeconomic justice.

Although the social gospel had no single formula for saving society, it tended to assert that Christians had clear moral choices to make in issues of economy, politics and the social order. Some social gospel thinkers went so far as to identify the Christian social order with such ideologies as democracy, socialism, the New Deal or the cooperative movement. "Peace" and "race" were perhaps the two most discussed issues among social gospelers, who were consistently known to repudiate war and racial discrimination. This was one of the main reasons King was tagged by many with the social gospel label.

When I asked King during our August 1966 interview about his belief or disbelief in an afterlife (in the context of being marked a social gospeler) given his all-consuming dedication to social justice on this present earth, he responded without hesitation: "I do not claim to know all the details about the furniture of heaven or the temperature of hell, but I definitely believe in an afterlife prepared by God for his people."

Thematic Examples Within King's Sermons

Good neighborliness. Whether explicitly stated or implicitly implied, the consistent overall theme of the sermons of Martin Luther King Jr. is that all peoples must live together as equal human beings in a brother-sisterhood or in what the noted philosopher-theologian Josiah Royce called the "Beloved Community."[45] Besides the theologians and social philosophers discussed above, this dominant theme probably finds its impetus also in Paul Tillich, concerning whom King wrote, "All theology, as he sees it, has a dual function: to state the basic truth of the Christian faith and to interpret this truth in the existing cultural situation. In other words, theology has both a 'kerygmatic' and an 'apologetic' function."[46]

Noticing a conspicuous absence of any explicit reference to Henry Nelson Wieman in King's sermons—particularly in view of several references to Paul Tillich and since Tillich and Wieman were joint foci in King's dissertation—I asked him if Wieman exerted any influence at all on his theological beliefs. His response was mildly negative; he further explained that Wieman's theology was somewhat humanistic, almost naturalistic, and as such was not entirely compatible with his own theology. He hastened to add, however, that Wieman had made valuable contributions to the overall body of theological knowledge.[47]

Here is a typical expression of King's perennial theme of brother-sisterhood:

> The real tragedy . . . is that we see people as entities or merely as things. Too seldom do we see people in their true humanness. A spiritual myopia limits our vision to external accidents. We see men as Jews or Gentiles, Catholics or Protestants, Chinese or American, Negroes or whites. We fail to think of them as fellow human beings made from the same basic stuff as we, molded in the same divine image. The priest and the Levite saw only a bleeding body, not a human being like themselves. But the good Samaritan will always remind us to remove the cataracts or provincialism from our spiritual eyes and see men as men. If the Samaritan had considered the wounded man as a Jew first, he would not have stopped, for the Jews and the Samaritans had no dealings. He saw him as a human being first, who was a Jew only by accident. The good neighbor looks beyond the external accidents and discerns those inner qualities that make all men human and, therefore, brothers. ("On Being a Good Neighbor")

Ordinarily, perhaps, a homiletician might criticize King for selecting one constant, never-wavering theme, because it may seem not to allow for the thematic variety that is thought to characterize the best preachers, especially in pastoral preaching. One must take into account, however, two considerations. First of all, notwithstanding that he continued in an official pastoral position with a local congregation whether in Montgomery or Atlanta, King's divine summons to advocate human rights on a grand scale compelled him to consider the world his parish.

Second, as James A. Winans reminds us that "a speaker's topic is often suggested, sometimes dictated, at least in a general way, by the occasion."[48] King, a universally known preacher championing the civil rights movement, was generally expected to address himself to that cause. Can one imagine someone inviting King to preach and not expecting him to expound on some aspect of the struggle? Surely the listeners would have been disappointed and felt cheated if King had ever ignored his consistent theme of human oneness. His first biographer, L. D. Reddick, noted that race relations constituted King's primary concern and expressed hope for the day when King's talented preaching would address other areas.

At one time King himself granted that the demanding schedule of civil rights activities had caused him to lead "a life of giving out and never stopping to take in." "I have lost freshness and creativity. I cannot write new speeches each time I talk, and it is a great frustration to have to rehash old stuff again and again."[49] Such healthy and wholesome self-analysis contributes to our appreciation of the greatness of the man.

Nevertheless, other Christian themes appear most frequently within his sermons; they may be considered reliable indicators of King's theology. My purpose here is not to offer an exhaustive analysis but to survey certain theological tenets and concepts common to his sermonic discourse: God, Jesus Christ, the church, the preacher, humankind (the Negro, the Caucasian), love, prayer, faith, good and evil.

God. King's most explicit expression of his doctrine of God is found in "God Is Able." Here God is described as a supernatural being who possesses the quality of omnipotence, that is, unlimited power. Noting several "threats" to God—(1) that God is being replaced by human scientific genius, space travel and mastery of the cosmic order, (2) that colonialism and segregation are necessary evils substantiated by history and (3) that problems and disappointments of life may crush humankind—King says that (1) God is able to sustain the vast scope of the physical universe, (2) God is able to subdue all the powers of evil (amid the contemporary cry that "God is dead," King declares that segregation is dying), (3) God is able to give us internal resources to confront the trials and difficulties of life.

As if to combat deism—the belief that God is Creator and final judge of humankind but in the interval remains aloof from, and completely beyond the range of, human experience—King says in "The Death of Evil upon the Seashore" that God sustains his world and its inhabitants:

> We must be reminded anew that God is at work in his universe. He is not outside the world looking on with a sort of cold indifference. Here on all the roads of life, he is striving in our striving. Like an ever-loving Father, he is working through history for the salvation of his children. As we struggle to defeat the forces of evil, the God of the universe struggles with us.

A similar picture of a Creator God is seen in "What Is Man?" Contending with atheism, "Antidotes for Fear" notes that "irreligion . . . would have us believe that we are orphans cast into the terrifying immensities of space in a universe that is without purpose or intelligence." Assuming that God fosters justice, freedom and love for the welfare of his creatures, how does King account for the existence of racial segregation and discrimination in a God-created and God-sustained world? The sermon "Shattered Dreams" answers:

> We as a people have long dreamed of freedom, but we are still confined to an oppressive prison of segregation and discrimination. . . . Must we conclude that the existence of segregation is a part of the will of God, and thereby resign ourselves to the fate of oppression? Of course not, for such a course would be blasphemy, because it attributes to God something that should be attributed to the devil.

In the sermons of King, then, God is the sustaining power in the universe whose presence assures the ultimate triumph of good over evil. As the One who provides human beings with inner resources to meet life's problems effectively, God works not separately but in cooperation with human faith to cast out all forms of evil from human beings' environment.

Jesus Christ. To King, Jesus Christ is divinity clothed in humanity. He has come to humankind for the purpose of revealing God. Posing an epistemological question, the sermon "Three Dimensions of a Complete Life" goes on to provide an answer:

> Where do we find this God? In a test tube? No. Where else but in Jesus Christ, the Lord of our lives? By knowing him we know God. Christ is not only God-like but God is Christ-like. Christ is the word made flesh. He is the language of eternity translated in the words of time. If we are to know what God is like, and understand his purposes for mankind, we must turn to Christ. By committing ourselves absolutely to Christ and his way we will be participating in that marvelous act of faith that will bring us to the true knowledge of God.

Typical expressions that may be taken as indicative of King's belief in a God-Christ are "our Lord and Master, Jesus Christ" and "God in Christ" (both from "Transformed Nonconformist"), "the Body of Christ" (referring to the Christian church, in "Paul's Letter to American Christians"), "God through Christ" ("Shattered Dreams") and "the gospel of Jesus Christ" ("How Should a Christian View Communism?").

Christ Jesus provides humankind with a divine epistemology. He constitutes

God in human flesh, living among human beings to demonstrate how we must live out basic virtues within moral relationships.

The church. In calling the church the body of Christ, "Paul's Letter to American Christians" portrays a mystical relation between the church and its Spiritual Leader. More than merely borrowing the term from the apostle Paul (1 Cor 12:27), King really believed the church actually constitutes the mystical body of Jesus Christ.

Concerning the church's environment, the sermon "Love in Action" declares that the church is the chief moral guardian of the community and must implore humanity to be "good" and "well-intentioned" and must extol "conscientiousness" as well as "kindheartedness." Not only does humanity look to the church for moral guidance but the church indeed should disconnect itself from the status quo (the tendency of society to be apathetic about appropriate change) and unequivocally address itself to economic deprivation and corrupt political and social systems ("A Knock at Midnight").

How must the church relate to the state? According to the same sermon,

> The church must be reminded once again that it is not to be the master or the servant of the state, but the conscience of the state. It must be the guide and the critic of the state,—never its tool. As long as the church is a tool of the state it will be unable to provide even a modicum of bread for men at midnight.

What leads to an irrelevant church, a church out of touch with its milieu? Having noted that the Protestant Reformation appropriately purged the stagnant medieval church, King speaks of an extreme element of Reformation theology in the Calvinistic doctrine of total human depravity, which encouraged an otherworldliness and thus a rather antisocial concern ("The Answer to a Perplexing Question"):

> This lopsided Reformation theology has often led to a purely otherworldly religion. It has caused many churches to ignore the "here" and emphasize only the "yonder." By stressing the utter hopelessness of this world and emphasizing the need for the individual to concentrate his efforts on getting his soul prepared for the world to come, it has ignored the need for social reform, and divorced relation from life. It sees the Christian gospel as only concerned with the individual soul. Recently a church was seeking a new minister and the pulpit committee listed several qualifications that he should possess. The first qualification was: "He must be able to preach the true gospel and not about social issues." This emphasis has led to a dangerously irrelevant church. It is little more than a country club where people assemble to hear and speak pious platitudes.

Further irrelevance ensues from the church's apparently typical stand (or lack of a stand) regarding war:

> In the terrible midnight of war men have knocked on the door of the church to ask for the bread of peace, but the church has often disappointed them. What more pathetically reveals the irrelevancy of the church in present-day world affairs than its witness regarding war? In a world gone mad with arms buildups, chauvinistic passions, and imperialistic exploitation, the church has either endorsed these activities or remained appallingly silent. During the last two world wars, national churches even functioned as the ready lackeys of the state, sprinkling holy water upon the battleships and joining the mighty armies in singing, "Praise the Lord and pass the ammunition." A weary world, pleading desperately for peace, has often found the church morally sanctioning war. ("A Knock at Midnight")

King does not hesitate to finger the Christian church, the spiritual body to which he unstintingly devotes his time and talent, as having had an active part in establishing racial segregation and discrimination. He charges in the same sermon: "It is to the everlasting shame of the American church that white Christians developed a system of racial segregation within the church, and inflicted so many indignities upon its Negro worshipers that they had to go out and organize their own churches." Putting its finger on the divisive and unchristian American system of a "white church" and a "Negro church," "Paul's Letter to American Christians" asks, How can segregation exist in the true body of Christ?

In appraising the Christian church in general, King does not fail to chide the so-called Negro church in particular. He brings to the fore two ineffective extremes often found in black churches:

> There are two types of Negro churches that have failed to provide the bread at midnight. One is a church that burns up with emotionalism and the other is a church that freezes up with classism. The former is a church that reduces worship to entertainment, and places more emphasis on volume than on content. It confuses spirituality with muscleality. The danger of this church is that its members will end up with more religion in their hands and feet than in their hearts and souls. So many people have gone by this type of church at midnight, and it had neither the vitality nor the relevant gospel to feed their hungry souls. The other type of Negro church that leaves men unfed at midnight is a church that develops a class system within. It boasts of the fact that it is a dignified church, and most of its members are professional people. It takes pride in its exclusiveness. In this church the worship service is cold and meaningless. The music is dull and uninspiring. The sermon is little

more than a nice little essay on current events. If the pastor says too much about Jesus Christ the members begin to feel that he is taking the dignity out of the pulpit. If the choir sings a Negro spiritual, the members bow their head in shame feeling that this is an affront to their class status. The tragedy of this type of church is that it fails to see that worship at its best is a social experience with people of all levels of life coming together to realize their oneness and unity under God. This church ends up losing the spiritual force of the "whosoever will let him come" doctrine, and is little more than a social club with a thin veneer of religiosity. When men have gone by this church at midnight they have either been ignored altogether because of their limited education or they have been given a lot of stale bread that has been hardened by the winter of morbid class consciousness. ("A Knock at Midnight")

According to "Transformed Nonconformist," the church has been weakened by diluting its gospel and conforming to the status quo of the world. The challenge is set forth:

Ever since that time [the apostolic era, first and second centuries A.D., when the church thrived in its primitive power] the church has been like a weak and ineffectual trumpet making uncertain sounds, rather than a strong trumpet sounding a clarion call for truth and righteousness. If the church of Jesus Christ is to regain its power, and its message its authentic ring, it must go out with a new determination not to conform to this world.

In brief, King's sermons reveal his serious dissatisfaction with, and hope for, the church. He believes the church should not be a thermometer, registering the temperature of majority opinion, but a thermostat, transforming and regulating through precept and example the temperature of society. As the mystical body of Christ and as God's supreme channel on earth for truth, righteousness, justice and peace, the church should serve as a moral conscience to society and should seek to respond to humankind's social, economic and political as well as spiritual needs.

The preacher. References to the ministerial profession in King's sermons sometimes reveal a dissatisfaction similar to that regarding the church. Preachers often conform when they should transform, they frequently preach sermons irrelevant to the real needs of their hearers, and they apparently feel safe when functioning within the physical and philosophical walls of the church building.

We preachers have often joined the enticing cult of conformity. We, too, have often yielded to the success symbols of the world, feeling that the size of our ministry must be measured by the size of our automobiles. So often we turn into showmen, distorting the real meaning of the gospel, in an attempt to appeal to the whims and caprices of the crowd. We preach soothing sermons that bypass the weightier matters of Christianity. We dare not say anything in our sermons that will question the respectable views of the comfortable members of our congregations. If you want to get ahead in the ministry, conform! Stay within the secure walls of the sanctuary. Play it safe. How many ministers of Jesus Christ have sacrificed truth on the altar of their self-interest, and, like Pilate, yielded their convictions to the demands of the crowd?

Further comments providing insight on King's concept of the ministry follow:

☐ The minister's sermon, disappointingly, is often "little more than a nice little essay on current events" ("A Knock at Midnight").

☐ The pulpit in many instances does not give us "objective and unbiased truth" ("A Tough Mind and a Tender Heart").

☐ "The most popular preachers are those who can preach soothing sermons on 'How to be Happy' and 'How to Relax.' Some have been tempted to re-translate Jesus' command to read 'Go ye into all the world and keep your blood pressure down and lo I will make you a well-adjusted personality.' All of this is indicative of the fact that it is midnight in the inner lives of men and women" ("A Knock at Midnight").

☐ The Christian preacher has a responsibility to discuss Communism with his congregation for three reasons: (a) Communism is believed in by almost one billion peoples of the world; communism is embraced by many as a religion and is such a force today as cannot be ignored.

(b) Communism is the only serious rival to Christianity. (Judaism, Buddhism, Hinduism, and Mohammedanism may stand as possible alternatives to Christianity but communism is the most formidable rival.)

(c) It is unfair and unscientific to condemn a system without first knowing what that system teaches and why it is wrong ("How Should a Christian View Communism?").

Other than the implied solutions accompanying the charges, the remedy preferred by King for the ministerial profession is general. He urges that preachers recapture something that early Christians had—they were aglow with a wholesomely radical gospel.

Humankind. King's estimate of human beings is dualistic. In "What Is Man?" he states that humankind is created in the "image of God," thereby possessing a rational capacity and the ability to fellowship with the divine; on the other hand, and true to his imputed theological position as a "moderate liberal,"[50] King admits in the same sermon that "man is a sinner" who possesses the God-bestowed "ability to choose between alternatives, so he can choose the good or the evil, the high or the low." The dualism in human nature (at once both good and bad) results, according to this sermon, from the fact that "he has misused his freedom" (this quite possibly is a reference to human sin in the Garden of Eden, or at least to the general concept of the Fall). Hence "some of the image of God is gone. Therefore, man is a sinner in need of God's divine grace."

That human beings are indeed free and fulfill God's purpose in life only by exercising "a voluntary choice" finds brief treatment in "The Death of Evil upon the Seashore."[51] How does King reconcile human freedom with the fatalistic brand of predestination? He does not. He simply recognizes certain inherent limitations upon human beings by virtue of their existence in time and space. The sermon "Shattered Dreams," elaborates:

> Since freedom is a part of the essence of man, the fatalist, in denial of freedom, becomes a puppet and not a person. He is right in his conviction that there is not absolute freedom, and that freedom always operates within the framework of pre-destined structure. Thus a man is free to go north from Atlanta to Washington or south from Atlanta to Miami. But he is not free to go north to Miami or south to Washington. Freedom is always within destiny. But there is freedom. We are both free and destined. Freedom is the act of deliberating, deciding and responding within our destined nature. Even if destiny prevents our going to some attractive Spain, there still remains in us the capacity to take this disappointment and do something with it. Fatalism doesn't see this. It leaves the individual stymied and helplessly inadequate for life.

"The Answer to a Perplexing Question" proffers a solution to the question why humankind cannot deliver itself from its moral, social, economic, and political evils. Emphasizing corrupt human nature as the major element of the problem, King says:

> The answer to this question is rather simple. Man by his own power can never cast evil out of the world. The humanist's hope is an illusion. It is based on too great an optimism concerning the inherent goodness of human nature. There are thousands of sincere and dedicated people outside the churches working unselfishly through various humanitarian movements to cure the world of its social evils. I would be the last to condemn these people because they have not yet found their way to God, for

I would rather that a man be a committed humanist than an uncommitted Christian. But so many of these dedicated people, having no one but themselves to save themselves, end up disillusioned and pessimistic. They are disillusioned because they started out with a great illusion. For them there is no sinner or no sin. Human nature is essentially good, and the only evil is found in systems and institutions; just enlighten people and free them from the crippling yoke of poverty, and they will save themselves. All of this sounds wonderful and soothingly pleasant. But it is an illusion wrapped in superficiality. It is a kind of self-delusion which causes the individual to ignore a basic fact about human nature.

More than fallenness, however, King also underscores the positive potential of humanity, and thus humankind's value in the reckoning of God:

Man, for Jesus, is not mere flotsam and jetsam in the river of life, but he is a child of God. Is it not unreasonable to assume that God, whose creative activity is expressed in an awareness of a sparrow's fall and the number of hairs on a man's head, excludes from his encompassing love the life of man itself? The confidence that God is mindful of the individual is of tremendous value in dealing with the disease of fear, for it gives us a sense of worth, of belonging, and of at-homeness in the universe. ("Antidotes for Fear")

It was not uncommon for King to shift from allusions to the general category of humankind and address himself to specific people (in terms of race), the "Negro" and the "Caucasian."

The negro. Making a broad application of the text that advises, "Be ye therefore wise as serpents and harmless as doves" (Mt 10:16 KJV), the sermon "A Tough Mind and a Tender Heart" offers the following admonition to African Americans with respect to the race problem:

This text has a great deal of bearing on our struggle for racial justice. We as Negroes must combine tough mindedness and tender heartedness if we are to move creatively toward the goal of freedom and justice. There are those soft minded individuals among us who feel that the only way to deal with oppression is to adjust to it. They follow the way of acquiescence and resign themselves to the fate of segregation. In almost every pilgrimage up freedom's road some of the oppressed prefer to remain oppressed. Almost 2,800 years ago Moses set out to lead the children of Israel from the slavery of Egypt to the freedom of the Promised Land. He soon discovered that slaves do not always welcome their deliverers. They would rather bear those ills they have, as Shakespeare pointed out, than flee to others that they know not of. They prefer the "fleshpots of Egypt" to the ordeals of emancipation. But this is not the way out. This soft minded acquiescence is the way of the coward. My friends, we cannot win the respect of the white people of the South or the peoples of the world if we are willing to sell the future of our children for our personal and immediate safety and comfort. Moreover, we must learn that the passive acceptance of an unjust system is to cooperate with that system, and thereby become a participant in its evil. Noncooperation with evil is as much a moral obligation as is cooperation with good.

There are those hard hearted individuals among us who feel that our only way out is to rise up against the opponent with physical violence and corroding hatred. They have allowed themselves to become bitter. But this also is not the way out. . . . It creates many more social problems than it solves. So I am convinced that if we succumb to the temptation of using violence in our struggle for freedom, unborn generations will be the recipients of a long and desolate night of bitterness, and our chief legacy to them will be an endless reign of meaningless chaos. There is still a voice echoing through the vista of time saying to every potential Peter, "Put up your sword." . . .

There is a third way open to us in our quest for freedom, namely, nonviolent resistance. It is a way that combines tough mindedness and tender heartedness. It avoids the complacency and donothingness of the soft minded and the violence and bitterness of the hard hearted. It is tough enough to resist evil. It is tender hearted enough to resist it with love and nonviolence. It seems to me that this is the method that must guide our action in the present crisis in race relations.

African Americans must not assume that their segregated and discriminated lot is providential. "Shattered Dreams" gives the following perspective: "Must we conclude that the existence of segregation is a part of the will of God, and thereby resign ourselves to the fate of oppression? Of course not, for such a course would be blasphemy, because it attributes to God something that should be attributed to the devil."

The caucasian. In an effort to palliate white people's fear of African Americans, King suggests a solution in "Antidotes for Fear":

If our white brothers are to master fear, they must depend not only on their commitment to Christian love but also on the Christlike love which the Negro generates toward them. Only through our adherence to love and nonviolence will the fear in the white community be mitigated. A guilt-ridden white minority fears that if the Negro attains power, he will without restraint or pity act to revenge the accumulated injustices and brutality of the years. A parent, who has continually mistreated his son, suddenly realizes that he is now taller than the parent. Will the son use his new physical power to repay for all of the blows of the past?

Once a helpless child, the Negro has now grown politically, culturally, and economically. Many white men fear retaliation. The Negro must show them that they have nothing to fear, for the Negro forgives and is willing to forget the past. *The Negro must convince the white man that he seeks justice for both himself and the white man.* A mass movement exercising love and nonviolence and demonstrating power under discipline should convince the white community that were such a movement to attain strength its power would be used creatively and not vengefully.

What then is the cure of this morbid fear of integration? We know the cure. God help us to achieve it! Love casts out fear.

The balanced life. King summons humanity to the balanced life. This has three dimensions: length (the inward drive to achieve one's personal ends and ambitions), breadth (the outward concern for the welfare of others) and height (the upward reach for God; "Three Dimensions of a Complete Life").

Having noted the similarity between the theme of this sermon by King and that of "The Symmetry of Life" by Phillips Brooks, I inquired of him whether there was a conscious relationship. He answered in the affirmative and stated that Brooks's sermon indeed had inspired him to develop the sermon "Three Dimensions of a Complete Life"; he volunteered that much of his preaching had been influenced by Brooks.[52]

Keith D. Miller cites this interview discussion of Brooks's homiletical influence and seeks to make a case of what he concludes is King's plagiarism and unwarranted borrowing of materials from a number of sources, including also the likes of Harry Emerson Fosdick, Howard Thurman, Wallace Hamilton and others.[53] Richard Lischer offers explanation and rebuttal by calling attention to the immense body of information available to preacher-seminarians, amounting to what I call a "public domain of universals" that, like many of the Negro spirituals, belong to no one in particular but to everyone. They are often attributed temporarily to the recent user who appears to be accomplishing most with them or glorifying them best.

How interesting and revealing it would be to interview Fosdick or Thurman or Hamilton and ask them of probable source antecedents to their very own sermons, which present-day critics claim were reservoirs for King. Lischer challenges us to consider whether we are crying fraud or foul at observable traces of "Jefferson's borrowings in the *Declaration of Independence* or Lincoln's reliance on Theodore Parker's 'of all, for all, and by all,' or Kennedy's well-publicized dependence on Theodore Sorenson."[54] Of course Miller's response might very well be "We ought to," but the larger reality, in my opinion, is more akin to Ralph Waldo Emerson's insight in *Quotation and Originality:* "When Shakespeare is charged with debts to his authors, Lander replies, 'Yet he was more original than his originals. He breathed upon dead bodies and brought them into life.'"[55] This is not to encourage everyone to enjoy "open season" on everyone else's material; however, we need to consider motive, time and circumstance, and at the appropriate moment acknowledge credit where credit is due.

Decades ago, long before public indictments of source usurpation by King, his instant affirmative response to my inquiry about the Brooks influence bespoke one devoid of intended pilferage and "sermon-lifting," especially when he further volunteered an admission of linear inspiration from Brooks beyond punctiliar impact on any one sermon. Homiletical theory has always encouraged *adapting* from other preachers without *adopting,* affirming them without aping them. Like any preacher taking his or her craft seriously, King doubtless assembled ingredients from a number of sources, but then he kneaded and worked and formed until he made his own loaf of bread.

Love. Although I have already highlighted the love ethic in the ministry of King, it appears appropriate to refer to this cardinal virtue again—this time in the immediate context of King's sermons.

It was pointed out earlier in this chapter (under the heading "Humankind") that King said love is the mastering remedy for the Caucasian's fear of the Negro ("Antidotes for Fear"). In the sermon "Love in Action," forgiveness is elevated as an active expression of love. "Loving Your Enemies" affords essentially the same treatment of love, emphasizing forgiveness as its empirical manifestation. However, in "Loving Your Enemies" King goes beyond what he calls the "practical *how"* of loving enemies to the "theoretical *why."* Assuming that the absence of love inevitably brings its opposite (hatred), King presents the following reasons for loving;

1. Hate multiplies hate; the endless cycle must be discontinued.

2. Hate leaves not only the hatred but the hater scarred and distorted.

3. Love is the only force capable of transforming an enemy into a friend.

4. Loving one's enemies is not only a commandment from God but also a prerequisite to knowing God.

The section "*Agape* Versus *Philia* and *Eros*" quoted King's remark in "Loving Your Enemies" that "in the Greek New Testament are three words for love . . . *eros* . . . *philia* . . . *agape*." I brought to King's attention that while the latter two words are indeed used fairly frequently by New Testament writers, *eros* does not occur even once. Why would King have made that erroneous statement? One possible explanation for this perhaps more academic than significant error may be that at Crozer Theological Seminary he did not enroll in any of the biblical Greek classes. According to Morton S. Enslin, while King took such courses as New Testament Life and Literature, The Gospels, and Greek Religion, records indicate that he did not take any Greek language classes.[56] When I interviewed King himself five months later, he reminisced about his Crozer days and confirmed what Enslin had said. He added that among his keenest "regrets" was that in all of his theological training he never enrolled in even one course in Greek.[57]

Because the word *eros* is so crucial for contrasting and heightening the meaning of the other two words for love, some preachers avoid King's technical error by saying something like "There are three popular words in the Greek language, two of which are found in the New Testament." At any rate, listening to King preach on any occasion or perusing his printed sermons reveals that *love* wins hands down as the most recurring theological theme found in his messages.

Prayer. King strongly believed in, consistently practiced and urgently advocated the experience called *prayer.* All biographies of the man record his testimony that prayer provided him the necessary inner fortitude to continue leading the Montgomery protest of 1956. A further indication can be found in the M. L. King Collection at the Boston University Library: King's recorded schedule shows that usually one to two (and sometimes three) days each week were devoted to "Silence and Meditation." His fervent desire, however, was that people would place prayer in a practical perspective.

Associating prayer with race relations, "The Answer to a Perplexing Question" first points out a misuse and then a suggestive right use of prayer:

> The idea that man must wait on God to do everything has led to a tragic misuse of prayer. He who feels that God must do everything will end up asking him for anything. Some people see God as little more than "a cosmic bellhop" that they will call on for every trivial need. Others see God as so omnipotent and man as so powerless that they end up making prayer a substitute for work and intelligence. A man said to me the other day: "I believe in integration, but I know it will not come until God gets ready for it to come. You Negroes should stop protesting and start pray-

ing." Well, I'm sure we all need to pray for God's help and guidance in this integration struggle. But we will be gravely misled if we think it will come by prayer alone. God will never allow prayer to become a substitute for work and intelligence. God gave us minds to think and breath and body to work, and he would be defeating his own purpose if he allowed us to obtain through prayer what can come through work and intelligence. No, it is not either prayer *or* human effort; it is both prayer *and* human effort. Prayer is a marvelous and necessary supplement of our feeble efforts but it is a dangerous and callous substitute. Moses discovered this as he struggled to lead the Israelites to the Promised Land. God made it clear that he would not do for them what they could do for themselves. In the Book of Exodus we read: "And the Lord said unto Moses, Wherefore criest thou unto me? Speak unto the children of Israel, that they go forward."

In King's thinking, prayer bears an important relation to peacemaking. The same sermon declares:

> We must pray earnestly for peace. But along with our prayers we must work vigorously for disarmament and suspension of nuclear tests. We must use our minds as rigorously to work out a plan for peace as we have used them to work out a plan for war. We must pray with unceasing passion for the emergence of racial justice. But along with this we must use our minds to develop a program and organize ourselves into mass nonviolent action and use every resource of our bodies and souls to end the long night of racial injustice. But along with our prayers we must work diligently.

Prayer, then, for King was a necessary Christian process, that of imploring God to act in behalf of humankind; but it must be accompanied by human cooperation and responsibility in use of work and intelligence.

Faith. Along with candid self-analysis, courage and love, faith provides a remedy for fear ("Antidotes for Fear"). Effectively contrasting the efficacy of human beings' religious faith with human trust in psychiatry and utopian hopes, King expounds:

> Abnormal fears and phobias that are expressed in neurotic anxiety may be cured by psychiatry; but the fear of death, non-being, and nothingness, expressed in existential anxiety, may be cured only by a positive religious faith.
>
> A positive religious faith does not offer an illusion that we shall be exempt from pain and suffering, nor does it imbue us with the idea that life is a drama of unalloyed comfort and untroubled ease. Rather, it instills us with the inner equilibrium needed to face strains, burdens, and fears that inevitably come, and assures us that

the universe is trustworthy and that God is concerned.

"Shattered Dreams" sees in faith a source of inner strength in the face of disappointments:

> In the final analysis our ability to deal creatively with shattered dreams and blasted
> hopes will be determined by the extent of our faith in God. A genuine faith will
> imbue us with the conviction that there is a God beyond time and a "Life beyond
> Life." Thus, we know that we are not alone in any circumstance, however dismal
> and catastrophic it may be. God dwells with us in life's confining and oppressive
> cells.

Faith seems to be, for King, a means by which human beings rely on a power beyond themselves. That power is supernatural, for that power is God. Our ability to meet adequately the issues of life stands in direct ratio to our reliance on the higher power.

Good and evil. The notion of dualistic forces in the universe, struggling for supremacy, is quite prevalent in the sermons of King. These forces are irreconcilable opposites and known as "good" and "evil"—"good" eventually to emerge as victor ("The Death of Evil upon the Seashore").

Is the existence of evil debatable? That is, could it be a mere figment of the imagination? In the same sermon, which is King's most extensive discussion of "good" and "evil," he maintains that while we debate the *origin* of evil, only a victim of superficial optimism would debate its *reality.*

What is the relationship of good and evil to humankind? As discussed under the heading "Humankind" earlier in this chapter, our nature itself is dichotomized by these forces, for we are at once creatures formed in God's image (good) and also sinners (evil). We must strive to cast evil (in all of its multiple forms) out of our midst. "But it will not be removed," admonishes King, "by man alone nor by a dictatorial God who invades our lives. It will be removed when we open the door and allow God through Christ to enter. 'Behold, I stand at the door and knock,' saith the Lord; 'if any man will open the door I will come in to him and sup with him and he with me'" ("The Answer to a Perplexing Question"). In this same sermon King proposes a way of overcoming a bad habit:

> What, then, is the way out? Not by our own efforts, and not by a purely external
> help from God. One cannot remove an evil habit by my resolution; nor can it be
> done by simply calling on God to do the job. It can be done only when a man lifts
> himself up until he can put his will into the hands of God's will as an instrument.

This is the only way to be delivered from the accumulated weight of evil. It can
only be done when we allow the energy of God to be let loose in our souls.

The force of "good" reveals itself in history in the form of justice, truth, righteousness and peace, while "evil" comes in the form of injustice, falsehood,
unrighteousness and war. King's concept of good and evil affords a basis for civil
disobedience, as is evident in the sermon "Loving Your Enemies": "We cannot in
all good conscience obey your unjust laws, because nonco-operation with evil is
as much a moral obligation as is co-operation with good."

Perfect optimism characterizes King's expectation of the inevitable defeat of
evil—particularly the ramifications of racial segregation and discrimination:

Looking back [at the 1954 Supreme Court decision to ban segregation from public
education], we see the forces of segregation gradually dying on the seashore. The
problem is far from solved and gigantic mountains of opposition lie ahead, but at
least we have left Egypt, and with patient yet firm determination we shall reach the
promised land. Evil in the form of injustice and exploitation shall not survive forever. A Red Sea passage ultimately brings the forces of goodness to victory, and the
closing of the same waters marks the doom and destruction of the forces of evil. . . .

Evil carries the seed of its own destruction. In the long run right defeated is
stronger than evil triumphant. . . .

As we struggle to defeat the forces of evil, the God of the universe struggles
with us. Evil dies on the seashore, not merely because of man's endless struggle
against it, but because of God's power to defeat it. ("The Death of Evil upon the
Seashore")

Walking hand in hand with Omnipotence, with such a vision as this, who could
preach anything less?

7
LANGUAGE
IN KINGLY
STYLE

And the Word was made flesh . . .
JOHN 1:14

All these things [he spoke] to the crowd in parables;
he did not say anything to them without a parable.
MATTHEW 13:34

Whenen Martin Luther King Jr. was asked to describe an excellent sermon, he noted that a sermon not only offers something valuable for the mind and heart but "paints an appeal to the imagination."[1] He was making direct reference to the best preachers' conscious choice of language. There has always been debate between extreme positions regarding the place language should occupy in preachers' craft—from Barth's advocacy of total disregard of any personal semantics to allow God room to speak for himself to charlatans' use of manipulative words that are full of sound and fury, signifying nothing. Somewhere in between is that effective and ethical employment of language spoken of by Cicero: it is the speaker's duty "to clothe and deck his thoughts with language."[2] Style, according to Hugh Blair, is "the peculiar manner in which a man expresses his conceptions, by means of language. . . . [It] has always some reference to . . . manner of thinking . . . and . . . is nothing else than that sort of expression which our thoughts most readily assume." Fundamentally, "style is *language;* language is a system of symbols called *words.* It is through words that communication is carried on."[3]

In terms of vividness, force, coherence, emphasis, appropriateness and concreteness, King's preaching was marked by a distinctive style. Style is the constituent of homiletics he meant by "an appeal to the imagination." As an English minor in college, King learned to wield language with beauty and facility; he acknowledged during his championing of human rights that the "eloquent statement of ideas is his greatest talent, strongest tradition, and most constant interest."[4]

In considering the language of King's sermons, we do well to use Lester Thonssen and A. Craig Baird's components of style as guidelines: (1) choice of words, (2) composition (or grammar) and (3) embellishment.[5] *Word choice* is essentially vocabulary, encompassing such qualities as correctness, aptness and clarity. A speaker seeks to select the best words for a particular preaching task; this is a highly individual matter touching on such variables as the speaker's knowledge, language facility, understanding of the preaching situation and the nature of the response desired. *Composition* is the orderly arrangement of the speaker's chosen words, involving structure, syntax and rhythm. *Embellishment,* as used here, covers the creative usage of language, principally though not solely through figures of speech.

Yardstick for Measuring Language

A usable approach to help in assessing the first two constituents of style, word choice and composition, has been developed by Rudolf Flesch.[6] His yardstick, a quantitative plan for measuring readability and understandability of a discourse, seems to follow the suggestion of I. A. Richards that in assessing the worth of a speech, critics should study its language microscopically.[7]

Flesch's system includes scales to assess *sentence length, words* and *personal reference* (or human interest). Combining totals in these three areas yields what he calls a "difficulty score," which determines the readability or comprehensibility of the sermon. We must understand, moreover, that the Flesch system for measuring communication effectiveness was popular and helpful and recommended during the King years and may serve our understanding today of how one particular window admitted light into a way of looking at the preaching effectiveness of the foremost preacher and leader of human rights during his lifetime.

The difficulty score is determined as follows: First, determine the average length of sentences and multiply that number by .1338. Second, take the number of affixes per 100 words and multiply that by .0645 (affixes are letters or

sequences of letters attached to beginning of words [called prefixes] and to ending of words [suffixes]; e.g., *anti*toxin, *by*stander, *para*phrase; activ*ate*, achieve-
ment, lemon*ade).* Third, add these two figures. Fourth, count the number of
personal references (or human-interest words) like names of people, personal
pronouns (except antecedents of inanimate objects) and other words denoting
humanity—man, woman, boy, girl and so on. (Flesch provides a guideline list of
such words on p. 73 of *The Art of Plain Talk*.) When the number of personal references per 100 words is multiplied by .0659, the result is a "Personal Reference"
score. Subtract this score from the sum of the first figures (sentence length and
affixes). Finally, subtract .75 and you will probably get a difficulty score ranging
from 0 (very easy to understand) to 7 (very difficult to understand).[8] Let me add
that once you do the basic addition, the multiplication tables are already and conveniently provided by Flesch for quick use throughout each step of the formula.
The three different factors employed (.1338, .0645 and .0659) to facilitate his
resultant scale determining difficulty are understood as statistical standard-devia-
tion figures assisting for possible margin of variation.

Analyzing King's Sermons by Flesch's Measures

From the sixteen sermons examined in this book, three were chosen for the purpose of applying Flesch's yardstick. To facilitate the probability that these three
sermons would be representative of the sixteen, required assumptions were
obtained such as "independence" (the choice of one sermon's having no bearing
on the choice of another to be included among the samples) and "randomization"
(each sermon's having an equal chance of being selected). To meet these criteria,
a number was assigned to each of the sixteen sermons, the numbers were placed
in a container, and then three were drawn (with replacement).[9] The sermons
selected were "Shattered Dreams," "The Man Who Was a Fool" and "Love in
Action."

Applying Flesch's measurements to the random sampling of three sermons by
King gave the results summarized in table 1.

Interpreting the three subscores from each of the three sermons according to
Flesch's "Quick Reference Chart," one sees that the sermons of King measure
"fairly easy" and "easy" in readability. This reflects his ability to target the comprehension of a potential 80-86 percent of adults in the United States. People at
typical fifth- and sixth-grade levels of understanding were able to comprehend
his sermons.

Word choice. Though the three sermons average a commendable 29.3 affixes per 100 words ("easy" in understandability), they do not quite equal the simplicity of the King James Version of the Bible, the word difficulty of which measures 20 affixes per 100 words (or "very easy"). It may be of interest to note that Flesch's own book, *The Art of Plain Talk,* has a word difficulty of 33 affixes per 100 words or "fairly easy"—less simple than King's sample sermons.

Table 1. Flesch's measurements

Sermon	Average sentence length in words	Affixes per 100 words	Personal references per 100 words	Difficulty score
"Shattered Dreams"	11.7 (easy)	32 (fairly easy)	7 (fairly easy)	2.42 (fairly easy)
"The Man Who Was a Fool"	15.4 (fairly easy)	27 (easy)	17 (easy)	1.93 (easy)
"Love in Action"	11.4 (easy)	29 (easy)	10 (fairly easy)	2 (fairly easy)

If these three sermons are typical of King's sermon in general, the overwhelming majority of his words may be described as simple. "Love in Action," for example, has a total of 3,353 words, 2,920 (or 87.1 percent) of which are one and two syllables in length (proper names were not included in the tally). Yet he also uses three-syllable words (249, or 7.4 percent) and words of four or more syllables (184, or 5.5 percent). Examples of the latter in "Love in Action" are *magnanimity, ignominious, retribution, schizophrenia, antithesis, dichotomy, retaliation, immutable, inexorably, uniformity, criminality, reverberates, rationalization, justification, pseudo-scientific, disillusionment, disarmament, annihilation* and *academician.* Occasionally unusual and even coined words find a place in King's sermons, for example *manyness* ("Antidotes for Fear"), *phobiaphobia* (if not coined, probably a misspelling of *phobophobia;* "Antidotes for Fear"), *humanness* ("On Beng a Good Neighbor") and *donothingness* ("A Tough Mind and a Tender Heart"). While as an academically trained clergyman King frequently used theologically and philosophically technical word symbols, in general (as indicated in the Flesch "word difficulty" score) his vocabulary was simple and informal and thus presumably conducive to listener comprehension.

King's meticulous and versatile use of words was one of the most outstanding elements of his oral discourse. His choice of words (in different sermons and occasionally within the same sermon) ranges from the theological ("What Is Man?"), scholarly ("The Death of Evil upon the Seashore") and philosophical ("How Should a Christian View Communism?") to the informal, folksy and down-to-earth expressions appropriate to a mass meeting rally. King was able to discuss with facility such technical and specialized topics as Platonism, Hinduism, Zoroastrianism, Judaism, Christianity and communism and yet also to communicate effectively with common people. As one reporter observed, "Many admit they don't always understand his words, but, as one of his congregation put it, 'We sure get the force of his meaning.' ('He knows how to speak to the Ph.D.'s and to the No D.'s.')"[10]

Walter G. Muelder affirmed the following in an interview on March 4, 1966:

> The amazing thing about Dr. King is his mastery of many forms of address. He is able to adapt the form and mode of address to varied audiences; he has versatility. His command of vocabulary ranges all the way from what can be understood by the most ignorant man on the street to the most sophisticated audience. . . . He is not tied to any one set of symbols or signs.

"Clear, forceful and adaptable," then, would characterize the Kingly choice of words in preaching.

Composition

"Direct and varied" would describe the sentence structure found in King's sermons. "Shattered Dreams," for example, comprises 255 sentences. The type of sentence form it uses most often is the simple sentence—70 percent of the total number of sentences. The declarative sentence purpose has the highest incidence, 92 percent.

King's custom of employing mostly simple declarative sentences indicates the value he placed on the quality of directness in style. Table 2 takes a broader view of the sentences of "Shattered Dreams."

The fact that King's sermons ordinarily contain all eight kinds of sentences (purpose: declarative, imperative, interrogative, exclamatory; form: simple, complex, compound, compound-complex) shows their variety and avoidance of monotony. Though his sermon preparation clearly involved conscious thought and planning, it was marked by an economy of effort. He employed accepted grammatical principles, governing such elements as tense, mood, number, gender and case. Yet since oral style is often less formal in structure than written style, syntactical elements of King's preaching (although grammatically correct) are often more informal than formal. Fragmentary or incomplete sentences, though sometimes powerful and forceful in oral discourse, seldom found a place in the oral discourse of King.

Table 2. Sentence composition in "Shattered Dreams"

According to Purpose	Total Number	Proportion to Total
Declarative	235	92.1%
Interrogative	9	3.5%
Imperative	6	2.4%
Exclamatory	5	2%
According to Form	**Total Number**	**Proportion to Total**
Simple	179	70.2%
Compound	30	11.8%
Complex	38	14.9%
Compound-Complex	8	3.1%

Conveying his emotional fervor, the prose of his composition is rhythmic without being metrical. An indication of his appreciation for rhythm and appropriate cadence is the high incidence of poetry quoted in his sermons. Of the sixteen sermons analyzed in detail here, fourteen (or 87.5 percent) include recitations from poetic works.

Embellishment

Vividness and imagery in the sermons we are considering lie principally in King's selective employment of sound, figures of speech and other rhetorical devices. A total of eighteen such elements have been found.

1. *Alliteration* (repetition of an initial sound or letter)

> Even the white religious leaders who have a heartfelt desire to open the door and provide the bread (of social justice) are often more cautious than courageous and more prone to follow the expedient path than the ethical path. ("A Knock at Midnight")

> Let us never feel that God's creative power is exhausted by this earthly life, and his majestic love is locked within the limited walls of time and space. ("Shattered Dreams")

2. *Anachronism* (as used here, a deliberate chronological misplacement)

With his own hands (the Good Samaritan in Christ's parable) he bound the wounds of the man and then set him on his own beast. It would have been easier to pay an ambulance to take the unfortunate man to the hospital, rather than risk having his neatly trimmed suit stained with blood. ("On Being a Good Neighbor")

3. *Anaphora,* also known as *epanalepsis* or *ephanaphora* (repetition of a word or words at the beginning of successive clauses)

Professor Bixler reminded us some years ago of the danger of over-stressing the well-adjusted life. Everybody is passionately seeking to be well adjusted; nobody wants to be maladjusted. . . . As for me, I must confess that there are some things to which I'm proud to be maladjusted. I never intend to become adjusted to the evils of segregation and the crippling effects of discrimination. I never intend to become adjusted to the moral degeneracy of religious bigotry and the corroding effects of narrow sectarianism. I never intend to adjust myself to economic conditions that will take necessities from the many to give luxuries to the few. I never intend to become adjusted to the insanities of militarism and the self-defeating effects of physical violence. ("Transformed Nonconformist")

4. *Asyndeton* (omission of conjunctive particles to express vehemence or speed or contrast)

Hatred and bitterness can never cure the disease of fear; only love can do that. Hatred paralyzes life; love releases it. Hatred confuses life; love harmonizes it. Hatred darkens life; love illumines it. ("Antidotes for Fear")

Who is my neighbor? . . . He is neither Jew nor Gentile; he is neither Russian nor American; he is neither Negro nor white. He is 'a certain man'—any needy man—on one of the numerous Jericho roads of life." ("On Being a Good Neighbor")

5. *Comparison* (linking by showing similarities)

[God's] boundless love supports and contains us as a mighty ocean contains and supports the tiny drops of every wave." ("Antidotes for Fear")

All labor that uplifts humanity has dignity and importance and should be undertaken with painstaking excellence. If a man is called to be a street sweeper, he should sweep streets even as Michelangelo painted, or Beethoven composed music, or Shakespeare wrote poetry. He should sweep streets so well that all the host of heaven and earth will pause and say, "Here lived a great street sweeper who did his job well." ("Three Dimensions of a Complete Life")

6. *Contrast* (linking by pointing out differences)

"I have learned," [Paul] said, "in whatsoever state I am, therewith to be content."
Paul did not mean that he had learned to be complacent. There is nothing in the life
of Paul which could characterize him as a complacent man. . . . Paul is not saying
that he had learned to dwell in a valley of stagnant complacency. Neither is he saying that he had learned to resign himself to some tragic fate. Paul meant that he had
learned to stand up amid the disappointment of life without despairing. He had discovered the distinction between a tranquil soul and the outward accidents of circumstance. ("Shattered Dreams")

7. *Enantiosis* (placing together or comparing things that are very different, so that
they set off and enhance each other)

Once a helpless child, the Negro has now grown politically, culturally, and economically. Many white men fear retaliation. The Negro must show them that they have
nothing to fear, for the Negro forgives and is willing to forget the past. The Negro
must convince the white man that he seeks justice for both himself and the white man.
A mass movement exercising love and nonviolence and demonstrating power under
discipline should convince the white community that were such a movement to attain
strength its power would be used creatively and not vengefully. ("Antidotes for Fear")

Each of us lives in two realms, the internal and the external. The internal is that
realm of spiritual ends expressed in art, literature, morals, and religion. The external
is that complex of devices, techniques, mechanisms, and instrumentalities by means
of which we live. These include the house we live in, the car we drive, the clothes
we wear, the economic resources we acquire—the material stuff we must have to
exist. There is always a danger that we will permit the means by which we live to
replace the ends for which we live, the internal to become lost in the external. The
rich man was a fool because he failed to keep a line of distinction between means
and ends, between structure and destiny. His life was submerged in the rolling
waters of his livelihood.

This does not mean that the external in our lives is not important. We have both
a privilege and a duty to seek the basic material necessities of life. Only an irrelevant religion fails to be concerned about man's economic well-being. Religion at its
best realizes that the soul is crushed as long as the body is tortured with hunger
pangs and harrowed with the need for shelter. Jesus realized that we need food,
clothing, shelter, and economic security. He said in clear and concise terms: "Your
Father knoweth what things ye have need of." But Jesus knew that man was more
than a dog to be satisfied by a few economic bones. He realized that the internal of
a man's life is as significant as the external. So he added, "Seek ye first the kingdom

of God and his righteousness; and all these things shall be added unto you." The tragedy of the rich man was that he sought the means first, and in the process the ends were swallowed in the means. ("The Man Who Was a Fool")

8. *Epiphonema* (a pertinent and instructive remark at the end of a discourse)

Fear knocked at the door. Faith answered. There was no one there. ("Antidotes for Fear")

9. *Erotesis* (the posing of a question to inject ardor and energy; the rhetorical question could probably be included here)

Can man be explained in such shallow terms? Can we explain the literary genius of Shakespeare, the musical genius of Beethoven, and the artistic genius of Michelangelo in materialistic terms? Can we explain the spiritual genius of Jesus of Nazareth in materialistic terms? Can we explain the mystery and the magic of the human soul in materialistic terms? ("What Is Man?")

Another thing that disturbs me about the American church is that you have a white church and a Negro church. How can segregation exist in the true Body of Christ? ("Paul's Letter to American Christians")

10. *The historical present* (description of a historical event as though it were taking place now)

The moment of testing emerges. Christ, the innocent Son of God, is stretched in painful agony on an uplifted cross. . . . Jesus lifts his thorn-crowned head and cries in words of cosmic proportions: "Father, forgive them; for they know not what they do." ("Love in Action")

11. *Irony* (saying the opposite of what is meant, in order to increase force and vehemence)

Even . . . preachers have often joined the enticing cult of conformity . . . [and] preach soothing sermons that bypass the weightier matters of Christianity. . . . If you want to get ahead in the ministry, conform! Stay within the walls of Christianity. Play it safe. ("Transformed Nonconformist")

The popular clergyman preaches soothing sermons on "How to be Happy" and "How to Relax." Some have been tempted to revise Jesus' command to read, "Go ye into all the world, keep your blood pressure down, and, lo, I will make you a well-adjusted personality." ("A Knock at Midnight")

12. *Metaphor* (removing of a word from its proper signification into that of another, thus suggesting an analogy or likeness between them)

Man is not a helpless invalid who is left in a valley of total depravity until God pulls him out; he is rather an upstanding human being whose vision has been impaired by the cataracts of sin and whose soul has been weakened by the virus of pride. But there is enough vision left for man to lift his eyes unto the hills, and there is enough of God's image left for man to turn his weak and sin-battered life toward the Great Physician, the curer of the disease of sin. ("The Answer to a Perplexing Question")

It would be both cowardly and immoral for you patiently to accept injustice. You cannot in good conscience sell your birthright of freedom for a mess of segregated pottage. ("Paul's Letter to American Christians")

Without God . . . life is a meaningless drama in which the decisive scenes are missing. But with him, we are able to rise from tension-packed valleys to the sublime heights of inner peace, and find radiant stars of hope against the nocturnal bosom of life's most depressing nights. St. Augustine was right: "Thou hast created us for thyself, and our heart cannot be quieted till it finds repose in thee." ("Three Dimensions of a Complete Life")

13. *Oxymoron* (combination of contradictory or incongruous words)

The church has often lagged in its concern for social justice and too often has been content to mouth pious irrelevances and sanctimonious trivialities. ("How Should a Christian View Communism?")

14. *Paramonasia* (words similar in sound or meaning are set in opposition to give antithetical force)

Let us never succumb to the temptation of believing that legislation and judicial decrees play only minor roles in solving this problem. Morality cannot be legislated, but behavior can be regulated. Judicial decrees may not change the heart, but they can restrain the heartless. ("On Being a Good Neighbor")

This universe is not a tragic expression of meaningless chaos but a marvelous display of orderly cosmos. ("Antidotes for Fear")

The trouble with Communism is that it has neither a theology nor a Christology; therefore, it ends up with a mixed up anthropology. ("How Should a Christian View Communism?")

15. *Prolepsis* (anticipation of objections in order to weaken their force)

Soft mindedness is also one of the basic causes of race prejudice. The tough minded always examine the facts before they reach conclusions; in short they post-judge. The tender minded will reach a conclusion before they have examined the first fact; in short they prejudge, hence they are prejudiced. All race prejudice is based on fears, suspicions, and misunderstandings that are usually groundless. So there are those who are soft minded enough to believe that the Negro is inferior by nature because of Noah's curse upon the children of Ham. There are those who are soft minded enough to believe in the superiority of the white race and the inferiority of the Negro race in spite of the tough minded research of anthropologists like Margaret Mead and Ruth Benedict revealing the falsity of such a notion. There are those who are soft minded enough to argue that racial segregation should be maintained because Negroes lag behind in academic, health and moral standards. They are not tough minded enough to see that if there are standards in the Negro they are themselves the result of segregation and discrimination. They are not discerning enough to see that it is both rationally unsound and sociologically untenable to use the tragic effects of segregation as an argument for its continuation. ("A Tough Mind and a Tender Heart")

Some of the most vigorous defenders of segregation are sincere in their beliefs and earnest in their motives. Although some men are segregationists merely for reasons of political expedience and economic gain, not all of the resistance to integration is the rear-guard action of professional bigots. Some people feel that their attempt to preserve segregation is best for themselves, their children, and their nation. Many are good church people, anchored in the religious faith of their mothers and fathers. Pressed for a religious vindication for their conviction, they will even argue that God was the first segregationist. "Red birds and blue birds don't fly together," they contend. Their views about segregation, they insist, can be rationally explained and morally justified. Pressed for a justification of their belief in the inferiority of the Negro, they turn to some pseudo-scientific writing and argue that the Negro's brain is smaller than the white man's brain. They do not know, or they refuse to know, that the idea of an inferior or superior race has been refuted by the best evidence of the science of anthropology. Great anthropologists, like Ruth Benedict, Margaret Mead, and Melville J. Herskovits, agree that, although there may be inferior and superior individuals within all races, there is no superior or inferior race. And segregationists refuse to acknowledge that science has demonstrated that there are four types of blood and that these four types are found within every racial group. They blindly believe in the eternal validity of an evil called segregation and the timeless truth of a myth called white supremacy. What a tragedy! Millions of Negroes have been crucified by conscientious blindness. With Jesus on the cross, we must look lovingly at our oppressors and say, "Father, forgive them; for they know not what they do." ("Love in Action")

16. *Restatement* (repetition in different words)

Now this numerical growth of the Church is not to be over-emphasized. We must not succumb to the temptation of confusing spiritual power with big numbers. Jumboism, as someone has called it, is an utterly fallacious standard in measuring positive power. An increase in quantity does not necessarily represent an increase in quality. A bigger membership does not necessarily represent a bigger commitment to Christ. ("A Knock at Midnight")

17. *Simile* (likening of one thing, action or relation to something of a different kind or quality)

The Hitlers and the Mussolinis may have their day, and for a period they may wield great power, spreading themselves like a green bay tree, but soon they are cut down like the grass and wither as the green herb. [The first words here, "The Hitlers and the Mussolinis," may also fall in the category of *eponym,* name so commonly associated with the attributes of the owner that it comes to symbolize those attributes.] ("Our God Is Able")

To believe that human personality is the result of the fortuitous interplay of atoms and electrons is as absurd as to believe that a monkey by hitting typewriter keys at random will eventually produce a Shakespearean play. ("The Man Who Was a Fool")

18. *Synecdoche* (using the name of the whole for the part or the part for the whole)

Frequently King used the term "the Negro" or "the white man" or "the Caucasian" when in fact he was referring to all members of the particular race.

In "Our God Is Able" King refers to the passing glory and power of "the Hitlers and Mussolinis," signifying the tyranny and exploits of all such tyrants.

Oral and Written Language Style

For some time now it has been common practice to recognize a distinction between spoken and literary style in public communication. Martin Luther King Jr. himself, as a serious practitioner of preaching, followed this tradition and employed a style that fostered "instant intelligibility."[11] In the preface of his published book of sermons, *Strength to Love,* he expresses his awareness of the distinction between oral and written style in the following words:

All of these sermons were preached during or after the bus protest in Montgomery, Alabama. . . . I have been rather reluctant to have a volume of sermons printed. My misgivings have grown out of the fact that a sermon is not an essay to be read but a discourse to be heard. It should be a convincing appeal to a listening congregation. Therefore, a sermon is directed toward the listening ear rather than the reading eye. While I have tried to rewrite the sermons for the eye, I am convinced that this venture could never be entirely successful. So even as this volume goes to press I have not altogether overcome my misgivings. But in deference to my former congregation, my present congregation, my close associates in the Southern Christian Leadership Conference, and my many friends across the nation who have asked for copies of individual sermons, I offer these discourses in the hope that a message may come to life for readers of these printed words.[12]

"Pilgrimage to Nonviolence," which appears in *Strength of Love* but which King says is not a sermon but an essay included at the urging of the publisher, has a readability difficulty score of 4.55, or "fairly difficult," by Flesch's measure. Given that three sample sermons proved to fall into the "fairly easy" and "easy" categories, it is evident that King indeed not only recognized but also practiced the distinctions between constructing a composition to be read and preparing one to be heard. The distinction is made not merely in use of language but also in objective, according to King's conception of the difference between sermons (the spoken word) and essays (the written word): "A good sermon differs from an essay in that an essay explains a subject, but a sermon appeals to people to make basic changes in their lives and to mend their ways so that they will be in harmony with the principles of God and Jesus Christ."[13]

In the main, it seems generally accepted that certain causal relationships exist between a speaker's style and his or her ultimate effectiveness, significant elements among these relationships include listener comprehension and listener attitudes. The sole major study during the King period, according to Jon Eisenson, Jeffrey Auer and John V. Irwin,[14] was done by Gordon L. Thomas, examining the effect of word choice in public address upon audience intelligibility.[15] Thomas's study found that a certain oral style enhances intelligibility by 10 percent. The eight elements of oral style Thomas discusses also may be said to characterize in reasonable quantity and quality the sermons of King: specific words, colorful words, informal and simple vocabulary, figurative language, personalization, informal syntax, questions and direct quotations.

And so Martin King, who as a very young boy once said to his mother, "I'm going to get me some big words," grew into mature use of language and became the effective epitome of the wise man's axiom that "a word aptly spoken is like apples of gold in settings of silver" (Prov 25:11).

8
SERMON DESIGN, PREPARATION & DELIVERY

He was a prophet, powerful in word and deed.
LUKE 24:19

Never man spake like this man.
JOHN 7:46 KJV

A s here considered, "sermon design" will not refer to the more formal homiletical options we often encourage and banter about such as "the Thematic Plan" or "the Jewel Plan" or "the Interrogative" or "the Hegelian" or "the Life Situation" or other developments intending to provide helpful movement and shape to the sermon.[1] Instead we will give attention to the general overall structure of sermons in the King repertoire. The philosopher and rhetorician Cicero taught that the speaker should "dispose and arrange his matter, not only in a certain order, but with a sort of power and judgment."[2]

King's Sermon Structure

The conceptualized structure of a King sermon generally conforms to the traditional three-part scheme of introduction, body and conclusion, although an occasional exception appears. For example, among King's personal papers at the Boston University Library I observed that the margin of a nonsermonic address titled "Civil Rights, the Central Issue of America's Growth" carried handwritten notations by King indicating the following outline:[3]

I. Introduction

II. Body and Historical Background

III. Recital of Evidence

IV. Conclusion

The student of homiletics and the student of rhetoric will recognize that this arrangement follows Aristotle's advice that if more parts than the "statement of the case" and the "proof" are needed in an address, the total number should not exceed four. Aristotle's parts are the exordium, the exposition or statement of the case, the proof and the peroration.[4] King's sermons do not divide into these four parts, but they do reflect the wisdom of another influential teacher of public address, Plato: a speech should be "put together like a living animal, having a head and body and tail." The King sermons usually have (1) an introduction ("head"), (2) a discussion ("body") of numbered points developed either deductively or inductively and buttressed by ethical, logical and emotional persuasion, and (3) a conclusion ("tail").

King confirmed my observation concerning the three-part arrangement of his sermons and added that the body generally contains three main points.[5] He also volunteered that his relatively consistent adherence to a three-point body was first influenced by Harry Emerson Fosdick. It is quite noticeable that his sermons usually follow either a *textual* development (that is, permitting the divisions of the Bible text itself to determine the sermon's structure) or a *topical* development (allowing the Bible text to provide a theme applied to the contemporary scene but devising his own disposition of points within the sermon) but hardly ever the ideal expository development.

An example of textual arrangement

Sermon: "Three Dimensions of a Complete Life"

Text: "The length and the breadth and the height of it are equal" (Rev 21:16)

Introduction

Body

I. "Let us turn first to the length of life . . ."

II. "So if life is to be complete it must move beyond length to the dimension of breadth . . ."

III. "Now one more dimension of the complete life still remains, namely, the height . . ."

Conclusion

An example of topical arrangement

Sermon: "The Death of Evil upon the Seashore"

Text: "And Israel saw the Egyptians dead upon the sea shore" (Ex 14:30)

Introduction
Body
    I. "A graphic example of this truth [that good eventually emerges as victor over evil] is found in the early history of the Hebrew people . . ."
    II. "The truth of this is revealed in the contemporary struggle between good in the form of freedom and justice, and evil in the form of oppression and colonialism . . ."
    III. "We must be careful at this point not to engage in a superficial optimism or to conclude that the death of a particular evil means that all evil lies dead upon the seashore . . ."
Conclusion

It might be said that the framework of King's sermons lines up very well with commonly accepted norms of sermon structure: title, Bible text, introduction, body and conclusion. Only one of his sermons, "Paul's Letter to American Christians," does not begin with a Bible scripture or text, probably because of its overall approach. It is rather allegorical in nature, inasmuch as King imagines what the apostle Paul might write in a modern epistle to contemporary America. The entire sermon resembles Scripture.

Although a thematic (purpose) sentence appears in each of the sermons studied, it does not consistently appear in any one division. The purpose sentence may appear in the introduction of one sermon, the body of another, the conclusion of another. Crystallizing the sermon's kernel thought or central idea, the thematic sentence is most frequently stated by King in the sermon body.

Introductions are generally five to eight minutes long, but this is not always the case. "A Knock at Midnight" introduces itself with only four sentences (a total of sixty-seven words)—the shortest of the introductions in King's sermon collection. The longest introduction comes in "The Three Dimensions of a Complete Life": approximately eighty sentences (and an approximate total of 860 words). Nevertheless, the rather lengthy introduction to this sermon, when I heard it preached at Howard University in 1961, did not seem to bore King's listeners or detract from the material presented in the body and conclusion. Nor when I heard him preach "A Knock at Midnight" at the Central Methodist Church (Detroit) in 1966 did its unusually short introduction produce abruptness; instead the brevity served as an attention-arresting device. The appropriateness of King's sermon introductions, whether they are long or short, probably results from the fact that they faithfully orient the audience toward the subject—not merely its general nature but also its relationship to audience needs and desires.

The body of King's sermons consistently contains identifiably separate yet coherent proofs and arguments, supporting main points that he almost never announces in advance. Whereas some speakers say, "There are three points I should like to share—number one . . . number two . . . and number three . . ." and then go back and develop each point, King simply presents his main points unannounced. Sometimes, however, he announced subpoints under a particular main point.

The conclusion to a King sermon usually consists of both a summarizing state-ment of his arguments in support of his central theme and an appeal to motivate his listeners to accept his propositions as a means of fulfilling their needs and desires. The conclusion usually ends in what might be termed an emotional manner, whether a statement reaffirming King's dedication to nonviolent civil rights endeavors or an apt quote from a poem, a hymn or a spiritual. In general, King's sermons evince a plan characterized by such qualities as unity, order, proportion and smooth transitions.

Readying the Material

When King entered his first pastorate in Montgomery in 1954, he spent as least fif-teen hours each week in sermon preparation for Sunday morning worship. His sys-tematic procedure usually began on Tuesday, when he began outlining ideas of what he wanted to say. On Wednesday he did necessary research and also thought of illus-trative material, life situations always being included. The actual writing of the dis-course took place on Friday, and writing was usually completed on Saturday night.[6] By Sunday morning he had gained thorough familiarity with the sermon content.

Although King said he wrote out his sermons before delivering them on Sunday morning, the Martin Luther King Jr. Collection includes a letter from a Tuskegee Institute student who requested a copy of "Three Dimensions of a Complete Life," which he had recently preached in the Tuskegee Chapel.[7] Though King had already preached this sermon the year before, 1954, in the Dexter Avenue Baptist Church, he said in response to the student that "Three Dimensions of a Complete Life" "was one of the sermons that I do not have written in manuscript form"; when he had a chance to write it out, he said, he would mail the student a copy.[8] Perhaps one should accept King's response at face value and conclude that this happened to be an exception to his writing out of his pulpit messages. Another possibility is that what King meant was that he had no extra copy for distribution.

King's meticulous approach to sermon preparation would be later modified, however, because of civil rights activities' increasing demands on his time. In 1966 King told me that his "current" practice of preparing his sermons was far from the rigid procedure of his pre-civil rights involvement. "I very seldom get to write out my sermons as I did in the past. I frequently have to be content with an outline."[9] He stated that his then-current practice was usually to begin thinking about his Sunday sermon at the beginning of the week, perhaps on Monday, and then to start writing an outline not earlier than about Saturday, one day before the sermon was to be delivered.[10]

Concerning the complex network of activities crowded into a typical week in King's life, Ernest Dunbar of *Look* wrote:

> During a recent week, he spoke at a fund-raising rally in White Plains, N.Y., on Tuesday. On Wednesday evening, he addressed similar rallies in two other New York towns. On Thursday, he met in Manhattan with fellow board members of the Gandhi Society, an organization that provides legal aid to Negro integration leaders; then consulted with publishers of a forthcoming book of King sermons, and flew to the West Coast to give lectures to the students at Los Angeles State and San Jose State Colleges. On Sunday, he went to Houston, Texas, for a fund-raising dinner. On Monday, he flew to Washington, D.C., to join other Negro leaders for a White House audience with President Kennedy on American policies in Africa. Afterwards, Kennedy and King met alone to discuss the continued bombing of Negro churches in Alabama. At the day's end, King returned to the Atlanta, Ga., headquarters of the Southern Christian Leadership Conference, of which he is president, to help organize an SCLC voter-registration drive in the South. Somewhere, during the day, he managed to write his biweekly column for a Negro newspaper and compose a sermon for his next church service. . . . King continues to cram his days with organizing demonstrations, fund-raising speeches, morale-building visits with backwoods Negroes, writing columns and delivering sermons.[11]

On one occasion in Montgomery in December 1955, King was faced with the predicament of having only twenty minutes to prepare an address, since civil rights affairs had consumed much more of his time than anticipated. What would he do? True to his customary approach, he prayed and then formulated an outline. Lacking time, he could do no more than sketch an outline in his mind. Relating the incident three years later, he remarked that the discourse had "evoked more response than any speech or sermon I had ever delivered, and yet it was virtually unprepared."[12] He said that for the first time he came to know pragmatically what the older preachers meant when they urged, "Open your mouth, and God will speak for you."[13]

Nevertheless, King did not permit this singular instance to affect his normal allotment of time for adequate sermon preparation. He declared, "While I would not let this experience tempt me to overlook the need for continued preparation, it would always remind me that God can transform man's weakness into his glorious opportunity."[14] This reference to God takes on vital significance when one recognizes that faith in God expressed through prayer consistently preceded and accompanied King's gathering and assessment of sermon materials.[15]

I witnessed this dependence on preparatory prayer when, at the Central United Methodist Church in Detroit during the 1966 Lenten season, I was privileged to be in the pastor's study with Dr. King. He had invited me there as a Ph.D. candidate he had approved to formally study his preaching. Before leaving the pastoral study for the pulpit, King and fellow clergymen bowed in prayer. For what, precisely, did they pray? Their petitions were for God to bestow upon King, the preacher of the hour, power and physical strength and effective oral persuasion to meet the hearers' needs.

Another indication of King's belief in and dependence on prayer in preparation can be seen in his weekly schedule. As noted earlier, among his personal papers at the Boston University Library, his appointment book shows that often two to three days each week were set aside for special "Prayer and Meditation."[16] There was no evidence that these days were spent solely (or even partially) in *sermon* preparation per se; however, King's prayer habit was a continual source of spiritual power and confidence and, in consequence, general sermon preparation.

Imparting the Message

There are four principal methods of delivering a sermon: extemporaneous, reading a manuscript, memorization and impromptu. The method normally employed by King was *extemporaneous*—that is, he organized his thoughts carefully into an outline and then acquired absolute command of the pattern of thought and controlling ideas. As exemplified below, King might, and did, preach the identical sermon twice, yet he used different words in some instances to express the same idea. Notwithstanding the fact that he would generally write out his sermons as a finished product, he never carried the full manuscript to the rostrum.

When asked if there was any conscious reason for his preaching without a manuscript (or even without notes or a written outline), King informed me, "Occasionally, I read a policy speech or an address for civil rights, but I never read a sermon. Without a manuscript, I can communicate better with an audience. Furthermore, I have greater rapport and power when I am able to look the audience in the eye."[17]

King's avoidance of written manuscripts in the pulpit may prompt the question, if he did not speak from a completely prepared script, why did he spend time writing it? Was not the process a waste of precious time? No. Writing out the sermon in preparation benefited King incalculably, mainly in three ways: (1) it promoted the analysis, synthesis and organization of materials, (2) it fostered careful selection of language and (3) it helped him familiarize himself with the organization and movement of ideas.

The three times I heard King preach, he held true to his customary practice of preaching without a sermon manuscript and even without notes of any kind. Two of these occasions were on a day when King delivered the same sermon twice, at a 10:00 a.m. service and a 12:00 noon service; this gave me an opportunity to observe King's mode of delivery by comparing the two sermon settings.[18] I recorded the two sermons on tape and then transcribed them.

The *content* of the sermon remained the same in terms of theme, controlling thought and overall movement of ideas. There were, however, marked variations in the delivery of those thoughts and ideas. Table 3 gives examples.

The purpose of table 3's comparison and contrast is to support the observation that he did not use a fully written out manuscript when he delivered a sermon and to demonstrate his masterful control over the main ideas and divisions of his sermons while altering the words used to express those ideas. Sometimes he also varied his supporting materials (as in the case of the statistics cited).

Clearly, King's extemporaneous mode of delivery promoted not only rapport with the audience (allowing him freedom from the constraints often imposed by a written-out manuscript) but also power, adaptability, flexibility, awareness of audience feedback and naturalness.

Visible Elements of Delivery

Physical bearing. To those who saw Martin Luther King Jr. for the first time, perhaps the most striking surprise was his relatively small stature. His sixty-seven-inch height did not afford him an imposing physique. A slight stockiness and an upright posture, however, suggested health and heartiness, confident bearing without brazen overconfidence. When King stood before an audience, he not only exuded such confidence but also inspired it in his congregation and thus did much to create an atmosphere quite receptive to his ideas.

Other physical assets of King included good motor control, poise, perennially

Table 3. Variations in King's Delivery of "A Knock at Midnight"

Sermon 1

1. Following the announcement of his sermon title, "A Knock at Midnight," King announced also the Bible text on which it was based. However, he gave only the name of the Bible book (St. Luke) and the chapter.

2. Among examples of the "midnight blackness" that King says characterizes the U.S. social order, he presented the state of Alabama: "In Alabama alone over the last few years, *some twenty-six* Negro and white civil rights workers have been brutally murdered. In most instances, most of the *people who committed the murders* are walking the streets today scot-free."

3. Turning to the North for another example, he said that in Chicago 97.7 percent of Negro people live in the ghetto; 41 percent of Negro families live in dilapidated rented housing; 90 percent of Negro students attend schools with more than 92 percent Negro enrollment; this, he deduced, means that more than 90 percent of Chicago schools are segregated. He said the unemployment rate of Chicago Negroes is three to one (three unemployed Negroes to every unemployed white) and that some 100,000 Negroes out of a population of one million are chronically unemployed.

4. Speaking of "midnight in the psychological order," King posed the

Sermon 2

1. He announced not only the Bible book and chapter but also the verses.

2.

"In Alabama alone over the last few years, *more than twenty-five* Negroes and white civil rights workers have been brutally murdered, and in most instances *the perpetrators of these evil acts* are walking the streets scot-free."

3. He began his enumeration of figures by citing not the 97.7 percent statistic but the 41 percent, proceeded to the 90 percent statistic of Negro students' attendance at the 92 percent racially segregated schools, and then mentioned the unemployment of 100,000 Chicago Negroes. Notice that he omitted both the 97.7 percent and three-to-one figures he had included in sermon 1.

4. Here he answered the question about popular works in psychology by

Sermon 1 (continued)

question "Today, what are the popular books in psychology?" He responded: "They are books entitled *Modern Man in Search of a Soul, Man Against Himself, The Neurotic Personality of Our Times*." Then he listed bestsellers in the area of religion.

5. There were several differences in wording, for example:

"I would have you think with me this morning from the subject . . . "

"the conflict in Vietnam"

"One hundred years ago, a great American, Abraham Lincoln, signed the immortal document which we know as the Emancipation Proclamation. This document was signed to free the Negro of the long night of chattel slavery."

"People are more frustrated and bewildered today than any period of human history."

6. King concluded by reciting words from the Negro spirituals "There Is a Balm in Gilead" and "We Shall Overcome."

Sermon 2 (continued)

listing *Man Against Himself, Modern Man in Search of a Soul* (note the reversed order) and *The Neurotic Personality of Our Time*. Then before proceeding immediately to list the religious bestsellers, he mentioned three depth psychologists: Sigmund Freud, Alfred Adler and C. J. Jung.

5.

"I would *like to preach* on the subject . . ."

"the *war* in Vietnam"

"One hundred years ago, Abraham Lincoln *issued and* signed the Emancipation Proclamation, *freeing* the Negro from the long night of chattel slavery."

"People are more frustrated, *disillusioned* and bewildered today than *at* any period of human history."

6. King used words from the same spirituals in conclusion but then quoted, as a final note, words from Job 38:7: "And when we believe this, 'the morning stars will sing together, and the sons of God will shout for joy.'" (Whereas Job uses past tense, King alters the tense to future.)

well-trimmed hair and mustache, youthful face with soft features, and clothes that were always in conservative good taste. In worship settings King followed the practice of preaching in an elegant black pulpit robe, which contributed to a worshipful and reverent atmosphere and platform dignity.

Bodily action. Very infrequently during any sermon did King use much physical motion. More often than not he remained in the very spot where he initially placed himself; but when he did shift, his movements appropriately punctuated his words. Occasionally to emphasize a point, he extended his right hand—sometimes palm up, sometimes finger pointing. Most often he was seen in a characteristic gesture of clenching the fist while bending and straightening out the elbow back and forth, often rapping the podium for emphasis.

Facial gestures were even less marked; a serious, placid countenance usually maintained itself even when he used humor. When his face did register a point he was setting forth, it was usually an expression conveying emphasis, resolution and determination.

One of his very strong physical avenues of delivery was eye contact. Looking directly at his audience while speaking not only served to awaken interest in his words but also helped him to remain cognizant of audience feedback (through the "call and response" that is prevalent in traditional black churches) and reaction.

While one might think there might have been room for more gestures during King's sermon delivery, it does not hold that King necessarily should have used them. His physical understatement was powerful, avoiding inanity and reflecting his poised, mild, tranquil personality.

Tone and Timbre, Accent and Adaptability

Within a very few moments after King began preaching, a listener was sure to become aware of at least two things: King was a Southerner and he made effective use of his voice. His articulation and pronunciation generally fit with what might be termed educated Southern expression. Although his vowels and consonants were usually enunciated very clearly, distinctly and unaffectedly, he was known to substitute a "d" sound for initial "th" in such words as "the," "this" and "that" when he thought it necessary for rapport. When the majority of his auditors are uneducated, he deliberately became a little folksy and informal. I never knew or heard, however, of King's mispronouncing a word by improper syllabification, regardless of the nature of the audience.

One of the marks of genius in King's effective preaching was his ability to adapt appropriately and persuasively to any congregation, whether it was Marsh Chapel (Boston University), Andrew Ranking Chapel (Howard University), Harvard Chapel, Riverside Church (New York), the Sunday Evening Club (Chicago) or a less liturgical, less formal and less polished congregation of predominantly unlettered people. Walter G. Muelder of the School of Theology at Boston University observed as much:

> When he is addressing the predominantly Southern Negro type audience, King's sermon is more rhythmic and emotional; yet I have never heard him use quite this technique when addressing the more sophisticated Boston audience for example. The amazing thing about King is his . . . [ability] to adapt . . . to varied audiences. He is a master-adapter.[19]

Muelder proceed to make a comparison between King and Billy Graham, the world-famous evangelist, on the point of adaptability: "King is a more profound leader than Billy Graham. Graham is the same everywhere. King adjusts."[20]

Based on the theory that speech is an "overlaid function"—that is, oral speech is produced biologically by muscles and structures that have other primary body functions—voice and health are very integrally related.[21] No small wonder, then, that King, endowed with near perfect health, should possess a dynamically forceful voice whose volume was invariably adequate.[22] As a speaker sensitive to his immediate environment, he varied his volume in a manner consonant with the subject, the occasion and the setting.

The *pitch* of his voice fell in the category of deep baritone, with a timbre of rich quality. At the beginning of a sermon his voice conveyed a minimum of emotion; then, as he progressed further into his message, his voice would rise and fall with the complete gamut of emotions—except that humor was usually executed via an idea or a turned phrase but never by any change in vocal quality or vocal pitch.

Voice *range* was unimpressively limited in King's oral communication. An analysis of several taped sermons disclosed that his pitch ranged on the musical scale from a high of A above middle C to a low of B below middle C, less than an octave, with the most consistent pitch of his public preaching voice operating between F-sharp and G. His optimum pitch, the level at which his voice normally performed best, would appear to have been about F.

Concerning the *rate* of his speaking, King began his sermons characteristically unhurriedly, deliberately, almost at a snail's pace, soon, however, increasing the rate to what may be considered "normal." His deliberateness in utterance was a distinct asset in his attempt to achieve understandability and maintain attention. He knew also how to make use of *pause,* meaningfully punctuating his pace.

His *duration* of speech sound was the factor that probably more than any other revealed his regional speech pattern. He was not just a Southerner but a preacher who had deep roots in the African American Baptist tradition. Furthermore, he was thoroughly familiar with and had acquired the relevant tones and rhythm that convey meaning to the black masses. The overall melody of his speech was commendably rhythmical without being metrical while transcending regional appeal and attaining universal effectiveness.

Al Kuettner, in the *The State Journal* of Lansing, Michigan (June 16, 1965), said that King was "gifted with a magnetic speaking voice"; Loudon Wainwright also applied an all-inclusive description when he said that King's voice was "compelling."[23]

9
CONCLUSION
King's Contribution
to Preaching & Theology

Now of the things which we have spoken this is the sum.
HEBREWS 8:1 KJV

*T*he purpose of our journey together has been to revisit Martin Luther King
Jr. as manifested in his sermons. Though no formal, lengthy comparisons or contrasts have been drawn to distinguish between the "sermon" and the "oration"
(such as his civil rights mass meeting speeches), inherent to our journey are the
following four variables setting the sermon apart as a unique discourse:

☐ The sermon is a medium of divine truth, the gospel as revealed in Jesus Christ.

☐ It is a biblically based message.

☐ It presupposes a setting of religious worship.

☐ The sermon assumes moral and spiritual motivation.

Focusing in depth on King's sermons contributes toward placing him in the
correct perspective as clergyman, a patron of the pulpit, rather than a political or
sociological figure, for he unwaveringly considered preaching his God-given
calling, while the latter he himself never claimed.

King's Development as a Preacher

King's early environment was significantly conducive to his choice of a career in
Christian ministry, for he was born into not only a Christian home but a family of
three generations of preachers. In his family the art of public address enjoyed a
cherished tradition; King himself began his preaching experience as a boy member of his father's Ebenezer Baptist Church in Atlanta.

Seriously and enthusiastically interested in perfecting his craft of public communication, King pursued academic excellence at Morehouse College and Crozer Theological Seminary, ultimately being awarded the Ph.D. in systematic and philosophical theology at Boston University in 1955. He practiced preaching while a student in all three of these academic institutions; while he was at Boston University, weekends often meant traveling to various cities to deliver sermons, the activity he loved best.

The theological framework of the King sermons reflects a moderate liberal and social gospeler whose principal doctrines and philosophies are provided by Jesus Christ, Henry David Thoreau, Walter Rauschenbusch, Mohandas K. Gandhi, Reinhold Niebuhr and G. W. F. Hegel. The thematic spectrum of the sermons covers such theological *topoi* as God, Jesus Christ, the church, the preacher, humankind, love, prayer, faith, good and evil, while the consistent underlying theme of every sermon is that human beings must live together in equal personhood. In the thinking of King, this kind of life together is cast as a prerequisite to an effectual relationship with God.

King's early propensity toward careful preparation and organization carried over into his approach to preparing his sermons. Generally his sermon preparation was highly systematic, though his increasing involvement in civil rights activities left him scant time for composing "new" sermons; consequently, sermon "preparation" often meant simply updating a previously preached discourse. Despite his extemporaneous mode of delivery, King usually followed the practice of writing out his sermons in full. His writing out his sermons accrued three advantages: (1) promoting the analysis, synthesis and organization of materials, (2) fostering thoughtful selection of language and (3) assisting him to familiarize himself with the sermon outline and the movement of ideas—hence with memorization.

Although King was relatively short of stature, he used his height to commendable advantage through an upright posture that suggested confidence. Among other physical factors conducive to effectiveness in his sermon delivery was his custom, particularly in his regular pulpit, of wearing a pulpit robe. Gestures, or bodily action, were few but timely; eye contact was one of his strongest assets. Vocal expression was distinctively but not distractingly Southern; articulation and pronunciation were clear and unaffected, although he adjusted and adapted depending on the immediate congregation. Vocal qualities (in terms of volume, pitch, range, rate and duration), too, proved quite adequate in his oral persuasion.

An extensive range of kinds of audiences—varying in educational, economic and social status—had the privilege of listening to the King sermons; yet they were generally "mixed," made up of people who held differing attitudes toward his convictions. King's facility for comfortably emoting with an audience doubtless grew out of his background and experience in black Baptist congregations.

What about the sermons themselves? They are rich with examples, narratives, statistics and quotations (or appeals to authority) as well as ethical, logical and emotional proofs. His ethical proofs were developed through establishing himself as a credible clergyman of competence, character and goodwill. Logical proofs came in the form of reasoning from example, analogy and causal relation. Emotional proofs consisted of appeals to a threefold desideratum of happiness, holiness and love. These three qualities provide the broad context in which King addressed such compelling motives as freedom, response, helpfulness, power and influence, reputation, security, new experience, self-preservation and property. Other psychological elements in his emotional proof are identification, suggestion, attention and the emotion of anger, granted release via the nonviolent demonstrations and marches that frequently followed his sermons. The organization of his sermon materials generally adhered to the trichotomous partition of introduction, body and conclusion with smooth transitions, unity, order and proportion.

Responses to King's preaching might be divided into (1) local, spontaneous responses, (2) local, delayed responses and (3) general, implied responses. The first kind of response consisted of involuntary reactions ("Amen, brother!" or a smile or nod of the head). The second takes in those expressions of support which King received orally or in letters and also responses in the form of participation in his campaigns for voter registration, voting, sit-ins, wade-ins, kneel-ins and so on. The third type of response came from organizations and governmental bodies: legislative measures, judicial decrees and executive orders.

Language style is a constituent of homiletics in which King surpassingly excelled. Perspicuity, forcefulness and adaptability characterized his word choice, while his composition and syntax were marked by correctness, variety and rhythm. A remarkable feature of the preaching of King was his adeptness at adapting and adjusting his language according to audience or occasion. He was widely known for his ability to express himself in thought forms and word symbols appropriate to an audience's level of education, status or religious commitment; and he made these adjustments with the greatest of facility. Embellishment of his content through the use of figures of speech and other rhetorical devices was a prevalent component of King's preaching; indeed he regarded it as necessary to "paint a picture to the imagination." For their skillful and fitting structures and imaginative language, King's sermons deserve a place among the nobility of sermons.

The ministerial calling of King may be described by a favorite term of Paul Tillich, "historical kairos"—a creative, critical moment bursting with possibilities for great things when a crucial decision has to be made; if the right decision is not made, development may be set back many years or an extraordinary length of time. In the case of King, the man and the moment met; he made a Christian decision in behalf of social, economic and political justice, and the world was changed.

A special *Life* issue, *2000 Years of Christianity: The Meaning of the Millennium* (December 1999), cited the Martin Luther King Jr. experience as a vitally significant episode in Christian history. This chapter in the history of the Christian church will continue in process of being written over and over again, through women and men of every generation who dare continue the gospel word in King's tradition.

When asked if their former student had made a difference in the world of his day, Boston University professors Walter G. Muelder, S. Paul Schilling and L. Harold DeWolf responded firmly that the Nobel Peace Prize winner had indeed contributed to his profession, both dogmatically and kerygmatically.

Muelder succinctly affirmed that King had "helped thousands of ministers to recover the relevance of preaching for our day" by showing the "continuity between the pulpit in the church and on the courthouse steps."[1] In other words, he continued, King has "taken preaching out of the sanctuary and has put it everywhere."[2]

Schilling agreed, noting that King had "forced Christians and Christian theologians to see the implication of their faith in God as suffering, victorious love for the human and social struggle of man."[3]

DeWolf was just as emphatic: "Dr. Martin Luther King Jr. has disclosed to great numbers of people the meaning and the power of the cross as a contemporary reality. Many under his leadership have come to the point where they, in love, would be willing to engage in activities that risk their lives. They are convinced that this is an avenue to take up their cross and follow Christ."[4]

Then, seemingly thinking of the institutional church, DeWolf posited that "nothing has done more to bring the Protestant churches out of their walls into the world during the last ten years than the Christian action branch of the civil rights movement which Dr. King heads."[5]

In the theological dimension, according to DeWolf, King "strengthened the trend in theology" toward "renewed involvement with philosophy" and with "reasoning in defense of Christian doctrine."[6]

To summarize, King's theological peers judge that he made a number of salient contributions to theology and our understanding of the Christian life:

1. He helped the clergy discover the relevance of preaching in our times by making a practical application of Christianity to the contemporary scene.

2. He led Christians (laypersons, theologians and pastors) to experience a fresh encounter with God and to understand that faith in God means also love for fellow human beings in their socioeconomic-political struggle. This includes exploration of the cross of Jesus Christ as having not merely historical meaning but present-age reality.

3. He assisted in strengthening a growing trend toward preachers' use of philosophy and formal reasoning to proclaim and defend Christian doctrine, the "good news" of salvation. (In our August 31, 1966, interview King noted that as a student of philosophical theology at Boston University he underwent intense discipline in formal logic.)

In King's day many Protestant leaders believed that the institutional Christian church as it then stood could not survive. In 1965 George Harris averred in a national journal that "the church can live again only when it abandons protective buildings, orthodoxy, bureaucracy—and takes its place in the daily world of doubt."[7] Though most religious leaders did not ride the "God is dead" bandwagon, many agreed that unless the church responded more honestly to human suffering, it would continue fading in a slow death of irrelevance, belying its divine claims.

Decades after Martin Luther King Jr.'s years of ministry, we have the same choice. The church *can* live and love again, and that more abundantly, for the mouth of the Lord has spoken it through the King who came preaching.

Appendix 1
KING SPEAKS
AT OAKWOOD COLLEGE
Huntsville, Alabama, March 2, 1962

This address represents King's typical speech delivered before civil rights mass meetings and is to be distinguished from his sermons preached to worshiping congregations. Even his speeches, however, almost inevitably included biblical allusions supportive of his call for human equality. Bracketed words represent audible responses of the audience.

Mr. Chairman, President Millet, and to the other distinguished platform guests, ladies and gentlemen. I don't think I can begin to tell you in words this evening how very delighted I am to be in this community and to see the warmth and the enthusiasm of your movement and the power and dynamic qualities of your leadership and the depth of your dedication and commitment to the goal of freedom and human dignity. And I can only say to you that I bid you Godspeed as you continue in this magnificent work, and I know that as a result of your labors and as a result of your struggles you will be able to make Huntsville a better community and a better city in which to live.

I certainly want to express my personal appreciation to the officers and members of the Community Service committee for inviting me to be here. And may I say as my colleagues, Wyatt Walker and Ralph Abernathy, have already said that the full resources of the Southern Christian Leadership Conference are with you in your struggle here. You have our absolute backing. You have our absolute support. And we want you to know that, and we want you to feel free to call on us. There is something about a movement that can never be outlawed. You can outlaw organizations, but you cannot outlaw a movement. And we want it clearly stated, and we want it clearly known that Alabama can outlaw the NAACP, it can outlaw CORE, and maybe they will try to outlaw the Southern Christian Leadership Conference, but there is a movement in the Negro community; and as Victor Hugo said some years ago that "there is nothing more powerful in all the world than an idea whose time has come." And the idea whose time has come today is the idea of freedom and human dignity. And as Ralph Abernathy has said, we do not plan to stop until we have our freedom. And we want you to know that you have our absolute support in all that you're doing.

Now I can never come back to the state of Alabama without feeling a great sense of at-home-ness. I am not a stranger in this state, for it was in this state that I struggled for 381 days with the 50,000 Negro citizens of Montgomery, Alabama. Montgomery, Alabama, is still a difficult community hardened in its attitudes, but one thing that we can say about Montgomery is the buses are thoroughly integrated; and Negroes can sit anywhere they want to. *[Applause]*

A few months ago, Prime Minister Macmillan of England was taking a trip through the great continent of Africa, and at one point he stopped along the way to make this significant statement: "The wind of change is blowing in Africa." In a real sense, the wind of change is blowing all over the world. It is blowing in our own nation. It is a mighty wind sweeping away an old order and ushering in a new order. Now we are all familiar with the old order that is passing away, because we have lived with it; and we've seen it in all of its dimensions. We've seen it in the form of colonialism and imperialism. And as you know there are approximately 2,700,000,000 people in the world. The vast majority of these people live in Asia and Africa, about 700,000,000 in China, about 500,000,000 in India and Pakistan, 100,000,000 in Indonesia, 220,000,000 in Africa, about 96,000,000 in Japan. For years these people have been dominated politically, exploited economically, segregated and humiliated by some foreign power. But there comes a time when people get tired, there comes a time when people get tired of being trampled over by the iron feet of oppression. And these people became tired, and they decided to protest, and as a result of that most of these people live in independent countries, and we see that the old order of colonialism is passing away and the new order of freedom and human dignity is coming into being.

But the thing I want you to see tonight more than anything else is that we've had an old order in our own nation in the form of slavery and then in the form of racial segregation. And we all know of the long history of this old order in the United States. It had its beginning in 1619 when the first slaves landed on the shores of this nation. They were brought here from Africa. And unlike the Pilgrim Fathers who landed at Plymouth a year later, they were brought here against their will. Two hundred and forty years the Negro was treated as a thing to be used not a person to be respected. The famous *Dred Scott* decision rendered by the Supreme Court in 1857 well illustrated the state of the Negro during slavery. This decision rendered by the Supreme Court said that the Negro has no right that the white man is bound to respect, that he is merely property subject to the dictates of his owner. Then after the Emancipation Proclamation issued by Abraham Lincoln in September of 1862, which took effect on the first of January, 1863—even after this, the Negro still confronted a system known as segregation. Living with these conditions, many Negroes lost faith in themselves. Many came to feel that perhaps they were inferior. Perhaps they were less than human. But thank God, something began to happen. Something happened to the Negro. Circumstances made it possible and necessary for him to travel more—the coming of the automobile, the upheavals of two world wars, the Great Depression. And so his rural plantation background gradually gave way to urban industrial life. His economic life was gradually rising through the growth of industry, the influence of organized labor, expanded educational opportunities, and even his cultural life was gradually rising through the steady decline of crippling illiteracy. And all of these forces conjoined to cause the Negro to take a new look at himself. Negro masses all over began to reevaluate themselves, and the Negro came to feel that he was somebody. His religion revealed to him that God loves all of his children and that all men are made in his image and that God somehow loves every man from a bass black to a treble white and all are significant on his keyboard. So the Negro could unconsciously cry out with the eloquent poet:

Fleecy locks and black complexion
    Cannot forfeit nature's claim;
Skin may differ but affection
    Dwells in black and white the same.
And were I so tall as to reach the pole
    Or to grasp the ocean at a span,
I must be measured by my soul;
    The mind is the standard of the man.

And with this new sense of dignity and this new sense of destiny, a new Negro came into being with a new determination to suffer, sacrifice and even die if necessary in order to be free. *[Applause]* Then something else happened. The Supreme Court of the nation rendered a new decision. In 1896, the Supreme Court had rendered what was known as the *Plessy* v. *Ferguson* decision, which established the doctrine of separate but equal as the law of the land, and we all know what happened as a result of this old *Plessy* doctrine. There was always a strict enforcement of the "separate" without the slightest intention to abide by the "equal." The Negro ended up being plunged into the abyss of exploitation, where he experienced the bleakness of nagging injustice. Then in 1954, the Supreme Court rendered a new decision. This decision said in substance that the old *Plessy* doctrine must go, that separate facilities are inherently unequaled, that to segregate a child on the basis of his race is to deny that child equal protection of the law. When this decision was rendered, seventeen states and the District of Columbia practiced absolute segregation in the public schools. But today, fourteen of these states and the District of Columbia have made some moves (now most of them have been only token moves), but they have made some moves toward integrating the schools, and there are only three states now trying desperately to hold out: the state of South Carolina, Mississippi, and the great sovereign state of Alabama. *[Mixture of mild laughter and applause]* But in a real sense, the old order is passing away. The wind of change is blowing it away. To put it figuratively in biblical language, we've broken loose from the Egypt of slavery; and we have moved through the wilderness of segregation, and now we stand on the border of the promised land of integration. And I know *[brief applause]* and I am convinced now as I stand before you tonight that old man segregation is on his deathbed, and the only thing uncertain about it is how expensive the South will make the funeral—the old order. *[Applause]* The wind of change is blowing.

Whenever anything new comes into history, it brings with it new challenges and new responsibilities. And it would be tragic indeed for us to stand idly by and notice this emerging new age in our nation and all over the world without meeting the concomitant responsibilities that come to us as a result of this emerging new age. And I would like to mention for the moments left the responsibilities that we have as a people, that we face as a nation, and that we face all over the world as a result of this new age that is coming into being. I want to suggest first that we are challenged to rise above the narrow confines of our individualistic concerns to the broader concerns of all humanity. In other words, we must develop a world perspective. We will not achieve brotherhood in America until enough people in America develop a world perspective. You see, this new age in which we live now is geographically one. This challenge is to make it spiritually one. Now the geographical oneness of this new age is come into being to a large extent through man's scientific ingenuity. Man through his scientific genius has been able to dwarf distance and place time in chains and even carve highways through the stratosphere, and our jet planes have compressed into minutes distances that once took days. I think that Bob Hope has adequately described this new jet age in which we live. He said it is an age in which it is possible to take a nonstop flight from Los Angeles, California, to New York City; and if on taking off in Los Angeles you develop hiccups, you will "hic" in Los Angeles and "cup" in New York City. *[Laughter]*

That's moving pretty fast. You know it is possible because of the time difference to take a nonstop flight from Tokyo, Japan, on Sunday morning and arrive in Seattle, Washington, on the preceding Saturday night; and when your friends meet you at the airport and ask you when you left Tokyo, you will have to say I left tomorrow. *[Mild laughter]* Now this is a bit humorous, but I'm trying to laugh a basic fact into all of us. It is simply this: man through his scientific genius has made of this world a neighborhood, and now through our moral and ethical commitment we must make of it a brotherhood. We must all learn to live together as brothers or we will all die together as fools. *[Applause]* This is what we will . . . [final word in this short sentence is indistinct due to both audience applause and King's slightly dropping his voice]. Every individual and every nation must see this interdependency that we face. All I'm saying is simply this, that all life is interrelated, and all men are caught in an inescapable network of mutuality tied in a single garment of destiny, and whatever affects one directly affects all indirectly. John Donne was right: "No man is a island entire of itself. Every man is a piece of the continent, a part of the main." And he goes on toward the end to say, "Any man's death diminishes me, because I am involved in mankind. Therefore, never send to know for whom the bell tolls, it tolls for thee." And until we come to see this all over the world, and until our white brothers come to see this, we will be miserable and we will end up with a cosmic elegy.

The second challenge that we face (and this is particularly true of those of us who have been on the oppressed end of the old order): we must achieve excellence in our various fields of endeavor. And may I say to every young man and every young woman here tonight (I see many students from the colleges, the high schools) let me say to you that doors are opening now that were not opened to our mothers and our fathers. Opportunities are coming now that did not come to our parents. The challenge we face is to be ready to enter these doors when they open. Ralph Waldo Emerson said in a lecture back in 1871 that "if a man could write a better book or preach a better sermon or make a better mousetrap than his neighbor, even if he builds his house in the woods, the world will make a beaten path to this door." This will become increasingly true. And so we must set out to do a job and to do it well. Discover your life's work and put your whole self there.

I know it so easy to use our oppression as an excuse for laziness, but we must make full and constructive use of the freedom we already possess. And we must rise up amid dark and desolate nights of oppression and plunge against these cloud-filled skies new and blazon stars of inspiration. This is our challenge, and this is our inspiration. And don't set out to do merely a good Negro job. I've seen people so often say that I want to be a good Negro this or a good Negro that. Now if you are setting out merely to be a good Negro schoolteacher or a good Negro doctor or a good Negro lawyer or a good Negro skilled laborer, you have already flunked your matriculation exam for entrance into the university of integration. *[Applause]* We must set out to do a good job. We must set out to do a good job and to do it so well that the living, the dead or the unborn couldn't do it any better. *[Applause]* And to carry it to one extreme, if it falls your lot to be a street sweeper, just go on out and sweep streets like Beethoven composed music. Sweep streets like Shakespeare wrote poetry. Sweep streets like Michelangelo carved marble and like Raphael painted pictures. Sweep streets so well that all the hosts of heaven and earth will have to pause and say, here lived a great street sweeper who swept his job well. *[Applause]*

This is what Douglas Mallock meant when he said:

If you can't be a pine on the top of the hill,
    Be a shrub in the valley—but be
The best little scrub on the side of the rill,
    Be a bush, if you can't be a tree.

If you can't be a highway, just be a trail,
    If you can't be the sun, be a star;
For it isn't by size that you win or you fail—
    Be the best of whatever you are. *[Applause]*

Now the third and final challenge is this. We're challenged to continue to engage in creative protest in order to bring the new age into being in its full sense. I want to underscore this. We are challenged to engage in creative protest, and I want to underscore this because there are still too many people who believe that . . . that things will work themselves out. You've heard this idea—just be patient, and just keep praying, and everything will be all right. Well, I believe firmly in prayer, and

I believe in patience, and at the same time I pray to God to save me from that patience which makes me patient with anything less than the best. And I say that we must engage in creative protest and realize that human progress never rolls in on the wheels of inevitability. It comes through the tireless efforts and the persistent work of dedicated individuals. And without this hard work, time itself becomes the ally of the insurgent and primitive forces of irrational emotionalism and social stagnation. We must help time, and always realize that the time is always right to do right. *[Applause]* We must see this.

And so we must continue to seek to get the right legislation. We need civil rights legislation right now all over the United States. I know the argument here. They say that you can't legislate certain things. You can't change it through the law. You hear this endlessly. They say it must be done another way. Well, it may be true that morality cannot be legislated, but behavior can be regulated. It may be true that the *[delayed applause]* . . . It may be true that the law can't make a man love me, but it can keep him from lynching me, and I think that's pretty important also. *[Applause]* So let us not overlook the significance of legislation, for it is true that we must depend on religion and education to . . . change bad internal attitudes. But we need legislation and court orders to control the external affects of bad internal attitudes. And so through legislation, we regulate behavior. It may be true that legislation cannot change the heart, but it can restrain the heartless; and this must always be done in society. And it is important that we get legislation, and we must continue to work through the courts to get meaningful court orders so we can clarify the law and make it clear that we're moving on.

Right here in the state of Alabama, one thing that I am concerned about now (and I have been talking in the last few days with some of the leaders of this state), it would be tragic indeed if Governor Patterson goes out of office without having to confront the challenge of a court order with Negroes going to integrated schools. *[Applause]* If he goes out of office without facing this *[extended applause]* . . . If he goes out of office not facing this, it will only intensify his arrogance. He will use it for his political aggrandizement and argue for years and years to come that he held off integration his four years in office, and hardly any politician in the state will have the courage to stand up. And I think it is the responsibility of the citizens of this state to get together and get some Negroes who have the courage to go to the University of Alabama and Auburn and some Negroes who will go to the public schools in the state of Alabama so that this will happen. *[Applause]* So we must work through the courts to get these decisions, but even after this we must realize that a court order can only declare rights—it can never deliver them. Rights are only delivered when the people themselves begin to act. Rights are only given life-blood, and the people en masse begin to move and to act; and if they don't act, the laws fade into oblivion. And I say that it is necessary for each of you here tonight to be something of individual creative obstetricians presiding at the birth of a new age, acting here and there, sitting-in, standing-in, riding-in or any kind of other "in" that's necessary to make integration a reality in this city and in this nation. *[Applause]* This is the challenge.

In other words, we must supplement what can be done through the courts with nonviolent direct action. I am still convinced that the most powerful weapon available to oppressed people in their struggle for freedom and human dignity is the weapon of nonviolence. This is a powerful method. It has a way of disarming the opponent. It exposes his moral defenses. It weakens his morale, and at the same time it works on his conscience. He doesn't know how to handle it. It leaves him frustrated. If he tries to beat you, you develop the power to accept it without retaliating. If he doesn't beat you, fine. If he throws you in jail, you go on in jail and transform the jail from dungeons of shame to havens of freedom and human dignity. *[Applause]* Even if he tries to kill you *[applause continues]* . . . Even if he tries to kill you, you develop the quiet courage of dying if necessary without killing. He doesn't know how to handle it. It leaves him frustrated. This is the power of this method. They know how to handle violence. They are experts in that. The minute we rise up with violence, they can call out the state militia, the National Guard and everything (you don't have a single Negro in the National Guard all over the South). They are experts in violence. *[Applause and mild laughter]*

When you stand up nonviolently, you become something of a creative powerful nonviolent anvil that will wear out many a spiritual hammer, and somehow they do not know how to deal with it. And another thing about it is that it makes it possible for you to struggle to secure moral ends through moral means. You don't have to worry about using immorality to achieve morality, but ends and means begin to cohere. One of the great discussions through philosophical and theological history has been over the whole question of means and ends, and there have been those from Machiavelli on down who argued that the end justifies the means. I think this is the ultimate weakness of communism. This is its ultimate tragedy—it believes that the end justifies the mean [sic], as Lenin used to say, any method (violence, deceit, lying) can be used as justifiable means to achieve the end of the classless society, but this is where nonviolence breaks with communism and any other movement that would argue that the end justified the means; because the end is preexistent in the means. And in the long run of history, destructive means cannot bring about constructive ends. The ends and the means must cohere. And so we can struggle with moral means in order to achieve moral ends. And the other thing about this method is that it says that it is possible for you to resist, stand up against an unjust system with all of your might and all of your strength, and yet you don't have to hate the perpetrators of that unjust system. This is powerful. We don't have to be bitter. We don't have to hate.

There is still a voice crying through the vista of time saying, "Love your enemies, bless them that curse you, pray for them that despitefully use you." And this is what we can say in our movement: our aim is not to defeat or humiliate the white man but to win his friendship and understanding. We know that the struggle in the South in the final analysis is not between black men and white men, but it is a tension between justice and injustice. It is a struggle between the forces of light and the forces of darkness. And let us say to our white brothers who are so worried about our advance that if there is a victory it will not be a victory merely for twenty million Negroes; but if there is a victory, it will be a victory for justice, a victory for freedom, a victory for democracy, and it will make a better nation for everybody because the pestering sore of segregation debilitates the white man as well as the Negro, and we are struggling to free him. *[Applause]* This is what our movement says. It is a powerful movement. It is a powerful expression, and somehow we come to the point in this nonviolent movement that we can look into the eyes of those who would seek to block our advance for freedom and say something like this: We will match your capacity to inflict suffering with our capacity to endure suffering. We will meet your physical force with soul force. Do to us what you will, we will still love you. We cannot in all good conscience obey your unjust laws, because noncooperation with evil is as much a moral obligation as is cooperation with good. And so throw us in jail, and we will still love you. Bomb our homes and threaten our children, and we will still love you. Send your hooded perpetrators of violence into our communities at the midnight hours, and drag us out on some wayside road and beat us and leave us half dead; and as difficult as it is, we will still love you. But be ye assured that we will wear you down by our capacity to suffer.

One day we will win our freedom. We will not only win freedom for ourselves. We will so appeal to your heart and conscience that we will win you in the process, and our victory will be a double victory. This is our message.

And I say to you as I move toward my conclusion that this method, this approach to the problem is not at all without successful precedent. It was used in a magnificent sense by Mohandas K. Gandhi to free his people from the political domination inflicted upon them by the British Empire, and it has been used in a marvelous way right here in the United States of America by hundreds and thousands of students right here in Huntsville and all over. And they have taken our deep groans and passionate yearnings for freedom and filtered them in their own souls and fashioned them into a creative protest which is an ethic known all over our nation. Whether you realize it or not, as a result of the nonviolent struggles of these students more than 150 cities of the South have integrated their lunch counters. And I say to you that this is nothing less than revolutionary.

We've also seen this powerful method in the Freedom Rides. Something has come from this Freedom Ride movement that we can all be proud of. We can look around now and see bus terminals integrated all over the South, and with a few scattered examples [sic: King probably meant "exceptions"] in Mississippi and here and there, most of the bus terminals have integrated, and we see a new day developing all over the United States of America all because of this method. And I say with this creative protest we will be able to bring into being this new age.

With all of these working together, we will be able to do something for God's kingdom. And I can only say to you tonight, go out with new, grim and bold determination to make of this community a better community to end the reign of segregation. God needs you. I am not able, and I will never be able, to convince everybody here tonight. Most of you will go back home not convinced that you must struggle for freedom, but if I can just convince a few people here tonight that God needs you. God needs you to work for him to help him make the kingdom a reality.

God needs you now, he needs you at this minute, he needs you at this hour. Who this evening will be a coworker of the Almighty God and set out to get your freedom realizing that freedom is the greatest thing in all the world? It's worth losing a job for. Freedom is worth getting killed for. Maybe before this struggle is over, some will have to get killed. If physical death is the price that some must pay to free their children from a permanent life of psychological death, then nothing can be more redemptive.

Yes, we must come to see once more and sing with our forefathers of old:

O, freedom! O, freedom! Before I'd be a slave,
I'll be buried in my grave;
And go home to my Father, and be saved.

This is what we need at this hour. It will not be easy. It will be difficult. Before
the victory is won, some may have to get scarred up a bit. Before the victory is
won, some more will have to go to jail. Before the victory is won, some will be
called bad names and misunderstood and dismissed as dangerous rabble-rousers
and agitators. Before the victory is won, some will be called communists and
Reds simply because they believe in the brotherhood of man. But we must go on
with the faith that we will overcome. And we will overcome, because God is on
our side. We shall overcome. The arc of the moral universe is long, but it bends
toward justice. We shall overcome because Carlyle is right: "No lie can live forever." We shall overcome because William Cullen Bryant is right: "Truth crushed
to earth will rise again." We shall overcome because James Russell Lowell is
right:

Truth forever on the scaffold,
Wrong forever on the throne;
Yet that scaffold sways the future,
And behind the dim unknown
Standeth God within the shadows,
Keeping watch above His own.

We shall overcome, because the Bible is right: "You shall reap what you sow."
And with this faith, we will be able to go out and bring this new age into
being. And this will be the day that we will be able to sing with new meaning:

My country, 'tis of thee, sweet land of liberty,
Of thee, I sing;
Land where my fathers died, land of the pilgrims' pride,
From every mountainside, let freedom ring.

And this must become literally true all over America. Freedom must ring from
every mountainside. And so I say this evening, let it ring from the mighty mountains of New Hampshire. Let it ring from the heightening hills of New York. Let it
ring from the prodigious Alleghenies of Pennsylvania. Let it ring from the snow-
capped Rockies of Colorado. Let it ring from the curvaceous slopes of California.
But not only that, from every mountainside let freedom ring. And so let it ring
from Stone Mountain of Georgia. Let it ring from Lookout Mountain of Tennes-

see. Let it ring from every hill and molehill of Alabama. From every mountain-side, let freedom ring. And when this happens, all of God's children—black men and white men, Jews and Gentiles, Protestants and Catholics—will be able to join hands and sing in the words of the old Negro spiritual, "Free at last, free at last. Thank God almighty, we are free at last!"

God bless you.

Appendix 2
THE ULTIMATE DOOM OF EVIL
*Central United Methodist
Church, Detroit, March 20, 1964*

Note that treatment of the theme of evil in this sermon bears resemblance to an earlier sermon, "The Death of Evil upon the Seashore," where King developed the topic from the death of the Egyptian army in Exodus 14:30. The latter is found in his book of sermons Strength to Love. *Bracketed words represent audible responses from the audience.*

Text: Psalm 37:1-2

This morning I would like to use as a subject from which to preach, "The Ultimate Doom of Evil." Our text is taken from a very familiar passage found in the Psalms: "Fret not thyself because of evildoers, neither be thou envious against the workers of iniquity. For they shall soon be cut down like the grass, and wither as the green herb."

There is nothing more obvious than the fact that evil is present in the universe. We may debate over the origin of evil, but only the superficial optimist would debate over its reality. Evil is with us as a grim, stark and colossal reality. The Bible is very clear in its affirmation of the reality of evil. And from the beginning of the Old Testament to the end of the New Testament, we read over and over again of the reality of evil. The Bible pictures evil symbolically as a conniving serpent which comes to inject a discord in the beautiful symphony of life in a garden. In the New Testament, it pictures evil as nagging tares disrupting the orderly growth of stately wheat. The prophets picture evil in aptly [sic] hypocrisy and tragic injustices. The Bible is clear in its affirmation of evil.

And certainly as we look around in our day, we see evil in all of its glaring and ugly dimensions. We see evil in tragic lusts and inordinate ambitions. We see it in high places where men are willing to sacrifice truth on the altar of their self-interests.

We see evil in racial injustice where men are willing to trample over other men with the iron feet of oppression. We see it in calamitous wars where battlefields are left drenched with blood and men by the hundreds and thousands are sent home psychologically deranged and physically handicapped. We have seen evil. We have seen it in all of its dimensions. And so that it seems that in the long history of mankind in the world, there is a tension, a conflict in the universe between good and evil.

Every great religion has seen this, every philosophical system. Platonic philosophy pictures it as a conflict between spirit and matter. Hinduism sees it as a tension between illusion and reality. Zoroastrianism sees it as a struggle between the god of light and the god of darkness. Traditional Judaism and Christianity see it as a tension, a conflict between God and Satan, that is, this tension at the center of the universe.

But Christianity goes on to affirm that in the long struggle between good and evil, good always emerges as the victor. Evil will ultimately be doomed by the powerful forces of good. This is the affirmation of Christianity. Good Friday may occupy the throne for a day, but ultimately it must give way to the triumphant beat of the drums of Easter. Evil may so shape events that Caesar may occupy the palace and Christ a cross, but one day that same Christ will rise up and split history into A.D. and B.C., so that even the life of Caesar must be dated by his name. "Fret not thyself because of evildoers, neither be thou envious against the workers of iniquity. For they shall soon be cut down like the grass and wither like the green herb."

A graphic example of this truth is pointed out by the dean of American historians, Dr. Charles A. Beard. Once he was asked how long and how many volumes it would take to summarize the history of the world. First he said, "Oh, I think I could do it in about ten volumes." And then he said, "I think I could do it in five." And he thought again, and he said, "Well, I think it could be done in one volume." Then after he thought again he finally said, "No, I think I can really do it in one minute by quoting four ancient proverbs." Each of these proverbs reveals that history makes it unmistakably clear that evil will be ultimately doomed. So let us examine each of these proverbs one by one and see how they give meaning to our basic theme: the ultimate doom of evil.

The first truth that history has to teach according to Dr. Beard is set forth in the proverb "Whom the gods would destroy, they must first make mad with power." Whom the gods would destroy, they must make mad with power. The Bible says the same thing in another way: "Pride goeth before destruction." "Whosoever exalteth himself shall be abased." This is saying in substance that when a man loses his head over his own importance he has taken the first step to his self-destruction. The process is easy to describe. An individual rises to the heights of significant leadership, and this individual makes an important contribution to the life of his nation or to the life of the world. He may be in a political position, he may be in some other position; and for a period he does a good job. He works hard, and he makes a significant contribution, and because of this people begin to praise him. They say nice, kind, flattering things about him. They tell him he's a great man. They give him awards, and they call him a hero. And then pretty soon it goes to his head. He gets a big head, he sticks his chest out, he becomes arrogant, and then he becomes centered in himself. He becomes a tragic victim of the disease of egotism, and he begins to say "I" and "my" so much that he loses the capacity to say "we" and "our." And then he's on the road that leads to his destruction. It is the long story of history: "Whom the gods would destroy, they must first make mad with power."

This is the story of the dictator. Most of the dictators in the history of the world started out with noble desires for their people, started out with humanitarian concerns, started out concerned about the problems of the masses of people. But somewhere along the way, they got the big head, they got chesty, and everything centered in them as they looked at it, and they were moving toward their doom. This was the story of Hitler. This was the story of Mussolini. This was the story of Batista of Cuba. This was the story of Peron. Everywhere you turn, you find the same story.

There was a man who lived not too long ago by the name of Napoleon, and as a very young man he rose to heights of power. In 1796 he went to the position of first consul with the power of a dictator. Still a young man in 1804, he rose to the position of emperor, and he came close to controlling the whole of continental Europe; but all of this went to his head. Napoleon became drunk with power, and he thought he could trample over men and nations because of his military genius. And along the way, something happened to Napoleon. Watch that same Napoleon as he began to weaken at the Battle of Leipzig in 1814. That same Napoleon came to his utter doom in 1815 at the Battle of Waterloo. And Victor Hugo said something very significant in *Les Miserables* when he talked about the Battle of Waterloo. He said Napoleon was defeated there because of God! Napoleon had been impeached before the Infinite, and his fall was decreed! He vexed God! In other words, God got disgusted with Napoleon. Waterloo is not merely a battle. It is a change of the front of the universe. Waterloo is not merely a point on the map. It is the symbol of the doom of *every* Napoleon! "Whom the gods would destroy, they must first make mad with power." "Fret not thyself because of evildoers, . . . for they shall soon be cut down like grass."

And our nation has to be careful. We have risen to great power and to great heights. We are the richest nation in the world, and there is the danger that we will get the big head in America because we are the richest nation in the world. There is the danger that we will conclude that our dollars can buy anything. Dollars can't buy friendship. *[Amen.]* We are seeing in Asia and Africa and South America many people by the millions who are saying in substance that we've got to believe in what you [sic] stand for, and we've got to believe that your powers are given through the fingers of compassion and concern. And without this, your dollars will mean nothing. "Whom the gods would destroy, they must first make mad with power."

The second truth that history reveals is expressed in the proverb "When it gets dark enough, you can see the stars." Sunlight always hides the depths of the heavens. You cannot see the Milky Way in daytime, but the darkness of the night unveils the North Star by which we can chart our course. "When it gets dark enough, you can see the stars." The darker it is, the more radiantly light shines. And this is a great truth of history. We've seen it running through the pages of history. . . . There was a John Bunyan caught in a dark situation in Bedford Prison. This was a dark and desolate situation, but somehow his mind broke through the bars and comprehended the light of truth; and he came back and scratched across the pages of history a *Pilgrim's Progress.* There was a man named Handel caught in the darkened condition of his wretched old age, his physical strength all but gone, his vision all but gone, his body broken, his creditors chasing him everywhere, because he was broke.

And yet, in this dark period, he lifted his mind's eye up to the high heavens and caught new insights and truth and came back and scratched across the pages of history the majestic words of the great *Messiah,* the glad thunders and the gentle sounds of the "Hallelujah Chorus." "When it is dark enough, you can see the stars." *[Amen.]*

I've seen this in my own life. I remember an experience which was a dark one. After one Saturday afternoon in Harlem, the city of New York, I was there autographing my first book; and a demented woman came and stabbed me with a Japanese letter opener. I was rushed to the hospital, and I never will forget the experience. The doctor said that that letter opener was so near my aorta, which is the main artery, that if I had simply sneezed, I would have died immediately. And so it was a very technical and difficult operation where they had to open the chest to get that blade out. It was a dark moment. It had its agonizing and painful moments, but I submit to you this morning that through that experience I came to know the truth of God more than any other time in my life. I experienced the meaning of God in human experience more in the darkest moment of my life than in any other time. "When it is dark enough, you can see *[you can see]* the stars."

Oh, this is what the New Testament talks about. It was dark when Jesus was born. Dark indeed, one of the dark moments of history, and yet the greatest life that history has every known came at that period. Phillips Brooks talks about it: "Yet in the dark streets shineth the everlasting light." "When it gets dark enough, you can see the stars."

And there is a further truth that history teaches. It is found in the proverb "The bee always fertilizes the flower that it robs." Think about that. "The bee always fertilizes the flower that it robs." The bee goes to the flower to get what is called nectar. It robs the flower of nectar. It's robbing the flower of nectar in order to make honey. But in process of robbing the flower of nectar, the bee gives off a substance called pollen; and it is that substance which fertilizes the flower and causes it to bud and come forth in all of its fragrance and beauty. "The bee always fertilizes the flower that it robs." It's taking something from that flower, it robs something from that flower; but in the process, it fertilizes the flower. *[Yes.]* It causes it to bud. And so from our evil, good emerges.

Today we're talking a great deal about peace all over the world. Where did this talk come from? Why are we concerned about peace? Where did all the talk about peace come from? Where but from the horrors of war? The bee of war robbed the flower of our civilization, those who had the bloom of youth on their faces, but the bee also fertilized the flower. We have a United Nations today, and it was because of the darkness of war, the darkness of the inhumanity of man to man, that we were able to fertilize the idea of a United Nations. By the men and women of the world, the nations of the world will come and sit down together in creative and meaningful dialogue. "The bee always fertilizes the flower that it robs."

Not too long ago, the bee of assassination robbed the flower of our nation of its president. That was a dark moment. But it is strange indeed that in robbing the

nation of its president, it fertilized the ideas of the president; and many of the
things that he stood up for will get through quicker now as a result of his assassination. "The bee always fertilizes the flower that it robs!" He stood up for a tax
bill, and they would still be arguing about that tax bill in Congress now. As a
result of the assassination of the president, the men of Congress came to see the
necessity of getting this bill through. He stood up for civil rights, and as a result
of that he was criticized and condemned by forces particularly in the South but
even in other sections of the country, and they were going all out to block that
bill. And they were using all of their resources to block that bill, but it is one of
the ironies of history that the man who succeeded him as president, the man who
is now calling for the passage of that bill and who says he will stand up for it as
president of this nation, is a man who was born in the South, a son of its native
soil! And never again can the Southern senators say that's one of those Northern
Yankees in the White House who doesn't understand our problem! *[Yeah, amen.]*
"The bee always fertilizes the flower that it robs!" *[Amen.]* The Civil Rights Bill
will get through quicker now. Things that President Kennedy stood up for will get
through quicker now. *[Amen.]* They tried to kill the man, but they couldn't kill his
ideas. *[Amen.]* They tried to kill Abraham Lincoln, but they couldn't kill his
ideas! "The bee always fertilizes the flower that it robs!" *[Amen.]* William Cullen
Bryant was right: "Truth crushed to earth will rise again." This is the long story of
history. "Fret not thyself because of evildoers. . . . For they shall soon be cut
down like the grass and wither like the green herb."

And there is another proverb I would like to leave with you that Dr. Beard
talked about. It is a beautiful one: "The mills of God grind slowly but exceedingly fine." The mills of God grind slowly but exceedingly fine. Right defeated is
stronger than evil triumphant. Why? Because "the mills of God grind slowly but
exceedingly fine." And there is something in this universe that Greek mythol-
ogy used to refer to as the goddess of nemesis. There is a process at work, and
in a . . . sense evil and injustice may seem strong for a time, but they cannot endure,
because all reality hinges on moral foundations. "Whatsoever a man sowest, that
shall he also reap." *[Amen.]* In the final analysis, life cannot be fooled. There is a
checkpoint in the universe, and somehow evil is its own restraint. Evil carries a seed
of its own destruction. "The mills of God grind slowly but exceedingly fine."

I've seen this also in my personal experience. I saw it in a beautiful way in
Montgomery, Alabama. You will probably remember the bus protest that took
place there several years ago starting on December 5, 1955, as a result of a coura-

geous, charming lady (who lives in this city right now) refusing to get up from her seat. I guess she said like Martin Luther said centuries ago, "Here I sit, and I can do none other, so help me God." *[Amens and light laughter]* That protest started and lasted some 381 days. I remember that after we had struggled some eleven months after we had walked the streets and used our transportation system which we had worked out and sharing rides with automobiles—our car pools that, incidentally, were made possible by contributions that many of you sent and people from all over the nation. And then after about eleven months, the mayor of Montgomery came out and said, "We're are tired of this mess now, *[Huh]* and we're going into court and seek to get rid of that car pool. We will seek an injunction to destroy it." He knew that this would probably destroy the movement. And I never will forget the day when that announcement came. It was a difficult day, and then came that morning when I received my subpoena to be in court. And all day Monday (I remember very vividly), I had certain thoughts running through my mind, and I began to ask questions to myself. How would we be able to sustain this movement now? How would the people be able to get around the city without our car pool if they are able to get an injunction against the car pool? And I began thinking about the fact that the people would probably lose faith in the leaders, that we had done all of this in vain, and they would begin to say, "You led us down a false road, you've led us down the road of defeat."

We were to have a mass meeting that Monday night, and I could hardly muster up enough courage to go to face the people to tell them what would happen the next morning in court, because I knew that once Judge Carter listened to the issues involved he would rule with the city. And all day I stayed in my den having conversation with myself and trying somehow to hear the word of God in a difficult situation. *[Amen.]* Finally the hour came for the mass meeting, and I developed enough courage to go out there, and I stood before that audience, and I tried to make my little speech. But my words didn't come out well that night. The only thing I can remember saying was that we have been engaged in the struggle for many months, and I looked at the audience and said we're going to court tomorrow morning, and the city will try to destroy the car pool and they will probably win the case. But the only thing I can say to you is that I don't know what will happen after that. But we've struggled all of these months with the feeling that God was with us in the struggle, and I'm convinced that even though I can't see it now, a way will be made out of no way. *[Amen.]*

It was a dark night, darker than a thousand midnights. I could hardly sleep that night even after I'd talked. I could see cool breezes of pessimism flowing around that audience, and I could see clouds of despair floating in the mental skies of all of the thousands of people who had assembled there. It was a dark night. *[Yeah.]* It was difficult.

And I got up that morning early and got with Ralph Abernathy and E. D. Nixon and . . . some others, and we started walking down to the courthouse. We got there, and I took a seat at the table as the chief defendant with the lawyers. And the attorney for the city started arguing that we had a real profit-making corporation, and that it was a public nuisance, and that we were operating without a license. Our lawyers argued brilliantly that this was just a volunteer share-a-ride plan and that it had no profit in mind at all. And I saw that Judge Carter was not thinking about what our lawyers were talking about. He had his mind made up. Toward twelve o'clock noon, I saw Commissioner Sellers move out of the courtroom. I looked over and I saw [the] major . . . move out of the courtroom. Then I looked at Judge Carter, and he started turning around on the bench; and I knew something had developed. And he looked out and said, "The court is recessed for fifteen minutes." I didn't know what was happening. It was still dark; it was still midnight in our lives.

Pretty soon somebody else moved out of the courtroom, and by that time R. Thomas from the Associated Press ran over to the table where I was sitting, and he had a piece of paper in his hand. He said, "Dr. King, this has come across the wire service, and I would like for you to read it and give me your comment immediately; because I want to get it right out." It was still dark, it was still midnight. I looked at that piece of paper, and it said, "This morning, the United Supreme Court unanimously declared bus segregation unconstitutional in Montgomery, Alabama." *[Amens and applause]*

I knew somehow that morning had come. *[Amens and continued applause]* I knew somehow that morning had come, and I started telling the lawyers around the table, and I started running around the courtroom talking to the people, letting them know what happened. And one of the faithful followers in the back of the courtroom shouted out, "Great God Almighty, the Lord done spoke from Washington." *[Laughter and tumultuous applause]* This is it. "The mills of God grind slowly but exceedingly fine."

Sometimes it takes 381 days, but "the mills of God grind slowly but exceedingly fine." And so this is what sustains me. Carlyle was right, "No lie can live forever." Somehow those who struggle for justice must be consoled by the fact that the arc of the moral universe is long, but it bends toward justice. Somehow we must see that there is great truth in the words of James Russell Lowell:

Truth forever on the scaffold,
Wrong forever on the throne;
Yet that scaffold sways the future,
And behind the dim unknown,
Standeth God within the shadow,
Keeping watch above his own.

"The mills of God grind slowly but exceedingly fine." *[Yeah.]* And there is a magnificent pendulum swinging in the universe between darkness and light. If we see that, we gain faith to carry on. *[Yeah.]* Our slave foreparents saw it swinging, and when they would think of the darkness of life and they would think of the agony of life, they would sing a song which says, "Nobody knows the trouble I've seen." They knew that morning would come, that daybreak would appear, and so they could sing another song, "I'm so glad that trouble don't last always." This is a faith that can keep us going. This is a faith that will cause us to adjourn the counsels of despair and bring new life into the dark chambers of pessimism.

And so when days become dark and nights become dreary and we go through those moments of the chilly winds of adversity blowing all around us and are forced to stand amid the surging water of life's restless sea, gain consolation from the fact that there is a God in this universe who is able to lift us from the fatigue of despair to the buoyancy of hope and transform dark and desolate valleys into sunlit paths of inner peace. This is our faith, and this is our hope, and this is what can keep us going in difficult and frustrating days. "Fret not thyself because of evildoers, neither be thou envious against the workers of iniquity. For they shall soon be cut down like the grass and wither like the green herb." "Trust in the Lord and do good, *[Amen.]* and he will give thee the desires of thine heart." *[Amen.]*

And now unto him who is able to keep us from falling, and to present us fault-less before our Father's throne, to him be power and authority, majesty and dominion now, henceforth and forevermore, world without end. Amen. *[Amen.]*

Appendix 3
THE PRODIGAL SON
Ebenezer Baptist Church,
Atlanta, c. 1966

This sermon is available to the public on audiocassette from the Southern Chris-
tian Leadership Conference (SCLC) office in Atlanta, Georgia. Bracketed words
represent audible responses from the audience.

Text: Luke 15:11-24

I turn today to one of the most familiar of all of the parables ever told by Jesus. It
is a parable that has, on the one hand, the tang of the human and, on the other
hand, the glow of the divine. George Murray, referring to this parable, said that it
is probably the most humanly touching and divinely inspiring story in all literature. I speak of the parable of the prodigal son. The story is a familiar one, but in
order to refresh your memories, I turn to the fifteenth chapter of the gospel as
recorded by St. Luke. And we read, "And he said," referring to Jesus, "a certain
man had two sons; And the younger of them said to his father, Father, give me the
portion of goods that falleth to me. And he divided unto them his living. And not
many days after, the younger son gathered all together, and took his journey into
a far country, and there wasted his substance with riotous living. And when he
had spent all, there arose a mighty famine in that land; and he began to be in
want. And he went and joined himself to a citizen of that country; and he sent him
into his fields to feed swine. And he would fain have filled his belly with the
husks that the swine did eat: and no man gave unto him." In other words, he
found himself after losing all having to work in a hog's pen. This was the only
place that he could live at that moment and the only place that he could eat. Then
the next verse comes with the glorious and even cosmic change in the life of this
boy. It says, "And when he came to himself, he said, How many hired servants of
my father's have bread enough and to spare, and I perish with hunger! I will arise
and go to my father, and will say unto him, Father, I have sinned against thee, I've
sinned against heaven and am no more worthy to be called thy son; make me as

one of thy hired servants. And he arose, and came to his father. But when he was yet a great way off, his father saw him, and had compassion, and ran, and fell on his neck, and kissed him. And the son said unto him, Father, I have sinned against heaven, and in thy sight, and am no more worthy to be called thy son. But the father said to his servants, Bring forth the best robe, and put it on him; and put a ring on his hand, and shoes on his feet: And bring hither the fatted calf, and kill it; and let us eat, and be merry: For this my son was dead, and is alive again; he was lost, and is found. And they began to be merry."

"For this my son was dead, and is alive again; he was lost, and is found."

This is a story, an arresting , beautiful, challenging story. This morning I want to challenge you to look at that boy and to see him not merely as a notorious character of a distant day. But I want you to look at him and see him as a faithful reflection of life everywhere. The prodigal sons and daughters still live today. And what is it in this story that we need to see? Why is it that this boy was a prodigal? And why is it that we still in so many instances remain prodigals?

First, the tragedy of this boy's life was that he dreamed a dream that could never come true. You know, it's a terrible thing to dream dreams that cannot somehow be ultimately structured into reality. Dreams are great, dreams are meaningful. And in a sense, all of life moves on the wave of a dream. Somebody dreams something and sets out to bring that dream into reality, and it often comes in a scientific invention. It often comes in great literature. It often comes in great music. But it is so tragic to dream a dream that cannot come true. This was that boy's tragedy. He dreamed a dream that pleasure was the be-all and end-all of life. He dreamed a dream that satisfaction of the senses is the end of existence. This is a dream that could never come true, and yet millions of people have dreamed that intriguing dream and in many forms and variations. They dream it still. It has never been more alluringly presented. And in the lacelike poetry of Omar Khayyam the Persian poet, he says on the one hand: "Come fill the cup; waste not your hour. Better be jocund with the fruitful grape than saddened after . . . a bitter fruit." Then in some of his other writings, he says, "You take the cash, and let the credit go, nor heed the rumble of a distant drum." "You don't trouble your mind about the future," says Omar Khayyam. "Who knows? Nor about the past, for who can change it?" And so he goes on to say, "The moving finger writes, and having writ, moves on. Neither peers nor wit can cancel out a line of it." And then he begins to say what life means, and it boils down to saying, "A book of verses underneath the bough, a jug of wine, a loaf of bread and thou."

This is the notion, you see, that pleasure is the end of life.

Now people follow this today in so many ways, running after this thrill and that thrill. Running after this experience and that experience. Running from this nightclub to that nightclub. Running from this tavern to that tavern. You've seen people like that. Somehow life for them is an endless round of trying to find the thrill. This is the dream that that boy dreamed. It was a tragic dream, but he dreamed it. It was tragic, because it couldn't come true. And somebody is asking this morning, I'm sure, "Why is it that the dream couldn't come true?" It couldn't come true, my friends, because thrills play out. Sensations are short-lived. Pleasures pale. And people who make commission of happiness and stake all of life's meaning on the senses find invariably that life grows duller and duller. This is always the case when one seeks to make pleasure the end of life.

But there is a second thing that I'd like to get you to see here, and that is that this boy allowed his worse self to take over his best self. You remember I read that point where the prodigal son while in that far country came to himself. And the passage read, "He came to himself." It's so important to see that. For that is a part of the basic meaning of this story. The prodigal was not himself in what he was doing. He was not his real self when he left home. He was not his whole self. He was not the self for which he was born. This tells us something about life. And I hope this morning we will search our souls and know that it tells us something about ourselves, and that is that each of us is two selves. The great burden of life is to always try to keep that higher self in command. They have written about it in literature. Shakespeare one day thought of the fact that there are halos within man and within human nature. He wrote in Hamlet: "What a piece of work is man! How noble in reason! how infinite in faculties! in form, in moving, how express and admirable! in action how like an angel! in apprehension how like a god! the beauty of the world! the paragon of animals!"

Later on, Shakespeare wrote *King Lear.* He knew that man had not only halos in his being, but he also had horns. So in *King Lear* he wrote: "Man is false of spirit, bloody of hand, a wolf in greediness, a lion in prey." This is human nature. Whenever we look at man real good, we see this division, and the real challenge of life is to work on it and say I am going to always keep the high self in command. John Oxenham wrote:

To every man there openeth
A Way, and Ways, and a Way.
And the High Soul climbs the High Way,

And the Low Soul gropes the Low,
And in between, on the misty flats,
The rest drift to and fro.
But to every man there openeth
A High, . . . and a Low (way).
[And] . . . every man decideth
[Which] way his soul [will] go.

And God grant this morning that each of us will choose the high way, that each of us will choose the way of truth, the way of beauty, the way of goodness. And every time that old lower self begins to act up and tell us to do wrong, let us allow that higher self to tell us that we were made for the stars, created for the everlasting, born for the eternity. The prodigal son's greatest tragedy was that he forget who he was, and so he allowed his worse self to take over.

The final point I want to bring out is the crux of this story, and that is this story does not only reveal to us the weaknesses of human nature, but it tells us about the strength of divine nature. Jesus didn't tell this story merely to tell us about the badness of man, but he wrote it to tell us about the goodness of God. *[All right.]* Jesus told this story to let us know that we are not orphans thrown out into the terrifying immensities of space with nobody concerned about us! Over and over again, I've walked out at night, *[Yeah.]* looked up at the stars as they bedeck the heavens like swinging lanterns of eternity. And something came to me and said these stars shine from that cold, serene and passionless height, totally indifferent to the joys and sorrows of men. Something caused me to say, "Oh no," for behind those swinging lanterns of eternity is a purpose that embraces all mankind, a God concerned about his children. And so you can't understand the story of the prodigal son without understanding that when Jesus talked about the father back home he was talking about God.

Look at that story for a minute. *[Yeah.]* The boy left home, wasted all of his money, all of his energy, all of his time, and he had nothing. And so he had to go to a citizen of another country. This citizen of the other country took him in, but he put him out there in a hog's pen. Think about it, a human being having to live with hogs. Something happened to that boy. Something deep down in his remembrance.

Seems that I can see that boy now getting ready *[Yeah.]* to try to get something to eat. He was hungry. Seems that I can see that boy reaching down to the ground now, bringing the food up that the hogs ate. When it got almost to his lips, it seems that I can see him throwing it away and saying to himself, "I'm not a hog. *[All right.]* I don't think like a hog, I don't talk like a hog, because a hog can't communicate with me. Basically, I don't smell like a hog, I don't live like a hog. and I have a father back home who has a lot of food! And I think he might have said he has thousands and thousands of cattle upon a thousand hills, and that's an awful lot of steak. *[Ha ha ha, yeah.]* Seems that I can see that boy saying, "I'm gonna rise now." *[Yes sir.]* He gets up. He gets a little speech he's going to give to his father, "I've sinned against thee. I am not worthy to be called your son. Make me as one of your hired servants!" *[Yeah.]*

Watch him as he goes back up the dusty road that he had once come down. *[Preach!]* Broke down in spirit, shabbily clad clothes all wrinkled and dirty, hasn't had a shave for weeks, *[Oh yes.]* he walks down that road with a little bag on his back! Nothing left in it! Going on back home! The beauty of it is—and this is the story—somebody was at home looking out afar. Before that boy got there, that father started running toward him. *[Yeah.]* Grabbed him! Kissed him! He turned around and said, "Now, we're going to have a divine party tonight! *[Yeah.]* Get the fatted calf! And I want you to put some shoes on his feet! And I want you to put a ring on his finger! And put some clothes on his back! And let's all of us be happy tonight, for my son who was lost is found again! *[Yeah.]* My son who was dead is alive now! *[Yeah.]* Let's make merry!"

Ah, this is the joy of life! Somebody has been away from home a long time. Somebody here this morning has strayed away to some dangerous and tragic far country. The more you do what you like, the less you like what you do. *[Yeah.]* This would be a tragic world if we could feel happy when we do what is wrong. This would be a tragic world if we would feel natural when we do the unnatural. But this is God's unbroken hold on us. Somebody this morning needs to come home. *[That's all right.]* Some nations need to come. God is speaking today. Seems that I can hear a voice crying through the vista of eternity saying, "America, there was a time that things looked good, you built ideologically a great structure. You were in your Father's house ideally. You put it on paper: 'We hold these truths to be self-evident that all men are created equal and endowed by their Creator with certain inalienable rights and that among these are life, liberty and the pursuit of happiness.' Beautiful America. But something happened to you. For some strange reason, you would not dwell in that house. *[Oh yeah.]* You went to a tragic far country. A far country of racism where even until this day, America, you leave twenty-two billion [sic] of your black brothers and sisters living outside of the sunlight of opportunity, *[Yeah.]* where even to this day, America, *[Yeah.]* as you stay there in that far country, you leave 22 billion [sic] of your black brothers humiliated, segregated, dominated politically. America, whenever you stray away from home a famine breaks out. *[Yeah.]* There's a famine in your nation today. You can't understand it. *[Tell it like it is.]* Every city in your country today is a literal powder keg: riots breaking out day in and day out and, America, you wonder what is wrong. *[All right.]*

You must be told, America, that a riot is the language of the unheard. And what is it that America has failed to hear? Failed to hear that the economic plight of the Negro poor has worsened! Failed to hear that the promises of freedom and equality have not been met! Failed to hear that large segments of white society are more concerned about tranquillity and the status quo than about justice and humanity! *[Yeah.]* This is it. A famine has broken out. *[Yeah.]* And that isn't the way to deal with this famine. It's a misguided outbreak, as I've said. Riots are socially destructive and self-defeating, and I will stand up and condemn them at every point; and at the same time I must condemn the conditions that make people feel so hopeless, *[Yeah.]* make them feel in such despair that they engage in this kind of misguided action.

America needs to hear something, and that is our summers of riots are caused by winter's delay. As long as the Negro doesn't get his freedom and long as he doesn't get it now, there's going to be tension all over this nation. There's a famine in this country, a moral and spiritual famine because somewhere America strayed away from home. And I can hear the voice of God saying, "America, it isn't too late. If you will only come to yourself. The cities are exploding today, America, but just come to yourself. You, you, you, you, you know, America, I have nothing to spare if you will follow my Spirit to help you solve your problem, if you will come back home, America. Now if you get your priorities right and you do that, America, if you come home, you can end poverty. You won't have . . . city in any city! You won't have a dilapidated Harlem in any city! You will not have a West Side and a South Side of slums in Chicago in any city, because you will be a home and home will get things right for you. And everybody will begin to love everybody and live as one big happy family."

Jesus is saying to America, "Come home." Speaking to somebody here this morning, I don't know your far country. It may be a bad temper. He's saying you ought to come home this morning. It may be excessive drink. He's saying you ought to come home this morning. *[Yeah, yeah.]* It may be something deep down within you that causes you to be jealous of people and hate people and be envious of people. He's saying you ought to come home this morning. May be a family program where you haven't been quite true to your wife or to your husband, but he's saying to you now you ought to come home this morning. May be you haven't given the attention that you should give to your children, but he's saying to you you ought to come home this morning. Somebody ought to come home this morning! Come home, come home, ye who are weary, come home. Softly and tenderly Jesus is calling, calling for you and for me.

When one will come home, something happens. In a sense, all the eternities will stand still and the angels will strike silent. Indeed, the morning stars will sing together, and the sons of God will shout for joy.

Appendix 4
NO ROOM
AT THE INN
Ebenezer Baptist Church,
Atlanta, c. 1967

This sermon is available to the public on audiocassette from the Southern Christian Leadership Conference (SCLC) office in Atlanta, Georgia. Bracketed words represent audible responses from the audience.

Text: Luke 2:7

There are numerous truths that come to all of us and many challenges that stand before us as we think about the meaning of Christmas. As we search the New Testament and reach the meaning of the Christmas story, we find so many things that should cause us to stand before the scrutiny of God and search our souls. There is a passage in the Gospels as recorded by St. Luke, chapter 4 [sic] verse 7, which tells us about a strange inhospitality to the Highest. It reads in very familiar words, "There was no room for them in the inn."

These words ring across the centuries. "No room for them in the inn." And I guess the words have special meaning for us today, because as we look back over the life of Christ, that was to be the Master's experience throughout his ministry. "No room." No room for his teachings in the minds of men. No room for his reforming zeal in the synagogue. Then with closed minds came that ultimate tragic event when he was crucified on the cross of Calvary. The writer of the fourth Gospel summarizes it in a piercing pathetic sense: "He came unto his own, and his own received him not." Inhospitality to the Highest. "No room."

I guess this text has meaning for us for another reason, and that is that somehow and in a real sense a crowded end of this story is an eternal parable of the human soul; and over some of the most shameful tragedies of human history hang these words: "No room." We see it in so many ways. We see it in the intellectual life. We see it in our closed minds. Years ago, Socrates sought to give birth to certain new and creative ideas which had come as a result of his philosophical delvings, and the Athenians of his day cried out, "No room." And they ended up making him drink the hemlock. Then centuries later, Galileo came along and came to certain insights about the universe, but there were those with closed minds in the ranks of the church who said in substance, "No room for your new ideas." But not only do we need to look in the realm of ideas, if we look in the social life of man, how tragic it reads! Go to South Africa today, and there you will see the millions of people pregnant with the idea and longing for freedom and human dignity, standing before the South African government, pleading for release; and yet an answer comes, "No room." Go to Rhodesia today, and there you will find Mr. Ian Smith crying out to the black people of Rhodesia, "No room." Come to the United States today, and still you will see millions of God's children who happen to be black covered up in slums and ghettos, having a desire to give birth to that great longing for freedom and to be in the mainstream of American life. But all too many realtors, all too many sophisticated Pharaohs whether they be North or South, are still saying, "No room." *[Well.]* And for years the Negro has been crying out for freedom, but in all too many instances the cry has been "No room."

And see what we've done to the nation because of the "no room in the inn" ethos and practice. Oh, who knows *[Yeah.]* but in the delta of Mississippi there's not some Einstein on the scene; but because of a lack of educational opportunities, this great possibility is blocked for years and centuries. Who knows but in the crowded segregated schools of Atlanta we don't have another Plato and Aristotle on the scene. Who knows but in the segregated schools of Crawfordville, Georgia, we may not have another Beethoven and Mozart on the scene. But because we have had a sign on the door of our nation reading "No room," so many creative gains have been blocked. And over some of the most shameful tragedies of human history hang these words: "No room."

Now let us look at that more closely, that text, and see what it says to us. First let us remember that the inn that Joseph and Mary went to to give birth to Jesus was really crowded. There's nothing in the story to say that the innkeeper was dishonest. The parents of Jesus were not turned down because of ill-will. The problem was all spaces were filled with other guests. Know how often we crowd Jesus out. This is it. It isn't that we mean to be disloyal to the Highest. It isn't that we consciously want to get rid of Christ. It isn't that we stand before the life and teachings of Jesus Christ and say, "Goodbye Christ, we're going to leave you now." But it's simply that we crowd him out. We become so involved with other things—our many responsibilities, our many, many duties here and there, the hurly-burly of everyday life; and unconsciously we end up crowding Christ out.

You know, one of the strangest things is that we crowd him more than ever before around the Christmas season. We are so busy giving and exchanging gifts. We're so busy getting in the crowded traffic and in the mad rush of the stores that we see Christmas as little more than a commercial holiday rather than a sacred holy day. And so often in our lives as we come to the Christmas season, we find ourselves saying in substance, "No room." We stand before great spiritual opportunities and great spiritual realities, but we're busy. And you know we've crowded Christ out, because we've become so involved in dealing with those things which we can see and those things which we can apply our five senses to *[Yeah.]* that we forget that ultimately it's the unseen that's real.

You remember the story that Jesus experienced later in his life. He had been in the temple. His parents had taken him up to Jerusalem, and they had been in the temple for several days, and then they started back to Nazareth. And you remember the story that the parents of Jesus, moving ahead, walked a whole day. It says, "They went a whole day's journey not knowing that Jesus wasn't with them." They were just busy. They had not taken time to look back.

And how many people this morning are just busy doing other things. We've become so involved in getting our big bank accounts, in getting our big cars, that we unconsciously forget to think about Jesus, and we forget to think about spiritual matters. We've become so involved in looking at the manmade lights of the city that we unconsciously forget to look at that great cosmic light that gets up early in the morning in the eastern horizon and like a symphony of motion paints its technicolor across the blue—a light that man could never make. We've become so involved in thinking about our radar and our televisions that we've forgotten to think about those great swinging lanterns of eternity and the stars that bedeck the heavens like shining silvery pins sticking in the magnificent blue pincushion—something that man could never make. We've become so involved in looking at our skyscraping buildings that we unconsciously forget to think about the gigantic mountains kissing the sky as if to bathe their peaks in the lofty blue—something that man could never make. We've become so involved in thinking that we can usher in a new order by our power that we forget to think about the divine dimension, and when we look back we discover that we've gone a whole day's journey *[Yes.]* not knowing that God is not with us and not realizing that we're without the spiritual presence of Christ. *[Great God.]* We crowd him out. The eternal pride of many of God's children is "no room."

Now the other thing you must see in that story is this. If this man had known who Jesus was, he would have made room for him, he would have rearranged things, he would have in some way made it possible for history's supreme character to be born in his inn. But the fact is he didn't know who he was. *[Yes.]* He wasn't spiritually sensitive enough to know who he was. And so often God wants to do something for our lives and great spiritual possibilities stand before us, but we are not spiritually attuned, we're not spiritually sensitive *[That's right.]* so that we know when it is there. The beautiful thing is that we must recognize that Christ does not always come in the high places. *[Well.]* His presence may be in the lowest places. And this man didn't know who he was because he thought that the parents would come accompanied by an army and accompanied by sounding trumpets. *[Well.]* He didn't recognize that a new kind of king was on the horizon. Not a king that came accompanied with great armies. Not a king that would come accompanied with all the bugles and all the sounds of the horns and the drums but a king that would be a humble servant, *[Yeah.]* a king that would say, "He that is greatest among you shall be your servant." That is where you find Christ, and that is why he's a new kind of king.

Napoleon toward his latter days, after he had gone through many military conquests and after he had come to the point of coming to his utter defeat at Waterloo, made this statement, "Caesar, Alexander the Great, Charlemagne and I have built great empires, but upon what did they depend? They depended upon force, but long ago Jesus built an empire that depended upon love; and even to this day millions will die for him." The innkeeper didn't realize that Jesus was a new kind of king. *[Yeah.]* He wasn't the king that they anticipated. He was a king that would just move out with the ammunition of love. He was a king that would put on the breastplate of righteousness and the whole armor of God *[Yes.]* and just start marching through history, and he's been marching now a long time. A new kind of king. And so we must know the coming of the Christ by the kind of kingship that he represents.

The other thing is, I suspect, that the real barrier to our welcoming Christ is ultimately sin. Think about it. There are things in our lives which must leave if Christ comes in. If Christ comes into our lives, greed must leave. If Christ comes into our lives, selfishness will leave. *[Yeah.]* If Christ comes into ours lives, hatred and malice will leave. And deep down within so many of us, we find tides of envy and jealousy capable of rising to flood proportions, but if Christ enters our lives they will leave. *[Yeah.]* If Christ enters our lives, race prejudice will leave. If Christ enters our lives, our vicious class systems will dissolve. If Christ enters our lives, war will end in the world, and men will "beat their swords into plowshares and their spears into pruning hooks, and nations will not rise up against nations, neither will they study war anymore."

Yes, we cry, "No room in the inn," because deep down within we don't want Christ in our lives. We want to do things like we've been doing them! *[Yes.]* We want to hold on to our old hatreds. We want to hold on to our old nationalisms. We want to hold on to our old and dilapidated patriotisms. We want to hold on to our idea of "my nation right or wrong," and we are not willing to give up this notion and say, "Humanity—this is what we are concerned about." We don't want Christ in, because when *he* comes in he lets us know that we've got to be better people! *[Yes.]* When he comes in our lives, he lets us know that we must go the second mile! *[Yes.]* When he comes into our lives, he lets us know that we must do unto others as we would have them do unto ourselves. When he comes into our lives, he lets us know that we can't commit adultery, that even he that looketh upon a woman with lust in his eyes has already committed adultery. When he comes into our lives, he lets us know that he who gives a cup of cold water to him who is in need is ready to enter the kingdom of God! We don't want him in our lives, because we want to do things like we used to do them. And when he gets into our lives, the things we used to do, we don't do them anymore.

And the final thing is that while we crowd him out, he takes us in. We crowd him out, he takes us in. Hear him as he cries out, "In my Father's house are many mansions. If it were not so, I would have told you." We crowd him out, he takes us in! "Behold, I stand at the door and knock. If you will open the door, I will come in to you and will sup with you and you with me." We crowd him out, he takes us in! *[Yeah.]* This is the beauty of the gospel: as we crowd Christ out, he's always taking us in. "Come unto me, all ye who labor and are heavy laden, and I will give you rest." We crowd him out, he takes us in. We crowd him out with our race prejudice, but he takes us in. "Out of one blood God made all men to dwell upon the face of the earth." We crowd him out, he takes us in. "In Christ there is neither Jew nor Gentile, bond nor free, male nor female, but we are all one in Christ Jesus." We crowd him out, he takes us in. And this is why he's the Lord of our lives today, because he takes us in, and this is why this morning all over the world can sing:

In Christ there is no east nor west,
In him no north nor south,
But one great fellowship of love
Throughout the whole wide world. [sic]

This is why we can hear another chorus crying out this morning:

Jesus shall reign where'er the sun
Doth its successive journeys run;
His kingdom spread from shore to shore
'Til moon shall wane and wax no more. [sic]

And this is why we can hear another chorus singing: "All hail the power of Jesus'
name." *[Yeah.]* And this is why we can hear another chorus singing:

Hallelujah! Hallelujah!
He's king of kings and lord of lords;
Hallelujah! Hallelujah!
The kingdom of this world shall become
the kingdom of our Lord and his Christ;
And he shall reign forever and forever
Hallelujah! Hallelujah!

We crowd him out, but he takes us in.

This is the challenge this morning. I call upon you to allow him to come into
your life. He will change it. He will give it new meaning. This is the Christmas
message. This is the meaning of it. And God grant that we will not allow on our
lives the sign reading "No room." For Christ is desirous of entering and giving us
a new bent and a new hold on life.

Appendix 5
KING'S USE OF SOURCES

Quotations and References in Sixteen of Martin Luther King Jr.'s Sermons

TITLE OF SERMON	BIBLE	OTHER LITERARY WORKS (Quoted)	(Referred to)	PERSONALITIES (Quoted)	(Referred to)
"A Tough Mind and a Tender Heart"	Matthew 10:16 Matthew 5:1-12 Matthew 26:52 Exodus 16:3	*Mein Kampf* by Adolf Hitler *Palace of Art* by Tennyson	*God the Invisible King* by H. G. Wells	French philosopher Hegel Elderly segregationist in the South Adolf Hitler Shakespeare (poetry) Aristotle	Nkrumah of Ghana Nehru of India H. G. Wells Tennyson Capernicus Galileo Darwin Margaret Mead (anthropologist) Ruth Benedict (anthropologist)
"Transformed Nonconformist"	Romans 12:2 Acts 16:12 Luke 12:15 Matthew 5:28 Matthew 5:10 Matthew 21:31 Matthew 5:44 Matthew 26:52 Matthew 25:40 Amos 5:24 Daniel 3:17 Mark 8:33	"Essay on Self-Reliance" by Emerson		Nietzsche Thomas Jefferson (2) James Russell Lowell (poetry) Abraham Lincoln King's six-year-old daughter John Bunyan	Paul McCarthy (ism) John Birch (Society) White Citizens Council Socrates Professor Bixler

TITLE OF SERMON	BIBLE (Quoted)	OTHER LITERARY WORKS		PERSONALITIES	
		(Quoted)	(Referred to)	(Quoted)	(Referred to)
"On Being a Good Neighbor"	Luke 10:29 (2) Luke 10:25 Luke 10:27 Luke 10:28 Exodus 20:13		Declaration of Independence Emancipation Proclamation	Himself (in conversation with Mrs. King)	Albert Schweitzer Abraham Lincoln Harry Emerson Fosdick
"Love in Action"	Luke 23:34 Matthew 18:21 Matthew 18:22 Romans 10:2 John 3:19			William Shakespeare (poetry) John Bowring (poetry)	Samson Socrates Saul (Paul) Copernicus Darwin Aristotle Ruth Benedict (anthropologist) Margaret Mead (anthropologist) Melville J. Herskovits (anthropologist) Dante
"Loving Your Enemies"	Matthew 5:33-35		"The Pathology of Race Prejudice" by Dr. E. Franklin Frazier Greek New Testament	Nietzsche Ovid (Latin poet) Plato Paul Napoleon Bonaparte Isaac Watts (poetry) John Oxenham (poetry)	Abraham Lincoln Elizabeth Cady Stanton H. G. Wells Paul
"A Knock at Midnight"	Luke 11:5-6 Luke 11:7 Psalm 30:5	Negro spiritual Negro spiritual Negro spiritual	*Man Against Himself* *The Neurotic Personality of Our Times* *Modern Man in Search of a Soul* *Peace of Mind* *Peace of Soul*	Harrison Salisbury William Wilberforce William Pitt Lord Aston Schopenhauer (philosopher) Shakespeare Ralph Bersedi	Darwin

TITLE OF SERMON	BIBLE (Quoted)	OTHER LITERARY WORKS (Quoted)	OTHER LITERARY WORKS (Referred to)	PERSONALITIES (Quoted)	PERSONALITIES (Referred to)
"The Man Who Was a Fool"	Luke 12:20 Luke 12:19 Luke 12:15 Matthew 6:32 Matthew 6:33		Paraphrase of portion of Psalm 23 (poetry)	Dr. George A. Buttrick Sir James Jeans (physicist) Arthur Balfour (philosopher) Jean Jacques Rousseau Alfred the Great G. K. Chesterton Asian writer	Herbert Spenser Darwin
"The Death of Evil upon the Sea-shore"	Exodus 14:30 Hebrews 12:11 Psalm 139:7-12		Emancipation Proclamation	Hinduism Zoroastrianism Judaism Christianity William Cullen Bryant Thomas Carlyle Shakespeare James Russell Lowell Tennyson (poetry) Winston Churchill Thomas Jefferson Abraham Lincoln Frederick Douglass Charles A. Beard (historian) Matthew Arnold Coretta Scott King	Mohandas K. Gandhi
"Three Dimensions of a Complete Life"	Revelation 21:16 2 Kings 5:1 Psalm 8:4 Matthew 22:37	*Peace of Mind* by Rabbi J. Liebman		Longfellow Ralph W. Emerson Douglas Mallock (poetry) John Donne	Aeschylus Sophocles Euripides Socrates Plato Aristotle Handel

TITLE OF SERMON	BIBLE (Quoted)	OTHER LITERARY WORKS (Quoted)	(Referred to)	PERSONALITIES (Quoted)	(Referred to)
"Three Dimensions of a Complete Life" *(cont.)*				Professor Sevekin Reinhold Niebuhr Plato Augustine	Ludwig van Beethoven (2) Bach T. Washington Marian Anderson George Washington Carver Ralph Bunche Michelangelo Shakespeare
"Shattered Dreams"	Romans 15:24 Jeremiah 10:19 Philippians 4:11 John 14:27	Christian hymn *Decline and Fall of the Roman Empire* by Gibbon Negro spiritual Christian hymn		Omar Khayyam (poetry) Paul Tillich	Schubert George Frederick Watts Mohandas K. Gandhi Woodrow Wilson Darwin Robert Louis Stevenson Helen Keller Handel
"What Is Man?"	Psalm 8:4-5	*Pilgrim's Progress* by John Bunyan *The Messiah Moral Man and Immoral Society* by Reinhold Niebuhr		Shakespeare Carlyle John Oxenham (poetry)	Shakespeare Beethoven Michelangelo
"How Should a Christian View Communism?"	Amos 5:24 Matthew 25:40 Luke 1:52-53 Luke 4:18-19 Isaiah 40:4-5	Poetry	*Communist Manifesto*	Lenin Paul Tillich William Temple (Archbishop of Canterbury) John Oxenham (poetry)	Karl Marx

TITLE OF SERMON	BIBLE (Quoted)	OTHER LITERARY WORKS		PERSONALITIES	
		(Quoted)	(Referred to)	(Quoted)	(Referred to)

"Our God Is Able"	Jude 24
	Isaiah 40:4
	John 14:24
		Les Miserables by Victor Hugo		Richard Swin-
				burne
				John Keats
				Prime Minister
				  Macmillan
				James Russell
				  Lowell (poetry)
				Paul L. Dunbar
				  (poetry)	

"Antidotes for Fear"	1 John 4:18 Proverbs 3:19	*Journal* by Henry David Thoreau *Confession* by Tolstoy Poetry (anony-mous)		K. Horney Shakespeare Angelo Patri Sigmund Freud Plato Aristotle Thomas Aquinas Epictetus Paul Tillich Erich Fromm Mother Pollard	Sigmund Freud

"The Answer to a Per-plexing Question"	Matthew
	  17:19
	Matthew
	  17:18
	Matthew
	  17:20
	Exodus 14:15
	Ezekiel 2:1
	2 Corinthians
	  5:17
	Revelation
	  3:20
		Origin of Spe-cies		Rousseau
				Condorcet
				  (French
				  humanist)
				Modern humanist
				Gabriel Marcel
				Tolstoi	

"Paul's Letter to Ameri-can Chris-tians"	Romans 12:2
	Galatians
	  3:28
	Acts 17:24, 26
	Romans 8:38-39
	Matthew
	  5:11-12
				Thoreau	the Epicureans
					the Stoics
					Plato
					Aristotle

TOTALS	70	21	12	87	69

Grand Total of "Quotes": 178

Bible Citations from Sixteen of Martin Luther King Jr.'s Sermons

OLD TESTAMENT   **NEW TESTAMENT**

Exodus
14:15
14:30
16:3
20:13

2 Kings
5:1

Psalms
8:4
8:4-5
30:5
139:7-12

Proverbs
3:19

Isaiah
40:4
40:4-5

Jeremiah
10:19

Ezekiel
2:1

Daniel
3:17

Amos
5:24 (twice)

Matthew
5:1-12
5:10
5:11-12
5:28
5:33-35
5:44
6:32
6:33
10:16
17:18
17:19
17:20
18:21
18:22
21:31
22:37
25:40 (twice)
26:52 (twice)

Mark
8:33

Luke
1:52-53
4:18-19
10:27
10:28
10:29 (twice)
11:5-6
11:7
12:15 (twice)

12:19
12:29
23:34

Romans
8:38-39
10:2
12:2 (twice)
15:24

2 Corinthians
5:17

Galatians
3:28

Philippians
4:11

Hebrews
12:11

1 John
4:18

Jude
24

Revelation
3:20
21:1

Notes

Chapter 1: A Homiletical Biography

[1]Martin Luther King Jr., "The UnChristian Christian," *Ebony* 20, no. 10 (August 1965): 77.

[2]See Lewis V. Baldwin, *There Is a Balm in Gilead* (Minneapolis: Fortress, 1991, pp. 160-228); James H. Cone, *Martin and Malcolm and America* (Maryknoll, N.Y.: Orbis, pp. 135-49); Taylor Branch, *Parting the Waters* (New York: Simon & Schuster, 1988), pp. 3, 695-96, 738-43.

[3]Personal interview with Martin Luther King Jr., August 31, 1966.

[4]Letter from Alberta King, September 7, 1966. This letter, which followed a telephone interview with Mrs. King, is in appendix I-N of Mervyn A. Warren, "A Rhetorical Study of the Preaching of Doctor Martin Luther King, Jr., Pastor and Pulpit Orator," Ph.D. diss., Michigan State University, 1966.

[5]Basil Mathews, *Booker T. Washington: Educator and Interracial Interpreter* (Cambridge, Mass.: Harvard University Press, 1948), pp. 50-51, 58, 91-92.

[6]Lerone Bennett Jr., *What Manner of Man: A Biography of Martin Luther King Jr.* (Chicago: Johnson, 1964), pp. 11-12.

[7]Ibid., p. 10.

[8]Asa Philip Randolph was featured on the cover of *Life* on September 6, 1963, as one of the minds behind the organization of the March on Washington, when over 200,000 African Americans and whites streamed into the nation's capital in support of the Negro's call for equal rights in the United States.

[9]Frederick Lewis Allen, *Only Yesterday* (New York: Bantam, 1931), pp. 226-42.

[10]Arthur S. Link, *American Epoch: A History of the United States Since the 1890s* (New York: Alfred A. Knopf, 1958), p. 296.

[11]William Hordern, *A Layman's Guide to Protestant Theology* (New York: Macmillan, 1955), p. 83.

[12]Ibid., p. 83. For a parallel consideration of the social activism of King and Fosdick, see Julius R. Scruggs, *Baptist Preachers with Social Consciousness: A Comparative Study of Martin Luther King Jr. and Harry Emerson Fosdick* (Philadelphia: Dorrance, 1978).

[13]Hordern, *Layman's Guide,* p. 84.

[14]In the Martin Luther King Jr. Collection at Boston University Library (consisting of his donation of personal papers) is a classroom essay he wrote while a student at Crozer Seminary entitled "An Autobiography of Religious Development." He gives a very intuitive and perceptive description of his spiritual pilgrimage, acknowledging what he considers his "natural" penchant for intellectual analysis, criticism and inquiry. Although King remembered having written the paper, in an interview with me on August 31, 1966, he indicated that he did not recall for which class it was written.

Another related type of material from a number of different sources is the ongoing series The Martin Luther King Jr. Papers Project, under senior editor Clayborne Carson. The first three volumes were published in l992, 1994 and 1997 respectively by University of California Press (Berkeley).

[15]L. Harold DeWolf, *Present Trends in Christian Thought* (New York: Association, 1960), pp. 77-97. See also Hordern, *Layman's Guide,* pp. 121-64.

[16]Martin Luther King Jr., *Strength to Love* (New York: Harper & Row, 1963), p. 6.

[17]The quotations in this paragraph are taken from DeWolf's *Present Trends in Christian Thought;* however, the same thoughts were also expressed to me in an interview with him on March 6, 1966.

[18]L. D. Reddick, *Crusader Without Violence: A Biography of Martin Luther King Jr.* (New York: Harper & Row, 1959), p. 86.

[19]Ibid., p. 51.

[20]"Man of the Year," *Time,* January 3, 1964, p. 13.

[21]Loudon Wainwright, "Martyr of the Sit-ins," *Life* 49 (November 7, 1960): 124.

[22]"Battle Against Tradition: Martin Luther King, Jr.," *New York Times,* March 21, 1956, p. 28.

[23]Reddick, *Crusader Without Violence,* pp. 2-3.

[24]Martin Luther King Jr., "Autobiography of Religious Development," typescript (paper written for a class at Crozer Seminary), undated, Martin Luther King Jr. Collection, Boston University Library.

[25]Bennett, *What Manner of Man*, p. 18.

[26]Ibid., pp. 18-19.

[27]Ibid., p. 18.

[28]Ibid.

[29]Reddick, *Crusader Without Violence,* p. 7.

[30]Wainwright, "Martyr of the Sit-ins," p. 124.

[31]Reddick, *Crusader Without Violence,* p. 8.

[32]William Peters, "The Man Who Fights Hate with Love," *Redbook* 112 (September 1961): 91.

[33]Wainwright, "Martyr of the Sit-ins," p. 132.

[34]Ibid., p. 124.

[35]Ibid.

[36]Martin Luther King Jr., *Stride Toward Freedom* (New York: Harper & Row/Perennial Library, 1964), p. 85. It should be noted that this is the paperback edition; the original hard-cover edition was published in 1958. Pagination of the two editions differs. All references in the present discussion are to the 1964 soft-cover edition.

[37]Ibid., p. 85.

[38]Carl T. Rowan, "Heart of a Passionate Dilemma," *The Saturday Review* 42 (August 1, 1959): 20-21. Rowan here reviews two biographical works, Francis L. Broderick's *W. E. B. DuBois: Negro Leader in Time of Crisis* and Reddick's *Crusader Without Violence.*

[39]Bennett, *What Manner of Man,* pp. 19-20.

[40]Confidential interview, December 7, 1965. (The interviewee preferred that his or her name not be mentioned.)

[41]Reddick, *Crusader Without Violence,* p. 54.

[42]Ibid., p. 61.

[43]Bennett, *What Manner of Man,* p. 25.

[44]Personal interview with Lloyd O. Lewis, December 7, 1965.

[45]Telephone interview with Benjamin E. Mays, February 15, 1966.

[46]Personal interview with Lewis, December 7, 1965.

[47]Telephone interview with Mays, February 15, 1966.

[48]Bennett, *What Manner of Man,* p. 28.

[49]Ibid.

[50]Ibid.

[51]Martin Luther King Jr., "The Purpose of Education," *Maroon Tiger,* 1948.

[52]Carter G. Woodson, *The History of the Negro Church* (Washington, D.C.: Associated, 1921), pp. 167-84.

[53]"Man of the Year," *Time,* January 3, 1964, p. 13.

[54]Reddick, *Crusader Without Violence,* p. 83.

[55]Confidential interview, March 1966.

[56]Personal interview with Martin Luther King Jr., August 31, 1966. In C. J. LaRue, *The Heart of Black Preaching* (Louisville, Ky.: Westminster John Knox, 2000), p. 126, King is placed among examples of African American preachers who balance sense and soul.

[57]Telephone interview with Benjamin E. Mays, February 15, 1966.

[58]Martin Luther King Jr., letter to Miss Joan Thatcher, August 7, 1959, in "Letters Received," Martin Luther King Jr. Collection, Boston University Library. This letter by King is with correspondence received from Joan Thatcher. Thatcher, publicity director of the Board of Education and Publication of the American Baptist Convention, Division of Christian Higher Education, had written to King

July 30, 1959. She said the American Baptist Convention was writing to "twenty persons who we feel are outstanding representatives of various Church vocations. Most of their names will be well known to Baptist young people. We are asking each of you to write a brief statement of 100 to 500 words describing your own call from God to the church vocations. These will then be quoted in a leaflet and in magazine articles we are preparing." The complete text of the Thatcher letter is found in the King Collection at Boston University Library.

[59]Bennett, *What Manner of Man,* pp. 27-28.

[60]"Crisis in the Making: U.S. Negroes Tussle with Issue . . . of Resisting a Draft Law Because of Racial Segregation," *Newsweek,* June 7, 1948, pp. 28-29.

[61]Ibid.

[62]Harry S. Truman, "Civil Rights Message to Congress," *Vital Speeches of the Day* 14 (February 15, 1948): 258-61.

[63]Bennett, *What Manner of Man,* p. 34.

[64]Personal interview with Morton S. Enslin, March 7, 1966.

[65]Telephone interview with Robert E. Keighton, March 6, 1966. At the time, Robert E. Keighton, professor emeritus of homiletics at Crozer Theological Seminary, was retired and doing an interim assignment at the Lansdowne Baptist Church in Lansdowne, Pennsylvania.

[66]King, *Strength to Love,* p. 137.

[67]Stephen B. Oates, *Let the Trumpet Sound: The Life of Martin Luther King Jr.* (New York: New American Library, 1982), pp. 33-34.

[68]Sankey L. Blanton, letter to Martin Luther King Jr., November 1, 1951, in "Letters Received," Martin Luther King Jr. Collection, Boston University Library.

[69]Edinburgh University official, letter to Martin Luther King Jr., November 1, 1951, in "Letters Received," Martin Luther King Jr. Collection, Boston University Library.

[69]Personal interview with L. Harold DeWolf, March 6, 1966.

[71]Personal interview with Walter G. Muelder, March 4, 1966.

[72]Personal interview with S. Paul Schilling, March 3, 1966.

[73]Ibid.

[74]Personal interview with L. Harold DeWolf, March 6, 1966.

[75]Ibid.

[76]Major J. Jones and Melvin Watson, letters to Martin Luther King Jr., in "Letters Received," Martin Luther King Jr. Collection, Boston University Library.

[77]Reddick, *What Manner of Man,* p. 88.

[78]Martin Luther King Jr., letter to L. Harold DeWolf, in "Letters Sent," Martin Luther King Jr. Collection, Boston University Library.

[79]These cities were culled from letters King sent expressing appreciation to pastors for their having granted him the opportunity to preach in their churches (Martin Luther King Jr. Collection, Boston University Library).

[80]L. Harold DeWolf, letter to Martin Luther King Jr., June 4, 1955, in "Letters Received," Martin Luther King Jr. Collection, Boston University Library.

[81]*The Case of Brown* v. *The Board of Education,* 347 U.S. 438, 1954.

[82]*The Case of Plessy* v. *Ferguson,* 163 U.S. 537, 1896.

[83]Ibid.

[84]*Case of Brown* v. *Board of Education.*

[85]Martin Luther King Jr., letter to leaders of Dexter Avenue Baptist Church, in "Letters Sent," Martin Luther King Jr. Collection, Boston University Library.

[86]King, *Stride Toward Freedom* , p. 2.

[87]Bennett, *What Manner of Man,* p. 49.

[88]With Dexter, as with many independently operated parishes, it was a policy first to invite several ministers to preach at different times and then to extend an official call based partially on the minister's ability to deliver effectively and satisfactorily the Word of God.

[89]Speech text in "Dexter Avenue Church," Martin Luther King Jr. Collection, Boston University Library.

[90]Ibid.

[91]Martin Luther King Sr., letter to Martin Luther King Jr., December 2, 1954, in "Letters Received," Martin Luther King Jr. Collection, Boston University Library.

[92]King, *Stride Toward Freedom,* pp. 10-11.

[93]Louis Lomax, *The Negro Revolt* (New York: Harper & Brothers, 1962), p. 111.

[94]Martin Luther King Jr., quoted in "Man of the Year: Never Again Where He Was," *Time,* January 3, 1964, p. 14.

[95]Carey McWilliams, "Miracle in Alabama," *The Nation,* March 3, 1956, p. 169.

[96]King, *Stride Toward Freedom,* p. 45.

[97]Ibid., p. 48.

[98]Bennett, *What Manner of Man,* p. 71.

[99]"Man of the Year," p. 27.

[100]Tom Johnson, "Rev. King Is Boycott Boss," *Montgomery Advertiser,* January 19, 1956.

[101]Bennett, *What Manner of Man,* p. 72.

[102]King, *Stride Toward Freedom,* p. 114.

[103]Ibid., pp. 114-15.

[104]Bennett, *What Manner of Man,* p. 79.

[105]Reese Cleghorn, "Martin Luther King Jr., Apostle of Crisis," *The Saturday Evening Post* 236 (June 15, 1963): 15.

[106]Ibid.

[107]Ibid.

[108]Lerone Bennett Jr., "From Booker T. Washington to Martin Luther King," *Ebony* 117, no. 1 (November 1962): 152-62.

[109]Bennett, *What Manner of Man,* p. 106.

[110]Cleghorn, "Martin Luther King Jr.," p. 15.

[111]Bennett, *What Manner of Man,* p. 187.

[112]Cleghorn, "Martin Luther King Jr.," p. 19.

[113]Bennett, *What Manner of Man,* p. 197.

[114]"The Big Man Is Martin Luther King Jr.," *Newsweek,* July 29, 1963, pp. 30-32.

[115]"Awards: The Youngest Ever," *Time,* October 23, 1964, p. 27.

[116]"Man of the Year," p. 13.

Chapter 2: King as Black Preacher & the Liberating Word

[1]E. Franklin Frazier, *The Negro Church in America* (New York: Schocken, 1963), p. 29. See also Albert Raboteau, *Slave Religion* (New York: Oxford University Press, 1978), p, 8.

[2]Frazier, *Negro Church,* pp. 27-28.

[3]James H. Harris, *Preaching Liberation* (Minneapolis: Fortress, 1995), pp. 12, 37, 40-41, 45, 46-48, 61.

[4]Mervyn A .Warren, *Black Preaching: Truth and Soul* (Washington, D.C.: University Press of America, 1977), pp. 3-4.

[5]Marty Bell, "Fire in My Bones: The Prophetic Preaching of Martin Luther King Jr.," *Baptist History and Heritage* 34, no. 1 (Winter 1999): 7-10.

[6]Flip Schulke and Penelope McPhee, *King Remembered* (New York: Pocket, 1986), p. 293.

[7]Mervyn A. Warren, "A Rhetorical Study of the Preaching of Doctor Martin Luther King, Jr., Pastor and Pulpit Orator," Ph.D. diss., Michigan State University, 1966, pp. 4, 11, 35, 116, 119, 124, 167, 174, 189, 210.

[8]Ellen G. White, *The Great Controversy* (Mountain View, Calif.: Pacific, 1950), p. 609.

[9]Personal interview with Martin Luther King Jr., August 31, 1966, Chicago. See also Warren, "Rhetorical Study," p. 167.

[10]Personal interview with Walter G. Muelder, March 4, 1966, Boston. See also Warren, "Rhetorical

Study," p. 166.

[11]Telephone interview with Benjamin E. Mays, February 15, 1966. It may be more than coincidental that the prophet Amos was mentioned as an example of the kind of ministry King emulated, for King himself was known to quote frequently and often predictably this prophet's words from Amos 5:24: "Let justice run down like waters, and righteousness as a mighty stream."

[12]Personal interview with S. Paul Schilling, March 3, 1966, Boston.

[13]Personal interview with L. Harold DeWolf, March 6, 1966, Washington, D.C.

[14]Martin Luther King Jr., "A Comparison of the Conceptions of God in the Thinking of Paul Tillich and Henry Nelson Wieman," Ph.D. diss., Boston University, 1955, p. 16.

[15]Richard Lischer, *The Preacher King: Martin Luther King Jr. and the Word That Moved America* (New York: Oxford University Press, 1995), p. 177.

[16]Anthony Campbell of Boston University, quoted in Dick Russell, *Black Genius and the American Experience* (New York: Carroll & Graf, 1998), p. 439.

[17]Yngve Brilioth, *A Brief History of Preaching* (Philadelphia: Fortress, 1945), p. 3.

[18]Keith Miller, "Alabama as Egypt: Martin Luther King Jr. and the Religion of Slaves," in *Martin Luther King Jr. and the Sermonic Power of Public Discourse,* ed. Carolyn Calloway-Thomas and John Louis Lucaites (Tuscaloosa: University of Alabama Press, 1993), p. 20.

[19]Henry H. Mitchell, *Black Preaching* (Philadelphia: J. B. Lippincott, 1970), p. 25.

[20]Ibid., p. 25.

[21]Carl E. Braaten, *New Directions in Theology Today,* vol. 2, *History and Hermeneutics* (Philadelphia: Westminster Press, 1966), pp. 139-40.

[22]C. K. Barrett, *Biblical Problems and Biblical Preaching* (Philadelphia: Fortress, 1964), pp. 28-29.

[23]W. E. Sangster, *The Craft of Sermon Construction* (Philadelphia: Westminster Press, 1951), p. 189.

[24]"Man of the Year," *Time,* January 3, 1964, p. 14.

[25]Martin Luther King Jr., "An Autobiography of Religious Development," typescript (paper written for a class at Crozer Theological Seminary), Personal Papers and Manuscripts, Martin Luther King Jr. Collection, Boston University Library.

Chapter 3: The Audience

[1]Carolyn Calloway-Thomas and John Louis Lucaites, eds., *Martin Luther King Jr. and the Sermonic Power of Public Discourse* (Tuscaloosa: University of Alabama Press, 1993). Although there are hints in this work that public address takes place in a number of contrasting settings, the overwhelming assumption seems to be that all King's messages (spoken and written and in all situations) were "sermons" or "sermonic"—a notion opposed by homileticians and those who specialize in matters of sermon construction and delivery. Practitioners of homiletics affirm the centrality of Bible exegesis, interpretation and application to a worshiping congregation if the message is to be a sermon. (Consult any volume on biblical preaching for a discussion of this concept.) Examples of a typical "speech" and contrasting typical "sermons" are found in the appendices of the present book.

[2]Aristotle, *The Rhetoric of Aristotle,* trans. Lane Cooper (New York: Appleton-Crofts, 1932), p. xxxviii.

[3]Carter G. Woodson, *Negro Orators and Their Orations* (Washington, D.C.: Associated Publishers, 1925), p. 10.

[4]Arthur W. Smith, *Rhetoric of Black Revolution* (Boston: Allyn & Bacon, 1969), pp. 69-70.

[5]E. Franklin Frazier, *The Negro Church in America* (New York: Schocken, 1963), p. 17.

[6]Carl E. Braaten, *New Directions in Theology Today,* vol. 2, *History and Hermeneutics* (Philadelphia: Westminster Press, 1966), pp. 13-14.

[7]Ruby F. Johnson, *The Development of Negro Religion* (New York: Philosophical Library, 1954), p. xvii.

[8]Jon Eisenson, Jeffrey Auer and John V. Irwin, *The Psychology of Communication* (New York: Appleton-Century-Crofts, 1963), p. 69.

[9]Ibid., p. 294. See also Lester Thonssen and A. Craig Baird, *Speech Criticism* (New York: Ronald,

1948), pp. 357-82.

[10]David Buttrick, *Homiletic: Moves and Structures* (Philadelphia: Fortress, 1987), pp. 77-78.

[11]John Mason Stapleton, *Preaching in Demonstration of the Spirit and Power* (Philadelphia: Fortress, 1988), pp. 16, 12.

[12]Studies by the Fund for Theological Education indicate that about 93 percent of black church pastors lack college or seminary education.

[13]Arthur Edward Phillips, *Effective Speaking* (Chicago: Newton, 1908), pp. 48-62. See also William Evans, *How to Prepare Sermons and Gospel Addresses* (Chicago: Moody Press, 1913), pp. 103-4.

[14]"Changing Theologies for a Changing World," *Time*, December 26, 1969, p. 45.

[15]F. H. Allport, *Social Psychology* (Boston: Houghton Mifflin, 1924), pp. 261-62.

[16]Martin Luther King Jr., *Strength to Love* (New York: Harper & Row, 1963), pp. 47-48.

[17]Elton Trueblood, *The Humor of Christ* (New York: Harper & Row, 1964), pp. 21, 33, 36.

[18]Personal interview with Martin Luther King, Jr., August 31, 1966.

[19]Ernest Dunbar, "A Visit with Martin Luther King," *Look*, February 12, 1963, pp. 92, 96.

[20]Robert T. Oliver, *The Psychology of Persuasive Speech* (New York: Longmans, Green, 1957).

[21]Phillips, *Effective Speaking*, pp. 48-62. It has been noted that in William Evans's homiletics text *How to Prepare Sermons and Gospel Addresses* Phillips's "Impelling Motives" remained intact.

[22]Oliver, *Psychology of Persuasive Speech*, p. 251.

[23]Irving J. Lee, "A Study of Emotional Appeal in Rhetorical Theory with Special Reference to Invention, Arrangement and Style," Ph.D. diss., Northwestern University, 1939.

[24]John A. Broadus, *On the Preparation and Delivery of Sermons* (New York: Harper & Row, 1944), p. 215.

[25]Ibid., pp. 215-16.

[24]Robert Penn Warren, *Who Speaks for the Negro?* (New York: Random House, 1965), pp. 372-73. As can be readily recognized, this quotation, particularly the third paragraph, contains very strong evidence of the tremendous ethos that accompanied King as a spiritual leader and spokesperson.

[27]H. L. Hollingworth, *The Psychology of the Audience* (New York: American Book, 1935), pp. 19-32.

[28]Oliver, *Psychology of Persuasive Speech*, pp. 85-88.

[29]Hollingworth, *Psychology of the Audience*, pp. 19-32.

[30]In a telephone interview with Martin Luther King Sr. on August 11, 1966, I was informed that absolutely no advertising was done for the first Sunday of the month (and sometimes third Sunday) when the younger King occupied the pulpit at Ebenezer Baptist Church. King Sr. added that these dates were generally known to "belong" to King Jr. and therefore attracted larger crowds than the Sundays when he was not preaching.

[31]Personal interview with Lloyd O. Lewis, December 9, 1965.

[32]Alan H. Monroe, *Principles and Types of Speech*, 5th ed. (Chicago: Scott, Foresman, 1962), pp. 280-302. More modern speech textbooks continue endorsing and teaching Monroe's "motivated sequence"; an example is Michael Osborn and Suzanne Osborn, *Public Speaking* (Boston: Houghton Mifflin, 1988), p. 361.

Chapter 4: The Content of the King Sermons, Part One

[1]Marcus Tullius Cicero, *De Oratore*, trans. J. W. Watson, Bohn Classical Library (New York: Harper & Brothers, 1890), p. 178.

[2]Kenneth G. Hance, David C. Ralph and Milton J. Wiksell, *Principles of Speaking* (Belmont, Calif.: Wadsworth, 1962), p. 62.

[3]T. Harwood Pattison, *The Making of the Sermon* (Chicago: American Baptist Publication Society, 1914), pp. 227-28.

[4]John A. Broadus, *On the Preparation and Delivery of Sermons* (New York: Harper, 1944), p. 76.

[5]Personal interview with Walter G. Muelder, Boston, March 4, 1966.

[6]Daniel C. Thompson, *The Negro Leadership Class* (Englewood Cliffs, N.J.: Prentice-Hall, 1963), p. 34.

[7]*Reader's Digest Almanac* (Pleasantville, N.Y.: Reader's Digest Association, 1966), p. 372. This particular group of Baptists, of whose parent body J. H. Jackson was president, is to be distinguished from the National Baptist Convention of America (C. D. Pettaway was president), which had a membership of over three million.

[8]"Man of the Year: Never Again Where He Was," *Time,* January 3, 1964, p. 14.

[9]Ernest Dunbar, "A Visit with Martin Luther King," *Look,* February 12, 1963, p. 96.

[10]Ibid., p. 94.

[11]L. Harold DeWolf, *Present Trends in Christian Thought* (New York: Association, 1960), p. 18.

[12]L. D. Reddick, *Crusader Without Violence* (New York: Harper & Brothers, 1959), p. 51.

[13]"Man of the Year," p. 14.

[14]Martin Luther King Jr., letter to Harry S. Truman, April 19, 1960, in "Letters Sent," Martin Luther King Jr. Collection, Boston University. The complete text of the letter is in this folder.

[15]Personal interview with L. Harold DeWolf, March 6, 1966.

[16]Other than in this sermon on communism, the first three of these points appear in at least two other sermons: "Paul's Letter to American Christians" and "A Knock at Midnight."

[17]J. Edgar Hoover, quoted in "Next: A National Police Force?" *U.S. News & World Report,* December 7, 1964, p. 44.

[18]Martin Luther King Jr., quoted in "Department of Justice: Off Hoover's Chest," *Newsweek,* November 30, 1964, p. 30.

[19]Editorial, *New York Herald Tribune* (n.d.), quoted in "Department of Justice," p. 30.

[20]"The Hoover-King Meeting," *Newsweek,* December 14, 1964, p. 22. See also David J. Garrow, *The FBI and Martin Luther King, Jr.: From "Solo" to Memphis* (New York: W. W. Norton, 1981), pp. 128-29.

[21]Charles E. Silberman, *Crisis in Black and White* (New York: Random House, 1964), pp. 148-49.

[22]Ibid., pp. 148-49.

[23]Dunbar, "Visit with Martin Luther King," p. 94.

[24]King's concept of violating existing unjust laws and willingly accepting the penalty, a clear outgrowth of his reading of Henry David Thoreau's *Essay on Civil Disobedience,* was not altogether a new approach to America's race problem. Among the religious voices addressing the question of Negro slavery in America immediately after the Civil War, Ellen G. White, leading spokesperson and prophetic voice of the Seventh-day Adventist denomination, also advocated civil disobedience in the following words: "When the laws of men conflict with the word and the law of God, we are to obey the latter, whatever the consequences may be. The law of our land requiring us to deliver a slave to his master, we are *not to obey;* and we must *abide the consequences* of violating the law" (*Testimonies for the Church* [Mountain View, Calif.: Pacific, 1948], 1:201-2).

[25]Martin Luther King Jr., *Stride Toward Freedom* (New York: Harper & Row/Perennial Library, 1964), pp. 83-85. Note on page 83 a discussion of nonviolence as the renowned theologian Reinhold Niebuhr envisioned it and related it to the Negro's struggle in America. SCLC, the civil rights organization headed by King, required the signing of a "commitment to nonviolence" form before one could participate as a demonstrator. A copy of the form is published in Lerone Bennett Jr., *What Manner of Man: A Biography of Martin Luther King Jr.* (Chicago: Johnson, 1964), p. 135.

[26]"King's Use of Pulpit Assailed," *State Journal* (Lansing, Mich.), September 11, 1965.

[27]Michael Eric Dyson, *I May Not Get There with You: The True Martin Luther King Jr.* (New York: Free Press, 2000), pp. 155-74.

Chapter 5: The Content of the King Sermons, Part Two

[1]Personal interview with Martin Luther King Jr., August 31, 1966.

[2]Robert T. Oliver, *The Psychology of Persuasive Speech* (New York: Longmans, Green, 1957), p. 251.

[3]Aristotle, *The Rhetoric of Aristotle,* trans. Lane Cooper (New York: Appleton-Century-Crofts, 1932), p. 8.

[4]Kenneth G. Hance, David C. Ralph and Milton J. Wiksell, *Principles of Speaking* (Belmont, Calif.:

Wadsworth, 1962), p. 62.

[5]Ibid., pp. 52-53, distinguishes among "instances," "illustrations" and narratives/stories by including instances and illustrations under the label of "examples" and defining them as follows: *Instances* are allusions or references to specific cases; they are not completely developed descriptions, nor do they contain the details of the case. *Illustrations* are fully developed instances or expansions of instances through the inclusion of pertinent details. The *narrative* (or *story*) includes real or fictional details that are generally arranged chronologically for the purpose of clarifying or proving a point. The narrative "differs from the example in that its details are arranged in a specific sequence, and its events are unfolded according to a plot or scheme that leads to a climax."

[6]It was during a personal interview with one of King's Boston University professors, L. Harold DeWolf, on March 6, 1966, that the charge was first brought to my attention. DeWolf directed me to a source of the charge, Joseph Washington's *Black Religion* (Boston: Beacon, 1964). On page 10 Washington criticizes King for a type of syncretism "due to the dominance of philosophy over systematic theology."

Parallel but not identical to this charge is another: that the language of King might include extensive borrowing without giving due credit to other sources, thus diminishing from his personal competence and creativity. For a discussion of this observation and an explanatory reply if not exoneration, see respectively Keith D. Miller, *Voice of Deliverance: The Language of Martin Luther King Jr. and Its Sources* (New York: Free Press, 1992), and Richard Lischer, *The Preacher King* (New York: Oxford University Press, 1995), pp. 108-18.

[7]Ellen G. White, *Acts of the Apostles* (Mountain View, Calif.: Pacific, 1911), pp. 235-36.

[8]Aristotle *The Rhetoric*, trans. Lane Cooper (New York, London: D. Appleton, 1932), p. 7.

[9]Norval Pease, "Charles E. Weniger's Theory of Speech and Homiletics as Revealed in His Teaching Procedures, His Writings and His Public Addresses," Ph.D. diss., Michigan State University, 1964, p. 7.

[10]Although I was given access to some unedited manuscripts of sermons by King, they bear the same titles as those he had published three years earlier in *Strength to Love* (New York: Harper & Row, 1963).

Chapter 6: The Themes of King's Sermons

[1]Personal interview with Walter G. Muelder, Boston, March 4, 1966.

[2]Milton Meltzer, ed., *Thoreau: People, Principles and Politics*, American Century Series (New York: Hill and Wang, 1963), pp. 35-36.

[3]Henry David Thoreau, *The Portable Thoreau*, ed. Carl Bode (New York: Viking, 1960), p. 111.

[4]Ibid., pp. 119-20.

[5]Ibid., p. 121.

[6]Ibid., p. 122.

[7]L. D. Reddick, *Crusader Without Violence: A Biography of Martin Luther King* (New York: Harper & Brothers, 1959), pp. 15-18.

[8]Martin Luther King Jr., *Stride Toward Freedom* (New York: Harper & Row/Perennial Library, 1964), p. 73.

[9]August Derleth, *Concord Rebel: A Life of Henry D. Thoreau* (New York: Chilton, 1962), p. 204.

[10]King, *Stride Toward Freedom*, p. 73.

[11]Ibid., p. 73.

[12]Ibid.

[13]Walter Rauschenbusch, *Christianizing the Social Order* (New York: Macmillan, 1912), p. 114.

[14]Ibid., pp. 357-58.

[15]Ibid., pp. 367-68.

[16]King, *Stride Toward Freedom*, p. 73.

[17]Martin Luther King Jr., *Strength to Love* (New York: Harper & Row, 1963), p. 138. Just as Thoreau created a term, "civil disobedience," to describe his protest, so Gandhi minted a Hindu expression,

satyagraha, to represent his protest philosophy. Disliking the term "passive resistance," Gandhi offered a prize for a better name embodying his new kind of mass-yet-individual opposition to unfair government. His cousin Maganlal Gandhi suggested *sadagraha*—meaning "firmness in a good cause." Mohandas Gandhi amended the suggestion to *satyagraha*—truth-force or love-force, being "strong not with the strength of the brute but with the strength of the spark of God." Gandhi said that *satyagraha* is "the vindication of truth not by infliction of suffering on the opponent but on one's self." In breaking civil law, one accepts (in good conscience) penalty for the violation. See Louis Fisher, *The Life of Mahatma Gandhi* (New York: Harper, 1950), p. 77.

[18]King, *Strength to Love,* p. 138.

[19]Louis Fisher, *Gandhi: His Life and Message for the World* (New York: New American Library/Mentor, 1960), p. 129. See also M. K. Gandhi, *Harijan,* July 7, 1940, quoted in *M. K. Gandhi: Non-violent Resistance,* ed. Bharatan Kumarappa (New York: Schocken, 1961), p. 176.

[20]King, *Stride Toward Freedom,* pp. 78-79.

[21]William Hordern, *A Layman's Guide to Protestant Theology* (New York: Macmillan, 1953), p. 147.

[22]Ibid., p. 148.

[23]Reinhold Niebuhr, *Moral Man and Immoral Society: A Study in Ethics and Politics* (New York: Charles Scribner's Sons, 1947), pp. 252, 171-72.

[24]Ibid., p. 252.

[25]Ibid., p. 253.

[26]Reinhold Niebuhr, *The Nature and Destiny of Man* (New York: Charles Scribner's Sons, 1941), pp. 186-87.

[27]King, *Stride Toward Freedom,* p. 80.

[28]Niebuhr, *Moral Man and Immoral Society,* p. 254.

[29]As noted in chapter one, King, before matriculating at Boston University, had been accepted for graduate studies at Edinburgh University in Scotland. When I asked King why he went to Boston instead, he replied that it was mainly because of his interest in philosophical theology and the presence of Dr. Brightman, a foremost teacher in this area, that finally tipped the scale in favor of Boston. Personal interview, August 31, 1966.

[30]Walter G. Mueder and Lawrence Sears, eds., *The Development of American Philosophy* (Boston: Houghton-Mifflin, 1960).

[31]Personal interview with L. Harold DeWolf, March 6, 1966.

[32]Hordern, *Layman's Guide,* pp. 85-86.

[33]King, *Stride Toward Freedom,* p. 82.

[34]Ibid.

[35]Dunbar, "Visit with Martin Luther King," pp. 92.

[36]King, *Stride Toward Freedom,* p. 86.

[37]Van A. Harvey, *A Handbook of Theological Terms* (New York: Macmillan, 1964), p. 14.

[38]King, *Stride Toward Freedom,* p. 86.

[39]Ibid.

[40]Ibid.

[41]Ibid., pp. 86-87.

[42]DeWolf, *Present Trends,* p. 18.

[43]Hordern, *Layman's Guide,* p. 94.

[44]Ibid.

[45]Ibid., p. 86.

[46]Martin Luther King Jr., "A Comparison of the Conceptions of God in the Thinking of Paul Tillich and Henry Nelson Wieman," Ph.D. diss., Boston University, 1955, p. 16.

[47]Personal interview with Martin Luther King Jr., August 31, 1966.

[48]James A. Winans, *Speech-Making* (New York: D. Appleton-Century, 1938), p. 49.

[49]Loudon Wainwright, "Martyr of the Sit-ins," *Life,* November 7, 1960, pp. 133-34.

[50]DeWolf, *Present Trends,* p. 18.

[51]In several sermons by King, Paul Tillich is a salient source for the doctrine of human freedom. In an all-inclusive declaration summarizing his concept of this doctrine, King proclaims: "Man, says Paul Tillich, is man because he is free" ("How Should a Christian View Communism?"). All other references to or quotes from Tillich on human nature in King's sermons pertain to Tillich's dogma of the "courage to be" or the incumbency upon human beings to determine to go on living, asserting and achieving in spite of roadblocks, obstacles and disappointments. (Sermons containing this concept include "Shattered Dreams" and "Antidotes for Fear.")

[52]Personal interview with Martin Luther King Jr., August 31, 1966.

[53]Keith D. Miller, *Voice of Deliverance: The Language of Martin Luther King Jr. and Its Sources* (New York: Free Press, 1992), p. 229.

[54]Richard Lischer, *The Preacher King* (New York: Oxford University Press, 1995), p. 112.

[55]Ralph Waldo Emerson, essay, "Of Quotation and Originality" (1875) quoted in *Bartlett's Familiar Quotations,* ed. John Bartlett (Boston: Little, Brown, 1980), p. 500.

[56]Personal interview with Morton S. Enslin, March 7, 1966.

[57]Personal interview with Martin Luther King Jr., August 31, 1966.

Chapter 7: Language in Kingly Style

[1]Personal interview with Martin Luther King Jr., August 31, 1966.

[2]Marcus Tullius Cicero, *De Oratore,* trans. J. W. Watson, Bohn Classical Library (New York: Harper & Brothers, 1890), p. 178.

[3]Hugh Blair is quoted in Kenneth G. Hance, David C. Ralph and M. J. Wiksell, *Principles of Speaking* (Belmont, Calif.: Wadsworth, 1962), p. 181.

[4]L. D. Reddick, *Crusader Without Violence: A Biography of Martin Luther King Jr.* (New York: Harper & Brothers, 1959), p. 11.

[5]Lester Thonssen and A. Craig Baird, *Speech Criticism* (New York: Ronald, 1948), pp. 416-23.

[6]Rudolf Flesch, *The Art of Plain Talk* (New York: Harper & Brothers, 1946).

[7]Marie Hockmuth, "I. A. Richards and the 'New Rhetoric,'" *Quarterly Journal of Speech* 44, no. 1 (February 1958): pp. 1-16.

[8]Flesch, *Art of Plain Talk,* p. 75.

[9]Hubert M. Blalock, *Social Statistics* (New York: McGraw-Hill, 1960), pp. 109, 393-94. In statistical analysis, "replacement" refers to the process of putting each sample back into the container after its withdrawal, thus permitting the original total number of samples to be in the container for each subsequent sample drawing. The replacement process is a prerequisite for independence and randomization.

[10]George Barrett, "Jim Crow, He's Real Tired," *New York Times Magazine,* March 3, 1957, p. 74.

[11]William N. Brigance, *Speech Composition* (New York: F. S. Crofts, 1937), p. 200.

[12]Martin Luther King Jr., *Strength to Love* (New York: Harper & Row, 1963), pp. ix-x.

[13]Personal interview with Martin Luther King Jr., August 31, 1966.

[14]Jon Eisenson, J. Jeffrey Auer and John V. Irvin, *The Psychology of Communication* (New York: Appleton-Century-Crofts, 1963), p. 301.

[15]Gordon L. Thomas, "Oral Style and Intelligibility," *Speech Monographs 23* (August 1956): 46-54.

Chapter 8: Sermon Design, Preparation & Delivery

[1]For very helpful discussions of formal designing of sermons, see James Earl Massey, *Designing the Sermon: Order and Movement in Preaching* (Nashville: Abingdon, 1980); Don M. Wardlaw, ed., *Preaching Biblically: Creating Sermons in the Shape of Scripture* (Philadelphia: Westminster Press, 1983); and Ralph Turnburn, ed., *Baker Dictionary of Practical Theology* (Grand Rapids, Mich.: Baker, 1967).

[2]Marcus Tullius Cicero, *De Oratore,* trans. J. W. Watson, Bohn Classical Library (New York: Harper & Brothers, 1890), p. 178.

[3]Martin Luther King Jr., "Civil Rights, the Central Issue of America's Growth," typescript in "Pro-

posed Speeches," Martin Luther King Jr. Collection, Boston University Library.

[4]Lester Thonssen and A. Craig Baird, *Speech Criticism* (New York: Ronald, 1948), p. 398.

[5]Personal interview with Martin Luther King Jr., August 31, 1966.

[6]Martin Luther King, Jr., *Stride Toward Freedom* (New York: Harper & Row/Perennial Library, 1964), pp. 11-12.

[7]Letter to Martin Luther King Jr., August 20, 1955, in "Letters Received," Martin Luther King Jr. Collection, Boston University Library.

[8]Martin Luther King Jr., letter to student in "Letters Sent," Martin Luther King Jr. Collection, Boston University Library.

[9]Personal interview with Martin Luther King Jr., August 31, 1966.

[10]Ibid.

[11]Ernest Dunbar, "A Visit with Martin Luther King," *Look,* February 12, 1963, pp. 92-94, 96.

[12]King, *Stride Toward Freedom,* p, 249.

[13]Ibid.

[14]Ibid.

[15]Ibid., pp. 3, 45, 49. See also Lerone Bennett Jr., *What Manner of Man: A Biography of Martin Luther King Jr.* (Chicago: Johnson, 1964).

[16]Martin Luther King Jr. Collection, Boston University Library. See also James H. Cone, *Martin and Malcolm* (Maryknoll, N.Y.: Orbis, 1997), pp. 67-69, 216; Stephen B. Oates, *Let the Trumpet Sound* (New York: Harper & Row, 1982), pp. 118-19; and John J. Ansboro, *Martin Luther King, Jr.: The Making of a Mind* (Maryknoll, N.Y.: Orbis, 1984), pp. 47, 134.

[17]Personal interview with Martin Luther King Jr., August 31, 1966.

[18]Martin Luther King Jr., sermons preached March 3, 1966, Central United Methodist Church, Detroit, during the Lenten season. Two worship services (10:00 a.m. and 12:00 noon) were held to accommodate the large crowds desirous of hearing King.

[19]Personal interview with Walter G. Muelder, March 4, 1966.

[20]Ibid.

[21]Virgil A. Anderson, *Training the Speaking Voice* (New York: Oxford University Press, 1957), p. 4. See also Robert T. Oliver and Rupert L. Cortright, *Effective Speech* (New York: Holt, Rinehart, 1961), p. 357.

[22]King considered himself to have been specially endowed with the gift of good health, according to his paper "An Autobiography of Religious Development" (for a class at Crozer Seminary), Martin Luther King Jr. Collection, Boston University Library.

[23]Al Kuettner, "Controversial Dr. King Target of Bitter Criticism," *The State Journal* (Lansing, Michigan), June 16, 1965, C-5; Loudon Wainwright, "Martyr of the Sit-ins," *Life* 159 (November 7, 1960): 124.

Chapter 9: Conclusion

[1]Personal interview with Walter G. Muelder, March 4, 1966.

[2]Ibid.

[3]Personal interview with S. Paul Schilling, March 3, 1966.

[4]Personal interview with L. Harold DeWolf, March 6, 1966.

[5]Ibid.

[6]Ibid.

[7]T. George Harris, "The Battle of the Bible," *Look,* July 27, 1965, p. 17.

Index

CREATIVE
CLOTHING CONSTRUCTION

CREATIVE
CLOTHING CONSTRUCTION

ALLYNE BANE

**associate professor of home economics
Ohio University**

SECOND EDITION

McGRAW-HILL BOOK COMPANY   New York   St. Louis   San Francisco   Toronto   London   Sydney

PREFACE

The prevailing thought today is that it is no longer necessary to sew because attractive clothing can be purchased on the ready-to-wear market for what our grandmothers would have considered a song. And with this thought comes the hypothetical question: Why should you make it when you can buy it for $7.98? And indeed why should you when, if you want to, you *can* buy it for $3.98? The American woman of today does not need to sew for reasons of economy; she can, no matter what her clothing budget, find attractive and serviceable merchandise on the market within her price range. However, even in this day, when efficient mass-production methods have created a shopper's paradise, there is a modest economic advantage in home sewing, providing the time required can be pared to a bare minimum. Many persons—and, I am sorry to say, many home economists —have clung to the emphasis on economy in home sewing and have, in the name of progress, balanced the budget by developing quick, shortcut methods to ensure the old economic advantage. And certainly if one is sewing in the $7.98 bracket, these timesaving methods are justifiable. Construction of pajamas, sport blouses, simple cotton dresses, and

children's play clothes is practical sewing and should be done in a minimum
length of time.

But this book is slanted in quite a
different direction. It is written with the
basic assumption that home sewing is a
rewarding and exciting experience and
that if it turns out to be practical, that
is just a happy little bonus. This book is
written for the girl or woman who sews
because she cannot keep from doing it,
for the person who sews with the need
and urgency with which the artist paints.
In other words, it is written for the
woman who chooses this particular "palette and brush" to express herself. We
do not ask the artist why he paints if he
does not plan to sell his product; we do
not put a price tag on artistic pursuits. I
propose that we in the field of home sewing make progress not by making a
declining economic necessity more practical but by developing the creative possibilities that have been hidden all too
long by an emphasis on economy.

The fact that pattern and fabric sales
have not diminished in these years when
home sewing has lost its economic
appeal and the fact that sales of expensive fabrics and patterns designed by
European *haute couture* designers have
increased are proof that many women
who sew today are quite different from
their counterparts of the early part of the
century. This book is written for such a
woman—the woman who loves good
fabric and exclusive design, the woman
who does not care how long it takes
because she loves every minute of it, the
woman who uses home sewing as a
means of creative expression. This
woman will want to make her suits and

coats and cocktail dresses (she will
probably buy the more practical items in
her wardrobe because they are not as
much fun to make) and will want to
achieve a result comparable to very expensive garments on the ready-to-wear
market. She will want to set her goals on
the couturier standard she could not
possibly afford to buy. Eventually as her
talents are developed, she will find that
sewing has become practical again; when
she is talented enough to make $10
worth of fabric look like $50, and this is
entirely possible, then home sewing will
pay higher dividends than it ever did.

As technology gains greater respect
in America every day, respect for the
so-called skills has fallen to an alarming
level. I am concerned about this undercurrent of disrespect for skills for many
reasons. Perhaps I can best condense my
thoughts by saying that I am convinced
that worthwhile leisure-time activity,
time-consuming leisure-time activity, is
essential to effectiveness on the job now
and that leisure-time happiness is more
important in the world of the ever-shorter
workweek and the ever-longer retirement
years than it has ever been. Leisure-time
pursuits must, if they are to be worthwhile and time-consuming, demand an
ample measure of creative skills, and a
respect for skills must be developed in
our productive years if it is to serve the
leisure needs of our retirement period.
Bearing these thoughts in mind, I have
written this book with respect for, and
pride in, the skill of home sewing and
with conviction that skill is not "busy-
work"—true skill is the result of thought
and understanding.

I regret that much of the current
advertising suggests that the advertisers
do not respect the intelligence of their
audience. You have probably all read or
heard that if you will just buy a sewing
machine, the rest is automatic. However,

those of you with the most limited experience already know that mastery of the sewing machine is the very easiest thing about home sewing. Another advertisement you may have read claims that an inexperienced woman made a lined coat in two hours; if you have had any experience at all, you discounted that story. Buying a sewing machine and a pattern does not automatically make you a couturier seamstress. Neither does manual dexterity—the ability to work well with your hands. Naturally this helps—but there is no substitute for knowledge, experience, and careful concentration while working. One current advertisement says something like this: "You are a clever girl, so how can you miss?" This book is written with the knowledge that you *can* miss. Home sewing is not easy; it takes concentrated thought, and we should be glad it does.

The successful costume, whether it is made at home or purchased on the ready-to-wear market, is a result of careful study in broad areas of learning. Artistic principles must be applied (by the designer or by the woman who sews) in the matters of choice of color, combination of colors, use of texture and texture contrasts, pleasing lines and appropriate lines for the individual figure, and effective proportion and good balance. The influences of fashion play a leading role in the ultimate success of a costume. The fabric (its fiber content, weave, finish, etc.) determines the character, use, and care of the garment. And these are just a few of the areas of study that come into play as a costume is created. I suggest that you visit the local library or begin now to build a modest library of books that will provide the foundation of knowledge needed for success in costume planning. Two books, one on clothing selection and wardrobe planning and another on fundamentals of textiles, are

indispensable. A book on the ways of the fashion world would be most helpful although less necessary than the other two because your fashion knowledge can be strengthened by studying current fashion magazines. In fact, the women's magazines are doing such a commendable job in the whole realm of consumer education that you can easily build an extensive and serviceable file, covering all the areas of knowledge I have mentioned, merely by clipping magazine articles over a period of time. It would be quite impossible to cover all this information in one book, so the scope of this book is limited to clothing construction; clothing selection, fashion, and textiles will be discussed only as they influence clothing construction.

I have an educated respect for the commercial pattern and the instruction sheet included with the pattern. So this book is in no way intended as a replacement for the instruction sheet but rather as a supplement to it. It is to be followed while you work, as is the instruction sheet. The two, the book and the instruction sheet, should be followed in all the steps of construction; for example, if the instruction sheet directs you to make bound buttonholes or put on a bias facing, refer to the book for the detailed directions that space limitations of the instruction sheet cannot allow.

The scope of the book is unique in that fundamentals are discussed in unusual detail. I have chosen to give very full directions for the construction details that appear most frequently and to elaborate on principles which can be applied in various circumstances. I have emphasized the "why's," for only if you understand the underlying why's will you be able to solve problems which are always new and always different with each pattern and each fabric. Space for these important elaborations was gained by omitting the construction details that are not used often. To illustrate, I have not included directions for making pockets; pocket details are unique to the particular design, and it is far wiser to follow the directions on the accompanying instruction sheet. This book is written in a less conversational style than the original *Creative Sewing* in hopes that the reader will not be too comfortable as she reads it but will instead read it as a technical book must be read.

I have been shocked (and embarrassed) by the changes that have taken place during the ten years since I wrote *Creative Sewing;* this edition is almost entirely rewritten. There have been drastic changes in patterns and sizing during these years. Almost everyone is lining almost everything now, and no mention of linings was made in the original book. This book includes a discussion of the traditional method of lining dresses, skirts, jackets, and coats. A very elegant method of lining dresses and skirts, which I have developed during the past ten years, is included for the most experienced reader. The complete interfacing is a new technique and an exciting one. The chapters on pattern alteration and fitting are entirely new. The many changes in new sewing machines, findings, and fabrics made it necessary to rewrite large sections of the book. Developments in fabrics make changes in construction processes urgently needed.

The challenge of constant change is the one dimension of home sewing that I find most rewarding as a classroom teacher and as a woman who sews her entire wardrobe. The solving of new problems is exciting and satisfying. But as an author who has learned how quickly the printed word, the frightening printed word, becomes obsolete, I am less enthusiastic about change! As I write I realize that some fabric or technique is in development and will be ready for the market before this book goes to press; I realize that some new fabric I discuss may prove unsatisfactory and be taken off the market. I must realize that some wonderful new "something" will soon change everything. But so it is. I can only emphasize that it is important to think each new problem through. If you will learn to understand the why's, you will be able to discriminate between what is right under particular circumstances and what is suddenly wrong because of new developments. Each new problem requires thought and research for the best solution. An excellent way to keep pace with current developments is to study articles in the magazine pattern books published by several pattern companies and available on newsstands and by subscription.

I am greatly indebted to Miss Jean Schubel, Clothing Extension Specialist with Michigan State University, for her valuable suggestions and constructive criticism on portions of the manuscript. I should also like to thank Mrs. Joe Collins who read my scribbles, cast a magic spell over the typewriter, and acted as my able and willing assistant throughout the preparation of the manuscript. I wish I could mention the names of all the persons—teachers, professional friends, students—who have given me a new perspective that has become a part of my teaching and a part of this book.

It is quite impossible, for there are so many of you. I have thanked you individually, and you are, as many of you know, given credit in my classroom for your contributions. I must say an especially affectionate "thank you" to my students, past and present, at Ohio University for the ideas and inspiration and happy times they have given me.

ALLYNE BANE

CONTENTS

CHAPTER 4

CHAPTER 5

CHAPTER 6

CHAPTER 7

CHAPTER 8

CHAPTER 9

CHAPTER 10

CHAPTER 11

CHAPTER 12

1

CLOTHING CONSTRUCTION AS CREATIVE EXPRESSION

The woman who makes her own clothes runs an entire factory single-handedly: she is the business manager, the designer, the fashion authority, the layout technician, the machine operator, and the presser all rolled into one. She must see that her "profits" exceed her expenditures; she must be an artist and must be wise enough in the ways of fashion to choose appealing and lasting designs, but she must be a scientist or a mathematician during the construction processes. Home sewing is, like clothing manufacturing, a combination of art and science, and for this reason it is at once demanding and rewarding. But the science of construction, important as it is, must be directed toward an ultimate artistic result. The function of the designer in the manufacturing company illustrates the importance of creative expression. Although the best designers are those who are both artists and technicians, there are many successful designers who have only artistic talents. When that is the case, a technical staff solves the scientific problems, but even so, every solution must be acceptable to the designer. Her function is not diminished; she oversees every operation in "queen-bee" fashion, for in the end the scientific decisions must result in an artistic costume. And so it must be in the one-woman "factory."

PLANNING
CREATIVE
CLOTHES

The successful designer is a student of fashion—of fashion as it is influenced by world events, cultural movements, and human nature. She spends hours in thought before she takes up her drawing pencil, and then she makes many sketches before she selects the right one. She thinks of the role this costume must play in the lives of her customers; she chooses fabrics that will meet the needs and desires of her customers in a particular season; she tests colors and color combinations with textures and texture combinations; she shops the vast market for just the right button or the perfect little braid trimming; she would not dare jump to decisions. She tests and experiments and studies the various effects achieved. And, if she is not entirely satisfied, she discards every idea and starts all over again. And so it must be in the home factory.

GET ACQUAINTED WITH YOURSELF

This may sound like an unnecessary precaution, but it is not. We might think we know ourselves, our taste in clothing, our likes and dislikes, but if we do not know the reasons why we make certain choices, we *do* need to get better acquainted with ourselves. It is not enough to say, "I've always worn blue." The important question is: Why? Is it because blue does nice things for your eyes or does it make you feel content and confident or are you, by chance, in a rut? If you will look for the answer with a fresh approach, you may well find that green does even nicer things for your eyes and you are much happier in pink and that, perhaps, you were in a rut!

These questions are mere suggestions that will, I hope, bring other questions to your mind: Which costumes in your wardrobe do you consider the most flattering? Do the compliments you receive indicate that others agree with you? Which costumes are the ones you wear most often? Which ones are chosen for the most special occasions? Are there some that seem to ensure social success and happy times? Are there some, the old favorites, you always choose for the working day that promises to be long and demanding? Are there some, perhaps very lovely things, that send you hurrying home for a change? These are but a few of the many questions you should ask yourself. But the most pertinent question is: Why? This question may require more thought than you might imagine, but an accurate answer will result in greater happiness and a more attractive wardrobe. Following are some of the "why's" you should consider.

the "why" may be involved with color You might like cool colors because warm colors make you feel conspicuous; a certain color may cast flattering tones on your skin; or a color, because of its psychological implications, may be a happy choice for you. Because color is the first characteristic of clothing that attracts attention, decisions concerning color must be weighed very carefully.

the "why" may be involved with texture A certain texture may feel pleasant to your touch; the very weight of the fabric may add to your personal comfort (some women prefer a lighter-than-air costume, and others like the sensation of weight); heavier, thicker fabrics may make you feel and look 10 pounds heavier; or perhaps you will need warmth for body comfort.

the "why" will frequently be involved with line The design lines of a costume can accent the most attractive features of the figure while camouflaging the less attractive lines. It is far better to approach the problems of figure from a positive viewpoint; concentrate on your advantages. If you have a problem figure, give careful thought to your problem but do not allow your mind to play tricks on you. Many women become so preoccupied with figure problems that they allow the figure to dominate their every wardrobe choice; be aware of this tendency, for too much emphasis on figure may result in a dull and monotonous wardrobe. Certainly figure faults should be heeded, but regardless of the problem, there should be some fun and excitement in your wardrobe, too. There are many women who are, unfortunately, dominated by imagined or outdated figure problems; get to know yourself well enough to know the difference between real and fancied problems. These two brief stories will serve to illustrate how important it is to keep figure problems in the proper perspective. I know a woman who, at forty-five, has a fashion figure that is the envy of all her friends. But she was many pounds overweight from her teens to her early forties. She remembers those days so well that she still thinks of herself as a very large

woman, and it has taken several years and many hours of conversation to convince her that she can wear gay colors and knit fabrics and sportswear and revealing evening dresses. This woman has an imagined, outdated problem. By contrast, another woman of my acquaintance has a petite figure that earned her father's adoration and made her the darling of the high school set. She learned to play up her advantage at a tender age, but the tragedy is that she still dresses in essentially the same mood at the age of fifty-eight. In her case, her figure is a new problem, and she does not realize it. These two stories, which could be multiplied by the thousands, will, I hope, encourage every reader to ask herself many questions and to search for accurate answers, on and beneath the surface of her thoughts, in the past as well as in the present.

the "why" may be a matter of fit The way our clothes fit is extremely important to their appearance and their comfort. Some women tend to wear clothing that is either too snug in every way or too snug in one area of the body. This tendency is a result of the mistaken idea that clothing which fits very close to the body has a slimming effect (unfortunately it does not), and so the larger woman often makes this mistake. And the too-snug fit in certain areas is a result of the very real problem of squeezing larger-than-average hips (or bust, etc.) into the average-size ready-made dress. The wise woman will study sizing information (Chapters 4 and 7 in this book) and will follow those accepted sizing standards, and the woman who makes her own costumes will alter her pattern to have a proper fit that will do the most for her figure.

However, there is a certain personal feeling in the matter of fit. Some women like wide belts, fitted midriffs, and tight skirts because of the feeling of security the "belted-in" fit gives them, while others will feel hampered and "chained" by the garment which meets the accepted standards of good fit. So one must strive for an acceptable fit and not wear clothing that "shouts" of misfit, while at the same time paying heed to individual preferences influencing personal comfort.

the "why" is always involved with the mood or personality of the costume Our clothes are a reflection of our feelings, our moods, and our individual preferences. Perhaps you prefer those costumes that promise attention (or even promise to be a sensation), or would you be embarrassed by what you would consider an obvious bid for attention? Perhaps costumes with dash and daring keep pace with your tempo, or do you feel that this kind of costume overpowers you? Perhaps you enjoy the gaiety of striking colors and unusual prints, or does that kind of gaiety seem superficial to you? There is no right or wrong answer to these questions of mood, but there is a right answer for the individual woman.

the pleasure derived from favorite costumes may be the result of a preference for a particular fashion trend Certainly the woman who is proud of her legs and the woman who loves to be free in her movements has been happy with the short, easy-fitting fashions of the early 1960s, while the woman with a tiny waist has been impatient, waiting for a chance to play up her best feature. However, if fashion trends have caused you unhappiness and discomfort, perhaps you have been too dependent on fashion. We need not be slaves to fashion so long as we stay within reasonable bounds. We cannot wear our skirts 4 inches shorter or longer than is currently the style, but we can wear them at a slightly different length and still look fashionable. We can break one rule if we do not break them all. We can wear a certain fashion so often and so long that it becomes our "uniform" and trademark, and if that fashion is artistically sound (the little Chanel suit is an excellent example), and if we vary it and polish it once in awhile, we can wear that beloved uniform for years.

The Chanel suit is a reminder of the old-friend versus new-friend preferences. Are your wardrobe favorites several years old, or are they, quite simply, your most recent purchases? Some women have confidence in the old standby ("I know what to expect of it," or "I always have a wonderful time when I wear it"), while others feel happy and confident in costumes of the current season ("It was my good luck to go shopping on the very day the new shipments came in"). There is no right or wrong philosophy concerning the age of "friends" in your wardrobe, but it is important that you realize the effect that the age of the costume has on your wardrobe preferences.

the "why" may be involved with the meaning clothing has for you An essential part of preplanning is this thorough understanding of wardrobe preferences. And it is obvious that we must think of the needs (additions or replacements) of our wardrobe. Additions and replacements are necessary to round out and complete our wardrobes, and these needs are based on very personal demands, personal reasons for wearing clothes. We wear clothing to keep pace with our social group and the activities of that group; we wear clothing to meet the demands of our careers and the careers of our husbands; we wear clothing to impress others because we feel the need to impress or because our position in society demands that we impress; we wear clothing for purely functional reasons (to be warm enough or cool enough, to ensure safety on our jobs); we wear clothing that meets our economic demands (sturdy enough to withstand wear, in colors and fashions with lasting appeal); we wear clothing that will make an immediate and lasting impression (a requirement of the traveling stylist, for example, who must leave her mark and has only an hour to do it); and we wear clothing with a quiet kind of charm required of those costumes that will be worn often (the "little black dress" worn by the saleswoman or by the woman who needs just one party dress). We wear clothing to meet physical and emotional needs: to lift our spirits (there is a great deal to be said in defense of the new hat), to see ourselves in new perspective, to put new life into the same old "grind." We dress to please ourselves, and we dress to please others. And these are but a few of the functions our wardrobes must serve.

the "why" may be involved with a need for creative expression The woman who makes her own clothing has additional wardrobe requirements, particularly if she sews as a form of creative expression and/or pleasure, as so many women do at the present time. The demands of creative expression and the pursuit of leisure-time pleasure are not always economically sound; the creative woman may well need an addition to her wardrobe for the simple reason that she needs to create and to relax with her hobby. *And there is no better reason for investing in*

a new costume! And the cost should not be considered solely a wardrobe expense; some of it is a leisure-time expense and should be considered in the same light as the expenses of gardening, painting, color television, and theater tickets. The creative woman is one part designer, and she may make a new costume because she thought of a new idea and must try it; she is also one part technician, and she may make a new costume because the construction involves new techniques that offer her the challenge she requires.

GET READY BEFORE YOU SHOP
The following are suggestions for the initial planning that should precede a shopping trip:

1 In review: Understand yourself, your wardrobe preferences, and the needs and functions your clothing must fulfill.

2 Be aware of current fashion trends and heed them well, but do not allow yourself to be enslaved by them. Make the current fashions work for you.

3 Be informed about the new fabrics and textile fibers and about all other recent developments in the field of textiles. Know what to expect of the new fabrics under the circumstances in which you will use them. Articles in recent women's magazines and the magazine pattern books published by many of the pattern companies will give an excellent capsule résumé of new developments.

4 Look your best for a shopping trip, paying particular attention to hair and make-up, for you will be testing various effects (colors, texture, etc.) before a mirror.

5 Have a note pad, some onionskin paper, and a box of colored pencils in your shopping bag.

6 Under many circumstances it is wise to carry any number of assorted items with you: samples of fabrics from your favorite costumes (if you are shopping for a coat) or a favorite glove or purse or shoe, if a costume is to be planned around accessories of fashion colors.

7 Study the information in Chapters 2 to 5 before shopping for a new costume. If you do not own the equipment required for efficient home sewing, it should be purchased immediately. Chapter 3, Commercial Patterns, will provide a basis for understanding the differences among the pattern companies and will correct several widespread fallacies concerning pattern sizing, yardage amounts, etc. You must determine your size and figure type by taking body measurements. Chapter 5, which covers the selection of pattern and fabric, includes sections on selection of linings, interfacings, and other supportive fabrics. It is imperative that you be well informed so that you need not rely on a saleswoman, who may or may not be competent and experienced.

8 Avoid last-minute decisions. We must plan the costumes we make at home just as carefully as a designer plans her line. The pitfalls of the last-minute purchase (just before the stores close, the day before an assignment is due, a few days before the costume will be worn) are responsible for many disappointments in home sewing. Planning well ahead of anticipated need will result in wiser choices; time to shop for the little touches will ensure greater success; and, certainly, ample time to construct the garment will result in a happy experience in creativity and in the relaxed frame of mind so necessary for high-quality workmanship.

Ideally, the woman who sews should work one season ahead, just as the designer does. This will add to the fun, for it allows one to dream of summer days while the snow drifts and to enjoy a happy change of pace by working with wool at the very time when the joys of summer fade.

SHOPPING CREATIVELY AND SUCCESSFULLY

The designer of ready-to-wear clothing spends a sizable percentage of her time "shopping the market." She visits fabric houses so that she will be aware of every new development in the textile field; she is in close touch with the manufacturers of findings and is as delighted with a showing of new buttons or braids as she is with the showings from abroad. She wants to see the current hat collections, and she is alerted by a new color, even if it appears in a bathroom rug or a late-model car. She comes to look, she stays to study, and she returns to her office to predict the future success of every new concept. If the prediction is promising, she experiments with the idea, refining it for her own uses, and only then adds it to her own collection. And the designer knows her competition very well. She learns lessons from his successes and his failures; she "borrows" his brilliant ideas; and she tries, if she can, to beat him at the game. And so must it be with the woman who sews.

SURVEY THE READY-TO-WEAR MARKET
The ready-to-wear market is your competition and can be an excellent source of inspiration. The remarkably high quality of the design and construction of most reasonably priced ready-to-wear makes

these clothes formidable competition indeed. It is wise to meet the demanding standards of your *top* competitor, the manufacturer of expensive, elegant ready-to-wear. The quality of the construction, even more than the quality of the fabric, is obvious in expensive costumes. Most of us do not wear truly exclusive ready-to-wear merchandise, and we are often unaware of the little touches, so simple to do, that are responsible for high standards. You should shop the exclusive departments to set your standards high and then "borrow" all the tricks and touches you will discover to add to your own collection.

Take advantage of the talents of the buyer in the department store, as well. She spends most of her budget on rather staple merchandise, while a much smaller percentage is allotted to current, exciting fashions. With this smaller collection of high-fashion costumes (some experimental, some avant-garde), she predicts "things to come"; these are the prestige items which are responsible for the fashion reputation of the store. The buyer, who must always strive for fashion prestige, advertises these newsworthy fashions in departmental and window displays. You should see and study all the displays because they show newsworthy fashion interpreted by a professional buyer and chosen especially for your area of the country and your community.

While you survey the market, take cues from the kind of ready-to-wear clothing you would buy. All too often the woman who buys imaginative merchandise loses courage as she buys a pattern and fabric and selects something she would never have purchased ready-made. This is a result of an understandable lack of courage, resulting from limited experience. There is something very revealing and intimate in the selection of any merchandise which will become a part of

your public image, and even greater intimacy is involved if you make the item as well. As you plan a costume you will make, try to retain the confidence you have as you buy a ready-made costume, and you will be, at the same time, acquiring some of the skills involved in making creative, exciting choices.

Before going to the fabric and pattern departments, it is well to browse through the accessory departments. Ordinarily you will not plan a costume around a hat or a purse, but under some circumstances you might. The findings department and particularly the button display may give you ideas; perhaps a decorative frog or an artificial flower will trigger your imagination. At any rate, a cursory examination of all fashion departments will give you an overall "feeling of the season" and will help provide background for a wise choice of wardrobe additions.

SURVEY FABRICS AND PATTERNS
Some women prefer to select the fabric and then choose a pattern that will be suitable, while others plan the costume around the pattern. There is no one right way unless it is to do both at once, which is, perhaps, the way we all do it whether we realize it or not. The best method is to survey both fabrics and patterns without making a final decision, to come to the final decision with both patterns and fabrics in mind (a good time for a coffee break), and finally to purchase the pattern and then the fabric.

Approach the fabric department with an open mind. It is a mistake to go to a certain display (the wool counter, for example), bypassing the brocades and the cotton suitings and the rayon prints.

See them all, even if you know you will buy wool; inspiration (an interesting color combination, the magic addition of a subtle texture accent) may come from an unlikely source.

The sources of inspiration can be extended if you have the imagination and courage to shop in the drapery and upholstery departments. Some of the satins and brocades lend themselves remarkably well to cocktail and evening wear; the nubby cotton tweeds make excellent summer coats; many of the drapery fabrics, particularly bold geometric designs, have the verve and gaiety that create excitement in sportswear; the subtle colors and interesting textures of some upholstery fabrics make them excellent choices for straight-lined coats and jackets. Often these fabrics offer an economical advantage, for many are woven in wider widths than similar fabrics in the dress goods department without a comparable increase in price.

The survey of patterns should be equally broad. Perhaps you have always bought patterns from a certain company, and perhaps you have been completely satisfied with your choices; even so, the pattern that proves to be your favorite of a lifetime might appear, this very season, in a pattern catalog you have never bothered to examine before.

The following practical suggestions are included for those who are novices or those who have difficulty visualizing the design in fabric and color. In order to study the effect of the fabric with contrasting accents of color or texture, the bolt of fabric can be carried to other displays in the department, and a short length can be extended for testing in combination with various other fabrics. A length of the fabric can be held up to the figure to test and study color or design before a full-length mirror. The sales staff will not object to these testing techniques; rather, they expect a customer to experiment and will, if time permits, help drape fabric on the figure in lines comparable to the lines of the design to be used.

Before making a final decision on the pattern design, it is well to copy on onionskin paper the several designs that interest you. This can be done quite quickly. It is well to record the pattern number, the catalog page number on which it appears, and the yardage amounts required for your particular size in various widths of fabric.

MAKE THE DECISION
And now it is time for a coffee break. This is indeed the time to find a quiet spot for concentrated thought before coming to a final decision.

TEST COLORS AND COLOR COMBINATIONS
If you are inexperienced or if you cannot visualize the effects of color and design, use colored pencils to test colors and color combinations on the pattern designs you have copied. There is no need to work for perfection; quick shading will usually suffice, and the effect of prints or checks, etc., can be simulated very quickly with simple lines on the sketch. My students make several copies of each sketch in this planning period so that they can test several ideas; this procedure is recommended for all inexperienced persons.

BE IMAGINATIVE WITH TEXTURES
If you have studied the ready-to-wear market, you have discovered that a shock-

ing combination of textures can result in a stunning costume. The designers of high-fashion merchandise know the rules of appropriate texture combination, but occasionally they break the rules with exciting results. I am reminded of one of the most newsworthy costumes designed by the late Claire McCardell; it was a cocktail or theater suit made of white duck (the same duck used for sturdy sportswear) lined in satin and accented with a collar and oversized lapels of black velvet. The rule book would frown on duck combined with velvet, but happily Miss McCardell knew how and when to break the rule. Of course you will want traditionally compatible combinations for most costumes you make, but be courageous enough to break the rules once in awhile.

MAKE IT PERSONALLY YOURS

This is the greatest advantage of home sewing, this intimate and distinctive touch that makes the costume a very personal thing. The clothes you make will be personally yours in many little ways. The size and design of the buttons, the particular belt you choose, the lining you use, even so minute a feature as topstitching (the width, the color of thread) —all these very small details will make this a personal costume. And of course the color and textures you choose will result in a costume that is uniquely yours.

There are, of course, more obvious ways of adding personal distinction to a costume. Companion pieces offer fertile opportunities to the imaginative woman. The go-with piece can be a hat, a purse, a stole, a belt to match a blouse, a tote-bag, or any one of a number of other "little" items. The companion accessory, if it is right, is a brilliant addition to the costume; if it is wrong, it brings down the whole costume with it. So the com-

panion piece must keep pace with and even surpass the costume. No one is fooled by the fabric envelope playing the role of a purse, and yet the same envelope, stiffened and padded professionally, would enhance the costume. Likewise, the hat based on a professional buckram frame (available at nominal cost in most large department stores) will add dollars in apparent cost to the total costume.

The companion piece will be a successful addition to the costume only if it is something that is currently fashionable and is being "done" by leading designers and worn by well-known fashionable women. This illustration will clarify the preceding statement. Ordinarily one could say that a little triangle of matching fabric, pretending to be a hat, would not keep pace with a lovely dress. And yet for a few seasons in the early 1960s the little triangular scarf was very fashionable, and one Paris designer, in presenting his 1963 fall collection, topped the entire collection, including the wedding gown, with these little triangles tied in interesting ways. The woman who would make a companion accessory should study the market and copy only the currently fashionable ideas.

THE TIME TO BUY

After you have experimented with ideas and have come to a studied decision, it is time to return to the fabric and pattern departments to make the final purchase. The time spent on careful planning will result in greater confidence as the purchase is made and in greater satisfaction as the costume is worn.

SUMMARY

The woman who sews must continue to use her imagination and artistic talents as she constructs the garment. In every chapter of this book, in every step of construction, there are opportunities for decisions of artistic concern. To illustrate, the following are a few examples of the opportunities for creative expression in just one construction detail, bound buttonholes: they can be made on a diagonal or vertical line, rather than on the usual horizontal line; they can be in contrasting color or contrasting texture; they can be triangular rather than the traditional rectangle; they can be spaced in groups of three or four in preference to the usual even spacing; etc. And this is just one of the construction details that lend themselves to an exercise in creative expression.

And so it follows that the woman who sews must keep her "palette and brush" close at hand and must continue to use creative talents throughout the entire adventure in home sewing.

EQUIPMENT
FOR
CLOTHING CONSTRUCTION

Much of the equipment needed for clothing construction can be found in almost any home, whether it is a mansion or a furnished room, for these items are indispensable to womankind. However, often the pair of scissors that has served ordinary household uses does not cut fabric well, and the straight pins that have served the occasional household purpose are not thin and sharply pointed enough for lovely fabrics. In the main, sewing equipment is not too expensive, but it is expensive enough so that most of us must acquire it over a period of years. Certain items are essential for beginners, and other specialized tools can be purchased as interest and ability in construction increase. See page 17 for a chart of essential items.

SHEARS
AND
SCISSORS

SCISSORS

Scissors are 6 inches or less in total length, whereas shears are more than 6 inches in total length. Steel scissors with well-sharpened blades and well-matched points are an essential piece of equipment. The scissors should be tested before purchase by cutting several types of fabrics and by making little clips in the fabric with the points. A good pair of scissors will cut right up to the tip end of the blade. The first pair of scissors bought for your sewing box should have 5-inch blades; these scissors can be used for cutting fabric and for cutting threads during the sewing process. A smaller pair with 3-inch blades is convenient (but not essential) to use for cutting threads and clipping seams.

SHEARS

These are used for cutting heavy fabrics such as coatings and upholstery fabric. They are worth the price to the experienced person but need not be included in basic sewing supplies.

PINKING SHEARS

These are so convenient that they are all but essential to every home sewer. These are shears used to finish seams on fabrics that do not ravel appreciably (they should not be used to cut out the garment). This is usually an expensive item (about $8), although some inexpensive models have recently appeared on the retail market. These less expensive pinking shears serve the purpose of the novice who will be using medium-weight fabrics, but the woman who does all her sewing will want a pair of sturdier ones. The upkeep on these shears is high because they must be sent back to the factory for sharpening.

TAPE MEASURE

The tape measure is an essential item. It should be very firm and sturdy so that it will not stretch with use. Some persons like the numbering to begin on opposite ends of the two sides, for that is more convenient to use, while others fear the inaccuracy that would result if such a tape measure twisted and so prefer to have the numbering the same on the two sides. The tape measure should be 60 inches long, with ⅛-inch divisions.

YARDSTICK

The yardstick should be finished to a satiny smoothness so that it will not snag delicate fabrics. It is useful for many purposes, from drawing lines on paper to drawing lines on fabric.

L SQUARE

The L square has a perfect right-angle corner, and each arm of the square is numbered in inches. Both arms are shorter than a yard. It is convenient for measuring hems and for measuring straight-of-material lines preparatory to cutting fabric. It is also helpful for trueing up fabric.

SIX-INCH RULER

A short ruler (6 or 12 inches) is essential for measuring small amounts. It should be kept close at hand at all times. Buy a ruler marked with 1⁄16-inch divisions.

GAUGES

The gauge is merely a measuring guide useful for measuring hems, widths of tucks and folds, topstitching lines, and seam allowances. Gauges can be made of cardboard; the cardboard backing that comes with seam binding and bias tape serves the purpose very well. The little plastic calendars used for advertising purposes make excellent gauges because they never wear at the edges. Metal gauges with an adjustable sliding marker are available for such measuring purposes.

HEM MARKERS

A professional skirt marker is more accurate than the yardstick in the hands of an inexperienced person. Two types are offered on the market: the pin marker and the chalk marker. The pin marker is usually favored because it is more accurate. The skirt hangs between the standard and a free arm, and when the free arm is pressed in place, it holds the skirt in a position to be pinned. The chalk marker is convenient because it enables a person to mark her own hemline.

MARKING
EQUIPMENT

TRACING WHEEL AND CARBON PAPER

The tracing wheel has fine needle-pointed edges for very fine lines or saw-toothed edges for more distinct lines. Carbon tracing paper is a waxed paper available in white and a variety of colors.

CHALK

There are several types of chalk available to serve the many purposes of marking. Ordinary blackboard chalk, sharpened to a fine point, gives the most distinct line on most fabrics; clay chalk (which comes in flat squares) can be used on flat-surfaced fabrics; and waxed chalk in flat squares or pencil form) is more effective on wools and nubby fabrics.

CHALKBOARD

The chalkboard is made with a base of poster board which has been painted with blue carpenter's chalk and covered with net. A blue line is made on the

fabric when a tracing wheel is used. The chalkboard makes a good surface for tracing because it keeps the tracing wheel from marring the table.

THREAD

The home sewer should have three or four spools of thread in a variety of colors in her sewing box to be used for basting and tailor's tacks. A special basting thread with a somewhat waxy surface permits the threads to be removed easily. Cotton sewing thread comes in a great range of sizes, from number 8 (very heavy for work on canvas, etc.) to number 100 (very fine). Numbers 40, 60, and 80 serve most household purposes, for these sizes are suitable for lightweight and medium-weight textures. Mercerized cotton thread, available in size A or number 50, serves most of the needs of the home sewer. Mercerized thread is more lustrous than cotton thread that has not been so treated. Silk thread is very expensive but gives a lovely lustrous effect. It is available in size A, which compares in size with the very fine number 80 or 100 cotton thread. Silk thread can be used for topstitched details on a garment, while another thread will be more economical for the seams. A sewing thread of nylon is made in size A, comparable in size to size A silk thread. Nylon thread will withstand a lot of heavy wear and is elastic, so it is a good choice for fabrics which have elasticity. But nylon melts at a low temperature and therefore should not be used on fabrics that must be ironed at high temperatures, such as cotton and linen.

The thread used for stitching a garment must of course blend in with the fabric and be inconspicuous. If the thread is just a shade darker than the fabric, it will blend in well; a good test is to lay a single strand of the thread over the fabric. If a fabric is plaid or printed, the color of the thread should match the dominant color of the plaid or print. If a print, stripe, or check is composed of equal amounts of two colors, the thread should match the darker color.

PINS
AND
PINCUSHIONS

PINS

The right choice of pins is most essential for good workmanship, speed, and convenience in sewing. It is truly amazing how much quicker the sewing processes go and how much less patience they require when pins slip easily into fabric. The number of pins is important too—always have at least 10 times more than you will ever need. Pins should be kept separately in a small box; the efficiency of the worker is impaired when other items such as threaded needles are put in the pin box. Pins come in three types: *bank* (a utility pin not suited to dress fabrics), *dressmaker* (a pin of medium diameter but quite suitable for most sewing needs), and *silk* (a very slender pin with a needle point to be used on delicate fabrics). Each type comes in a variety of sizes. Dressmaker and silk pins can be purchased in most notions departments. Buy them in ¼-pound boxes. Silk pins are the most expensive but a real joy to use. Number 9 *sharp* needles can be used

in place of pins on fabrics such as satin or velvet, for these fabrics are easily marred with pins. Glass-headed pins are gaining in popularity; the colored heads are an advantage.

PINCUSHIONS

Many persons prefer to use pins directly from a box, while others prefer the pincushions. A pincushion should be made of felt or wool and filled with wool, hair, or powdered cork; cotton filling is not satisfactory. A pincushion that can be held to the wrist with an elastic strap is very convenient. A few thicknesses of wool fabric wrapped around the large center arm of the machine make a convenient pincushion for use at the machine.

THIMBLES

The thimble should fit the second finger of the predominant hand snugly but not so tightly as to be uncomfortable. The depressions on the outside should be quite deep and sharply cut for the best service.

NEEDLES

Needles come in packages of *assorted sizes* (of which sizes 5 through 10 are the most useful) or *solid sizes* with one size to a package (of which sizes 7, 8, and 9 are most useful). There are many types of needles, but *sharps* and *crewel,* or embroidery, needles are used for most general sewing; sharps have small round eyes, while crewel needles have longer eyes that are easily threaded. Needles vary in length as well as diameter; longer needles are more convenient for long stitches, and vice versa. In general, better work can be done with a small, fine needle, providing the eye is large enough to accommodate the thread and the material is not too heavy. In general, use a small needle for fine details on fine fabrics and a larger one for heavier fabrics.

PRESSING
EQUIPMENT

IRONS

The utility iron weighing 3 pounds or more is satisfactory for pressing most fabrics. The iron with automatic controls is safer and more convenient to use and is well worth the additional cost. A steam iron is a great help, and although it is expensive, the woman who sews a great deal will want one eventually. Some steam irons require distilled water because tap water clogs and rusts the inside of the iron. The combination steam-and-dry iron is a wise choice for the consumer.

FILTER JAR

This item is an essential for use with the steam iron that requires distilled water. Tap water is poured into a plastic squeeze jar, and the filter is put into place. The filter makes ordinary tap water safe for use in the steam iron.

IRONING BOARD

The ironing board should be a comfortable height for the worker and should be solidly built. It should be well padded with great care (a ridge or wrinkle in the ironing board will mark fabric) with cotton padding or a folded wool blanket. The cover should be fresh and clean at all times. Muslin or duck makes an excellent covering, providing it has been boiled or washed several times to remove the sizing; starch or other sizing adheres to the surface of the iron. Special ironing-board covers made of asbestos, which will not scorch, are available on the market in sizes to fit most ironing boards. Covers which have been treated with a scorch-resistant finish are easier to keep clean than the asbestos ones and are less apt to leave lint on dark colors. There are many types of covers and pads available on the market; the choice is unlimited, and the quality is consistently high.

SLEEVE BOARD

The sleeve board is a small ironing board to be used for pressing small units of a garment; one end is tapered, and the other is rounded like the eased-in cap of a sleeve. This board should be padded and covered as carefully as the ironing board is.

SEAM BOARD

The seam board is a padded board, pointed at one end and mounted edgewise on a wooden base. It is essential for pressing hard-to-reach seams. A modified seam board can be made at home with a tightly rolled magazine covered with muslin.

TAILOR'S HAM

The tailor's ham is shaped somewhat like an egg and measures about 10 by 14 inches. It is indispensable for pressing darts and curved seams (such as the seam over the hip in a slim skirt). Cushions in a variety of sizes are available in some notions departments, but the woman who sews can make her own with little time and effort. Cut two ovals in the desired size from heavy muslin or duck. Seam them together, leaving an opening of about 5 inches. Turn right side out. Stuff the cushion tightly and smoothly with small scraps of wool. Whip the opening edges together.

PRESS MITT

The press mitt is similar to, although smaller than, the tailor's ham and is made to slip over the hand. It too can be made at home, although it is inexpensively priced in most notions departments. The mitt is often too flat to be useful, but it can be easily opened to add additional stuffing for a more rounded contour.

PRESS CLOTHS

The press cloth should be heavy for heavyweight fabric (drilling or duck) and lighter (such as thin muslin) for thinner fabrics. It is essential that there be no starch or other sizing in the press cloth (boil the cloth in soap and water to remove it) because sizing sticks to the iron, burns, and rubs off on fabric. Use a piece of wool as a press cloth when pressing the right side of wool garments. Chemically treated press cloths are available on the market. Transparent press cloths, which allow seams and darts to show through, are available; silk organza is very effective if a lightweight press cloth is desired.

MISCELLANEOUS

SCOTCH TAPE

A small container of Scotch tape is indispensable for many uses in home sewing. It is especially useful in making pattern alterations because the altered pattern can be handled and folded so much more conveniently than a pinned pattern. The new Magic Mending variety is preferred because it will take pencil markings.

TICKER TAPE

A roll of the familiar adding-machine tape will have a surprising number of uses and is most convenient for use in pattern alterations.

SEAM RIPPER

This handy little item, available in a variety of sizes, not only is excellent for ripping seams but also is a great aid in removing basting stitches.

EYELET TOOL KIT

This kit, priced at $1, is well worth the cost. It contains a supply of eyelets and a tool which punches holes and sets the eyelet into place.

SEWING BOXES AND TRAYS

A great array of sewing boxes is available. They are attractive and fitted out in a magnificent fashion. However, the plastic trays are far less expensive and perhaps more convenient. The plastic cases for thread and bobbins are a boon to good organization.

AIDS FOR THREADING NEEDLES

For the person who likes fine needles even if her eyes are weak or her hands unsteady, these aids will be most welcome. The needle threader has a thin wire hook which can be inserted very easily into the eye of the needle. The thread is inserted through the wire loop, which is of ample size, and then the loop is pulled back through the needle. The needle threader can be used at the machine, too. A special needle for hand sewing has an easy-threading feature; there is a double eye through which the thread can be pulled into position. Many persons will like this needle, even though occasionally the thread pulls out while the needle is being used. This is no great disadvantage because it can be rethreaded so easily.

THE MACHINE
AND
ATTACHMENTS

There are many good machines on the market, each with its own desirable features and advantages. It is advisable to buy from a nationally known manufacturer because his sale is backed by his reputation and continued service of the machine. The accessibility of repair service should be taken into consideration.

TABLE AND PORTABLE MODELS

The choice between the table and portable models depends on customer preference. The person who travels and the person who is in temporary living quarters will prefer the portable model because of its light weight, small size, and ease of handling. However, the table model is more sturdy, the working surface is more convenient, and it is made ready for use by merely lifting the top. The person who sews a great deal will prefer the table model.

REGULATION AND DELUXE MODELS

The conventional-model machine does straight stitching and sews forward and backward. I use such a machine, and with three attachments that cost less than $15, I make all the important items in my wardrobe and also do slipcovers and draperies; I feel no need for a more deluxe model. My educated guess is that 90 per cent of machine work is involved with straight stitching. The deluxe model, which zigzags and makes impressive decorative stitches, is much more expensive, and despite the exuberant advertising claims, it does not solve all the problems of home sewing. It does not solve a single problem that is not concerned with decorative stitches. The decorative stitches, exciting as they are, are very limited in scope; they are pretty on little girls' dresses, on kitchen curtains, in certain topstitched details, on informal table linens, and in appliquéd designs. The consumer must decide whether she can afford the extra price, which is considerable, for those limited uses. The zigzag

feature is of great value in finishing seams and for stitching on knits or the new stretch fabrics; buttonholes can be made without an additional attachment. However, there are machine models available, less expensive than the deluxe model, that have a zigzag feature but do not have the decorative stitching features; in my opinion these semideluxe models are more practical for most consumers.

ATTACHMENTS

A box of attachments is included with the machine, but they are in general the less expensive ones. An adjustable zipper foot is an absolute essential. The buttonhole attachment is a wise investment.

CHART OF EQUIPMENT FOR CLOTHING CONSTRUCTION

essential items	helpful items for later purchase
scissors with 5″ blades	
tape measure	scissors with 3″ blades
yardstick	shears
6″ ruler	L square
gauges	pinking shears
tailor's chalk	pin marker
assorted colors of thread	tracing wheel and carbon paper
¼ lb of dressmaker pins	chalkboard
assorted needles	silk pins
thimble	steam iron
lightweight iron	filter jar
ironing board	sleeve board
seam board	tailor's ham
machine	buttonhole attachment
zipper foot	eyelet tool kit
seam ripper	
Scotch tape	

COMMERCIAL PATTERNS

The successful commercial pattern is a complex product, and it creates unique and formidable problems for the manufacturer. Three factors place heavy burdens on the manufacturer: (1) This product is purchased because of confidence in the company and the appeal of a fashion sketch, and it cannot, in any way, be examined or tested by the consumer before she buys. (2) The product sells for a modest price, most frequently for $1 or less, but it becomes the foundation for additional sales which could easily exceed $50. (3) The pattern is merely a means toward an end, the first step in a series of do-it-yourself activities, and it is the only step over which the company can exert any control; yet the ultimate result—the finished product, which is so dependent on the talents of the do-it-yourself-er—is the criterion that determines the success of the original product and the reputation of the company. The vicious circle is complete as that reputation becomes the basis for future sales.

I wish space limitations did not prevent me from elaborating on the remarkable standards upheld by the well-known pattern houses; it was a thrilling professional experience to be associated with two of these companies and to learn for myself that they spare no amount of money or effort to produce a product as nearly perfect as is humanly possible. I can assure the reader that the pattern company cannot afford even small mistakes. One example will, I hope, suffice to illustrate the frightening responsibility placed on the staff. During the three years I worked for two of the large pattern houses, there was only one serious mistake made. The yardage amount for size 18 in view 2 for 39-inch fabric (just one of the approximately 30 yardages stated in the chart) was given as 3⅝ yards instead of 3⅞ yards, which was correct. The mistake was of limited scope, to be sure, and was the result of a typographical error. But that mistake cost the company a whopping $10,000. I am confident that every person in the company remembers those details as vividly as I do, even though the incident happened almost twenty years ago. I hope this example will serve to assure the reader that mistakes cannot be allowed; the staff works under tremendous pressure, for each one knows how serious the slightest mistake can be.

Correcting a mistake is not a simple matter of refunding the price of the pattern. A mistake involves the nominal price of the pattern and the price of fabric (thousands of yards) from which the customers will cut; the company is responsible for the total price (which might be $5 and could easily be $50) of an original purchase of a mere $1. The reliable pattern company guards its all-important reputation by employing such a complete-refund policy. This mushrooming problem is further aggravated by the do-it-yourself-er who may be careless in a hundred different ways, any one of

which could result in failure and every one of which she may blame on the pattern company. The company must be absolutely confident that each pattern can withstand even undeserved criticism.

Four pattern companies enjoy the greatest popularity earned by their fine reputations. The Big Four of the pattern industry are Simplicity, McCall's, Butterick, and Vogue, and you may be confident that each of these companies is jealous of its good name and that each pattern is backed by that fine reputation. There are many other companies (some quite good, some questionable) that have not enjoyed the time-tested popularity of these four. Every one of the Big Four makes an excellent and accurate pattern and deserves your utmost confidence; every one is proud of its international favor and will guard its reputation with continued vigilance.

COMPONENTS
OF
A GOOD
PATTERN·

Each individual customer has her own idea of what constitutes a good pattern. All customers want the accurate pattern I have discussed above, but each has her own personal standards for a pattern; one person will say a pattern is good only if it is quick and easy, another will consider it good if it is difficult enough to challenge her, and another places styling high on the list of desirable qualities. Each company makes a variety of styles in the hope of pleasing every taste in styling as well as in construction techniques, and each company specializes somewhat in the tastes of a particular group. For example, Simplicity is especially interested in pleasing the young person who is not yet an expert in construction, while Vogue satisfies the more sophisticated customer who prefers unusual cut and high fashion. Many persons consistently buy the designs of a particular company, while others play the field.

There are other, less obvious components of a good pattern. The sketch for the counter catalog is a most pertinent piece of artwork, for it is this sketch that makes the sale. That fashion sketch must be more than appealing; it must be honest and accurate. It *is* an honest sketch, although it is pictured on a fashion figure (taller, slimmer), as is all advertising art. Another sketch of the design, the line drawing that appears on the envelope back and on the instruction sheet, is perhaps more accurate, simply because the absence of color and texture allows lines to show more distinctly.

The $10,000 mistake illustrates that yardages must be accurate if a pattern meets the high standard required. These yardages are worked out on large tables as economically as possible. The layout artist might work days to test out the most economical layout and might discard the labors of a week if she finds a better method at the end of that week. The customer can buy the yardage stated with confidence that it is correct. The instruction sheet and all other instructions (on the printed pattern, on the envelope) must be correct and, in addition, must be understood by the average customer if the pattern is to result in a successful finished product. Each of the Big Four

companies does an excellent job of instruction.

To review, the good pattern is an accurate pattern, in a design appealing to the customer; it is accurately presented in the counter catalog, the yardages are accurate, and the instructions are reliable and easily understood. It is important that the reader believe that the pattern company does an excellent job, for only if she does will she follow her pattern and read the directions. Respect for the pattern is essential to success.

NOTE   However, if a fabric is chosen that is different in character from the fabrics suggested, the competent seamstress will need to modify the construction techniques.

FALLACIES CONCERNING COMMERCIAL PATTERNS

A great percentage of the common complaints about patterns are the result of the inadequacies and inexperience of the do-it-yourself-er. Because the complainers are so legion and vociferous, a detailed defense is required. These complaints are most detrimental when heard by the inexperienced person because they lead to distrust of her pattern and to the mistakes and inaccuracies that result from such distrust. The most frequent and dangerous fallacies are the following.

"PATTERNS ARE NOT RELIABLY SIZED"
Typical complaints are, "I bought a size 12 the last time and it fit perfectly, but this time the size 12 didn't fit at all," or "I buy a size 14 in Butterick, but a size 14 Vogue is not the same size," etc., etc. These statements are not true. All patterns in the Big Four group are sized according to measurement standards of the Pattern Fashion Industry, which results

in a standardized fit that is completely reliable. These complaints are made by persons who have gained or lost weight or by persons who made a mistake cutting one of the patterns or because of a special circumstance. Every pattern made by a major company, which in turn is based on the standard measurements of the Pattern Fashion Industry. Because all major companies use these measurements, their basic patterns are remarkably alike, really almost identical. If size 12 is your size, it is the right size for any pattern of any of the Big Four pattern companies.

"THE PATTERN CALLS FOR ⅛ TO ¼ YARD MORE FABRIC THAN IS REALLY REQUIRED"

This complaint is perhaps the most frequent and the most dangerous. It is not true; the experienced, knowledgeable customer does not believe it. However, there are many reasons why the customer might be convinced that her complaint is honest, and her sincerity makes her complaint the more serious. The following are reasons why a customer might cut the pattern from less yardage than the pattern states:

1 She might have bought the fabric amount for a narrower width of fabric but cut it, perhaps unknowingly, from a wider width of fabric. To illustrate, one of my students bought the amount of 54-inch fabric her coat required, but her fabric was 60 inches wide; in her case the 6-inch advantage in width was so great that she was able to cut a skirt as well as a coat. This advantage in width may turn out to be great in one pattern, but in another, because of the shape of pattern pieces, there may be no advantage at all. The advantage exists, but it is nebulous and unpredictable.

2 Often the customer who makes this complaint has decided to make shorter sleeves

or to omit the big patch pockets or to cut her facings from lighter-weight fabric, etc. Any change or omission of design will, of course, result in a saving of yardage.

3 The short woman who alters her pattern can make fabric savings that might be considerable, so her complaint might be honest with no true reflection on the accuracy of the yardage charts. But even this statement must be questioned; each layout influences the saving on that particular problem. I give my classes an assignment that proves this point. They are given one particular pattern alteration and are required to figure the saving in yardage on the 19 layouts of the pattern we selected. The saving varies from ⅛ to ⅜ yard, depending on the layout. So this legitimate saving must be figured for the particular layout to be used; the customer must not generalize that, because of her height, she can always save ¼ yard.

4 The person who is the smallest size of the size grouping for the layout she will use (the size 12 in a layout pictured for sizes 12, 14, and 16) has a slight advantage in width which might result in a saving of fabric in some cases but which will not consistently result in a saving.

5 The do-it-yourself-er who complains about yardage amounts often cuts a pattern piece off grain, a "sin" the experienced person would not commit. Cutting on a crosswise grain, instead of lengthwise as instructed, can often result in fabric economy but will as often result in an unsatisfactory garment. Unfortunately the mistake of off-grain cutting does not show up immediately; the tragedy of it is revealed after repeated launderings or

dry cleanings, long after the mistake could be corrected.

6 If a pattern requires 3 yards and a mere ½ inch of fabric length, the pattern company must state a requirement of 3⅛ yards. But the customer who sees what appears to be an extra ⅛ yard of fabric is often convinced that an extra amount was added for good measure.

7 There is one legitimate saving that can sometimes (but not always) be made by the very competent person. With tricky folding and by intricately changing the folding of the fabric as each piece is cut or by cutting one piece at a time on a single thickness of fabric, the competent person can sometimes economize on yardage while following the rules of accurate cutting. But this complicated folding and refolding could not be pictured on the layout, and even if it could, it would be too difficult for the average customer to understand. The pattern company must state a yardage amount that is most economical in a layout that can be effectively drawn and easily understood.

"THE INSTRUCTIONS WERE ALL WRONG— I KNOW A MUCH BETTER WAY TO DO IT"

This complaint might well be considered a legitimate one. There are often better ways of doing a particular construction detail, and there are sometimes additional construction details that would be advisable. But the experienced person (the one who makes this complaint) should consider the problems of the pattern company before she destroys trust and confidence in the pattern for her less experienced friends. The instructions must be written for the elusive "average customer," and she is not experienced.

The talented writer in the instruction sheet department knows all the finest tricks, you may be sure. But she must write correct techniques that can be understood by the novice, she must not confuse the average customer, and she must write directions that can be best pictured in a sketch. She must necessarily compromise. Her instructions are not wrong; they are entirely right under the circumstances under which she works. Improve on them, if you are experienced, but rely on them with complete confidence if you are a novice. Respect for directions is absolutely essential during the learning period.

HOW A PATTERN IS MADE

Each month the designer reviews sales information and decides which 30 or 40 designs to discard and replace during the month. A staff of artists, directed by the designer, designs the new collection. The patternmakers (the most respected and highly paid artisans in the industry) work from a designer's sketch and, using the company's basic pattern as a guide, make the pattern. The pattern is tested first in paper and then in muslin; it is tested on a dummy made to conform to Pattern Fashion Industry standard measurements and is action-tested on a human figure if the design requires special movement. At each stage in the procedure, the design must meet the exacting standards of the designer. When the pattern meets her final approval, work begins in several departments.

The grading and layout department, the instruction sheet department, and the art department work simultaneously on the pattern. The grader sizes the pattern up and down from the original size 12 or 14. The graded sizes are used by the layout department to figure yardages. In the instruction sheet department, the writer directs every phase of the work involved with the finished sheet. She writes the copy, directs the artist so that the sketches are accurate and are pictured in the best way, writes the information which appears on the printed pattern, and plans the required pattern markings. Typists, paste-up artists, and inkers complete the staff. Each step of the procedure undergoes exhaustive checking and rechecking. The art department prepares the line drawings, the sketch for the catalog and the envelope front, and any other advertising artwork desired. Then these three departments submit their work for a final review and coordination, which results in the consistency and accuracy the pattern company must attain. Work completed in this creative phase of the procedure is shipped to the manufacturing plant, where it is processed, packaged, and mailed. The entire procedure, from the design office to the retail store, requires almost six months.

DIFFERENCES
IN
PHILOSOPHY

There are two distinct philosophies of dress reflected by designs of the pattern houses, and, of course, there are shadings between the two. The most common philosophy in the pattern business, as in the whole business community, is based on mass approval and sales; this is the philosophy of the average customer. The average customer is a farmer's wife, a schoolgirl, a secretary, and a teacher. She lives in the country and the city; she lives in America and the whole world. She is fourteen and fifty. She is indeed elusive,

but she is consistent in some respects. She is making her first or perhaps her second garment. She is a busy person who steals hours for sewing from a busy schedule. High fashion is not required of her, and she does not have fashion daring. She makes her less important garments and buys her cocktail dresses, suits, and coats ready-made. This average customer is responsible for probably 90 per cent of pattern sales. Simplicity, Butterick, and McCall's, of the Big Four group, and Advance-Sew-Easy cater to this woman.

A contrasting philosophy is reflected in the designs of Vogue and, to a considerably lesser extent, in the designs of Spadea and Modes Royale. These companies cater to the woman who is more fashion-conscious, to the professional dressmaker or the experienced customer, and to the woman who knows good design, loves good fabric, and sets her goal at a couturier level. She is willing to spend more time and effort; probably fashion plays a larger role in her life.

The prices of patterns reflect the philosophy of the company and its customers. The companies catering to the mass market can maintain lower prices because less work is required on the less complicated designs and because mass sales allow a smaller profit margin per pattern. The price of some Vogue patterns ($3.50) might seem exorbitant, but it includes (1) the cost of the design, which was imported from the fashion centers of Europe and carries the name of an internationally known designer; (2) the costs of labor to create and manufacture the much more complicated patterns; and (3) a necessarily higher profit margin per pattern because of the limited market potential. The higher price is not outrageous; the exclusive design is well worth the price to the customer who insists on high fashion.

The special features offered by each pattern company further emphasize differences in the philosophies of their customers. All the major pattern houses offer designs for every age group and every wardrobe need in addition to such novelty sections as costumes, doll clothes, and accessories. The following special features ensure additional customer satisfaction.

VOGUE

Young Fashionables Gay, young designs for the teen-ager or the young at heart. They require a minimum of experience.

Mrs. Exeter designs A collection of costumes appropriate for the mature woman, offered in designs flattering to the heavier figure.

Paris Original models High-fashion designs purchased from successful Parisian designers. They feature intricate cut and elaborate construction and are for the experienced customer.

International Couturier designs Imported from well-known designers of Spain, Italy, and England. They are highly styled and intricately cut and are for the experienced customer.

Vogue Americana Designs A collection of designs in the American mood by designers who have won acclaim in the ready-to-wear industry.

BUTTERICK

Learn to Sew patterns A series of very quick and easy patterns planned for class-room projects or for the person who will teach herself. The lessons progress in a logical sequence of learning experiences.

Quick and Easy designs (some labeled Very Quick and Easy) Patterns with a minimum amount of detail and a small number of pattern pieces. They are for the beginner or the person who must spend a minimum length of time.

McCALL'S

(Easy to Make) Quickie patterns Comparable to Butterick's Quick and Easy patterns.

Adjust for You patterns A collection of patterns with two sets of cutting lines so that one might cut along a larger pattern for the skirt and a smaller pattern for the bodice, and vice versa.

NOTE At the time of writing, these patterns have not been available long enough to have established a record of customer approval.

junior petite sizes An ample number of designs cut in the new size grouping so ideal for the mature but diminutive figure.

New York Designers' Collection Plus A group of designs from very successful American designers and American fashion houses.

SIMPLICITY

How to Sew patterns A wide choice of patterns in simple designs intended for classroom use or as an aid to effective self-instruction.

Jiffy styles Comparable to Butterick's Quick and Easy designs.

junior petite sizes An ample collection of the new size grouping for mature but small-boned figures.

American Casual designs A collection of informal costumes and coordinates. They are simple in cut and relatively easy to execute.

The miscellaneous features or customer services listed for each of the major companies is not an exhaustive list and fortunately for continued progress in the home sewing field, the list can never be entirely up-to-date. Contrary to popular opinion that sewing never changes, new ideas in all of the industries related to home sewing (patterns as well as fabrics, notions and machines) appear on the market with such rapidity that the home sewing enthusiast must be constantly alert to something new. The wise customer will keep abreast of developments by reading the pattern-book magazines offered by all of the major companies for newsstand sale and by looking through all of the pattern catalogues at least every few months. All of the major companies listed on page 24 are pace setters and all are dedicated to solving old problems with new solutions and to meeting the changing needs of the woman who sews. While most new innovations are so helpful that one wonders why someone didn't think of them years ago, the customer must guard against blind acceptance of every new idea; the wise customer will weigh the disadvantages and the advantages of a new idea with her individual needs in mind.

THE MINOR PATTERN COMPANIES

Spadea This company does not "travel with the pack." It is the only company which manufactures a perforated pattern; the last of the major companies to give up perforated patterns did so in 1956. Spadea advertises "ready-to-wear sizing," but the problem is that the measurements on which the patterns are based were decided by Spadea alone for Spadea patterns only. Since the sizing change of January, 1968, patterns from all of the major companies are sized very

much like ready-to-wear. The advantage of a pattern from the major companies over a Spadea pattern is that the major houses all use standard body measurements established by the Measurement Committee of the Pattern Fashion Industry. Therefore the customer is assured of consistent sizing in patterns from all of the major companies. At the time the standards were set up, Spadea did not accept an invitation to participate in the decisions; educators and customers alike continue to hope that Spadea will conform to the standards of the Pattern Fashion Industry in the near future. Until that time, the customer cannot assume that her size in a Spadea pattern is identical to her size in any pattern from all of the major companies, and she cannot assume that the pattern alterations she usually makes will be correct for Spadea patterns. Rather she must study the special measurement charts provided in the Spadea catalogues and approach a sizing decision and a decision on pattern alterations as completely different and new experiences.

The instruction sheet and layouts are not presented with the clarity one can expect from the larger companies and there is evidence that the quality of pattern making is not entirely reliable. This company is not as devoted to educating the consumer as are the major companies. The experienced person will find that instructions are adequate and will possibly recognize and be able to correct the shortcomings of instruction and patternmaking, but these patterns cannot be recommended for beginners. The designs are highly styled; the company apparently caters to the customer with more sophisticated tastes than the average customer, who will prefer a Butterick, McCall's or Simplicity but who is far less fashion conscious than the Vogue devotee.

Modes Royale Modes Royale makes a limited collection of designs for women but does not offer the scope, in terms of age or figure differences, that the larger companies do. Prior to January, 1968, when the major houses used uniform sizing based on Government Bureau of Standards measurements, Modes Royale conformed to the same sizing standards. But, like Spadea, this company did not accept an invitation to participate in the discussions which resulted in the new sizing standards. Educators are hopeful that this company will conform to the new standards even if representatives did not take part in the committee decisions.

Instructions on these patterns are brief, which fact in itself indicates that the company does not cater to the average customer and is not particularly interested in the education field. The styles are quite dashing with the kind of design interest that is based largely on intricate detail; I cannot resist adding that the designer seems to be "button happy."

inexpensive newspaper patterns These patterns are so very inexpensive that one must question their quality; the price is ridiculously low. Furthermore, the name of the company, if it appears at all, is not featured prominently; this fact alone should make the buyer beware. It is foolish economy to save little more than a quarter (the newspaper pattern is as low as 15 cents, and similar designs made by reliable companies are available for 50 cents) on a purchase which will mushroom into several dollars. These patterns are not recommended under any circumstances.

4

SIZING
OF
COMMERCIAL
PATTERNS
AND
SELECTION
OF
CORRECT
SIZE

The preceding chapter emphasized the fact that pattern companies must be reliable in every phase of the creation and manufacture of the pattern. Perhaps consistency of size is of greater concern to the customer than any other consideration. The major pattern houses make consistently sized patterns (consistent within the company itself and consistent with sister companies) because these major companies set their sizing standards according to identical body measurements.

SIZING STANDARDS

The Measurement Standard Committee of the Pattern Fashion Industry has established standard body measurements which have been adopted by all the major pattern companies (Butterick, McCall's, Simplicity, and Vogue). The advantages of consistent sizing are so numerous that all the major companies cooperate with each other to make consistent sizing possible. The minor companies did not take part in the committee decisions but educators and customers alike continue to hope that they will adopt the sizing standards in the near future.

Each pattern company has a dress form in one size of each figure grouping (size 10 or 12 is used for the misses figure), and that dress form is made to specifications of the measurement standards of the Pattern Fashion Industry. Each company makes a basic pattern to fit the standard dummy, and because the companies who conform to the standard are working on dress forms of identical size, the resulting basic patterns are remarkably alike. Since the basic pattern is the foundation for all the designs in the collection, all patterns of all major companies are consistent in size. The woman who sews may be assured that when her pattern size and figure type are established, all designs from companies using measurement standards of the Pattern Fashion Industry will give comparable results. Furthermore, she may be sure that the pattern alteration required on one pattern will be correct for patterns from other companies who conform to the established standards.

1 **the sizing change effective in January, 1968** Prior to January, 1968, all the major houses sized patterns consistently by using Government Bureau of Standards measurements. The consistent sizing was a great advantage to the customer, but the Bureau of Standards measurements were such that the customer usually required a pattern one size larger than she wore in ready-to-wear. This resulted in some confusion. The customer was hesitant to order a size 14 pattern when she thought of herself as a size 12, her size in ready-to-wear. In order to make pattern sizes correspond more closely to ready-to-wear sizing, a sizing change was initiated in January, 1968. All designs since that date have been made with standard body measurements developed and approved by the Pattern Fashion Industry. With this change the customer will probably wear the same size in a pattern that she buys in ready-to-wear.

2 **comparison of "new sizing" and the former sizing based on bureau of standards measurements** The new sizing does not result in an appreciable difference in fit. A comparison of new sizing measurement charts with those on an old pattern will reveal that body measurements are very much alike and that the main difference is that the measurements have been given a smaller size "tag." The customer will continue to buy dress, blouse, suit, and coat patterns by bust size but she will find that a bust size of 34, formerly requiring a size 14 pattern, will require a size 12 if the pattern appeared after January, 1968.

There are a few changes in measurements but they are not extensive. Waist sizes in the new sizing are somewhat smaller. In Misses', Women's, and Junior figure types, hip measurements are slightly smaller (about ½ inch) in some sizes. Figure types remain the same except that the former Teen, Pre-Teen, and Sub-Teen figure types have been replaced with one new figure type called the Young Junior/Teen Figure type and labeled "new size range" within a red circle. The "new sizing," labeled within a red box, is used for designs for the fashion minded group (the Young Junior/Teen age group and older), whereas the sizing of Men's and Boys' patterns remains the same; likewise Toddlers', Children's, and Girls' sizes have not been changed.

3 **problems of the transition period** During the years 1968 and 1969 (when patterns sized by former standards and those sized with the new sizing standards will both appear in counter catalogs), the customer must be especially careful to buy patterns according to her bust size. The new sizing appears in a red chart in the catalogs while the former sizing is shown in a blue chart. There will be no confusion if the customer will buy the size required for her bust measurement.

NOTE The reader must understand that the special symbol for new sizing, boxed as it is (on a background of red on patterns and in the catalogs), will not be necessary after the transition period is over. Likewise the need for charts in two different colors will diminsh as the transition is completed.

SLIGHT DIFFERENCES IN SIZING OF PATTERNS FROM DIFFERENT COMPANIES

FACTORS THAT DETERMINE SIZE

1 **body size** Body size is consistent from all the major companies because it is based on measurement standards established by the Pattern Fashion Industry. *This is, however, the only factor of size controlled by measurement standards.*

2 **amount of livability (room to move and live in)** Average livability amounts are listed on

page 179. Each garment needs more size than mere body size, depending on the action of particular parts of the body. This component of size is not decided by standard measurements (it differs too much with the costume) but is left to the discretion of each designer. Her opinion might differ from the opinion of another designer, but it differs amazingly little. All designers must be, by training and because of their artistic talent, good judges of (a) the amount of livability required for action and movement and (b) the amount of ease required for atractive, becoming fit. One designer might think 3 inches is the right amount of livability at the bust of a fitted dress, while another might think it should be 3¼ inches; however, their opinions differ so slightly that one is truly unaware of them as a garment is worn.

3 **style fullness** All garments must have the two factors listed above. Some garments have yet another component, style fullness. Style fullness is the extra size or fabric needed to make the garment look a certain way; it is obvious in such features as the gathered skirt, the batwing sleeve, and the peg-top skirt. This component of size differs greatly from design to design, and each designer must judge the amount of fullness required for each particular design. This factor, more than any other, makes it seem that patterns differ in size, but even so, they do not. Each is based on the same body size, and if the customer buys her proper size she will be assured of (a) the proper amount of livability and (b) the ideal amount of style fullness, both decided by a talented designer.

RELIABILITY
OF
PATTERN
SIZE

Patterns are reliably sized, but it is perhaps understandable why a customer might have doubts that seem to her well-founded. There are several reasons:

1 She may know very well that she has always worn patterns in size 12 and that they fit perfectly as long as she cuts them ½ inch wider at the side edges. She may not realize that a ½-inch addition may make the difference between a size 12 and a size 14 and that the pattern in the correct size would fit better in many little ways than an altered pattern.

2 She may have been wearing her clothing too tight because her standards are not as educated as those of the trained designer. In other words, she may have been "stealing" some of the livability size and using it for body size. The livability amount at the bust of a fitted dress is about 3 inches in the opinion of experts, but one could "get into" the dress if her size were 2 inches larger than the pattern. The dress would be judged a poor fit by an expert, although the inexperienced person might be satisfied with it.

3 She may have, perhaps without realizing it, always made garments with a great deal of style fullness, such as the shirtwaist, which is a popular beginning project. If considerable style fullness is involved, one can steal enough of it to make an additional 4 or 5 inches of body size. Using this style fullness for body size is a serious mistake; there must be style fullness to give the design the character for which it was selected. But again an unknowing person might be honestly unaware that she had not achieved the proper effect.

4 She may have changed in size since she made the last garment; the size change may be an overall change, or it may be a change in distribution of flesh. Many women are unaware of gradual weight changes. It is advisable to take new body measurements before cutting each garment if there is any possibility of figure change.

THE TRUE TEST
OF PROPER SIZE
AND
FIGURE TYPE

The only accurate test is to make a garment with a dart-fitted bodice, regulation set-in sleeves, and a straight skirt. All the large pattern companies offer a basic pattern of this description. Such a basic dress, made in inexpensive fabric, is a wise choice as a first project. This is a good test for size and figure type, required pattern alterations, and fitting requirements. When the best solution is attained, the customer can buy that size and make those alterations on any of the patterns from the major pattern houses.

FIGURE TYPES
AND STANDARD MEASUREMENTS
AS ESTABLISHED BY THE
PATTERN FASHION INDUSTRY

Size is but one consideration; proper fit will result only if the pattern is purchased in the correct size and in the proper figure type. The Pattern Fashion Industry has established several types of figures, and these in turn are offered by all the major pattern companies. Selection of the best figure type is a more difficult matter, and some experimentation will be necessary. Ready-to-wear is similarly typed into figure groups, and the figure type you have found best for you on the ready-made market will probably be right in a pattern, too. The description of several figure types follows:

JUNIOR

Figure about 5'5", with high bust quite well developed, shorter-waisted than misses

standard body measurements

Size	5	7	9	11	13	15
Bust	30	31	32	33½	35	37
Waist	21½	22½	23½	24½	26	28
9" Hip	32	33	34	35½	37	39
Back waist length	15	15¼	15½	15¾	16	16¼

JUNIOR PETITE

Figure about 5'1", fully developed but small-boned and diminutive, shorter-waisted than juniors

standard body measurements

Size	3	5	7	9	11	13
Bust	30½	31	32	33	34	35
Waist	22	22½	23½	24½	25½	26½
7" Hip	31½	32	33	34	35	36
Back waist length	14	14¼	14½	14¾	15	15¼

MISSES'

Figure about 5'6", fully developed, longer-waisted than juniors

standard body measurements

Size	6	8	10	12	14	16	18
Bust	30½	31½	32½	34	36	38	40
Waist	22	23	24	25½	27	29	31
9" Hip	32½	33½	34½	36	38	40	42
Back waist length	15½	15¾	16	16¼	16½	16¾	17

WOMEN'S

Figure an extension of the misses' type cut in sizes for the larger, more mature figure, normal waist length

standard body measurements

Size	38	40	42	44	46	48	50
Bust	42	44	46	48	50	52	54
Waist	34	36	38	40½	43	45½	48
9" Hip	44	46	48	50	52	54	56
Back waist length	17¼	17⅜	17½	17⅝	17¾	17⅞	18

HALF SIZES

Figure about 5'3", fully developed but shorter in all ways than misses' and women's, narrower shoulders and wider hips (compared with bust) than misses'

standard body measurements

Size	10½	12½	14½	16½	18½	20½	22½	24½
Bust	33	35	37	39	41	43	45	47
Waist	26	28	30	·32	34	36½	39	41½
7" Hip	35	37	39	41	43	45½	48	50½
Back waist length	15	15¼	15½	15¾	15⅞	16	16⅛	16¼

These are the figure types that will fit most girls and women. There are many other figure categories, and although each company does not make every one, all the following are available from one or more of the companies:

Children	4–8
Girls	7–14
Infants and toddlers	½–3
Chubbies	8½C–14½C
Young junior/teen	5/6–13/14
Boys	1–14
Men	32–46 (chest)

THE PROPORTIONED PATTERN

The major pattern houses offer a limited collection of somewhat basic patterns in proportioned lengths for the short, average, and tall figure. The yardage charts state yardage differences for the three heights, and the pattern includes pattern pieces for each figure. It sounds like a wonderful idea, and indeed there are some advantages. However, the solution to problems of height is not as simple as the advertisements would lead the novice to believe. These patterns are based on the assumption that a tall figure is tall in every portion of the body and that a short figure, similarly, is short all over. Unfortunately, this is not true. A woman might be 6 feet tall, but her torso might be short; the short girl might have longer arms and a longer torso than her 6-foot friends. Such cases are too frequent to be ignored. The proportioned pattern is a convenience, but each section of the pattern should be tested on the figure. A short girl might well discover, for example, that she should use the average-length bodice, the longer sleeve, and the shorter skirt.

SELECTION
OF SIZE
AND
FIGURE TYPE

1 Take bust, waist, and hip measurements over a slip and the undergarments you usually wear. Blouses, dresses, suits, and coats are purchased by bust size (regardless of even very large hips). Separate skirts, slacks, and shorts may be purchased by either waist or hip size. It is wise to buy these patterns (skirts, etc.)

for the larger of your two measurements and fit in the garment at the smaller-than-average area. This statement is true for slacks and skirts, but the original statement that other patterns are purchased by bust size is very important in the selection of all other patterns. There are a few exceptions (mainly the small-boned persons who have a larger-than-average bust) when it might be advisable to buy one size smaller than bust size; consider any exception to the general rule with caution. The small-boned person might buy the smaller pattern and then alter her pattern, as described on page 85, to compensate for her larger-than-average cup size. The diminutive person might prefer a "greatcoat" in a size smaller than her bust size indicates; a coat cut with exaggerated fullness tends to engulf the slight figure, and in this case it is advisable to steal some of the style fullness for body size.

2 Read the description of the figure types and select the one best describing your figure. A complete listing of figure types, and often a word description, appears in the back pages of the counter catalog.

3 Ideally, choose a basic dress for a first project as an aid in testing size, figure type, and pattern alteration. However, this is not necessary if the customer will measure and alter her pattern carefully, as described in Chapter 7.

4 Perfect your sizing decision by keeping records of pattern alterations: Were they right? What should be done next time? Try another size or figure type if that seems advisable. With careful records, you should be established in the correct size and figure type by the second and certainly by the third project. Surely it goes without saying that during this testing period it would be well to use relatively inexpensive fabric.

5

SELECTION
OF
PATTERN
AND
FABRIC

Fortified with well-laid plans, a decision of size and figure type, an understanding of the merits and philosophy of various pattern companies, and a knowledge of the special offerings of each pattern company, the customer is prepared to select the design.

SELECTION
OF
PATTERN

It is well to survey the fabric offerings of the season and the store for inspiration before selecting the pattern, although some women prefer to choose the pattern and get fabric inspiration from it. It is advisable for a novice to leaf through several counter catalogs, although the experienced person may well go directly to her one favorite catalog. All customers should read the information in the yardage chart and any word description that might appear with the fashion sketch for a more accurate appraisal of the design. The ambitious person should select a design that will challenge her abilities—something new in construction detail that will involve new learning.

The customer is allowed to examine the pattern envelope before purchase and should request to do so. Although she cannot remove the paper pattern from the envelope, she can look over the instruction sheet, and by studying it and the information on the envelope back, she can make a more satisfactory purchase.

THE ENVELOPE FRONT

The beginner should select one view of the design as shown on the envelope front and carry it through without variation. The experienced person often decides to use this feature of one view and that feature of another, but if so, she should understand the subsequent problems of yardage, cutting, and construction. If a pattern lends itself to the use of plaid, it will be pictured in plaid in at least one view on the envelope front, and the novice who wishes to use plaid should buy only a pattern so pictured.

THE ENVELOPE BACK

The line drawing on the back of the envelope reveals structural lines of the design more clearly than the fashion sketch. A word description will appear on the envelope back; it should be read carefully, for it will reveal those features difficult or impossible to distinguish on the sketch. It might state that it is a two-piece dress (and perhaps the fashion sketch looks all of one piece) or that the shoulders are slightly dropped or that the pocket is a simulated one. A scale drawing of the pattern pieces will appear on the envelope back or on the instruction sheet. The pattern pieces reveal difficulty of construction and estimated time requirements to the experienced person. The novice is helped some simply by using the number of pattern pieces as a guide; in general few pattern pieces (six instead of a possible twenty or more) indicate ease and speed of sewing. The number of markings (dots, notches) on the pattern is a criterion for judgment also. The notions and findings are listed on the back of the envelope.

Notions should be purchased as soon as the pattern and fabric have been selected; quite apart from the obvious saving in shopping trips, it is very discouraging to be in the mood to sew and to lack the necessary supplies. Appropriate fabrics for the design are listed under "Suggested Fabrics" on the envelope back. The person with developed taste will not need this help, but the novice or the person who is less competent in selecting compatible patterns and fabric will find these suggestions invaluable. Special notes appear on the back of the envelope; such information as "napped fabrics not suitable" or "diagonal weaves not suitable" can make all the difference between success and failure.

One very important note appears on many patterns; it reads, "Extra fabric is required for matching plaids and balancing large designs." Each plaid or large design, by size or nature, requires a different amount of extra fabric for matching purposes; the pattern company could not give a yardage amount that would be right for all purposes. Therefore the chart states the amount of fabric required for cutting the pattern pieces, and the customer must figure the extra required for her particular plaid. Estimating yardage for matching plaid is discussed on page 99.

The words "with or without nap" appear in the yardage chart and, as used here, refer to all fabrics which have an up and down. These are fabrics, like corduroy or velvet and napped woolens, which show shading differences when worn unless all pattern pieces are cut in the same direction. In general such a layout requires more yardage. A more detailed discussion of napped and pile fabrics appears on page 98.

THE YARDAGE CHART

Figure 1 pictures a typical yardage chart. The chart includes a variety of information which can be used for many different purposes; the customer must study the entire chart. By reading the chart up and down she obtains the necessary information. It is well to circle the amount of yardage needed; as an example, the chart is circled for size 14, version A, 39-inch fabric. Four factors determine the amount of yardage required: (1) the version, (2) the size of the pattern, (3) the width of the fabric, and (4) the nature of the fabric (napped, plaid, one-way design, etc.).

Individual pattern alteration and fabric choices make it necessary under certain circumstances to estimate special yardage requirements. Such cases are listed below with page references for detailed directions:

to estimate yardage for an altered pattern see page 97 The saving in yardage for the shortened pattern and additional fabric for a lengthened pattern are figured from the layout to be used; in some cases a new layout must be made.

to estimate yardage for a new layout see page 96 If the fabric width selected is not listed in the yardage chart, this will be necessary; a salesperson cannot figure this accurately without making a layout.

to estimate yardage for changes in design see page 97 If the customer wishes to cut some pieces of a contrasting fabric or if she combines views of the pattern, new layouts are required.

to estimate yardage for plaids see page 99 Extra fabric must be added to the amount stated in the yardage chart; this must be

Yardage

Diagonal fabrics are not suitable.
No allowance for matching plaid or stripes.

Misses Size	8	10	12	14	16
Bust	31½	32½	34	36	38
Version A					
39" Without Nap†	3 1/2	3 5/8	3 5/8	3 7/8	4
45" Without Nap†	3 1/8	3 1/4	3 1/4	3 1/2	3 5/8
Version B					
39" Without Nap†	3	3 1/8	3 1/4	3 3/8	3 3/8
45" Without Nap†	2 1/4	2 3/8	2 3/8	2 5/8	2 3/4
Version C (cut crosswise)					
35" Without Nap†	2 5/8	2 3/4	2 7/8	3	3 1/8
45" Without Nap†	2 1/8	2 1/8	2 1/4	2 1/4	2 3/8
54" Without Nap†	1 3/4	1 3/4	1 7/8	1 7/8	2
Underbodice					
35" or 39"	1 3/8	1 3/8	1 3/8	1 3/8	1 3/8
Petticoat A					
39"	2 1/8	2 1/8	2 1/4	2 1/4	2 1/4
1" ribbon for waist-band	7/8	7/8	7/8	1	1
14" dress zipper.					
Length of dress at center-back from natural neck-line	39 3/4	40 3/4	41 1/4	41 3/4	42 1/4

Width at lower edge of Version A in size 14 is 116" (about 3 1/8 yards).

Width at lower edge of Version B or C in size 14 is 41 1/2" (about 1 1/8 yards).
3" Hem allowed on Version B and C.

†Without nap or pile or with a two-way design.

Fabric Suggestions

Crepe - Chiffon - Surah - Faille Crepe - Georgette
Wool Crepe - Sheer Woolen - Cotton Broadcloth
Linen - Pique

Typical Yardage Chart
with yardage for Size 16,
Version A circled

FIGURE 1

estimated for the particular plaid and the particular layout.

to estimate yardage for napped fabrics see page 98 Fabrics which have an up and down (referred to as "with or without nap" on the pattern envelope) require a layout with all pieces laid in one direction; if this layout is not included with the pattern, one must be made.

ASSISTANCE FROM THE STORE PERSONNEL

The staff in the pattern and fabric departments are willing to answer questions from the customer, but it is unfair to expect too much of a salesgirl's time. Furthermore, many salesgirls have had neither the formal training nor the experience which would enable them to give competent answers to technical questions. Probably most customer questions are involved with estimating special yardage amounts (the very problems just mentioned), and there is no quick, easy answer to any of those questions. The experienced salesgirl will confess that she does not know for sure but will, if you wish, give an educated guess. As the customer learns more about home sewing, she will ask fewer questions of strangers and at the same time will learn to rely with confidence on the talented members of the sales staff.

SELECTION
OF
FABRIC

The scope of this book does not include a study of textiles, although such knowledge is essential for success. It is assumed that the reader has taken the suggestion in the Preface and has armed herself with a fundamental knowledge of textiles from a reliable and recent source.

REPUTATION OF THE STORE

The reputation of the store or merchant is perhaps the first guarantee toward any wise purchase. The store which stands back of its merchandise with a sound refund policy, the store that thinks of tomorrow's sales while making today's transactions, is the only store an inexperienced person should shop. These merchants play a fair game. Unfair practices exist in every business, and the fabric market is no exception. For example, this summer I learned that a certain specialty shop rewraps fabric on empty bolts to gain the questionable advantage of the information on the end of the bolt. The case in point was a wool-nylon blend which had been wrapped on an empty bolt which read "100 per cent virgin wool." This merchant was known for his low prices—small wonder! Large department stores would not jeopardize their nationwide reputations with malpractices of this sort; their future depends on continuing business. But the unscrupulous merchant, especially in a city location, can make a reasonable profit on transient sales alone. The person who knows textiles well can shop anywhere with safety; the novice would do well to stay on the beaten path to the department store.

INFORMATION ON THE BOLT

Information given on the end of the bolt of fabric includes the fiber content by percentage, the finishes used, and the width of the fabric; often there are other statements ("drip-dry," "needs little or no ironing," "less than 1 per cent shrinkage," etc.) that are most helpful aids to the consumer. In addition there is often a hangtag, which contains suggestions for care and other pertinent information. The customer should check the width of fabric herself; the salesgirl makes human errors and might state a width incorrectly.

EXAMINATION OF FABRIC

The customer has every right to examine fabric carefully; the wise buyer examines the entire length of fabric before it is cut from the bolt. Flaws in weaving or dyeing can occur without the knowledge of the merchant who purchased from a reliable fabric company. Loose threads on the underside are no disadvantage usually, but they do suggest an inspection of the area from the right side. If fabric has been on display in or near a window, evidences of sun fading may appear. Fabrics left on display shelves for long periods of time may show their age with dust or fading at the fold or selvedge edges. The customer must be cautious, the more so during clearance sales, for it is just such damaged goods that carry the more attractive prices at that time.

TENTERING PROBLEMS

Many of the easy-care finishes we insist on today are achieved with a resin-treating process; the fabric is subjected to high temperatures, and this seals the lengthwise and crosswise threads in the position they hold during the process. The finishes are wonderful, but there are disadvantages. The process of tentering fabric, rather like blocking curtains on a stretcher, should result in a fabric with lengthwise and crosswise threads in perfect right-angle position. However, the tentering process is not that carefully done, especially in less expensive fabrics. Actually, a 1-inch variation is considered acceptable to most fabric finishers. If the fabric is off grain when treated with the resin finish, the grain is permanently set and cannot be corrected. This is no great disadvantage in plain colors because the

fabric will not change with washing and therefore will hang well during a lifetime of wear. However, if the resin-treated fabric is a woven plaid, the crosswise stripe will not be at right angles and cannot be straightened into the right-angle position required for matching crosswise lines. This condition is evident before fabric is purchased; if a stripe on the upper layer of folded fabric lies on itself on the lower layer, the fabric is perfectly tentered. If the stripe on the upper layer angles off as much as ½ inch, the customer must realize that if the remarkable resin finishes were used, her fabric can never be straightened; no matter how clever she is, the plaid will not match. It is well to confine your purchase of plaids to those fabrics that have not been resin-treated.

Fabrics that do not have the miracle finishes can be straightened, but they require effort and result in a loss of yardage. If a poorly tentered fabric has been cut rather than torn from the bolt, the customer must buy extra yardage to compensate for the subsequent loss. Unfortunately, poorly tentered fabrics are often cut from the bolt (even those that could be torn with safety) because then the quality of tentering is not so evident to an inexperienced person. But the wise customer can learn to judge the quality of tentering. If she can see the weave at all, she will sense the direction of the crosswise threads; they should be very close to a right-angle position with the lengthwise threads. If the fabric is not resin-treated, the lines need not be in perfect right-angle position, for these fabrics can be straightened. Figure 2 shows bolts of fabric as they appear in the store.

Figure 2a pictures fabric that is in quite a good position with perhaps a 1-inch variation from the right-angle position, while Figure 2b pictures fabric poorly tentered with what might be as much as a 4- or 5-inch variation. The fabric in Figure 2a is a wise buy if it is not resin-treated or if it is resin-treated but featured in a plain color or an allover print, but it is a poor purchase if it is resin-treated and features some kind of woven

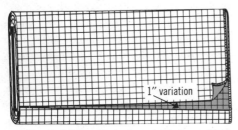

a Bolt of fabric illustrating tentering with a minimum of variation. It is a wise purchase if it has not been resin-treated; if it has been resin-treated, it is acceptable if it does not feature a woven crosswise stripe.

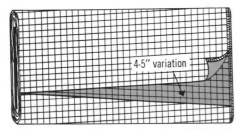

b Bolt of fabric illustrating very poor tentering. It is an unwise purchase if it has been resin-treated, but if it has not been resin-treated, it is acceptable if straightened. There will be a ⅛-yard fabric loss.

FIGURE 2

crosswise stripe. The fabric shown in Figure 2b, if it misses as much as 3 to 5 inches, is really not a wise buy at all. If, however, it is very inexpensive and has not been resin-treated, a customer might decide to purchase it, but she must realize that she will lose some yardage (the amount of the variation as she straightens this fabric) and that it might require professional blocking before it is ready for cutting. She must add the cost of an extra ⅛ yard of fabric and the possible cost of professional blocking (roughly 50 cents per yard) to the original cost of the fabric. She may well decide it is wiser to put the extra money into better fabric.

EXTRA FABRIC FOR STRAIGHTENING AND PRESHRINKING

If fabric is poorly tentered it must be straightened (see page 52), a process which will decrease the yardage by the amount of off-grain variation. If that variation exceeds 1 inch, the customer would be wise to purchase an additional ⅛ yard of fabric in order to compensate for the loss.

One of the great advantages of sewing at home is that we can preshrink fabric before making up a garment, thereby ensuring adequate size and length for the lifetime of the garment. Preshrinking adds to the cost of the garment (1) because of the possible loss of yardage which must be compensated for, (2) because of the time required to do the process at home, and (3) because of the expense (about 50 cents per yard) of having fabric professionally preshrunk at the cleaners. In every case this is time and money well spent, an economy in the long run. Most washable fabrics have undergone this process in their manufacture; a statement to that effect, very possibly given by percentage, will appear on the bolt of fabric. Even so, it is advisable to put fabric which will be washed through the identical washing process under which the garment will be washed and dried. I am sure the reader is aware of the greater amount of shrinkage that results from the automatic drying process as compared with the loss when clothing is dried by natural means. Fabric carrying the label which reads "no more than 2 per cent shrinkage" should be preshrunk for best results. Two per cent of 1 yard is about 7/10 inch; that means the average skirt length can shrink about ¼ inch after it is washed. This amount is not great and probably is nothing to worry about in quickly constructed, staple, and/or loosely fitted garments, but such a loss would be very disappointing to the discerning person if the costume were an important one.

Likewise, those fabrics which will be dry-cleaned should be put through the drycleaning process before they are made up. Wools which carry a label stating that they have been preshrunk can shrink when pressed or cleaned; again the amount of shrinkage is limited, but the demanding customer would be wise to ensure her investment in time and money by spending the additional 50 cents per yard to have the fabric put through the cleaning process.

Preshrinking is absolutely essential for both fabrics in the lined garment. In the lined garment two fabrics must act as one; preshrinking will make this possible. It is entirely possible that the lining might shrink in the crosswise direction while the fabric for the garment might shrink in a lengthwise direction, and the professional dry cleaners could not prevent the disastrous results after the garment is made up.

It is impossible to state the exact amount of extra fabric required for preshrinking purposes because each fabric will, of course, respond in a different manner. An estimate of an additional ⅛

yard for a 3-yard length of fabric should be sufficient for most fabrics of average to high quality. Less expensive fabrics, loosely woven fabrics, and crepes will probably shrink more than high-quality and firmly woven fabrics. Fabrics that have not been preshrunk during manufacture will probably shrink more.

APPROXIMATE YARDAGES FOR BASIC GARMENTS

Although the wisest and most economical way to buy fabric is to buy exactly the yardage required for the garment to be made (in other words, pattern and fabric on one buying trip), many persons like to buy fabric lengths to be used at future times. This is not really wise and certainly cannot be entirely safe, but there are circumstances (sales or buying trips abroad) when it would be well to have a few estimates as guidelines. The reader who likes to buy ahead would be wise to make a little chart of estimated yardages, based on her size, including several widths of fabric. A few minutes with a pattern catalog would enable her to make a simple little chart which she could carry in her wallet at all times. A chart similar to the one shown below, listing the kinds of garments she will probably make in the future, would be brief, workable, and as accurate as an estimate could be.

	35"	39"	45"	54"	60"
long-sleeved blouse					
sheath dress with sleeves					
straight skirt					
suit					

GOOD
FABRIC CHOICES
FOR
THE BEGINNER

It is advisable to master the art and science of clothing construction on fabrics that are easy to handle before attempting more difficult projects.

In general, fabrics that are closely woven and firm are more easily handled than the loosely woven fabrics, which will stretch; therefore plain and twill weaves, being the firmest weaves, are better choices for the beginner than satin or crepe weaves. Fabrics with a high thread count (*thread count* means the number of lengthwise and crosswise threads per square inch) are firmer and easier to work with than fabrics with a low thread count.

The fiber content is a consideration. Cottons and linens are quite easy to work with, whereas most other fabrics require greater care in cutting, sewing, and pressing. The others are not "off limits" for the beginner, providing the type of weave does not add to the problem. Cottons are the least expensive fabrics, and most beginners feel more confident in choosing them as first projects. On the other hand, I have known students who are so challenged and intrigued by more difficult and more expensive fabric that they do better work than they do on fabric that is easily handled.

Some persons are discouraged by using a white cotton or linen fabric because it naturally soils during the construction process. And almost any beginner is discouraged by the lint picked up by very dark colors, especially black, in wool or other fuzzy fabrics. First garments might better be chosen from the middle range of colors.

Some fabrics that are easy for the beginner to work with are cotton broadcloth, butcher's linen, chambray, dimity, dress linen, stiff faille, gabardine, handkerchief linen, Indian Head, percale, poplin, seersucker, taffeta, and tweed. The beginner should avoid the following:

1 Stripes or plaids that must match and large designs that must be balanced
2 Satins, crepes, and other heavy or limp fabrics that give and stretch as they are being constructed
3 Any pile fabric, because these require special care in cutting and pressing
4 The plastic fabrics, which offer a variety of problems in construction
5 Dark colors in a woolen fabric, since woolen fabrics in these colors are most difficult to press because they are so easily marked with an iron
6 Novelty fabrics, especially in rayon, because they ravel a great deal
7 Butcher's rayons with thick threads and a low thread count because they ravel considerably
8 Sheers because all seams and darts show on the outside and no minor mistake can be hidden
9 The fur fabrics because these are pile fabrics and create, because of their thickness, greater problems than velvet or corduroy
10 The stretch fabrics because they are in the experimental stage and because each will differ greatly, thereby creating its own problems, and each will require special testing

REVIEW
OF WISE
BUYING
PRACTICES

41

SELECTION OF
PATTERN AND FABRIC

1 Buy from a reliable department store or merchant.
2 Have a fundamental knowledge of the fabric to be purchased. Be a well-educated consumer.
3 Study any tags on the bolt of fabric and study the information on the end of the bolt. See this information for yourself. It is not advisable to ask the salesgirl for her opinion on matters of importance (such as "Do you think this fabric will shrink?"), for she may not be a good judge. Do not ask her such questions as "Is this fabric Sanforized?" A verbal assurance is not a guarantee.
4 Check the width of the fabric yourself before it is cut from the bolt. The salesgirl could make a mistake between 35- and 39-inch fabric.
5 Examine the fabric as it is being measured for flaws, sun shading (if the piece has been in the window), wrinkles, etc. This should be done before a length is cut from the bolt.
6 Examine the fabric for the quality of tentering.
7 Buy additional fabric (over and above the amount stated in the yardage chart) for matching plaid or balancing large designs, for straightening poorly tentered fabric, and in order to allow for shrinkage.

SELECTION
OF
LINING
FABRICS

NOTE A chart to aid in selection of linings and other supporting fabrics appears on page 49.

PURPOSES OF A LINING

The purposes of a lining are many and varied. Understanding the reasons for using a lining will strengthen the reader's ability to select an appropriate lining for a particular fabric and use. These purposes are listed below with a few examples which will serve as a guide for wise selection of lining fabrics.

1 **to add body and weight to limp fabrics** A smooth cotton (such as percale) can be used to line shorts or slacks made of dress-weight fabrics to give these fabrics the body and weight of a heavier fabric, like tarpoon cloth, that is more suitable for these garments. The added weight of a sheath lining in a silk dress will allow the silk to hang more beautifully, especially in a slim skirt.

2 **to prevent wrinkles** The layer of lining fabric acts as a cushion to reduce creasing as it is worn or folded for packing.

3 **to prevent stretching** If the lining is a firmly woven fabric that will not stretch appreciably, it will help prevent woolens, crepes, and knits from stretching with wear. Skirt sections of a garment are most in need of lining to serve this purpose. Any garment or any portion of a garment (the fitted midriff section) that will fit close to the body will retain its shape better if lined with a firm fabric of proper weight and texture.

4 **to give greater comfort; to feel pleasant next to the body** Any scratchy, rough fabric (such as the drapery fabrics) will be less irritating to skin if lined with a soft

fabric. One whose skin is irritated by a particular fabric (many are somewhat allergic to wool) may wear that fabric comfortably if it is lined.

5 **to enhance the appearance of sheers**   A lining of soft crepe in skin-color beige under a sheer or lace fabric creates a bare-underneath illusion that is often desirable for evening wear. A lining of any color under a sheer hides the unattractive effect of slip and bra straps. A colored lining under a sheer or lace can create a variety of moods. For example, contrast the psychological effect of black lace over rich red and over pale blue.

6 **to double as an interfacing as an aid to building a silhouette**   Silk organza can be used to line the bouffant skirt of a silk dress, thereby serving a lining-interfacing purpose. Taffeta used in an A-line skirt will hold the silhouette line and will have the smooth surface one likes in a lining.

7 **to add to the aesthetic appeal of the costume**   The lining in a skirt or dress, even if it is hidden from the public view, is a means of personal satisfaction to the wearer. If the wearer gets a "lift" from her favorite color as she slips on a dress, her confidence while wearing the dress is increased. The lining of a coat or jacket is a part of the costume and must be selected with as much thought as is given to the selection of the coat fabric itself. The lining in coats and jackets (and the special lining for dresses and skirts discussed in Chapter 27) hides raw seams in the garment and adds tremendously to its beauty.

BUYING HINTS

1 Preshrink lining fabrics under the identical circumstances under which they will be laundered or dry-cleaned. Buy an extra ⅛ yard to compensate for possible loss in yardage.

2 The following general rule for selection is an extremely important one: Select a lining that will be subordinate to the fabric of the garment; this means that it should be lighter in weight and of a softer hand so that it will not dominate the character of the costume. A wool dress should look and act like wool, crepe should be soft and drapable, and lace should behave as it is expected to behave. If a garment is lined with a fabric that is stiffer and heavier, the resulting costume takes on the character of the stiffer, heavier fabric. I elaborate this point because so many garments on the ready-to-wear market are lined in taffeta that it is no wonder the average customer follows that lead, but the truth is that taffeta is used not because it is a wise choice, but because it is inexpensive and easy to manage under manufacturing conditions. Examples of lining fabrics that will be subordinate are (*a*) sheath lining, a limp, firmly woven but lightweight fabric which is made of rayon or silk for soft woolens, lace, and sheers and which is made of cotton for washables of light to medium weights; (*b*) medium to heavy crepe (soft, drapable, less firmly woven) for use with heavy woolens, velvets, etc.; and (*c*) a limp satin for use in jackets and coats.

EXCEPTION TO THE GENERAL RULE   If, in addition, the lining is to act like an interfacing to build out a silhouette, then it must have the dominant character of taffeta, etc.

3 Select a lining fabric that feels pleasant to the touch—a smooth, soft fabric, whether it is cotton, rayon, or silk. The

feel of the lining is especially important in a jacket or coat, but it adds a pleasurable sensation in all garments.

4 Select a lining fabric that is not sticky, that will hang freely on the body, and that will not adhere to girdle or slips. This is a more important consideration for the jacket or coat that must slip on and off easily; in these garments a somewhat slippery surface is desirable. The rayon sheath linings are ideal for this reason, whereas cotton tends to cling. I do not recommend silk linings in dresses and skirts because they are very sticky; most persons find them sticky to the touch as well.

5 Select a lining that will "keep pace" with the garment. The lining must last the lifetime of the garment, and it is a foolish economy to buy a low-quality lining that may shred and pull out at the seams and shorten the life of the garment. Replacement of a dress or skirt lining done by the traditional method (caught in the seams of the garment) is all but impossible; the jacket or coat lining is easily replaced by comparison. The thin, sleazy sheath lining offered at the lowest price on the market is acceptable for lightweight garments but will not withstand heavy wear or the pull against heavy fabric. A good test of wearing qualities can be made before purchase. Scrape your fingernail hard against the threads near the cut edge; hold it up to the light to see whether the threads have shifted and separated noticeably, for if they have, the lining is not a wise purchase. Not only must the lining keep pace in wearing qualities, but it also must be consistent aesthetically with the garment itself. The obviously cheap lining, especially in a jacket or coat, is a very expensive mistake; if the lining cheapens a $50 suit to the $25 standard (and it can do just that), the lining was expensive indeed.

6 If the lining is to be of contrasting color or a design or plaid, test the lining fabric under the fabric of the garment. If the garment is to be made of a loosely woven fabric or a lightweight fabric or if it is in a pastel color, the lining may show through appreciably. One must be especially careful of a design or plaid underneath a fabric of light color; differences in intensity of color in the design are apt to cast a muddy, spotted appearance over the garment.

7 If the lining is to control stretch, put pressure on the fabric in both the lengthwise and the crosswise directions by pulling it firmly between the hands. The crepes, although attractive and pleasant to the touch, will stretch more than firmly woven, flat fabrics.

8 Buy a lining of good quality but do not feel that it must be expensive. For example, good-quality rayon sheath lining is about one-half the price of a comparable silk and every bit as good (I prefer it). The only thing silk has in its favor, in my opinion, is snob appeal. Likewise, one of the highest-quality rayon crepe or satin linings for suits or coats will be less expensive than the least expensive silks and would be a wiser choice. It is wiser to put additional money into quality fabric for the garment and to buy a high-quality lining in the medium price range.

9 Be practical but do not neglect the aesthetic appeal of the lining. Have fun, be imaginative. Reread page 6 and try your wings.

THE BONDED FABRICS

A limited number of fabrics are available with a lining fabric bonded to the fabric from which the garment will be cut; one very popular one is an inexpensive flannel in a wide range of attractive colors with a bonded lining of an identical color. This idea has obvious advantages but these fabrics are recommended only with reservations. However, they serve some uses well. Obviously they quicken and simplify the construction process. They are quite acceptable for staple skirts, slacks, and shorts. But these fabrics separate sometimes in cleaning (or sections of the total area separate), and they have other disadvantages. The seams and hems will be bulky and must necessarily remain so, whereas the separate lining seams can be staggered to decrease bulk. Furthermore, there are many areas in a garment where a lining is not needed and is not desirable (collars, cuffs, pocket flaps, facings). This fabric can serve to illustrate that the consumer must always be wary of the new idea that sounds so wonderful on the surface; each time an innovation appears on the market, the wise consumer will think the whole problem through carefully before deciding to buy.

SELECTION
OF
INTERFACING
FABRICS

An interfacing is an underfacing—an extra piece of fabric that will lie between the facing and the outer section of the garment. It is not usually cut of the fabric of the garment but is cut from some fabric that is strong, stiff, and firm, because the main purpose of an interfacing is to add stiffness, strength, and body to the fabric. Although an interfacing is hidden from view, it plays a leading role in the ultimate success of a garment.

PURPOSES OF AN INTERFACING

1 **to keep the fabric of the garment from stretching** Some fabrics stretch more than others; outstanding examples are crepes, woolens, and jerseys, but almost any fabric will stretch somewhat under constant strain. Naturally, stretching causes a misfit, so it must be prevented. Use of an interfacing at those places on a garment (such as neck and front edges, pocket edges, etc.) where strain will occur will prevent stretching and increase the beauty and usefulness of the garment.

2 **to add stiffness and body to limp fabrics** Such fabrics as voile, batiste, tissue gingham, lace, etc., need extra weight to enhance their natural beauty. Although sheer fabric is lovely, it must not be too limp. These fabrics are interfaced in those portions of the garment where limpness is a liability. The most outstanding example of this purpose of an interfacing is net interfacing used in lace garments—often an entire bodice and even whole sections of a skirt are interfaced to give more strength and body to the lace.

3 **to add stiffness and body to certain portions of a garment** Most collars and cuffs and pocket flaps must be stiff and perky to give the desired effect. Sometimes an entire pocket or yoke must be stiffened so that it will give the flat, firm effect desired. Belts and waistbands must be stiff and firm as well as strong, so they are always interfaced. Sometimes whole skirts are interfaced to add stiffness for a more *bouffant* effect.

4 **to act as a cushion for bulky seams** If a seam is bulky, it will show an unattrac-

tive ridge on the right side when it is pressed. A bumpy, bulky seam edge is unprofessional-looking and detracts seriously from the beauty of the finished garment. The seams of a heavy fabric are more bulky of course, so an interfacing is essential to cushion those seams from the garment. Bound buttonholes are necessarily bulky, so an interfacing is always used in any portion of the garment where bound buttonholes appear.

5 **to build an unusual silhouette** An unusual silhouette is any line that differs from, and stands out from, the body. The A-line and the bell-shaped skirts are good examples. Such a line must stand out from the body, and most fabrics must be supported with a stiff, firm fabric to retain such an unusual silhouette. It may be just one section of a garment that stands away from the body—then that section must be interfaced. The use of an interfacing in an entire skirt is another example of building an unusual silhouette with an interfacing foundation.

SUITABLE INTERFACING FABRICS

NOTE A chart to aid in selection of interfacings and other supporting fabrics appears on page 49.

There are a variety of fabrics that may be used for interfacing. They will all have two qualities in common: they will be firm and closely woven, so that they can keep the garment from stretching, and they will add a certain amount of stiffness. The heavier the fabric of the garment, the heavier the interfacing must be in order to hold the fabric in place and support its weight. Following is a list of good interfacing fabrics with suggestions for the use of each.

lawn This is a sheer, lightweight, but firm cotton fabric. Since it is washable, it

is excellent to use for sheer washables such as batiste, voile, tissue gingham, and lightweight chambray. It can be used for other sheer, lightweight fabrics such as net, Bemberg, crepes, etc.

nylon net Nylon net is a washable net which retains most of its crispness through washing and dry cleaning. Nylon net can be used for any of the fabrics listed under "Lawn" and, in addition, is excellent to interface lace and sheer nylon fabrics.

NOTE Cotton net loses its crispness when washed or dry-cleaned, and therefore it is not acceptable as an interfacing. However, nylon net will melt or fuse under high temperatures, so it should not be used for those cottons or linens which need extreme temperatures.

muslin Muslin is a firm cotton fabric made in a plain weave. There are many grades and weights of muslin, and for that reason it is one of the most adaptable fabrics for interfacing. The lightweight muslins give body and firmness to the fabric but will not add stiffness. Heavier weights can be used for suits and coats. Muslin interfacings should be preshrunk.

hair canvas Hair canvas is a firm fabric with hair added to give it extra crispness and stiffness. This fabric is not usually used in a washable garment, but it dry cleans exceptionally well. It is one of the better interfacings for wool dresses, suits, and coats. Lightweight canvas is available in a dress weight, and some of them can be washed.

all-wool (or wool with a small percentage of goat's hair) hair canvas This hair canvas has many of the qualities of the traditional cotton canvas but is more pliable and takes a softer roll; it is available in more than one weight, but in general it is lighter in weight than its cotton counterpart. It is lovely to work with and is especially desirable for softly tailored wool costumes. However, it is about double the price of cotton canvas, and usually the additional cost is warranted only for the person whose skill has developed to a couturier level.

NOTE If wool hair canvas is used as a complete interfacing in a jacket or coat, it adds warmth to the garment and serves as an interlining.

nonwoven interfacings These fabrics have struck the public fancy, and consequently too many persons buy them without considering any other interfacing. This is regrettable, for these are dominant fabrics which will tend to make the resulting costume act like the interfacing rather than allowing it to retain the character of the fabric of the garment. For this reason their use is limited to those circumstances when a dominant interfacing is required—for example, to build out a bell-like silhouette. These fabrics do not mold to the body and tend to show a hard line at cut edges. They are ideal when a flat, firm effect is required, for example, in French cuffs, band trims, and waistbands or belts.

miscellaneous interfacing fabrics There are many excellent interfacings on the market, known to the customer by trade names, and of course there will be new ones introduced each year. The best way to become acquainted with these fabrics is to browse through the selection in the store, testing all the fabrics in the hand and in combination with the fabric to be used for the garment. Read the information on the bolt for details and special features; also, an informed sales staff should be prepared to answer questions about new fabrics. One such fabric on the market at present, known by the trade name Siri, comes in three weights for various uses and is an excellent interfacing. Undercurrent is a new interfacing fabric that promises to be very effective.

INTERFACINGS WITH SPECIAL FEATURES

1 "Iron-on" interfacings are available in woven and nonwoven types; one is made especially for use with wools. These interfacings have a gluelike back which will adhere to fabric under heat and pressure. The advantages are (*a*) the interfacing need not be basted into place if accurate work is done at the ironing board and (*b*) two fabrics bonded together to act as one are slightly stiffer than the same two fabrics handled independently. The disadvantages are (*a*) slippery fabrics are more difficult to manage at the ironing board, so press-on methods may result in less accuracy than basted methods; (*b*) if a wrinkle is accidentally pressed in the interfacing or the fabric of the garment, the mistake cannot always be corrected; (*c*) these interfacings do not adhere to all fabrics, and sometimes certain areas do not adhere; (*d*) the interfacing may separate with continued washing or dry cleaning; and (*e*) these interfacings are not suitable for loosely woven or thin fabrics.

2 The nonwoven interfacings are made with a bias feature, which is a misnomer, for a nonwoven fabric does not have a bias direction. This feature, which is claimed to make the nonwovens more

pliable, is questionable in my mind. If pliability is required, it seems advisable to use a pliable woven interfacing.

3 As this book is being written, a new interfacing concept is under consideration. Discussion must be limited other than to state that it is a woven interfacing which will be "cut on the bias"—in other words, a strip of bias. It is intended for use in stretch fabrics and promises to be excellent for knits or any garment in which weight or body is required and stretch control is not.

BUYING HINTS

1 Have the interfacing to be used in washable garments preshrunk under the identical circumstances under which the garment will be washed and dried. The professional drycleaning process will not shrink interfacing fabrics.

2 Reread step 2 on page 42, which emphasizes that lining, and interfacing fabrics as well, should ideally be subordinate fabrics. With this rule in mind, be wary of choosing a nonwoven interfacing because it tends to dominate even in the lighter weight and even with the so-called bias feature. Examples of good interfacing fabrics that are subordinate are (a) all-wool hair canvas for a softly tailored wool dress, (b) lightweight muslin or percale in medium-weight cotton garments and heavier-weight muslin in medium-weight woolens, and (c) a firm voile in wool chiffon or in silk or rayon crepe.

EXCEPTION TO THE GENERAL RULE If the interfacing is to be used to build out a silhouette, a more dominant fabric (one of the nonwovens, for example) should be chosen.

3 If the garment is to be made of a loosely woven fabric of any color, of a lightweight fabric, or in a light color, the color of the interfacing becomes an issue. Test to see whether color shows through. In-

terfacing fabrics are black, white, or a natural beige. However, lightweight cotton dress fabric, cotton percale, Undercurrent, and Indian Head are available in a full color range, and one of these four fabrics will solve most interfacing problems.

4 The interfacing plays a leading role in ultimate success, but even so, it need not be expensive. For example, hair canvas is more expensive in two ways (it costs more per yard and is narrower in width) than muslin; there are circumstances under which hair canvas is the wiser choice, but on the other hand, muslin is adequate for almost every purpose.

5 The complete interfacing (underlining or backing) discussed in Chapter 13 is an exciting, relatively recent idea imported from the fertile minds of Parisian designers. Some patterns plan for it and state yardage amounts for it (surely more and more will), but others state the lesser yardage for the traditional interfacing method. If the customer intends to do the complete interfacing in a pattern that has not planned for it, she will need to do a layout to determine yardage (see page 96).

SPECIAL NOTE Vogue patterns feature the complete interfacing and refer to it as "backing." Almost all the Paris Original and International Couturier jackets are completely backed, or interfaced. Vogue intends the backing for jackets to be a relatively lightweight interfacing, and then an additional heavier fabric is used for a traditional interfacing, in addition to the backing. The heavier interfacing, used just for portions of the garment, is referred to as "interfacing" on the envelope back. If the garment is a dress, the backing, as suggested by Vogue, should be a firm lining fabric rather than an interfacing fabric because in dresses, the backing in Vogue patterns doubles as a lining.

SELECTION
OF
UNDERLINING
FABRICS

NOTE These are also referred to as "backing" or "complete interfacing." A chart to aid in selection of underlinings and other supporting fabrics appears on page 49.

There is a fine line of distinction between the supporting fabrics which are interfacings, underlinings, or linings. An interfacing adds body, and so does an underlining, but in general, the typical interfacing might add slightly more body and more stiffness than the underlining; this is true in dresses when the interfacing is perhaps heavier and stiffer than the underlining for a dress. However, the jacket might be completely interfaced, in which case the interfacing itself becomes an underlining, and so the interfacing serves both purposes. In this case the complete interfacing is cut and constructed in exactly the same manner as the underlining.

This same fine line of distinction exists between underlinings and linings. The underlining, if cut of a smooth, silky fabric, provides additional body and, at the same time, acts as a lining. In this case the construction techniques used are identical, for in each case the supporting fabric (whether it is called an "underlining" or a "lining") is basted to pieces of the garment before construction begins.

It is impossible to make a definite statement of the differences among the three supporting fabrics, but in general, it is safe to say that the underlining is quite light in weight compared with the fabric and that its main function is to add a small amount of body to the fabric of the garment. But one must keep in mind that the purpose of the underlining can be modified and extended to achieve the desired results.

EXPLANATION
OF CHART
FOR SELECTION
OF SUPPORTING FABRICS

The chart on page 49 should be an aid in the selection of all supporting fabrics. The reader will notice that there is an overlapping of suggestions, which is understandable because the functions of these supporting fabrics will be in many cases similar and in some cases identical.

SELECTION OF SUPPORTING FABRICS

	INTERFACING	UNDERLINING (backing, complete interfacing)	LINING
WEIGHT			
light	lawn, batiste, lightweight muslin, permanent-finish organdy, nylon net, same fabric as garment if garment is washable	China silk; rayon marquisette; lightweight sheath lining in cotton, rayon, or silk; nylon net; nylon sheer; Siri; Undercurrent	China silk, acetates in lightweight sheath linings, soft cottons for washables, Siri with smooth finish
medium	dress-weight hair canvas, wool hair canvas, medium-weight muslin, percale	lightweight muslin, percale, same fabric as garment if garment is washable	acetates in medium-weight crepes, satins, or twill; satin-back crepe; silk satin or crepe
heavy	heavy-weight muslin, Indian Head, heavyweight hair canvas	any of the interfacings listed at the left if extra body is desired	any of the linings listed for medium-weight fabrics; also Milium if warmth is desired; for novel effects, brocades, quilted fabrics, or fur fabrics
CHARACTER			
subordinate— to add body	any of the above when used combined with a fabric slightly heavier in weight	any of the above when combined with a fabric slightly heavier in weight	any of the above when combined with a fabric slightly heavier in weight
dominant—to create shape and build silhouette	any of the above when combined with a fabric slightly lighter in weight also nonwoven interfacings	any of the above when combined with a fabric slightly lighter in weight also nonwoven interfacings and taffeta	any of the above when combined with a fabric slightly lighter in weight; also taffeta
COLOR			
if fabric is firmly woven	of little consequence; white, natural, or black acceptable	of little consequence; white, natural, or black acceptable	matter of personal choice, but it must match the color of the garment if fabric is loosely woven and if no underlining is used
if fabric is loosely woven	should match in color; use batiste, percale, Indian Head	should match in color; use batiste, sheath lining, percale, Indian Head, Undercurrent	

PREPARATION
OF
FABRIC
FOR
CUTTING

BASIC
TERMS

There are certain basic terms that will be used frequently in many connections in clothing construction. See Figure 1. The meanings of these terms should be memorized and should become a working part of your vocabulary.

selvedge The selvedge (sometimes spelled "selvage") is the finished edge of the fabric running lengthwise on the bolt of fabric. There is a selvedge on both lengthwise edges of woven fabric. The selvedge is woven differently, with stronger threads than the rest of the fabric. In good fabric the selvedge is about ½ inch wide and very firmly woven, while on the other hand in poor fabric it is narrow and more loosely woven.

lengthwise threads These are the threads running parallel to the selvedge. The lengthwise threads are stronger as a rule than the crosswise threads, and for this reason garments are cut in such a way that the lengthwise threads run lengthwise on the body. The words "straight-of-material," "straight-of-fabric," and "lengthwise grain" are used on the pattern to designate the direction of the lengthwise threads. Fabrics will not stretch when pulled in a lengthwise direction.

crosswise threads These are the threads running at right angles to, or perpendicular to, the selvedge. These threads are usually slightly weaker than the lengthwise threads, although they will not stretch noticeably. Sometimes the layout will show a pattern piece laid so that the straight-of-material line lies in a crosswise direction. This is done only on pattern pieces where maximum strength is not required or if crosswise stripes are featured in the design.

true bias True bias is the diagonal of a perfect square of fabric. The bias line makes a 45-degree angle with the lengthwise and crosswise threads. The outstanding characteristic of the bias line is its elasticity. Any diagonal line on the fabric is bias and will stretch somewhat, but the maximum amount of stretch and give is obtained only with the true bias line.

TO
EVEN
FABRIC

Some fabrics can be torn from the bolt, while others must be cut. If fabrics are cut from the bolt, they should be cut carefully along a crosswise thread. However, this is time-consuming, and most

salesgirls cannot take the time required, excepting for very expensive fabrics; instead, they usually cut the fabric approximately at right angles to the selvedge with no regard for the crosswise threads. Figure 2a shows fabric cut from the bolt, and Figure 2b pictures fabric torn from the bolt. Notice that the crosswise threads in Figure 2a do not run parallel to the cut edge. This fabric must be evened as described in the next paragraph. The fabric shown in Figure 2b has been torn from the bolt, as evidenced by the fact that the crosswise threads are parallel to the torn edge and little ends of lengthwise threads extend over the torn edge. This fabric does not require evening.

METHODS OF EVENING FABRICS

There are several ways fabric might be evened, and one should choose the fastest method that will ensure satisfactory results.

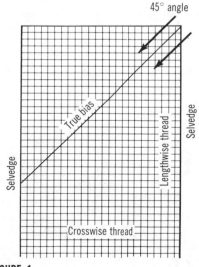

FIGURE 1

1 Very loosely woven fabrics, fabrics with a woven crosswise stripe (such as a stripe or plaid), or fabrics with some prominent crosswise threads (such as some novelty weaves) can be evened very quickly by cutting along a visible crosswise thread. These threads in a loosely woven fabric (even in a plain color) are quite easy to follow, although results may not be entirely flawless; raveling out a few threads will correct slight errors.

2 In some fabrics that are more firmly

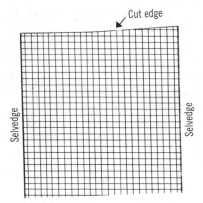

↖ Cut edge

Selvedge

Selvedge

a Fabric cut from bolt

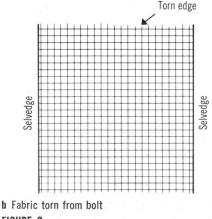

↙ Torn edge

Selvedge

Selvedge

b Fabric torn from bolt
FIGURE 2

woven, the crosswise threads can be followed quite well if the fabric is held up to the light by an assistant. One can see the threads better and, with care, can cut along the threads with reasonably accurate results. The errors can be corrected by raveling out excess threads. This method is not a wise choice unless the threads can be readily seen.

3 Clipping into a selvedge and then tearing the fabric is the very easiest and quickest method, but one should use caution because some fabrics do not tear well; in some fabrics the lengthwise threads snag and distort to damage the fabric. This method must be tested. Fabrics made in a plain weave usually tear well, whereas the novelty, jacquard, and satin weaves will be damaged by tearing.

4 The most time-consuming method but the one that is entirely safe for any fabric is pictured in Figure 3. Clip into the selvedge near the cut edge of the fabric through a single thickness. Pull out a crosswise thread and continue pulling it until it puckers up the fabric. Then cut along this puckered line. Ravel out another thread and continue across the width of the fabric. This procedure is easy or difficult depending on the nature of the threads. A strong, smooth crosswise thread in a loosely woven fabric can be pulled for perhaps half the width before it breaks; a weak, sticky, wooly thread in a tightly woven fabric may break when the puckered line is only ½ inch long.

TO STRAIGHTEN
FABRIC—
CORRECTION
OF FABRIC GRAIN

NOTE Resin-treated fabrics cannot be straightened; they must be cut in the condition in which they were purchased.

When the fabric is evened, fold it in half lengthwise with selvedge edges together. See Figure 4. If the ends of the fabric (the crosswise threads) lie on top of each other and form a right angle with the selvedge, as they do in Figure 4a, the fabric is on grain. If the ends of the fabric miss each other and do not make a right angle with the selvedge, as seen in Figure 4b, the fabric must be straightened.

Open up the fabric and place it on a square or rectangular table; flaws of tentering will show up readily in contrast to the square corners of a table. Figure 5 pictures three examples of poorly tentered fabrics. The flaw shown in Figure 5a, in which the crosswise threads take a diagonal direction across the entire width, is most common. Figure 5b shows an example of a fabric that is in good condition in some areas but needs attention in others. Figure 5c shows crosswise threads out of line, changing direction at the center line, where the fabric was folded. By pulling along bias lines in the direction required (study the arrowed lines in the sketches), the crosswise threads can be pulled into line. Move along about 6 inches between each bias line, and always pull on the true bias line for maximum results. Test the fabric on the table top to check results; Figure 6 pictures fabric properly straightened. Sometimes fabrics must be stretched several times and the pressure increased before they are in proper condition. Any fabric can be straightened with less effort when it is wet.

Selvedges may be out of line, or fabric may have been folded inaccurately. When fabric is folded lengthwise, selvedge edges should lie on top of each other, or if they do not, they must be parallel to each other. See Figure 7. Figure 7a shows selvedges out of line, and Figure 7b pictures the correction with

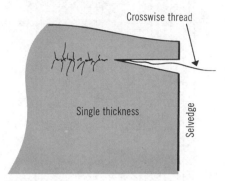

FIGURE 3

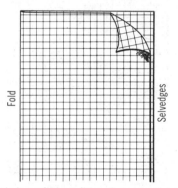

a Fabric in perfect condition. Crosswise threads at right angles to lengthwise threads.

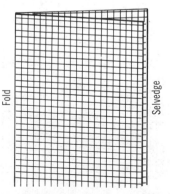

b Poorly tentered fabric that must be straightened.
FIGURE 4

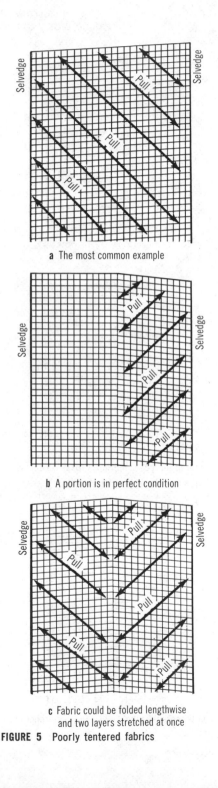

a The most common example

b A portion is in perfect condition

c Fabric could be folded lengthwise
and two layers stretched at once

FIGURE 5 Poorly tentered fabrics

all edges basted in proper position; use long (1- to 1½-inch) basting stitches.

TO
PRESHRINK
WASHABLES

Fabrics that will be laundered should be preshrunk for predictable results. Washables should be preshrunk under the identical circumstances under which the garment will be washed and dried; the strength of the soap or detergent and the temperature of the water are considerations. If the garment will be dried in an automatic dryer, the fabric should be processed in the dryer. If the fabric will be dried on a line, be sure it is hung straight, with crosswise threads along the line and selvedge edges together.

Fabric must be ironed in such a way that it remains true and straight. Place it on the ironing board with selvedge edges at right angles to the length of the board. Iron in the direction of the lengthwise threads but never push the iron in a bias direction; ironing along diagonal lines gives a pebbly, bumpy appearance to the fabric because threads have been shifted out of line.

TO
PRESHRINK
WOOLENS

Many good-quality woolens purchased from a reliable dealer will not shrink appreciably if professionally dry-cleaned. Some carry a label such as "ready for the needle" or "no preshrinking necessary." These statements are not entirely reliable, although certainly the fabric will shrink less than a fabric that does not carry such a label. The bargain wool from an unknown merchant should certainly be preshrunk, and it is a wise economy to preshrink all fabrics which will be dry-cleaned; the wise person who sews will take every precaution to ensure ultimate satisfaction.

Professional dry cleaners will preshrink wool at a nominal cost (50 cents per yard is average), and usually the saving in time is well worth the cost to many busy women. Prepare the fabric for preshrinking by evening and straightening it and basting ends and selvedges together. The home process includes rolling the woolen in a wet sheet and allowing it to remain for about eight hours and then pressing the fabric. Read Chapter 17, Pressing Techniques. The large-surface irons at the professional shop ensure a more satisfying result than home pressing with the smaller iron.

NOTE The coin-operated drycleaning machines may use a stronger cleaning solution than the pro-

fessional dry cleaner. If garments will be cleaned by self-service, preshrink the fabric by the same method

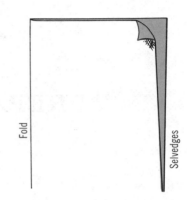

a Selvedges not parallel; fabric inaccurately folded

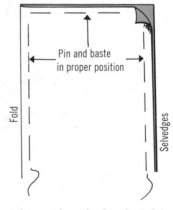

b Corrections made and edges basted in proper position

FIGURE 7

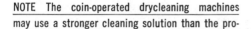

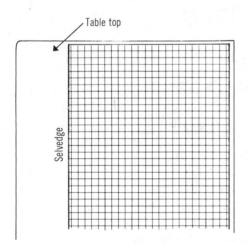

FIGURE 6

PREPARATION
OF
PATTERN
FOR
CUTTING
AND
PATTERN
ALTERATIONS

There is something so exciting about a
new pattern and new fabric that it is no
wonder if you simply cannot wait to get
started. Probably like most people you
will have an almost uncontrollable urge
to "get it cut out today." It would be
wonderful if one could get off to exciting
business on this first wave of enthusiasm. But if you do cut the pattern without preliminaries, the discouragement
and difficulties in fitting which might
arise later will be magnified. Clothing
construction is a delight from beginning
to end if it is done each step of the way
so that the whole project (from cutting

to fitting and finishing) moves along smoothly and successfully. The preparation of the pattern is very essential, and although the measuring and pattern alteration described here will take some amount of time now, these preliminaries will save time and trouble in the long run.

GENERAL SUGGESTIONS

1 Sort out the pattern pieces and place them in logical piles—skirt pieces, bodice pieces, lining pieces, etc., together. Separate those pieces which are not required in the view you are using, fold them up, and put them back in the envelope. There is a statement or a listing of pattern pieces for each view on the layout side of the instruction sheet. Check this list very carefully.

2 Pattern pieces should be pressed with a warm iron to remove the creases; this makes for more accurate cutting. Pattern pieces should be hung over a hanger as soon as they are pressed and should not be folded up again until the fabric is cut.

3 Any pattern piece that is not cut on the fold has a straight-of-material line indicated. This straight-of-material line will be placed on the lengthwise threads of the fabric. It is indicated with a printed line about 5 or 6 inches long. It will be advantageous later if this line is as long as possible. So place a yardstick along the line or the perforations and extend the straight-of-material line to the edges of the pattern (Figure 1). Do this on all pattern pieces.

4 If you are working in a room with a group of friends or in a classroom, put your name on each pattern piece.

NOTE The cutting line on the pattern is a solid line, the heaviest line on the pattern. The seam-

lines, usually ⅝ inch inside the cutting lines, are drawn in broken lines. Each pattern piece will have an excess margin (see Figure 1, in which the margin is shown in broken lines) which is not part of the pattern but merely an aid for accurate work in the manufacturing process. Do not take time to trim off this margin; it will fall away as the fabric is cut. For the sake of clarity, these margins will not be pictured hereafter.

TAKING BODY MEASUREMENTS

See Figure 2. Body measurements should be taken over the undergarments that will be worn with the costume. The tape measure should be held flat against the body for snug, but not tight, measurement. The tape should be parallel to the floor. Whether someone takes these measurements for you (recommended) or you do it yourself in front of the mirror, accurate measurements will result only if the body is viewed from both the front and

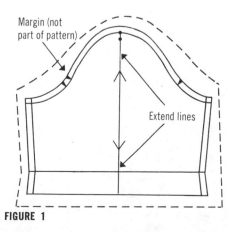

Margin (not part of pattern)

Extend lines

FIGURE 1

the side to check the position of the tape measure. If you have someone assisting you, she should work at eye level for even more accurate results. The 3-inch hipline is especially difficult to measure because of the rounded contours in this portion of the body; it is necessary to be very careful that the tape does not slip up in the back.

Three measurement and alteration charts are included: a dress chart (page 66), a skirt chart adaptable to shorts and slacks (page 65), and a jacket or coat chart (page 67). A copy of the appropriate chart should be made for each garment to be constructed; the classroom teacher will probably want to run off mimeographed copies. Select the appropriate chart and record body measurements in parts 2 and 3 of the chart.

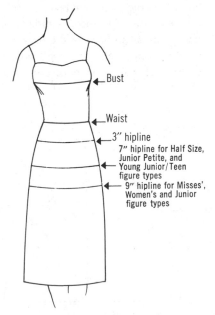

FIGURE 2

EXPLANATION OF MEASUREMENT AND ALTERATION CHARTS

If patterns are properly tested on the figure and accurate body measurements are compared with measurements of the pattern, it is possible to figure pattern alteration so that little or no fitting is required. By keeping a record of alterations made and making notes of recommended changes in future garments, it is possible to attain such accuracy that women with problem figures can eventually sew without basting, if basic lines remain somewhat similar. Fitting is the most difficult step in clothing construction for the experienced person and the novice (and the author), so every care should be taken to make fitting easier. Pattern measurement and alteration are not easy and are time-consuming, especially when one wants to "get on with it," but alterations are infinitely easier than fitting and should not be carelessly done.

The measurement and alteration charts are divided into three parts:

part 1 Pattern measurements involved with length and proportion are checked, not really by measurement, but by pinning the pattern together and testing it on the figure. This method is never used as a test for width or allover size because the paper will not bend around the body to give an accurate test.

part 2 Some measurement involved with width or size can be checked by comparison with the body-measurement chart. The chart includes body measurements for the bust, waist, and 7-inch or 9-inch hipline (see Figure 2).

part 3 Certain important measurements in width and allover size must be made by measuring the actual pattern because no comparable measurement is stated in the measurement chart. The 3-inch hip-line and the biceps line of the sleeve must be checked by measuring the pattern.

PART 1: TESTS ON THE FIGURE

pinning the pattern together Bodice pieces, skirt pieces, and sleeve pieces must be pinned together as they will be sewn; if in doubt, look through the instruction sheet for the construction order. Pin in the darts and fold in the tucks and pleats. Turn under one shoulder edge on the seamline and lap it to the seamline of the corresponding shoulder.

CAUTION A common mistake is to fold along the cutting line and bring it to the corresponding cutting line. This mistake is caused by the worker confusing the excess margin with the seam allowance.

Pin in the hems along designated hemlines in sleeves and skirts. Pin the underarm seam of the sleeve but do not pin the underarm seams of the bodice and skirt; the pattern, if pinned at the sides, will not shape around the body well. If the design has a high, round neckline, clip into the seam allowance at the neck edge to allow the pattern to "hug up" to the neck. Do not pin the bodice and skirt together because they can be tested more easily separately. Do not pin sleeve in armhole.

The tests on the figure should be done over the undergarments that will be worn with the garment. Put a tape measure around your waist; the lower edge of the tape will designate the waist position.

tests for the bodice, jacket, or coat Have an assistant hold the pattern to your body, observing the following precautions: the shoulder line must lie on the

top of the shoulder, the center-front and center-back lines should be in the proper position, and the neckline should fit the neck in the way it was intended for the particular design. The assistant should grasp one hand firmly over the shoulder so that the pattern cannot shift while the tests are made.

NOTE The following directions for testing the position of the waistline are written for the smooth-fitted garment. Some designs have extra length and are intended to blouse. If so, extra length should be allowed for blousing.

1 Smooth the pattern down over the front and bust area and notice the position of the waist seamline (seamline, not cutting line). Compare it with the position of the lower edge of the tape. This test will determine whether the bodice-front length must be altered. Estimate the alteration and record it on the chart.

2 If there is an underarm dart, it should be on a level with the high point of the bust. If it falls above or below the bust, record the required alteration on the chart.

3 Being careful to keep the pattern on the shoulder in the same position, smooth the back pattern down over the shoulders in the center-back area. Notice the position of the waist seamline (seamline, not cutting line) and compare it with the position of the lower edge of the tape. This test will determine alterations required for back length. Estimate the alteration and record it on the measurement chart.

NOTE Other features that have to do with proportion (pocket flaps, band trims, etc.) can be pinned in place and examined for effect at this time.

tests for the sleeve These tests have a certain margin of error, but it is not great and is no greater than that of any other method that might be used to test sleeve length. Have an assistant slip the sleeve over your arm and bring it up to the position it should take (this is the margin of error)—try to hold the seamline in the sleeve cap in the position it will take on the body.

NOTE Sleeves that gather to a cuff must have sufficient length to allow for the bloused effect. The cuff should be pinned on the sleeve during this test to ensure the desired results.

1 With the hem pinned up, study the total sleeve length and if in doubt about the effect, experiment with different lengths at this time. Record the desired alteration on the chart.
2 If this is a fitted sleeve, there will probably be an elbow dart. It must be located at the elbow level to give shape for the elbow. Bend your arm slightly so that your assistant can test the dart position. Record the estimated alteration on the chart.

tests for skirts, slacks, and shorts Wear shoes with a heel height like that of the shoes you will wear with the garment. Have an assistant hold the skirt pattern to your body so that the seamline at the waistline (seamline, not cutting line) rests on the lower edge of the tape.

1 With the hem pinned up, study the skirt length and if in doubt, experiment with different lengths at this time. Record the desired alteration on the chart.

2 Shorts or slacks must be tested for total length and also for length of the crotch seam. Tuck the pattern between your legs; the crotch seam should fall about 2 inches below the body. These patterns may need alteration in length in the torso area. Estimate the alteration, do the alteration, and retest on the figure for accuracy.

PART 2: COMPARISONS WITH THE BODY-MEASUREMENT CHART
This part of the chart is very easy to fill in, for it involves merely a comparison of measurements and then figuring the differences for the required alterations. The two following points need clarification.

concerning waist measurement The chart states that waist measurements should not be decreased by pattern alteration. This does not mean that the waist will remain too large in the finished garment; it simply means that the waist will be adjusted by fitting rather than by pattern alteration.

concerning the hipline measurement Hip measurements in the body measurement charts refer to the fullest part of the hip —7 inches below the waist for shorter figure types (Half Sizes, Junior Petites, and Young Junior/Teens) and 9 inches below the waist for longer torso figure types (Misses', Women's, and Juniors).

If every figure were average, comparison of the three measurements in the measurement chart with actual body measurements would establish pattern alterations. Average figures gradually taper from bust to waist and then curve out to the fullest part of the hip. For these figures, pattern alterations at bust, waist, and full-hip level would take care of all problems.

However, individual figures present serious problems not indicated by measurements at these three levels. The fullest part of the hip may not be at the same level as on the average figure. In bell-shaped figures, full-hip measurements may be 3 inches below the waist, requiring alteration at that level. Protruding hipbones or pads of fat create similar problems between the waist and lower hip levels. A short torso figure (Half Size, Junior Petite, Young Junior/Teen) may have thigh problems requiring alteration below the measurement chart's 7-inch hip level. If so, the short person must consider even lower hipline measurement. A roll of fat in the midriff area will cause alteration problems not indicated by the three measurements on the body measurement charts. Larger than average arms will cause sleeve alteration problems. It is therefore necessary to test additional levels on the pattern by comparing actual pattern measurements with body measurements.

PART 3: TESTS MADE BY TAKING ACTUAL PATTERN MEASUREMENTS

Taking actual pattern measurements (with seams, darts, tucks, and pleats folded in as they will be in the garment) is more difficult than the procedures in Parts 1 and 2. See the measurement alteration charts, pages 65–68. The figure's problem area must be measured and then recorded in the chart. Since it must allow for livability, the total measurement needed will exceed the body measurement. Body size plus livability must be recorded in the "measurement needed" column and the amount compared with the pattern's actual measurements to establish alterations. Minimum livability amounts have been indicated for the 3-inch hipline and the biceps line of the sleeve. These amounts differ with the type of garment. A 1-inch minimum at the 3-inch hipline is required for dresses or skirts; more is needed for shorts, slacks, jackets, or coats. The charts

provide space in which to record measurements of any figure level presenting problems.

the problem of style fullness The issue of style fullness as a component of pattern size was discussed earlier but bears repetition at this time. Pattern size is a result of three components: (1) body size, (2) room to live in (livability), and (3) style fullness (in some designs). The measurement and alteration charts cannot include the style-fullness factor because it varies so much from design to design. Style fullness must be given attention for each particular design and will be discussed in more detail on page 63.

to measure the actual pattern

1 Figure 3 shows the typical straight, fitted skirt which has no style fullness. This is the simplest skirt to measure and illustrates the general principles of pattern measurements. The darts, the center-back pleat, and the seam allowances have been shaded to illustrate that they are not a part of the finished size of the pattern; these are the areas that should not be measured because the garment will be sewn on those lines. The basic general rules are as follows: measure to fold lines, to pleat lines, to center lines, and to dart and tuck lines.

Most patterns are made for half the body, so all measurements must be doubled. Therefore, A plus B plus C plus D doubled equals the 3-inch hip measurement. E plus F doubled equals the 9-inch hip measurement.

Record these amounts in part 3 of each chart in the column headed Measurement of Pattern.

2 The technique of measurement is the

same regardless of the number of pieces which must be meaured. Figure 4 pictures the pattern of a typical six-gore skirt which has no style fullness.

NOTE Six-gore skirts might have style fullness at the 9-inch hipline if they are very flared designs.

The general rules are followed; note that the pattern is measured to center lines

and to seamlines only. Therefore, *G* plus *H* plus *I* plus *J* doubled equals the 3-inch hipline. *K* plus *L* plus *M* plus *N* doubled equals the 9-inch hipline.

3 The matter of style fullness complicates the problem. Figure 5 shows a skirt with style fullness created by loose tucks at the waist instead of a snug dart fitting. The dashed lines do not appear on the pattern; notice, then, that no lines appear on the pattern at the 3-inch hipline. One might measure straight across the pattern, assuming all the width was available for body and livability amounts, and this is a very common error. The impor-

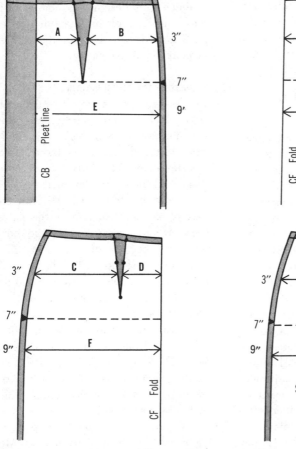

FIGURE 3 Measuring the 3- and 9-inch hiplines on a fitted skirt

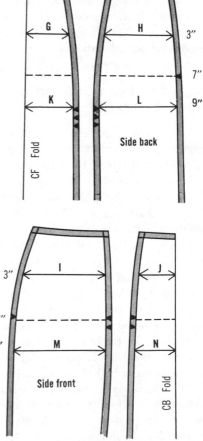

FIGURE 4 Measuring the 3- and 9-inch hiplines in the six-gore, princess-line skirt

tant thing to understand is that there must be additional size for style fullness and that if extra size is not allowed, the garment simply will not have the style it should; for example, if the style fullness of loose tucks or gathers is used for body size, the tucks or gathers poke out and form a shelf or wrinkle below the waist.

Style fullness must be folded in, thus making an allowance for it, and then the pattern must be measured for body size and livability size. In Figure 5 the tuck lines have been extended on the pattern to illustrate that loose tucks are really long darts that have simply not been sewn to the tip. Extend the tuck lines on your pattern, as shown in the sketch, to a point where the lines converge. See Figure 6. Fold in the tucks on the extended lines and pin in place; by so doing, you have made an allowance for the required style fullness. Then take measurements across the shaped pattern: line O doubled equals the front skirt measurement at the 3-inch hipline, and line P doubled equals the front measurement at the 9-inch hipline. Add this to the back skirt measurement and record this amount in part 3 of each chart in the column headed Measurement of Pattern.

It is impossible to give enough examples of style fullness to cover every possible design. The woman who sews must study a basic example (such as the skirt in Figures 5 and 6) and, using these general principles, apply them to each new situation.

4 The biceps line of the sleeve is a line at right angles to the straight-of-material line, located at the base of the sleeve cap. See Figure 7. The actual pattern measurement is taken from seamline to seamline.

The sleeve might be in two sections, as it is in the raglan sleeve or the two-piece tailored sleeve so often found in

suit and coat patterns. The principle is exactly the same. The two-piece tailored sleeve is shown in Figure 8. The base of the sleeve cap (the biceps line) begins at the underarm position in the Under

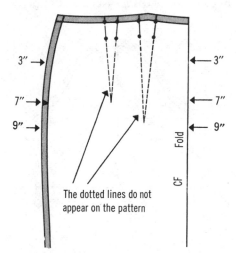

The dotted lines do not appear on the pattern

FIGURE 5 The skirt front with loose pleats for style fullness

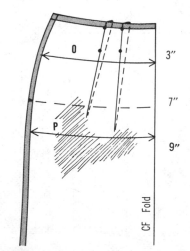

FIGURE 6 Measuring the skirt front with style fullness folded in

Sleeve section, as shown. It is at right angles to the straight-of-material line and continues across the Upper Sleeve section at the same level on the lengthwise seamlines. These two measurements combined compose the biceps measurement. Record the biceps measurement in part 3

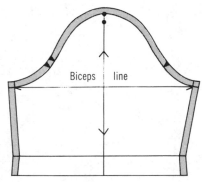

FIGURE 7 Measuring the sleeve

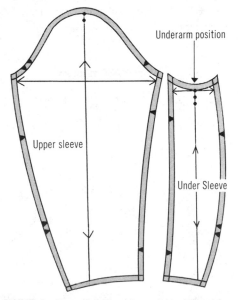

FIGURE 8 Measuring the biceps line of the two-piece sleeve

of each chart in the column headed Measurement of Pattern.

INTRODUCTION
TO
PATTERN
ALTERATIONS

If a pattern is purchased in the correct size and figure type, pattern alterations can be kept to a minimum. The alterations included here are those which (1) are required most frequently and (2) can be executed without danger of "destroying" the accuracy of the pattern. Many books will include more complicated alterations, but some are so difficult that it would take a professional patternmaker to execute them with scientific and predictable results; such alterations have not been included. "Play it safe" is a good motto for the woman who makes her own clothes. This does not mean that it is wise to cut a pattern far too large or too long, but it does mean that it is far smarter to make it a little larger and a little longer, as you first begin to sew, when you are still not sure of your requirements. Strangely enough, many persons hate to add size to a pattern, often insisting that they know they will not need it (a statement rarely fortified by fact). This is such a foolish mistake; it is so much better to add some size to the pattern as a safety measure and then baste the garment, if desired, along the original seamline of the pattern. That is playing it safe. If a garment is too small when basted for a fitting, it takes two or three times longer (or more) to make it larger than it takes to fit in a garment that is too large. The saving in time is only one issue; the garment that is "let out" is not as good or serviceable because the seams are inadequate in width.

MEASUREMENT AND ALTERATION CHART
FOR SKIRTS, SLACKS, AND SHORTS

PART 1
CHECK THE FOLLOWING BY PINNING THE PATTERN TOGETHER
AND TESTING ON THE FIGURE

	ALTERATION REQUIRED
LENGTH OF SKIRT (slacks or shorts)	lengthen or shorten? _____
LENGTH OF CROTCH SEAM (slacks and shorts)	lengthen or shorten? _____

PART 2
CHECK THE FOLLOWING BY COMPARING YOUR MEASUREMENTS
WITH THOSE GIVEN ON THE BODY–MEASUREMENT CHART

	YOUR BODY MEASUREMENT	BODY–MEASUREMENT CHART	ALTERATION REQUIRED
WAIST			increase? _____ (do not decrease by pattern alteration)
FULLEST PART OF HIP			increase or decrease? _____

PART 3
CHECK THE FOLLOWING BY TAKING ACTUAL PATTERN MEASUREMENTS

	YOUR BODY MEASUREMENT	MEASUREMENT REQUIRED	MEASUREMENT OF PATTERN	ALTERATION REQUIRED
3″ HIPLINE		your body measurement plus 1″ is _____		increase or decrease? _____
SPACE FOR INDIVIDUAL FIGURE PROBLEMS		your body measurement plus livability amount is _____		increase or decrease? _____

NOTE This chart is adaptable for slacks and shorts, but in part 3 in the column headed Measurement Required, the measurement needed is 1″ more for slacks and shorts: 2″ at the 3″ hipline unless stretch fabric is being used.

MEASUREMENT AND ALTERATION CHART
FOR DRESSES

PART 1
CHECK THE FOLLOWING BY PINNING THE PATTERN TOGETHER
AND TESTING ON THE FIGURE

	ALTERATION REQUIRED
BODICE—FRONT LENGTH	lengthen or shorten? _____
POSITION OF UNDER-ARM DART	raise or lower? _____
BODICE—BACK LENGTH	lengthen or shorten? _____
SLEEVE LENGTH	lengthen or shorten? _____
POSITION OF ELBOW DART	move up or down? _____
LENGTH OF SKIRT	lengthen or shorten? _____

PART 2
CHECK THE FOLLOWING BY COMPARING YOUR MEASUREMENTS
WITH THOSE GIVEN ON THE BODY—MEASUREMENT CHART

	YOUR BODY MEASUREMENT	BODY—MEASUREMENT CHART	ALTERATION REQUIRED
BUST			increase or decrease? _____
WAIST			increase? _____ (do not decrease by pattern alteration)
FULLEST PART OF HIP			increase or decrease? _____

PART 3

CHECK THE FOLLOWING BY TAKING ACTUAL PATTERN MEASUREMENTS

	YOUR BODY MEASUREMENT	MEASUREMENT REQUIRED	MEASUREMENT OF PATTERN	ALTERATION REQUIRED
3″ HIPLINE		your body measurement plus 1″ is_____		increase or decrease?_____
SPACE FOR INDIVIDUAL FIGURE PROBLEMS		your body measurement plus livability amount is _____		increase or decrease?_____
BICEPS LINE OF SLEEVE		your body measurement plus 2″ is_____		increase or decrease?_____

MEASUREMENT AND ALTERATION CHART
FOR JACKETS AND COATS

PART 1

**CHECK THE FOLLOWING BY PINNING THE PATTERN TOGETHER
AND TESTING ON THE FIGURE**

	ALTERATION REQUIRED
POSITION OF WAISTLINE	lengthen or shorten above waist?_____
POSITION OF UNDER-ARM DART	raise or lower?_____
SLEEVE LENGTH	lengthen or shorten?_____
POSITION OF ELBOW DART	move up or down?_____
LENGTH OF JACKET OR COAT	lengthen or shorten?_____
POSITION OF POCKETS	move up or down?_____

PART 2
CHECK THE FOLLOWING BY COMPARING YOUR MEASUREMENTS
WITH THOSE GIVEN ON THE BODY–MEASUREMENT CHART

	YOUR BODY MEASUREMENT	BODY–MEASUREMENT CHART	ALTERATION REQUIRED
BUST			increase or decrease?_____
WAIST			increase?_____ (do not decrease by pattern alteration)
FULLEST PART OF HIP			increase or decrease?_____

PART 3
CHECK THE FOLLOWING BY TAKING ACTUAL PATTERN MEASUREMENTS

	YOUR BODY MEASUREMENT	MEASUREMENT REQUIRED	MEASUREMENT OF PATTERN	ALTERATION REQUIRED
3″ HIPLINE		your body measurement plus a minimum of 2″ is_____		increase or decrease?_____
SPACE FOR INDIVIDUAL FIGURE PROBLEMS		your body measurement plus livability amount is _____		increase or decrease?_____
BICEPS LINE OF SLEEVE		your body measurement plus a minimum of 2″ is_____		increase or decrease?_____

NOTE   The amounts listed in part 3 in the column headed Measurement Required are absolute minimums. Many coats and jackets will require more size, especially if they are loose and boxy.

Keeping records of pattern alterations and their results is the way to perfect your requirements. If this is done for several garments, your requirements will be established to such an extent that you need not go through any of the pattern-measurement steps. One of my students with a problem figure was able, over a period of time, to make such accurate pattern alterations that she could sew without basting or fitting. She worked scientifically and kept records for perhaps four or five garments, and then she "had her number." And this girl truly had a problem figure. She was a size 16 in the bust and had no shoulder problems, but she had a thick waist, and as I remember, she had to add 4 inches at the waist. Her hips required an additional 6 inches, and she was short-waisted. Her scientific techniques resulted in a tremendous saving of time in the lifetime of sewing she will do. I tell this story to illustrate that scientific pattern alterations, although time-consuming now, are an important investment in economy of time over the long run.

Pattern alterations solve problems of length and width or of overall size; in contrast, fitting is involved with the more difficult problems of shape. The alterations included here are treated in four sections: the first section covers alterations in length; the second, alterations in width; the third, alterations for upper arms and shoulder height; and the fourth (more advanced and complicated), pattern alterations involved with changing the shape of the garment.

BASIC RULES

1 The alterations are pictured for the important structural pieces of the pattern. The lesser pieces are not pictured (in this book, on the instruction sheet, or in any reference), and one must alter all corresponding pieces in like manner. For example, alterations in bodice length must be made to front facing pieces, a band trim, etc. If a jacket has been lengthened, the lining piece must be lengthened, etc. It is wise to place all pieces that will fit the same part of the body on top of each other in the position they will take; for example, place the altered jacket front on a table and then go through the entire pattern for the pieces that will fit under the jacket front. These might be the front-facing pattern, the front-interfacing pattern, and the front-lining pattern. Having them all in one pile will guide you in making all corresponding alterations accurately.

2 If an addition in width or length is made, the sketches show a strip of paper Scotch-taped to the pattern. Pins might be used, but the Scotch tape—especially the Magic Mending tape, which will take pencil lines—is far better and more convenient. It is very important to use an extra strip of paper when adding length and a very serious mistake to assume that you will remember, for example, to cut each skirt piece longer. Perhaps you will remember to cut pieces longer, but perhaps you will miss just once; it takes only one miss on merely one edge to ruin a garment. It is a temptation to use the extra margin on the pattern to draw lines for adding width, but this practice can be a dangerous one; the pencil lines you can draw on tissue paper are not as dark as the cutting line of the pattern, and they might be overlooked. Furthermore, one is so accustomed to cutting along the dark blue cutting line of the pattern that one tends to continue cutting along that line unless there is an obvious reminder, such as an extra strip of paper. It is better to play it safe and add the strips of paper.

ALTERATIONS FOR CHANGING LENGTH

There are two ways of lengthening or shortening patterns: (1) Taking a tuck to shorten or inserting a strip of paper to lengthen is the method that must be used for pattern pieces that are not rectangular. Examples are the fitted bodice pieces and the fitted sleeve. (2) By adding on to or cutting away the pattern at the lower edge, rectangular pieces can be altered. Examples are the very straight skirt, the boxy jacket or coat, and the roll-up sleeve. Printed information on the pattern shows which of the two methods is recommended; pieces that must be altered by method 1 will have lengthening-shortening lines drawn on the pattern in the proper position, and pieces that can be altered by method 2 will be so designated by writing the words "lengthen or shorten here" near the lower edge of the pattern.

to shorten a pattern piece by the tuck method
See Figure 9. Draw a ruler line parallel to the lengthening-shortening line on the pattern to mark off the amount of decrease desired. Crease along this line and bring it to the lengthening-shortening line; Scotch-tape in place. Note that the side edge of the bodice front has been distorted; it was originally a ruler-straight line (labeled *XY* on sketch). Diagonal lines which have become distorted must be straightened. A new ruler-straight line must be drawn between points *X* and *Y* (this line is not drawn to avoid confusion

in the sketch). The more diagonal the line and the greater the amount to be lengthened or shortened, the greater the distortion will be; Figure 10 pictures the two pieces of a bodice front which illustrates this point. The double-notched edges are very diagonal, and a greater alteration has been used. This distortion must be corrected; in this case the original lines were slightly curving ones, so the correction should be made by working with a curving line, cutting off a bit of the wider section and adding on a bit to the narrower one, as shown in the dashed lines at the side of the Bodice Front piece.

to lengthen a pattern piece by inserting an extension strip   See Figure 11. Draw parallel lines on a strip of paper (ticker tape is very convenient) to mark off the desired amount of increase. Cut the pattern apart along the lengthening-shortening lines. Scotch-tape the upper section of the pattern to the strip of paper with the cut edge of the pattern along one pencil line on the paper. *Important step:* with a ruler extend the straight-of-material line or the center fold line of the pattern on

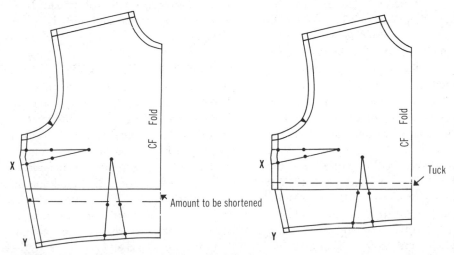

FIGURE 9   Shortening a pattern by the tuck method

the strip of paper. Place the lower part of the pattern along the remaining pencil line with the straight-of-material line or the center fold line meeting the vertical line (the line extended from the upper piece). Scotch-tape in place. Diagonal lines will be distorted similarly to those in the shortened pattern. (Reread the foregoing paragraph on the shortened pattern and study those sketches.) The distortion of line XY, in this case a ruler-straight line, must be corrected with a new ruler-straight line between those points.

to alter bodice length different amounts in front and back It is not at all unusual for a figure to require different amounts of alteration in bodice length in the front and the back; it is, as a matter of fact, a more common alteration than the equal front-back alteration. Examples are: (1) The full-busted person with a straight back will need more length in front and less in back; (2) the person with round shoulders will need extra length in back but not necessarily extra length in front; and (3) the person whose waistline dips down in the back (rather than dipping

slightly in front, like the average figure, for which the pattern was made) will need more length in back and not necessarily extra length in front.

The problem is that each piece must

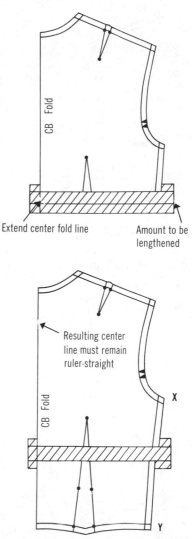

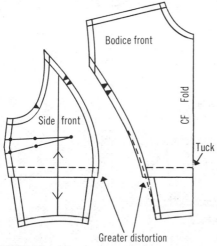

FIGURE 10

FIGURE 11 Lengthening a pattern by inserting an extension strip

be altered the same amount across the entire width so as not to distort the all-important grain lines of the pattern, but the pieces must be of identical length at the side edge. The following alteration solves the problem with truly remarkable results. A variation in front and back length is a gradual thing; this alteration results in a gradual correction without destroying the accuracy of the original pattern.

See Figure 12 for two illustrations of the method.

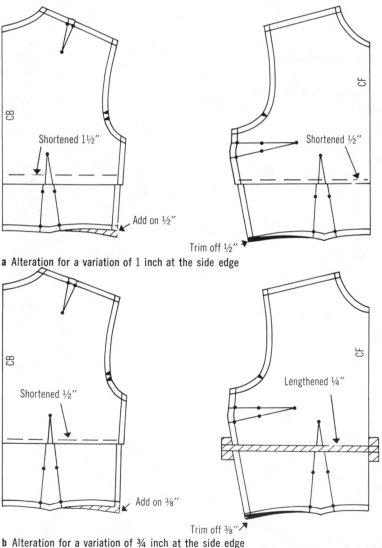

a Alteration for a variation of 1 inch at the side edge

b Alteration for a variation of ¾ inch at the side edge

Figure 12

GENERAL RULES THAT WILL SERVE UNDER ANY CIR-
CUMSTANCES Alter each pattern piece in length
as it requires. Figure the variation in length at
the side edge. Beginning and ending at the dart
position (about 3 inches from center front and
center back), add one-half of the variation to the
shorter edge and trim off one-half of the variation
from the longer edge.

The problem sketched in Figure 12a
is that of a figure that is short-waisted in
front and back, but shorter in the back.
The variation is 1 inch at the side edge,
so that ½ inch must be added to the
shorter edge (the back) and ½ inch
trimmed from the longer edge. Notice
that the evening-off alteration at the side
edge is made along the same curving
lines of the original pattern, thus retain-
ing the original character of the pattern.
Figure 12b illustrates an alteration where
one piece is lengthened and the other
shortened. The general rules stated above
will solve the problem, no matter what
alteration is required.

to alter a pattern piece at two different levels
The fitted sleeve pictured in Figure 13
must be the proper length, and the dart
must be at elbow position. The example
shows the alteration for a person who
needs to add a total of 1½ inches in
length; however, more of that length is
in her lower arm, and therefore the alteration done as shown will result in
proper elbow position. It is entirely possible that one might need to lengthen a
pattern below the elbow and shorten it
above.

NOTE If the elbow dart is only slightly (perhaps
½ inch) off position, it can be drafted into the
new position, as explained in the following section.

Shorts or slacks (and skirts) may require alteration at two levels. The length
of the torso must be taken into considera-

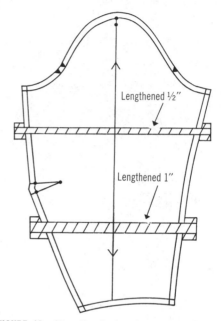
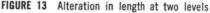

FIGURE 13 Alteration in length at two levels

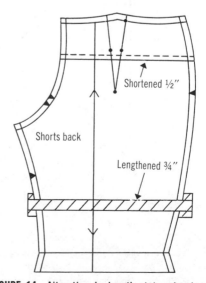
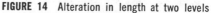

FIGURE 14 Alteration in length at two levels

tion, and therefore the pattern may need an alteration above the hipline, as shown in Figure 14, and also below the hipline because of a problem of length.

to redraft the position of the underarm dart
Figure 15 pictures an alteration for lowering the position of the dart; the procedure would be the same if the dart needed to be raised. Draw in new dart lines in the desired position (shown in broken lines in Figure 15a) so that they will be at a level with the high point of the bust; by making the new dart lines parallel to the original lines, the resulting dart will be the same width as the original. The "jog" of a dart is shaped as it is so that when the dart is stitched, the edges between the dart lines will fall with cut edges even along the cut edge of the seam. Each new dart needs its own jog. See Figure 15b. Crease along the lower line of the new dart and bring the crease to the remaining line; pin in place. The seam will be distorted somewhat and will look more distorted than it really is because of the extension of the jog of the original dart. With the dart folded in, draw a new ruler-straight line between points X and Y. Cut along this line with the dart folded in. Then release the folded-in dart. The jog of the new dart will be properly shaped.

NOTE This technique can be used in any place on the pattern where a small change in dart position is required.

to alter length by adding to, or cutting away from, the lower edge This method of lengthening or shortening a pattern is very quick and easy, and so it is a wise choice, providing it will result in a good pattern. The uses are somewhat limited to those patterns that are based on a rectangular shape. Figure 16 shows two such patterns, and of course the slim,

New dart lines

CF Fold

X

Fold in new dart

CF Fold

Y

Draw new ruler-straight line **XY** with new dart folded in; cut pattern along this line

FIGURE 15 Redrafting dart position

straight skirt is another excellent example. However, in the skirt, one must use some caution. Figure 17 pictures a perfectly rectangular skirt, but it has a pleat extension at the center back. If one were to shorten this skirt a great amount, the pleat would be so short that it would look unattractive; lengthening at the lower edge would be less serious. Ideally, sizable alterations are made above the pleat line in a skirt like this, so as to retain the intended proportions of the pleat.

Because this method is so easy, one would wish that it could be used to lengthen or shorten the very flared skirt, as pictured in Figure 18. To alter this skirt by the tuck or extension-strip method creates a serious distortion of the diagonal lines (as seen in the sketch), which must be corrected and which adds to the complication of such an alteration. If a slight alteration is required, it is certainly more expedient to do it at the lower edge. However, large alterations create the following problems: (1) If a great amount of length is trimmed away from the lower edge, the skirt is not as flared as it was intended to be. Perhaps this would be of no importance to some persons, but others would want the maximum flare. (2) If a great amount of length is added, the skirt gets progressively wider and therefore more flared. This would not be a disadvantage usually, but the skirt pattern might become so wide that it would not fit on the width of fabric. If these two problems exist, the pattern must be altered by the tuck or extension-strip method.

ALTERATIONS FOR ADDING WIDTH

These alterations are methods of adding allover size for the figure that is quite average in shape but is slightly larger or smaller than average in certain parts. Three general rules result in accuracy. Understanding each and following

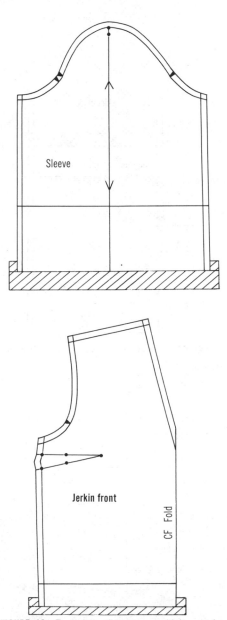

FIGURE 16 Examples of patterns which can be lengthened or shortened at the lower edge

CREATIVE
CLOTHING CONSTRUCTION

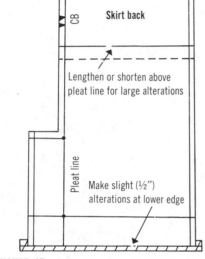

FIGURE 17 Alteration for skirt with pleat extension

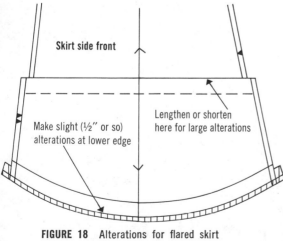

FIGURE 18 Alterations for flared skirt

through with each of the three will ensure a remarkable measure of success. The examples used are mainly skirts because it is assumed that the pattern was purchased in the proper bust size. Only one example of bust alteration will be used, and it will be a small (1-inch) alteration because if more than that is required at the bust, the pattern should be in the next larger size. All the examples given can be worked in the same manner for a decrease or increase in size. The illustrations will show an increase because this results in a more understandable sketch and because, unfortunately, many more persons need to add size to hiplines anyway!

rule 1: alter one-fourth of the desired amount on each side edge "Side edge" means not the two side edges of each pattern piece but the edge of any pattern piece that will be at the side of the body when worn. See Figure 19, which illustrates this rule with the alterations for a figure that is slightly larger than average at the waist and hip levels, becoming increasingly larger in the lower part of the body. Note that the identical alteration was made to the front and back; to alter all-over size, make identical alterations on corresponding edges.

NOTE A most common error is to alter one-half rather than one-fourth of the desired amount. But keep in mind that most patterns are made on the half and will therefore be cut twice, so that an alteration of one-fourth will result in the desired amount when the complete garment is cut.

rule 2: make identical alterations on all corresponding edges See Figure 20, which illustrates this rule. In this example, 1 inch is added to the bust size, 2½ inches are added to the waist size, and the hiplines are normal. Any alteration at the waist requires an identical alteration to the bodice and skirt pieces and to belt length, as well. An alteration at the underarm seamline to alter bust size has altered the length of the armscye curves, and an identical alteration must be made so that the armscye curves of the sleeve will be the proper adjusted length. The same would be true if the armhole edges were finished with a facing; then facing ends would have to be altered in an identical manner. These examples must serve as a guideline for all alterations made. Each pattern is different, and each problem must be thought out carefully.

rule 3: altered lines must be in character with the original pattern lines "In character" does not mean that the altered line should be identical to the original but that it should be similar enough to the original so that it is not a "surprising" line. The character of the original line at the side edge of a skirt is that it curves slightly above the 7-inch hipline and is

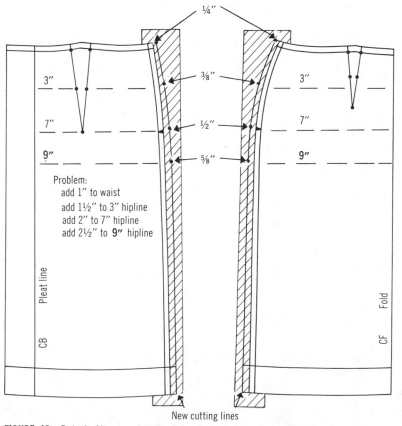

FIGURE 19   Rule 1: Alter one-fourth of the desired amount on each side edge

a ruler-straight line below the 7-inch hip-line. After alteration, the corrected line must curve slightly (not abruptly), and it must be a ruler-straight line below that curve. In most patterns, the original pattern line curves above the 7-inch hipline and is ruler-straight below because in the average figure, for which the pattern was

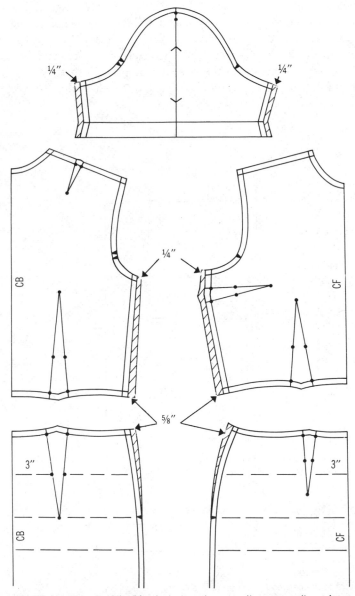

FIGURE 20 Rule 2: Make identical alterations on all corresponding edges

made, the high point of the hip curve is near the 7-inch line. However, many figures differ; the bell-like figure may curve out the maximum amount at the high hip, the 3-inch level; the figure with thick thighs may curve out the maximum amount at the lower hip, the 9-inch level. So "in character" means that the side edge should curve slightly above the high point of the hips (3, 7, or 9 inches) and should be a ruler-straight line below that point.

See Figure 21 for three examples; in each case the front skirt is pictured, and the back skirt would be altered in identical fashion. This rule is needed more in skirt patterns than in any other pattern because of the three hiplines, which are so close together and so close to the waist, and because each of these four levels may require a different alteration.

The sketch on the left in **Figure 21a** shows the alteration problem marked off with dots and a broken line on a strip of paper Scotch-taped to the pattern edge. This figure is average in that the high point of the hip is the 7-inch hipline, but the figure is larger than average. Examine the broken line, and you can easily see that it does not "make sense"—it is not in character with the original. The sketch on the right shows the problem solved with a slightly curving line above the high point of the hip and a ruler-straight line below. In this case, the line tapers back to the original line at the lower edge because the fact that the 9-inch hipline is normal indicates that the figure does not have large thighs, and that extra width is not needed in the lower area.

The sketch on the left in Figure 21b shows the alteration problem marked off with dots and a broken line on a strip of paper Scotch-taped to the pattern edge. This figure has a longer torso and the high point of the hip is at the 9-inch

hipline and the figure is larger than average size at that level. The broken line is not in character. The sketch at the right shows the problem solved with a slightly curving line above the high point of the hip and a ruler-straight line below. In this case the additional width was added in the lower area of the skirt because the extra required at the 9-inch hipline indicates that there is a thigh and leg problem and that this figure probably needs extra size all the way down.

The sketch on the left in Figure 21c shows the alteration problem marked off with dots and a broken line on a strip of paper Scotch-taped to the pattern edge. This is the bell-shaped figure, very round at the upper hip level. The broken line is not in character. The sketch at the right shows this problem solved with a slightly curving line above the high point of the hip and a ruler-straight line below. In this case the line tapers back to the original line at the lower edge because the fact that the 9-inch hipline is normal indicates that the figure does not have large thighs and that extra width is not needed in the lower area.

This problem is more complicated than the other two, and it involves another rule:

RULE If one must add more than ½ inch at each side edge (2 inches of total size) at the 3- or 7-inch hipline, an addition must be made to the waistline in order to keep the corrected line in character with the original.

This must be done even if the figure does not require extra size at the waist, as the illustrated problem shows. Note that the amount added is about one-half the

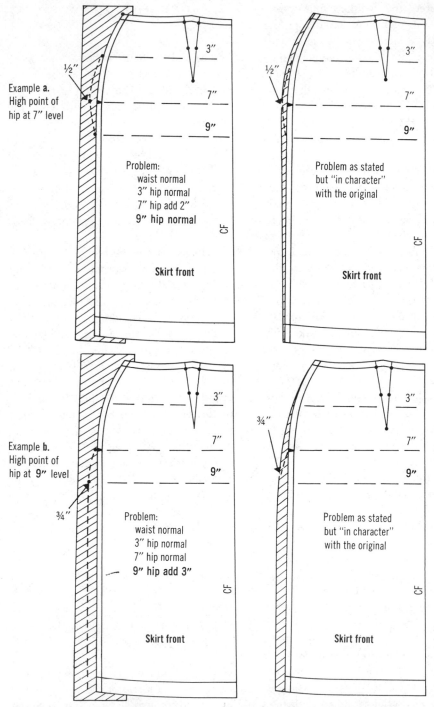

Example **a.**
High point of
hip at 7" level

½"

3"

7"

9"

Problem:
   waist normal
   3" hip normal
   7" hip add 2"
   9" hip normal

CF

Skirt front

½"

3"

7"

9"

Problem as stated
but "in character"
with the original

CF

Skirt front

Example **b.**
High point of
hip at **9"** level

¾"

3"

7"

9"

Problem:
   waist normal
   3" hip normal
   7" hip normal
   9" hip add 3"

CF

Skirt front

¾"

3"

7"

9"

Problem as stated
but "in character"
with the original

CF

Skirt front

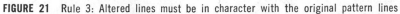

FIGURE 21   Rule 3: Altered lines must be in character with the original pattern lines

amount that was added at the 3-inch hip-line; the rule is that enough must be added so that the line curves slightly (not abruptly) above the 3-inch hipline.

If the waist did not require an increase, this alteration would make the waistline too large. However, this extra waist size is a great advantage in fitting the figure that is more rounded than average because this figure needs extra darts to give the extra shape required in the rounded area. (Much more will be said of this in Chapter 15, Fundamentals of Fitting.) See Figure 22, which pictures this alteration completed on the front and back pieces of the skirt. For the 1-inch addition at the 3-inch hipline, an addition of about ⅝ inch at the waistline would be wise. Now draft in a new

dart, ⅝ inch wide and 3 inches long, as shown. It is impossible to say exactly where this dart should be located. Darts create shape and should be located to create shape where the figure is most shapely. For such bell-shaped figures, an educated estimate is to locate the dart about 2 to 2½ inches from the original side seamline. This certainly will suffice for the time being; this dart should be basted in for a first fitting. During the fitting, the position can be changed, and the dart can be lengthened or shortened as the individual figure requires.

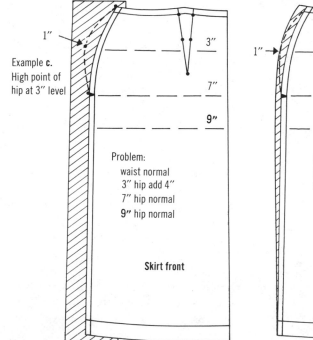

1"

Example **c.**
High point of
hip at 3" level

3"

7"

9"

Problem:
  waist normal
  3" hip add 4"
  7" hip normal
  9" hip normal

Skirt front

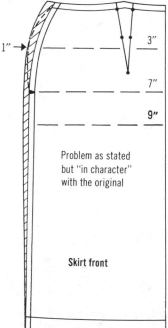

Add about half the addition made at 3" hipline

1"

3"

7"

9"

Problem as stated
but "in character"
with the original

Skirt front

FIGURE 21 continued

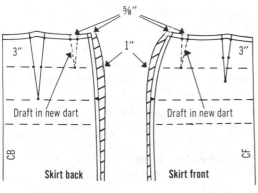

FIGURE 22

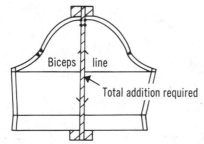

a To increase biceps line a very small amount (½ inch)

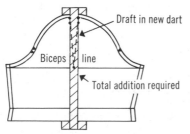

b To increase biceps line a small amount (under 1 inch)

FIGURE 23

ALTERATIONS FOR UPPER ARMS AND
SHOULDER HEIGHT

to increase the biceps line for the figure with heavy arms Heavy arms create a regrettable problem because extra width must be added; then the cap of the sleeve is fuller, and the result is a somewhat gathered sleeve cap. And of course the greater the amount added, the more gathered the effect. These alterations avoid that problem.

Figure 23a shows a simple method of inserting an extension strip which is quite acceptable if the addition will be no more than ½ inch, particularly if the fabric eases well (crepes, knits, soft woolens). The shoulder position should be marked halfway between the original shoulder markings at the top of the sleeve cap.

Figure 23b pictures another solution, the wiser choice for an addition of about 1 inch for fabrics that do not ease well. The method is identical but with one addition. Draft in a dart in slightly curving lines as shown. The dart position will act as a shoulder-line marking. This dart will be sewn in and will appear in the finished garment. This method might meet with some resistance from the reader, but its great advantages far outweigh the one disadvantage that one does not often see a dart in this position in a sleeve (it is not unheard of, however). The addition of this dart makes it possible to have the width required at the biceps line and yet have no extra fullness to ease into the armhole; the dart is far, far less objectionable than a gathered-looking sleeve. The woman with a heavy-arm problem is so happy to have it solved with a resulting smooth-fitting sleeve that she will not give a second thought to an extra dart line.

Figure 24 pictures an alteration that

is a wiser choice when large additions (2 inches is not unusual) are necessary. It will result in a seam at the center of the sleeve—again far less offensive than a sleeve that looks very gathered because of an additional 2 inches eased into the armhole. As a matter of fact, many designs feature a seam at the center of a sleeve, so this seam will not be at all objectionable to the eye. The alteration is shown in two steps: Figure 24a shows the sleeve pattern cut apart at the center of the sleeve and strips of paper Scotch-taped to both center edges. An addition of half the amount desired on each center edge will result in the total amount required. Notice that an addition was made, parallel to the center lines below the biceps line, and then the line was curved off to the original shoulder marking at the top of the sleeve. Again this is an alteration which provides the size where it is needed and retains the original amount of ease at the cap of the sleeve; this sleeve will fit smoothly, without gathers. Figure 24b shows the addition of a ⅝-inch seam allowance on the corrected lines. Trim along the new cutting line. Cut two of each pattern piece.

to alter shoulder height for squarer-than-average shoulders Figure 25 shows the bodice-front, bodice-back, and sleeve patterns to be altered. The desired increase in height is added at the outer, armhole edge of the bodice pieces and gradually tapers back to the original shoulder line at the neck edge. That same increase is added at the top of the sleeve cap and gradually tapers back to the original pattern line at the notch position (about 3 inches from the underarm seamline).

to alter shoulder height for sloping shoulders This alteration would be done in a way similar to that for adding height, except

that the excess would be trimmed from, rather than added to, the pattern; again lines would return to the original at the neck edge in the bodices and in the notch position in the sleeve. This alteration is not pictured; it seems wiser to take care of this correction in fitting for the first several projects. When the amount of excess height is determined, one would feel free to trim off this amount from the pattern pieces before cutting.

to alter shoulder width See Figure 26, which pictures bodice-front and bodice-back pieces properly altered for addi-

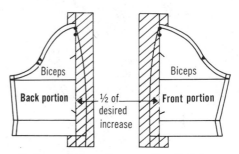

a To increase biceps line more than 1 inch

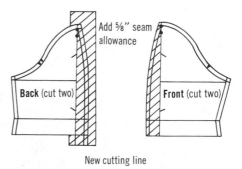

New cutting line
b Finished pattern with corrections made
FIGURE 24

tional width. Slash into the patterns from the shoulder line (about 2 inches in from the armhole edge) to the armhole seamline at approximately the notch position. Use an extension strip to gain the extra width. Pivot the small section out from the notch position to achieve the desired increase. This will distort the shoulder line very slightly, and it should be straightened with a ruler. The same method in reverse will decrease shoulder width. The bodice back is pictured in

Figure 27. Cut to the notch position and lap out the excess width; the bodice front would be altered in an identical manner. This alteration will result in a very slight distortion of the shoulder line; straighten it with a ruler.

ALTERATIONS THAT CHANGE SHAPE AS WELL AS SIZE

WARNING The alterations included in this section are remarkably effective ones and will result in improved fit, but they are more complicated, and each one requires an educated guess. So every alteration included in this section must be tested in muslin before cutting into good fabric. However, after one of these alterations has been made on three or four garments, it will be perfected,

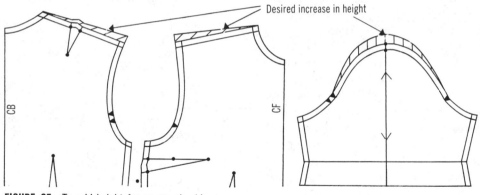

Desired increase in height

FIGURE 25 To add height for square shoulders

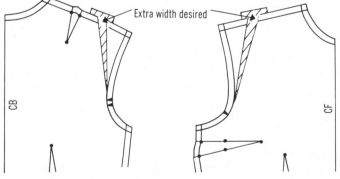

Extra width desired

FIGURE 26 To add width to shoulders

and then the alteration can be made with confidence and without prior muslin testing.

The following alterations are included: for a bust with larger-than-average and smaller-than-average cup size, for rounded shoulders and very straight shoulders, for hips that protrude in the back and for hips that are very flat, and for the figure with a larger-than-average tummy.

In each of these alterations, there is an issue of size, but more importantly, there is an issue of shape. Ordinarily problems of shape are solved in fitting rather than pattern alteration, but if they can be solved by pattern alteration, it is a great advantage. Shape is created in a garment mainly by dart fittings. The principle of the dart (discussed in more detail on page 178) is this: *The greater the curve, the wider the dart required to fit it; the smaller the curve, the narrower the dart required to fit it.* As we make these pattern alterations, we are concerned with this principle.

But shape is difficult to pinpoint in scientific measurements. One can see that a bust is larger than average (or hips are flatter, or a back is more rounded), but it is much more difficult to say how much the size of a curve varies from average. The bust larger than average is the most serious figure problem in my estimation, for it is one that cannot be solved completely if a garment has been cut, and so the alteration for the larger-than-average bust is the most valuable one. A discussion of the problem of shape in the bust will make an excellent illustration for all the other shape problems because it is the one that varies the greatest amount. The pattern has been made for an average bustline, which is really relatively small—an A or B cup size. So the person who wears a larger cup size is larger

than average; diagonal ripples (beginning at the bust and angling to the waist or armhole) are a sure indication that the bust is larger than average.

The alteration problem would be simple if an estimate could be based on cup size alone, but there is another factor involved in bust shape. Posture plays a large part. The person who holds herself erectly adds chest size to her bust curve; a Jr.-A cup size and an erect posture may result in a figure that is average, just as a D cup size and a sagging posture may result in average shape. It is this ambiguous factor of posture that makes any estimate included in these alterations just an educated guess. Muslin testing is absolutely necessary until the guess has been established in scientific amounts.

to increase width of dart for larger-than-average bust See Figure 28a. Draw a line through the center of the under-bust dart, extending it to the shoulder line. Slash along this line to the seamline (not the cut edge) at the shoulder line.

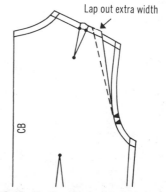

FIGURE 27 To decrease width of shoulders

See Figure 28b. Spread out the pattern and place a strip of paper underneath. Spread the pattern an estimated amount. The following amounts are mere guidelines: spread ½ inch for a C cup size, spread ¾ inch for a D cup size, and add about ½ inch to each of these amounts for the very erect figure. Scotch-tape the extension strip in place.

See Figure 28c. Draft in a new dart from a point midway between the original lines at the tip and ending on the original lines at the waistline edge. The figure problem has been solved in two ways at once: (1) size is added where it is needed and (2) a larger-than-average dart is created to give the proper amount of shape where it is needed. The length of the shoulder line has not been changed at all because the slash was made only to the shoulder line; therefore, the shoulder edge of this altered pattern will fit the back shoulder edge of the original

pattern. Note that the waistline measurement of the pattern has not been changed, but the pattern will have more shape because of the wider dart, and it will have more size at the bust, as can be seen in the shaded section in the sketch.

Test in muslin, using this altered pattern and the bodice-back pattern. If the guess is not correct, the pattern can be realtered by adding more dart width or by decreasing dart width as required.

Figure 29 pictures this same alteration in a pattern with a French dart. Notice in this case that the slash line down the center of the dart has touched the center-front line, and that line, which was ruler-straight, has been distorted by spreading the pattern. Center-front lines must remain ruler-straight, and therefore this line must be corrected as shown. If a garment had only an underarm dart, this same problem would occur.

to increase width of dart for rounded shoulders or protruding back hips See Figure 30, which pictures the completely altered bodice-back and skirt-back patterns. The general principle of increasing size and

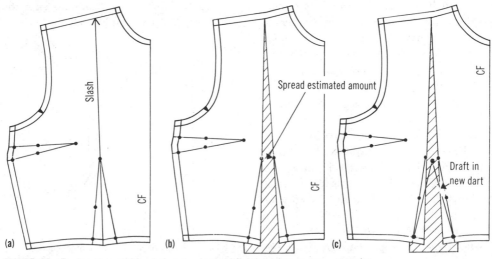

(a)   (b)   (c)

FIGURE 28 To increase width of dart for bust with larger-than-average cup size

shape, as described for the bust, can be applied to any part of the figure. More than ½ inch extra size is rarely needed at the shoulder area, but serious problems of protruding hips (which are usually posture problems) might require as much extra spread at the hipline as 1 or even 1½ inches. A front skirt could be altered in the same manner to accommodate the very rounded tummy.

Test these patterns in muslin, and if the estimate is not correct, the pattern can be realtered, allowing the pattern to spread a greater or lesser amount at the shoulder or hip level.

to decrease width of dart to create less-than-average shape This type of alteration can be worked in reverse. Figure 31 pictures a bodice back altered for the straighter-than-average figure. A slash is made through the center of the dart. The pattern is lapped over in the shoulder area, and this results in a narrower dart. Most figures that are quite straight would still require a dart about ½ inch wide at the lower edge, but extremely straight (ram-

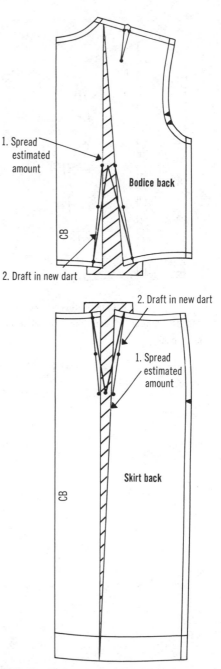

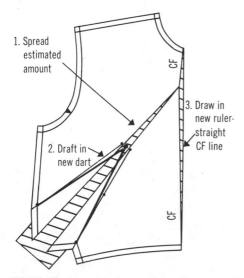

FIGURE 29 An alteration which distorts the center-front lines

FIGURE 30 To increase width of dart for round shoulders and protruding back hips

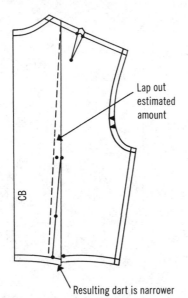

Lap out
estimated
amount

CB

Resulting dart is narrower

FIGURE 31 Alteration for the straighter-than-average back

rod) figures might require the entire width of the dart removed. The bodice front could be altered in this same manner for the bust curve smaller than average. A back skirt could be altered in the same manner for very flat back hips.

Test in muslin using the altered pattern. If the estimate is not correct, the pattern can be realtered by adding to the dart width or by decreasing it still more.

LAYOUTS
AND
CUTTING

NOTE Directions for estimating special yardage requirements appear on pages 96 to 100. Included are (1) directions for making a new layout for a width of fabric not stated in the yardage chart, (2) directions for making a layout for sections of a design in contrast, (3) directions for estimating the extra fabric or the saving in fabric that results from alterations in pattern length, (4) directions for making a layout or changing an existing layout for napped or pile fabrics, and (5) directions for estimating the extra fabric required for the purpose of matching plaid.

Now that the fabric is evened and grain lines corrected and the pattern measured and altered, it is well to cut all the fabric to be used (the garment, the lining, the interfacing, contrasting fabrics, etc.) during one long cutting session. Use a large table and line the fabric up with the table so that it is always a rectangular shape with square corners; this positions the lengthwise and crosswise lines properly. If the fabric is slippery and tends to take a wobbly line on the table, it can be Scotch-taped to the table in just enough places to keep it in position. Unusually slippery fabrics can be pinned to rectangles of tissue paper, which will keep them in line.

A common question is: "Do I have to follow the layout exactly as it is? Can't I make up my own?" Refer back to pages 21 and 22 to review the discussion on yardage amounts and layouts. The inexperienced person should follow the layout letter for letter and line for line, for she does not have the experience at this time to improvise. However, the competent, experienced person may see better solutions, and if so, there is no reason why she cannot use them. It is always well to compare your layout very carefully with a layout in the pattern to be sure that (1) you have included all the necessary pattern pieces (check them off on the pattern layout to be sure), (2) you have cut all pieces the proper number of times (some pieces are laid on twice, such as a collar, and some pieces are laid on several times, such as pocket flaps if there are many pockets), and (3) all pieces which should be on the fold are placed on a fold line. If you have done this and have the pattern pieces placed with the straight-of-material lines parallel to the selvedge, your improvised layout is quite acceptable.

SELECTION
OF
LAYOUT

The layout should be selected by considering the same four factors which influenced the amount of yardage required. They are (1) the view of the design to be used, (2) the size of the pattern, (3) the width of the fabric, and (4) the nature of the fabric (plaid, napped, one-way designs, etc.). Take great care in selecting the correct layout, and then circle it with a pencil line to make it stand out from the others.

HEADINGS OF LAYOUTS

There are many layouts on the pattern, and if you are making a complicated garment that will include interfacing, underlining, and lining as well as the fabric for the garment itself, you may be using several of the layouts. Read the headings before beginning work. I have seen careless persons cut interfacing pattern pieces out of lining fabric because they failed to read the heading of the layout.

TYPICAL
LAYOUTS

Fabric can be folded in any one of several ways to make it accommodate a particular pattern in the most economical way. Some of the most common layouts are shown in Figure 1. In those layouts requiring folded fabric, the right side of the fabric should be folded inside, as shown.

lengthwise fold This is the easiest layout to work with, for it is folded just as the fabric was folded when purchased. The two selvedge edges are together, and the fold runs parallel to the selvedges in the directions of the lengthwise threads. (Figure 1a.)

crosswise fold This layout is used when pattern pieces are too wide for a lengthwise fold. The fabric is spread open and then refolded on a line at right angles to the selvedges in the direction of the crosswise threads. Note that selvedges are together. (Figure 1b.)

open This layout is made with a single thickness of fabric as stated on the layout chart. It is used for asymmetric designs mainly. It is more difficult to work with, for there is twice as much cutting to do and it is more difficult to cut through a single thickness of fabric. So this layout is avoided by the pattern companies unless it proves to be most economical. (Figure 1c.)

combination There can be a combination of two or three of the common layouts used to lay out one pattern. The layout shown combines lengthwise- and crosswise-fold layouts. (Figure 1d.)

combination This sketch shows a combination of crosswise-fold and open layouts. (Figure 1e.)

double fold This layout is used when many pattern pieces must be cut on a fold. The fabric is spread open and then refolded so that the selvedge edges meet each other. (Figure 1f.)

Learn to study each line of the layout carefully—each line is important. The layouts are necessarily small in order to fit into the limited space on the instruction sheet. But all necessary information is given; it does, however, require a special technique to learn to "read" lines well.

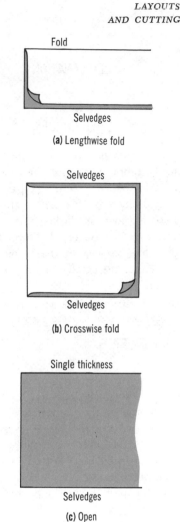

(a) Lengthwise fold

(b) Crosswise fold

(c) Open

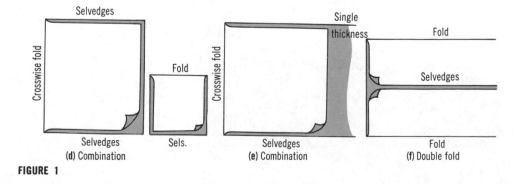

(d) Combination

(e) Combination

(f) Double fold

FIGURE 1

EXPLANATION
OF
LAYOUT
TECHNIQUES

1 If the same pattern piece must be laid on the fabric twice, it is shown once outlined in solid lines and again outlined in dashed lines (Figure 2). If the pattern piece is shown in dashed lines, the pattern must be reversed (turned over). This can be seen in the layout by the position of the notch or notches.

NOTE A pattern company may use dashed lines as have been used in these sketches, or it may use a system of shading to show the reverse position of the pattern.

2 If a pattern piece must be cut on the fold, it is usually placed on the fold edge of the fabric, or the pattern itself may be folded over on the fabric as shown in Figure 3. In this case the pattern is shown in solid lines. All edges of it, except the fold edge, should be cut, and then the pattern should be turned over to the reverse position (shown in dashed lines) and cut.

3 Sometimes a pattern piece is shown extending beyond the edge of the layout as shown in pattern piece B in Figure 4. You will notice that the edge over which the piece extends is always a fold edge. This means that after piece A is cut, the fabric can be spread out flat and will be twice the width as shown in the layout. Pattern piece B will fit on the fabric now. Note that one piece of B is shown in solid lines and the other in dashed lines to show that the pattern must be reversed.

4 Figure 5 shows pattern piece C lying outside the fabric. A note accompanies the layout to explain how to cut the pieces.

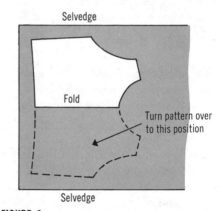

Selvedge

Fold

Turn pattern over to this position

Selvedge

FIGURE 3

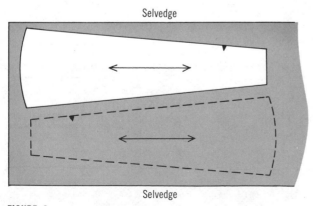

Selvedge

Selvedge

FIGURE 2

Note that the fabric is on the fold, which means that there is a double thickness of fabric. The note explains that only one C and one D piece are required. This means that when all other pieces have been cut, the fabric should be spread out to a single thickness, and then there will be enough fabric in the two layers to cut one each of C and D.

5 Sometimes a pattern piece has what is called a *cutoff line*. For example, one view may require a full-length sleeve, while another view of the same design has a short sleeve; the pattern will probably have only one sleeve, with a cutoff line for the short-sleeve view. Cutoff lines are shown in dashed lines on the layout, as shown in Figure 6.

6 Each pattern piece is separated on the layout so that it can be easily distinguished. See Figure 7 and note the spaces between the pattern pieces. This does not mean that there really is extra space there—there may be, and there may not be. The layouts picture what appears to be extra space because if the pieces were shown as close together as

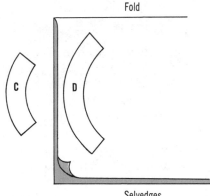

FIGURE 5

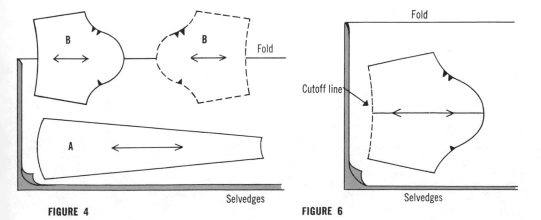

FIGURE 4

FIGURE 6

they should be placed, it would be very difficult for the novice to understand the layouts. Do not assume there is extra fabric.

GENERAL RULES FOR LAYING ON THE PATTERN

1 Use a large table for cutting. The table should be as wide as the fabric and as long as is available. There are cutting boards on the market that will protect the table and increase its size somewhat.

2 If an open layout (single thickness of fabric) is used, place the fabric right side up on the table and place the pattern pieces right side up on the fabric (unless a dashed line indicates that the pattern should be reversed).

3 The pattern must be so placed that the straight-of-material lines on the pattern lie parallel to the selvedge edges of the fabric.

4 Place all pattern pieces on the fabric ex- actly as the cutting layout shows. Notice the position of notches on the layout and see that your pattern is placed in an iden- tical position.

5 Place large pieces on the fabric first and fit small pieces in later.

6 If a combination layout is used, always lay out those pieces on the lengthwise fold first and then cut the fabric and re- fold it to cut the crosswise layout.

7 Lay the pattern pieces as close together as possible; do not leave as much as ¼ inch between pieces. Remember that the pattern company figured yardages as eco- nomically as possible.

8 First quickly lay out all pattern pieces in the approximate position. Then go back and perfect the layout as described in the following paragraphs.

MEASURING STRAIGHT–OF–MATERIAL LINES

The straight-of-material lines are placed on the pattern in such a position as to ensure maximum wearing qualities and to obtain the desired effect. They were drawn very scientifically by an expert patternmaker; it is very important to the success of the finished product that these lines be placed so that they fall on the

Selvedge

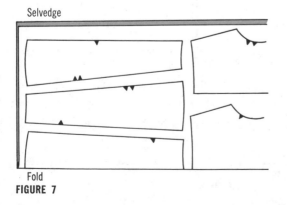

Fold
FIGURE 7

lengthwise threads of the fabric. Measure with an L square or a ruler as shown in Figure 8; measure from the extended straight-of-material lines and place a pin at the upper and lower edge of the pattern. Every pattern piece has either a straight-of-material line or a line marked "place on fold"; the place-on-fold line must be placed on lengthwise threads also. So if a pattern piece must be turned over along the fold line, as illustrated by the collar in Figure 8, the fold line must be parallel to the selvedge.

PINNING
ON
THE PATTERN

When the straight-of-material lines have been pinned in place accurately, more pins must be added to hold the whole pattern in place accurately. Pins should be placed close to the cutting line (no more than ¼ inch away) and approximately at right angles to the cut edge (Figure 9). The number of pins depends on the contour of the pattern piece and the nature of the fabric. More pins are needed on curved edges than on straight edges; more pins are needed on slippery fabrics than on firm, stiff fabrics. In gen-

eral, pins placed every 3 or 4 inches will prove satisfactory.

CUTTING
THE FABRIC

CUTTING NOTES
Certain cutting information is written in the form of a note which may appear in a separate boxed-in section close to the layouts or which may be given as notes

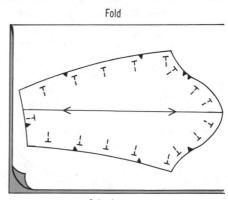

Fold

Selvedges

FIGURE 9

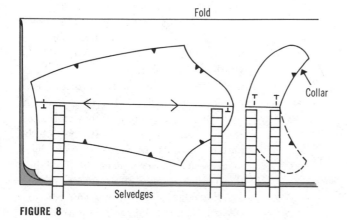

Fold

Collar

Selvedges

FIGURE 8

with an individual layout. Look for these notes and read all of them carefully.

CUTTING TECHNIQUES

Do not lift the fabric off the table; keep one blade of the shears resting on the table. Use long slashes with the cutting scissors in preference to short, choppy ones. Never use pinking shears for cutting out a garment, for they are too difficult to handle and there is a danger of inaccuracy with such bulky scissors. Cut exactly along the pattern line or the altered pattern line. Inaccurate cutting

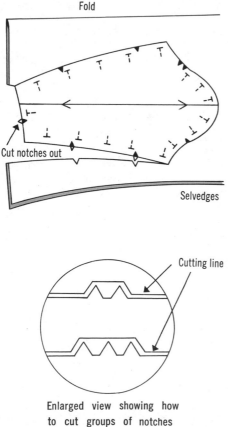

Fold

Cut notches out

Selvedges

Cutting line

Enlarged view showing how to cut groups of notches

FIGURE 10

can make the difference between one size and another. Curves are especially important, so cut them with great care. There are notches on the edge of the pattern to aid in the construction of the garment. These notches are cut in on the pattern as shown in Figure 10. It is a good idea to cut them out, as shown, when the fabric is cut. They are more noticeable that way, and the seam allowance remains complete for use in fitting.

When all pieces have been cut, fold them over a hanger to prevent wrinkling. Always keep the pieces on a hanger when they are not in use to save pressing time.

FIGURING SPECIAL YARDAGE REQUIREMENTS

FOR A FABRIC WIDTH NOT GIVEN ON THE PATTERN

See Figure 11. Figuring a whole layout is a difficult problem that can be handled well only by the experienced person; the beginner should never undertake it but should instead select a pattern that gives the yardage amount for the width of fabric she wishes to use. The problem should be done just as it is done by the pattern company. A long table serves the purpose best. First experiment to see what type of layout (lengthwise fold, crosswise fold, or combination) is most economical. Use yardsticks to mark off the width of the fabric on the table. Place the pattern pieces on the table as economically as possible, observing place-on-fold lines and straight-of-material lines. It is advisable to check with one of the pattern layouts to be sure you have placed each pattern piece on the fabric the correct number of times. By measuring the edge of the table, you can discover how much fabric is required.

CAUTION Be sure to double measurements if a
crosswise-fold layout is used.

97

LAYOUTS
AND CUTTING

FOR SECTIONS OF A DESIGN IN CONTRAST

The best way to figure yardage for separate pieces is to do it at home just the way it is done by the pattern company. Figure 12 illustrates the method of doing a layout; it shows how to obtain the yardage amount for contrasting collar and cuffs. Be sure to allow for the number of pieces required (two collars, four cuffs, etc.). By measuring the edge of the table, you can discover how much fabric is required.

lengthened 2 inches. There will be a saving of 2 inches in the area where *A* and *B* are cut, another saving of 2 inches in the area where *C* and *D* are cut, and a saving of 1 inch in each area where the bodices are cut—a total saving of 6 inches. But lengthening the sleeve 2 inches gives a saving of only 4 inches. Inches must always be figured in ⅛-yard divisions because fabrics are cut in ⅛-

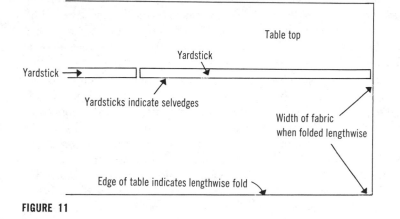

FIGURE 11

FOR A LENGTHENED OR SHORTENED PATTERN

Figure 13 shows a sample layout for a basic dress composed of a six-gore skirt, a fitted bodice, and a short sleeve. It will be used as an example for several problems. If your pattern has been altered considerably in length, select the layout to be used and then figure the amount of extra fabric required or the amount that might be saved by figuring on that particular layout. Two sample problems are discussed below as an aid toward understanding the general principles involved.

problem 1 Skirt pieces shortened 2 inches, bodice pieces shortened 1 inch, sleeve

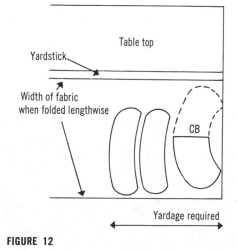

FIGURE 12

yard divisions. There are 4½ inches in ⅛ yard, so this person cannot save ⅛ yard of fabric if she uses this layout.

problem 2 Skirt pieces lengthened 3 inches, bodice pieces shortened 1 inch, sleeve lengthened 2 inches. This problem requires 3 inches of extra fabric in the area where *A* and *B* are cut and another 3 inches of extra fabric where *C* and *D* are cut. There will be a total saving of 2 inches where the two bodices are cut, so a total of 6 inches extra is needed for the skirt; however, 2 inches is saved on the bodices, and therefore 4 inches extra is required thus far. Add to that an additional 2 inches for lengthening the sleeve, and the answer is an extra 6 inches required for this person with this layout. There are 4½ inches in ⅛ yard and 9 inches in ¼ yard, but this person will have to buy the extra ¼ yard.

This method is a quick one that can be done in the store, but it is a method that does not work for every layout. Sometimes a layout is very complicated, with pattern pieces dovetailed in such a way that it is quite impossible to figure yardage requirements so simply. For such intricate layouts, the only safe solution is to make a new layout as described on page 96, using the altered pattern pieces.

FOR NAPPED OR PILE FABRICS

These fabrics have a different appearance and color if the tops of all pieces are not laid in the same direction. If layouts of the pattern have not been planned for napped fabrics, it is likely that some pieces will be laid in opposite directions because the pattern fits in more economically that way. See Figure 13 and notice that pattern pieces *A*, *C*, and *G* are placed with the tops in a direction opposite to that of all the other pattern pieces; this layout is not suitable for napped fabrics, and therefore the heading reads "for 36-inch fabric without nap."

As one makes a layout for napped fabrics, it is well to follow a layout on the instruction sheet for the size, width of fabric, and view to be used and then to change only those pieces that must be changed.

Figure 14 shows the sample layout corrected for use with a napped fabric. Pieces *A*, *C*, and *G* had to be moved so that the upper edges would be in the same direction as the upper edges of the other pieces. This example indicates why more fabric is usually required for napped fabrics. Compare the position of the sleeve in the two layouts. In the corrected layout, the straight lower edge of the sleeve does not fit in as well with the shoulder edge of piece *F* as it did when it could be turned around the other way, and piece *C* creates a problem in this corrected layout because it does not fit into the width of the fabric as it did be-

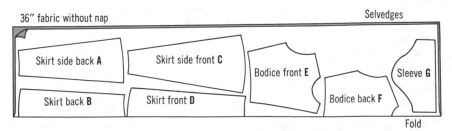

36" fabric without nap — Selvedges

Skirt side back **A** — Skirt side front **C** — Bodice front **E** — Sleeve **G**

Skirt back **B** — Skirt front **D** — Bodice back **F**

Fold

FIGURE 13 Sample layout

fore. This might be a serious problem and could require a considerable amount of extra material, depending on how much the pattern piece extends over the fabric. It can be pieced if the amount is small and if the piecing seam will fall in the hem. However, if the piecing seam will show, an entirely new layout must be made, and it will, of course, require even more extra fabric.

FOR PLAID OR LARGE DESIGN

Additional fabric over and above the amount given on the pattern is needed to match plaids or stripes or to balance large designs. This fact is stated clearly on the pattern envelope. Even if a design is shown in plaid and a special layout for plaid is included, extra fabric is needed for matching. The reason for this is that plaids vary in size and type, each with its own matching problems, and the pattern company cannot possibly give a yardage amount that would allow for matching any and all plaids the customers might choose. There are two types of plaids—even and uneven (Figure 15). *Even plaids* are in squares or rectangles, and each quarter of each unit is identical with the others, so that when you start from the center of any block, the stripes of color on either side will match. These plaids are much easier to match than uneven plaids, and they should be the choice of the novice. *Uneven plaids* may be in perfect squares, but more often the

block is rectangular. Each quarter of each block has a different design made by the colored stripes. These plaids are much more difficult to match and should never be attempted by the beginner.

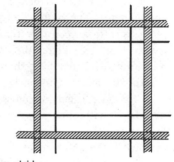

a Even plaid

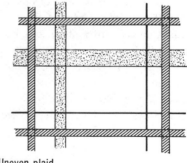

b Uneven plaid
FIGURE 15

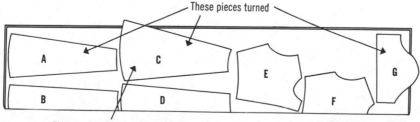

This may be pieced under some circumstances   Extra fabric required
FIGURE 14 Sample layout altered for napped or pile fabrics

More extra fabric is required for matching uneven plaids. In addition to the type of plaid, the size of the block influences the amount of extra yardage needed for matching. A very small, 2-inch block requires little extra yardage, whereas a larger block (5 and even 6 inches) requires much more. The number of pattern pieces is also a consideration. A pattern with 4 pieces will require much less extra yardage for matching than the pattern with 20 pieces. Obviously it is impossible to give exact amounts for matching plaids with such diverse considerations to be taken into account. The customer must make an estimate—from a minimum of ¼ yard for even plaids of medium size for a design with few pattern pieces up to 1½ yards and even more for a large uneven plaid in a design with many pattern pieces. A good plan is to buy plaid in a nearby store and cut it immediately, so that if your estimate was short you can buy more fabric before it is sold out.

A sample problem will help illustrate the principles mentioned above. Refer back to the sample layout in Figure 13 and study the layout for a plaid of 3-inch squares. Each time pattern pieces are placed in an area (*A* and *B* are placed in the same area), there is a chance that extra fabric will be required for matching. Even at the very left end of the layout, as the first pieces are placed down, there is a chance that some fabric will be lost in order that the plaid unit may be started off right at the waistline. Count the spaces between the units and count one at the beginning end for the number of times extra fabric might be required; in the sample layout, the number is a total of five times. Each time there is a possible need for extra fabric, the amount needed might be almost as much as the size of the unit of plaid. In this problem almost 3 inches of extra fabric might be needed five times; thus a total of 15 inches of extra fabric is the answer that would be completely safe. However, not that much extra will be needed because it is most unlikely that the maximum amount of extra fabric would be needed each time; sometimes the plaid will fall so that no extra fabric is required. So a good rule is to estimate the maximum amount that might be needed and then buy about half that much extra fabric. In this problem, 7 inches of extra fabric would undoubtedly be sufficient, and so an extra ¼ yard would be a good educated estimate.

MARKING
FABRIC
AND STAY
STITCHING

All patterns have markings which are all-important and which must be transferred to the fabric. The printed patterns have markings in the form of lines (either solid or broken) and dots of varying sizes. The lines may be for the making of pleats, darts, and tucks, or they may be an indication of fold lines or center lines. All printed patterns have the seam-lines drawn in with a broken line ⅝ inch in from the cut edge of the pattern. On many of these lines and at other important construction points, there are dots which indicate various exact points which are important to the excellent construction of the garment. All these dots and at least some of the lines must be transferred to the fabric. All center lines should be marked with long basting stitches (see page 123).

METHODS
OF
MARKING

The various methods of marking are described below. First read the evaluation of each method, in which advantages and disadvantages and recommended uses are discussed. Then decide which method is best for a particular use.

TAILOR'S TACKS

Little tufts of thread appear on both sides of both thicknesses of the fabric. This is the only method of marking that marks both sides of the fabric, and therefore it has many advantages; for example, darts are sewn from the inside, or wrong side, of the fabric, and pleats are laid in from the right side, or outside, of the fabric. Tailor's tacks are made in a different color for each size or shape of marking, and this makes certain construction details infinitely easier to do. This is especially important in Vogue patterns because they have four different sizes of markings and because they have more intricate pattern lines to be marked. Most people think this method takes longer; perhaps I do not agree because I want all the advantages it offers. This method is recommended for use on Vogue patterns, on any pattern with complicated pattern lines, and for couturier methods of sewing.

to make tailor's tacks See Figure 1. It is very important to use a different color of thread for each size of marking. Have needles threaded with each color to be used so that it will be convenient to do all markings on a pattern piece at one time. Choose colors that contrast to the color of the fabric; avoid the use of dark, bright colors of thread that might fade on light fabrics. Use a double thread. To tailor-tack the usual two thicknesses of fabric, take a very small stitch through the center of the marking, catching both

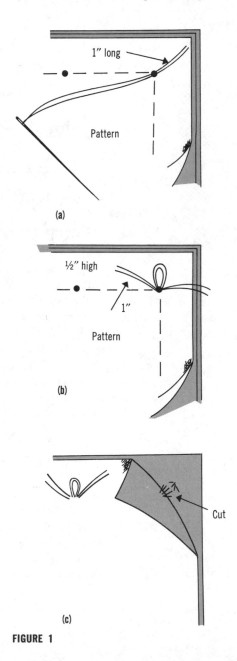

FIGURE 1

thicknesses of fabric; leave an end of thread about 1 inch long (Figure 1a). Take another very small stitch through the center of the marking, leaving a loop of thread ½ inch high. Cut off thread, leaving ends of 1 inch (Figure 1b). Do not cut the loop of thread. To remove the pattern, slip one hand under the pattern and hold the little threads as you lift the pattern off; this is a relatively simple job because the stitch has weakened the paper so that it usually lifts off without disturbing the threads. Separate the two thicknesses of fabric and cut the threads; this will leave a tuft of thread on each piece (Figure 1c).

To tailor-tack only one thickness of fabric, take a very small stitch through the center of the marking, leaving ends of thread about ½ inch long (Figure 2a). Remove the pattern, and see that such a simple stitch leaves a tuft of thread on the one thickness of fabric (Figure 2b).

TRACING WHEEL AND CARBON

Carbon sheets are available in several different colors, and when used with the tracing wheel, a colored line can be traced to the wrong side of the fabric. This must be done on the wrong side only, and therefore this method is ideal for use on those garments that have basic structural details composed of darts and seams, both of which are stitched from the wrong side. There is danger that traced lines may show through to the outside on some light-colored lightweight fabrics. This method does not allow for a different color of marking for the various sizes of pattern markings. It is recommended for beginners on simple patterns when using fabrics heavy enough so that the traced lines will not show through to the outside.

The carbon should be in a color contrasting to the fabric. Remove the pins from a portion of the pattern. Assuming

the fabric has been folded right sides together, put a piece of carbon paper face up on the table. Slip another piece of carbon between the pattern and the fabric, with the face of the carbon toward the fabric (Figure 3). Repin the

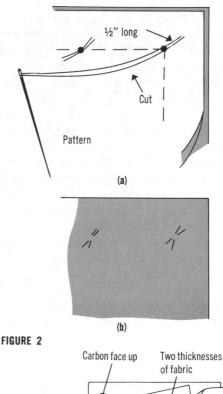

FIGURE 2

FIGURE 3

pattern. Then run the tracing wheel along the seamlines and dart lines of the pattern. Handling the wheel takes some practice, so try it out on some scraps of fabric.

TAILOR'S CHALK OR LEAD PENCIL

Chalk or pencil can be used to draw lines on fabric after the pattern has been removed. It is well to make the tips and ends of darts and any other important markings with tailor's tacks and then remove the pattern for sketching in ruler-straight lines with chalk or pencil. A pencil may be used on the wrong side of the fabric only; chalk can be used on the right side of some fabrics (test to be sure it will rub off). This is recommended as an auxiliary marking method. Pencil is ideal for use when making a muslin copy or for marking medium-weight cotton fabrics. The pencil line or chalk line should not be heavy and wide; it is more accurate if it is fine and sharp.

to use chalk or pencil Figure 4 shows the tips and ends of darts marked with tailor's tacks and any straight line drawn with

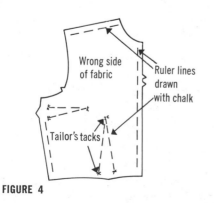

FIGURE 4

chalk or pencil. Use a ruler for drawing lines and draw lines on under side of fabric.

STAY STITCHING

A paper pattern is accurately and perfectly cut, and if the fabric is cut carefully along the edges of the pattern, an accurate copy of the pattern will be achieved. However, because of the nature of fabric, any edge that is cut on the bias or on a slightly bias line will stretch as soon as the pattern has been removed. If it does not stretch from the mere weight of the fabric, it is possible that you might stretch it as you work with it. This stretching will be noticed particularly in crepes and other heavy, slippery fabrics; it happens to some extent on all fabrics except the boardlike ones, such as taffeta and canvas. The purpose of stay stitching is to keep the bias curved edges of a garment from stretching—in other words, to ensure that the fabric will retain the exact measurements and shape of the pattern.

EDGES THAT MUST BE STAY-STITCHED

A basic garment is illustrated in Figure 5. Study it as you read the following rules:

1 Stay-stitch edges that will stretch as a garment is fitted. Examples: necklines, armholes, waistline edges of a fitted bodice or skirt.
2 Stay-stitch edges that are slightly bias and will stretch. Examples are armholes, necklines, zipper edges, and waistline edges.
3 Stay-stitch edges that will be handled a great deal during construction. Examples are the neck edge as a collar is applied and the opening edge of a skirt as the zipper is inserted.

1 Some fabrics stretch more readily than others. Included in this category are knits, crepes, sheath lining fabrics, the stretch fabrics, and any heavy fabric, such as a heavy wool coating, which stretches from its own weight. These fabrics should be stay-stitched. However, the stiff, boardlike fabrics such as tarpoon cloth, ticking, and taffeta do not stretch, and little or no stay stitching is required for them.

2 The ability of the individual is a factor to consider. The novice, who will work longer on each construction detail and who does not know as yet how to handle fabric properly, must stay-stitch to compensate for her temporary inexperience. The experienced person who has learned a certain elusive "something" about handling fabric can work with very stretchy fabric with a minimum of stay stitching.

if in doubt   There is no reason for being too concerned about whether or not to stay-stitch a particular edge. In most cases, if one is doubtful, stay stitching should be done; there is an important exception (explained below), but other than that, it will do no harm to stay-stitch an edge that does not require it. The following is a list of edges that need not be stay-stitched; reasons are given so that these might serve as principles to apply to a great variety of pattern pieces.

1 Edges cut on the lengthwise or crosswise threads need not be stay-stitched because those edges stretch very little, if at all. Examples are the side seams and waistline edges of a gathered or pleated skirt.

2 Outer edges of facings (unnotched edges) need not be stay-stitched because these edges will not be sewn to any other edge and need not be controlled so perfectly.

3 The cap of the sleeve need not be stay-stitched because it will be sewn to the armhole edge of the bodice, which will be stayed, and thus the sleeve is controlled by the armhole.

4 The lower edge of the garment need not be stay-stitched because it will be brought into perfect control when the hem is put in.

EDGES THAT MUST NOT BE STAY–STITCHED

The purpose of stay stitching is to prevent stretching, and therefore stay stitches are required on slightly bias edges. But notice the words "slightly bias." See Figure 6. If an edge is true bias or almost true bias, it was purposely cut that way to achieve a certain effect. A bias line drapes well and folds well and stretches; some designs require those qualities, and to stay-stitch bias lines would destroy that very desirable feature. The Bodice Front pictured in Figure 6 is such an ex-

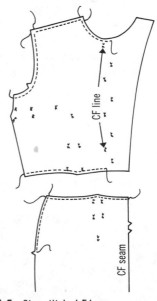

FIGURE 5 Stay-stitched Edges

ample. Note the direction of the straight-of-material line. This is the pattern for a cowl-neck bodice; the cowl neckline drapes and falls in limp folds. So the neck edge of the pattern, a true bias line, should not be stay-stitched. However,

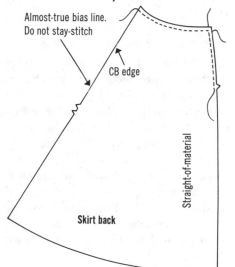

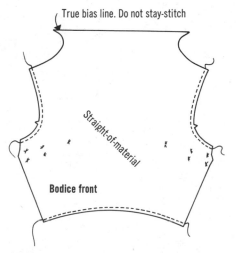

FIGURE 6

the armhole and waistline edges, which are slightly bias and which will fit close to the body, should be stay-stitched.

The Skirt Back shown in Figure 6 is another example when stay stitching would harm the finished effect. Note the direction of the straight-of-material line, and you will see that, by comparison, the center-back edge is very bias, almost true bias. In a flared skirt of this sort, the entire weight of the skirt is going to fall free from the body; most fabrics will stretch, and there is nothing one could do to prevent it. If the edge were stay-stitched, the seam itself would not stretch; however, the rest of the skirt would stretch anyway, and the seam would then look puckered. So skirts with bias edges are hung full length on a hanger before they are basted to allow them to stretch a maximum amount before work is begun on those pieces.

DIRECTIONS FOR STAY STITCHING

As soon as the garment is cut, either just before or just after the tailor's tacks are made, remove one pattern piece at a time and prepare to stay-stitch the necessary edges. See Figure 5.

Stay stitches are made through only one thickness of fabric. The stitches are done by machine with a stitch long enough to pull up if it becomes necessary to draw in the fabric to make it return to the size of the pattern, and at the same time the stitch must be short enough to serve the purpose of holding the edge firmly. In most fabrics except the very heaviest of wools, this stitch should be about 1/10 inch long (10 stitches per inch). In heavy wools the stitch might have to be 1/8 inch long (eight stitches per inch) in order to be long enough to pull up.

Use thread that matches the garment —the same thread you will use for the stitching of seams. The reason for this is that stay stitches do not need to be removed after the garment is finished, and a matching color will make the garment look more attractive from the inside.

The stay stitches must be placed outside the seamline, in the seam allowance. They may be placed anywhere from ⅛ to ½ inch from the cut edge. Most authorities give ⅛ inch as the correct placement because of this advantage: If you should have to let out the seams of the garment, these stitches would not show and would not have to be removed. The ⅛-inch measurement works very well on fabrics that are not too limp and slippery. Stitches ½ inch from the cut edge have the great advantage of giving control where it is needed most—very close to the seamline. This is of great importance in slippery rayons and silks, where control is badly needed at the seamline. Decide for yourself which measurement best suits your problem.

Since the stitching is done through one thickness of fabric and since the machine is keyed to stitching through at least two thicknesses of fabric, and since a longer stitch than usual is being used, the fabric is apt to pucker. This can be counteracted by a firm, gentle pull on the fabric as it comes through the machine. How much to hold it and whether to pull it slightly depends on the fabric. To find out, stay-stitch one edge of a piece, holding the material so that it comes out of the machine with no puckers. Then lay the pattern piece back on the fabric and see whether that stay-stitched edge is just like the pattern. If the fabric is now shorter than the pattern,

that is your cue to hold it more firmly as it moves through the machine; if the fabric measures more than the pattern, hold it less firmly than you did.

Stay-stitch each edge of the fabric with separate threads, as shown, leaving short (½ inch or so) ends of thread; each edge can then be adjusted in length as it may require without changing any other edge that may measure the proper amount.

important test Always put every pattern piece back on the fabric and check every edge to see that it has retained the same measurements as the paper pattern. If an edge is too long, pull up the bobbin thread until that edge measures exactly the same as the pattern. If an edge has been drawn up and is too short, loosen the stitches and cut them if necessary in order to achieve an exact copy of the pattern.

A BRIEF REVIEW

Stay-stitch any bias edge, except the long, almost true bias edges. Use matching thread and stitch with a stitch about ¹⁄₁₀ inch long. Place stitches ⅛ to ½ inch from the cut edge. Cut threads at each corner. Always test every piece and every edge of every piece with the original paper pattern.

HOW
TO
READ
THE CONSTRUCTION
SIDE
OF
THE INSTRUCTION
SHEET

The instruction sheet must be small enough to be handled conveniently during construction. This puts a limitation on the size of the sheet and means that the instructions must necessarily be brief. Because of this, writers of how-to information (whether it concerns clothing construction, laying a tile floor, or making furniture) use what I call "telegram English" to conserve space. Technical writing is brief and concise, and *every* word in the sentence, every comma, and every period are important. The little frills of wording that add color and clarity must be dispensed with. It is this terseness, this brevity that causes most people to think that directions are difficult to read. We are so accustomed to reading with a short-story technique, sliding over a few words here and condensing a paragraph there, that technical writing seems new and strange and difficult. True, it is more difficult than light reading, but it can be mastered so that it becomes easy. It is your most difficult job in learning to sew, this weighing of every word in a sentence. However, once you have mastered the technique, you will be able to make any garment you desire—make it easily and beautifully.

I firmly believe that the ability to read and follow directions is more important to success than a natural gift for sewing. I have seen rank beginners who progressed from a simple cotton dress to a lined suit as a second project; and in every case those persons were the ones who read directions well. I have known persons quite awkward with their hands who turn out beautiful garments because they read directions well. Truly this is the secret of success—train yourself, make yourself read directions, and value your instruction sheet.

Instructions are complete only if you read the directions and study the sketches carefully. The two go together; sometimes it is impossible to understand directions by reading alone and equally impossible to sew well by following the sketches only. Sometimes words are little or no help, and the drawings must explain the construction. This is called in pattern-company lingo *letting the drawing carry it*—meaning the drawing tells the story. By *letting the write-up carry it*, details which are impossible to draw are explained with words. And so written directions and drawings are dependent on each other. Unfortunately, too many persons take the lazy way out and make the garment by following the drawings

only. This is a serious mistake. It might work for one design, perhaps for many, but the time will come when a garment will be ruined because the written directions were not followed too.

The writer cannot include fitting in the instruction sheet. First of all, she could never anticipate all the problems her millions of readers would encounter with their individual figure faults. But more important is the fact that the issue of fitting would so complicate the sheet that it is considered entirely unwise to include it. Therefore, the directions read "Join seams," "Stitch darts," etc. Usually there is no mention of basting. The reader must realize that she must baste and fit and that when her fitting problems have been worked out, she can return to the instruction sheet and follow the construction procedures.

WRITTEN DIRECTIONS

The writer in the instruction sheet department has heavy responsibilities, for she is held responsible for all the directions (the written copy, the sketches, and the information on the printed pattern). She is, without exception, unusually talented in the science of clothing construction. She must write correct directions. But she must think of far more than that. There are many accepted and correct ways to arrive at a finished garment. The writer must decide which way is easiest, quickest, and most correct. She must write the directions in such a way that the accompanying drawings will be easy to follow. She must decide which method of several can be best described so that the reader will understand. She must write directions so that the majority of readers (those elusive "average persons") will understand them; yet she writes for a diversified clientele. She must consider what type of fabric the majority of customers will use. She must consider all these factors and even more. She must lead you to finish the garment correctly, economically, and easily, and with her wide experience in the field, she knows better than the home sewer which method will best do all three things. Follow her lead if you are a novice; improve on her techniques if you are truly experienced.

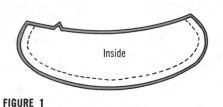

Inside

FIGURE 1

Inside

FIGURE 2

TELEGRAM ENGLISH TERMS

Some persons have difficulty reading the instruction sheet because they do not understand some few words that are used; probably these words are unique to clothing-construction directions. Some of the most common telegram English terms are defined and explained below. They are used so frequently that it is important to memorize them now, so that they become a working part of your vocabulary and so that you need not falter when you meet them in print.

face means place two identical pieces together, right sides together; baste and stitch on the designated edges An example of the use of the word "face" is given below in the terse wording of the instruction sheet.

Figure 1: "Face collar leaving notched edge open." This means place two collar pieces together, right sides together; baste and stitch on all edges but the notched edge.

join means place two corresponding edges together, right sides together; baste and stitch as indicated "Join" and "face" mean almost the same thing; notice that "face" is used when two identical pieces are involved, while "join" is used when two similar pieces are seamed together. Two examples of the use of the word "join" are given below in the terse wording of typical sewing directions.

Figure 2: "Join side seams leaving left side open below notch." This means place right sides together, baste, and stitch the entire right side seam and stitch the left side seam as far down as the notch.

Figure 3: "Join facing to neck edge, matching shoulder seams." This means place right sides together with shoulder seams matching, baste, and stitch at neck edge.

clip means cut with the tip of the scissors at right angles to the edge to within ⅟₁₆ inch of stitching, or it may mean cut with the tip of the scissors to within ⅟₁₆ inch of a designated point Two examples of the use of this word are given below in typical brief wording.

Figure 4: "Stitch seam. Clip curve." This means cut with the tip of the scissors at right angles to the edge to within ⅟₁₆ inch of the stitching. A clip is just a cut with no wedge of fabric cut out of the seam. However, a cut does not show up well in a sketch. In Figure 4 some clips are drawn as cuts, and they are not very noticeable. Because of this, the artist separates the fabric a little bit to catch the eye of the reader. Many persons who look only to the sketch and who do not read directions interpret the clips as notches; however, written directions should be followed to the letter. If the directions read "clip," it is to be a clip and not a notch, even if the sketch may lead you to believe otherwise. Remember, the artist always separates the fabric when she pictures a clip.

Figure 5: "Clip to corner small o." This means cut with the tip of the scissors diagonally into the corner to within ⅟₁₆ inch of the small o.

trim means cut off some of the seam allowance parallel to the edge Sometimes the instruction sheet will state the amount to be trimmed away, but more often the amount is not stated, so general rules must be followed.

Trimming seams is a truly necessary step if professional results are desired; this technique is discussed in great detail on pages 133 and 134. A word of warning: Some persons confuse the definitions of the terms "clip" and "trim." They remember that ⅟₁₆ inch is involved in one of the definitions and trim seams that close to the stitching. A seam may be

clipped at right angles to the seamline as close as ⅟₁₆ or ⅛ inch, but one must not trim parallel to the seamline as close as ⅟₁₆ or ⅛ inch.

turn under and stitch means turn under ¼ inch on the raw edge and stitch close to the

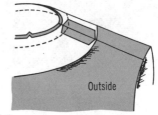

Outside

FIGURE 3

These lines do not catch attention

Outside

The artist shows clips like this

FIGURE 4

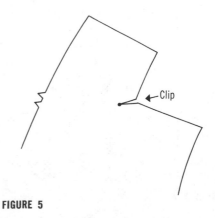

←Clip

FIGURE 5

fold edge   The pattern instructions do not state the amount to be turned under, but it is ¼ inch unless otherwise stated. Two examples of the use of these words are given below in typical instruction-sheet wording.

Figure 6: "Turn under and stitch long unnotched edge of facing." This means

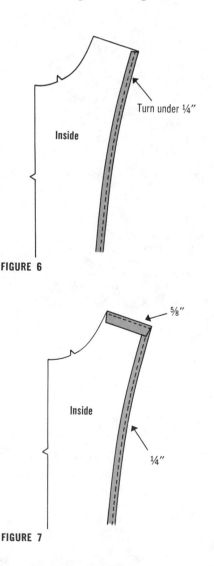

FIGURE 6

FIGURE 7

turn under ¼ inch and stitch close to the fold edge.

Figure 7: "Turn under seam allowance on shoulder edge and ¼ inch on long unnotched edge of facing and stitch." This is a case where there is an exception to the general rule of ¼ inch.

hem means turn under twice, encasing the raw edges and using the full seam allowance, and sew by hand or machine   If the directions read "Hem edges," you should assume that only the seam allowance is to be used for the hem. If the hem is to be wider, the directions will state the width or will instruct you to "turn up hem along hemline."

miter means join fabric in a seam at a corner by taking out a triangular piece   The directions may read, "Join facing to neck edge, mitering corner." The beginner really needs much more direction than that, but there is not space enough on the instruction sheet to take care of every little detail. How to miter corners is discussed on page 323.

notch out fullness means cut out triangles of fabric in the seam allowance   Fullness must be notched out of any seam with an outside or convex curve so that the seam allowance will lie flat. Perhaps the most common use of notching is on the outer curved edges of collars and cuffs, as shown in Figure 8.

reinforce corner means machine-stitch along the seamline to strengthen a corner that will be clipped later   See Figure 9. The directions read, "Machine-stitch along seamline for about 1 inch each side of small o." Reinforcing corners is another important step that is handled with necessary brevity on the instruction sheet. This issue will be covered in detail on page 118.

ease in fullness means to work in a slightly longer edge so that it becomes the length of a shorter edge   A common example is given below.

Figure 10: "Join shoulder edges, easing back to fit between notches." The notches must be matched and pinned into position, and then, rather than stretch the shorter edge, the slight amount of extra length should be worked in. The sketch does not show the ease because it is such a slight amount.

TECHNIQUES
USED
IN DRAWING
CONSTRUCTION DETAILS

The drawings on the instruction sheet are far more accurate and helpful than most persons realize. Notches and markings are shown in their proper position. Every detail is very carefully drawn in. These drawings require careful study. Again you must acquire the habit of "reading" every line. Certain general techniques, used by all pattern companies, are given below.

1 All drawings on the instruction sheet are in scale and are accurate in that they are exactly like the pattern pieces themselves. The diagram of pattern pieces (shown on the envelope back and repeated on the layout side of the instruction sheet) is a photostatic copy of the actual pattern pieces. It is a similar photostatic copy which the artist uses as she makes the sketches for the instruction sheet. Knowing this, you will trust the drawings more and will learn to rely on them for valuable help.

2 If you have difficulty understanding a particular point in construction, hold the garment in exactly the same position that is shown in the sketch. You will find this

an immediate help. The sketches are shown for the right side of the garment, so it is a good idea to do the construction of the right side before you do the left.

3 Every pattern company has some method of distinguishing between the right and wrong sides of the fabric. Most of the companies are now shading the right side of the fabric and leaving the wrong

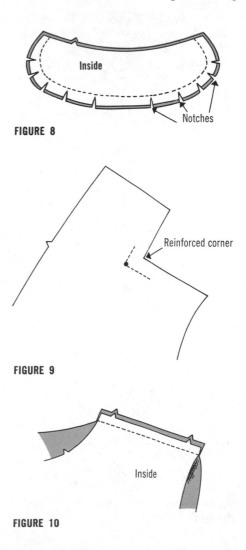

FIGURE 8

FIGURE 9

FIGURE 10

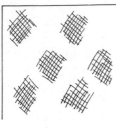

Methods of showing interfacing fabric

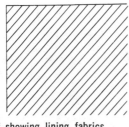

Method of showing lining fabrics
FIGURE 11

side the basic color of the paper. Check each pattern to see the system that company uses. If shading is not used, the word "inside" or "outside" appears on each sketch.

4 All pattern companies have ways of distinguishing among the fabric of the garment, the interfacing pieces, and the lining pieces. Although the policies of the pattern companies vary somewhat, interfacings are usually shown in patches of checks, dots, or flecks, as illustrated in Figure 11. Linings are quite consistently shown shaded with diagonal lines. Since the fabric of the garment has no lines through it, you are able to distinguish interfacings, linings, etc., very easily. Become aware of these small tricks in the drawings. A glance is not enough; study the sketches.

5 Basting stitches are shown as long stitches in the sketches, while machine stitching is shown as shorter stitches.

6 Notches and markings on the pattern are pictured in the sketch. There is no excuse for sewing the wrong seam because each seam has a different positioning of notches and the artist pictures the proper number and position of notches in her sketch. These important notches and markings are pictured in the sketch involved with that step, but they do not usually appear thereafter.

7 Often the writer and the artist decide that there is some virtue in picturing the construction when it is in the process of being done but not yet complete. Three examples appear in Figure 12. The person who looks only at the pictures is very confused by this practice because she wonders just how far to stitch the collar, how far down to stitch the seam, etc. Bear in mind that the instruction sheet gives very precise information; if stitching must end at a certain point, a marking appears on the pattern at that point. The written directions are more valuable

than the sketches, and if one must take a choice, the writings should be favored, for in cases like those pictured in Figure 12 the written directions would have read as follows: for Figure 12a, "Join unnotched edges of collar"; for Figure 12b, "Join side seams"; for Figure 12c, "Topstitch ¼ inch from finished edge of cuff."

IMPORTANCE OF FUNDAMENTAL KNOWLEDGE

Every truly successful garment is based on a firm foundation of simple, fundamental rules, followed scientifically. The little things, such as clipping or trimming seams, make all the difference in the world. Learn these fundamentals now. In every case, this chapter has been far too brief; many of the points covered here need elaboration. The following chapter, which is devoted entirely to fundamentals, will strengthen the points covered in this chapter and will provide a sound foundation for mastering the more difficult construction techniques to follow.

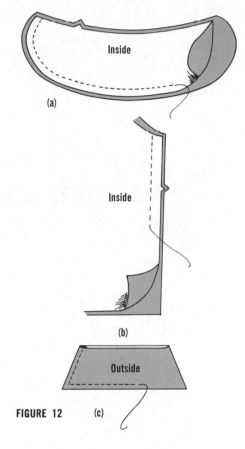

FIGURE 12

FUNDAMENTALS
OF
CLOTHING
CONSTRUCTION

This chapter includes a great variety of information, all of which must be understood in the very early stages of work on a garment. Unfortunately, it seems that one must know almost everything before beginning work, for each design is different: one design requires a certain bit of information, and another requires something quite different. In most cases the information given here is that which is needed very early in the game. But I have also included certain construction techniques that are so basic that they are not even mentioned on the instruction sheet; the instruction sheet department assumes that certain basic information is known by everyone, and although the reader might disagree, she must understand that it would be quite impossible for an instruction sheet to contain every bit of information she might conceivably use.

Study these fundamental techniques now, for they are very basic to success.

These pages will be referred to many times in the remainder of the book. When a reference is made to these pages later on, reread and study that section of this chapter again. Actually, as you work you will refer to this chapter so often that it would be well to mark it with a strip of seam binding or a bookmark so that you can turn very quickly to these pages.

CARE
OF FABRIC
DURING
CONSTRUCTION

Fabric should be handled in such a way that it is kept in good condition, avoiding wrinkles and creases from the time it is purchased to the time the garment is finished. This will mean that it need not be pressed as often, which will result in a saving of time and less wear on the fabric as well. But there is a more important reason for handling fabric well, and that is the effect the condition of the fabric has on the worker. If the fabric is wrinkled and looks unsightly, the standards of the worker lower, and she becomes discouraged. Clothing construction requires patience, and at every step in the procedure, the worker should strive toward habits that will encourage and aid her enthusiasm.

As soon as the fabric is purchased, it should be removed from the package and hung on a hanger in a strip as wide and as long as the closet height will allow. Most wrinkles that have formed in the package will fall out, and usually the fabric will not require pressing before cutting.

When the fabric is cut and before pattern pieces are removed, it should be laid out on a flat surface or hung on a hanger. Lightweight and medium-weight fabrics can be hung on a hanger without

tearing the paper pattern, but heavy coating should be laid out flat on a bed or table. As long as the fabric is in separate pieces while it is being marked and stay-stitched, all but the very small pieces should be hung on the hanger between working periods. The student who will

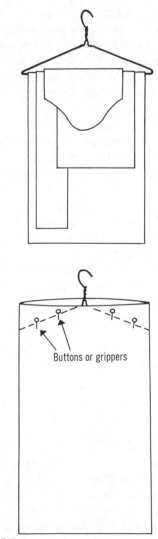

Buttons or grippers

FIGURE 1

need to carry her work across campus can avoid losing pieces by devising some sort of pillowcase covering for a hanger. Figure 1 pictures a very convenient coverall. It might be a pillowcase, or it could be a special covering made of denim, pillow ticking, or tarpoon cloth. Buttons and buttonholes or grippers placed in a line that takes the shape of the hanger will keep the pillowcase in place and will be easy to slip on and off the hanger. This covering will look more attractive on campus, will be a protection against the weather, and will prevent loss of pattern pieces.

While in construction, the garment should be hung on a padded hanger (skirts on skirt hangers) as soon as possible. This can be done very early in the construction process, almost as soon as the first seams are basted. The garment should be pinned in place—at center-front or center-back openings—so that it will not slide off the hanger.

During construction the worker should learn to keep her fabric as flat as possible on the table, smoothed out in an orderly fashion. She should have on her worktable only those parts of the garment she is working with at the time. She should never work with fabric folded up in her lap.

REINFORCING
CORNERS

There are points of construction which require a clip directly down to the seamline. The seamline must be reinforced at this point before clipping to prevent weakness and eventual raveling and ripping. Such points include the tip end of a gusset opening, the corner of the shoulder line and neckline seam in a collar cut in one with the bodice, and other points too numerous and varied to mention. This step is one of the very first construction processes.

Vogue patterns contain a great number of these clip points, and the more intricate the pattern, the greater the number. This is a basic construction detail, so basic the pattern may not mention it. But if directions for clipping are given, the points must always be reinforced by one of two methods, even if this is not mentioned on the instruction sheet. These points are reinforced before any basting is done on the garment. Go through the entire instruction sheet and look for all the points that are clipped or slashed before a seam is sewn, for it will save a great deal of time to do all reinforcing at the same trip to the machine. Think about the wear each point will receive, take your fabric into consideration, and then choose one of the two methods of reinforcement given below.

SIMPLE METHOD OF REINFORCEMENT
See Figure 2. This is suitable for points that will not get a great deal of wear and pull as the garment is worn and for fabrics that do not ravel. An example of a point that will not get a great deal of wear is the point which will be under the collar in a collar cut in one with the bodice, as pictured. Use a short stitch at the machine (17 to 22 per inch) and machine-stitch just inside the seamline for about an inch each side of the marking, stitching directly through the marking. Be careful to make a distinct point (do not retrace any stitches) because a cut must be made to within $\frac{1}{16}$ inch of that point. The point can now be clipped; however, it is well to avoid making the clip until the very time it is required for construction purposes. In fabrics that do

not ravel at all, such as felt or some of
the napped coatings, this method of reinforcement can also be used for points
that will get considerable wear.

VERY SECURE METHOD OF REINFORCEMENT

See Figure 3. This method will be used
more often, for it is required for points
which will get strain and which will pull
when the garment is worn and for fabrics
that ravel. The outstanding example of a
point that will get tremendous strain is
the slashed opening for a gusset. An extra
scrap of fabric is used for reinforcement;
this fabric will not be seen in the finished
garment, and so it does not need to be
of the fabric of the garment. It is well to
use a lighter-weight fabric, but it should
be closely woven. Lightweight interfacing, organdy, or sheath lining fabrics can
be used; one can use the fabric of the
garment if that fabric is light in weight.
Place the scrap of fabric (about a 2-inch
square) right sides together over the
point to be clipped or slashed in such a
way that at least ½ inch of the scrap
extends outside the seamline, as shown
in the sketch. Pin in place.

CAUTION A common mistake is to place this
scrap on the wrong side of the fabric; it must be
placed on the right side in order that it can turn
to the wrong side later.

Use a short stitch (17 to 22 per inch) at
the machine and machine-stitch along the
seamline, making a distinct point at the
marking. Be very careful not to retrace
stitches because a cut must be made directly to the marking. When this point is
clipped, the scrap of fabric is turned to
the inside, and it "acts like" a seam allowance at the point where there really is no
seam allowance. (Refer to the directions
for constructing a gusset on page 237 to
see how this scrap of fabric aids construction.) The clip or slash can now be made
any time it is required in the construction

process. It is well to avoid making cuts
of this sort until they are required in the
construction process.

BASTING

Remember that the instruction-sheet
writer must assume that the garment will

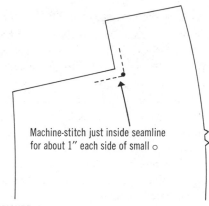

Machine-stitch just inside seamline
for about 1" each side of small o

FIGURE 2 Simple reinforcement

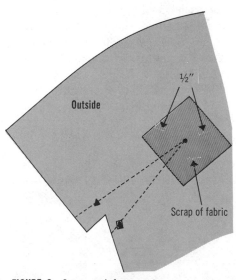

½"

Outside

Scrap of fabric

FIGURE 3 Secure reinforcement

fit, and therefore she does not include basting in her directions. The worker must, however, baste structural pieces for fitting purposes (explained in detail in Chapter 15), and she must baste certain construction points to hold them in place for accurate stitching. Careful basting results in the high-quality standards the creative woman desires.

PREPARATION FOR BASTING

See Figure 4. All seams or darts must be pinned prior to basting. The pins should be placed at right angles to the line to be basted because, first of all, the seam is controlled far better and the seam can bend and give as it is basted. In addition, one can baste right across the pins without removing them and then remove them all at one time; this is a very small saving in time, but it adds up to a great deal over a lifetime of sewing. The pin should catch a very small area of fabric right on the seamline so that the fabric is controlled well at the very place where control is needed. Compare the length of the pin in Figure 4 to the amount of fabric caught up by the pin; excellent control results if the pin catches in only about ⅛ inch of fabric, but in thick fabrics this amount may have to be ¼ inch.

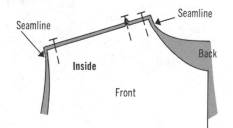

Seamline

Seamline

Inside

Back

Front

FIGURE 4

To pin two seam edges together, first pin one end and then the other; then match any points (such as notches or pattern markings) and pin in between these established points. Place patterns with long edges (such as skirts) flat on a table to pin them properly. In Figure 4 the ends of the seam and the notch position have been pinned; now the seam is ready to be pinned in between those points. The number of pins varies, and it is no virtue to use too many. A good rule is to use the number required to hold the seam securely and keep cut edges even. If this is a long, straight seam in firm fabric, pins every 5 inches would be sufficient, but if it is an intricately curved seam in slippery fabric, it may require pins every 2 inches or even every half inch.

THE PURPOSES OF BASTING

The purpose the basting is to serve will determine the method to be used. If the purposes of basting are understood, one can vary the length of basting stitches and save valuable time. The purposes are:

1 **to hold the garment together for a fitting** Basting threads must be fastened very securely at those points (such as waistline edges) that will get strain during fitting. When basting stitches are to be used for fitting purposes, they must be short enough and secure enough to hold the seams together as well as machine stitching would. That is essential for all seams that will be held close to the body during fitting (such as side seams of the bodice, darts, side seams of a close-fitting skirt as far down as the hipline, etc.); here, the stitches should be about ¼ inch long. On the other hand, if a seam will fall free from the body (such as the seams in a full, flaring skirt), the basting stitches need not be small (perhaps ½ to

¾ inch). Do not use a short stitch when a long one would serve the purpose.

2 **to hold two pieces of fabric together to keep them from slipping during stitching** During machine stitching the top layer of fabric tends to push forward because of the pressure of the machine foot, so the two edges must be basted to ensure accuracy. The length of the basting stitch which will serve this purpose varies with the fabric. Heavy fabrics (such as thick woolens) need short basting stitches (¼ inch) to keep them in line; flat, stiff fabrics (such as taffeta) will stay in place if a long stitch (½ to ¾ inch) is used. Then, too, certain construction requires shorter stitches. For example, attaching a collar requires a short stitch (a scant ¼ inch) because a small amount of slippage at that point would be serious, whereas a small amount of slippage on a side seam would be far less serious.

3 **as a guideline for topstitching** Many persons find that they are able to topstitch more accurately if they have a good basted line to follow. For this purpose the stitches need to be just short enough to make an accurate line and hold that line during stitching. They would vary in length from ¼ to ½ inch.

4 **to mark a line** There are certain lines on the garment (mainly center-front and center-back lines) that should be marked with a basting thread, so that they may be referred to easily while the garment is in construction. In that case a long stitch (1 inch) is desirable because it is easier to see.

5 **as an aid to pressing** Pleat lines and finished edges of collar and facings must be basted (¼- to ⅜-inch stitches) to keep them in the proper position until they are pressed.

Thread for basting should be in a contrasting color so that it can be seen more readily and removed more easily. Leftover spools of thread provide an excellent variety of colors, and regular sewing thread is quite acceptable for basting. It is wise to have a spool of nylon or silk thread for basting those edges which are basted as an aid for pressing. Regular sewing thread leaves an unattractive mark on fabric after it is pressed (it can be removed by steaming after the threads are removed), but silk thread is less apt to leave a mark. It is advisable to use silk for basting fabrics which are easily marked, such as satin.

THE SECURITY OF A BASTING THREAD

A single thread is used for basting, and there is no circumstance under which it is advisable to use a double thread. Security and strength of basting depend on two factors: the length of the stitch and the frequency with which the thread is reinforced with smaller, firm backstitches. See Figure 5.

TYPES OF BASTING STITCHES

even basting This is a firm basting used where there will be strain during fitting, for seams in heavy or crepey fabrics that slip during machine stitching, and as a guideline for topstitched details. See Figure 6.

Use a single thread of a contrasting color. Secure the thread as you begin by taking several small, firm stitches at the end of the seam. Make the running stitches about ¼ inch long. If the seam is long and if a strong seam is desired, secure the thread every few inches with small, firm stitches. Secure the thread well at the end of the seam.

uneven basting This is a less secure but faster basting method used where there is little strain during fitting; for seams in stiff, flat fabrics that do not slip during machine stitching; and as a guideline for stitching straight, long seams. See Figure 6.

Use a single thread of a contrasting color. Secure the thread as you begin by taking several small, firm stitches at the end of the seam. Make two stitches ¼ inch long and then make a long stitch ¾

to 1 inch long and repeat. Secure the thread well at the end of the seam.

machine basting This is done with a long stitch and is used on any edge except those involved with intricate construction. It is preferred by persons who handle fabric better at the machine than by hand. It can be used on any fabric that is not marred by the pressure of the machine foot as it sews over pins.

This is done with a contrasting thread. The machine should be set at the longest possible stitch. Because of the adjustable pressure foot on all recent machine models, the machine can sew over pins if they have been put in at right angles to the seam to be sewn. Machine basting has the great advantage of saving time. However, machine stitches do take

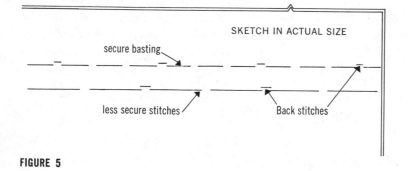

secure basting

SKETCH IN ACTUAL SIZE

less secure stitches   Back stitches

FIGURE 5

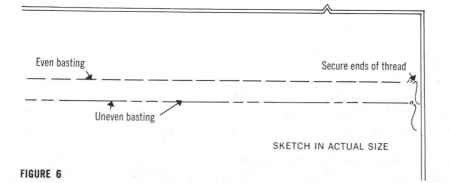

Even basting   Secure ends of thread

Uneven basting

SKETCH IN ACTUAL SIZE

FIGURE 6

more time to remove than hand stitches, especially in heavy fabrics. The machine should not be used for basting on such fabrics as satin because the needle marks might show after the thread has been removed. There is also some danger that the needle point might be slightly dulled by hitting the edge of a pin, and if this happens, the needle will immediately begin to snag any delicate fabric.

marking basting   This does nothing more than mark a line, and it is used to mark center-front and center-back lines.

This basting is done with a single thread in a contrasting color, and it is usually done on a single thickness of fabric. A long stitch should be used because it will define a line more clearly. Secure the thread as you begin by taking several small, firm stitches at the end of the line. Then take a long stitch (about ¾ to 1 inch) on the right side of the fabric and a short stitch (¼ inch) on the wrong side of the fabric. Secure the thread well at the end of the line.

slip basting   This is very time-consuming, but it must be used when working with

a plaid or striped fabric, where it is necessary to work from the right side of the fabric in order to match stripes properly. See Figure 7.

Use a single thread of a contrasting color. Turn under the seam allowance on one piece and lap it over to the seamline on the other piece. Secure the thread as you begin; work from the right side. Take a short stitch on the seamline of the under piece. Slip the needle through the fold of the upper piece and repeat. A seam basted from the right side in this manner can be stitched accurately from the wrong side. Secure the thread well at the end of the seam and do reinforcing backstitches often.

pin basting   This is a substitute for basting. Seams are not basted at all but are pinned and stitched. This method is favored by the quick-sewing advocates, but it has more limitations than they

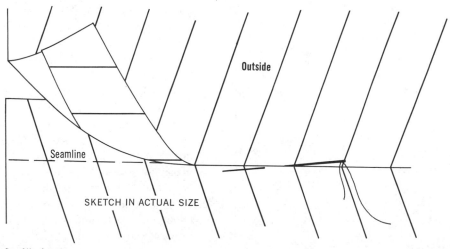

Outside

Seamline

SKETCH IN ACTUAL SIZE

FIGURE 7   Slip basting

claim. It can be used safely under the following circumstances:

1 The person who can handle fabric well at the machine and who can stitch a straight line without a basted guide is able to machine-stitch after pinning only.
2 The person who has a perfect straight-size figure does not need to baste for fitting purposes. And the person who has perfected her figure problems by careful pattern alterations, tested over a period of time, does not need to baste for fitting purposes.
3 Fabrics that do not shift out of line under the pressure of the machine foot (flat, firm fabrics) and fabrics that are somewhat stiff can be stitched accurately after being pin-basted.
4 Fabrics which are not marred by stitching over the pins and which are not delicate and easily snagged with a slightly dull needle can be stitched after being pin-basted.
5 Certain seams in any garment made of a firm fabric can be stitched without bast-

ing because fitting would not be done by altering the seam. Examples are seams in an all-around gathered skirt, seams that fall on the inside fold of a pleat, and the underarm seams of a full gathered sleeve.
6 Construction details that are not intricate can be done by this method.

Obviously this method has its shortcomings, and the person who wishes to do high-quality work will use it with caution.

BASTING DARTS

A common mistake many inexperienced persons make is to stitch all darts without basting them for a fitting; this person assumes she can do all fitting in the seams. This is a serious misconception, for actually darts are changed more often than seams during fitting. Darts control shape, which varies tremendously from figure to figure, whereas seams are more involved with allover size. It is very important to baste darts for fitting purposes.

The line on which the dart is basted and stitched plays a large role in the ultimate success of the garment. Most darts are ruler-straight lines, which means that the dart becomes increasingly narrower at the tip. The most common error in basting and stitching darts is shown on the left in Figure 8; the correct dart line is pictured on the right. The faulty dart line is simply not thin enough at the tip, and the garment will not fit the body curve smoothly. To get the "feel" of basting dart lines properly, fold the paper pattern at the center of the dart; notice how slim the dart becomes at the tip and then try to simulate this line in basting. Placing a strip of paper along the markings as you baste or drawing in a light pencil line will be an aid to accurate work until you are experienced enough to baste and stitch darts accurately without a guide.

Figure 9 pictures a curving dart,

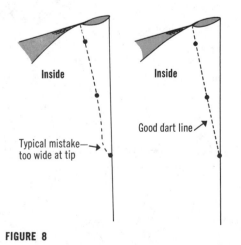

Inside   Inside

Good dart line ↗

Typical mistake—→
too wide at tip

FIGURE 8

which is used sometimes in the skirt front or in a skirt where a dart replaces the curving side seam. Notice that the tip is even slimmer in this case and that the curve must be a smooth, even line.

GATHERING AND EASING IN FULLNESS

If one long edge is to be sewn to a shorter edge, the longer edge must be gathered or "eased in." If the long edge is much longer than the shorter edge, it must be gathered; if it is only slightly longer, the term "ease" is used. The longer edge is drawn up to the desired length with gathering stitches, which should have the following characteristics:

1 Gathering stitches must be perfectly even in length. The best way to ensure even gathers is to stitch by machine. However, hand stitches are needed when very heavy fabrics must be drawn up into a very small area because in that case a longer stitch than is possible on the machine is required. If hand stitches are used, take the greatest care to make them even.

2 Gathering stitches must be as short as possible and yet long enough so that the material can be drawn up to the proper length. The gathering stitch must be longer than the stitch used for sewing seams because only then is it possible to draw up the fabric by pulling a bobbin thread. Small stitches make tiny, even gathers; long stitches draw up so much fabric that the result is a tucked effect. For gathering purposes, the machine can be set to sew with from 6 and up to 12 stitches per inch, depending on the fabric used. The heavier the fabric, the longer the stitch must be. It is well to test-stitch

a scrap of fabric to determine what length of stitch to use. Here are a few general suggestions to be used as a guide:

12 stitches per inch for:
georgette
chiffon
net

10 stitches per inch for:
voile
nylon
sheers
batiste

8 stitches per inch for:
rayons
rayon crepes
most medium-weight cottons

6 stitches per inch for:
heavy wools
stiff fabrics

3 Gathering stitches should be made so that the gathers fall at right angles to the seam and are very well controlled.

Notice Figure 10a, which pictures one row of gathering pulled up. See that some of the gathers fall at right angles to

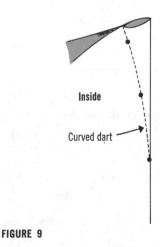

Inside

Curved dart

FIGURE 9

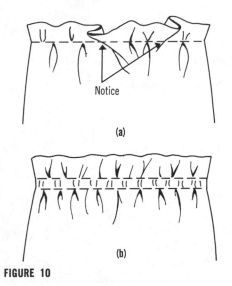

Notice

(a)

(b)

FIGURE 10

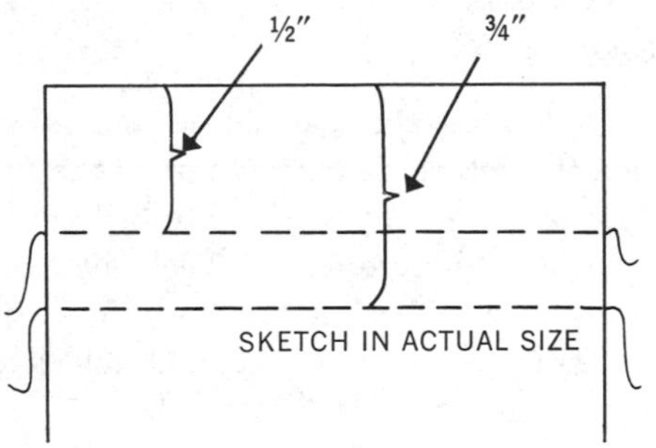

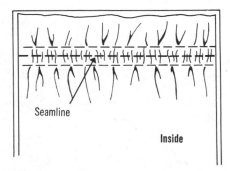

½″ ¾″

SKETCH IN ACTUAL SIZE

FIGURE 11

Seamline

Inside

FIGURE 12

the seam and that at other points the gathers fall every which way. There is not sufficient control at the seamline. Then see Figure 10b, which pictures two rows of gathering stitches pulled up. Notice how even and straight the gathers are. If the bobbin threads are pulled up at the same time, it is possible to keep the gathers in line and to make sure that they fall at right angles to the seamline.

Gathering stitches should be so placed that they control the fabric best for stitching; the best control is needed at the seamline.

GENERAL RULE Place one row of gathers on each side of the seamline, ⅛ inch from the seamline.

This means that the two rows will be ¼ inch apart, which is close enough to control the fabric well. All commercial patterns use a ⅝-inch seam allowance, so the gathering rows would be placed ½ and ¾ inch in from the cut edge, as shown in Figure 11.

There is an important exception to the rule given above, and it has to do with the lower row of stitches. There are some fabrics (satin is an example) in which needle marks show even after the threads have been removed. Pressing will erase the needle holes in most fabrics. You must test your fabric to see that needle marks will disappear with pressing. *If the needle marks remain after the fabric is pressed, all gathering stitches must be kept in the seam allowance. In that case, put one row of stitches on the seamline and the other ¼ inch outside the seamline.*

If the general rule can be followed, the stitching will fall between the two rows of gathering stitches. Figure 12 illustrates what perfect control there is at the seamline. Notice that the lower row of threads will show from the outside of the garment. This row of stitches can be easily removed by pulling the bobbin thread.

When the bobbin threads have been pulled up the desired amount, wind them around a pin. This will hold the gathers until the seam is basted (Figure 13).

EASING IN FULLNESS

See Figure 14. If the amount of extra length on one edge is very slight, the excess can be worked in with pins as described in method 1. If there is a greater amount of length to work in and if the fabric is quite stiff, gathering stitches will be an aid; see method 2.

method 1 Pin the two edges together at the ends of the seam and at the notches. Keep the longer edge uppermost as you work. There will be only a small amount of fabric to be eased in. It can be done by distributing the fullness evenly as pins are put in. Use more pins than usual. When the fullness is so well distributed that it lies flat on the under piece, baste with small stitches. When the seam is stitched and pressed, the small amount of ease will hardly show.

method 2 Put in two rows of stitches, just as you would for gathers. Pull up the bobbin threads until the two pieces to be joined are the same length. Pin and baste with small stitches. Stitch the seam and press as directed.

SEAMS
AND
SEAM
FINISHES

The purposes of a seam finish are (1) to finish raw edges to prevent fraying and (2) to make the inside of the garment more attractive. Of the two, the first is by far the more pertinent. A seam cut

along the straight or crosswise threads of the fabric will fray more than a seam cut on the bias. Each time you work with a new fabric, test a scrap of it to determine how much fraying will occur. Cut it on the straight and cross of the material and pull at the edges with your finger-

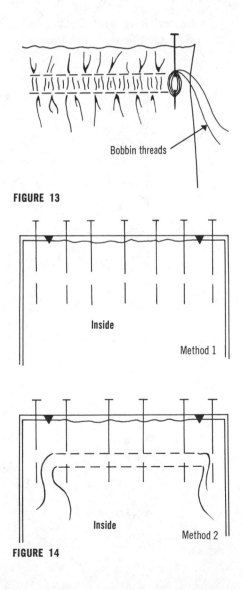

Bobbin threads

FIGURE 13

Inside

Method 1

Inside

Method 2

FIGURE 14

nails. If the entire length of a thread pulls away from the fabric, the fabric will fray very badly; if it is almost impossible to pull some of the threads from the fabric, there will be little fraying. In general, the seam finish which is the quickest to do and which will add the least amount of bulk to the seam is the one to use, if it is sufficient to prevent fraying. The more complicated finishes, the time-con-

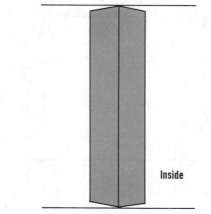

FIGURE 15

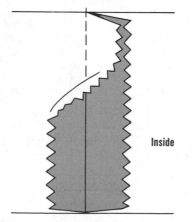

FIGURE 16

suming ones, and the finishes that add bulk are used for problems of serious fraying.

NOTE Any garment that is lined by a method which hides all raw seams (such as jackets and coats always, and dresses and skirts if they are lined by the method described in Chapter 27) will not require seam finishes; the lining prevents rubbing and wear on the seams, and they will seldom ravel appreciably.

plain This is the seam that is used for most functional seams in a garment, such as side seams of a bodice or skirt, underarm seams of a sleeve, etc. A seam pressed open is the least bulky of all seams. Place right sides together and cut edges even. Baste and stitch along the seamline. Press seam as stitched and then press open (Figure 15).

pinked This is the quickest finish to do and the one that is the least bulky, so it is preferred above all others, providing it will prevent the fabric from fraying. Always test a scrap of fabric with a pinked seam before deciding to use another finish. If pinking will prevent threads from pulling away from the fabric as you pick at it with your fingernails, by all means use this method of finish. Immediately after a seam is stitched, trim off about ⅛ inch of fabric with the pinking shears, which will result in a seam of ½ inch finished width. Then press the seam open. Each seam should be pinked and pressed before crossing it with another (Figure 16).

French The French seam is a very secure and neat seam finish, and it leaves no raw edges exposed. It is used only for dainty baby garments and delicate lingerie. This seam is acceptable on sheer fabrics only because it is one of the bulkier seam finishes. Notice in Figure

17 that this seam requires two stitchings. A seam that must be stitched twice on the machine is apt to pucker and will necessarily be stiffened by the additional stitching. This seam can be made ⅛ or ¼ inch wide, depending on the effect desired.

See Figure 17a. Place wrong sides of the fabric together.

CAUTION You are accustomed to placing right sides together.

Have cut edges even. Baste along the seamline. Stitch ⅛ or ¼ inch from the seamline, as desired. Trim close to

the stitching. Remove basting and press the seam toward one side.

Figure 17b. Place right sides of the fabric together, creasing the fabric along the seam. Stitch ⅛ or ¼ inch from the edge, as desired, thus encasing all raw edges. Press the seam to one side.

flat-fell See Figure 18. This seam is used on men's shirts, some severely tailored women's garments, and shorts and slacks. Like the French seam, it encases all raw edges. It is very time-consuming because it is done on the right side of the garment

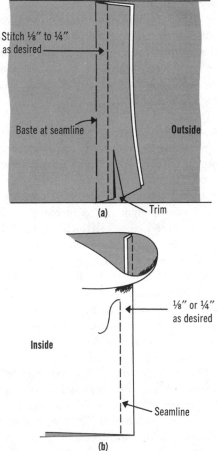

FIGURE 17

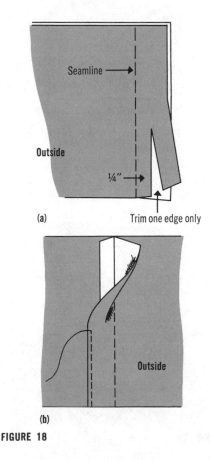

FIGURE 18

and must be very accurate. A false flat-fell seam, which gives almost the same effect but which is much easier to do, will be described later.

See Figure 18a. Place wrong sides of the fabric together.

CAUTION You are accustomed to placing right sides together.

Have cut edges even. Baste and stitch along the seamline. Trim one edge ¼

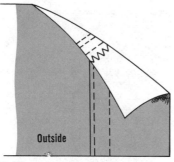

FIGURE 19

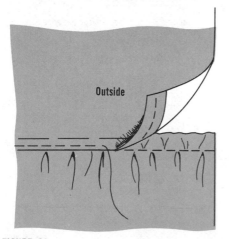

FIGURE 20

inch from the stitching. Press the seam toward the trimmed edge.

See Figure 18b. Turn under ¼ inch on the remaining raw edge and stitch it down to the garment. This takes time because all work must be accurate; the two rows of stitching, which will be part of the design, must be perfectly even.

false flat-fell The flat-fell seam is very strong and serviceable, gives an attractive tailored effect, and encases all raw edges. The false flat-fell seam can serve all these purposes except that it does not encase raw edges. It saves a great deal of time and is much easier to do. It is quite acceptable on most women's garments. See Figure 19.

Place right sides together and cut edges even, and stitch a plain seam. Press the seam to one side. From the outside or right side, stitch close to the seamline and then add another row of stitching ¼ inch from the first.

topstitched This seam is used for tailored effects usually. It is often used for stitching yokes to bodices and is very often used for stitching a plain edge to a gathered edge. See Figure 20. This seam is less conspicuous if the machine stitching is placed close (1⁄16 inch) to the fold edge. For more tailored effects, the stitching can be done ¼ inch from the fold edge. Turn under the seam allowance on one edge and press or baste. Lap the fold edge of this piece to the seamline of the other piece and baste. Topstitch the seam as desired.

Often a curved edge must be topstitched. An example of a bodice yoke is given in Figure 21, and another outstanding example is a curved pocket which must be topstitched to the garment. Turning under a curved edge presents additional problems. The curve must be smooth and even, and this is difficult to achieve. The first essential is to baste under this edge with small basting stitches placed ⅟₁₆ inch from the fold. Ripples in the seamline should be notched out as shown in Figure 21. Then the seam will lie flat, and it is prepared for topstitching to another edge.

zigzag The zigzag feature on recent-model sewing machines is very helpful for finishing seams. This is an ideal method of finishing seams because it is quick to do and prevents raveling without adding great bulk to the seam. The stitches are placed close to the cut edge, but the length and width of the stitch must be tested out on scraps of fabric. If the stitch is too wide, it tends to roll up the fabric and make a ridge; this is more apt to happen in limp, lightweight fabrics. As an example, heavy wool could probably be finished with a stitch almost ¼ inch wide, whereas rayon crepe would roll up if a stitch wider than ⅟₁₆ inch were used. See Figure 22.

bound Rayon bias seam binding should be used. This seam finish, incorporating seam binding to encase the raw edges, is used to finish the seams of unlined jackets and coats. If the work is done carefully and if the seam binding matches well in color, a most attractive result is obtained. This finish is used for seams of heavy woolen fabrics that fray badly. It does add a certain amount of bulk because of the thickness of the seam binding. Many persons will try to encase the raw edges by folding the binding over the seam and stitching in one operation. It is all but impossible to obtain a good result that way. Notice Figure 23. The binding should be stitched first to the underside of the seam, as shown on the right-hand side of the sketch. Then fold the binding over and stitch on the upper side of the seam. This work should, of course, be

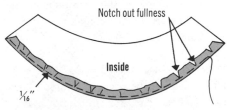

Notch out fullness

Inside

⅟₁₆ "

FIGURE 21

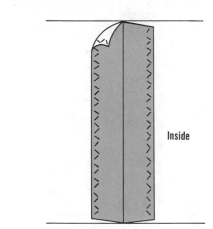

Inside

FIGURE 22

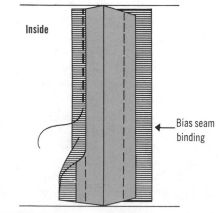

Inside

Bias seam binding

FIGURE 23

very accurate so that the resulting seam will be an even width. There is a danger of getting the binding on too tight and thereby drawing up the seam; sometimes it is necessary to baste first in order to avoid this.

turned under and stitched See Figure 24. This finish can be used on unlined coats and jackets and for finishing fraying

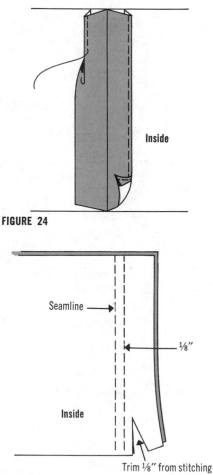

Inside

FIGURE 24

Seamline ⟶

⅛″

Inside

Trim ⅛″ from stitching

FIGURE 25

seams so long as the fabric is not too heavy. It is a bulky and stiff finish. Turn under ¼ inch on each seam edge and top-stitch close to the fold. Work accurately so that the resulting seam will be an even width.

a seam finish for sheers See Figure 25. Seams will show through a sheer garment. For this reason and because a sheer garment should look delicate, a narrow seam is desired. By pressing a seam in one direction instead of pressing it open, a narrower finished width can be obtained. The ideal finished width of a seam for sheers is ¼ inch. Because this is so narrow, it is advisable to double-stitch the seam to prevent fraying. Certainly the seams of a sheer cannot be bound because the binding would show through. In some fabrics pinking is not acceptable because the jagged edge would look unattractive.

With right sides together and cut edges even, stitch the seam along the seamline. Add another row of stitching ⅛ inch outside the first. Trim ⅛ inch from this final row of stitching. Then press the seam in one direction, and the desired ¼-inch width will have been obtained. Shoulder and underarm seams should be pressed toward the front, and center-front seams should be pressed toward the right side.

piped seams, plain and corded Piping or cording a seam stiffens it and gives an added decorative touch. Such seams are used in slipcovers, for outlining yoke lines, to add a decorative finish to waist-lines of children's garments, to emphasize the seams in a tiered-ruffle skirt, etc. Bias strips about 1½ inches wide are needed; see pages 250 and 251 for directions on cutting and joining bias strips.

See Figure 26. For plain piping, fold the strips in half lengthwise, wrong sides together. Run a marking basting ¼ inch from the fold edge. For corded piping, wrap bias around the cord and baste close to the cord.

See Figure 27. To apply piping, with right sides together place the basted line of the piping along the seamline to be piped. Pin and baste with small, firm stitches.

See Figure 28. Place together the right sides of the two pieces to be joined and stitch the seam in the usual manner. The piping will be caught in the seam and will give added emphasis to the seam.

NOTE If corded piping is used, a cording foot or zipper foot must be used to stitch the seam.

TRIMMING SEAMS—REDUCING BULK IN SEAMS

There are two types of seams in a garment. Structural seams are those which hold the large units of a garment together; examples are side seams of skirt and bodice, shoulder seams, armhole seams, and waistline seams. These seams are exposed to friction against the body as the garment is worn and are therefore apt to fray and wear. For this reason, these seams should remain the full ⅝ inch wide; they are not trimmed unless a very slight amount is trimmed off with pinking shears. Another type, called *encased seams*, do not get wear and strain because they fold back on themselves (encasing the raw edges); they will never be exposed to sight or wear and therefore will not fray. Examples are outside edges of collars and cuffs and any faced edge, such as the front edge or the neck edge after a neckline facing has been stitched and turned to the inside. These seams should be trimmed to a narrower width to reduce bulk.

to trim encased seams See Figure 29, which pictures an encased seam in actual

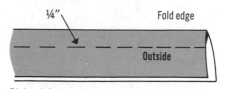

¼" Fold edge

Outside

a Plain piping

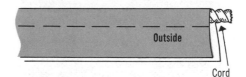

Outside

Cord

b Corded piping
FIGURE 26

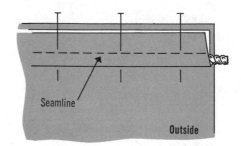

Seamline

Outside

FIGURE 27

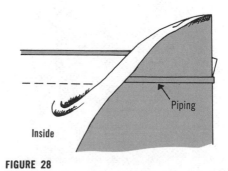

Piping

Inside

FIGURE 28

size. Encased seams usually include a third layer of fabric, an interfacing, which is indicated by shading on the sketch. Because this seam will turn back on itself, it will be very bulky at an edge which is very noticeable in a garment; actually there will be four thicknesses of fabric plus the interfacing right at the edge after this seam folds back. In order to reduce the bulk, encased seams are trimmed in a "staggered" fashion so that there will be no sudden "jump off" of thickness; instead, the thickness will gradually taper off from four thicknesses, to three, and finally to just two. All encased seams except those in very sheer fabrics should be trimmed in this way.

to trim corners of encased seams See Figure 30, which pictures an encased seam properly trimmed. The sketch is in actual size.

When an encased seam is turned to the inside, there is a great deal of bulk at the corners. Corners must be trimmed down so that they are as flat as the rest of the seam. As soon as the seam is stitched and before it is turned to the inside, trim the corners off to within 1/16 inch from the corner of the stitching.

GENERAL RULE Trim the corners in such a way that the two angles formed between the stitching and the cut edges equal the one angle formed by the stitching.

to trim corners of cross seams See Figure 31. When one seam is stitched across another or when a seam crosses a dart, there will be a great deal of bulk at the joining point. Figure 31a pictures the situation, and Figure 31b shows the corners of the cross seam trimmed away; the seam should be trimmed to 1/16 inch from the stitching lines. This removes one thickness of fabric and makes an amazing difference; the seam will now lie much flatter.

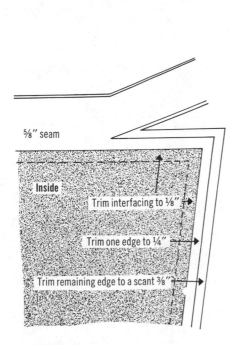

5/8" seam

Inside

Trim interfacing to 1/8"

Trim one edge to 1/4"

Trim remaining edge to a scant 3/8"

SKETCH IN ACTUAL SIZE

FIGURE 29 How to trim encased seams

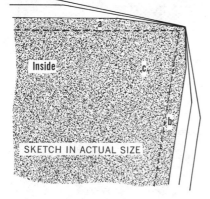

Trim to 1/16" of stitching

Inside

c

a

b

SKETCH IN ACTUAL SIZE

Rule: angle **a**
plus angle **b**
equals angle **c**

FIGURE 30 How to trim corners of encased seams

to reduce bulk of seams in hem area See Figure 32. The idea of staggered seams can be applied to the situation where one structural seam lies on top of another, as is the case in the hem. The identical situation is true when a facing seam lies directly on top of a structural seam in the garment, such as the shoulder seam of the facing and the shoulder seam of the garment. Both edges of the seam in the hem or facing area should be trimmed to ⅜ inch; staggered seams are ever so much smoother because of the gradual tapering off of bulk.

to decrease bulk in darts See Figure 33. A dart pressed in one direction will create three thicknesses of fabric in the area in which it lies. If the fabric is heavy, this will result in an unattractive bulkiness which is even thicker because a fold edge is more bulky than two cut edges. If a dart measures ½ inch wide when folded (or ⅜ inch wide in thick fabrics), it should be slashed and pressed open. It

can be slashed down to a point where the fold edge of the dart is about ¼ inch from the stitching line; this will mean that there will be a seam allowance of ¼ inch at the narrowest point. In wide darts, this might be quite close to the tip, but in narrow darts it might be quite a distance from the tip. A little diagonal clip through one edge will allow the dart edges to be pressed open and the tip to be pressed in one direction.

See Figure 34. If a dart is very wide (the under-bust dart is usually wide), trim ⅝ inch from the stitching line of the dart before pressing the dart open.

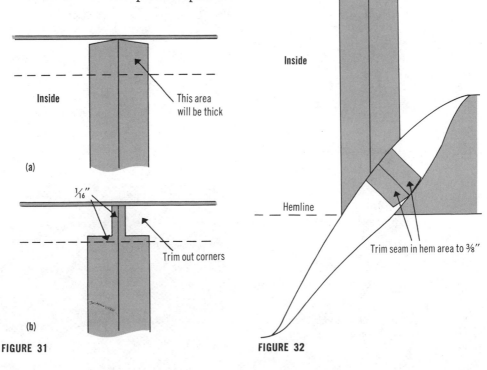

Inside

This area
will be thick

(a)

¹⁄₁₆″

Trim out corners

(b)

FIGURE 31

Inside

Hemline

Trim seam in hem area to ⅜″

FIGURE 32

TREATMENT OF FINISHED EDGES OF ENCASED SEAMS

Edges of encased seams are important edges because they appear at conspicuous places on the garment and are usually involved with the design which is intended to catch the attention. These edges are the edges of collars, cuffs, pocket flaps, and front or back opening edges if a separate facing is used. Every care should be taken that the seam line will not be unsightly. To prevent this,

these seams are rolled slightly to the underside of the garment as shown in Figure 35. Rolling them just 1/16 inch to the inside will hide the seam in most fabrics, but in some very heavy fabrics they may have to be rolled underneath as much as 1/8 inch in order to hide them entirely. This is an important step and one the instruction sheet department assumes you know. Directions will read, "Trim seam, turn, press," and it is assumed the worker will follow through on this basic technique. These edges must be basted in preparation for pressing,

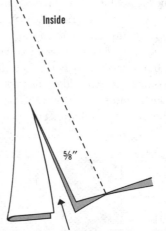

Trim wide darts to 5/8" from stitching

FIGURE 34

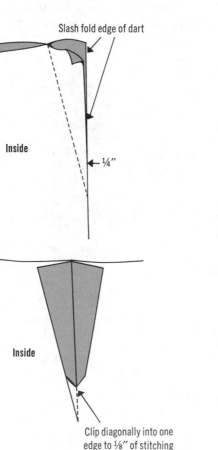

Slash fold edge of dart

Inside

1/4"

Inside

Clip diagonally into one edge to 1/8" of stitching

FIGURE 33

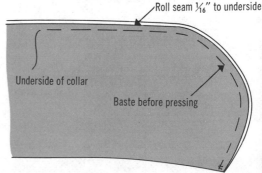

Roll seam 1/16" to underside

Underside of collar

Baste before pressing

FIGURE 35

even in quick-sewing methods. On the rare occasions I do quick sewing (a housecoat, perhaps), I do the whole process without basting, including setting in sleeves, but even so, I feel that these edges of encased seams must be basted.

THE MOST ESSENTIAL
HAND
STITCHES

The four types of stitches described here will solve almost every purpose of hand sewing because each can be modified somewhat to serve a particular purpose. Stitches can be made shorter and reinforced more often for greater strength; they can be longer and looser for an inconspicuous effect. Avoid "sewing the style out" of a garment with stitches too short or too tight. Many persons feel that they are doing a good job if they use very little stitches, but on the contrary, the beauty is being impaired for no good reason; in most cases hand stitches do not have a heavy job to do. Oversewing is what might be called "nailing it down" —the garment will look rather like a building with all the inside framework showing. A far better practice is to make hand stitches as long and as loose as they can possibly be and still hold the edges

securely enough. Easy, "lazy" stitches will make the construction less obvious, will make the garment look as if it "just grew"; an easy-does-it touch gives a professional result.

THE WHIPPING, OR HEMMING, STITCH

The whipping stitch is used for hemming purposes with a short stitch for narrow hems and bias facings and a longer stitch for hems of traditional widths. This is the quickest way to hem a garment, and although it looks less attractive on the inside than the blind stitch, which will be described later, it is quite acceptable for most hemming purposes. Figure 36 pictures a whipping stitch (¼ inch long) in actual size.

This stitch is done with a single thread of matching color. Working from right to left with the needle, catch one or two threads of the fabric and one or two threads along the fold of the hem. Be sure the stitches are inconspicuous on the right side of the fabric. It is well to take an additional fortifying stitch every few inches through the hem only. When

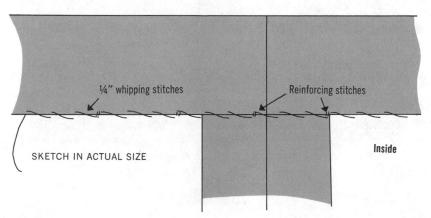

¼" whipping stitches   Reinforcing stitches

SKETCH IN ACTUAL SIZE

Inside

FIGURE 36

this stitch is used as a hemming stitch, the stitches should be ½ inch apart. If it is used for a whipping stitch, the stitches should be ¼ inch apart.

THE SLIP STITCH

The slip stitch is used for the finest construction on hems of traditional widths. It is very attractive because long floats of thread are hidden from view, but it is far more time-consuming than the whipping, or hemming stitch. The fact that threads are hidden from view means that they will be less apt to catch in jewelry or the heel of a shoe. Figure 37 pictures the slip stitch in actual size.

This stitch is done with a single thread of matching color. Working from right to left with the needle, catch one or two threads of the fabric and slip the needle into the fold of the hem for about ½ inch. Then take up a few threads of the fabric and repeat. Be sure the stitches are inconspicuous on the right side of the fabric. It is well to take an addi-

tional reinforcing stitch every few inches through the hem only.

THE CATCH STITCH

The catch stitch is used to hem down any raw edge, so that it is used to secure cut edges of interfacing pieces and is used for every hem and facing edge in the lined garment if the lining is constructed like the jacket or coat lining, which hides all raw edges. This stitch is not used for thin, sheer fabrics because thread marks press through to the outside. The catch stitch is illustrated in actual size in Figure 38.

This stitch is done with a single thread of matching color. Working from left to right, take a small stitch in the hem or facing (about ¼ inch from the raw edge) and then take a small stitch in the fabric, always holding the needle so that it points toward the left. Repeat, taking even stitches so that there is always an identical slant to the thread. Be sure the stitches are inconspicuous on the right side of the fabric.

THE BLIND STITCH

The blind stitch is used when a hand stitch must be used on a finished seam-

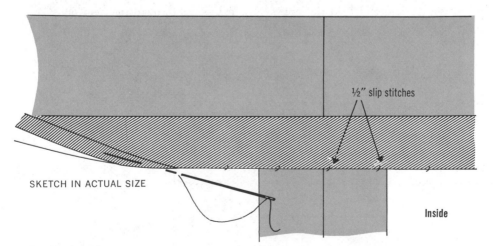

½" slip stitches

SKETCH IN ACTUAL SIZE

Inside

FIGURE 37

line and the construction requires the most inconspicuous stitch. This stitch is used for securing the seam of a bound buttonhole, for sewing in shoulder pads, and for other purposes too numerous to mention. This stitch is not pictured, so these directions must be followed by word description only. The stitch is done from the right side of the garment, with a single thread in matching color.

The stitches are usually placed right in a seam, and the work is done from the right side of the garment. Working from right to left, bring the needle up through the seam from the wrong side. Then take the smallest stitch possible (just a thread or two) in the seam and slip the needle under the seam. Do not pull the stitches too tight. Then bring the needle up again along the seamline and repeat. The length of the stitch varies with its uses from ¼ to ½ inch.

SHOULDER PADS

Fashions in shoulder lines change, so that there are times when the shoulder pad is a tremendously important issue and other times when it is almost unheard of. Some readers may remember that shoulders were high and wide in the

1940s, and of course the shoulder pad had to work the miracle. Of course pad manufacturers follow the fashions, so that pads which will give the current fashion effect are always available. In years when the natural line is favored, the pads are very thin. The woman who makes her own clothing should follow the lead of the best designers; if they use shoulder pads, she should use them.

Pads do serve purposes other than those involved with fashion; pads can camouflage figure faults, so that one might use them even if they are not currently fashionable. The person with one shoulder lower than the other can use a pad in the lower shoulder and remove the padding from the pad cover to use for the higher shoulder. The person with sloping shoulders can build up her shoulders to look more attractive. The person with narrow shoulders can use pads as a foundation to extend her shoulder line. And the person with bony shoulders that do not have a smooth line can use a pad (perhaps composed of nothing more than stiffening) to straighten her shoulder line.

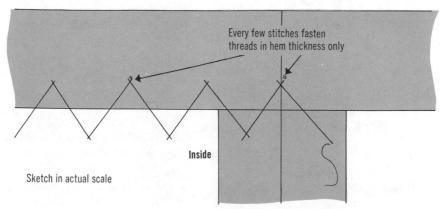

Every few stitches fasten threads in hem thickness only

Inside

Sketch in actual scale

FIGURE 38

The pad must be used for the very first fitting and in each subsequent fitting.

There are two styles of shoulder pads, *square* and *round*. See Figure 39. The square pad has a sharply defined angle at its outer edge. It is used for all garments with the usual set-in sleeve and regulation armhole. The round pad has a smooth, even curve at its outer edge. It is used for any garment which does not have a regulation armhole; for example, it is used for raglan sleeves, sleeves cut all in one with the bodice,

sleeves with a dropped armhole seam, etc.

There are four sizes of shoulder pads. Each is available in the round or square style. The size is determined by the amount of space the pad covers on the body and by the thickness of the pad. See Figure 39. The sizes are blouse, dress, suit, and coat, and the amount of space the pad covers on the body and the height of the pad increase from blouse to coat. Blouse and dress pads are covered with fabric, usually white or black, and need not be covered with the fabric of your garment, unless you prefer to do so just to add a nice touch to the inside of a garment or for a better effect in a sheer garment. Suit and coat pads are not covered with fabric and can be used only in lined garments. If you wish to use them in unlined garments, they must be covered.

Notice that all the pads cover a triangular area on the body except the coat pad. Coat pads are made with a squared line in front but have the usual diagonal line in back. This square shape in front allows the pad to cover a greater area, to fill in the hollow between the shoulder and the bust, and to give a better tailored effect.

TO SET IN SQUARE SHOULDER PADS

See Figure 40a. From the inside place the shoulder line of the pad under the shoulder line of the garment, allowing the pad to extend the desired amount beyond the armhole seam. Pin the pad in place at this point.

See Figure 40b. Turn the garment right side out. From the outside pin the other end of the pad in place, making sure that the shoulder line of the pad lies along the shoulder line of the garment.

Now hold the garment in the position it will take on the body, and smooth the fabric over the pad. Place a pin at each

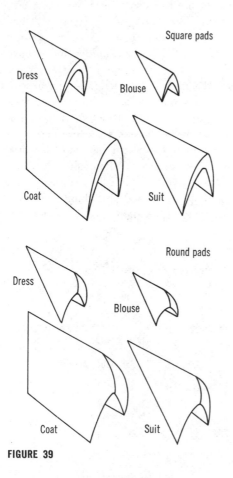

Square pads

Dress

Blouse

Coat

Suit

Round pads

Dress

Blouse

Coat

Suit

FIGURE 39

of the remaining corners of the pad. Try on the garment for a fitting. See that the fabric is not rippled up and that it lies smoothly over the pad.

See Figure 40c. Reread the directions for blind stitching on page 138. The pad is sewn in from the right side of the garment so that it can be held in the position it will take on the body. Therefore the blind stitch is used. The pad

should be blind-stitched along every seamline it touches. The stitches should be ½ inch long, and they need not go through the entire thickness of the pad, so long as they catch into part of it. If you are very careful not to pull them too tight, the stitches will not show.

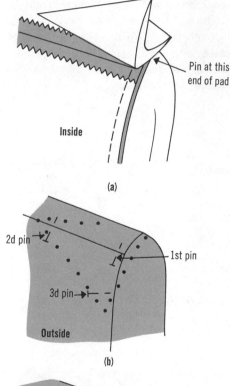

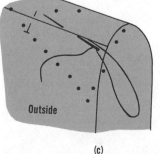

FIGURE 40 How to set in square pads

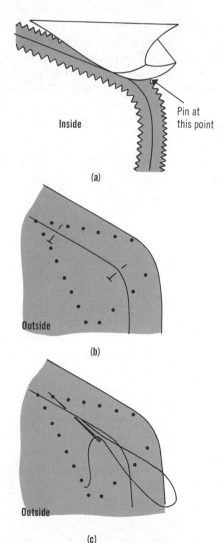

FIGURE 41 How to set in round pads

TO SET IN ROUND SHOULDER PADS

See Figure 41a. From the inside, place the shoulder line of the pad under the shoulder line of the garment. Pin the pad in place at this point. The shoulder line in this type of garment may be a seam, or it may be a dart. Usually there is a marking on the pattern to mark the position for the end of the pad.

See Figure 41b. Turn the garment right side out. From the outside, pin the other end of the pad in place, making sure that the shoulder line of the pad lies along the shoulder line of the garment. Try on the garment for a fitting. Check to see that the pad gives the desired width to the shoulders. The pad can be adjusted to whatever width is required.

See Figure 41c. Reread the directions for blind stitching on page 138. The pad is sewn in from the right side of the garment so that it can be held in the position it will take on the body. The pad should be blind-stitched along every seam it touches. The stitches should be ½ inch long, and they need not go through the entire pad, so long as they catch into some of it. If you are very careful not to pull them too tight, the stitches will not show.

12

PROBLEMS
OF
SEWING
WITH
VARIOUS
TYPES
OF
FABRICS

This chapter is planned as a résumé of
the basic problems involved with the
great variety of fabrics on the market.
Although some information, pertinent to
a particular fabric, appears here and at
no other place in the book, the primary
purpose of this chapter is to act as a
clearinghouse—as a review to aid in easy
reference to other parts of the book.

PROBLEMS
OF SEWING
WITH
WOOL

1 Reread the information given on pages 37 and 38 concerning tentering problems in fabrics; wool is often tentered a few inches off grain and must be straightened. It is advisable to have wools, particularly inexpensive ones, preshrunk before cutting.

2 Wools offer no particular problems in cutting, although the very heaviest may have to be cut one layer at a time to obtain an accurate cut edge. The pattern can be pinned to both layers of fabric, but the scissors can be slipped between the two layers to cut first the top layer and then the under layer of that edge.

3 Wool stretches and must be stay-stitched on slightly bias and curving lines; see page 106. If the wool is very heavy, almost like a coating, stay stitches are not enough to prevent stretching at the waistline edge during fitting; then it is well to baste a piece of cotton-twill tape along the waistline to hold that edge until the waistline seam is stitched or a waistband is attached.

4 Because of its thickness, wool tends to push out of line at the machine; the top layer pushes forward. Reread the entire section on Basting on pages 119 to 125. Baste spongy wools with small stitches and reinforce often. When stitching at the machine, decrease the pressure of the machine foot by making an adjustment on the machine.

5 Most wool garments must be interfaced with a partial or complete interfacing. Reread Selection of Interfacing Fabrics on page 44 and study Chapter 13, Methods and Techniques of Interfacing.

6 Many wool garments will be lined. Reread Selection of Lining Fabrics on page 41. There are two methods of lining included for dresses and skirts. One is the traditional method, which is quite easy and should be the choice of the beginner; see Chapter 14. A more elegant but much more difficult method is given in Chapter 27; this chapter includes linings for coats and jackets.

7 The seams of unlined jackets and coats should be finished by one of two methods: turned under and stitched (page 132) or bound with rayon bias seam binding (page 131).

8 Because of the thickness of wool, seams must be trimmed and the bulk decreased in every way possible. The whole section entitled Trimming Seams—Reducing Bulk in Seams on page 133 is essential reading.

9 The edges of encased seams must be rolled to the underside as described on page 136. In thick fabrics these edges may be rolled under as much as ⅛ inch if that is necessary to conceal them.

10 Edges of facings are never finished by the turn-under-and-stitch method, even though this is mentioned in the instruction sheet. See Figure 1 for three acceptable finishes for inner edges of facings. The seam-binding finish is traditional and will be preferred by many who will feel that the other two methods give an unfinished appearance. Actually, the other two finishes are quite acceptable and in a way are preferred because both result in a flatter finish and a more attractive appearance from the outside of the garment. The zigzag stitch can be used plain, or for a very nice touch, one of the decorative stitches might be used; the scalloped stitch pictured lends itself very well to this use.

11 Hems for lined garments such as coats

and jackets (or dresses and skirts lined by a similar method that hides all seams) remain raw and are catchstitched. The stitch is described on page 138, and the hem construction is described on page 296. Hems that will be exposed should be finished with rayon bias seam binding; hem construction is given on page 295.

12 Wool responds beautifully to heat and moisture, and for this reason it is one of the most satisfying fabrics to work with. However, its beauty can be easily destroyed by poor pressing. Wool must be treated as a living thing, for mistreatment makes it hard, stiff, and dead-looking. Bad pressing flattens the fibers, stiffens them, removes the natural elasticity of the fabric, and causes a shine. Read Chapter 17.

NOTE The looped mohairs create an additional problem. Sometimes the loops catch in the presser foot of the machine. A strip of tissue paper placed over the seam edge and fed into the machine with the fabric will prevent this problem.

PROBLEMS
OF SEWING
WITH
SILK

1 Many of the silk fabrics are slippery and difficult to control.

If the fabric is lightweight and limp, it may be so slippery that it will not lie in a rectangle on the cutting table. It can be kept in line for cutting by pinning it to a large sheet of tissue paper or by Scotch-taping it to the table.

2 Silk is easily snagged with a slightly dull pin or needle. Use silk or dressmaker pins and small needles. The machine needle should be of a smaller size than that customarily used. Always test-stitch each time you use the machine because a slightly dull machine needle causes serious snagging.

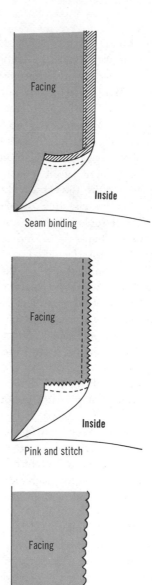

Seam binding

Pink and stitch

Plain or decorative zigzag stitch

FIGURE 1 Finishes for facing edges in wool

Many of these fabrics must be stitched with finer thread than is customarily used. This is particularly true of sheers and taffetas. If a test seam does not press open well or if the thread in the seam causes an unattractive ridge, the thread is too heavy. Silk or nylon threads are an excellent choice because they are fine.

3 If silk is used for a jacket or a tailored dress, it will require the extra body of an interfacing to be effective. Reread Selection of Interfacing Fabrics on page 44 and study Chapter 13, Methods and Techniques of Interfacing. For jackets and bodices of tailored dresses, the complete interfacing would be a wise choice.

4 A lining may be used to serve somewhat the same purposes as an interfacing. Reread Selection of Lining Fabrics on page 41. Directions for linings are given in Chapters 14 and 27.

5 Because these fabrics are thinner than average, additional pressure on the machine foot may be required. If maximum pressure will not keep thin fabrics from sliding, strips of tissue paper inserted into the machine with the fabric will aid in stiffening the edge for proper stitching.

6 Seams may fray and will probably require some kind of seam finish; see page 127. Avoid heavy, bulky finishes (bound, turned under and stitched) because inside construction details press through and show on the outside of these delicate fabrics.

7 Edges of facings and hems can be finished by the turned-under-and-stitched method or with seam binding. Test seam binding before using it; on fairly sheer fabrics in light colors, the seam binding shows through.

8 Silk creates special pressing problems be-cause it water-spots so readily. It can be pressed with a steam iron if it is protected with a dry press cloth or a sheet of tissue paper. But care must be exercised that no water drips from the steam iron (be sure steam has formed before starting to use the iron) and that there is no moisture in the ironing-board cover.

9 Silk shows perspiration stains very easily, and because it is a warm fabric (insulating) it tends to increase perspiration. During fittings it is well to take the precaution of tucking a facial tissue under the arms, and, even if you have no perspiration problem with other fabrics, dress shields are a wise precaution.

PROBLEMS OF SEWING WITH RAYON, NYLON, DACRON, AND THE SO-CALLED MIRACLE FABRICS

The man-made fibers offer an infinite variety of possibilities for interesting and serviceable fabrics. The fact that these fibers can be combined into a great variety of blends makes the whole family of the miracle fabrics so large as to defy description. Continuing research constantly broadens the scope and alters the characteristics of these fabrics. For all these reasons it is impossible to predict the problems an individual fabric will present. All the suggestions given for silk fabrics would have merit for most of these fabrics, although as a total family group these fabrics do not in general water-spot and stain from perspiration as readily as silk. Reread all the suggestions above and suspect that each might be helpful in these fabrics also.

Each new fabric or new blend requires a certain amount of research to solve the particular problems it presents. Test-stitch on the machine; experiment with length of stitch, tension, pressure on the machine foot, and methods of handling the fabric. Approach each new construction activity with caution; assume that a new approach may be needed.

Washing, ironing, and pressing require experimentation. Use scraps of fabric to test pressing techniques. In general the miracle fabrics require little ironing; however, this very fact may mean that seams will not lie as flat as they should. Perhaps more moisture or pressure will be required. Some of these fabrics will water-spot; test pressing will point out such problems. In general these fabrics must be pressed at a low temperature setting; many of them will fuse or melt if the iron is too hot.

These suggestions are intentionally ambiguous, for they must be very general and evasive. It is hoped the ambiguous nature of all these remarks will serve as a constant reminder that sewing with these fabrics is an adventure into the unknown. Experimentation is the only safe solution.

PROBLEMS
OF SEWING
WITH SHEERS
AND LACE

1 Many sheers, especially the limp ones, are "creepy" and difficult to control. They may not lie in a rectangle on the cutting table. They can be kept in line for cutting by pinning them to a large rectangle of heavy tissue paper or by Scotch-taping edges to the table.

2 The yarns from which sheers are made are of course very delicate; they can be snagged easily with a dull pin or needle. Use silk dressmaker pins (or small needles to take the place of pins) and small needles for hand sewing. The machine needle must be of a smaller size than average. Test-stitch for best results

and always test-stitch each time you use the machine because a slightly dull machine needle causes serious snags that often pull across the whole width of fabric. A fine thread, preferably silk, must be used for machine stitching.

3 Interfacing is not usually used in sheer garments because it would destroy the see-through quality desired in sheers. However, linings are sometimes used to serve an interfacing purpose, and they are preferred to an interfacing because they enhance the appearance of the fabric. Reread Selection of Lining Fabrics on page 41. Sheers and lace garments should be lined by the traditional method described in Chapter 14.

4 Because these fabrics are so thin, additional pressure on the machine foot will certainly be required. If the maximum amount of pressure will not keep them from slipping under the machine foot, strips of tissue paper inserted into the machine with the fabric will increase the bulk for proper stitching.

5 Seams on sheers are not pressed open because they would appear unattractively wide. They are pressed in one direction only; shoulder and side seams should be pressed toward the front, and center-front seams should be pressed toward the right side. Seams should always be narrow. French seams (page 128) can be used, but a better seam for fabrics that do not ravel appreciably is given under A Seam Finish for Sheers on page 132.

6 Darts should appear as a slim, narrow line. See Figure 2. This dart is handled exactly like the seam finish for sheers. Add an additional row of stitching ⅛ inch outside the dart line. Trim ⅛ inch from this last row of stitching for a dart

which will be an attractive ¼ inch wide.

7 Edges of facings and hems should be done by the turn-under-and-stitch method. Seam binding cannot be used, of course, because it would show an unattractive opaque line.

If the sheer skirt is based on a rectangle (the full, gathered skirt), the width of the hem is much wider than that of the traditional hem. The hem should certainly be 4 inches wide as a minimum, and many smart costumes on the ready-made market feature hems from 8 to 12 inches in width, or a double hem.

8 The slip worn with a sheer is truly part of the costume. Ideally each sheer dress (if not lined) should have a slip made especially for it. The fabric of the slip should be heavy enough to be shadow-proof, and the lines of the slip should conceal all undergarments; be especially careful that the slip is cut in lines that will hide the upper edges of the bra. The lower edge of the slip should be measured with the same care used for an outside garment; the slip should be hung about ½ inch shorter than the dress.

9 If shoulder pads are in fashion and are to be used, they should be covered with the fabric of the slip or of the lining.

10 Reread the section on the miracle fabrics, paying particular attention to pressing problems, discussed in the second paragraph.

PROBLEMS OF SEWING WITH PLAIDS

A plaid or striped fabric is more difficult to cut and sew than other fabrics, and it should be avoided by the novice. However, even plaids are much easier to work with than uneven ones (the differences between the two are explained on page 99), and so although I do not recommend their use for the beginner, suggestions for cutting and sewing even plaids are given below.

1 **buy an even plaid with the design woven in** The right and wrong sides will look alike. Avoid buying a plaid that has been printed on the fabric (the wrong side will look faded when compared with the right side). A printed plaid will match only if it has been printed on perfect grain; this happens so rarely that it is well to avoid the printed plaids.

2 **buy a pattern featured in plaid on the envelope** Plaid fabrics require special layouts, and only those patterns featured in plaid will include the necessary cutting diagrams.

3 **buy more fabric than the amount stated on the envelope** The amount stated on the envelope is the amount needed to cut the pattern, but you must allow extra for matching the plaid. Make an estimate using the suggestions given on page 100.

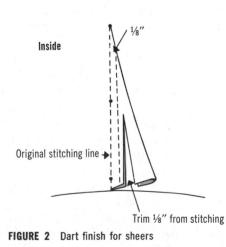

Inside

⅛″

Original stitching line →

Trim ⅛″ from stitching

FIGURE 2 Dart finish for sheers

4 **how to fold fabric for cutting** Select a layout on the instruction sheet for your pattern size, fabric width, and view. Then fold the fabric in that way. Now the fabric must be lined up so that the blocks of plaid in the upper piece lie directly over the blocks in the lower piece (Figure 3). Place pins every few inches to hold the two thicknesses in the proper position.

5 **placement of the pattern on the plaid is the most important and difficult problem** The way the plaid is cut determines to a large extent the beauty of the finished garment. It is this problem that the beginner will find so great because she does not have the experience necessary to visualize how the finished garment should look.

Figure 4 shows a simple design laid on an even plaid; the beginner should choose a design with simple lines and few pattern pieces. Of course, each design offers different matching problems, so the sketch and this discussion must necessarily be general. Study the layout very carefully as you read the suggestions given below.

a Every plaid has a dominant line (usually a wider line in a darker color); in the sketch, the heavier lines are the dominant ones. Center-front and center-back lines of the pattern should fall on dominant lines or midway between dominant lines. Notice that the center lines of the bodice front and bodice back lie over a dominant line. Because the bodice back is cut on the fold, the fabric was folded lengthwise on a dominant line. This rule applies to any center line to be cut on the straight-of-material—bodice, blouse, skirt, collar, facing, yoke, etc. If you prefer to have the center lines midway between dominant lines, the fabric must be folded in such a way that the

fold will fall between the dominant lines.

b Notches which will match each other must lie on the same crosswise stripe and on the same lengthwise stripe, if possible. In Figure 4, the notches have been numbered, and matching notches have been given corresponding numbers. See notch 1 in the two skirt pieces. Notice that notches 4 and 5 in the sleeves are laid on the same stripe as notches 4 and 5 in the bodice front and bodice back; one stripe of the plaid should circle the body in that area. Notch 1 in the skirt pieces is on the side seams, and notice that they lie on the same vertical and horizontal stripe. Notches 2 and 3 in the skirt

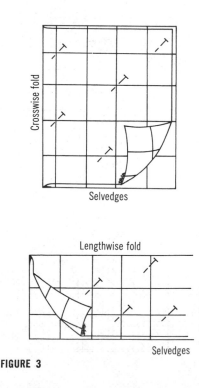

FIGURE 3

pieces are on center seams, which will not match another edge.

c The waistline and lower edges of the skirt pieces must fall in identical positions on the plaid.

d A straight hemline, such as the one at the lower edge of the sleeve, should fall at the lower edge of a dominant stripe, so that the finished hem will fall at the lower edge of the widest, heaviest stripe; this gives better balance to

the design. The same is true for hemlines of pockets or hemlines of straight, gathered, or pleated skirts.

CAUTION Be sure to put the hemline, not the lower cut edge of the pattern, on the dominant stripe.

e Certain pieces may be cut on the bias (see the band collar and flap) for an added decorative touch. The stripes on these pieces will run diagonally and will give subtle contrast. Notice that they are laid so that the dominant stripes cross each other at the center line.

f Notice that one edge of the bodice

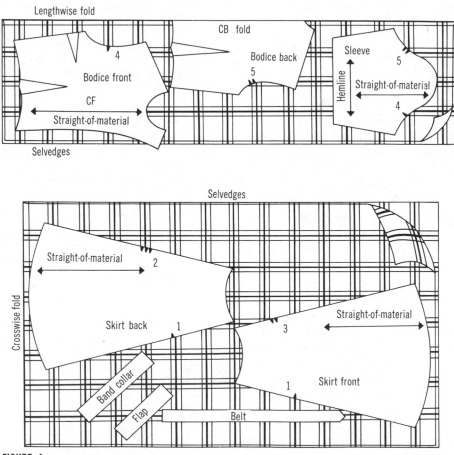

FIGURE 4

front extends over the selvedges of the fabric. There will be times when this is necessary in order that the pattern may be laid on so that it will match; in the sketch it was necessary in order that the center-front line could fall on a dominant stripe. Of course you must not make a piecing seam in a prominent position, but there are corners where piecing would not be noticeable. For example, the piece extending in the sketch is the facing section and will be underneath when the garment is finished. Plaids can be pieced very satisfactorily, and if they are matched and basted by slip basting (described on page 123), the piecing is most inconspicuous.

g The waistline edges of the bodice and skirt should be placed in such a way that the dominant stripes progress smoothly from bodice to skirt. Note that the lower edges of the bodice pieces in Figure 4 fall somewhere near a dominant line (they will not fall exactly on a stripe); the skirt pieces in the sketch are also placed approximately on a dominant stripe. Now note that the belt is cut on a dominant stripe. This is to ensure that the blocks of design will remain about the same size in spite of the unavoidable break in the design in the waistline area.

h Facings should identically match those edges of the garment to be faced.

6 **slip basting is required in order to match plaid perfectly** See page 123 for detailed directions.

PROBLEMS
OF SEWING
WITH
STRETCH FABRICS

Ready-made garments in stretch fabrics have been on the market for several

years, and now yard goods are offered on the fabric market in ever-increasing variety. The stretch fabrics promise to have an exciting future, and they are certainly adding an interesting new dimension to fashion. However, I feel compelled to emphasize that these fabrics have a future but do not have much of a past. This is something each woman who sews must understand. They are new and relatively untried; the manufacturers are experimenting to such an extent that the fabric on the market today may be very different from the fabric offered next season. One must understand that any promising innovation must be tested, not just once, but each time a different fabric is encountered.

The sewing of these fabrics involves problems that are quite easily solved; one need not be frightened of them so long as important techniques are tested. Because they are intended for comfort and action, these fabrics lend themselves best to the staple garment in basic lines—slacks, sport blouses and jackets, etc. Neither action nor comfort is quite as important in the very highly styled, intricate designs featured in International Couturier and Paris Original patterns, and I would not advise the use of these fabrics for any garment that is intricate and is apt to be costly in time and money. So long as these fabrics are in the experimental stage, it seems wiser to use them for less expensive garments that can be made quickly.

Although the sewing problems can be solved quite easily, there is concern about other problems. The matter of recovery is not entirely predictable; surely the reader has discovered that some of the ready-made garments increase in size with washing and dry cleaning. The fabric has not entirely recovered, and although some of the stretch characteristic remains, the fabric has actually lost some of its stretchability, just as elastic eventually wears out. This problem has not been great in slacks, for example, and perhaps I am too critical of this problem. My concern is for the interfaced, lined garment (a tailored jacket, for example) when recovery of the fabric, the lining, and the interfacing would have to be almost identical to create a compatible whole. In most cases, the reader would be wise to confine her sewing on stretch fabrics to those garments that do not require elaborate interfacings or linings, but on the other hand, she should keep an open mind about the future of stretch fabrics; the compatibility of fabrics may be completely predictable in the very near future.

The amount of stretch bears consideration. Those fabrics that stretch a relatively small amount are less experimental than those which have a tremendous amount of stretch. I have seen a wool fabric that would double in width with the slightest pressure of the fingers—it had far, far more stretch than one would ever need in width and far more than a knit garment would have. Fabric with this amount of stretch should be purchased with caution and with the realization that it might prove unsuccessful over a period of time.

There are three types of stretch fabrics available: (1) warp stretch, or lengthwise stretch, also called "action" stretch, which is ideal for ski pants and slacks with a stirrup strap; (2) filling stretch,

or crosswise stretch, also called "comfort" stretch, which would add to the comfort of sport blouses and jackets; and (3) two-way stretch, which is required of bathing suits. The information on the bolt of fabric should include the type of stretch, the amount of stretch by percentage, and the recovery by percentage. This information should be used to select the fabric to serve the purposes intended.

The problems of sewing are largely those of ensuring that seams intended to stretch can do so and of controlling those seams where stretch is undesirable.

1 The fabric may have been somewhat extended or stretched as it was rolled on the bolt. Allow it to relax for about twenty-four hours before cutting. Support the fabric on the cutting table (with chairs, etc.) because the weight of the fabric itself will distort the total length.

2 The pattern should be purchased in the usual size because, in general, the garment should fit exactly as it would if it were made of nonstretch fabric. However, when using a fabric with a warp, or lengthwise, stretch for slacks or pants which are to have a stirrup strap, the crotch area and leg area should be altered to a slightly shorter length than is required for the figure; the fabric will then have to stretch, and it is this small amount of stretch that gives these garments their characteristic trim appearance.

3 Machine stitching is the greatest problem. The needle must be smaller than one suitable for nonstretch fabrics of comparable weight. The important issue is that the stitch must have elasticity so that threads will not break as the fabric stretches. Test stitching each new fabric is an essential step; the stitch is elastic enough if it does not break when the seam is stretched to maximum length.

An elastic stitching line can be achieved in several ways:

a The zigzag stitch set at a narrow width (a scant ⅟₁₆ inch or so) is very elastic. Although the seam will not press quite as flat, the resulting elasticity is worth this slight disadvantage.
b Nylon or silk thread has more elasticity than any other thread so it should be the choice for all stretch fabrics.
c Short stitches are more elastic than longer ones; use about fifteen stitches per inch.
d The tension of the two machine threads should be equally balanced but should be looser than that used on a comparable nonstretch fabric.

4 Any seam that must give structural support to the garment and therefore must not stretch must be stayed with cotton-twill tape or straight rayon seam binding. Those seams are the shoulder seams, the upper armhole seam between the notches, neck edges, and waistline seams.
5 If an interfacing is used, it would be well to cut it on the bias, with the straight-of-material line of the pattern placed parallel to a true bias line on the interfacing. The bias cut will allow the interfacing to stretch somewhat and "keep pace" with the garment. Study Chapter 13, Methods and Techniques of Interfacing; use the partial interfacing method.
6 If the garment is lined, use a stretch lining fabric. Select a fabric which stretches in the same direction as the garment and which has a comparable percentage of stretch and return.
7 If a filling, or crosswise, stretch fabric is used, the hems must be elastic. The raw edge should be overcast by hand or with the zigzag stitch. The handwork should be done with catch stitches (page 138), for this stitch is the most elastic, or the tailored-hem construction can be used.
8 Scraps of fabric should be pressed to

determine the best method. The fabric should be pressed following the rules for pressing fabrics of the particular fiber content involved.

PROBLEMS OF SEWING WITH NAPPED AND PILE FABRICS

NOTE Special suggestions for working with fur fabrics appear in step 12.

A very broad use is made of the words "napped fabrics" on the envelope back and on the layouts on the instruction sheet; these words are used to refer to napped fabrics, pile fabrics, and other fabrics (such as prints) with a distinct up and down. Napped fabrics are soft wool fabrics which are napped (brushed up) after they are woven. They include suede cloth, broadcloth, and flannel. Pile fabrics are fabrics woven in such a way that cut ends of threads produce a furry or hairy effect. Outstanding examples are velvet, corduroy, and velveteen. Both napped and pile fabrics show shading differences depending on the way they are cut. *Velvet and corduroy should be cut so that the pile is running up in order to achieve a rich effect, while napped fabrics should be cut with the nap running down.* The nap or pile must run in one direction on a garment, and this means that a special layout (with all pattern pieces laid in one direction) is required; this type of layout requires more fabric. If napped textures are included among the "Suggested Fabrics" listed on the envelope back, the yardage chart will include napped fabrics, and there will be special layouts on the instruction sheet. It is unwise for the novice to make a garment of a napped or pile fabric with a pattern that does not suggest these fabrics, for it means that she must estimate the extra fabric required and must create her own special layout.

The designs on some fabrics have a distinct up and down and therefore must be cut with all pattern pieces laid in one direction. For designs of that sort, the "with nap" yardage and layout should be

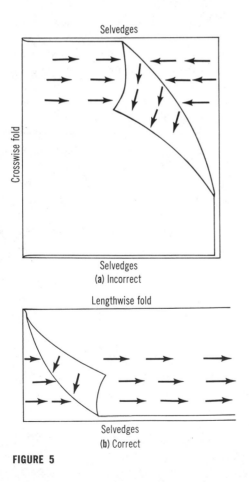

Selvedges

Crosswise fold

Selvedges
(a) Incorrect

Lengthwise fold

Selvedges
(b) Correct

FIGURE 5

used. In fact, some pattern companies point out this similarity by giving yardages for fabric "with nap or one-way design" and "without nap or one-way design."

1 These fabrics create cutting and layout problems.

They must always be cut on a lengthwise fold or open layout. See Figure 5. Arrows indicate the direction of the nap. Figure 5a shows a crosswise fold, which is incorrect for pile or napped fabrics. See the direction of the arrows; the nap or pile runs in opposite directions on the folded piece, so two pieces cut from these two thicknesses of fabric would have the nap running in opposite directions. Figure 5b, a lengthwise fold, shows a correct fabric fold for napped fabrics. Note that the nap runs in the same direction on the two thicknesses of fabric.

If the fabric must be spread out to its full width and two thicknesses are required, it must be prepared as shown in Figure 6. The layout on your instruction sheet will look like Figure 6b and will include a note similar to the one given here. Fold fabric on a crosswise fold as shown in Figure 6a. Cut along the fold. Now turn one piece around so that the right sides face each other with the nap running in the same direction.

To see which way pile fabric should be cut, hold the fabric up to your body and look down at it. Turn it the other way and look down at it. Decide which looks richer—there will be a noticeable difference, unless you have one of the new erect pile fabrics. Then lay the pieces on the fabric so that they will be cut with the pile running in the desired direction.

2 Refer back to To Figure Yardage for Napped Fabrics on page 98. This discussion points out that all pattern pieces must be laid on so that the top of each

piece is at the same end of the fabric. The top should be placed in the direction which will achieve the desired result.

3 The fake furs, because of their thickness, may have to be cut one layer at a time to obtain an accurate cut edge. The pattern can be pinned to two layers, but the scissors can be slipped between the two layers to cut first the top layer and then the under layer of that edge.

4 Pile fabrics tend to push out of line under the pressure of the machine foot; the top layer tends to push forward. Reread the entire section on Basting on pages 119 to 125. Decrease the pressure of the machine foot; use a slightly longer stitch and a slightly looser tension.

5 Many of the garments will be interfaced with a partial or complete interfacing. Reread Selection of Interfacing Fabrics on page 44 and study Chapter 13, Methods and Techniques of Interfacing.

6 Many of these garments will be lined. Reread Selection of Lining Fabrics on page 41 and study Chapters 14 and 27 for lining techniques.

7 Seams of dresses, skirts, and unlined jackets and coats made of pile fabrics (not napped) must be finished to prevent fuzz and little bits of yarn from continuing to fray from the seams. Binding with rayon seam binding (page 131) is the only successful finish.

8 Because of the bulk of these fabrics, the whole section entitled Trimming Seams —Reducing Bulk in Seams on page 133 is essential reading.

9 Edges of facings are never finished by the turn-under-and-stitch method even though this is mentioned on the instruction sheet. These edges should be bound, like the seams, with rayon bias seam binding.

10 Hems for lined garments such as jackets and coats (and dresses and skirts lined by a similar method that hides all seams)

remain raw and are catchstitched or finished by the tailored-hem construction. The stitch is described on page 138, the catchstitched-hem construction on page 296, and the tailored-hem construction on page 294. Hems that will be exposed should be finished with rayon bias seam binding; hem constructions appear on page 295.

11 The pressing techniques used for napped and pile fabrics are described on page 208. The important point to remember is

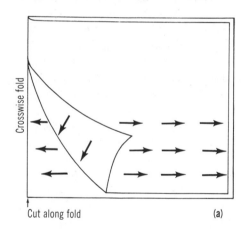

Crosswise fold

Cut along fold   **(a)**

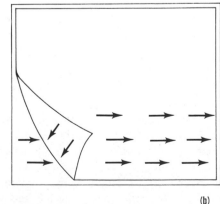

(b)

FIGURE 6

to avoid crushing the pile with the pressure of the iron.

12 The fur fabrics present all the problems of the pile fabrics and a few additional ones. Because these fabrics are unusually bulky, special attention must be given to pattern selection; there should be no pleats or gathers and preferably no collars or cuffs or pocket flaps, and the sleeve should be cut in one with the garment. In short, the most basic design is recommended.

These are pile fabrics and must be cut all in one direction, by a "with nap" layout. In addition, many of the furs have prominent markings which make it necessary to match the designs on the fabric, rather as one would match a plaid. Because of their extremely thick nature, each piece should be cut separately, never using a fold or double thickness of fabric.

Encased seams are very bulky, so it is wise, if it is at all possible, to cut facings from another fabric that is firm but flat by nature; a lightweight wool flannel is a compatible fabric, but it would have to be chosen in a near-matching color or an obviously contrasting one. If the facings must be cut of the fur fabric, do not sew the seams in the traditional manner but instead baste the cut edges together, wrong sides together, and use a bias trim or braid to encase the raw edges.

While basting and stitching seams, push the pile away from the seam and try to get the stitches down to the backing without catching in many of the hairs. If hairs are caught in the stitching, they can be pulled out by lifting gently with a pin. Always strive to avoid the "chopped off" look of hairs caught into the seam or hairs clipped off at the seam. Test-stitch to become adept at handling this problem.

Buttons and buttonholes should be avoided, except for fabric loops, made of a compatible fabric, which could be used to fasten buttons. Decorative hooks or braid loops or frogs are better fastening devices.

PROBLEMS OF SEWING WITH SUEDE

The problems of sewing with suede are varied and complex, requiring experience in several areas of clothing construction. The expense of suede, coupled with the difficulty of handling it, rules out experimentation, and only the experienced person should undertake a project as ambitious as this.

1 Suede is purchased in skin form, and so it is irregularly shaped. A pattern must be selected that will fit on the irregular skins, and the number of skins required must be estimated for the particular pattern pieces involved. The pattern should be of a simple design because collars, cuffs, encased edges, and complicated construction lines create difficult problems.

2 Pin marks and basting and stitching lines mar the suede, and so no fitting adjustments can be made on the garment. For this reason, the costume must be made up in muslin to test the fit and any corrections transferred to the pattern before the suede is cut.

3 Suede has no grain or direction, and so pattern pieces can be laid on in any manner required by the shape of the skins. However, some attention must be given to shading differences in the suede; select the most uniform and attractive

skins for the front and sleeves. Lay the pattern on and cut a single layer at a time; take care to reverse the pattern when cutting it a second time.

The pattern cannot be pinned in place unless pins are confined to the area of the seam allowance. The pattern should be placed on the wrong side and affixed to the skins with Scotch tape or magic mending tape. Markings should be made on the wrong side with pencil or chalk.

4 Seams can be basted if the stitches are placed within the seam allowance. Test-stitch on little scraps to ensure the best results with machine work. The machine needle should be large (3 or 4), and stitches should be relatively long—8 to 10 per inch. Suede stretches easily, so be careful not to put pressure on it as it passes through the machine.

5 Some miscellaneous points are as follows: A preshrunk seam tape can be used to reinforce seams that will get considerable strain. Seam allowances should be

trimmed to ⅜ inch. Corners must be rounded off because the suede will not turn into a point or corner. Interfacings can be used if desired.

6 Pressing suede is a problem and should not be undertaken until tests have been made on scraps. The iron should be moderately warm, the board should be covered with brown wrapping paper, and the suede should be pressed from the wrong side. Avoid great pressure with the iron. For encased edges that are especially heavy, place several layers of paper over the seam and tap lightly with a flat piece of wood, used as a hammer.

7 Hems cannot be secured by hand stitches but must be fastened with rubber cement or a liquid adhesive suitable for leather.

8 Suede garments should be lined; read Selection of Lining Fabrics on page 41.

METHODS
AND
TECHNIQUES
OF
INTERFACING

An interfacing is an underfacing, an extra piece of fabric that will lie underneath the outer sections of the garment and will be hidden from view by facings or linings. It is usually not cut of the fabric of the garment but from some slightly stronger and firmer fabric, for the main purpose of the interfacing is to add body to the garment. Review Selection of Interfacing Fabrics on page 44, paying special attention to the purposes of the interfacing.

Although the interfacing is hidden from view, it plays a leading role in the ultimate success of the garment. The more experienced the seamstress, the more she relies on interfacing to achieve the effect she desires. Many inexperienced persons (or just impatient ones who want to hurry) decide to omit the interfacing, and this is a serious mistake. One is led to believe that it is all right to omit the interfacing because some patterns state that it is optional. The pattern company makes this statement on those patterns which are simple and which the rank beginner or the woman who prefers quick and easy methods will probably buy. The staff of the pattern house realizes the interfacing is important, but the statement is made as a concession to the average customer, who is very inexperienced. Those persons who want to attain a high-quality product will assume the interfacing is essential rather than optional.

An excellent illustration of the importance of an interfacing is found in Vogue Paris Original patterns. It is not unusual to see a large percentage of the space on the instruction sheet devoted to techniques of interfacing. However, Vogue has a practice that is confusing to the beginner even if it is in harmony with the basic Vogue philosophy. Vogue assumes the customer has knowledge of fundamentals. And so sometimes Vogue fails to include the most basic interfacing (a strip of interfacing underneath bound buttonholes is absolutely essential) while at the same time using one-half of a column to give details for an interfacing responsible for silhouette. I mention this regrettable practice in particular because actually Vogue, being the most fashion-conscious pattern company, does the finest job with interfacings.

The instruction sheet for every pattern gives directions for cutting and using interfacing, but Vogue places more emphasis on interfacing. The other companies include the basic, most essential interfacings, and this basic step should not be ignored. With increased experience the customer will want to add even more interfacings. The most basic interfaced areas are collars, cuffs and pocket flaps, belts and waistbands, front or back opening edges, neck edges, and any

area where bound or machine buttonholes will be made. Interfacing requirements vary with the design, of course.

METHODS

1 The partial, or traditional, interfacing method, as its name implies, is one in which portions of the garment are interfaced. In general these portions are those listed in the preceding paragraph. This is the method used on most garments from most of the pattern companies for dresses, blouses, and brief little tops. Techniques involved with this method are described on page 163.

2 The complete interfacing method, as its name implies, is one in which the whole garment is interfaced. Methods of cutting and construction for an underlining or backing are identical to methods used for this complete interfacing. This method is relatively new, but it will surely gain in popularity because it is a very exciting innovation. This method is being used more and more often in jackets and coats, and it lends itself very well to tailored dresses and brief overblouses. Techniques involved with this method are described on page 164.

It would be well to look ahead to Figures 7 and 9 in this chapter for an understanding of the difference between these two methods. The woman who sews should make her own decision about such matters as this; she need not follow the directions of the pattern if her fabric or her personal preferences suggest another method. To better understand the advantages and disadvantages of each, consider the two methods applied to the various purposes of an interfacing:

1 **to keep the fabric of the garment from stretching** The partial interfacing keeps certain sections from stretching, while the complete interfacing controls the whole garment.

2 **to give stiffness and body to limp fabrics** The partial interfacing stiffens certain sections only but does not create a whole garment with increased body and stiffness.

3 **to give stiffness and body to certain portions of the garment** The partial interfacing does this, and if this is the purpose for which the interfacing is intended, the partial interfacing is quite sufficient.

4 **to act as a cushion for bulky seams** The partial interfacing cushions most of the bulkiest seams in the garment, and so it is adequate for this purpose.

5 **to build an unusual silhouette** In this case the complete interfacing is essential.

It is obvious that the complete interfacing has many advantages, and it will be the choice of many persons for more and more uses. It requires more fabric and increases the total cost of a garment of course, but the experienced person with high standards will think that the money is well spent. It may well be that the pattern companies will decide, for reasons of economy and simplicity, to favor the partial interfacing, as most of them do at this time. The woman who decides to use the complete interfacing must do her own layout to figure yardage amounts and must think through the cutting and sewing techniques for each new design, bearing in mind the basic principles given in this chapter.

BASIC
CONSTRUCTION TECHNIQUES
FOR BOTH METHODS
OF INTERFACING

when interfacing is caught in with the stitching of a seam In this case it must be trimmed to decrease bulk. See Figure 1. The seam should be trimmed as soon as it is stitched and before it is pressed. For seams that will not get a great deal of strain (all encased seams and seams in partial interfacings), the interfacing should be trimmed down to ⅛ inch from the stitching line. For the structural seams of a complete interfacing (shoulder and side seams, etc.), which will get strain as the garment is worn, the interfacing should be trimmed to ¼ inch from the stitching.

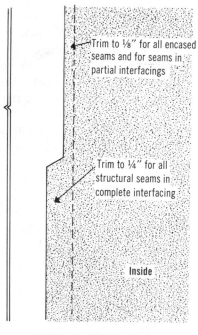

Trim to ⅛″ for all encased seams and for seams in partial interfacings

Trim to ¼″ for all structural seams in complete interfacing

Inside

SKETCH IN ACTUAL SIZE

FIGURE 1

to sew a seam in interfacing before it is placed in the garment Here the lap-and-stitch seam is used. See Figure 2. The seam is much flatter than the traditional seam, where edges fold back on themselves. The directions will read, "Lap seamlines and stitch." When seamlines are matched, the total lap-over is 1¼ inches (two ⅝-inch seam allowances). Stitch along the seamline. Trimming is not pictured in the sketch, but the seam edges should be trimmed to ¼ inch from the stitching line to reduce bulk.

if interfacings must be pieced This is quite all right because the piecing seam does not press through to the right side of most fabrics. It should be done by the lap-and-stitch method. The traditional seam is not used in interfacing under any circumstances.

to sew a dart through interfacing and fabric in one operation A few precautions will result in a smooth dart line. See Figure

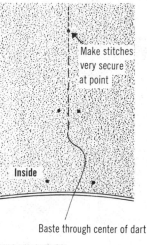

Make stitches very secure at point

Inside

Baste through center of dart

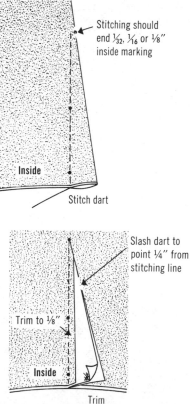

Stitching should end ⅟₃₂, ⅟₁₆ or ⅛" inside marking

Inside

Stitch dart

Slash dart to point ¼" from stitching line

Trim to ⅛"

Inside

Trim

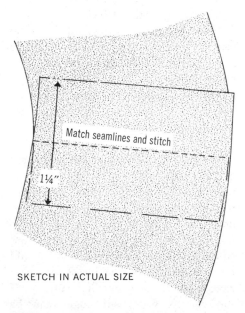

Match seamlines and stitch

1¼"

SKETCH IN ACTUAL SIZE

FIGURE 2 Lapped seam for joining interfacing pieces

FIGURE 3 To sew a dart through interfacing and fabric in one operation

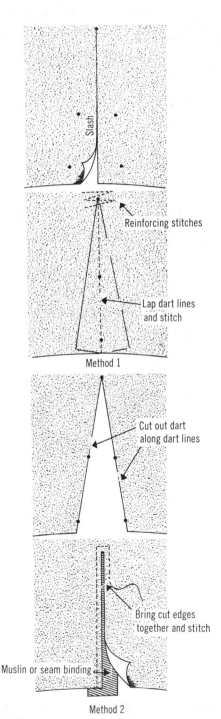

Slash

Reinforcing stitches

Lap dart lines
and stitch

Method 1

Cut out dart
along dart lines

Bring cut edges
together and stitch

 Muslin or seam binding

Method 2

FIGURE 4

3. When two thicknesses are stitched at the same time, there is a danger that the fabric underneath will slip out of line and that, in fact, the stitching will not catch through the under piece at the tip of the dart. To avoid this, baste down the center of the dart lines, making very secure stitches at the point; the two fabrics will now act as one.

The dart is stitched in the traditional manner with one exception: notice in the center sketch that the stitching line does not touch the fold edge at the tip as the stitching for a dart usually must for a smooth dart line. The reason for this is that the stitching must end at the fold edge of the fabric for the garment, which is underneath the interfacing as the dart is being stitched. Test-stitch a sample dart to determine how far away from the fold edge of the interfacing to end the stitching in order that the stitching will end at the point of the fabric for the garment. The heavier the fabric of the outer garment, the greater the distance must be; ⅛ inch is a maximum that would be required for thick wools.

The dart should be slashed down the center to a point where the fold edge is ¼ inch from the stitching line so that it might be pressed open. The interfacing should be trimmed ⅛ inch from the stitching line, and this must be done before the dart is pressed open.

to sew a dart in interfacing before it is placed in the garment Two methods might be used. See Figure 4. Method 1 is comparable to the lap-and-stitch seam. Slash down the center of the dart line to the point of the dart. Lap dart lines and stitch. The point will be weak and should be reinforced with machine stitches zigzagged rather like mending stitches. If the dart is wide, cut edges can be trimmed to ¼ inch from the stitching lines.

Method 2 has the advantage of a stronger point. Trim out the dart along dart lines. Bring dart lines together, cut edges even, and baste and stitch over a strip of muslin or seam binding.

to reduce bulk at corners of encased seams
Trim the corner point of the interfacing to ⅛ inch inside the seamline at the corner. See Figure 5. The point will, when faced and turned, be more definite.

THE PARTIAL,
OR
TRADITIONAL,
INTERFACING

Directions for cutting will appear on the instruction sheet. The suggestion for cutting the collar interfacing, pictured in Figure 6, is different from that which will appear on the pattern, but it is a desirable improvement and is therefore recommended for the beginner and the experienced person alike. If the collar is not a stand-up or band collar but will roll in a gentle curve, the shaping qualities of a bias interfacing would be very desirable. Place the center-back line of the pattern along a true bias line on the interfacing, cut one portion, and then fold the pattern over on the bias line and cut the remaining half. The interfacing will be handled no differently during construction, but it will mold into more graceful curving lines.

The instructions on the instruction sheet are very good, but a few remarks for emphasis will be helpful:

1 Occasionally a rectangular strip of interfacing is required. If so, the directions for cutting will be given in one of two places: in the cutting notes on the layout side of the sheet or within the text of the construction details.

2 Interfacing pieces are basted to the inside of the piece of the garment involved, cut edges even. See Figure 7, which pictures a bodice front and front interfacing. The fabrics should be placed flat on a table, smoothed out, and then pinned for basting. The basting stitches need not be short; it is well to place the stitches about ½ inch from the cut edge so that they can be easily removed when a seam is stitched on the ⅝-inch line.

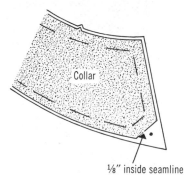

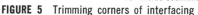

⅛″ inside seamline

FIGURE 5 Trimming corners of interfacing

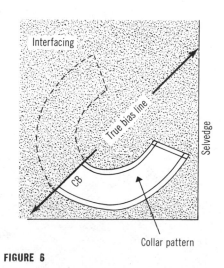

Collar pattern

FIGURE 6

3 There are times when the directions will state that certain edges should be catch-stitched. If an edge of interfacing touches a fold line, as it does in the lower sketch of Figure 7, that same edge must be secured with catch stitches. See page 138 for directions for doing the stitch.

Study construction techniques on page 160.

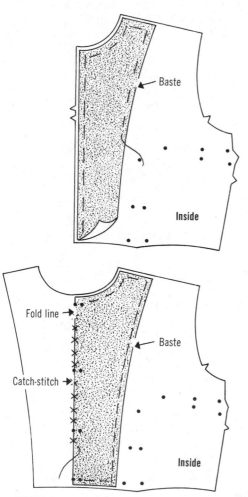

Baste

Inside

Fold line →

Baste

Catch-stitch →

Inside

FIGURE 7

THE COMPLETE INTERFACING (UNDERLINING OR BACKING)

Figure 8 pictures the structural pattern pieces of a boxy jacket. Portions which should be cut of interfacing are shaded in the sketch. Study these cutting suggestions very carefully; many readers will want to use this method, and a large number of patterns do not include directions. In general, the entire body of the garment is cut of interfacing, but hems and facings are not cut of interfacing as an aid toward decreasing bulk. The general rule is: *Cut interfacing to ⅛ inch inside hemlines and fold lines and in every other way cut it exactly like the structural pieces of the pattern.*

The sleeve may or may not be completely interfaced in this method. If the purpose of the interfacing is to add body to fabric that is otherwise too light in weight for the garment (for example, wool chiffon is too light in weight for a jacket), then the sleeves should be interfaced. If the purpose of the complete interfacing is to give more consistent body to a bodice or jacket than a partial interfacing could, and if the fabric is heavy enough for the purpose (for example, tweed is heavy enough for a jacket), then the sleeves need not be interfaced. The interfaced sleeve will be slightly stiffer, and the person who is very active might like the softer, freer feeling of a sleeve that is not interfaced.

Figure 9 pictures the preparatory step in the construction of the complete interfacing. The fabric must be flattened out on a table and the two pieces smoothed out to an accurate position before pinning the interfacing in place. The basting stitches need not be short, and it is well to place them about ½ inch from the cut edge so that they can be easily removed when a ⅝-inch seam is stitched. Notice that all edges are basted in place and that those cut edges falling at fold lines and hemlines are catchstitched in place. See page 138 for directions for catch stitching. At this time, the basting stitches through the center of the dart are done; see page 161.

Other sections of the garment—the collar, cuffs, pocket flaps, belt, etc.— should be interfaced just as they are in the partial interfacing method. Refer back to Figure 6 for a suggestion for cutting the collar interfacing (if the collar is rolled) that is different from the directions for cutting given on the instruction sheet.

Vogue pioneered the complete interfacing method and is, at this time, using it far more than the other companies. It is featured in practically all suit jackets and in many coats in the Paris Original and International Couturier patterns. A discussion of how Vogue handles the interfacing is in order. The cutting directions given here are slightly different from, and have a certain advantage over, the Vogue cutting directions; I recom-

mend that the reader make the small change in cutting and apply the principles given here to Vogue patterns.

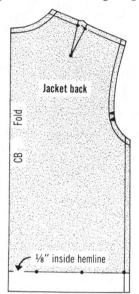

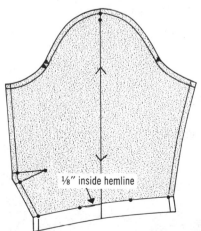

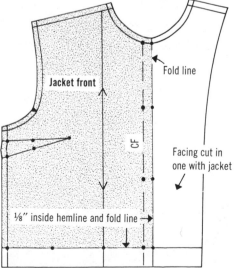

FIGURE 8 Pattern with shaded sections indicating how to cut complete interfacing

Vogue cuts the entire structural parts of the garment in interfacing; in other words, the Vogue interfacing is truly complete. The difference between these cutting directions and the Vogue directions is that these directions omit the interfacing in hems and facings cut in one with the garment and result in a smoother line and less bulk at hem edges.

At this time, Vogue uses the term "backing" to mean a complete interfacing in jackets and coats and the term "interfacing" for an additional, partial interfacing. Vogue intends for the backing to be a lightweight interfacing fabric, while the additional interfacing in certain portions of the garment is of traditional weight. Vogue also uses backing in many dresses, and in this case the backing doubles as a lining and should be chosen in a more lininglike fabric.

The directions in this book do not suggest two layers of interfacing, as many Vogue patterns do. If a proper weight of interfacing is used (heavier than Vogue's backing), one interfacing is sufficient. If, however, a small amount of body is desired in the body of the garment and much more stiffness in certain areas, the two interfacings are recommended.

Study construction techniques on page 160.

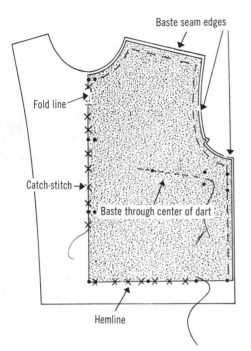

Baste seam edges

Fold line

Catch-stitch

Baste through center of dart

Hemline

FIGURE 9

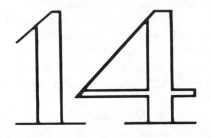

THE TRADITIONAL METHOD OF LINING DRESSES AND SKIRTS

SPECIAL NOTE The construction details given in this chapter are also applicable to the construction of underlinings and backings. The underlining, or backing, suggested by some patterns for dresses, skirts, etc., acts, in most cases, like a lining. The backing is cut and handled in a way that is exactly like this traditional method of lining.

The method of lining described in this chapter is one in which the lining is caught in with the seams of the garment so that the fabrics of the garment and of the lining act as one. In this method, raw seams show on the inside of the garment. This is the method of lining skirts, dresses, etc., often used by manufacturers for ready-made garments and by the pattern companies. I have seen it in the skirt of a suit which retailed for $400, which should prove that it is a most acceptable method of lining. Another method, described in Chapter 27, does result in a more exciting finish, for in that method the entire dress or skirt is lined like a jacket or coat, with no seams exposed. It might be well to glance through the sketches in this chapter and those in Chapter 27 for a quick comparison of the two methods. There is no question that the one finished like a jacket lining is the more elegant; it is used infrequently on the ready-made market in garments of superior quality. However, that lining is far, far more difficult to do and is included in this book for the experienced person; the novice or the beginner who is working without an instructor would be wise to choose the simpler method given in this chapter.

COMPARISON OF THE TWO METHODS

TRADITIONAL METHOD

In this method, which is described in this chapter, the lining and fabric act as one.

advantages This method is quite easy to do and requires little extra time. Any fitting problems are taken care of in one operation. There is a minimum of handwork. It controls stretch better than its alternative. The dress can be altered easily (that is why it is used almost ex-clusively in ready-to-wear), and hem length can be changed with little difficulty. Pressing and washing or dry cleaning are no great problem, providing the fabrics have been preshrunk. It gives a very attractive finish and serves most of the purposes of a lining very well. It can serve as an interfacing too if a stiff fabric is used to build out a silhouette. It looks professional if for no other reason than its similarity to lining in expensive ready-to-wear.

disadvantages Its disadvantages have to do with the fact that the lining is caught in with the seams. Seams will be bulkier, they will not press as flat, and they will be exposed and so may require special seam finishes. Hems will be more prominent because seam binding must be used and hemming stitches must be taken through two thicknesses of fabric. If the fabrics have not been preshrunk and if one should shrink more than the other, the results can be disastrous; sometimes the only solution is simply to cut the lining out of the garment. However, this last disadvantage, which is the greatest one, can be prevented by preshrinking both fabrics before they are cut. It is not as elegantly finished on the inside as the alternate method.

DRESS OR SKIRT LINING HANDLED SEPARATELY FROM THE GARMENT

This lining is handled like a jacket or coat lining. It is described in Chapter 27.

advantages The greatest advantage of this method in my opinion is that it is wonderful-looking, exciting, glamorous. To many experienced persons who set their standards high, this advantage alone will be the deciding factor. There are other advantages. All seams are hidden from view and friction, so they will not ravel and need not be finished. The hem can be left raw and catchstitched, and this results in an inconspicuous hem. Seams in the lining are sewn separately so that they press well, and the seams of the garment can be pressed flatter. One need not wear a slip with a garment lined by this method, and so there need not be unattractive folds of a slip to mar the beauty of the costume. And because seams are separate and lower edges are handled in such a way that there can be a "shift" in length, the problem is far, far less serious if the two fabrics do not react the same in dry cleaning.

disadvantages This method requires more time for stitching, handwork, fitting, and pressing; it may almost double the time required to make the garment (a fact that is no disadvantage to the woman who sews as a creative outlet, however). This method does not control stretch quite as well as the traditional method. Alterations and even changes in length are time-consuming and far more difficult to execute. Pressing the finished garment is more difficult, and for this reason it is not recommended for washables; the dry cleaners do an excellent job of pressing. The greatest disadvantage of this method is not obvious from glancing at the directions in this book. The examples of this method used in Chapter 27 are staple designs which serve instructional purposes best. However, depending on the design, this method can be easy, very difficult, or absolutely impossible. Each garment presents problems at pleats, edges that are gathered or pleated, and zippers, and it is common problems of this sort that I have included in Chapter 27. Skirts are usually quite basic and offer few problems, but dresses, especially Paris Original and International Couturier designs, can require tremendous experience. The order of construction of the garment must be changed

drastically in complicated designs, and the person who undertakes this method must be one who is experienced enough to "write" her own directions. Students working under an instructor could undertake this method, and all but the most inexperienced could use this method on a simple dart-fitted garment—skirt, slacks, or dress.

Both methods are good, and both are professional-looking. One is more elegant and far more difficult. If the reader would like to aim toward the lining comparable to that of a jacket, first select a dart-fitted skirt, then move on to a dart-fitted dress, and then try a dress with gathers in the front skirt; if all these ventures are successful, try your hand at a complicated pattern.

No matter which method is chosen, it would be well to reread Selection of Lining Fabrics on page 41 before proceeding. Preshrinking the fabric of the garment and the lining is absolutely essential in both methods.

CUTTING
THE TRADITIONAL
LINING

This lining is very much like a complete interfacing; it is cut in a similar way and constructed in a similar way. Figure 1 pictures a basic dress in which there are darts, a tuck, a pleat, and a facing cut in one with the bodice. The lining is cut exactly like the structural pieces of the garment with two exceptions: (1) cut the lining to ⅛ inch inside hemlines and fold lines, and (2) if there is a pleat that will be stitched down to a certain point, do not cut the entire pleat but add only a seam allowance of ⅝ inch beyond the pleat line.

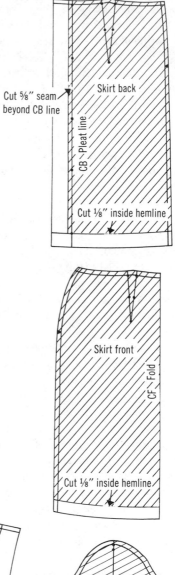

CONSTRUCTION DETAILS FOR THE TRADITIONAL LINING

BASTING

In this method of lining, the lining is basted to the underside of the fabric pieces as the very first step of construction. Figure 2 pictures a lining front basted to a bodice with a facing cut in one. It is important that the pieces be smoothed out flat on a table before the lining is pinned in place. The basting stitches should be reasonably secure, probably ¼ long, and secured every few inches. If the basting stitches are placed ½ inch in from all cut edges, they can be easily removed when a seam is stitched on the ⅝-inch line. The one edge which will not be held in a seam is catchstitched along the fold line (see page 138 for directions). Note that the tuck lines and

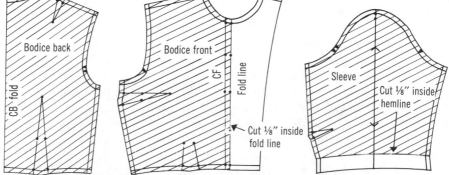

FIGURE 1 How to cut the traditional dress lining

the center of the dart lines have been basted; these steps will be discussed in the next few paragraphs.

TREATMENT OF DARTS

See Figure 3. When two thicknesses of fabric are stitched at the same time, there is a danger that the fabric underneath will slip out of line and that, in fact, the stitching will not catch through the under fabric at the tip of the dart. To avoid this, baste down the center of all dart lines, making very secure stitches at the point; the two materials will now act as one.

The dart is stitched in the traditional manner with one exception: notice in the center sketch that the stitching does not touch the fold edge at the tip as the stitching of a dart usually must for a smooth dart line. The reason is that the stitching must be a slight distance from the fold in order to be right at the fold on the fabric which is underneath. Test-stitch a sample dart to determine how far from the fold this stitching should end in order to be correct on the outside of the

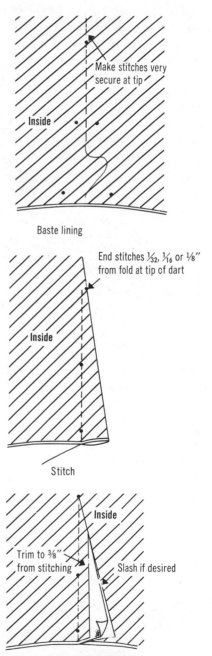

Baste lining

End stitches 1/32, 1/16 or 1/8" from fold at tip of dart

Stitch

Trim and press open if desired

FIGURE 3 Treatment of darts in lining

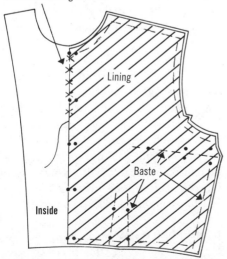

FIGURE 2 Basting the traditional lining

garment. The heavier the fabric of the outer garment, the greater the distance must be; ⅛ inch is a maximum that would be required for thick wools.

If the lining fabric and the fabric for the garment are rather thin, the dart can be considered finished at this time and can be pressed in one direction. It will be a more attractive garment from the inside if darts are not trimmed. However, in thick fabrics there is a value in

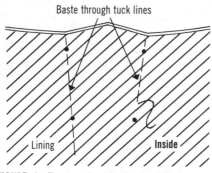

Baste through tuck lines

Lining   **Inside**

FIGURE 4 Treatment of tucks in lining

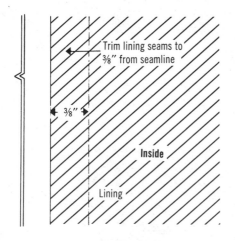

Trim lining seams to
⅜″ from seamline

⅜″

Inside

Lining

SKETCH IN ACTUAL SIZE
FIGURE 5 How to decrease bulk in seams

slashing darts and pressing them open. The dart is slashed to a point where the fold is about ¼ inch from the stitching of the dart. If the dart is slashed and the edges of the lining will be raw anyway, it is a good practice to trim the lining just as seams will be trimmed, down to ⅜ inch from the stitching line; this will aid in decreasing bulk.

TREATMENT OF TUCKS

See Figure 4. Tuck lines should be basted for the same reason that center lines of darts are basted. Basted tuck lines make the two fabrics act as one, and the tuck can be folded or stitched much more accurately.

TREATMENT OF SEAMS

Figure 5 is in actual size. After a seam is stitched and before it is pressed, the lining seam should be trimmed down to ⅜ inch from the seamline in order to stagger the seam allowance and decrease bulk in the seam area. The raw edges of the lining need not be finished, even if the fabric ravels, because they will be covered eventually by the seam of the garment and will therefore get little friction. Do not trim these seams with pinking shears because they are awkward to use and dangerous under these circumstances.

The seams of the garment will be exposed on the inside and, depending on the nature of the fabric, may require a seam finish. It is well to use as flat a finish as possible because these seams are necessarily bulky anyway. Pinking or zigzagging should be the preference, although bound seams will be more sturdy for cases of serious raveling. See page 127 for seam finishes.

TREATMENT OF PLEATS

Figure 6 illustrates the pleat construction. Notice that the stitching at the center-back pleat line caught in the seam allowance of the lining fabric as the pleat was stitched. Directions will indicate where the stitching for the pleat is to end; in this illustration it ends at the second medium dot from the lower edge, and below that point the lining and pleat are free. Make a clip directly to the end of the stitching as shown. Turn under ⅝ inch on the free edge of the lining; pin and baste. This edge must be sewn to the fabric of the garment at a place where the stitches could show on the right side. The stitch must be very inconspicuous, catching in just a thread of the fabric; it need not be a tight stitch, and it need not be reinforced because its purpose is simply to hold the edge of the lining in place.

TREATMENT OF HEMS

If the lower edge of the lining has been basted to the garment, remove that basting before the hem is measured. It is very important that the lining and garment hang as one, so that one of the pieces is not slightly different in length. Before the hem is measured, have an assistant pin the lining to the garment at a level about 4 or 5 inches above the hemline, allowing the two sections to hang as they "want to." The assistant can, at the same time, measure skirt length. But as soon as the garment is removed from the figure, the upper pin line should be basted as shown in Figure 7. Now as the hem construction is done, the worker is assured that the lining hangs properly down to the basting line, and she need only smooth out the lower few inches. If the lining should extend below the hemline, it must be trimmed so that it is about ¼ inch above the hemline; do not be alarmed if the lining is shorter, providing it is long enough so that the hem allowance will cover it.

Hem construction is given on page

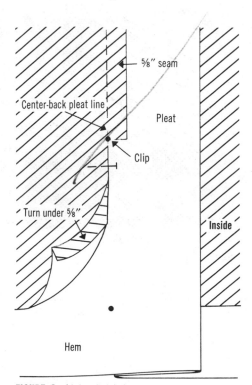

FIGURE 6 Lining finish for pleat lines

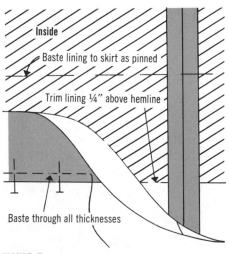

FIGURE 7

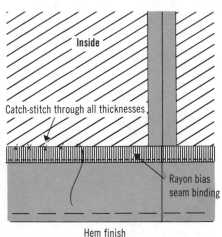

Catch-stitch through all thicknesses

Inside

Rayon bias
seam binding

Hem finish

FIGURE 8 Hem finish

295 for a straight skirt or a flared skirt; in any case, the hem should be finished with rayon bias seam binding, as shown in Figure 8. The hand stitches must go through two thicknesses—the lining and the garment—and for this reason, they will tend to be more conspicuous than stitches which go through just one thickness. Therefore it is well to use the catch stitch because it is an elastic stitch, which makes it less conspicuous (directions for the catch stitch are given on page 138).

FUNDAMENTALS
OF
FITTING

Fitting is the most difficult step in clothing construction. One reason for this is
that fitting problems must be seen and
felt and executed on an actual garment
on a particular figure; they cannot be
mastered entirely from the written word.
There are so many variables in fitting—
the figure, the fabric, the design, and the
purpose for which the garment is intended. A writer cannot write directions
for fitting that will solve every individual
problem. However, there are general
principles that will be of tremendous
value as a foundation for application to
the ever-new problems the woman who
sews will meet.

GENERAL
SUGGESTIONS

FACTORS THAT DETERMINE FIT

figure problems In general, figure faults
of the larger-than-average figure are min-
imized by a slightly looser, easier fit. A

psychological effect is created by the garment that is too tight on a large figure —the observer has a feeling that the person has gained more weight, and so she appears larger than she really is. Unfortunately, all too many large persons have a very different opinion; so many think they must make a garment tighter than average in order for their figure to look trim. This is not true; rather, the garment that fits with slightly more freedom gives a subtle effect that the wearer has lost weight recently. This principle can be applied to a particular part of the body; if any part of the body (the bust, the thighs, etc.) is larger than average, the best way to hide the fault is to allow more size than average during fitting. This suggestion does not work in reverse; the person who is too thin will appear to have lost still more weight in a garment that is fitted with great freedom. The thin person will look much better in a trim fit.

A person with a high tempo who moves more quickly than the less active person must have greater freedom in fit.

type of fabric The type of fabric has a bearing on the way a garment should be fitted. Very heavy fabrics must not be fitted too tightly or they will feel too binding; fabrics that are stiff and wrinkle seriously (taffeta, for example) do not lend themselves to straight-line skirts, but if they are used for that type of skirt, they must be fitted more loosely to prevent as much wrinkling as possible. Limp, flexible fabrics such as crepes and knits can be given a more snug fit and still be comfortable to wear.

design and purpose The design dominates the whole fitting sequence. If a pattern has been purchased in the proper size, the pattern company will have allowed the proper amount of freedom for movement and the extra size for style fullness. This point was emphasized in the chapter on sizing and needs little mention at this time. The design influences the purpose of the garment, of course. In general, sport clothes are fitted with more freedom than street clothes, and evening clothes are often fitted quite snugly because the figure-revealing quality of a snug fit is in good taste in the evening. And a garment which will be worn often and over extended lengths of time must be fitted with slightly more freedom than the garment which will be worn for occasional short lengths of time.

LEARN TO BE CRITICAL

It is so easy to decide that a garment fits and let it go at that in order to avoid time-consuming fitting and basting alterations. But one of the greatest advantages of doing your own sewing is the individual fitting one can achieve; it is foolish to decide it is good enough and to let it pass. Be critical. Think of the problems you encounter in ready-made garments—are they always too long-waisted, too tight across the bust, etc.? If so, expect the same problems in the costumes you make. Compare your figure with that of a lucky friend who wears a straight size, and think how your figure differs from hers—are you more round in the shoulders, are your thighs larger, etc.? This, too, will be an aid to pointing out your figure faults. It is well to read this entire chapter, and as each new figure fault is described, suspect that you might have that fault. Look for trouble now, before the garment is finished.

FITTING CAN BE COMPARED TO PATTERN ALTERATION

Fitting is done in fabric rather than in paper, but in many ways these two activities are similar. It would be well to review pattern alterations at this time. For example, if you did not alter the size of your skirt and do not know how this alteration is done scientifically, and if then you find you must alter the skirt in fitting, rereading the section on pattern alteration will be of great help.

PREPARATION FOR A FITTING

It is important that you keep your enthusiasm for the garment you are making and that you manage to encourage yourself in every way. An excellent way to nourish enthusiasm is to look your best at all fitting sessions. Wear makeup and have your hair combed. Do not, for example, try on a suit jacket over your pajama pants! Wear the girdle and bra you will wear with the garment; it is impossible to guess what the girdle and bra will do to your figure. Contrary to popular opinion, a girdle does not change hip size appreciably, even if it does make hips firmer. A tight girdle may decrease hip size on a figure with soft flesh, but it will increase size someplace on the body—perhaps at the waist or in the midriff or thigh area. Tight girdles *change figures more than they decrease size,* so it is of utmost importance to wear the girdle for every fitting. The strapless, boned bra changes the position and size of the bust. Wear the shoes you will wear with the garment or at least wear shoes of the same heel height. Heel height creates changes in posture, which in turn changes the figure. Finally, in preparation for a fitting, place a strip of muslin or Pellon firmly around your waist; this will be used to support the skirt during fitting.

PREPARATION OF GARMENT FOR FITTING

If shoulder pads are to be used, they should be pinned in place for every fitting. Turn up and pin hemlines in place (sleeves, jackets, skirts) along the hemline indicated by the pattern. This may not turn out to be the desired length, but it will be very nearly right, and the garment will look more attractive for the fitting (another way of keeping up enthusiasm). Center lines should be marked with a marking basting, and if this has not been done, do it at this time (marking basting is described on page 123. If the costume has a front buttoned edge, turn under the right front along the fold line and baste in place with long running stitches; if there is a back buttoned edge, turn under the left back along the fold line and baste. If there is a front or back zippered opening, turn under one edge on the seamline and baste. At the side opening edges, turn under the front edge on the seamline and baste in place. Basting fold lines and one edge of zippered openings makes it much easier to pin those edges in place on the figure and will result in greater accuracy as well.

The garment should be put on the figure right side out, and therefore all fitting should be done from the outside of the garment. Fitting is more difficult to do with the garment right side out, but it is done in this way because then the right half of the garment is on the right half of the figure, and the left half of the garment is on the left half of the figure. The two sides of the figure can be fitted differently, if the figure requires that kind of attention. However, it is much easier to fit if the garment is wrong side out, and if the figure is balanced, there is no reason why this cannot be done; of course, the fitted garment should be tested, right side out on the figure, before permanent fitting decisions are made.

THE PRINCIPLE
OF
DART
FITTING

There is no one principle in the whole field of clothing construction that is of more consequence than the "principle of the dart": *A dart creates shape in the area surrounding the tip of the dart. The wider the base of the dart, the greater the shape created; the narrower the base of the dart, the smaller the shape created.* This sounds simple, but it is well to fold a dart in a piece of paper and notice the amount of shape it creates; now fold in a much larger dart and notice the shape it creates. If the figure has a larger-than-average curve at a particular point, it will require a larger-than-average dart to fit that curve; a smaller-than-average curve will require a smaller-than-average dart. This knowledge will be of great help in fitting, for *fitting is largely a matter of perfecting the shape of a garment.* Fitting does perfect size; however, this is relatively easy to do, whereas perfecting shape is a more difficult matter. Because darts control shape, it is obvious that they will be changed often in fitting. Darts can be changed in width in order to increase or decrease the shaping created, they can be lengthened or shortened

to create shape at a higher or lower level on the body, and the direction can be changed so that the high point of the dart is located near the curve on the body. These subtle changes in darts make up the subtleties of fitting.

You will remember that waist size is not decreased by pattern alteration, even if measurements indicate that a decrease is needed. The reason for this is that it is a great advantage in fitting to have extra size in the waist, for at this time, the waist size can be decreased in various ways as demanded by the individual figure—at the side edges, at all darts, or at some darts—or part can be decreased at the darts and the remainder at the side edges. In other words, as the size is decreased, the shape also is improved.

At every check point in fitting, keep this principle of the dart in mind, for it will be used often.

THE FIRST
FITTING

PREPARATION
Basic structural darts and seams should be basted. The bodice and skirt should be separate units for this fitting. Facings, sleeves, and collars will not be included.

NOTE The altered lines in the sketches, when they appear as pin lines during fitting, are shown in dotted lines; the original seamlines are shown in solid lines.

POINTS TO BE CHECKED
Overall size of bodice or jacket, overall size of skirt, direction of center lines of skirt, direction of side seamlines of skirt, position and direction of darts, amount of shape created by darts, slant of shoulder lines, size of buttons, width of belt, and similar details, as dictated by the design, should be checked. Support the

skirt by pinning it to the muslin or Pellon strip at your waist.

to test overall size of bodice or jacket This can be done simply through observation by the person with a developed sense of fitting. The novice may need the extra help of a few generalities for a garment with no style fullness. Pinch out the excess fabric that is not required for your body size; the amount you can pinch out is the amount of livability in the garment. *The following are recommended livability amounts for typical garments:*

1 For a strapless dress, about 1 inch
2 For a sleeveless sundress or slim sheath dress, about 2 inches
3 For the typical dart-fitted dress with a set-in sleeve, about 3 to 4 inches
4 For a jacket or blouse with a set-in sleeve, about 5 to 8 inches

Remember that the above amounts are for livability only and do not take into consideration size for style fullness, which varies with each design. Another test for the inexperienced person is to put on a similar costume in which you have been comfortable and happy, pinch out the excess in that costume, and then compare it with the excess in the one under construction.

One should anticipate that no change in overall size will be necessary at the bust (or certainly very little change) if the pattern was bought according to bust measurement, but changes in size at the waist would not be surprising because the pattern was not purchased according to waist size.

Seams can be pinned in or let out to change size. Turn back to page 75 to see the same change being made on a pattern; the two processes are quite similar. Make a note to make the same fitting change on any corresponding edge; see

Figure 20 on page 78, which illustrates this step as a pattern alteration and which will be helpful as a guide for fitting alterations as well.

to test overall size of skirt Although the experienced person with a "good eye" can judge this point by observation alone, the novice may need the extra help of a few generalities that apply to garments with no style fullness. Pinch out the excess fabric that is not required for body size; the amount you can pinch out is the amount of livability in the garment. *The recommended livability amounts at the three hip levels are listed in the measurement charts and should be 1 inch at the 3-inch level and 2 inches at the 7- and 9-inch hip levels.* But remember that these amounts are for livability only and do not take into consideration size for style fullness, which varies with each design. The inexperienced person can compare this skirt with a similar and favorite skirt in her wardrobe by pinching out the excess in that skirt and comparing it with the excess in this. Seams can be pinned in or let out to change size. Turn back to page 75 to see the same change being made on a pattern; the two processes are quite similar. Make a note to make the same fitting change on any corresponding edge; see Figure 20 on page 78, which illustrates this step as a pattern alteration and which will be helpful for fitting alterations as well.

to test direction of center lines of skirt See Figure 1. Center lines should fall in a plumb line at right angles to the floor, ending midway between the legs. If the center line veers off to one side, this indicates that one hip or one side of the figure is larger than the other or that one leg is shorter than the other, which creates the same situation. Notice in the sketch that the center line veers toward the larger half of the figure and that as it does, it causes the skirt to stand out farther from the leg on the larger side.

See Figure 2 for the fitting correction. The skirt must be lifted at the waist on the smaller side until the center line falls in the proper position. Pin the waist in position, gradually tapering back to the original waist position on the larger side. Undoubtedly the smaller side will require a size alteration too, as shown in the sketch; there may be excess size just through the upper hip levels, or in extreme cases, excess size may appear all the way down to the lower edge.

Figure 3 shows this alteration, transferred to the inside of the garment, with the side seam basted and a marking basting at the waistline to indicate the new and corrected waistline seamline.

This problem does not exist as often in the bodice, and when it does it is usually the result of one shoulder sloping more than the other. This problem can

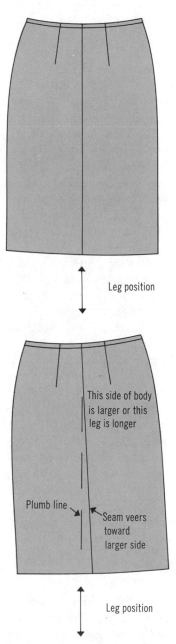

Leg position

This side of body is larger or this leg is longer

Plumb line

Seam veers toward larger side

Leg position

FIGURE 1

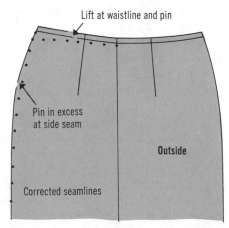

Lift at waistline and pin

Pin in excess at side seam

Outside

Corrected seamlines

FIGURE 2 To correct a slant in center lines on the figure

be corrected with shoulder pads (page 139).

to test direction of side seamlines of skirt
Figure 4 pictures three figures from the side view. The upper sketch pictures a side seamline hanging properly and dividing the body beautifully. The other two show flaws in the direction of the side seam. As in the case of the center seam, the side seam slants in the direction of the part of the body that is larger than average, so that if the line slants toward the back, probably the back hips are too large, and if it slants toward the front, one would first suspect that the hipbones or stomach was larger than average. But another issue is involved: if the waistline of the figure dips more than average in front, this will tend to cause the side seam to veer toward the back, and if the waistline dips more than average in back, the side seam will veer toward the front. If the side seam slants, suspect one or both of these problems: a curve larger than average or an unusual dip in waist position.

The illustration shows one problem that is most common: the side seam that slants toward the back caused by hips

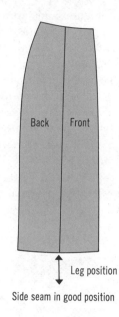

Side seam in good position

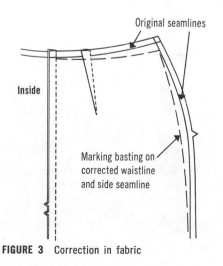

FIGURE 3 Correction in fabric

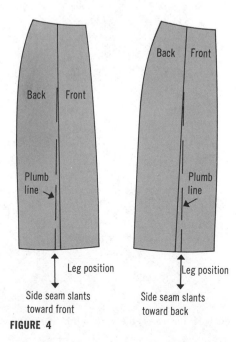

FIGURE 4

larger than average or a dipping waist in the front. Figure 5 pictures the solution for the figure with hips larger than average. Notice that the width of the darts has been increased to create more shape for the larger-than-average curve. If this is the problem, this correction will bring the side seam into proper position. The correction is pictured as it would be basted in fabric, after having been transferred to the inside.

Figure 6 pictures the solution for the figure with a front-dipping waistline. The skirt must be lifted up at the waist until the side seam falls in the proper position; perhaps the front darts will have to be lengthened if the skirt must be lifted an appreciable amount, and it is possible that both faults may exist on the figure and that the back skirt darts should be increased in width as well. The correction is transferred to the fabric with a marking basting to indicate the new, corrected seamline.

The principle of fitting the skirt with seams slanting forward is exactly the same; front darts may need to be increased in width, or the skirt may need to be lifted in the back to establish a new seamline at the waist.

To correct a side seam that curves at a certain level (the wobbly seam), see the two illustrations of Figure 7; in one sketch the seam curves toward the back at about the 3-inch hip level, and in the other the curve is toward the front in the thigh region. When a side seam curves, this indicates that at a certain level either the front or back of the figure is larger than average; the seam curves toward the trouble point, the part of the body that is larger than average. In the illustrations, one figure is larger than average in the back and probably has a

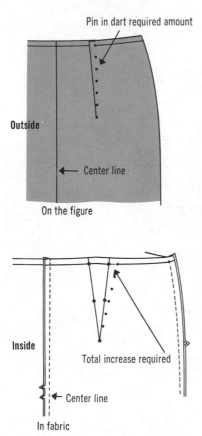

FIGURE 5 Increasing the width of back skirt darts

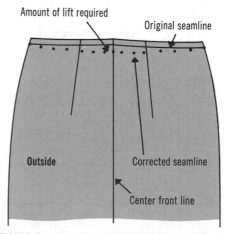

FIGURE 6 Correction for front-dipping waistline

pad of fat just below the waist in the back, and as the sketch shows, the seam curves toward the trouble area. The other figure has thighs larger than average, as indicated by the seam which curves toward the front.

Figure 8 pictures the solution of the seam curving toward the back in the 3-inch hip area. In Figure 8a, the side seam must be ripped out in that area. Then turn under the front edge on the original seamline and pin. Lap this pinned edge over the back skirt, allowing the extra size where it is needed. Pin in place. In this problem, it may be that the figure will require an extra little dart, just above the pad of fat, that will create more shape for the larger-than-average curve. Before the pins are removed, put a marking-basting line on the back skirt along the new, corrected seamline.

Figure 8b pictures the back edge with the marking-basting line indicating the new seamline. Notice that additional size has been obtained in the 3-inch hip

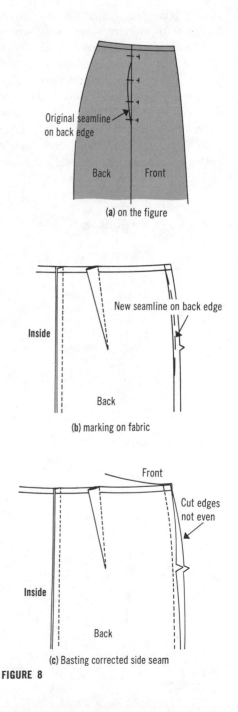

Original seamline on back edge

Back   Front

(a) on the figure

Inside

New seamline on back edge

Back

(b) marking on fabric

Front

Cut edges not even

Inside

Back

(c) Basting corrected side seam

FIGURE 8

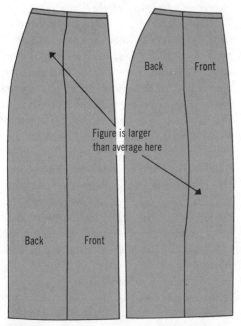

Back   Front

Figure is larger than average here

Back   Front

FIGURE 7   Examples of curving, wobbly seams

area. Figure 8c shows the side seam basted into position; notice that there is now less seam allowance on the back skirt at this level and that the front and back edges are not cut edges even. This alteration is sometimes difficult because of insufficient seam allowance on the edge which must be let out. The person with figure flaws of this nature should anticipate this fitting and add extra size to her pattern hereafter.

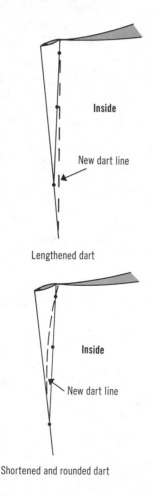

Inside

New dart line

Lengthened dart

Inside

New dart line

Shortened and rounded dart

FIGURE 9

to correct position and direction of darts   The dart can be drafted into a new position—higher or lower on the body in the case of horizontal darts or farther from the center front or center back in the case of vertical darts. This is done during fitting exactly as it is done in a pattern alteration, as shown in Figure 15 on page 74. Simply remove the basting stitches from the original dart and pinch in a new dart of the same width at the desired position, pinning on ruler-straight lines.

to correct amount of shape created by darts   A dart can be lengthened or shortened to create shape at a higher or lower level on the body. Figure 9 shows corrected lines of a lengthened dart and a shortened dart after it has been basted into place. The shortened dart has been rounded out as well; this outward curve is very helpful for front hip darts on rounded figures because it allows slightly more size at the 3-inch hip level and at the same time fits the body better because its curve matches that of the body.

The width of the dart can be altered in order to create more shape for larger-than-average curves or less shape for smaller-than-average curves. Figure 10 shows how to change width by pin fitting darts. Rip out the original dart. Retain the original dart line nearest the center front or center back by folding along the original dart line and bringing the folded line to the desired position. Therefore, the change in width alters the dart line nearest the side edge, as shown in the sketch. The dart line nearest the centers must be retained in order to preserve the original proportions of the design.

No matter where the dart appears, certain flaws indicate a need for a change in width and the resulting improvement in shape. If the garment stands away from the body at the tip of the dart (if you can easily pinch out a bit of fabric at the high point of the curve), this is an indication that the existing dart has created too much shape for your figure and that you have, at that point, a smaller-than-average curve; the dart must be decreased in width. If diagonal ripples form, beginning at the high point of the curve and angling in *any diagonal* direction, this is a sure indication that you have, at that point, a curve larger than average; the dart must be increased in width.

to test the basic darts General fitting standards are given, and each dart listed can be altered by following the general rules above.

The *front underarm dart* should be on a level with the bust point, ending about 1 to 2 inches from the high point of the bust. It may take a somewhat diagonal line according to the design, but the tip of the dart must be in line with the high point of the bust.

The *front waist dart* must angle toward the high point of the bust ending about 1 to 2 inches below the high point of the bust.

The *back bodice waist dart* should slant in the direction of the high point of the shoulder and should end about 1½ to 2 inches below the high point of the shoulder.

The *front skirt dart* should slant in the direction of the high point of the curves. These darts must be changed often because they are placed in the proper position for the average figure and yet figures vary so greatly. It is not unusual for the figure to demand that the dart be moved from its position about 3 inches from the center front to a position quite near the side edge in order to create shaping for prominent hipbones. It is not unusual for the figure to require

an additional dart (which can be drafted into whatever position the figure requires) in the skirt front, especially on the figure that is very rounded at the 3-inch hip level.

The *back skirt dart* should end about 1 or 1½ inches above the high point of the hip curve. Again the rounded figure may require an additional dart to create shaping for pads of fat at the 3-inch hip level.

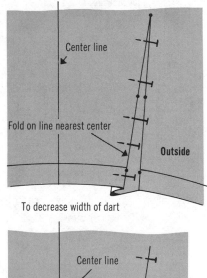

To decrease width of dart

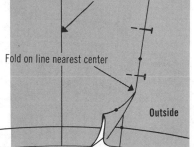

To increase width of dart

FIGURE 10 Enlarged views showing how to pin-fit darts on the figure

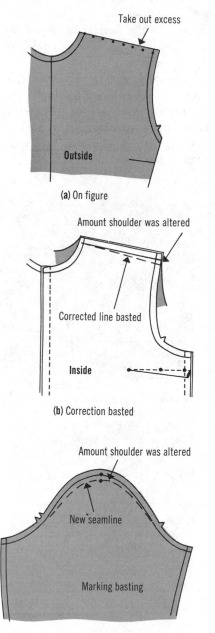

Take out excess

Outside

(a) On figure

Amount shoulder was altered

Corrected line basted

Inside

(b) Correction basted

Amount shoulder was altered

New seamline

Marking basting

(c) Marking basting to correct sleeve cap

FIGURE 11 Correction for sloping shoulders

to correct ripples that form in the skirt just below the waist If a ripple forms all the way around the skirt in the area directly below the waist, the skirt is too small for the figure. Perhaps it is too small all the way down, but certainly it is too small at the 3-inch hip level. The side seams should be ripped to allow the skirt to settle down on the body, and then the seams can be let out the required amount.

If a ripple forms in just one area of the skirt—below the front waist or below the back waist—this is an indication that the waistline of the figure dips more than average in the area where the ripple forms. Refer back to Figure 6 to see this problem explained. The skirt must be lifted up on the body in the area where it ripples, and a new waist seamline must be marked at the corrected position.

to correct slant of shoulder lines If shoulders slope more than average, the garment will stand up from the shoulder line, and the excess can be easily seen. See Figure 11. The excess should be pinned out at the outer edge, gradually tapering back to the original seamline at the neck edge, as shown in Figure 11a. This correction transferred to the inside and basted is shown in Figure 11b. Because there is now less height in the shoulders, there must be a corresponding alteration on the cap of the sleeve; if the shoulders are lowered ½ inch, the seamline at the cap of the sleeve must be lowered ½ inch. Put in a marking basting to indicate the new, corrected line in the cap of the sleeve by following the directions shown in Figure 11c.

If shoulders are more square than average, the shoulder seam must be ripped and the extra height gained at the outer edge by using some of the seam allowance. See Figure 12. The new seamline should gradually taper back to the original seamline at the neck edge, as

shown in Figure 12a. This alteration
transferred to the inside and basted is
shown in Figure 12b. A similar adjustment in height must be made in the
sleeve. Put in a marking basting on the
cap of the sleeve to indicate the corrected
line by following directions shown in
Figure 12c. This fitting alteration is exactly the same as the pattern alteration
shown in Figure 25 on page 84.

**to test size of buttons, width of belt, and
similar details, as dictated by the design**
This is the time to experiment with buttons for size, number, and type. Cut
circles of fabric or paper, depending on
the type of button to be used. Circles of
self fabric will give the effect of covered
buttons, while circles of paper or contrasting fabric will give the effect of
contrasting buttons. Experiment with different sizes of circles and test to see
whether a different number of buttons
looks better on your figure. The pattern
has been made in good proportions for
the average figure, but a very small person might want fewer or smaller buttons,
while the larger person may prefer more
or larger buttons.

Fold the fabric belt into various
widths to experiment with belt width.
Try contrasting belts you might have in
your wardrobe. Again, as with buttons,
the proportions of the figure and individual preferences can dictate changes in
the width suggested by the pattern.

Any design details—pockets, pocket
flaps, band trims—should be tested at
this time for attractive proportion. Be
very sure to pin under seam allowances
so that tests are made with these details
in the size they will appear when the
garment is finished.

BASTING THE FIRST FITTING CORRECTIONS
Transfer the pin-fitted lines to the inside
and baste along the corrected lines.

Rip seam and let
out seam allowance

Outside

(a) On figure

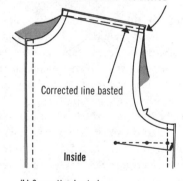

Amount shoulder was altered

Corrected line basted

Inside

(b) Correction basted

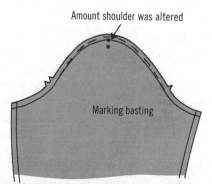

Amount shoulder was altered

Marking basting

(c) Marking basting to correct sleeve cap

FIGURE 12 Correction for square shoulders

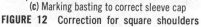

These lines will need some perfection because it is very difficult for the fitter to make ruler-straight lines and smooth curves with pins. Examine the original line of the garment and then make the fitting corrections in such a way that the resulting line is in character with the original; if the line was originally ruler-straight, perfect the pin lines of fitting so that they are ruler-straight, etc.

Although the fitter has probably pinned both sides of the figure, it would be unusual if her correction lines were identical on the two sides; it is much easier for the person who bastes to see that the corrections on the two halves of the body are equal. Of course, if the figure is different on the two sides, the corrections should not be identical.

After the corrections are basted, the garment must be tested again on the figure to be sure that in making the two sides identical and perfecting pin lines, the fit has been retained as desired. Perhaps certain small fitting details will need refitting at this time. *Make notes to make corresponding changes on any edge of any piece of the garment that will be affected by changes made during this fitting.*

KEEP RECORDS

Record all the changes made by this fitting; state what was done, exactly how much a line was changed, etc. If a change was rather great—for example, if all skirt seams were let out ¼ inch—make a note to add that much more to the next pattern as a pattern alteration. If a change was subtle, it is better to alter the pattern the same way the next time and incorporate the subtle change in basting the next garment for the first fitting. After several garments are made and records kept on each one, pattern alterations (plus little subtleties of basting) can result in a garment that fits so well that eventually, if desired, it could be sewn together without fitting.

THE SECOND FITTING

PREPARATION

The structural darts and seams are stitched, the seam finish (if one is to be used) is done, and the seams and darts are pressed well. The waistline seam, sleeves, and collar should be basted in place for the fitting; if the waist seamline of the skirt or the armscye line of the sleeve was changed during the first fitting and a new seamline was marked, use the corrected seamlines at those edges.

POINTS TO BE CHECKED

Length of bodice, width of shoulder, set of sleeve, size and length of sleeve, and design lines of collar should be checked at this time.

to check length of bodice If the bodice length is not correct, any changes must be made by ripping the seam. Assuming that the skirt hangs properly, no change will be made in the seamline of the skirt; it will be basted on the original seamline or, if that line was corrected during the first fitting, on the corrected seamline. All the change would be made on the bodice. Rip the waist seam. Turn under the skirt edge on the proper seamline and pin. Then lap that pinned edge over the raw edge of the bodice to the desired level. Test for comfort and movement as well as appearance. This means that there might well be a varying seam allowance on the lower edge of the bodice —the seam will vary if one portion of the bodice needed more alteration than the other. Another method more suitable for some designs is to try on the bodice (with sleeves and collar in place) and tie a cord around the waist. Move and bend until the proper amount of livability and style fullness is established and then mark the bodice waistline with pins or chalk by using the cord as a guide.

See Figure 13. Put a marking basting on the bodice to mark the position of the desired seamline. Remove pins. The figure illustrates a bodice which was too long in the back—note the marking-basting line. Now baste the bodice to the skirt again, placing this corrected line in the bodice along the established seamline in the skirt. Understand that cut edges will not be even after this alteration; this seam must now be basted with seamlines matching, and the cut edges will not be even. Baste and refit to test for perfection.

If the bodice is too short, only a small amount of extra length can be obtained by using the seam allowance. The very most would be an extra ⅜ inch, leaving a ¼-inch seam allowance, which would be a minimum. If this should happen, see Figure 14. Lap a strip of seam binding over the right side of the bodice edge a scant ¼ inch. Stitch in place. The stitching has reinforced the small seam allowance, and the seam binding will act as seam allowance as the seam is basted.

to test width of shoulder If shoulders are wide or too narrow, only the bodice pieces are involved; the problem has nothing to do with the sleeves, and no corresponding alteration would be made on them. See Figure 15. If shoulders are too wide, pinch out a little tuck along the shoulder line to bring the armscye line to the desired position (this tuck is only a temporary fitting aid). Rip out the sleeve and measure the amount of the tuck (a ¼-inch tuck removes ½ inch

of width). Put a marking basting on the bodices, beginning at the original seam allowance at the notch position and gradually bringing the line in the desired

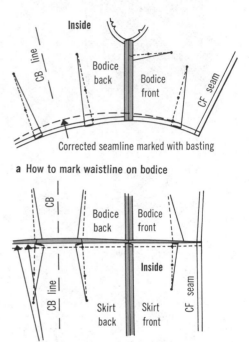

Corrected seamline marked with basting

a How to mark waistline on bodice

Cut edges are not even at waist seam

b How to baste corrected waistline seam
FIGURE 13

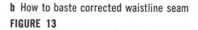
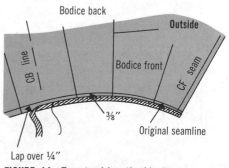
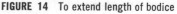

FIGURE 14 To extend length of bodice

Pin in tuck to bring armhole to proper position

Outside

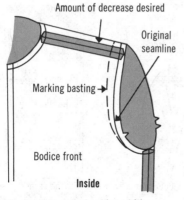

Amount of decrease desired

Original seamline

Marking basting →

Bodice front

Inside

FIGURE 15 To decrease shoulder width

Let out seam for more width

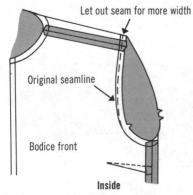

Original seamline

Bodice front

Inside

FIGURE 16 To increase shoulder width

amount at the shoulder. Then rebaste the sleeve, using the original seamline of the sleeve and this new line on the bodice; the upper portion of the seam will not be cut edges even—the bodice edges will extend beyond the cut edges of the sleeve. Fit again to perfect the correction.

If shoulders are too narrow, there is only a limited amount of extra width that can be gained by using a portion of the seam allowance; an extra ⅜ inch is an absolute maximum. See Figure 16. Put a marking basting on the bodices, beginning at the original seamline at the notch position and gradually bringing the line out the desired amount at the shoulder. Then rebaste the sleeve, using the original seamline at the sleeve and this new line on the bodices; the upper portion of the seam will not be cut edges even— the sleeve edge will extend beyond the cut edge of the bodice. Fit again to perfect the correction.

to test size and length of sleeve The elbow dart should be in line with the elbow to create shape for the elbow as it bends. It can be raised or lowered; see Figure 15 on page 74, which illustrates this correction as a pattern alteration. The fitting alteration can be handled in a similar manner.

The sleeve cannot be changed in width at the point where it joins the bodice without changing the size of the bodice as well, so it is unwise to consider an alteration in width at that level. However, the sleeve seam can be taken in beginning at the biceps line and gradually tapering in at the lower edge. See Figure 17. If the seam is tapered in, as shown in the sketch, it must angle out below the hemline in order that the upper edge of the hem will fit the portion of the sleeve it must fit when the hem is in place. Two sketches illustrate the right and wrong way to taper in a sleeve.

The proper length is a matter of design and personal preference. Certainly any sleeve that is not intended to be full length can be made whatever length the wearer desires. To test for the length of the full-length sleeve, bend the elbow and bring the arm to waist level. In this position, the lower edge of the sleeve should be at the base of the thumb, where the wrist bends. A certain amount of variation is possible to achieve the desired effect when the arm is in a natural position.

to test design lines of collar There is relatively little one can do to change the set of a collar on the bodice; certainly, such changes should be made by an experienced person. However, it is possible to make slight changes in the design by altering the outside edge of the collar. Even if the collar is faced, it can be turned wrong side out again, and the outer edges can be narrowed or changed slightly in shape.

KEEP RECORDS
Reread the paragraph with this heading on page 188 and make similar records of these alterations.

THE FINAL FITTING

The garment is finished excepting for stitching in the zipper and hanging the hem.

NOTE The three fitting sessions described here are the minimum needed, with careful planning, for a basic garment. It is entirely possible that additional fittings will be required for intricate designs before the garment is ready for this final fitting.

to test appearance of zipper Refer to the zipper directions for additional informa-

tion. The most common problem with the zipper is that a little roll or bump of fabric will form at the lower end of the zipper. This is caused by the fact that the side edges were stretched as the zipper was basted in. Remove the basting and ease the fabric up on the zipper tape as explained in the zipper directions. Retest on the figure before stitching.

Another common problem is that the garment stands away from the body, as if the skirt were too large at the point

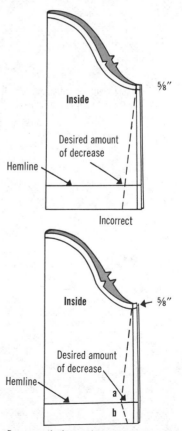

Proper method — angle **a** must equal angle **b**
FIGURE 17 To taper in sleeve

where the zipper ends. This is apt to happen on the figure which has a hollow at the 7-inch hipline (and quite a number of figures do). The hollow causes no trouble until the zipper is sewn in because it is the stiffening of this area that makes the flaw obvious. See Figure 18. The zipper must be removed and a very slight amount taken from the seam

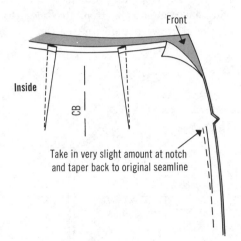

FIGURE 18

at that point, gradually tapering back to the original seamline. The corresponding side edge on the right half of the garment may not require this change because it is entirely likely that the hollow will cause no trouble on a seam that has not been stiffened by a zipper. The zipper must be set in again, using the slightly different seamline near the lower end.

to hang hem   Refer to the general notes and hem directions in Chapter 26; detailed directions appear on those pages.

ADDITIONAL FITTINGS

Lined garments require additional fittings, of course. The jacket or coat lining cannot be fitted to the figure. It is fitted to the finished jacket after the front and neck edges of the lining are basted to the jacket; a second fitting is required to hang lining hems. The separate skirt and dress linings, made like jacket linings, can be fitted to the figure to test overall size, and they too must be fitted when edges are basted in place to the garment and again to establish hem length.

MACHINE STITCHING

There are many makes of sewing machines on the market, and although there are striking similarities among them, each differs slightly in threading and adjustment. The best way to learn about your machine is not through a book of this kind but by reading and studying the excellent instruction book that comes with the machine; the illustrations are clearly drawn, and all aspects of operation are explained in detail. The purpose of this chapter is to enlarge upon and emphasize certain fundamental principles.

FEATURES OF NEW MACHINES

THE ZIGZAG FEATURE
The machine that zigzags and makes decorative stitches has practical uses as well. The zigzag stitch can be adjusted to the proper width to finish seams, finish inner edges of facings, and also finish

raw edges of hems if the fabric does not ravel seriously. The zigzag stitch is elastic and can, if set at a very narrow width ($\frac{1}{32}$ to $\frac{1}{16}$ inch), be used for stitching seams in knits and stretch fabrics. The same narrow setting can be used for any seam which requires elasticity such as the crotch seams in slacks and shorts and seams in very snug-fitting bathing suits. The simple zigzag stitch, set very narrow, can be used for topstitched details on wool tweeds and similar fabrics; the line of stitching will show more clearly, and if the stitch is tested and set properly, the effect is very attractive. The decorative stitches used on inner edges of facings and on hems of delicate, feminine fabrics give a flat and very pretty effect.

THE SELF–WINDING BOBBIN

An innovation is the machine with a plastic bobbin that is wound in the bobbin case from thread on the top spool. The clear plastic allows one to see the amount of thread remaining on the bobbin, and of course there is a saving of time as the thread does not need to be removed from the machine and rethreaded after filling the bobbin. The bobbin does not hold as much thread as the traditional bobbin, but it is no trouble to wind it more often. There is no adjustment for the bobbin tension, which is controlled automatically by a proper setting on the top tension. The machine has the usual type of adjustment for the top tension. This machine is so new at this writing that an evaluation of its merits after extended use cannot be included.

The information given in this section applies to all machines, the traditional and the reel machines (self-winding bobbin), with one exception: the information on bobbin tension does not apply to the reel machine because, as stated above, the bobbin tension is automatically controlled.

The two threads used in the machine, the top thread and the bobbin thread, must be held in tension to keep them from feeding through the machine at too great a speed. The tension is achieved by the upper thread's passing between two adjustable disks and the bobbin thread's passing around an adjustable hook in the bobbin case. There is usually a numbered guide to help in adjustment of the upper tension; the lower tension is adjusted by a screw on the bobbin case. Proper tension adjustment of the two threads ensures a firm and secure interlocking of the threads within the fabric. Figure 1 shows well-balanced tension between the two threads. Note that the threads interlock at the center of the two thicknesses of fabric. This seam will be strong and will withstand a great deal of strain.

TENSION ADJUSTMENT

Each fabric offers special tension problems largely due to the thickness of the fabric. In general, heavy fabrics require a looser tension than lightweight fabrics. This means that the tension of both threads must be adjusted for each different fabric. Always test-stitch on a sample of fabric before doing any stitching on the garment. And test-stitch on the same number of thicknesses of fabric that will be used when stitching on the garment. The usual seam consists of two thicknesses. Examine the samples. Is the interlocking of threads embedded in the fabric so that no loops of thread are visible? Is the fabric flat with no evidence of puckering? If so, the tension is well balanced for that particular fabric. If something is wrong, study the following paragraphs and sketches to determine the cause.

upper tension too loose If the upper tension is too loose (Figure 2), the upper thread is fed through the machine too fast and therefore passes through the two thicknesses of fabric, and *the interlocking of threads is visible on the underside of the fabric.* Note in Figure 2a that the interlocking of threads is on the underside and that the bobbin thread lies parallel to the fabric. Figure 2b pictures an even more exaggerated case; here the upper tension is so loose that actual loops of upper thread are visible on the underside.

Very often a mistake in threading the machine causes this bad balance of tension. It was mentioned earlier that two disks control the upper tension. It is possible to pass the thread in front of or behind the two disks, in which case the thread is not held in tension at all. This is a very common mistake because the machine, viewed from the usual sitting position, appears to be threaded properly, and the mistake can be detected only by leaning forward and looking down on the disks. If the upper tension is too loose, always check the threading first, because no adjustment of the disks will help if the thread does not pass between them. If it is threaded properly, tighten the tension regulator and test-stitch until well balanced tension is achieved.

bobbin tension too loose If the bobbin tension is too loose (Figure 3), the bobbin thread is fed through the machine too fast and therefore passes through the two

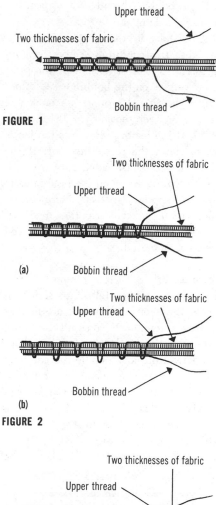

Upper thread

Two thicknesses of fabric

Bobbin thread

FIGURE 1

Two thicknesses of fabric

Upper thread

(a) Bobbin thread

Two thicknesses of fabric

Upper thread

Bobbin thread

(b)

FIGURE 2

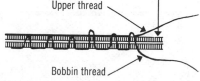

Two thicknesses of fabric

Upper thread

Bobbin thread

FIGURE 3

thicknesses of fabric, and *the interlocking of threads is visible on the upper side of the fabric.* Note in the sketch that the interlocking of threads is on the upper side. Under exaggerated circumstances, loops of bobbin thread will appear on the upper side of the fabric.

A mistake in threading the bobbin can cause this condition. Since the bobbin thread is held in tension by the pressure of a hook on the bobbin case, failure to pass the thread around the hook will cause a lack of tension on the bobbin thread. If the bobbin tension is too loose, always check the threading first. If the bobbin has been threaded properly, adjust the tension screw on the bobbin case, using the special very small screwdriver which is included with the machine. Test-stitch again until a well-balanced tension is achieved.

tension too tight   If the stitching of a test seam puckers up the fabric, as shown in Figure 4, one or both threads are held at too great a tension. If you pull the fabric in the direction of the seam, one or both threads will break. Examine the stitching closely to determine what adjustment is needed. If the interlocking of threads is not visible, this means the tensions are in balance, even though they are too tight, and that *both* are too tight. If the interlocking of threads is visible on the

top side of the fabric, the *upper* tension is too tight. If the interlocking of threads is visible on the underside of the fabric, the *bobbin* tension is too tight. Make the required adjustments and test-stitch until well-balanced tension is achieved.

THE MACHINE NEEDLE

SIZE AND APPROPRIATE USES

Each machine has a size range of needles for use with various fabrics. The needle size and thread size are determined by the weight of fabric used; heavy fabrics require a heavier needle and stronger thread. If the needle breaks, the size is too small for that particular fabric. If the thread wears and eventually breaks, the needle is too small for the thread. If the needle snags the fabric, it may have a defective point or it may be too large for that particular fabric. If needle marks are prominent in the fabric, the needle is too large. The instruction book for your machine will include a chart of needle sizes and appropriate uses. Consult this chart, and always keep a supply of various sizes for the many purposes your machine will serve.

HOW TO INSERT THE NEEDLE

The upper end of a machine needle is flat on one side and rounded on the other. As the needle is inserted, the flat side must face the particular correct direction for that machine. Machines vary in this respect, so you must study your own instruction book for the proper placement of the needle. In general the grooved edge faces the direction of the last thread guide.

CONDITION OF THE NEEDLE

The point of a needle can become dull with heavy use or from hitting a hard object (such as a pin). If this happens,

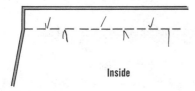

Inside

FIGURE 4

the needle will snag threads of the fabric and the fabric will pucker. Delicate fabrics are most influenced by a dull needle. Test stitching will determine the condition of the needle.

RESULTS OF INCORRECT INSERTION OF THE NEEDLE

If the needle has been threaded from the wrong direction or if the needle is inserted in the machine incorrectly, the stitches will not interlock properly; sometimes only a few stitches in every inch will interlock, as shown in Figure 5. Sometimes no stitches will interlock; often the thread will merely slip out of the needle. If any one of these stitching mistakes occurs, check the threading of the needle (shown clearly in the instruction book) and then check the placement of the needle.

ADJUSTMENT OF PRESSURE ON MACHINE FOOT

The foot of the machine must rest solidly on the fabric with enough pressure to keep the fabric in line and yet must not exert so much pressure that the fabric cannot travel smoothly through the machine. A screw, usually on the top of the machine just above the foot, can be adjusted for pressure. Although some few thick fabrics may require unusually heavy pressure, in general thick fabrics must have less pressure and thin fabrics greater pressure. Test stitching will indicate how the fabric moves along under the foot; if it seems to lag or if stitches tend to pile up, the pressure is too tight and the screw should be loosened; if the fabric is not stable as it passes through the machine, tightening the screw will increase the pressure and solve the problem.

LENGTH OF STITCH

All machines offer a wide range of stitch lengths to serve the many purposes of stitching and the many varieties of fabric. There are some slight differences among machines, but in general the range is from 6 to 30 stitches per inch. The stitch adjuster is numbered in some way to aid in easy adjustment. It is very important to use the correct stitch length for each purpose of stitching because the stitch length not only determines the strength and performance of a seam but also influences the appearance of the garment. For example, you can cheapen a garment with a stitch that is too long simply because the inexpensive ready-to-wear garments on the market are made with long stitches.

FACTORS THAT INFLUENCE LENGTH OF STITCH

fabric The heavier the fabric, the longer the stitch must be, and the thinner the fabric the shorter the stitch must be. Whereas 10 stitches per inch might hold a heavy woolen securely, 15 to 18 stitches per inch would be better for a flat, sheer fabric. To test the length of stitch for a particular fabric, stitch a test seam, press

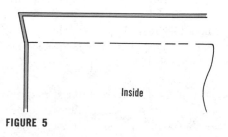

Inside

FIGURE 5

it open, and then gently pull the fabric at right angles to the seam. Does the seam spread apart and reveal stitches? Then the stitch is too long. For elastic fabrics (jersey and crepe are examples), a shorter stitch is required because a short stitch is more elastic and will allow the seam to give as those fabrics require.

purpose of stitching The shorter the stitch, the stronger a seam will be, so that a seam stitched with 20 stitches per inch will resist more wear than a seam stitched with 6 stitches per inch. However, if the stitch becomes too short (such as 1/30 inch long), the seam can be weakened; 30 stitches per inch means 30 punctures of the needle in the fabric.

A general rule is: *The shorter the stitch, the stronger the seam, up to the point where the stitch is so small that it punctures the threads of the fabric.* However, general rules are only guidelines, and experimentation is always wise.

This general rule should be applied to all machine stitching. Ask yourself: How strong must this particular seam be? For example, the crotch seams of shorts or slacks get great strain. Ideally these seams should be somewhat elastic. Then stitch them with a short stitch (possibly 22 stitches per inch depending on the fabric), and they will be both strong and elastic. By contrast, the seams in a gathered skirt will get very little wear and would be strong enough if they were stitched with 12 stitches per inch.

special uses Machine stitches may be used to gather or ease in fullness. In that case the factor of strength is not impor-

tant, but it is important that the stitch be long enough so that it can be drawn up. A detailed discussion of length of stitch as it applies to gathering or easing in fullness is given on page 125. The problem of stitch length as it applies to stay stitching is described on page 106. Machine basting requires a long stitch that can be removed easily (discussed on page 122). The important requirement for topstitching for decorative effects is that the desired effect be achieved. Before doing topstitching on the garment, test several stitch lengths (using the same number of thicknesses of fabric as the garment will have) to determine which length is most attractive. In general, topstitching requires a longer stitch than the seams of the garment, largely because topstitching is usually done through at least three thicknesses of fabric as compared with the usual two thicknesses of a seam.

Because so many factors influence stitch length, it is impossible to state definite rules to follow. A few generalities are given below, but you must interpret them with your own fabric and purpose in mind.

6 stitches per inch for:
  machine basting
  gathering heavy fabrics
8 to 10 stitches per inch for:
  gathering medium-weight fabrics
  stay stitching heavy-weight and gathering
    medium-weight fabrics
10 to 12 stitches per inch for:
  seams on thick, heavy fabrics
  gathering lightweight fabrics
  stay stitching lightweight fabrics
12 to 15 stitches per inch for:
  seams on medium-weight fabrics
15 to 18 stitches per inch for:
  seams on lightweight fabrics
18 to 22 stitches per inch for:
  seams requiring elasticity and strength

1 Before you are ready to stitch, each seam must be properly pinned and basted. Refer to page 120 for detailed directions on preparation of fabric for basting and stitching.

2 Prepare several units for stitching before going to the machine. Much time can be saved if you plan fewer trips to the machine. Arrange your pile of pieces so that similar jobs can be done at one time. For example, do the machine gathering on all pieces before changing the length of stitch for another type of work.

3 Certain equipment will be needed at the machine, and it should be well arranged on the right end of the machine top and ready for use. Necessary equipment is:

> box of pins or filled pincushion
> needle and basting thread
> gauges
> scissors (preferably small ones) for clipping threads
> scraps of fabric
> instruction sheet (folded for convenient use)

4 Always test-stitch with the machine to check threading, the size and condition of the needle, the balance of tension, and the length of stitch. Remember that each fabric makes a different demand on the machine, so adjustments may be needed. Always test-stitch under the identical circumstances under which the stitching will be done; use the same number of thicknesses of fabric and interfacing as the seam of the garment will have. Test stitching will save much time and trouble, so do not neglect to do it each time the machine is adjusted.

5 Examine each seam before sewing to determine whether or not one edge of the seam will be more difficult to manage than the other. Curved, clipped, bias, and eased edges require more care than a flat, straight edge, so the four types of edges mentioned are "difficult." Always keep the more difficult edge uppermost when stitching so that you can better control it. Usually seam edges are more or less identical, and in that case it does not matter which edge is uppermost. Always keep the bulk of the garment to the left of the machine whenever possible.

6 Support the weight of the fabric well. Small pieces will lie on the machine top very nicely, but large units (such as an almost-completed dress or a slipcover) need extra support to keep them from falling away from the machine and causing too much strain on the needle. A chair drawn up to the machine will serve the purpose nicely. Always adjust fabric so that a portion (6 or 12 inches, depending on the seam) of the seam is in a position to be stitched, stitch that portion, and then adjust another segment of the seam. Intricate seams must be stitched in shorter segments (2 or 4 inches) than straight seams. Never try to stitch more than a 1-foot segment before adjusting the fabric again. If the fabric is well supported and adjusted at the machine, it is possible to sew a straight seam with just the slightest touch of a finger to guide the fabric. Pulling and tugging at the fabric while the machine is in motion causes an uneven, wobbly stitching line.

7 The machine will operate at several speeds. An intricate seam should be stitched slowly, and it is well to have the right hand poised near the big balance wheel when intricate stitching is required, because most persons find it helpful to stop or slow down the machine by controlling the balance wheel with the hand. A long, straight seam can be

stitched at top speed, and you will find that the increased speed actually helps to make a smooth, even stitching line, if the seam is straight and free from complications. Everyone should acquire perfect control of the machine at high or low speeds. Although it is more difficult to keep proper control at the lower speeds, it is possible to practice until you can go so slowly you can count each stitch. The novice should practice on scraps of fabric until she gains experience and proficiency.

8 When a seam, a dart, a tuck, or a pleat must be crossed by another seam, the joining point becomes very thick, containing four to six thicknesses of fabric as compared with the usual two thicknesses in a seam. If the fabric happens to be heavy too, the problem of stitching is greatly increased. As you approach such a thick portion, lift the pressure foot of the machine slightly to help it up to the higher level, and then continue stitching.

9 There are two measuring aids on the machine foot. One of the prongs of the foot is ¼ inch wide, and the other is ⅛ inch wide. These are very helpful for topstitching especially, because those two measurements are so frequently used. There is a little metal attachment that you can purchase for some machines that will aid in measuring seam allowances. And the use of a cardboard gauge is most valuable. Do not guess at amounts—measure and be sure.

10 Most of the newer machine models can stitch backward as well as forward. Backstitching is an excellent and quick way to fasten thread ends at the end of a seam. In lieu of backstitching, the old reliable square knot must be used. Not all seams must be secured with a knot or backstitching; do not tie knots or backstitch when it is not necessary, because it is a waste of time. If a seam end will be crossed by another seam, the threads need not be fastened by a knot or backstitching; *only those seams or stitching lines that will not be crossed by another seam need to be fastened.* The ends of darts, tucks, or pleats are the most common places where a secure fastening is required.

17

PRESSING
TECHNIQUES

Pressing is quite as important as the quality of construction to the ultimate beauty of a garment. Indeed the professional presser in a manufacturing establishment is one of the highest-paid workers, more highly paid than the operator who sews the garment. There are many tricks to the pressing trade, each one easy enough to do at the proper stage during construction. The pressing suggestions in this chapter are just as important as the construction details and should be studied as carefully. A knowledge of pressing will do a great deal toward making your home-sewn garment come up to the high standards of good ready-made garments.

DIFFERENCES
BETWEEN
IRONING
AND PRESSING

Ironing is a process by which the iron is pushed along the fabric in the direction of the lengthwise or crosswise threads. The ironing process is used for washable garments after they have been constructed. "Wash and iron" go together, and "sew and press" go together. *Pressing* is a process by which the iron is lifted up and set down on the fabric in a series of up-and-down movements that progress in the direction of the lengthwise and crosswise threads. The pressing is used for garments that have been wrinkled, for all fabrics that are not washable, and for all garments during the process of construction. Ironing flattens the fibers in the fabric and will cause a shine on many fabrics; it is important to *press* all fabrics that will be dry-cleaned, so that their natural beauty will be retained.

DANGER OF OVERPRESSING

Naturally many pressings will harm the fabric somewhat. It is understandable that pressing flattens fibers, and overpressing (too often, too hard, too hot) will weaken the fabric, flatten it, and eventually make it shiny. Overpressing means that the fabric has been pressed with too hot an iron, with too great a pressure, or too many times. It is easy enough to check the temperature of the iron by test pressing. The suggestions for handling fabric, given on page 117, will greatly reduce the number of pressing operations.

GENERAL
SUGGESTIONS

the ironing board must be in good condition

First of all, the cover should be made of a fabric with no sizing (starch, etc.) because sizing sticks to the iron, burns, and then rubs off on fabric. The cover should be clean and free from dye marks. The board should be smoothly padded, and the cover should be smooth and tight; a ridge or wrinkle on the ironing board will mark the fabric of the garment.

each new fabric must be tested by using scraps to determine the best procedure to follow

You must know at what temperature to set the iron, the amount of moisture required to make seams and edges flat without shrinking the fabric, and the amount of pressure needed to give a flat finish without harming the appearance of the fabric. Because today's market is replete with the greatest variety of fabrics, because new fibers and fabrics are introduced every season, and because many of the new fabrics are made of a combination of two or more fibers, it is impossible to predict with true accuracy how a fabric will react to pressing. *Testing is of utmost importance.* Always test on a scrap of fabric large enough so that one-half of it can be pressed while the other half is left as purchased as a standard to follow. For example, if moisture spots the fabric, it will be more noticeable if one-half of the scrap is in its original condition. If moisture shrinks the fabric, it will be easily detected by a puckered line between the pressed area and the original. Changes in color and appearance of the fabric can be seen more accurately this way. Test several methods to determine which is best for your particular fabric.

the use of a press cloth is very important

The press cloth must be made of an unsized fabric because sizing sticks to the iron and burns. The weight of the press cloth should be similar to the weight of the fabric—a heavy press cloth is needed for heavy fabrics, and a lightweight press cloth for lightweight fabrics. The press cloth may be dry for some fabrics, particularly if the steam iron is used, and it may be damp (with varying degrees of dampness) for other fabrics. A press cloth may be dampened by one of two methods: (1) A wet sponge can be rubbed on the press cloth until the desired amount of moisture is achieved, or (2) the press cloth can be dipped in water, wrung out, and then pressed until the desired dampness is attained. Notice that the word "damp" is used; a wet press cloth is seldom used because it will shrink fabric. Some fabrics can take more moisture than others before shrinking occurs—this must be tested on a scrap of fabric. The press cloth must be uniformly damp so that no part of the fabric will shrink more than any other part. Sometimes fabric must be shrunk (described on page 206), and then the press cloth must be very wet. Several thicknesses of the press cloth (two, three, or even four) should be used when pressing on the right side of the fabric because this will create steam without leaving a print of the iron. Unattractive marks of the iron show on wool or pile fabrics more readily than on other fabrics, so great care must be taken when pressing these fabrics. It is an excellent idea to use a large scrap of the wool of the garment for a press cloth on that garment to prevent a shine.

A steam iron saves a great deal of pressing time. Usually a dry press cloth will suffice, and no press cloth is required for cottons and linens. The advertisements for some steam irons proclaim that no press cloth is needed and that you can safely iron on the right side of the fabric without a press cloth. Do not take these claims too seriously. Any steam iron is safer to use without a press cloth than a dry iron, but the steam iron will leave some mark on the fabric if it is used on the right side of the garment. Use a press cloth and always press on the wrong side, even when using a steam iron. Most steam irons release a standard amount of

steam or moisture, and therefore the worker does not have control over the amount of moisture the iron releases. If there is no steam-release adjustment, the press cloth is essential because a dry cloth would reduce the amount of moisture and a damp press cloth would increase the moisture. There are steam irons available with a steam-release adjustment, and if you own one of these, controlling moisture outlet is a simpler matter.

As soon as a seam is stitched, the basting threads, pins, and all tailor's tacks that will not be used again should be removed. A seam cannot be pressed flat with bastings in, and pins, if pressed over, leave an ugly mark on the fabric. The seam should be finished by pinking or some other seam finish before it is pressed.

When an edge, such as the fold edge of a pleat or the edge of a collar, is folded under, the basting threads must be left in until light pressing is done. Heavy basting threads will press a mark into the fabric which will be noticeable when the bastings are removed. These marks can be prevented by using a fine cotton or silk thread for basting such edges. Thread marks can be removed by using several thicknesses of a damp press cloth on the right side of the fabric and holding the iron against the press cloth with the entire weight of the iron supported by the hand. The steam from the press cloth will remove the marks.

There is no more important rule for pressing than to "press as you go." Press every seam before crossing it with another. First of all, pressing each seam as you go makes for easier construction. And certainly pressing can be done more effectively and more easily while the garment is in small sections. If a garment is pressed properly as you go, the final pressing will be child's play and will require only a matter of minutes. If pressing is neglected during construction, the final pressing can take an hour or more, and even then results will be disappointing.

Always press on the wrong side of the fabric. The original appearance of the fabric is retained if the iron is not placed on the right side of the fabric. And of course seams and darts are not revealed on the right side and can be pressed properly only from the wrong side. A certain amount of "touching up" will be necessary on the right side of the fabric, but it should be very little. This rule applies for ironing washables too. Always

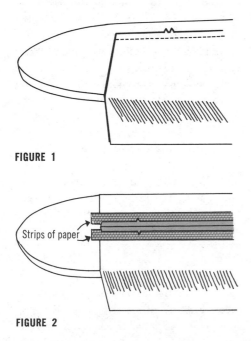

FIGURE 1

FIGURE 2

iron a washable on the wrong side, taking care at that time that darts, tucks, and seams are pressed well. Then do only final touching up on the right side.

Remember that pressing is an up-and-down process. Always lift the iron and set it down, progressing in the direction of the lengthwise or crosswise threads. Use as much pressure as the fabric requires. Never push the iron over the fabric as you do in ironing.

Allow some of the moisture to remain in the fabric after it has been pressed. Pressing until all moisture is removed from the press cloth causes the fabric to dry out and become deadened. This suggestion is especially important for wool fabrics. As you press, lift the press cloth occasionally to allow steam to escape. Be sure there is some steam still escaping when you finish pressing. Damp fabric will muss and wrinkle easily, so it is essential to hang up that section of the garment and allow it to dry by natural means before working with it again. Plan your work so that you can do something else for fifteen minutes or more while the fabric dries.

SEAMS

Always press seams together and flat first, as shown in Figure 1. This flattens out the stitching line and makes it easier to press the seam open later.

Sometimes the seam allowance will press through and cause an unattractive ridge or line; this will happen most often with wools and other heavy fabrics. The mark of a seam can be prevented by slipping strips of paper (ticker tape is convenient to use) under the seam before pressing, as shown in Figure 2.

A lapped or topstitched seam should be pressed before it is stitched and again after it is stitched and the bastings have been removed. It is a good idea to press the edge that will be lapped as soon as it is basted under and before it is basted to the other piece; a better, straighter, more accurate line can be achieved.

Keep seams ruler-straight on the board. Use a yardstick to check if your eye is not well trained. If a seam is pressed in a wobbly line, that inaccurate line is retained and the seam may never hang properly on the body.

Use a tailor's cushion to press curved seams such as those in the hip region of a slim sheath skirt (Figure 3). Darts, too, are better pressed over a tailor's cushion because a curved, molded line is desired at the tip of the dart. By pressing over a rounded surface, those portions of the garment that will fit a curve on the body are molded and shaped to conform to the figure.

GATHERS

Fabric should be pressed before it is gathered. Then if it is handled carefully and hung on a hanger when not in use, that area of the garment will require little, if any, pressing. If it must be pressed, let the gathered edge curve around the end of the ironing board, smooth out one area, and press with the tip of the iron pointing toward the gathered edge (Figure 4).

DARTS AND TUCKS

The instruction sheet states or illustrates the direction in which darts and tucks should be pressed. The general rule is: *Press vertical darts toward the center front or center back and press horizontal darts down.* However, there are exceptions to the rule, depending on the design, so you must always consult the instruction sheet.

Place the tip of the dart or tuck at the end of the ironing board so that one area of the piece is flat on the board while the rest of the piece hangs off the board, as shown in Figure 5. This will

enable you to press the dart right up to its tip. Use of the tailor's cushion as shown in Figure 3 is advisable for pressing darts that should be molded to fit a curve of the body.

PLEATS

The entire length of the pleat should be basted before pressing is done; it is impossible to get an accurate, true line without basting. The thickness of a pleat

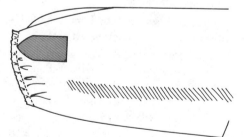

FIGURE 3

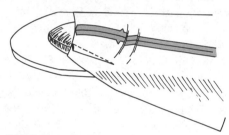

FIGURE 4

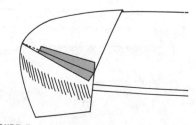

FIGURE 5

will mark through to the right side of the garment and cause an unattractive ridge or line, particularly in heavy fabrics. This can be prevented by inserting a strip of paper (any plain paper but never newspaper print) under the fold of the pleat before pressing (Figure 6).

Press to within 6 inches of the lower edge and remove bastings. The 6-inch unpressed edge will make the hem easier to put in. When the hem has been finished and pressed, baste the remaining fold edge of the pleats and press.

HEMS

The hem should be pressed from the wrong side until a flat, hard edge is achieved. Then the bastings should be removed, and the hem should be touched up with the iron from the right side.

SHRINKING OUT FULLNESS

If an edge has stretched or if an edge must be eased to another edge (such as the back shoulder to the front shoulder or the front skirt to the front bodice), the fullness can be shrunk out so that it is not noticeable, providing the fabric is such that it will shrink. Wools, crepes, and limp fabrics shrink more easily and satisfactorily than hard-finished cottons,

taffetas, and other stiff, firm fabrics. Fabrics that waterspot cannot be shrunk. Fabric will shrink with the application of a great deal of moisture, so a press cloth must be used, and it should be as wet as possible for best results. The iron is held against the press cloth, but the weight of the iron should be supported with the hand so that steam, rather than pressure, accomplishes the shrinkage. After the fullness has been shrunk out (and it may require more than one processing), press the fabric in the usual manner.

It is necessary to shrink out the fullness of an eased hem. The lower edge of such hems is a curved line. The problem here is to shrink the hem without shrinking the fabric directly underneath the hem; this means that a cushion of some sort must be inserted between the hem and the garment. A piece of cardboard about 8 inches long and 4 inches wide, cut in a curved line similar to the hemline, will serve the purpose nicely (Figure 7). Slip the shaped cardboard under the hem as shown in the sketch and proceed to shrink out the fullness as described above.

If two edges of different lengths must be joined together, one edge must ease to the other. Two outstanding examples are shoulder edges, where the back shoulder edge is often ½ inch longer than the front shoulder edge, and front waistline edges (if the skirt is a fitted one), where each half of the skirt front is ½ inch wider than each half of the bodice front. Although this easing is necessary for a beautiful fit, the edge should not look gathered; if the fullness is shrunk out, the fit will be retained but the edge will be flat and smooth. Gather the longer edge and draw up the gathers to the desired length. Place the edge over the tailor's cushion and smooth out the garment until it curves around the cush-

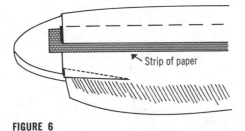

Strip of paper

FIGURE 6

ion (Figure 8). Then proceed to shrink out the fullness as described above.

THE FINAL PRESSING

Because all seams, darts, and edges, and actually all portions of the garment, have been pressed well during construction, there is little to do in the way of final pressing. The main purpose of a final pressing is to remove those folds and wrinkles caused by working with the garment. Many of them will fall out if you allow the garment to hang for a few hours after you have finished working with it. Pressing should be done following the general suggestions given earlier in this chapter and using the method which has proved best for your fabric.

For those costumes that will play leading roles in your wardrobe, a professional job of pressing when the garment is finished is well worth the cost. The large-area irons and the pressure and steam control available at the professional establishment result in a more finished appearance. The cost is relatively nominal—about 75 cents for a coat or suit and about 50 cents for a dress.

PROBLEMS OF PRESSING VARIOUS FABRICS

CAUTION "Blends" are fabrics made from a combination of fibers; two fibers, such as cotton and rayon, can be twisted together to make one yarn, or one set of yarns (lengthwise, for example) can be made of one fiber, while the other set of yarns can have a different fiber content. For this reason, pressing directions must be combined, and compromises must be made. It is very, very important to test-press on scraps of fabric before pressing on the actual garment, no matter what fabric is used, but that general rule is even more important when a blend is used.

COTTON AND LINEN

These are the easiest fabrics to press and therefore are an excellent choice for the beginner. No press cloth is required, and thus the pressing process is simplified. The iron should be set at a high temperature. Take care when pressing a cotton or linen garment that has seam binding on some edges; seam binding is usually made of acetate rayon, which cannot be pressed at such a high temperature.

SILK

Many silks (particularly silk prints) can be pressed without a press cloth, although all must be tested to see that the heat does not dry out the fabric too much and to see that iron marks do not show

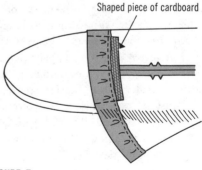

Shaped piece of cardboard

FIGURE 7

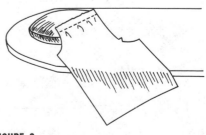

FIGURE 8

(they probably will on the darker colors). Most silks water-spot, and for this reason they are difficult to handle. Make sure your hands are not wet and that no water drips from a steam iron. A damp press cloth cannot be placed directly on the fabric for this reason; two or three layers of tissue paper between the fabric and the press cloth will prevent water spotting. If the fabric can be pressed without steam but some protection is needed to keep iron marks from showing, tissue paper or brown paper can be used instead of a press cloth.

RAYON, NYLON, DACRON, AND THE SO-CALLED MIRACLE FABRICS

In general these fabrics must be pressed at a low temperature; if pressed at too high a temperature, the threads melt and fuse, creating a hard, stiff mass, or a whole area of the fabric may melt and stick to the iron, leaving a hole in the fabric. A press cloth or paper, placed over the fabric, is a precaution against excessive heat. These fabrics, particularly, must be test-pressed to determine the problems involved. Refer to page 202 for more information on the problems of pressing these fabrics.

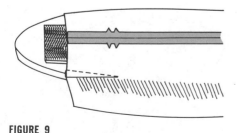

FIGURE 9

WOOL

Although wool is the most satisfactory fabric to press because of its excellent response to heat and moisture, precautions must be taken to retain its life and natural beauty. Wool shines easily, and this must be avoided by (1) always pressing on the wrong side, (2) always using a damp press cloth, (3) always pressing and never ironing, and (4) always leaving some moisture in the fabric to dry by natural means. The dark colors in wool will shine more readily than the lighter colors. If a scrap of wool fabric is placed on the ironing board and then the garment placed face down on it, there is even less chance that the fabric will shine. To remove an unsightly shine, use several thicknesses of a dampened cloth and hold the iron against the press cloth, supporting the entire weight of the iron with the hand. While the fabric is still damp and steaming, brush the area lightly to pick up the ends of fibers and remove the shine.

PILE FABRICS

Pile fabrics such as velvet, velveteen, corduroy, and velours require special pressing procedures to keep the pile erect. A needle board, which has a flat surface from which wire points project, is a great help (see Figure 9). But it is an expensive item, and most beginners will feel that its limited use makes the price prohibitive. The needle board is placed on the ironing board, and the napped fabric is placed face down on it. A slightly damp press cloth should be used, and most of the weight of the iron should be supported by the hand; the steam, rather than pressure, accomplishes the desired result. If a needle board is not available, place a scrap of pile fabric right side up on the board. Then place the garment right side down so that the two napped surfaces face each other. Use a heavy, slightly damp press cloth and support the weight of the iron with the hand. The steam, rather than pressure, will accomplish the pressing, but the napped surfaces will not be flattened. Brush the nap lightly while it is still

damp, and the original beauty of the fabric will be retained.

SELECTING
BUTTONS
AND
CONSTRUCTING
BUTTONHOLES

Buttons and buttonholes, although usually utilitarian in nature, often serve a design purpose as well, and certainly any buttoned closing on the front is a part of the design. Buttons and buttonholes are little "touches" that make a big difference. They deserve careful thought.

SELECTION
OF BUTTON SIZE
AND
DESIGN

The fashion sketch on the front of the pattern envelope pictures a button of the appropriate size. There are several factors to be considered. A large woman can use a larger button than a small woman. If there are many buttons, they must be smaller than if there is just one or two. The button must be in proportion to the length of the edge it is near. For example, the button on a huge pocket can be much larger than the one on a tiny pocket. The designer of your commercial pattern is an expert at such matters of beauty and proportion, so it is well to buy a button comparable in size to the button pictured in the sketch. Usually the exact button size is not stated on the pattern, so that each woman may have her choice. It is wise, however, to select a button not too different from that pictured or from one which would fit the buttonhole markings of the pattern. During the first fitting it is well to cut circles of paper or matching fabric to simulate contrasting or covered buttons and to test the size and number on the figure. Experiment with different sizes of circles and numbers of buttons.

PURCHASED BUTTONS

The design of the button is largely a matter of personal choice. If the buttons are to serve a strictly utilitarian purpose (for example, those on the front of a shirtwaist), they must not be too unusual; if there are many buttons, an unusual design will give an overdecorated effect. If, however, there is only one big button, its purpose is decorative and it can be of an elaborate design. If purchased contrasting buttons are to be used, it is well to take the bodice or jacket front to the department store so that the buttons can be tested under the circumstances under which they will be used. Or a large scrap of fabric (as long as the bodice or jacket front) will serve the purpose quite well. If the buttons are sold singly and are not on cards, they can be pinned to the scrap of fabric for a very accurate test. Buttons can add dollars in apparent cost to the garment, and by the same token they can cheapen the costume. It is foolish economy to

think of button cost as a separate item—to think, for example, that you must spend 10 cents for the button because 75 cents sounds so very expensive. The cost should be compared with the total cost of the garment; for example, a $15 costume investment becomes, with three buttons at the above prices, either $15.30 or $17.25. It would be false economy to ruin a $15 costume to save about $2.

SELF-COVERED BUTTONS

The button covered with the fabric of the costume is the frequent choice of the designer of ready-made costumes and the frequent choice of the woman who sews, as well. These buttons have great advantages: they are "safe" choices, for one cannot go very far wrong by choosing any one of the various types on the market. The button will be appropriate in color and texture, and it will harmonize with the garment. There is little or no chance of overdecoration. They look professional because the designer of ready-made costumes uses them so frequently. In addition to these advantages, they are not particularly striking and so are a wise choice for a row of several buttons of utilitarian function; yet they are pretty and attractive, and so they do add a nice touch to the design. And they are very much less expensive than a good-quality purchased button.

The metal frames are available at notions counters, so that one can cover buttons at home. The alternative is to have them professionally covered through your department store or Singer shop. In my opinion, it is wiser to have these buttons covered because the large machines used professionally can get a much better grip on the fabric than one can at home, and the buttons will be more serviceable. It takes just a few days to have the buttons covered, and a little preplanning will enable the woman who sews to have the more sturdy buttons without having to delay finishing her costume. Actually, the button-covering kits cost almost as much as professionally covered buttons; this fact is surprising to many persons who feel that if you do it yourself, you will surely save money. It so happens that the price of a large combination button-covering kit in our local five-and-ten is higher than the price of having the same button professionally covered. The woman who sews must realize that she is saving little, if any, money by covering her buttons; she is saving only the few days it takes to have them professionally covered.

Professionally covered buttons are available in a large variety of designs that add subtle interest to the costume. Study Figure 1 to see the infinite variety of effects that can be achieved through the style of the button, the choice of fabric, and perhaps the use of contrasting thread or decorative rim. In each case these are subtle effects and will not overdecorate the costume, even if there are many buttons. The chart illustrates the wisdom of choosing something with a little bit of interest in preference to the plain round button; in fact, it is this interest which I think is so worthwhile and which makes me favor the professionally covered button over the self-covered do-it-yourself type. The more interesting buttons cost just a few cents more each. The chart shows just one button size; however, all these buttons come in many sizes, and

Plain covered button

Combination button with narrow rim and flat center — can be made all in self fabric or one section can be in contrast

Combination button with wide rim and rounded center — can be made all in self fabric or either section can be in contrast

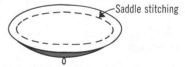

Saddle-stitched button — stitches can be in matching or contrasted color

Usual combination button with gold or silver metallic cord covering the seam

Button with contrasting rim of metal (silver or gold), plastic (in basic contrasting colors), or white or smoke pearl (sometimes available)

FIGURE 1 Button designs

there are other button designs as well. Square designs often enhance the plaid dress, and of course the traditional half-ball button is the choice for loop-and-button closings.

It is well to have one or two extra buttons covered to replace those which will get constant heavy use.

After the buttons have been purchased, double check your choice by pinning them to the garment before making the buttonholes. It would be wiser to buy a different button now if you have made a mistake than to ruin the effect of the costume with the wrong design or size of button.

BUTTON SUBSTITUTES

The decorative frog used on Oriental costumes can be used in place of buttons, but these frogs should be used sparingly on the costume to avoid an overdecorated effect. The corded strip of self fabric knotted into a ball-like shape makes an attractive, different button. A half bow of self fabric, to be pulled through the buttonhole like a button, is a nice touch if there is need for just one button.

NOTE Suggestions for sewing on buttons appear on page 227.

GENERAL
NOTES
ON
BUTTONHOLES

Just as buttons are a part of the design, so are the accompanying buttonholes. In fact, buttonhole construction (if the buttonholes are bound) is so important that it quickly "separates the men from the boys"; professionals use buttonholes as a quick standard for judging one's ability in the area of clothing construction. So buttonholes which serve only a functional

purpose have an important role to play, and buttonholes can be an outstanding design feature. Usually the buttonhole is functional, and so it is done with matching thread for the machine-worked types and with self fabric for bound, corded, and looped types.

However, buttonholes and buttons can become the outstanding design feature. See Figure 2 for examples of ways buttons and buttonholes, in various shapes and colors, can add tremendous interest to the costume. Of course the more unusual suggestions pictured must be used sparingly and only on simple costumes so that this effect is the only important design feature.

PLACEMENT ON GARMENT

Buttonholes are placed on the right front of women's garments. If the buttonholes are in the back, they should be placed on the left back. Buttonholes are placed on the left front for men's garments. The rule concerning placement of buttonholes on front openings of men's and women's garments is very rigid. I had never seen the rule violated until very recently, when a famous manufacturer of man-tailored shirtwaists and blouses for women brought out some that were buttoned like a man's garment. This exception to the rule was used by the manufacturer to emphasize the man-tailored look.

Buttonholes are usually placed at right angles to the finished edge because the button then holds more securely. If there is a band-type trim at the finished edge, buttonholes must be made parallel to that trim and are therefore parallel to the finished edge on the center line.

Diagonal buttonholes can be sewn by the machine or bound method in matching or contrasting color

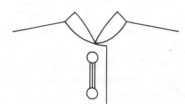

Long, wider-than-usual buttonhole, hand-sewn at center for two buttons—button or buttonhole can be in matching or contrasting color

Triangular bound buttonholes in matching or contrasting color

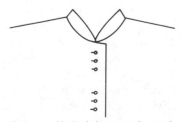

Buttons and buttonholes grouped — can be sewn by the machine or bound method in matching or contrasting colors

FIGURE 2 Buttons and buttonholes as a design feature

TYPES OF BUTTONHOLES AND APPROPRIATE USES

hand-worked	**1** for baby clothes
	2 for sheer lingerie made of very delicate fabric
	3 for mannish-tailored coats (made with buttonhole twist on very heavy coating fabrics)
	NOTE Directions for making hand-worked buttonholes are not given in this book because of the limited use of this method of construction.
machine-worked	**1** for utility garments of all kinds, housecoats, pajamas, work clothes, etc.
	2 for casual wear—sports blouses, beach coats, etc.
	3 used almost exclusively for children's wear
	4 for fashions with a mannish-tailored look
	5 for men's and boys' clothes
	6 for daytime cotton dresses and summer-weight suits; for costumes that are not especially expensive or "important"
bound or two-piece corded	**1** for significant costumes made of any fabric but sheers (adds apparent cost to cotton daytime dresses, for example)
	2 for all wool garments except those intended to be mannish in appearance
	3 for any buttonhole that contributes to the beauty of the design
loops—plain and corded	**1** for any edge that has only a seam allowance to work with—may be front, back, or sleeve opening
	2 in preference to a zipper at neck and sleeve openings to give a couturier touch
	3 traditionally used at back and sleeve openings of wedding dresses

Otherwise the parallel position is not recommended because the button unbuttons too easily.

MARKINGS ON PATTERN

Figure 3 shows the method of marking buttonholes on the pattern. Notice that the buttonhole mark begins about ⅛ inch over from the center line; this allowance is made so that when the button is buttoned, it will fall at the center line. Only one end of the buttonhole is marked on the pattern because the length of the buttonhole, as marked on the pattern, is not necessarily correct for the button each customer will choose; she will decide the length for herself.

to respace buttonhole markings for an altered pattern The buttonhole markings on the pattern will be correct and no respacing will be necessary if (1) the pattern has not been altered in length, (2) a plaid or design repeat does not require respacing or (3) the number of buttons has not been changed. But lengthening or shortening the bodice pattern will disturb the even markings on the pattern, and they must be respaced. Retain the original marking for the upper and lower buttonholes and respace markings in between. In plaids and designs with prominent repeats, the markings should be respaced with respect to the design.

As an added precaution for garments with a waistline seam, baste the garment and fit it to be sure the waistline position is correct. For example, the bodice may be too long-waisted, in which case the lower buttonhole marking may be too close to the waistline. In that case the lower buttonhole could be omitted.

Garments with no waistline seam (such as blouses, princess-line dresses, and fitted suits) must be fitted before the buttonholes are made. This is of the utmost importance because in such garments, one buttonhole must fall exactly at the waistline to ensure a good fit. Missing this point by even ½ inch would affect the fit of the garment. So while fitting the garment, place a pin exactly at the waist in front and use this marking for one of the buttonhole positions. It is often necessary to respace buttonholes in garments with no waistline seam for this very reason.

In snug-fitting bodices, one buttonhole should be directly in line with the fullest part of the bust; a relocation of buttonhole markings may be necessary for the person whose bust is higher or lower than average.

In designs that button down to the

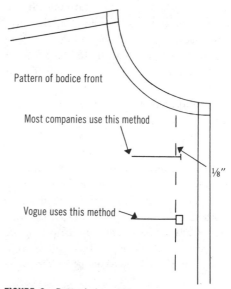

Pattern of bodice front

Most companies use this method

⅛"

Vogue uses this method

FIGURE 3 Buttonhole marking

hem, lengthening or shortening a skirt can necessitate alteration of buttonhole markings. Notice that the lower buttonhole marking in such a skirt is at least 5 or 6 inches from the hemline of the pattern. A button closer to the lower edge would spoil the beauty of the skirt. During a preliminary fitting, pin the hem at the approximate length desired. If this makes the lower buttonhole too close to, or too far from, the lower edge, respacing is required. And remember, if markings are respaced in the skirt, they must be changed accordingly in the bodice.

WAYS IN WHICH BUTTONHOLES MUST BE EVEN

1 They must be an equal distance from the finished edge. The finished edge is the edge of the garment when it is sewn and finished; this may be a fold line if the garment has a facing cut all in one with the garment, or it may be a seamline if a separate facing piece must be seamed to the garment. In all directions given in this chapter, the term "finished edge" will be used, and you must study your pattern to see whether that means fold line or seamline in your case.
2 They must be an equal distance apart.
3 They must be even in length.
4 They must be even in width.

In addition to these four ways in which buttonholes must be even, keep in mind that if there are buttonholes in both the skirt and the bodice, they must be equally spaced and identically sized. A very good rule is to make all buttonholes for the entire garment at the same time.

The length of the buttonhole is determined by the particular button size and need not be the same as given on the pattern. However, if you have chosen the buttons wisely, the length of the buttonhole will not vary greatly from that given on the pattern.

GENERAL RULE Diameter plus height of button equals length of buttonhole.

You may test this by cutting a slash in a scrap of fabric and passing the button through it. The button should go through the opening easily with no undue strain on the fabric. But the general rule is an excellent guide. The length of the buttonhole as achieved by taking these measurements is the minimum length required; sometimes a buttonhole made this minimum length will appear to be too short for the button (this is apt to happen with a heavy-looking button), and if it does appear too short, the buttonhole can be made longer than this minimum length.

MACHINE–WORKED BUTTONHOLES

1 Read General Notes on Buttonholes on pages 213 to 216. The only marking needed for machine-worked buttonholes is the mark nearest the center-front line. It is well to replace the tailor-tacked markings with a pencil dot at this time (Figure 4). Machine-worked buttonholes have so many stitches so close together that it is too difficult to remove the threads of tailor's tacks after the buttonhole is stitched; the pencil dot will be hidden under the stitches. Use a ruler to mark the dots and be sure that they are an equal distance from the finished front edge and are evenly spaced.
2 Always test-stitch on the machine before putting on the buttonhole attachment. Be sure that it is threaded properly and

that the tension is regulated correctly. Carefully read the directions for your particular attachment. There will be some way of adjusting the length of the buttonhole, and there will be some way of adjusting the bight (Figure 5). The bight is the width of the stitch formed. Some attachments have a means of adjusting what is called *space*, which is the amount of fabric left between the two rows of stitching.

Practice making buttonholes on a scrap of fabric like the fabric of your garment. This will give you confidence, will allow you to get the "feel" of the attachment, and will give you the needed opportunity to adjust the attachment to your particular fabric.

3 Mistakes made on the machine with the attachment can be very difficult to correct. Buttonholes have so many stitches that they are all but impossible to remove. A few precautions can save trouble later:

a Be very sure the machine is threaded properly. The test sample will serve that purpose. But remember to examine the bobbin stitching, too.

b Have plenty of thread on the top spool as well as on the bobbin. If either the top or bobbin thread runs out while the buttonhole is in process, serious troubles result.

c Always make three perfect samples in a row before attempting the buttonholes in your garment.

d Do not run the machine too fast, especially around the ends, where there are more stitches. If the machine runs too fast, the threads will break.

e It is not a good idea to sew around the buttonhole twice. A double stitching causes so many stitches to fall at one place on the fabric that the fabric is necessarily weakened. Then, too, there is too great a chance for threads to

break as the needle is forced in between stitches. Double stitching makes the buttonhole stiff and less pliable. However, double stitching can be used when it is necessary to get a strong contrast in color between the fabric and the thread; for example, white buttonholes on a red blouse should be stitched twice to get a more definite white line.

f The plate of the buttonhole attachment, the part that rests on the fabric to hold it securely under the machine, is very rough on the side that touches the fabric. If fabric is delicate and easily snagged, if it is fuzzy and sticky, or if the total edge is very thick, a piece of paper inserted with the fabric as it is slipped under the plate will prevent snags on the fabric. The paper

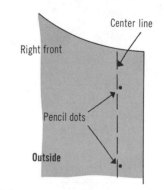

FIGURE 4

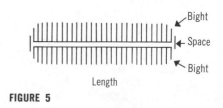

FIGURE 5

slips out easily after the fabric is in position.

NOTE See page 227 for directions for sewing on buttons.

BOUND BUTTONHOLES WITH CORDING FEATURE

CAUTION A test buttonhole, and perhaps more than one, must be made to determine the proper width and length problems due to the nature of the fabric. Raveling and weak corners are serious problems, and one must know what to expect before work is begun on the garment.

1 Read General Notes on Buttonholes on

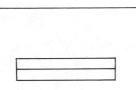

Good

Too wide

FIGURE 6

pages 213 to 216. Buttonholes must be slim-looking to give a professional appearance. Figure 6 shows good and poor proportions in two sizes of buttonholes. To our fashion-conscious eyes, the too wide ones look unattractive, too big for their purpose, and unsightly.

2 To ensure accurate measuring of all four ways in which the buttonholes must be even, a paper pattern will be made with the necessary lines drawn on it. This pattern will then be pinned in the correct position on the garment, the machine stitching will be done through the paper, and the paper will be torn away. Ticker tape is ideal for this purpose, but any strip of paper 3 or 4 inches wide can be used. Short pieces can be stitched together on the machine or pinned together to obtain sufficient length. Cut a piece of paper 3 or 4 inches wide and long enough to cover all buttonhole markings on the pattern.

3 To make the paper pattern, use the pattern as a guide and transfer the measurements of the buttonhole markings to the strip of paper as shown in Figure 7. Use a ruler, make sure that all lines are parallel, measure accurately, and use a fine pencil for best results. By drawing the lines shown in Figure 7, you have made the buttonholes even in three of the four ways: an equal distance from the finished front edge, an equal distance apart, and equal in length.

4 Draw another horizontal line about ¼ inch beneath the first line to make the buttonholes even in width. Reread step 1 for help in deciding exactly how wide they should be. Draw this last line so that the buttonhole is in beautiful proportion (Figure 8).

5 *If bound buttonholes are used, the garment must be interfaced. The interfacing must be basted to the wrong side of the garment before the buttonholes are started. Be sure to understand the differ-*

ence between interfacing and facing; interfacing is basted in place at this time, while the facing will not be used until step 15 is completed.

6 Cut 3-inch squares of fabric on the bias to be used as the binding for the buttonhole. Usually the binding squares are of self fabric, but they can be of a compatible fabric in a contrasting color if desired. See Figure 9. Center a square over each buttonhole marking, with one edge of the square along the finished edge of the garment, as shown. Pin in place with right sides together.

7 Place the paper pattern over the squares

of fabric; have the long cut edge of the pattern along the finished front edge of the garment and see that the top and lower buttonhole markings on the pattern fall in the same position as the top and lower markings on the garment (Figure 10). Pin in place carefully.

8 See Figure 11. Test the machine for tension, etc. Use matching thread and set the machine to sew about 17 to 22

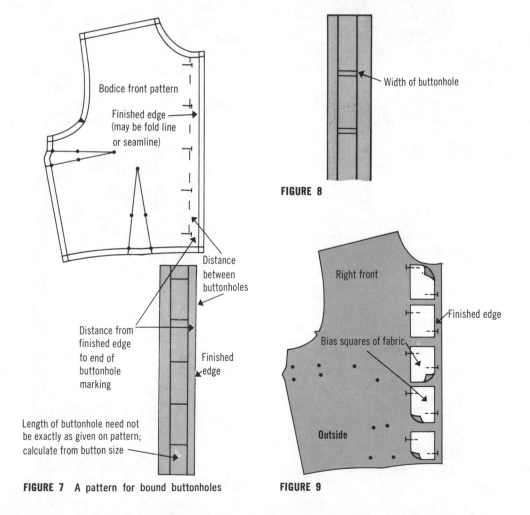

Bodice front pattern

Finished edge → (may be fold line or seamline)

Width of buttonhole

FIGURE 8

Distance between buttonholes

Distance from finished edge to end of buttonhole marking

Finished edge

Length of buttonhole need not be exactly as given on pattern; calculate from button size

Right front

Finished edge

Bias squares of fabric

Outside

FIGURE 7 A pattern for bound buttonholes

FIGURE 9

stitches per inch. Begin stitching the small rectangles at one corner. Count stitches at the ends so that all buttonholes for a garment will have exactly the same number of stitches in width, since

a difference of one stitch can make a great difference in the resulting size; leave the needle down in the fabric as you pivot the corners. Double-stitch for a few stitches so that knots will be unnecessary.

9 Carefully tear the paper pattern away from the stitches. See Figure 12. Using small sharp scissors, cut down the center of the buttonhole to within ¼ inch of the ends. Then cut diagonally to each corner. You must cut the corners directly to the machine threads. If you should cut the stitches by accident, restitch the corner before proceeding. Cut only one buttonhole and finish it before cutting the others.

Now turn the binding through the slash to the wrong side of the garment. It should lie flat with no puckers at the corners. If it does not lie flat, forming a perfect rectangle, turn the binding back to the right side again and clip into the

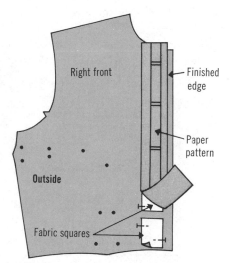

FIGURE 10

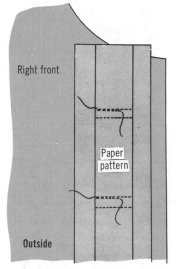

FIGURE 11

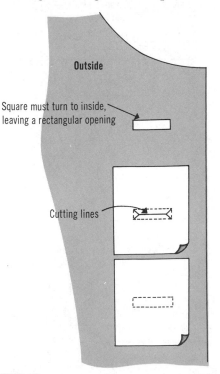

FIGURE 12

puckered corner; it puckers only if it has not been clipped to the corner.

10 See Figure 13. Turn the garment to the wrong side. Flip up one edge of the binding and notice the small seam. That seam has a tendency to lie toward the buttonhole, but it must be forced to lie away from it as shown. In order to hold the seam in the correct position, catch it down to the interfacing with small hand stitches.

NOTE In some fabrics that ravel badly, these hand stitches tend to ravel the seam even more. It is better to press this seam in the correct position when working with such fabrics.

11 The advantage of a corded buttonhole is that the lips will be rounded instead of flat, and thus the buttonhole will be more serviceable. The two-piece corded buttonhole (directions following on page 224) is the most professional buttonhole, but it is far, far more difficult to make than this one, and results are less predictable. But the cording feature included in these directions results in a buttonhole so nearly like the corded ones that there is no need to consider that more difficult construction. The cord used for this purpose should be pliable and of a diameter not to exceed ⅛ inch. Cut the cord in 3-inch lengths.

See Figure 14. Pin one edge of the binding flat against the garment and work with only one lip of the buttonhole at a time. Lay the cord inside the stitching line as shown. Do not attempt to pin it—it must be held in that position with the fingers.

12 See Figure 15. Working from the right side of the garment, wrap the binding around the cord firmly, and using no pins, blind-stitch along the seam of the buttonhole, encasing the cord; blind stitches should be a scant ¼ inch long and should be pulled quite firm. This

step is easier than it sounds, for the cord is a great aid in keeping the lip of the buttonhole even in width. When one

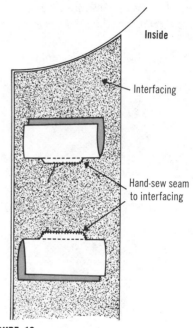

Inside

Interfacing

Hand-sew seam to interfacing

FIGURE 13

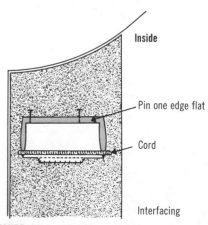

Inside

Pin one edge flat

Cord

Interfacing

FIGURE 14

edge is finished, place the cord in the remaining edge and repeat the process. From the wrong side fasten the ends very securely, passing the stitches through as many thicknesses of fabric as possible without allowing them to show on the outside.

13 Figure 16 illustrates the common flaws

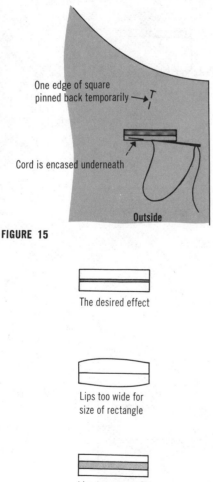

One edge of square pinned back temporarily → T I

Cord is encased underneath

Outside

FIGURE 15

The desired effect

Lips too wide for size of rectangle

Lips too narrow for size of rectangle

FIGURE 16

in buttonhole appearance and the reason that testing is absolutely necessary. In this method with the cording feature, the width of the lips of the buttonhole was controlled by the size of the cord; you were directed to wrap the fabric firmly around the cord for a firm, trim edge. The desired effect is a buttonhole with edges almost meeting at the center, as shown in the top sketch. If the rectangle is too narrow for the size of cord and the thickness of fabric used, the edges will bow out and the resulting buttonhole will be fat and heavy-looking. A thinner cord must be used, or the original rectangle must be made wider. If the edges do not meet each other (see the lower sketch), the cord must be thicker or the original rectangle must be narrower. Make corrections and retest before proceeding; these tests take precious time, but a beautiful row of buttonholes is well worth it.

14 Hold the lips of the buttonhole together with diagonal basting stitches; pull them only tightly enough to hold the buttonhole in a perfect rectangle (Figure 17). These stitches should be left in until the garment is finished and should be taken out only when the buttons are put on.

15 Trim the binding strips to ½ inch from the stitching on the long edges and ¼

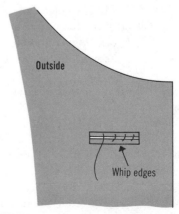

Outside

Whip edges

FIGURE 17

inch on the ends (Figure 18). Press the buttonholes carefully from the wrong side. This is the last good opportunity you have to press them. Whip the edges of the binding strip to the interfacing.

16 Return to the instruction sheet of your pattern and follow it until you are directed to finish the underside of the buttonholes. By this time the facing will be in place. See Figure 19.

step a Baste the facing to the garment around the buttonholes. From the right side stick a pin down through the center of the end of the buttonhole or use a pin at each corner to outline the rectangle.

Glance through steps b and c but do not do them before reading this entire paragraph. As the sketches show, fabric will be cut and must be turned under with very little seam allowance. Raveling is a serious problem, and this step should be tested on scraps of fabric, using the test buttonhole, before work is begun on the garment. To prevent raveling and to make the remaining steps very much easier, clear fingernail polish can be used; it is applied very carefully to just that area underneath the rectangle of the buttonhole. It must be applied lightly so that it does not penetrate through all thicknesses of the fabric. This is easier to do than it sounds, and although the polish discolors the fabric, if it is applied only under the buttonhole, the stained area will be turned to the inside and will not show. There are no resulting bad effects after washing or dry cleaning ordinarily, although one would be wary of using this method with light-colored silks and similar fabrics without pretesting.

Apply the polish and allow it to harden before proceeding with step b.

step b Cut to within ¼ inch of the pin (through the facing only) and then diagonally to the corners, thus making cuts

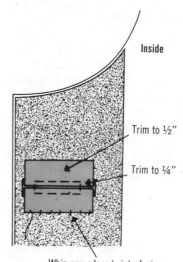

Inside

Trim to ½"

Trim to ¼"

Whip raw edges to interfacing

FIGURE 18

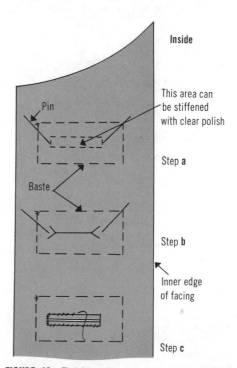

Inside

Pin

This area can be stiffened with clear polish

Step **a**

Baste

Step **b**

Inner edge of facing

Step **c**

FIGURE 19 Finishing the underside of buttonholes

exactly like those made previously, as the buttonhole was made.

step c Turn under the raw edges with the needle and carefully hem the turned-under edges to the binding. Handle this work most delicately, for the seam is very small and there are no protective stitches to prevent raveling. Press.

NOTE See page 227 for how to sew on buttons.

TWO–PIECE CORDED BUTTONHOLES

NOTE These directions are relatively brief compared with those for the bound buttonhole because they are written for the experienced reader. Read step 1, page 218, for ideas on proportions and size

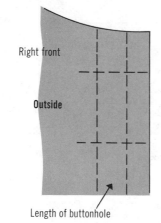

Right front

Outside

Length of buttonhole

FIGURE 20

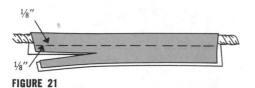

⅛″

⅛″

FIGURE 21

of buttonhole. It would be helpful to read all the directions for bound buttonholes for additional background material.

1 Read General Notes on Buttonholes on pages 213 to 216. Run a marking basting through the buttonhole markings nearest the center-front line. Decide on the desired length and put in a marking basting parallel to the first. Mark placement of buttonholes with a cross basting (Figure 20). It is *very* important that these lines be straight, well defined, and carefully measured. If your fabric does not show needle marks, it is well to do this basting by machine, for machine stitches make a better guide.

2 The cord used for this purpose must be small and pliable. One or two strands of four-ply knitting yarn make an excellent cord. Cut pieces of cord in 3-inch lengths; two pieces will be needed for each buttonhole.

3 Cut bias strips of fabric 3½ inches long and ¾ inch wide; two strips will be needed for each buttonhole. Wrap the bias strip around a piece of cord and baste close to the cord; be sure the bias is held quite tightly around the cord; baste with small, firm stitches. The corded edge should not exceed ⅛ inch in width. Prepare all strips to be used in the same manner; be sure all are identical when finished. Trim seam ⅛ inch from basting (Figure 21).

4 If corded buttonholes are used, the garment must be interfaced. The interfacing must be basted to the wrong side of the garment before the buttonholes are started.

5 Place corded strips on the right side of the fabric over buttonhole guidelines, with cut edges of strips meeting at the basted buttonhole line; allow ends of strips to extend equally beyond each of the vertical guidelines. Baste in place. A cording or zipper foot must be used when stitching by machine. Stitch along basted lines (⅛ inch each side of center line), using about 17 to 22 stitches per inch; end stitching exactly in line with guidelines. Tie knots to fasten threads (Figure 22).

6 Cut down the center of the buttonhole to a point about ¼ inch from the end of the stitching. Then cut diagonally to the ends of the stitched lines as shown in Figure 23.

7 Turn the strips through the slashed opening to the wrong side. Handle this step

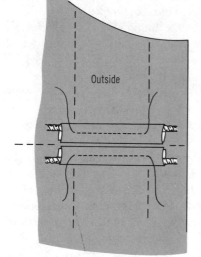

FIGURE 22

very carefully, for the ends of the buttonhole will fray easily. Flip up the end and notice the little triangle there. Sew this triangle to the strips with very small, firm hand stitches, being careful to sew right down to the base of the triangle (Figure 24).

8 Trim off extending ends of cord. Press. Finish the underside of the buttonhole by following step 16 on page 223.

NOTE See page 227 for directions for sewing on buttons.

CORDED FABRIC LOOPS FOR BUTTONS

Fabric loops are padded either with the thickness of a seam or with a small limp cord. The first kind is easier to do; the corded ones are more attractive. Loops are used on only those garments which

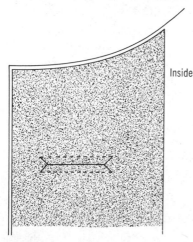

FIGURE 23

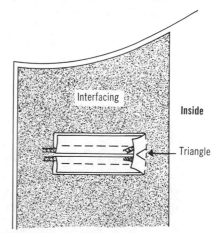

FIGURE 24

have a separate facing piece, since it is advisable to have a seam to conceal the raw ends; the facing is put on when step 5 is completed. The buttons used for this fastening are usually small and ball-shaped.

1 The dainty limp cord needed can be made of two or three strands of four-ply knitting yarn. Cut strips of cord 5 inches long. Cut strips of bias fabric 10½ inches long and 1 inch wide.

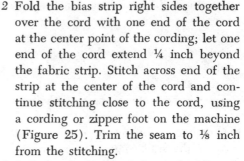

¼"   Center of cord

Inside

FIGURE 25

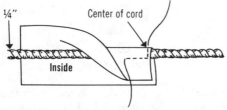

FIGURE 26

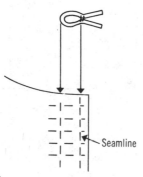

Seamline

FIGURE 27

2 Fold the bias strip right sides together over the cord with one end of the cord at the center point of the cording; let one end of the cord extend ¼ inch beyond the fabric strip. Stitch across end of the strip at the center of the cord and continue stitching close to the cord, using a cording or zipper foot on the machine (Figure 25). Trim the seam to ⅛ inch from the stitching.

3 Pull the short end of the cord and push the fabric along, thereby pulling the tubing over the free cord. Trim off the excess cord (Figure 26).

4 Place the buttons on the right front and decide on the number to be used. Buttons should be pleasingly spaced, with no more than ¼ to ½ inch between them. Therefore, the number of loops required is entirely dependent on the size of button used. Run a marking basting along the seamline at the front edge. Use cross basting to mark the spacing for the loops (Figure 27).

Experiment with the size of loop needed for the button. Tack one tube into a loop and push the button through it; it should be a snug fit, but not so snug as to cause undue strain on the button or the loop. When the size is correct, put another row of marking basting the required distance from the seamline as shown in Figure 27.

5 The loops may be attached in one of two ways, as shown in Figure 28. The finished appearance is slightly different. In both cases notice that the loops and the spacing of them are controlled by the guidelines. They must be basted to the seamline with very firm, small stitches because the thickness makes them difficult to control and they will slip out of place easily during stitching. Trim off the excess length of the loops.

6 Return to the instruction sheet of the pattern and follow it for directions on how to put on the facing. See

the directions below for marking position of buttons and sewing on buttons.

MARKING
POSITION
OF BUTTONS

Always give the garment a thorough final pressing before putting the buttons on. When the buttonholes are finished, the instruction sheet will read, "Lap right front over left, matching centers, and sew on buttons." To do this, pin the right front in position with center lines matching and with any cross lines matching; for example, the neck edges must be even, the waistline edges even, etc. To mark the position of a button, put a pin straight down through the end of the buttonhole nearest the center line (Figure 29). Mark the position of one button and sew that one on; and continue. If you mark the position of all buttons at once, there is a great danger of having to do several over because one mark was inaccurate.

SEWING
ON
BUTTONS

When a garment puckers after the buttons are fastened, it is because there is not enough room beneath the button for the thickness of the right front. Most buttons must have what is called a *shank* on the underside. The shank may be a metal loop attached to the underside of the button; if the button is flat or has a self shank made of fabric, a thread shank must be made. The purpose of the shank is to allow room for the right front, and therefore the length of the shank is de-

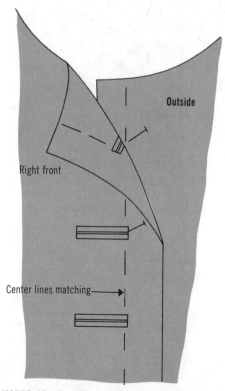

FIGURE 29   To mark position for buttons

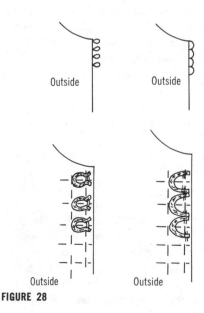

FIGURE 28

termined by the thickness of the fabric. For very flat fabrics (voile, nylon sheer, etc.) no shank is needed; for heavier fabrics the shank may be ⅛ inch long and sometimes as long as ¼ inch on heavy suits and coats. The right front is usually composed of two thicknesses of fabric and one thickness of interfacing; there is even more thickness if bound or corded buttonholes are used.

The thread used for this purpose should be as heavy as possible without being out of keeping with the nature of the fabric and the design. Buttonhole

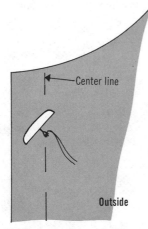

FIGURE 30 Button with metal shank

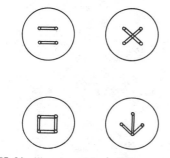

FIGURE 31 Ways to sew on buttons

twist, a heavy waxed thread, is excellent for tailored garments. Any regular sewing thread can be strengthened by pulling it through a piece of paraffin. Use a double thread with a small, compact knot. The color should match the fabric, except in cases where a contrasting color is desired for decorative reasons.

to sew on a button with a metal shank Work from the outside of the garment. Even the knot is placed on the outside because it will be hidden by the button, whereas it would look unattractive on the facing side. From the outside take a small stitch (1/16 inch) at the desired point (marked with a pin), catching through all thicknesses. Take another stitch to secure the knot. Take several small overhand stitches, catching in the metal shank. Fasten thread securely by taking several small stitches through one thickness of fabric only (Figure 30). Button this button, mark the next, and continue.

to sew on a button with eyes Buttons for rather tailored garments may have either two or four eyes. The button with four eyes can become a subtle design feature, for the thread can be inserted through the eyes in various ways (Figure 31).

This button is flat with no shank, and so one must be made with thread. This is done by sewing over a match (or similar object of the desired size) to make the stitches looser than they otherwise would be. From the outside take a small stitch (1/16 inch) at the desired point (marked with a pin), catching through all thicknesses. Take another stitch to secure the knot. Place the match over the button and bring the needle up through the eyes of the button. Take several stitches through the button and over the match. See Figure 32.

Remove the match and lift the button to pull the threads tight against the button; a shank of threads will appear beneath the button. Wind the thread around and around these threads and fasten thread securely.

NOTE For a flat button with no eyes and no shank, follow these directions with but one exception—place the match underneath the button.

REINFORCEMENT FOR BUTTONS

When a button will get great strain, it should be reinforced by placing a smaller flat button on the underside (the facing side) and sewing the two in place with the same stitches (Figure 33). The extra button will prevent the fabric from tearing under strain. If a button must be placed on one thickness of fabric, it will be insecure, and the fabric will eventually stretch and tear. This problem is handled by reinforcing the button position with a small scrap of matching fabric or a piece of seam binding or cotton-twill tape.

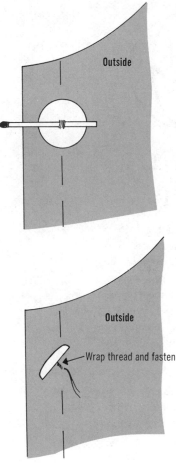

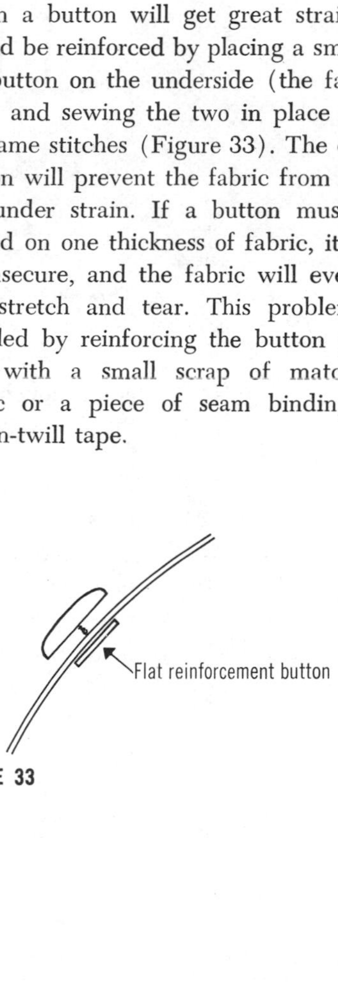

Outside

Outside

Wrap thread and fasten

FIGURE 32

Flat reinforcement button

FIGURE 33

THE SET-IN SLEEVE

The set of the sleeve plays a big role in the ultimate success of the garment. Perhaps no other step in construction can add so much to, or detract so much from, the final professional appearance (bound buttonholes, zippers, and sleeves are perhaps the three most important techniques to master). The directions on the instruction sheet must necessarily be brief, and perhaps this is the reason setting in sleeves is such a great problem for so many women who sew. Actually it is not difficult if several very simple little tricks are employed. These directions are written in great detail and should be followed step by step as the construction proceeds.

HEIGHT OF SLEEVE CAP

Figure 1 pictures three sleeve patterns which are identical except that they vary in cap height. Cap height is the distance from the biceps line to the shoulder marking. The sleeve that is called the *regulation set-in sleeve* has a cap with the greatest height and is a very comfortable sleeve to wear. This is the sleeve included in basic garments and most women's costumes. However, because of the height of the cap, this sleeve has more ease and is therefore the most difficult of the three to set in. About 1½ to 2 inches of extra length in the cap must be eased in as this sleeve is set into the armhole. The sleeve for a dropped shoulder line has a shorter cap, as illustrated, because the shoulder of the garment extends over the shoulder, providing some of the necessary length. If the shoulder line of the garment extends about ½ inch, the cap of the sleeve can be ½ inch shorter. The sleeve with the shortest cap (the action sleeve) is comparable to the sleeve in men's shirts and is used for shirtwaists and shirtlike blouses; it is the most comfortable one to wear. It has so little ease that one is hardly aware of it during construction; this is the easiest sleeve to work with.

NOTE The two-piece sleeve, used in many suits and coats, is no different in the cap area from the typical one-piece sleeve pictured. It can vary

in cap height just as this sleeve does. These directions can be used for setting in the two-piece sleeve—the only difference is that an underarm marking on the sleeve (instead of a seam) will match the underarm seam of the garment; notches and all other markings will be exactly like those on this sleeve.

SETTING IN THE SLEEVE

See Figure 2. Run two rows of machine gathering stitches between the notches; follow directions on page 125. Join the underarm seam of the sleeve.

See Figure 3. Compare the proportions of your sleeve cap with the patterns pictured in Figure 1 and then assume that your sleeve will have about the amount of ease stated for the most comparable sketch. Before pinning in the sleeve, draw up the bobbin threads to obtain the approximate amount of ease

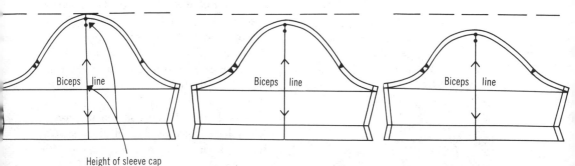

Biceps line

Biceps line

Biceps line

Height of sleeve cap

Regulation sleeve cape (about 1½ to 2 inches ease between notches)

b Shorter cap for slightly dropped shoulder line (about ¾ to 1 inch between notches)

c Still shorter cap used in mannish, tailored blouses (about ½ to ¾ inch ease between notches)

FIGURE 1

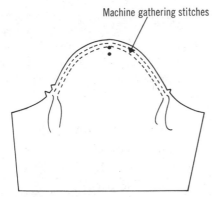

Machine gathering stitches

FIGURE 2

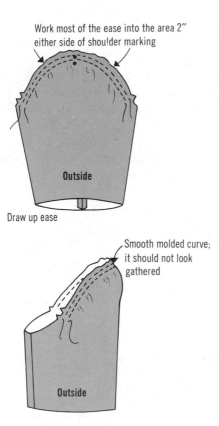

Work most of the ease into the area 2"
either side of shoulder marking

Outside

Draw up ease

Smooth molded curve;
it should not look
gathered

Outside

Test by holding into position with fingers

FIGURE 3

desired, distributing the ease equally on the front and back edges of the sleeve. Work in most of the ease in the very uppermost part of the sleeve cap, in the area about 2 inches on either side of the shoulder marking, as shown by the sketch.

To check your work, hold your fingers under the sleeve cap (to simulate a shoulder) as shown in the lower sketch and see that the sleeve looks smooth and molded. It should not look gathered, and if it does, it has been drawn up too much. Be sure that it is not drawn up too tightly because if it is, the remaining steps of construction will be more difficult. Do not fasten threads because this is just a temporary "guess"—the exact amount of ease will be determined when the sleeve is pinned to the armhole of the garment. It is helpful if this guess is quite accurate, and with experience it is possible to judge the right amount of ease with great accuracy.

See Figure 4. Work with the garment turned wrong side out. With right sides together and cut edges even, locate the sleeve in the armhole at four matching points: underarm lines, the two notch positions, and the shoulder position. First pin the area between and below the notches. Do not be surprised if the sleeve seems too big for the garment at that area, for there is often about ¼ inch of ease between each notch position and the underarm position of the sleeve; it is so slight and so easy to work in that the instruction-sheet directions seldom mention it, and the worker might well be unaware of it herself.

See Figure 5. This sketch pictures a trick that makes setting in sleeves very much easier. The trick has to do with the way the work is held. Hold the garment and the sleeve in such a position that the sleeve takes the outside curve over your fingers; notice that the ease works in so magically that it almost seems to disappear. Adjust the ease, pulling up or releasing the gathering threads as required, but be careful not to draw the gathers up too tightly. Pin in place, cut edges even. Baste with small stitches that are firm but not so tight that they draw up the garment. Test the seam for tightness by putting your hands into the armhole and gently pulling the sleeve against your hands. If you are aware of stitches "cutting in," the basting is too tight, and the thread should be clipped at several points to release it.

Turn the garment right side out and examine your work. Be sure the garment has not been drawn up with the seam. The upper edge of the sleeve should not look gathered—you should hardly be aware of the excess fullness. Fit the garment to check hang of sleeve and width of shoulder line. Make necessary adjustments and refit.

Machine-stitch the seam with the sleeve side up, so that you can better watch the eased edge. Stitch over the basting very slowly and carefully because at this time, careless stitching can cause tucks to form. Remove bastings and gathering threads.

See Figure 6. Most structural seams of the garment are not trimmed down in width, but the armhole seam is an exception. It should be trimmed down to a ⅜-inch width so that the sleeve can fall naturally over the shoulder (a ⅝-inch seam allowance would force the sleeve to stand out that far beyond the armhole and would make the shoulders seem too wide). The ripples formed in the cap of the sleeve as the seam is turned toward the sleeve make the sleeve cap bulky; to prevent this, notch out the ripples until the seam *lies* flat and smooth, as shown in the sketch. The armhole of the garment should be the size of the seamline for maximum comfort, and to achieve that size, the seam must be

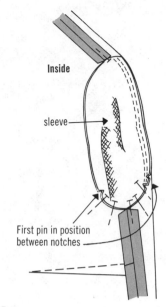

Inside

sleeve

First pin in position
between notches

FIGURE 4

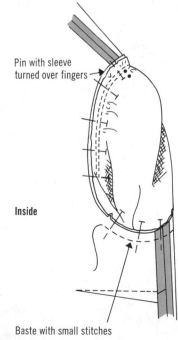

Pin with sleeve
turned over fingers

Inside

Baste with small stitches

FIGURE 5

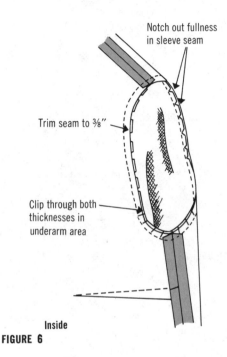

Notch out fullness
in sleeve seam

Trim seam to ⅜″

Clip through both
thicknesses in
underarm area

Inside

FIGURE 6

clipped almost to the stitching in the underarm area, as shown.

The sleeve seam turns toward the sleeve. Avoid pressing the seam if the seam *lies* in that direction without having been pressed. If the seam must be pressed, press just the seamline, allowing the iron to extend only about ⅛ inch over the seamline into the sleeve; this will avoid a series of flat surfaces which the iron would otherwise create and allows the sleeve to retain the natural roll that gives it a professional appearance.

NOTE Refer to the instruction sheet for special directions. The sleeve for a garment with a dropped armhole must sometimes be pressed open rather than toward the sleeve, as these directions read.

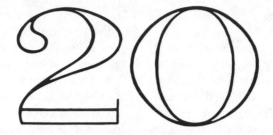

GUSSET
CONSTRUCTION

A gusset is a diamond-shaped or triangular piece set into the underarm area of a garment with a sleeve cut in one with the body of the garment. Its purpose is to make the garment fit well and look trim, while at the same time providing extra spread for arm movements. A garment with a gusset can be fit more snugly to the body than a similar design without a gusset. Because of its aid to smart fit, the gusset, in one of many guises, appears often in highly styled Vogue patterns. Gussets vary so much that about all they have in common is that they have at least one square or one pointed corner that must be set into a slash in the bodice. Figure 1 pictures four examples of the most common gusset patterns. The diamond-shaped piece is the traditional gusset and is the most difficult to do because it has four corners, two of which are set into slashes in the bodice. The half gusset is the simplest to do and appears in easy-to-make designs. By cutting two halves for each side, the resulting gusset is very much like the traditional gusset (with the addition of just a seam down the center). However, the half gusset is much easier to do because each half is set in before the underarm seam is joined.

A gusset can be combined with a portion of the body of the garment, as shown in the two right-hand sketches. The piece will have a pointed end and will extend in boxlike fashion to become the underarm section of the bodice or an underarm section of the sleeve; notice the markings on the pattern which designate the underarm position. This gusset is easier than the traditional gusset for

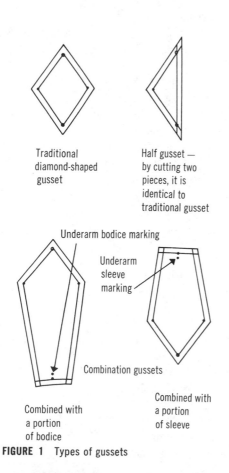

Traditional diamond-shaped gusset

Half gusset — by cutting two pieces, it is identical to traditional gusset

Underarm bodice marking

Underarm sleeve marking

Combination gussets

Combined with a portion of bodice

Combined with a portion of sleeve

FIGURE 1 Types of gussets

the simple reason that it has one less corner.

No matter what shape the gusset takes, there are certain general principles which hold the key to success. These principles will be discussed in detail in this chapter. No matter what shape the gusset takes, it has certain corners that are set into slashes in the body of the garment and other corners that are set into points formed by the joining of two seams; the most difficult corners to do are those which are set into slashes in the garment. In every illustration used in this chapter, the difficult points are marked with small o's and the easier corners with large O's. I have chosen to write about and sketch the traditional gusset in great detail because it is the most difficult and because it illustrates all the general principles involved in all gussets.

If the pattern you are working with is different, follow the instruction sheet for the little differences and follow these directions for general principles. The one most difficult step, that of basting and machine stitching the gusset, is shown in Figure 6, and as an aid to constructing the half gusset and combination gusset, the same step is pictured in Figures 9 and 10.

Only two markings—small o's and large O's—have been used in these sketches, but your pattern may have used other markings. For example, Vogue uses four different markings for the four corners. You should, of course, follow the marks on your pattern, using these sketches as an illustration of principle.

See Figure 2, which pictures a bodice front with typical lines for gusset construction. The main principle to understand is that the pattern piece for the gusset has ⅝-inch seam allowances on all edges (see Figure 1), whereas the stitching lines on the bodice converge, and therefore there is a varying seam allowance on the bodice; when the slash is made down the center of the stitching lines, the seam allowance on the bodice varies from perhaps ½ or ⅜ inch at the widest point to no allowance at all at the point. When two edges with different seam allowances are sewn together, they must be sewn with seamlines matching, rather than with cut edges even, as one usually sews. This is the principle which so many people do not understand. To repeat: *Gussets are constructed with seamlines matching, not cut edges even. Only on the gusset piece will the seam be an even width.*

CONSTRUCTION
OF
TRADITIONAL
GUSSET

See Figure 3. The very first step of construction (before seams are basted) is the reinforcement of the points that will be slashed. Reread Reinforcing Corners on page 118. This is done by placing a scrap of fabric on the outside of the garment, allowing it to extend ⅝ inch outside the stitching lines, as shown. Lining fabric or a lightweight interfacing fabric is a good choice; the fabric will not show when the garment is finished. Machine-stitch with short stitches (15 to 20 per inch) and with matching thread along the stitching lines, as shown, catching in the scrap of fabric; do not retrace stitches at the point because a cut must be made directly to the point.

Your pattern directions will tell you to cut to the point at this time. It would be wiser to cut only partway, to about 1 inch from the point at this time, so that there is no chance of the seam fraying while the garment is basted and fitted (these garments are fitted before

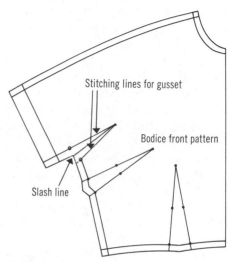

Stitching lines for gusset

Bodice front pattern

Slash line

FIGURE 2

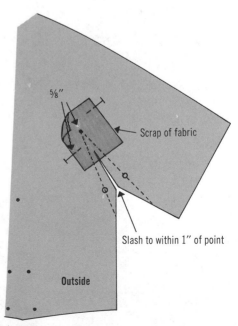

⅝"

Scrap of fabric

Slash to within 1" of point

Outside

FIGURE 3

the gusset is put in). When the fitting is done and the side seams have been stitched and pressed, slash directly to the point of the reinforced lines just prior to putting in the gusset.

See Figure 4. This sketch shows another very important step. As the underarm seams of the bodice and sleeve are stitched, the stitching must end directly at the marking and must not extend all the way up to the cut edges. Note that the stitches go to the large ○ and are secured with backstitching. This is a very common trouble point; the instruction sheet will read, "Join underarm seam below large ○." The word "below" is very important, and it is easily overlooked in brief, telegram English termi-nology. Let me repeat: Stitch only to the marking at the ends of the underarm seams and backstitch to secure the threads.

See Figure 5. All the remaining sketches picture the gusset opening as it would look if the arm were held at shoulder level and the body viewed from the side. Notice that the scrap of fabric turns to the inside and acts as a seam allowance at the point which otherwise would have no seam allowance at all. Note the little openings at the ends of the two underarm seams; these openings will act as clips as the gusset is set in, and without them, setting in a gusset would be all but impossible.

See Figure 6. The sketch shows the gusset basted in place; it would, of course, be pinned before basting. The little scrap of fabric, which is a great aid in sewing, covers up some points I wish to show, and so I have included the scrap

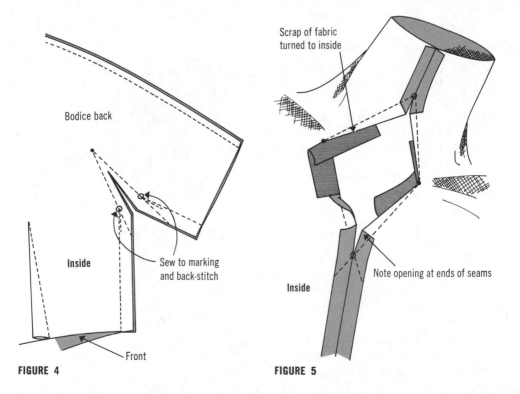

Bodice back

Inside

Sew to marking
and back-stitch

Front

FIGURE 4

Scrap of fabric
turned to inside

Inside

Note opening at ends of seams

FIGURE 5

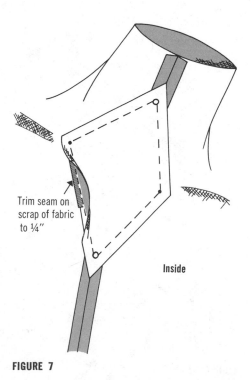

Inside

Gusset

Scrap of fabric not
pictured on this point

FIGURE 6

at one point to illustrate how it would look in place and have left it out of the drawing on the other side as an aid to showing the construction more clearly; do understand that a scrap of fabric must be used to reinforce each slashed point.

This drawing illustrates the principle of seamlines matching, rather than the usual cut-edges-even construction. Study the sketch carefully (particularly the right half) and see that the gusset edge, with its ⅝-inch seam allowance, extends beyond the slashed edge with its varying seam allowance. Pull the scrap of fabric to the inside and use it like a seam allowance. With right sides together and small o's and large O's matching, pin the gusset to the slashed edges, having seam-

Trim seam on
scrap of fabric
to ¼"

Inside

FIGURE 7

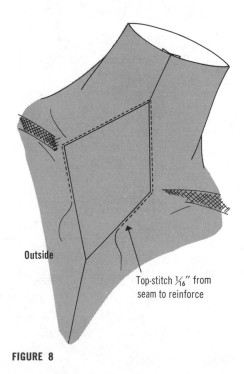

Outside

Top-stitch ¹⁄₁₆" from
seam to reinforce

FIGURE 8

lines matching (not cut edges even). Pin and baste very securely, especially at all corners. Stitch just inside the reinforcing lines from the bodice side, leaving the needle of the machine down as you pivot around each corner; all edges can be done in one continuous stitching if the unit is pivoted around the needle.

See Figure 7. Trim the edges of the scrap of fabric down to about ¼ inch. Press the seam toward the bodice as shown. The gusset is finished and should wear well for most special-occasion clothing. However, even though the slashed points are as secure as they can be made,

weakness does exist at these points. To strengthen these points on workaday clothing, the gusset seam can be top-stitched as shown in Figure 8. This will strengthen the points considerably, but the stitching line will make the seam more prominent.

CONSTRUCTION
OF
HALF
GUSSET

Figure 9 shows the basting and stitching of the half gusset and compares with Figure 6. The point is constructed in the same manner, but the half-gusset piece is set in before the side seams are basted or stitched; notice how much easier it appears. When the two halves have been inserted, the entire underarm of bodice,

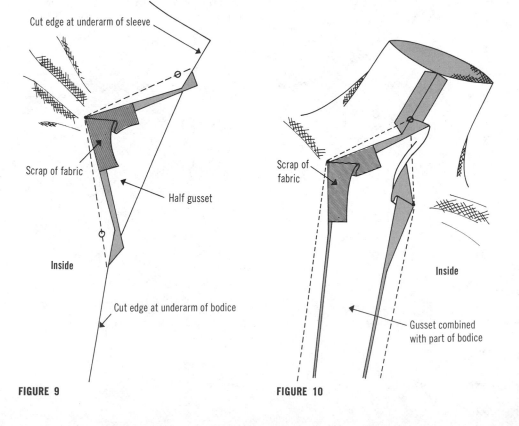

Cut edge at underarm of sleeve

Scrap of fabric

Half gusset

Inside

Cut edge at underarm of bodice

FIGURE 9

Scrap of fabric

Inside

Gusset combined with part of bodice

FIGURE 10

gusset, and sleeve are sewn in one easy operation.

CONSTRUCTION OF COMBINATION GUSSET

Figure 10 pictures a gusset combined with a portion of the bodice; a gusset combined with the sleeve would be exactly like this, turned upside down. This sketch compares with Figure 6; note how much easier this one is with just one less corner.

NOTCHED-COLLAR CONSTRUCTION FOR JACKETS AND COATS

The notched collar of a suit or coat is constructed very differently from a similar collar on a blouse or dress; it is so different that this is probably the most confusing construction detail in a suit or coat. For this reason these directions are given in great detail. Actually, each step in the process is simple, but each must be done with measured accuracy before proceeding to the next. The collar is attached in a different manner because, in this way, it is possible to press the neck seams open, thus distributing the great bulk of that seam over a larger area. The directions on your instruction sheet will be essentially like these, probably exactly like these, but they are given in a very condensed form.

See Figure 1. Machine-stitch ½ inch

from the neck edge of the jacket or coat between the tailor tacks which mark the placement for the end of the collar; use about 15 stitches per inch and see that the row of stitches is exactly ½ inch from the raw edge. Machine-stitch ½ inch from the neck edge of the two front facing pieces in the same manner. Clip down to this row of reinforcing stitches about every ½ inch, as shown. This step is usually not included on your instruction sheet, but it is an excellent idea—not only for this collar but as a preparatory step for attaching any collar to any type of garment. The stitches reinforce the neck edge for clipping, and the clips release the seam allowance so that it can "give" and shape to the lines of the collar.

In all sketches in this chapter, a large O is used as the marking for the placement of the end of the collar, and two small o's are used to designate shoulder position. Most pattern companies use this marking, although it is possible that your particular design may have another size or shape of marking here; if so, the construction is just the same.

See Figure 2. There should be a corresponding marking at the front corner of the collar patterns; if there is not, put one in at this time. It is located, as shown, at the meeting point of the seam-lines on the front corners of the neck edge (the neck edge is the notched edge). Examine the two collar patterns to better understand why this kind of construction has so many advantages. Place the Under Collar pattern on top of the Upper Collar pattern with neck edges (notched edges) meeting. Notice that the Upper Collar pattern is wider

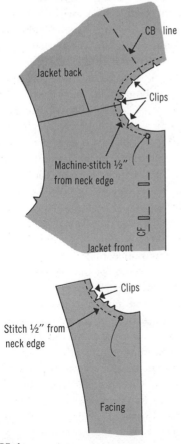

FIGURE 1

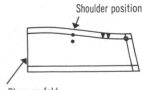

a Upper Collar pattern

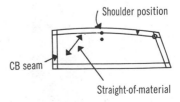

b Under Collar pattern
FIGURE 2

by ⅛ to ¼ inch; this enables the Upper Collar of the garment to bend around the Under Collar with width enough to take the outside curve. Note the straight-of-material line in the Under Collar, which causes the center back of the Under Collar to fall on a bias line; this bias cut of the Under Collar allows it to bend more easily and to take the inside curve as it is worn. Usually, although not always, the Under Collar pattern has a center-back seam, while the Upper Collar is placed on a fold line at the center back. Notice that the two neck edges have different notch markings; the Jacket Front pattern has corresponding notch markings to

match the Under Collar, and the Facing pattern has corresponding markings to match the Upper Collar.

See Figure 3. Baste the Under Collar (the Under Collar has been interfaced) to the jacket or coat, right sides together, and cut edges even with center backs, notches, and large ○'s matching. This seam is so thick that very, very secure basting stitches are required to hold the Under Collar in place accurately. Notice how the clips at the neck edge of the garment spread out to take the shape of the Under Collar neck edge.

The Upper Collar is attached to the Front Facing pieces in the same manner, with the one exception that usually there is no back facing. Baste the Upper Collar to the Front Facings, right sides together and cut edges even, with notches and large ○'s matching; usually there will be a shoulder marking, too, that must be matched to the shoulder line of the facing.

Check your work very carefully before stitching. The measurement from the large ○ to the edge of the lapel at the four corners involved should be equal; it will be if you have worked accurately. If these measurements vary so much as ⅛ inch, correct them at this time. They will eventually become the important lapel extensions, and since they will be so near each other as you wear the garment, any slight variation will show noticeably.

Stitch these seams as basted, with the following precaution: The machine stitches must end at the large ○ and must be secure, so backstitch exactly to the large ○ and then proceed around the neck edge to the other large ○ and backstitch. Do this as you sew the Under Collar to the garment and the Upper Collar to the Front Facing pieces.

See Figure 4. This is probably the bulkiest seam in the whole garment; read Trimming Seams—Reducing Bulk in

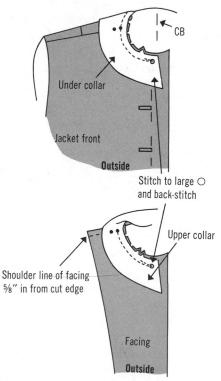

FIGURE 3

Seams on page 133. After trimming the interfacing and the bulk from cross seams, trim the neck seam of the Under Collar and garment to about ½ inch. Allow the seam of the Upper Collar and Front Facing to remain ⅝ inch in width; by so doing, these two seams, which will eventually lie on each other, are staggered so that they will not be so bulky.

These seams must be pressed open, and because they are so curved, this is difficult to do. It is wise to baste them open first. See that they *lie* flat; if they do not, clip wherever necessary. The seam of the Under Collar and garment is naturally the more difficult to press open because of the interfacing: it can be whipped down to the interfacing as a further aid to keeping it flat.

Press the seams very well, for this is the last opportunity you will have to press them. Use a tailor's cushion and press small segments of the seam at a time, using any curve on the tailor's

cushion that is the correct shape for a particular segment of the seam.

See Figure 5. Pin the Upper Collar and Facings over the Under Collar and garment, with right sides together and cut edges even, matching notches, large O's, and center lines. All these raw edges must now be basted and stitched, but do the collar stitching first and later on do the lapel and front edges.

Before stitching the seam, examine

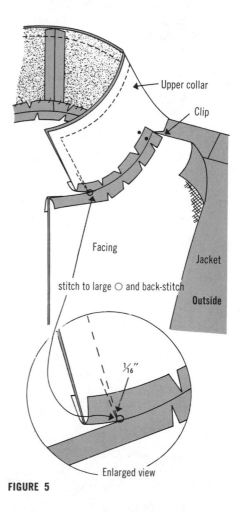

FIGURE 5

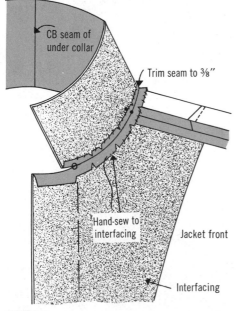

FIGURE 4

the enlarged view very carefully. The collar should be stitched on the seam-line, and the stitches should end at the large ○, but if they are placed just ⅟₁₆ inch outside the large ○, as shown (note that the stitching line is not centered in the large ○), the corner will turn very much better. Notice that the neckline seams are pressed up and are caught in with the stitching of the collar seam.

a Desired effect

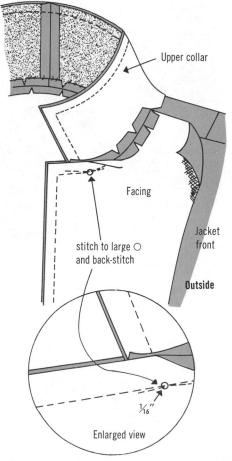

Upper collar

Facing

stitch to large ○ and back-stitch

Jacket front

Outside

⅟₁₆″

Enlarged view

FIGURE 6

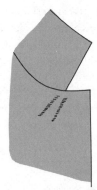

b Corner tight and puckered—one seam stitched too far

c Upper edge of lapel stitched at wrong level
FIGURE 7

Stitch the entire collar seam, backstitching at large ○'s, as shown. This is an encased seam, and the seam edges should be trimmed in a staggered fashion. Clip the neck edge of the Upper Collar to the seamline at the shoulder edge, as shown.

See Figure 6. Flip up the seam of the lapel in preparation for stitching the front and lapel edges. Before stitching, examine the enlarged view very carefully. The stitching, as it approaches the large ○, must be on a level with the stitching of the neck seam, but stop the stitches and backstitch about $\frac{1}{16}$ inch from the large ○, as shown. This will ensure a corner that will turn easily and *lie* flat. Stitch these edges, backstitching at the large ○'s, as shown.

See Figure 7. Before trimming this seam, turn the collar and facing to the inside to see whether the corner of the collar and lapel will turn into a flat, square corner. If it puckers and appears tight, one of the stitchings (the collar or the front and lapel) went a stitch or so too far; a stitch or so must be removed. If the lapel does not make a smooth, even line with the collar seam, the stitching of the lapel was not on a level with the stitching line of the collar and must be ripped and moved up to the seamline. When the desired effect is achieved, trim the front seam in a staggered fashion.

See Figure 8. The raw neck edge of the collar and the shoulder edges of the facing are not turned under; they remain raw because the lining will cover them. Baste these edges, cut edges even, to the neck and shoulder seam of garment. Hand-sew them in place with running

stitches and matching thread, keeping these stitches just outside the seamline (about ½ inch from raw edges), so that the lining will cover them.

NOTE The lower front corner of jackets and coats is very bulky when the hem is turned up. Special directions for decreasing bulk at these most important corners are given on page 298 and are incorporated in the directions for the catchstitched hem. Facing edges and hems for lined garments are always left raw and secured with catch stitches. Directions for doing catch stitching are given on page 138.

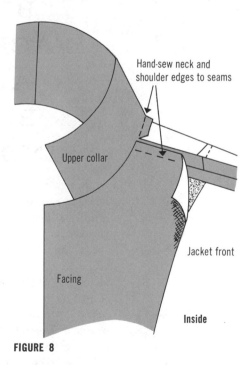

Hand-sew neck and
shoulder edges to seams

Upper collar

Jacket front

Facing

Inside

FIGURE 8

FITTED FACINGS, BIAS FACINGS, AND BIAS BINDINGS

A facing is a piece of fabric used to finish a raw edge; it is turned to the inside so that it is not visible as the garment is worn. A fitted facing is one that is the size and shape of the garment edges to be faced; therefore, the fitted facing must be cut from a pattern piece. A bias facing is one made of strips of fabric cut on the bias so that they can ease and stretch to take the shape of the garment edges to be faced; therefore, the bias facing does not require a pattern piece. The two facings, bias and fitted, serve the same purpose under ordinary circumstances, and so either type can be used. However, in general the fitted facing adds more in apparent cost to the garment (expensive ready-to-wear usually has fitted facings, and inexpensive ready-to-wear often has bias facings), and so the fitted facing is basically the wiser choice. Under the following circumstances, the bias facing or binding is preferable to a fitted facing: (1) in sheer fabrics for a delicate effect, (2) if a narrow collar is featured and a wider facing would be objectionable, and (3) in sheer fabrics when the double bias binding, used as a trimming, looks neat and attractive.

Most patterns will include fitted facings because they are the nicer finish. However, in simple-to-make designs, when a greater number of pattern pieces is discouraging to the novice, the pattern company may suggest bias facings in an attempt to make the pattern seem easier to make. This is regrettable because although there is less cutting involved when bias facings are used, the construction of the bias facing is far more difficult than that of the fitted facing. There is another reason the pattern companies sometimes suggest bias facings: they do it because many inexperienced persons think bias facings are very easy, and so the pattern company plays the game. The truth is that bias facings are very easy to do incorrectly and very difficult to do properly. The problem of the bias facing is that a strip of fabric must be molded and shaped to a curved edge, and this is not really easy. A fitted facing, since it is cut in the proper shape, can be very easily seamed to fit a shaped edge. The bias facing requires less fabric because it can be cut from scraps.

The fitted facing has many advantages except for sheers, and so if patterns for fitted facings are not included, the woman who wants a professional result is able to construct her own facing.

TO MAKE A PATTERN FOR A FITTED FACING

See Figure 1, which pictures a basic pattern and illustrates the principles of making fitted facings for any edge. A piece of tissue paper should be placed over the pattern so that the facings can be copied. All facings are the shape of the edge to be faced. Neck facings should be about 2½ inches wide from cut edge to cut edge; this results in the traditional 2-inch-wide neck facing. Armhole facings are usually a bit narrower than neck facings and so are made about 2 inches wide from cut edge to cut edge, resulting in the traditional 1½-inch-wide facing.

The grain line of facings should be identical to that of the garment; notice that the straight-of-material lines in the armhole facings are drawn parallel to the center lines, which are the straight-of-material lines in this pattern. A facing which is to face an edge which was cut on the fold, such as the center front in this illustration, is also cut on the fold.

The facing patterns are then cut from the fabric and seamed at shoulders and underarms, just as the garment was. They can be applied, cut edges even and seams matching, to the edges of the garment in a very simple operation.

to make a one-piece fitted facing for armhole edges See Figure 2. The armhole facing can be cut in two pieces, as was shown in Figure 1, or the front and back facing patterns can be combined into a one-piece pattern. This one-piece pattern is the one most often included with a pattern, if facing pieces are included. After the facing patterns have been made, lap

the seamlines at the shoulder edges (a total lap-over of 1¼ inches) and Scotchtape in place. Construct a straight-of-material line at right angles to the shoulder line, as shown.

to make a fitted facing for a darted edge   See Figure 3. The facing must be the size and shape of that edge after the dart is sewn in, and so the dart must be folded into the pattern and pinned in place before the facing pattern is copied off.

TO CUT AND JOIN
BIAS STRIPS
FOR FACING
OR BINDING

Fold scraps of fabric so that crosswise threads lie on top of lengthwise threads;

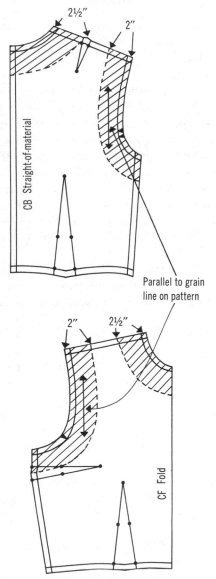

FIGURE 1   How to make fitted facing patterns for neck and armhole edges

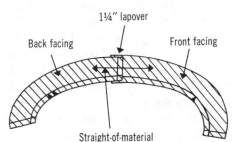

FIGURE 2   How to make one-piece armhole-facing pattern

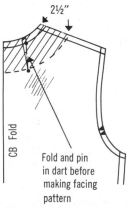

FIGURE 3   How to make facing pattern for a darted edge

the resulting diagonal line will be the true bias line. Crease along this line or draw a pencil line on the fabric. Mark off strips of the desired width as stated on the instruction sheet of your pattern, parallel to the bias line, as shown in Figure 4.

See Figure 5. Because bias strips are usually cut from scraps of fabric, more often than not they must be pieced to obtain sufficient length. Cut square across the ends of the strips. In order that the piecing seam may be on the straight grain, place two strips right sides together in the position shown. Stitch diagonally across the strips along a thread of the fabric, beginning and ending stitching at corners. Trim to ¼ inch from the stitching line.

The left-hand sketch in Figure 6 pictures the resulting seam as it should appear when trimmed. The seam takes a diagonal line on the bias strip and is stitched on the straight-of-material line. The right-hand sketch shows a seam made at right angles to the bias strip; this means the seam was stitched on a bias line. This is incorrect, for the bias seam will stretch and not lie flat; this is a very small matter, perhaps, but to an experienced eye one seam is right and the other wrong.

TO APPLY BIAS FACINGS

Directions for the application of an armhole facing are given in great detail, and the principles included can be applied to any edge that is to be faced. The problem is always one of shaping the bias strip in such a way that it fits flat to the garment on the larger curve, which is the inner curve, and of easing

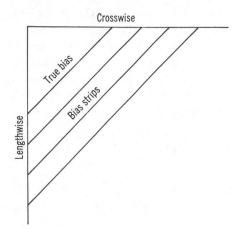

FIGURE 4   How to cut bias strips

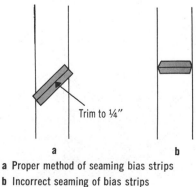

FIGURE 5   How to join bias strips

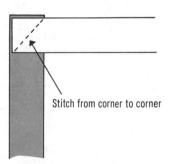

a
b

a Proper method of seaming bias strips
b Incorrect seaming of bias strips
FIGURE 6

in the extra length on the shorter curve, which is the seamline. The sharper the curve involved, the more ease will be required at the seamline in that area.

See Figure 7. Turn under ¼ inch on one edge of the bias strip and press in place. If pressing is not sufficient to hold the edge under, baste along this edge.

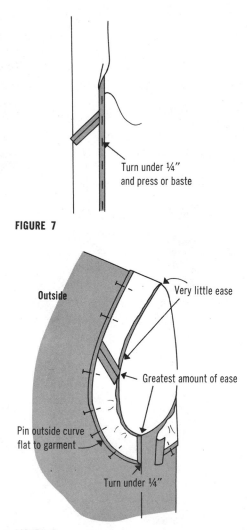

Turn under ¼″
and press or baste

FIGURE 7

See Figure 8. Place the bias facing to curved edge, having right sides together and cut edges even. Now note that the bias must be long enough to take care of the larger curve (which is the inner edge), and therefore it will be too long for the shorter curve (which is the cut edge). This means that it will have to be eased in to fit the shorter curve at the cut edge. Pin the bias on this larger curve so that it lies flat on the garment, and at the same time keep the cut edges even. Turn under ¼ inch at the underarm seam.

See Figure 9. Now pin the cut edges together, easing in the bias to fit; use lots of pins because the excess must be eased in very well and must eventually lie flat on the garment. Notice that more easing is done on the sharper curve, which in this case is the underarm region. Remove pins from outer edge.

See Figure 10. Baste along the seamline, using very small stitches so that the bias will lie flat with no tucks formed at the seamline. Stitch along bastings. Because this will be an encased seam, it should be trimmed to ¼ inch. Because

Outside

Very little ease

Greatest amount of ease

Pin outside curve
flat to garment

Turn under ¼″

FIGURE 8

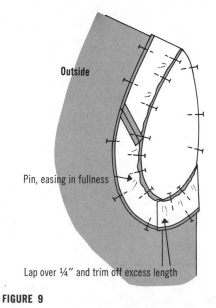

Outside

Pin, easing in fullness

Lap over ¼″ and trim off excess length

FIGURE 9

this is an inner curve, the seam must be clipped often—preferably every ½ inch.

See Figure 11. Turn facing to inside. Baste finished edges. Whip inner edge in place with ¼-inch stitches, being sure stitches are inconspicuous on the right side of the garment.

applying a neck facing with no collar offers exactly the same problem as facing the armhole It can be done by following those directions along with the instructions for your pattern. Just a little discussion will be helpful. You have learned that the facing must be long enough to fit the outer curve and must be eased to fit the shorter curve at the cut edge; you know that the sharper the curve, the greater the amount of ease needed. Study the neckline curve in Figure 12. In front it is a smooth, even curve; directly back of the shoulder line, the neck curve is very sharp; and for about 1½ inches on each side of the cener back, the neck is almost a straight line. This means that there will be a moderate amount of ease at the front neck, more ease directly back of the shoulder, and very little ease across

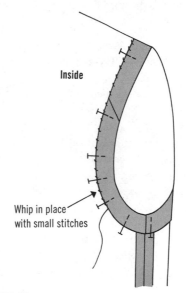

Inside

Whip in place
with small stitches

FIGURE 11

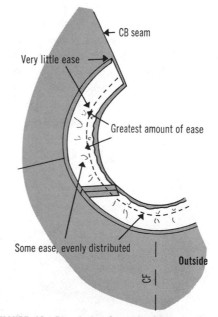

Outside

Baste with small secure stitches

FIGURE 10

← CB seam

Very little ease →

Greatest amount of ease

Some ease, evenly distributed

Outside

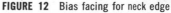
CF

FIGURE 12 Bias facing for neck edge

the center back. Keep this in mind as you fit the facing in place.

applying a neck facing over a collar offers a greater problem The problem is that the bias must be shaped to fit the garment exactly as described in the foregoing paragraph. But it must be placed on top of the collar (which is shaped differently), and therefore it is difficult to estimate the amount of ease needed. The person who has shaped many neck edges with bias will probably be able to estimate the correct amount and distribution of ease, but the beginner will not be able to do this. These suggestions will solve her problem: Before putting on the collar, shape the bias facing to the neck edge and pin (do not baste) in place as shown in Figure 12. With pencil or tailor's tacks, mark the center front, center back, and shoulder positions on the bias strip. Study the amount and distribution of the ease. Remove the bias facing. Then baste the collar in place and place the bias facing over the collar, locating centers and shoulder markings in the proper position. Ease in the bias

strip between the markings in the manner pretested.

TO
APPLY
BIAS
BINDINGS

The bias binding finishes a raw edge, as does the facing, but it has an additional design purpose. It is handled in such a way that a narrow band trim shows when the garment is worn. It can be a single bias binding if a heavy fabric is used or a double bias binding if the fabric is thin and sheer.

to apply the single bias binding The seam allowance on the edge to be bound is usually ¼ inch. Check your pattern to find the amount allowed; if a ⅝-inch seam is allowed, trim the edge down so that only a ¼-inch allowance remains. Cut bias strips 1 inch wide and join strips to obtain the desired length. Purchased bias binding is a timesaver and can be used on a cotton garment if a contrast in color is desired.

See Figure 13. With right sides together and cut edges even, join bias to raw edge in a ¼-inch seam. For a bias binding, the bias must not be eased to

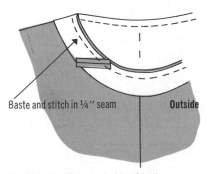
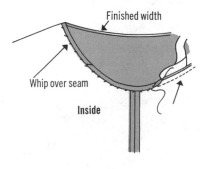

Baste and stitch in ¼″ seam   **Outside**

Finished width

Whip over seam   **Inside**

FIGURE 13 The single bias binding

the neck edge but must be flat to the edge; it is a good idea to stretch the bias slightly as it is applied.

Press seam up toward binding. Wrap binding over seam, turn under ¼ inch on remaining raw edge, and whip over seam. Be sure the hand stitches do not show on the right side; keep the finished width perfectly even.

to apply the double bias binding The seam allowance on the edge to be bound is usually ¼ inch. Check your pattern to find the amount allowed; if a ⅝-inch seam is allowed, trim the edge down so that only a ¼-inch allowance remains. Cut bias strips 1½ inches wide and join the strips to obtain sufficient length.

See Figure 14. Fold bias in half lengthwise, wrong sides together, and press. With right sides together and cut edges even, join bias to raw edge in a ¼-inch seam. For a bias binding, the bias must not be eased to the neck edge but must be flat to the edge; it is a good idea to stretch the bias slightly as it is applied.

Press seam up toward binding. Wrap bias over seam and whip fold edge of bias over seam. Be sure the hand stitches do not show on the right side; keep the finished width perfectly even.

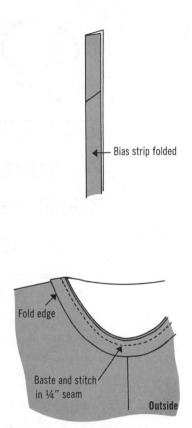

Bias strip folded

Fold edge

Baste and stitch in ¼″ seam

Outside

FIGURE 14 The double bias binding

FINISHING
THE WAISTLINE
SEAM

In years when a nipped-in waist is fashionable, the fit of the waistline must be very snug because under these circumstances, the waistline seam will get greater strain than any other seam when the garment is worn.

In addition, it must support all or a good portion of the weight of the skirt. It is especially important for that seam to be strong and to be finished in such a way that it will never stretch. Mere stitching of the seam will not give sufficient strength, so it must be reinforced with seam binding, grosgrain ribbon, cotton-twill tape, or belting. Note that all the above-mentioned are woven on the straight-of-material, so that they cannot stretch. Any of the finishes listed above adds a quality touch to the garment.

NOTE All materials used for waistline stays must be preshrunk.

The choice of waistline stay depends on the weight of the fabric and on the actual weight of the skirt. A heavy fabric requires a heavier waistline stay; a light-weight fabric can be controlled with a lightweight stay. Thus grosgrain ribbon is a good choice for heavy wools, and seam binding is a good choice for taffeta, cottons, and most medium-weight to lightweight fabrics. Cotton-twill tape is light in weight but strong and is used only on the most functional garments (playclothes, housedresses, etc.), since it looks more functional than attractive. Since the waistline must support all or part of the weight of the skirt, the particular skirt design becomes an influencing factor in the choice of a stay. Some skirts hang with their full weight from the waistline (such as the unpressed pleated skirt), while others rest on the body at the hipline (the sheath skirt); those which fall from the waistline place a far greater strain on the waistline seam, and if the loose-fitting skirt is made of heavy fabric, the strain is still greater. So a heavy wool skirt with unpressed pleats or gathers will require the heaviest stay, which is grosgrain ribbon or belting; the same skirt made of silk organdy could be supported with a lightweight stay such as seam binding.

The color of the waistline stay is of some importance, since it can add to the beauty of the inside of the garment. Seam binding and grosgrain ribbon are available in a large variety of colors, and they should be of a matching or harmonizing color. Cotton-twill tape and belting are available in only white and black.

The waistline stay can be either machine-stitched to the waistline seam or tacked to the vertical seams and darts as an inner belt. The easier and quicker construction is the machine-stitched method, and it can be used for most garments. The inner belt is advisable under two circumstances: for designs to be worn without a belt in which the

waistline seam must be pressed open and for garments with no waistline seam in which there are only vertical seams.

THE MACHINE–STITCHED STAY

NOTE Seam binding, grosgrain ribbon, and cotton-twill tape can be machine-stitched to the garment; if the garment is so heavy that belting is required, it is always applied as an inner belt.

See Figure 1. Baste the waistline seam according to directions on the instruction sheet. Fit the garment to check the fit of the waistline. Make any necessary alteration. As a preparation for putting in the zipper, check to see that the side opening edges are equal, both above and below the waistline.

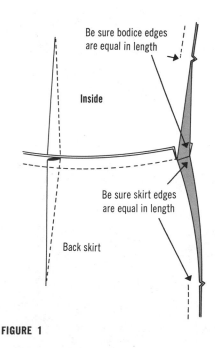

FIGURE 1

Stitch the waistline seam as basted. Remove bastings. Most waistline seams are pressed up toward the bodice because the whole skirt hangs better that way. However, some are pressed down toward the skirt for particular reasons. See the instruction sheet for pressing directions for your particular garment. If the bodice seam is bulkier, the seam is pressed down; if the skirt seam is bulkier, the seam is pressed up.

NOTE   If the seam is pressed up, the seam bind-ing is stitched to the skirt side of the seam; if it is pressed down, the binding is placed on the bodice side. The directions that follow are written for the seam pressed toward the bodice.

See Figure 2. Place the seam binding on the skirt side with one edge on the stitching line of the waistline seam. Set the machine needle in place and put the foot of the machine down. Now adjust the first few inches of binding so that it just touches the stitching line of the seam. You will find that it is very easy to hold the binding in place without basting. Stitch very close to the edge of the binding. Then adjust a few more inches of the binding and continue stitching the entire seam.

The waistline seam must be trimmed narrower than the binding—trim one edge to ¼ inch and the other to ⅜ inch, using the regular cutting scissors.

Press the waistline seam up. The upper edge is loose and will stay in place in most fabrics. However, if the fabric is heavy or if the seam is unusually bulky, the binding will not stay in place with mere pressing. Then it is better to tack the upper edge to vertical seams and darts, being careful that the stitches do not show on the right side.

See Figure 3. If a garment has a front or back buttoned edge or if the garment is very heavy and grosgrain ribbon is being used, it is well to leave part of the stay free so that it can be hooked in place. Figure 3 pictures an opening edge with a facing; note that the machine stitching is done only to a point about 1 inch from the inner edge of the facing. This kind of construction can be used for a zippered opening also in fabrics that are very heavy; in that case, the stitching should end about 2 inches from the opening edge.

Allow extra length at the end. Turn under about 1 or 1½ inches of length

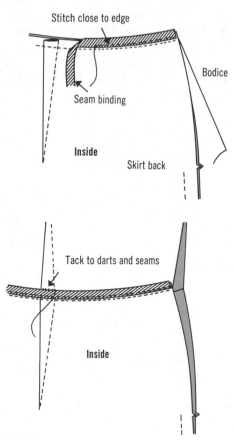

FIGURE 2

and hem one end. Do the same for the other end, measuring to be sure one hemmed end will lap over the other ½ inch when the garment is finished. Fasten the ends with hooks and straight eyes (directions are on page 319).

THE INNER BELT

The inner-belt construction is used whenever the fabric is so heavy that belting is required, and it is used in those cases when there is no waistline seam or in cases when the waistline seam must be pressed open. The inner belt is made for heavier fabrics, and so only grosgrain ribbon and belting are suitable; if the garment is one in which seam binding is strong enough for support, then the machine-stitched method is used.

See Figure 4. Turn under about 1 to 1½ inches on one end and hem in place. Place the grosgrain ribbon around the body and allow the hemmed-over end to

extend ½ inch over the unfinished end. Turn under the unfinished end at that point and hem that end in the same manner. Hooks and peats are used to fasten the belt, and they must be placed in such a way that the ends of the belt lap over each other ½ inch; directions for sewing on hooks and peats appear on page 319. The inner belt is then placed on the inside of the garment with the lower edge at the waistline level. Tack the belt to vertical darts and seams, being careful that stitches do not go through to the right side.

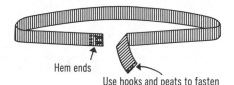

Hem ends

Use hooks and peats to fasten

a Preparation of inner belt

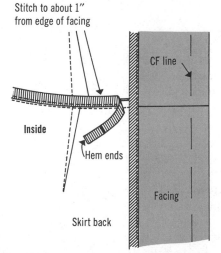

Stitch to about 1″ from edge of facing

CF line

Inside

Hem ends

Facing

Skirt back

FIGURE 3 Waistline stay for buttoned front or back opening

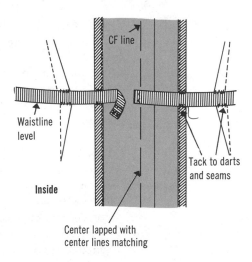

CF line

Waistline level

Inside

Tack to darts and seams

Center lapped with center lines matching

b How to apply inner belt
FIGURE 4

ZIPPER
CONSTRUCTION
AND
BOUND
PLACKETS

GENERAL
NOTES
ON
ZIPPERS

The information given in this section must be read and understood before doing any zipper construction discussed later in the chapter.

TYPES OF ZIPPERS AVAILABLE

There are many types of zippers in varying weights and lengths and with features to serve every purpose. The instructions on the envelope back will state what type and length of zipper is required for that particular design. Certain specialty stores make zippers to order, so that unusual lengths (such as the zipper used in zipped-in coat linings) can be obtained.

dress The dress zipper has a bridge top stop as well as a bottom stop. It is available in 10-, 12-, and 14-inch lengths.

skirt The skirt zipper has a bottom stop and an automatic self lock at the upper edge to keep it closed securely while being worn. It is available in 7- and 9-inch lengths.

separating This type has no bottom stop, so that it can be separated. It has an automatic self lock at the upper edge. It is available in medium weights for jackets, blouse fronts, etc., in 12-, 16-,

18-, and 20-inch lengths. It is made in heavier weight for coats in 14- to 22-inch lengths.

neck This type has a bottom stop and an automatic self lock at the upper edge. It is available in 4- to 10-inch lengths in a light weight and in 12- to 26-inch lengths in a heavier weight.

TYPES OF ZIPPER CONSTRUCTION AND EVALUATION

CONSTRUCTION	USES	COMMENTS
REGULATION (stitching about ½ to ⅝″ from opening edge; see Figure 1)	skirt side opening, dress side opening, skirt back opening, dress back opening; preferred method for most uses	hides the zipper completely; although it is more complicated to construct, most persons can do a better job of topstitching when using this method, and the topstitching is the most conspicuous step
SLOT–SEAM (stitching ¼″ on either side of opening edge; see Figure 1)	often used in back opening edges, used for very short openings such as the opening in a full-length fitted sleeve, and used in bulky fabrics that do not hold a crease; sometimes used for heavy fabrics to reduce bulk; can be used for all purposes listed for regulation zipper if this construction is a fashionable one at the time	is less complicated to construct than regulation zipper but is much more difficult to topstitch perfectly because stitching lines are so close and little flaws are magnified; is slightly less bulky; is not usually the preferred method because zipper teeth show to some extent
VISIBLE (teeth of zipper exposed; see Figure 1)	must be used at any place where there is no seam allowance to work with; used as an aid to design at any place (pockets, etc.) where the zipper is used as a decoration	not recommended excepting for the rare circumstances listed. NOTE Construction not included in this book because of its limited use.

trousers This zipper has a bottom stop and an extra serviceable self lock at the top. The length is 11 inches, and the weight is usually heavy.

slipcover This type has a bottom stop and an automatic self lock. It is available in 24-, 27-, 30-, and 36-inch lengths in a heavy weight. The tapes are wider than usual.

Types of zipper construction are pictured in Figure 1, but there are various

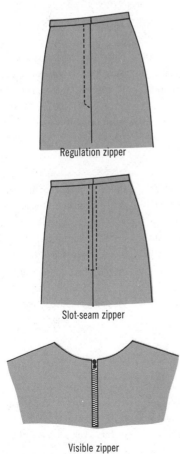

Regulation zipper

Slot-seam zipper

Visible zipper

FIGURE 1

means of achieving the pictured effects. Methods of construction vary most for the regulation zipper. The construction that is currently very popular is shown on the zipper folder, and for this reason it will not be discussed in this book. The construction for the regulation zipper included here is more difficult perhaps, but it has certain advantages that make it, in my opinion, the preferred method. The main advantage is that the zipper can be basted and tested on the figure for perfection of fit before stitching is done; in the simpler method, if there is a subtle mistake it cannot be seen until the zipper is stitched, and therefore correction of mistakes in that method is much more difficult. The simpler method works very well for cottons and lightweight fabrics and does not work as well for very heavy fabrics; the more complicated method included in this book works well for any type of fabric. The novice may want to use the simpler directions on her zipper package, but the woman who hopes for truly professional results will probably prefer the methods described in this book.

FACTORS DETERMINING LENGTH OF ZIPPER
The length of zipper included in your pattern is correct, and there is no reason to question that length under ordinary circumstances. However, there are personal considerations that enter the picture. The longer the zipper, the more easily the garment will slip on and off the body, and so a longer zipper might be desired for unusually sticky and heavy fabrics, for fabrics that muss seriously as they are handled, for the person who is handicapped, or for the person who insists on comfort in dressing. However, the length of the zipper cannot be changed so drastically that it looks very different from the effect our eyes are accustomed to seeing (for example, a

12-inch zipper in a skirt would make it easier to put on, but it would look ridiculous). In general, one can extend zipper length in the bodice at the underarm because the extra length does not show there, and in general one must be wary of extending the zipper much more than 7 inches into the skirt because our eyes are very accustomed to seeing the zipper end at the 7-inch line.

If bodice length has been altered more than 1 inch, a different zipper length would be advisable. And other figure faults might make a change in length advisable. The very large-busted person with a very small waist will find that a longer zipper, with the extra length in the bodice portion, will allow her to put on and take off dresses with a great deal more ease. The very short person may find that a 7-inch zipper in a skirt looks too long on her, and she may wish to use a slightly shorter opening.

There is a trend toward using a 9-inch zipper in skirts, slacks, and shorts, and some patterns state the 9-inch length rather than the traditional 7-inch length. The reason for using the 9-inch zipper is that a person with larger-than-average hips can slip the skirt over her hips as her slimmer friends do; in other words, this is a practical zipper length. The 9-inch zipper does not look as nice, it does not create as attractive proportions on most figures, and it looks conspicuous on the short person. It would be wise to question the 9-inch skirt zipper and perhaps decide to buy a 7-inch one instead. Certainly the person with an average figure has no need for the longer zipper, and for the truly important costumes it would be better to favor the more beautiful 7-inch length, even if it means having to take the skirt over the shoulders when dressing. The 9-inch zipper, then, is recommended for clothing that is more practical than decorative; it is the necessary length for shorts and slacks for any person with larger-than-average hips in relation to waist size.

GENERAL RULES FOR ZIPPER CONSTRUCTION

These rules, which include beginning steps as well as the final step of machine stitching, apply to every zipper construction. Read them now for the preliminary general information and refer to them later, as will be suggested at certain steps in the construction details.

1 Before proceeding with the zipper, check opening edges of a dress side opening or edges of an opening with faced edges to be sure that the two edges are the same length. Pin the opening edges together, as if you were preparing to baste a seam. If the edges are not equal, make whatever corrections are necessary at this time.

2 The zipper edges are basted in place and, in the case of regulation zippers, will be fitted before they are stitched. These basting stitches must be very secure (small, ¼-inch stitches reinforced every ½ inch or so) so that the heavy edges are held securely and will not slip during stitching and so that they are held securely for fitting.

3 Side-opening zippers require more careful attention to fit than back-opening edges because the side opening is often a curved line and might, therefore, have stretched. It is assumed that the opening edges have been stay-stitched, and if they have not, they should be stay-stitched before proceeding with the zipper (see page 104). Two mistakes may be noticed in fitting after the zipper is basted. One is that the garment may

stand out from the body as if it were too large at the level of the lower end

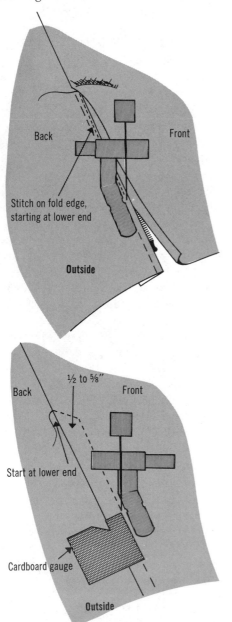

Back   Front

Stitch on fold edge, starting at lower end

Outside

Back   ½ to ⅝″   Front

Start at lower end

Cardboard gauge

Outside

FIGURE 2 Stitching the regulation zipper

of the zipper; this problem is explained on page 191. The other is that there may be a little bump or ripple (or sort of miniature shelf) formed directly below the zipper; this indicates that the opening edges have beeen stretched as they were applied to the zipper, and the zipper must be rebasted, easing those edges slightly to the zipper. The easing operation is explained in the skirt and dress zipper directions.

4 Stitching at the machine is an important step because this part of the construction is visible. Some general rules are illustrated in Figure 2, which pictures the regulation zipper, and Figure 3, which pictures the slot-seam zipper.

a Always machine-stitch from the bottom up to prevent pushing the fabric into a ripple at the lower end. Note in the case of the slot-seam zipper (Figure 3) that this means that the zipper should be stitched in two operations, rather than in a continuous stitching.

b A zipper foot must be used, and the adjustable foot, which can be moved from one side of the needle to the other, is an essential. Notice in Figure 2 that the foot is on the left side of the needle as the back edge is stitched and on the right side as the front edge is stitched. The foot of the zipper must be away from the metal part of the zipper. Because the zipper foot has only one foot, it is slightly less steady than the regular stitching foot. It is well to test-stitch to get the "feel" of the zipper foot.

c Test-stitch to check length of stitch and tension of the machine. Be sure there is sufficient thread on the spool and bobbin before proceeding.

d The zipper must be stitched from the outside, but you will find that by turning the garment wrong side out, the stitching can be done more easily on the right side. There is no sketch to illustrate this position, but if you turn the skirt wrong side out, you will quickly see how this aids machine stitching on the top side.

e The zipper should be zipped up while machine work is being done because this keeps the whole area in better control.

f Notice that a cardboard gauge is used to ensure even topstitching. Most persons find this is a greater help than following basting lines. The gauge must be held firmly in position before stitching; it cannot be moved at the same time the machine is moving. It is a good idea to practice stitching with the gauge to get the feel of handling it; remove the top thread from the needle and practice on the garment for best results.

g Notice in Figure 2 that the front edge of the regulation zipper is flipped up so that the stitching is placed right along the fold of fabric on the back edge, just $\frac{1}{16}$ inch from the fold. Notice that this machine stitching falls inside the marking-basting line; thus the stitching will not show when the garment is worn.

REGULATION ZIPPER
FOR SKIRT
SIDE OR BACK
OPENING

NOTE In all sketches, the back and front of the skirt are labeled for the side-opening zipper. Underneath each label the words "right back" and "left back" appear as the situation would be for a back-opening zipper.

Read General Notes on Zippers on page 260. The zipper should be put in when the vertical seams have been finished and pressed and before the waistband is applied.

See Figure 4. The side opening edges should be ¾ inch longer than the metal part of the zipper. If the opening is not the correct length, correct it now.

Cut a piece of seam binding ½ inch longer than the opening. Lap it ¼ inch over the raw front edge and stitch it in place with stitches very close to the edge of the binding. The purpose of this binding is to extend the seam allowance of the front edge; the back seam allowance is wide enough.

NOTE The garment should be turned right side out while the zipper is put in. Because the opening edges are often bias, handle the garment carefully to avoid stretching the fabric.

See Figure 5. Turn the front opening edge to the inside along the seamline and baste in place. Press. Run a marking-

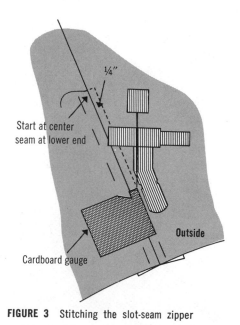

FIGURE 3 Stitching the slot-seam zipper

basting line along the seamline of the back.

See Figure 6. Turn under the back

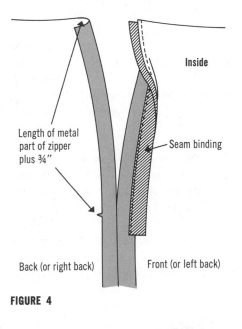

Length of metal part of zipper plus ¾"

Inside

Seam binding

Back (or right back)

Front (or left back)

FIGURE 4

opening edge ⅛ inch (or 3⁄16 to ¼ inch in spongy or heavy fabrics) beyond, or outside, the seamline and baste in place. Press. Hold your work in the same position as shown in this sketch and see that it looks just like the sketch.

See Figure 7. Pin the zipper on the inside of the skirt with the metal tab ¾ inch down from the upper edge, thereby leaving an ample allowance for stitching the waistline seam. Lap the back opening edge over the zipper with the fold edge close to the zipper teeth. Here is a very helpful trick for side-opening zippers: Hold the zipper and the skirt in the position it will take on the body. From the waist down, your body curves outward, and the zipper and skirt must curve that way too. Study the particular curve of your body, and then hold the zipper in that curve as you pin the back edge in place. Because the side edges of the skirt are often bias, there is a great danger of stretching the opening edges as you work. Be careful not to—in fact, it is a good idea to ease the skirt slightly (perhaps ⅛ inch) while pinning it, to

Outside

5⁄8"

Marking basting at seamline

Turn on seamline and baste

Note basting meets end of stitched side seam

Front (or left back)

Back (or right back)

FIGURE 5

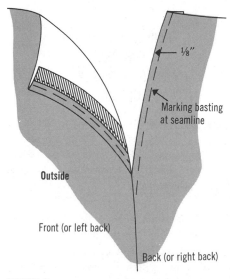

⅛"

Marking basting at seamline

Outside

Front (or left back)

Back (or right back)

FIGURE 6

counteract the almost inevitable stretching. Baste the edge with small, firm stitches. Trim off the excess tape even with the waistline edge of the skirt.

If, when the garment is fitted, there is a ripple directly below the zipper, return to this step and rebaste, easing up the fabric even more as it is pinned to the zipper.

See Figure 8. Lap the front edge over the zipper so that the fold edge (which is the seamline) meets the marking-basting line on the back (which is the seamline). Notice that the front laps over the back and hides the zipper completely. As you did with the back, hold the skirt and zipper in the position it will take on the body (an outward curve if it is a side-opening zipper) and pin the front edge in place. Baste with firm, small stitches about ½ inch from the seamline. Have the stitches take a diagonal direction at the lower end; be careful not to baste across the metal part of the zipper.

Fit the skirt. See that the zipper lies flat on the body. The most common defect of zipper construction is the formation of a ripple at the lower end. This means that the opening edges have been stretched. If this happens, rebaste the zipper, easing the skirt as needed.

Reread and study step 4 on page 264 and then machine-stitch.

REGULATION ZIPPER
FOR DRESS
SIDE
OPENING

Read General Notes on Zippers on page 260. The zipper should be put in as soon as the waistline seam is stitched; seam binding should be applied to the seam, and the waistline areas should be pressed thoroughly. Turn the garment

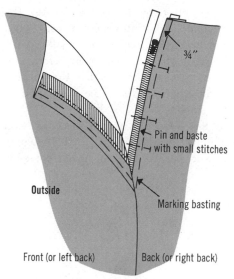

¾″

← Pin and baste
with small stitches

Outside

Marking basting

Front (or left back)　　　Back (or right back)

FIGURE 7

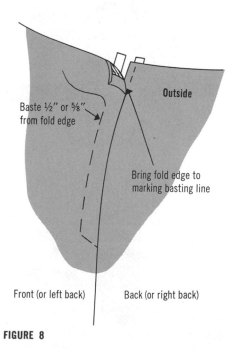

Baste ½″ or ⅝″
from fold edge

Outside

Bring fold edge to
marking basting line

Front (or left back)　　　Back (or right back)

FIGURE 8

inside out and pin the opening edges together. The front and back opening edges must be the same length; the waistline seams must meet. If corrections are necessary, make the small adjustments in the waistline seam before proceeding. Check to see that the opening is the same length as the metal part of the zipper.

See Figure 9. Cut a piece of seam binding 1 inch longer than the opening. Lap it ¼ inch over the raw front edge

and stitch it in place, with stitches very close to the edge of the binding. The purpose of this binding is to extend the seam allowance of the front edge; the back edge does not need an extension.

NOTE The garment should be turned right side out while the zipper is put in. Because the opening edges, especially in the skirt, are often bias, handle the garment carefully to avoid stretching the fabric.

See Figure 10. Turn the front opening edge to the inside along the seamline and baste it in place. Run a marking-

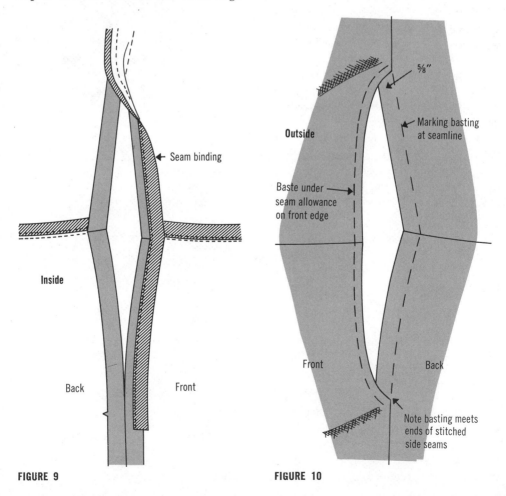

← Seam binding

Inside

Back   Front

FIGURE 9

⅝"

Outside

← Marking basting at seamline

Baste under → seam allowance on front edge

Front   Back

Note basting meets ends of stitched side seams

FIGURE 10

basting line along the seamline of the back edge.

See Figure 11. Turn under the back opening edge ⅛ inch (or 3/16 to ¼ inch for spongy or heavy fabrics) beyond, or outside, the seamline and baste in place. Press. Hold your work in the same position as shown in this sketch and see that it looks just like the sketch.

See Figure 12. Place the zipper on the inside of the dress and lap the back edge over the zipper with the fold edge close to the teeth of the zipper; place the tab end of the zipper at the upper end of the opening. Here is a helpful trick: Hold the zipper and the dress in the

position it will take on the body. As far down as the waistline, your body is more or less a ruler-straight line. Hold the zipper and dress in that way and pin the back edge over the zipper. But from the waistline down, your body curves outward, and the zipper and dress must curve that way too. Study the particular curve of your body and hold the zipper in that position as you pin the back edge over the zipper. Because this side edge

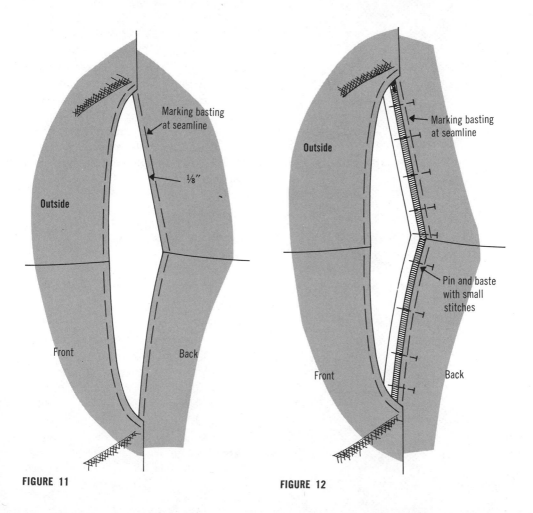

FIGURE 11   FIGURE 12

of the skirt is slightly bias, there is a great danger of stretching the skirt as you handle it. Be careful not to—in fact, it is a good idea to ease the skirt slightly (perhaps ⅛ inch) while pinning it to avoid the almost inevitable stretching. Baste this edge with small, firm stitches. Fasten it securely at the waistline, where the greatest strain in fitting will be.

If when the garment is fitted there is a ripple directly below the zipper, return to this step and rebaste, easing up the fabric even more as it is pinned to the zipper.

See Figure 13. Lap the front edge over the zipper so that the folded edge (which is the seamline) meets the marking-basting line on the back (which is the seamline). Notice that the front laps over the back and therefore hides the zipper completely. As you did with the back, hold the zipper in the position it will take on the body (straight above the waist, curved out below) and pin in place. Baste with small, firm stitches about ½ inch from the seamline. Have the stitches make a diagonal line across the end and be careful not to baste across the metal part of the zipper.

Fit the dress. See that the zipper lies flat on the body. The most common defect of zipper construction is the formation of a ripple at the lower end. This means that the skirt edges have been stretched in the process. If this happens, rebaste the lower part of the zipper, easing up the skirt the necessary amount.

Refer to step 4 on page 264 and then machine-stitch.

REGULATION ZIPPER
FOR FACED
NECK
OPENING

Read General Notes on Zippers on page 260.

See Figure 14. The zipper construction starts with the application of the neck facings, which must be done in a manner slightly different from the usual. The directions on the instruction sheet will read, "Face neck and back edges, stitching left back in a ⅝-inch seam and stitching right back in a ½-inch seam." This wording is very brief, and it does not explain this step in sufficient detail.

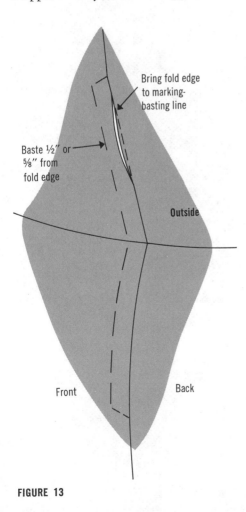

Bring fold edge
to marking-
basting line

Baste ½" or
⅝" from
fold edge

Outside

Front   Back

FIGURE 13

Make a ¼-inch clip into the lower edge of the facings about 1 inch over from the back edge; then turn up ¼ inch at the lower edge of the facing. This additional step finishes off the raw edge which will lie over the zipper when the garment is finished. Now notice that the neck and the left back seams are stitched the usual ⅝ inch but that the right back seam is stitched the narrower ½ inch; notice that the turned-up edge of the facing is caught in with the seam.

See Figure 15. Lap a strip of seam binding ¼ inch over the left back edge and stitch close to the edge as shown; this step is necessary to extend the seam allowance somewhat on that edge. The right back needs no extension.

See Figure 16. Baste under the ⅝-inch seam allowance on the left back edge. Run a marking-basting line along the seamline (⅝ inch from the cut edge) on the right back edge—notice that because that edge was stitched in a ½-inch seam, the marking basting will be ⅛ inch from the finished edge near the neck. This construction is very much like that for the skirt zipper from this step on; it would be well to refer back to the section on the skirt zipper on page 266, beginning with the directions for Figure 6. Turn under the right back edge ⅛ inch

beyond the marking-basting line and baste in place all the way down the length of the zipper.

See Figure 17. Lap the right back over the edge of the zipper, with the folded edge close to the teeth of the zipper, and pin and baste in place; place the metal tab ¼ inch down from the upper finished edge.

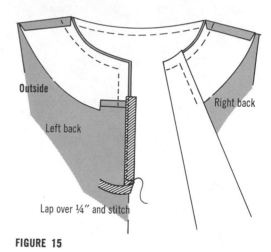

FIGURE 15

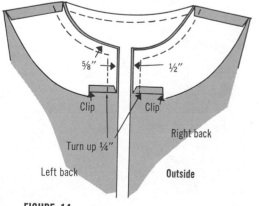

FIGURE 14

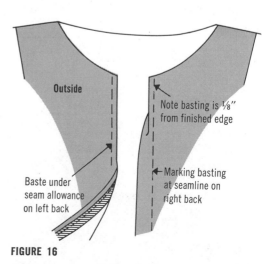

FIGURE 16

hook and eye. Directions for sewing on hooks and eyes appear on page 319.

SLOT–SEAM ZIPPER FOR SKIRT SIDE OR BACK OPENING

See Figure 18. Read General Notes on Zippers on page 260. Turn the garment inside out and pin the opening edges together. Check to see that the length of the opening is ¾ inch longer than the metal part of the zipper. Baste the opening edges along the seamline with small, firm hand stitches or, better still, with a long machine stitch. Press the seam open.

See Figure 19. Place the zipper on the inside of the garment with the right side of the zipper to the wrong side of the garment. Place the tab end of the zipper ¾ inch down from the upper edge, thereby leaving sufficient allowance

From this point on, refer back to the section on the skirt zipper on page 266 and continue with the directions for Figures 7 and 8. When the zipper has been stitched, fasten the upper edge with a

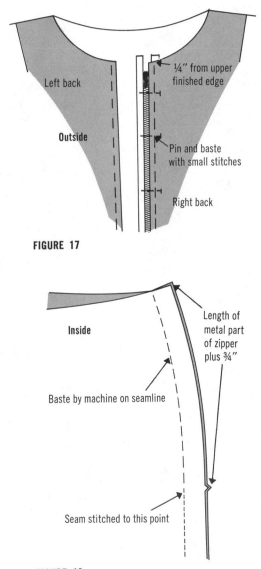

Left back

Outside

Right back

¼" from upper finished edge

Pin and baste with small stitches

FIGURE 17

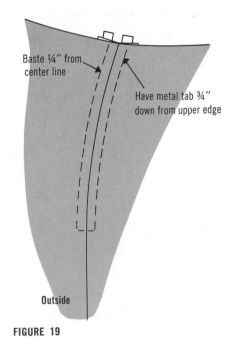

Baste ¼" from center line

Have metal tab ¾" down from upper edge

Outside

FIGURE 19

Inside

Length of metal part of zipper plus ¾"

Baste by machine on seamline

Seam stitched to this point

FIGURE 18

for that edge to be finished later. Pin in place, being very careful to keep the center of the zipper over the seamline. Trim off the tape ends even with the upper cut edge.

From the outside, baste the zipper in place with stitches ¼ inch from the seamline. Use small, firm stitches. Be careful not to baste across the metal part of the zipper as you baste across the end.

Refer to step 4 on page 264 and then machine-stitch.

SLOT–SEAM ZIPPER
FOR FACED
NECK
OPENING

Read General Notes on Zippers on page 260. See Figure 20. The zipper construction starts with the application of the neck facings. There is one additional step given here that is not usually included on the instruction sheet: Make a ¼-inch clip into the lower edge of the facings about 1 inch over from the back edge; then turn up ¼ inch on the lower edge of the facings. This additional step finishes off the raw edge which will lie over the zipper when the garment is finished. Now stitch the neck and back

edges in a ⅝-inch seam, catching in the turned-up edge as shown.

See Figure 21. The seam will have been stitched up to a point designated on the pattern; often this zipper extends

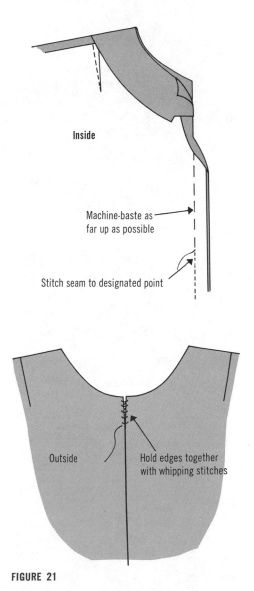

Inside

Machine-baste as far up as possible →

Stitch seam to designated point

FIGURE 21

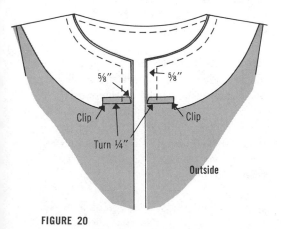

FIGURE 20

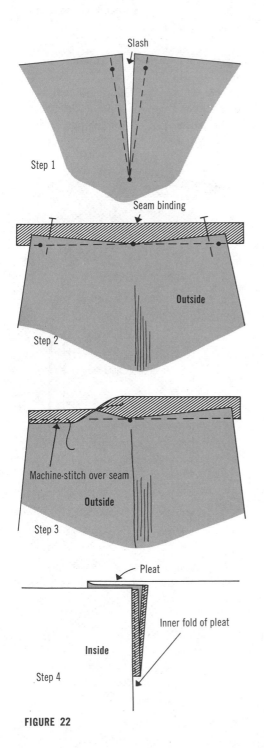

Step 1

Slash

Step 2

Seam binding

Outside

Step 3

Machine-stitch over seam

Outside

Step 4

Pleat

Inner fold of pleat

Inside

FIGURE 22

entirely down the length of the bodice and for a distance into the skirt. The sketch shows a shorter opening, but the longer opening would be done in exactly the same manner. Machine-baste from the end of the stitched seam up as far as possible toward the neck edge (about an inch from the lower edge of the facing). Press basted seam open. Then from the outside use whipping stitches to draw the finished edges together as shown.

The zipper is then put in exactly like the skirt zipper on page 272 with one exception: the metal tab is placed ¼ inch down from the upper finished edge (¾ inch down for the skirt), and after the zipper is stitched, the upper edge should be fastened with a hook and eye. Directions for sewing on hooks and eyes appear on page 319.

SLASHED PLACKETS

SLASHED PLACKET FINISHED WITH SEAM BINDING See Figure 22. This finish for opening edges is rarely used except for the opening in an all-around pleated skirt. The opening falls at the inner fold of the pleat in a position where it is completely hidden and is so inconspicuous that no snaps are needed to close it. The slash line will be marked on the pattern.

step 1 Machine-stitch a triangle, beginning ¼ inch each side of the slash line and tapering to a point at the end of the slash line. Now this stitching line will become the seamline. Notice that there is a varying seam allowance—from ¼ inch down to almost nothing. Slash to within 1/16 inch of the stitched point.

step 2 Hold the slashed opening in the position shown; notice that the stitched line becomes a straight line. There will be a fold of fabric formed in the garment, but there should be no fold at the seamline. Cut a piece of binding slightly longer than the slashed line. Place it on the inside of the garment so that one edge of the seam binding laps over the stitched line just ¹⁄₁₆ inch. Pin in place. Study the sketch carefully. Notice the irregularity of the seam allowance. Stitch the seam binding in place by stitching directly over the original stitches.

step 3 Fold the seam binding in half lengthwise and stitch the remaining edge over the seam, encasing the raw edge. Be sure to keep the stitches close to the finished edge of the binding. Press.

step 4 Although the pattern instruction sheet may not direct you to form the pleats immediately, the sketch shows how the opening edges will look when the pleat is formed. From an inside view as shown, the bound edges fall on the inner fold of the pleat, thus being safely hidden from view.

SLASHED PLACKET FINISHED WITH SELF FABRIC
See Figure 23. This placket can be used in places where it might show when the garment is worn; it is used most frequently for the opening in a sleeve with a cuff. A slash line and stitching lines will appear on the pattern.

step 1 Machine-stitch a triangle along the stitching lines. Slash to within ¹⁄₁₆ inch from the stitched point. The stitching lines become the seamline; notice that the seam allowance varies from ¼ inch down to nothing at the point.

step 2 Hold the slashed opening in the position shown; notice that the stitched line becomes a straight line. There will be a fold of fabric formed below the

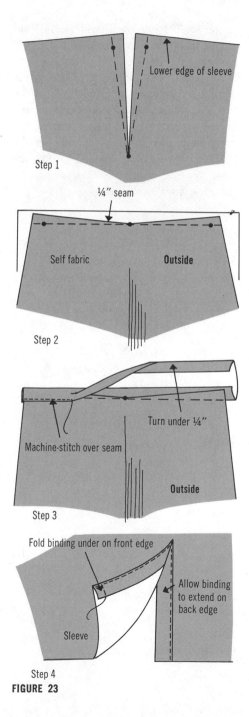

Step 1

Lower edge of sleeve

¼" seam

Self fabric — Outside

Step 2

Turn under ¼"

Machine-stitch over seam

Outside

Step 3

Fold binding under on front edge

Allow binding to extend on back edge

Sleeve

Step 4
FIGURE 23

center point, but there will be no fold at the seamline. Cut a strip of self fabric 1¼ inches wide and slightly longer than the slashed edge. Place it to the inside of the garment with the right side of the binding strip to the wrong side of the garment. Place the stitching line of the garment ¼ inch from the cut edge of the binding strip, thus making a ¼-inch seam on the binding. Stitch along the stitching lines as shown.

step 3 Press the seam up. Turn under ¼ inch on the remaining raw edge of the binding, lap the turned-under edge ¹⁄₁₆ inch over the seam, and machine-stitch in place.

step 4 This sketch shows how this placket is handled for a sleeve opening. The binding is allowed to extend on the back edge and is turned under along the seam on the front edge. The front edge therefore has something to lap over as the placket is used; the sleeve opening does not require snaps, but the placket could be snapped if circumstances warranted.

BELT
AND
WAISTBAND
CONSTRUCTION

GENERAL
NOTES
ON
BELTS

The belt is another little detail that is
deceptively simple in itself and yet very
important to the professional appearance
of the costume. The woman who sews
can make her own belt, or she can have
it professionally made at a department
store or Singer shop. She must balance
the cost of having the belt covered (perhaps $1.25 to $1.75) against the length
of time required to make a truly professional belt and the nominal cost of supplies; this length of time might well be
two hours, but the cost of supplies is as
low as 20 cents. It is entirely possible to
make a belt as professional-looking as
those made by the belt companies, providing the buckle is professionally covered. However, that adds more to the
cost of covering the belt yourself, and so,

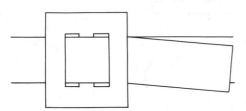

The slide buckle with no prong and no eyelets is appropriate to use on very dressy garments. The belt may need hooks and peats to hold it securely.

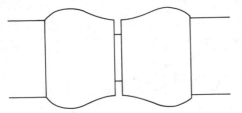

The two-piece buckle is the most formal type and lends itself well to cocktail and evening costumes.

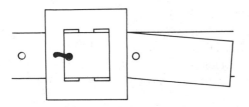

The slide buckle with a prong gives a more tailored effect and holds the belt securely in place. Eyelets must be used.

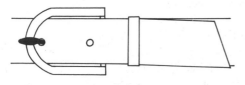

The half buckle with a prong looks best on tailored garments. Eyelets and a fabric belt strap are required.

FIGURE 1 Types of buckles

in general, one might say that the saving in money is not worth the time involved.

There are a variety of belt kits on the market which contain all supplies needed, including the buckle. But again, as in the case of covered buttons, one cannot achieve the firm and lasting grip of fabric on a buckle covered at home, as is possible in the professional establishment where heavy clamping machines ensure a more secure buckle. The only buckle offered in kits that can be covered as well at home is the wire frame one that is covered with a narrow loop of fabric (this buckle is the one illustrated in the lowest sketch of Figure 1). In all other cases it would be advisable to have the buckle professionally covered.

If the belt is covered at home, it can be done with belting, which can be trimmed to the desired width, or, for a softer effect, a heavy Pellon can be used. Directions for such a stiffened belt, which will look entirely professional, are given on page 281, and similar directions for a contour belt are given on page 282. This is the only belt construction that ensures a truly professional result and therefore is the only one included in this book. There are other methods of making belts. The most common is the interfaced belt, in which a strip of fabric is folded lengthwise, stitched, and turned. This is the belt construction that is often described on the instruction sheet, for it is the simplest and least time-consuming, and so the pattern company favors it for the average customer. It is not a good belt; it is not trim and stiff enough to hold its shape well, and it is not recommended. However, if this belt is desired (and it might be for washable patio dresses or sundresses), sufficient directions are given on the instruction sheet.

TO DECIDE ON WIDTH OF BELT AND BUCKLE

The fashion sketch on the pattern envelope shows a belt width that the trained designer considers best for the design; the pattern piece for the belt will result in an attractive belt for the average figure. However, a slight change in belt width might be a great advantage with certain figures. Fold the fabric into various widths to test the effect on the figure; examine several widths to decide which is best for your particular figure.

You must have noticed how often in these pages the good ready-made dress has been cited as a guide to home-sewing standards. This applies also in the case of the belt. Study the belts of fashionable, good ready-made dresses. Notice how often the very trim, narrow belt (a mere ½ inch wide) is used. Notice how seldom you see a 1½-inch belt; it misses the point a bit, for it is neither narrow enough to be trim nor wide enough to be dashing. Notice that a 2½-inch width is more often used for designs requiring a wide belt. These generalities should help you.

Of course, personal preference and comfort must be considered. Some persons feel more comfortable in a narrow belt because that spells freedom to them; others like the feeling of security a wider belt gives. But in general, make a narrow belt ½ to ¾ inch wide and make a wide belt 2 to 3 inches wide.

After you have decided on the approximate belt width, select the buckle (whether it is a purchased one or a frame to be covered) before actually making the belt. The belt must be ⅛ inch narrower than the buckle slots, and if the belt is made first, it might not fit the slots perfectly. See Figure 2.

TO CHECK BELT LENGTH

A belt should be at least 7 inches longer than is required to reach around the body. The words "reach around the body" are very important. Many persons make a belt 7 inches longer than their waist measurement and find to their disappointment that the belt is not long enough. This is because the width of the belt determines how much length is required to reach around the body. For example, a belt ½ inch wide will rest on the body at the waistline and so will require the waist measurement to reach around the body, whereas (to exaggerate a point) a belt 5 inches wide will rest on the body at a point about 5 inches above the waist, where the measurement is considerably larger than the waist. For this reason, a belt length should be checked with the pattern folded to the width it will be when finished, and then the pattern should be tested on the body. At this time see that there is at least a 7-inch overlap. It is much better to make a belt too long; it can easily be trimmed off.

TO PUT IN EYELETS

The eyelets for a buckle with a prong are put in before the buckle is attached. Figure 3 shows an interesting comparison between two belts and buckles identical in every way except the positioning of the eyelets, and it serves to illustrate the effect of "little" mistakes. In the upper sketch, the eyelets have been put in too close to the end of the belt, and to

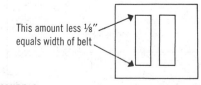

This amount less ⅛" equals width of belt

FIGURE 2

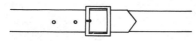

Eyelets too close to end of belt;
buckle fastened in wrong eyelet

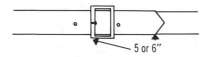

5 or 6″

Proper effect

FIGURE 3

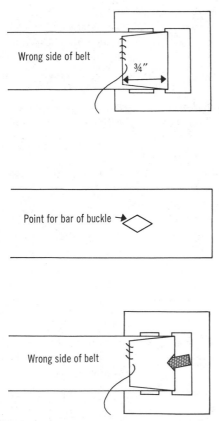

Wrong side of belt

¾″

Point for bar of buckle →

Wrong side of belt

FIGURE 4

exaggerate the situation, the buckle has been fastened into the eyelet nearest the end, thereby resulting in an overlap of perhaps 3 inches. Compare that sketch with the lower sketch, in which the eyelets are properly positioned and the buckle properly fastened into the middle eyelet. Notice that the first sketch gives the impression that the person has gained weight or that she is so thick in the waist that she needs every bit of length she can possibly achieve. This is another little detail, but the sketches illustrate that little details matter very much.

The middle eyelet should be about 5 or 6 inches from the end of the belt, but that position can be perfected by placing the buckle over the belt and testing various positions. Two additional eyelets are placed about ¾ to 1 inch on either side of the center.

Eyelets made with the buttonhole or satin stitch in matching thread give a very subtle, delicate touch to the belt. The professional belt is available with either metal or thread eyelets. Metal eyelets might be preferred for more practical clothing. The woman who sews can make her own thread eyelets, and there is a wonderful eyelet kit available for about $1 that will enable her to set in metal eyelets.

TO ATTACH THE BUCKLE
See Figure 4.

for a buckle with no prong Put the end of the belt around the center bar of the buckle. Pin the end in place, and fit to be sure the length is correct. Sew in place from the wrong side with firm hand stitches. Notice that the belt end is turned back only ¾ inch. See page 319 for directions for sewing on hooks and peats.

for a buckle with a prong Fasten the buckle on the belt end, using the middle eyelet. Now wrap the belt around the body to find the point on the unfinished end where the bar of the buckle touches. Cut a diamond-shaped hole in the belt end at this point. These cut edges need not be finished.

Put the end of the belt around the center bar of the buckle with the prong inserted through the opening. Sew the end of the belt in place on the wrong side with firm hand stitches.

TO MAKE A FABRIC BELT STRAP

See Figure 5. Cut a piece of fabric on the lengthwise grain 1 inch wide and 1 inch longer than the width of the belt. Baste under ¼ inch on the long edges. Fold in half lengthwise, encasing the raw edges, and machine-stitch close to the edges.

Wrap the strap around the belt in a position approximately 1½ inches from the buckle; allow enough room for the belt to slide through. Hand-sew the raw edges to the inside of the belt.

THE STIFFENED BELT

This belt is very professional-looking, for it closely resembles the belt with a leather backing used on purchased garments. The stiff belting or Pellon keeps it from folding over and becoming rope-like, and so this belt construction is the only desirable one for a wide belt. These directions differ from those usually given on the instruction sheet, and therefore additional notions are required. Preshrink the belting or Pellon and grosgrain ribbon to be used, if the belt will be washed. Read General Notes on Belts on page 277.

The supplies needed are a yard of belting trimmed to the desired width, or enough heavy Pellon to cut a strip the

desired width and about a yard long, and a yard of matching grosgrain ribbon the width of the finished belt.

See Figure 6. Shape one end of the stiffening into the desired shape. Be sure that this shape suits the design of the garment. Cut the stiffening the necessary length to reach around the body with an overlap of at least 7 inches.

Cut a strip of matching fabric (cut carefully on the lengthwise grain) 1 inch wider and 1 inch longer than the stiffening.

Holding the belting in a curved position as it will be on your body when you wear it, lap one edge of the belt fabric ½ inch over the stiffening and baste in place firmly. Still holding the belt in a curved position, wrap the fabric around the stiffening. Keep it firm and evenly tight and be careful that the crosswise threads are not pulled off grain. Pin it in

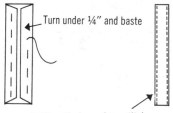

Turn under ¼" and baste

Fold lengthwise and top-stitch

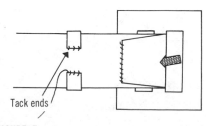

Tack ends

FIGURE 5

place over the stiffening and baste the remaining edge in place. Baste the ends in place as shown.

From the outside, machine-stitch all

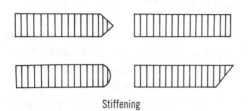

Stiffening

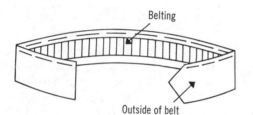

Belting

Outside of belt

Baste and then top-stitch

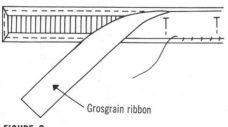

Grosgrain ribbon

FIGURE 6

edges of the belt, using a slightly longer stitch than was used for the seams of the garment. Personal preference will determine how close to the edge these stitches should be. Do not make them closer than ⅛ inch because there is too great a danger of not catching in the stiffening. For a more tailored effect, they could be placed as far as ¼ inch from the edge.

To finish the raw edges on the underside, pin grosgrain ribbon to the belt, turning under the ends of the ribbon at the belt ends. Still keep the belt in a curved position. Whip all edges of grosgrain ribbon in place with hand stitches about ¼ inch apart. See page 279 for detailed directions for attaching the buckle, inserting eyelets, and making a belt strap.

THE CONTOUR BELT

Read General Notes on Belts on page 277. As the name implies, the contour belt is shaped to the body so that it will rest quite naturally at the waistline, dipping down somewhat in the back. It is usually slightly wider at the back. If it is a wide belt, the contours show up more than on a narrow belt, where the contours are hardly discernible when worn. This belt takes more time to make than the straight belt with belting as a backing.

A pattern piece will be given, and you will be directed to cut two by this pattern. One of the pieces will be used as a facing on the wrong side of the belt and will not be seen when the belt is worn. For this reason it is permissible and wise, when using heavy fabric, to cut one of the belts of thinner fabric, such as taffeta.

The pattern may tell you to interface the belt, or it may tell you to use crinoline or buckram for a heavier, stiffer belt. These directions have been written for the stiffer belt, and buckram is used for a backing. Buckram can be purchased in most yard goods departments.

See Figure 7. Trim off the seam allowance of the paper pattern. Pin the trimmed pattern on the buckram and cut out the pattern, cutting along the original seamline of the pattern.

Place the fabric belt over the buckram and wrap the edges around the buckram. Baste the edges. Topstitch from ⅛ to ¼ inch from the edges, as desired; use a longer stitch than was used for stitching seams in the garment. Personal preference will determine how far from the edge to stitch. A belt looks more tailored if the stitching is ¼ inch from the edge; for dressier effects, the stitching should be closer to the edge.

Using the piece which will become the belt facing (it may be of dress fabric or of a lighter-weight fabric if the dress fabric is heavy), turn under all edges 1/16 inch more than the seam allowance and baste all edges. Now trim this seam allowance down to ⅜ inch.

Pin the belt facing over the wrong

side of the belt. Notice that it will fall just inside the belt edges. Hand-sew the belt facing in place with stitches ¼ inch apart; be careful that the stitches do not show on the right side. For directions for attaching the buckle, inserting eyelets, and making a belt strap, see page 279.

GENERAL NOTES ON WAISTBANDS

Figure 8 illustrates issues involved with fastening the waistband. The waistband must have an overlap on one end. This overlap, if put on the back edge of the waistband, will lap under the garment and will result in a clean line as shown in the upper sketch; this is the preferred method. The extension can be put on the front edge of the band, which will result in the effect shown in the second sketch;

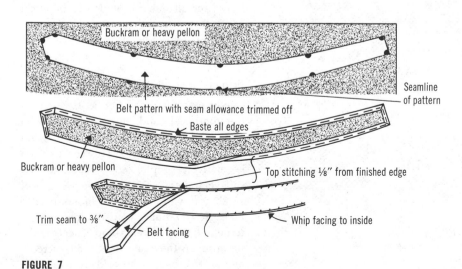

Buckram or heavy pellon

Belt pattern with seam allowance trimmed off

Baste all edges

Seamline of pattern

Buckram or heavy pellon

Top stitching ⅛" from finished edge

Trim seam to ⅜"

Belt facing

Whip facing to inside

FIGURE 7

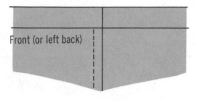

Extension for lapover on back edge
of waistband — preferred method

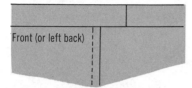

Extension for lapover on front edge
of waistband — acceptable but
not recommended

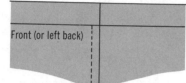

Fastening with hooks and peats —
safe choice for any use

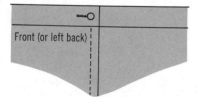

Fastening with machine-worked buttonhole
and button for tailored garments

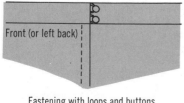

Fastening with loops and buttons
for decorative effects

FIGURE 8

the line at the side edge is not as clean, and although this method is not wrong, it is not recommended. For a back-opening skirt, the overlap is placed on the right back.

The waistband can be fastened with hooks and peats, which add no detail at all to the outside of the garment and which result in an uncluttered look that is always safe. The waistband can be fastened with buttons, as illustrated, to achieve the desired effect.

TO DECIDE ON WIDTH OF WAISTBAND

Read To Decide on Width of Belt and Buckle on page 279, for many of those suggestions can be used for the waistband. Surely you have noticed how many ready-to-wear skirts are made with waistbands about 1¼ to 1½ inches wide, and indeed how often this same width is used by the pattern companies. This width is not necessarily the best width—it is used so frequently because it is easily handled in manufacturing and by the average woman who at home. Actually a narrower waistband (¾ to 1 inch) is very much smarter, especially for special costumes, but it is slightly more difficult to handle. The narrower band is preferred for all but the obviously practical uses, sturdy sport garments, garments made of unusually heavy fabric, and skirts worn with very short jackets.

METHODS OF MAKING WAISTBANDS

The waistband most frequently used is the interfaced band; this band is used on most ready-to-wear and is included with most pattern directions. This construction is relatively simple and is handled with sufficient detail on the instruction sheet so that it will not be included in this book. It is a bulky construction; the interfacing is relatively limp (necessarily, because of the way it is constructed), and so this band may fold over and become somewhat ropelike with wear. It is also very apt to stretch with use. Therefore, it is not the best construction for truly professional results. The stiffened band, included in these pages, is far superior to it, but again, like all the couturier touches, it does require more time.

The skirt waist can be finished with a band of grosgrain ribbon or belting that is turned to the inside so that it does not show at all on the outside when the garment is worn. These directions are included on the instruction sheet for those designs for which the designer feels the concealed band is the wiser choice; because of its limited use, directions are not included in this book. This band is the least bulky of all waistbands, and since no band shows, the resulting effect is uncluttered and understated.

THE STIFFENED
WAISTBAND

See Figure 9. The stiffening for this band should be a heavy Pellon. The Pellon is cut to the desired finished width (no seam allowances). When the width has been decided, shape the end as desired. Then rule off parallel lines on the Pellon and cut a strip 3 or 4 inches longer than your waist. To decide proper length, wrap the strip around the body and pin in a position that is a comfortable fit for a waistband. Now let it slip just ¼ inch, making it ¼ inch longer than was comfortable; this little extra allowance is required to make up for thicknesses of fabric that will be involved in the finished skirt. Mark a point where the end of the band meets the band. Now add an additional 1½ inches of length for a lap-over and trim off any excess length.

Cut a strip of skirt fabric 1 inch wider and 1 inch longer than the strip

of stiffening. Wrap the fabric around the stiffening as shown, turning under ½ inch on all edges. Baste.

This waistband has the great advantage of fitting exactly as you want it to fit; it will never stretch, it will be firm and will not roll over, and it has the very great advantage of creating a minimum of bulk. However, it does have one disadvantage that makes it more difficult to apply. It does not have notches to match

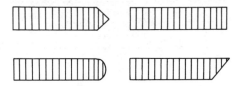

Shape ends of stiffening

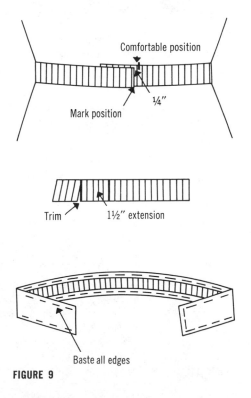

Comfortable position

Mark position   ¼″

Trim   1½″ extension

Baste all edges

FIGURE 9

to the skirt as the pattern does. This is no great disadvantage for the person who must adjust waist size because she cannot use the notch markings anyway, but the person who is a perfect size could use the pattern notches. Some method must be devised to locate points on the waistband that will match to the skirt.

The person who is exactly the size of the pattern and who has not altered her skirt by pattern alteration or fitting can transfer pattern markings to this waistband as shown in Figure 10. Remember that the pattern includes seam allowance and that the prepared waistband has had seam allowances turned under. Place the waistband pattern along the prepared fabric waistband and put thread markings along the edge in the notch positions. These markings, then, will match to the notches in the skirt.

The person who is not a perfect size

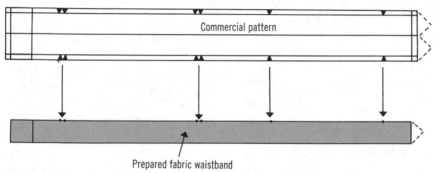

FIGURE 10   For straight-size figure when no alterations have been made

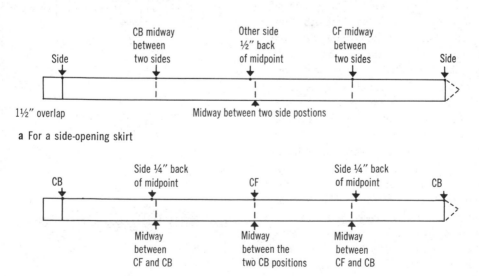

a For a side-opening skirt

b For a back-opening skirt
FIGURE 11

and who has altered her skirt by pattern alteration or fitting can locate matching points (centers and sides) as illustrated in Figure 11. The upper sketch pictures the waistband for a side-opening skirt, and the lower sketch pictures the back-opening skirt. This problem is more complicated because the front and back waist measurements are not equal—the front waist measures 1 inch larger than the back waist on the average figure. The steps must be done in the following order.

FOR THE SIDE–OPENING SKIRT

1 Find the midpoint between the two side positions at the ends of the waistband.
2 Put a tailor's tack ½ inch back of this midpoint. This designates the right side position.
3 Now mark midpoints between the side positions to obtain center-front and center-back lines.

FOR THE BACK–OPENING SKIRT

1 Find the midpoint between the two center-back positions. Put a tailor's tack at this point, which designates the center-front line.
2 Find the midpoint between center fronts and center backs. Put tailor's tacks ¼ inch back of these midpoints. These points designate the side positions.

TO APPLY WAISTBAND

The waistband should be basted to the skirt, matching centers and sides. The matching points just established will work well for the average figure, but it is possible that the problem figure will need to move points during fitting; be sure to do identical fitting on the two sides of the body.

See Figure 12. The sketch is labeled for a skirt side opening, but underneath the words "front" and "back" appear the

words "left back" and "right back" for use with a back-opening skirt.

Lap the waistband ⅝ inch over the upper edge of the skirt; have one end of the band even with the front edge of the skirt, thereby leaving the overlap to extend beyond the back edge. Baste the band to the skirt with secure stitches.

Try the skirt on for a fitting to see that it hangs properly from the waist and to see that the band length is correct. Make adjustments if necessary.

Machine-stitch ⅛ inch (never closer) from all edges of the band, catching in the skirt; use a longer stitch than was used for the seams of the garment.

NOTE If the skirt is to be lined with a separate lining, the lining should be set in at this time.

See Figure 13. To finish the raw edges on the underside, pin grosgrain ribbon to the band, turning under the ends of ribbon at the ends of the band. Whip all edges of grosgrain ribbon in

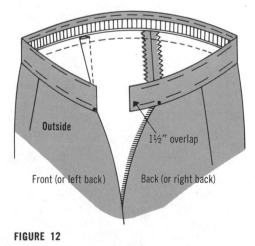

Outside

1½" overlap

Front (or left back) Back (or right back)

FIGURE 12

place with hand stitches ¼ inch apart.
Fasten with buttons and buttonholes or
hooks and straight eyes. See page 319 for
directions for sewing on hooks and
straight eyes.

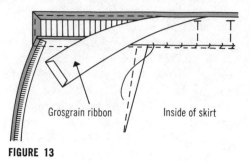

Grosgrain ribbon   Inside of skirt

FIGURE 13

HEM
CONSTRUCTION

The width of the hem and the method of hem finish used are two more small details that are of great importance to the success of a costume. Almost everyone, even persons who do not sew or who do not consider themselves at all perceptive when it comes to matters of dress, will sense any deviation from the normal hem width. The fact that skimpy hems are used in very low-priced ready-to-wear because of the obvious saving in yardage is reason enough to strive for the proper hem width as a way of adding a quality touch to the garments we make at home. And of course it is obvious to all readers that the length of a garment can enhance the individual figure. And so the length of the garment and width of the hem must be given careful thought.

GENERAL
NOTES
ON
HEMS

FACTORS INFLUENCING WIDTH OF HEM

fashion and precedent set certain standards
There are logical and scientific reasons

why hems are made a certain width; the designers of quality ready-to-wear consider the why's, and therefore many of them use approximately the same hem width. And so in a way, certain widths become fashionable. There is another way that fashion enters the picture: hem widths should be in good proportion to the total length of the garment (the hem in a bolero jacket is not as wide as the hem in a skirt of mid-calf length), and in the case of skirts, the hem must consequently be narrower in those seasons when very short skirts are fashionable than it is when a longer skirt length is preferred.

the type of fabric makes certain demands
One of the purposes of the hem is to add weight to the garment so that it will hang well, and so it follows that a wider hem will create more weight for the garment made of flimsy, lightweight fabric. In general, heavy fabric can have hems up to ½ inch narrower than average, and lightweight fabrics can have hems up to ½ inch wider than average.

the type of garment is a factor The particular type of garment calls for a certain hem width simply because of precedent, based on all the factors mentioned in this section.

the size and height of the wearer are considerations If the hem is to create good proportions with the total length of the garment, a slightly wider-than-average hem width can be used for the tall girl, and a slightly narrower-than-average hem width can be used for the short girl. A good general rule is this: Follow the general rules for hem widths stated below; however, the person who is 5 feet tall can make her hems about ½ inch narrower than average, and the person who is 5 feet nine or ten inches tall can add about ½ inch to hem widths.

GENERAL RULES FOR HEM WIDTHS
All the following are estimates based on the figure of average height (about 5 feet 6 inches tall). These rules are good guidelines, but each problem must be given individual consideration. The discerning person will keep up with trends on the high-quality ready-to-wear market and be ready to accept new ideas as they are introduced.

½-inch finished-hem width is used for:
extremely flared sheer dance dresses in daytime or floor length
blouses
slips and petticoats
aprons and similar very functional garments
ruffles (hem ¼-inch wide preferred)

1-inch finished-hem width is used for:
short sleeves
shorts
very brief jackets
circular skirts in stiff fabrics that do not ease well

1½-inch finished-hem width is used for:
circular skirts in most fabrics
three-quarter- and full-length sleeves in dresses, jackets, and coats
waist-length and near-hip-length jackets
slacks

2½-inch finished-hem width is used for:
sheath dresses in all weights of fabric
straight skirts
gathered and pleated skirts (based on a rectangle)
three-quarter- and full-length coats

3- to 4-inch finished-hem width is used for:

sheer dresses in daytime length (as an absolute
   minimum width)

floor-length, straight-line dinner and ball gowns

5- to 10-inch finished-hem width is used for:

sheer fabrics in full-skirted garments (if based
   on a rectangle)

PREPARATION FOR HANGING THE HEM

The hem is hung during the last fitting;
refer back to Chapter 15, Fundamentals
of Fitting, on page 177. The undergarments and shoes you will wear with the
costume should be worn at this fitting. If
you will wear a belt, be sure to use it
(or a belt of the same width) when the
hem is hung.

Before putting on the garment, turn
up the hem allowance and pin in place.
This length may not be correct, but it
will be close to right and will be an aid
to establishing the desired length. Put
the garment on and be critical of the
length. Test out other lengths by turning
up slightly more or less hem (do not
measure—this is just an estimate). When
you are satisfied with the estimated
length, the hem can be measured.

HANGING OR MEASURING THE HEM

The hem can be measured with a yardstick, an L square, or a pin marker; the
pin marker is recommended. Have an
assistant hang the hem. She should test
along the estimated hemline and find a
"happy medium" hemline (the estimated
hem will not be entirely accurate).
Ideally the assistant should work at eye
level; the best solution is for the assistant
to sit and the wearer to stand on a table.
The wearer must stand straight and
especially steady, being careful to hold
her head in a normal position, especially
if the garment is a free-hanging one
(dropping the head when wearing a
boxy full-length coat changes the hem-

line considerably). Pins should be put in
every 4 or 5 inches for a straight skirt
and every 3 or 4 inches for a flared skirt;
it is of no advantage to use more pins,
and there is an added danger that a
longer length of time spent will result in
less accuracy because the wearer gets
weary and unsteady.

The measured hemline must be
tested for appearance. The garment can
be taken off, and the wearer can pin up
the hemline and then dress again, or the
assistant can pin up the hem as she finishes her work. This latter method is
really easier unless the skirt is very full
or flared or the hem is very wide. In
either case, the pins holding the hem in
position should be put in at right angles
to the hemline so that the hem falls in a
limp, natural manner, and there should
be a sufficient number of pins so that the
hem will stay in the proper position.

**criticize the measured hem; look for optical
illusions**   The hemline must appear to be
parallel to the floor, but the fact that it
has been measured parallel to the floor
is no assurance that it will look even.
And the important issue is that the hemline must *look* right (*being* right is less
important). Sometimes, for elusive reasons of figure or posture or design, a
garment which really is parallel to the
floor appears uneven. If this happens
(and it does frequently), the optical illusion must be corrected.

Frequent optical illusions are these:
(1) The garment may look longer in the
back, beginning perhaps at the side seam
(it can, of course, appear longer in front,
but this does not happen often); this
may be the result of posture or a result

HEM FINISH AND APPEARANCE
AND APPROPRIATE USES

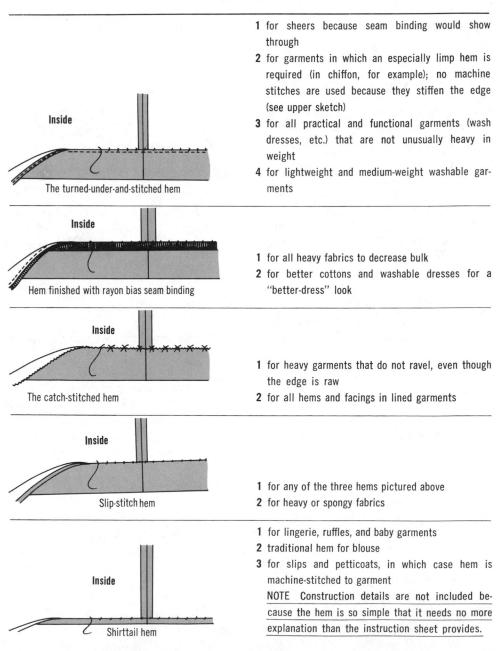

The turned-under-and-stitched hem

1 for sheers because seam binding would show through

2 for garments in which an especially limp hem is required (in chiffon, for example); no machine stitches are used because they stiffen the edge (see upper sketch)

3 for all practical and functional garments (wash dresses, etc.) that are not unusually heavy in weight

4 for lightweight and medium-weight washable garments

Hem finished with rayon bias seam binding

1 for all heavy fabrics to decrease bulk

2 for better cottons and washable dresses for a "better-dress" look

The catch-stitched hem

1 for heavy garments that do not ravel, even though the edge is raw

2 for all hems and facings in lined garments

Slip-stitch hem

1 for any of the three hems pictured above

2 for heavy or spongy fabrics

Shirttail hem

1 for lingerie, ruffles, and baby garments

2 traditional hem for blouse

3 for slips and petticoats, in which case hem is machine-stitched to garment

NOTE Construction details are not included because the hem is so simple that it needs no more explanation than the instruction sheet provides.

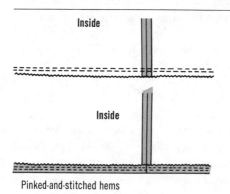

Pinked-and-stitched hems

1 for lower edge of blouses to reduce bulk
2 upper sketch shows a hem is least bulky and can be used if the fabric does not ravel appreciably
3 the lower sketch shows a hem which is slightly more bulky but which is still a nice flat finish. This hem can be done in a wider width with many rows of stitches, as a decorative detail.

NOTE Construction details not included in this book.

of fullness in the back—a pleat, etc. (2) Whenever a garment has concentrated fullness of pleats or gathers (no matter where that fullness is), there is a tendency for the garment to look longer in that area. (3) The garment may look longer on one side if the wearer has one leg longer or one hip larger than the other; this garment may need a correction in both front and back for a few inches on either side of the side seamline (the correction may extend as far as the center-front and center-back lines).

No matter what the illusion, correct it by making an estimate of the amount of correction required and testing the results. Figure 1 shows the method of correction; the illustration is one of apparent extra length in the back. Note that the original line of measuring pins is not removed but is retained as a guide; note that the correction is gradual and that eventually the corrected line returns to the original (in this case at the side-seam position). Now test on the figure to see whether the hem appears even; continue

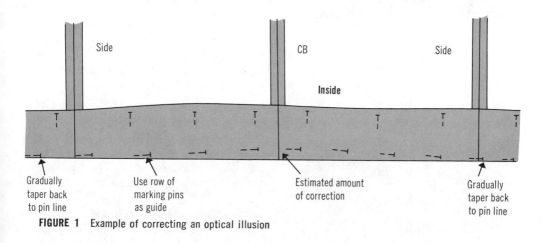

Gradually taper back to pin line

Use row of marking pins as guide

Estimated amount of correction

Gradually taper back to pin line

FIGURE 1 Example of correcting an optical illusion

testing until the hem appears parallel to the floor before proceeding with hem directions.

THE TAILOR'S HEM

NOTE Study the entire section entitled General Notes on Hems on page 289, paying special attention to Preparation for Hanging the Hem and Hanging or Measuring the Hem on page 291. If there is a pleat in the skirt with a seam falling on the inside fold of the pleat, see page 299 for directions for handling this seam.

See Figure 2. The tailor's hem is pictured in two sketches as it would appear in (1) a hem employing seam binding

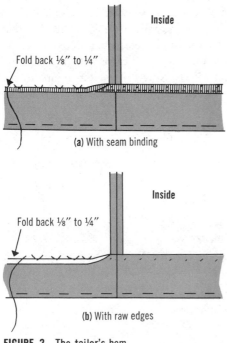

(a) With seam binding

(b) With raw edges

FIGURE 2 The tailor's hem

and (2) a hem with raw edges exposed. The tailor's hem is, in reality, a method of doing the hand stitches and is characterized by stitches placed ⅛ to ¼ inch under the edge of the hem. Because the stitch does not extend over the edge of the hem, the upper edge of the hem is free, which results in a flat, inconspicuous finish. This stitch (or the catch stitch) is the ideal choice for spongy or heavy fabrics.

The slip stitch or blind stitch (described on page 138) should be used. The upper edge of the hem is folded back ⅛ to ¼ inch so that the stitches fall under the edge. These stitches should be loose and "easy" for the most inconspicuous results.

THE TURNED–UNDER– AND–STITCHED HEM

NOTE Study the entire section entitled General Information on page 289, paying special attention to Preparation for Hanging the Hem and Hanging or Measuring the Hem on page 291 If there is a pleat in the skirt with a seam falling on the inside fold of the pleat, see page 299 for directions for handling this seam.

See Figure 3.

step 1 Perfect the measured pin line by putting in pins at right angles to the fold edge. Baste ⅛ inch from the fold edge with ½- to ¾-inch-long stitches to hold the hemline in a secure position.

step 2 Make a cardboard gauge the desired width of the hem. With chalk or pencil, put a marking line on the hem parallel to the fold edge. Trim ¼ inch from the marking line as shown.

step 3 Turn under ¼ inch and machine-stitch ¹⁄₁₆ inch from the fold edge as

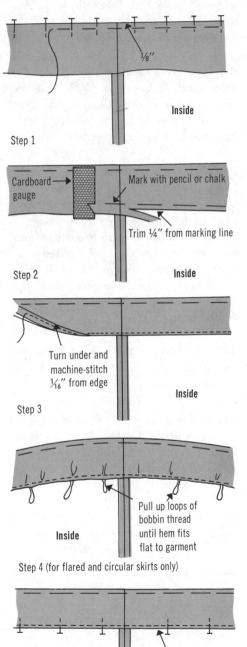

Step 1

Cardboard gauge

Mark with pencil or chalk

Trim ¼" from marking line

Inside

Step 2

Inside

Turn under and machine-stitch ¹⁄₁₆" from edge

Inside

Step 3

Pull up loops of bobbin thread until hem fits flat to garment

Inside

Step 4 (for flared and circular skirts only)

Inside

Pin in place

Step 5

FIGURE 3

shown; if the skirt is flared or circular, make these stitches about size 8 to 10 per inch, for they will serve the purpose of gathering threads in the next step.

step 4 *For flared or circular skirts only.* Put a pin through one of the bobbin stitches every few inches and draw up the edge slightly by pulling out loops of thread as shown. This will draw in the upper edge of the hem; adjust the ease and pull up the thread until the hem fits flat to the garment. As the hem is hand-hemmed, the loops can be tucked underneath.

NOTE If the fabric cannot be eased in, the fullness can be darted out with small darts spaced as needed.

step 5 Pin the upper edge of the hem flat to the garment.

NOTE Hand hemming stitches are discussed and shown in actual size in the section entitled The Most Essential Hand Hemming Stitches on page 137.

THE HEM
FINISHED
WITH RAYON
BIAS SEAM BINDING

NOTE Study the entire section entitled General Notes on Hems on page 289, paying special attention to Preparation for Hanging the Hem and Hanging or Measuring the Hem on page 291. If there is a pleat in the skirt with a seam falling on the inside fold of the pleat, see page 299 for directions for handling this seam.

See Figure 4.

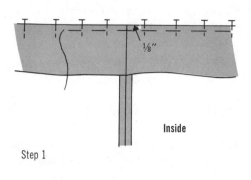

⅛"

Inside

Step 1

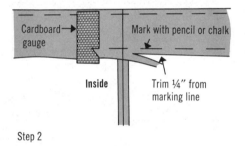

Cardboard gauge

Mark with pencil or chalk

Inside

Trim ¼" from marking line

Step 2

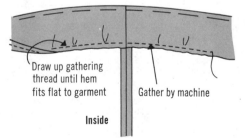

Draw up gathering thread until hem fits flat to garment

Gather by machine

Inside

Step 3 (for flared and circular skirts only)

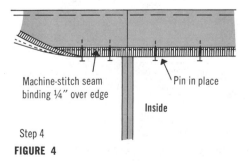

Machine-stitch seam binding ¼" over edge

Pin in place

Inside

Step 4

FIGURE 4

step 1 Perfect the measured pin line by putting in pins at right angles to the fold edge. Baste ⅛ inch from the fold edge with ½- to ¾-inch-long stitches to hold the hemline in a secure position.

step 2 Make a cardboard gauge the desired width of the hem. With chalk or pencil, put a marking line on the hem parallel to the fold edge. Trim ¼ inch from the marking line as shown.

step 3 *For flared or circular skirts only.* Machine-stitch (with stitches about size 8 to 10 per inch) ¼ inch from the raw edge as shown. Put a pin through one of the bobbin stitches every few inches and draw up the edge slightly by pulling out loops of thread as shown. This will draw in the upper edge of the hem; adjust the ease and pull up the thread until the hem fits flat to the garment.

NOTE If the fabric cannot be eased in, the fullness can be darted out with small darts spaced as needed.

step 4 Baste rayon bias seam binding ¼ inch over the cut edge. Machine-stitch binding in place with stitches as close to the edge as possible. Pin the upper edge of the hem flat to the garment.

NOTE Hand hemming stitches are discussed and shown in actual size in the section entitled The Most Essential Hand Hemming Stitches on page 137.

THE CATCHSTITCHED
HEM
WITH
RAW EDGES

NOTE Study the entire section entitled General Notes on Hems on page 289, paying special attention to Preparation for Hanging the Hem and Hanging or Measuring the Hem on page 291. If there is a pleat in the skirt with a seam falling on the inside fold of the pleat, see page 299 for directions for handling this seam.

See Figure 5.

step 1 Perfect the measured pin line by putting in pins at right angles to the fold edge. Baste ⅛ inch from the fold edge with ½- to ¾-inch-long stitches to hold the hemline in a secure position.

step 2 Make a cardboard gauge the desired width of the hem. With chalk or pencil, put a marking line on the hem parallel to the fold edge. Trim ⅛ inch from the marking line as shown.

step 3 *For flared or circular skirts only.* Machine-stitch as shown, using a long stitch. Put a pin through one of the bobbin stitches every few inches and draw up the edge slightly by pulling out loops of thread as shown. This will draw in the upper edge of the hem; adjust the ease and pull up the thread until the hem fits flat to the garment. As the hem is hand-hemmed, the loops can be tucked underneath. This gathering line should, however, remain in the hem.

step 4 Pin the upper edge of the hem flat to the garment. If you are making a jacket or coat, see the following section on finishing the lower front corner before securing the hem with hand stitches.

NOTE Hand hemming stitches are discussed and shown in actual size in the section entitled The Most Essential Hand Hemming Stitches on page 137.

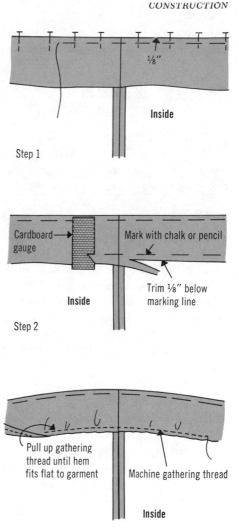

Step 1

⅛″

Inside

Step 2

Cardboard gauge · Mark with chalk or pencil

Inside · Trim ⅛″ below marking line

Pull up gathering thread until hem fits flat to garment · Machine gathering thread

Inside

Step 3 (for flared and circular skirts only)

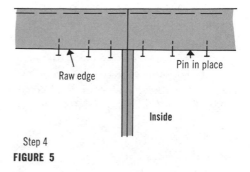

Raw edge · Pin in place

Inside

Step 4
FIGURE 5

HANDLING
LOWER FRONT CORNER
OF JACKETS
AND COATS

NOTE These directions result in a flatter finish at these bulky corners. These suggestions are recommended for high-fashion clothing but are not recommended for garments for growing children.

The front corners of jackets and coats present a problem because of the great bulk in that area when the hem is turned up and the facing is turned back; there will be four thicknesses of fabric at that point, and that is too much. This is true of vent-back openings and buttoned sleeve openings. As an aid to decreasing bulk, corners are handled as shown in Figure 6.

step 1 Fold the facing to the inside as shown. Check to see that the hem marking line in the facing falls on the hemline of the jacket; if it does not, correct it at this time. Make a clip in the garment hem 1 inch from the inner edge of the facing as shown.

step 2 Pull the facing out as shown. Press the seam open to a point about 1 inch above the hemline. Then, beginning at the clip, trim out some of the hem allowance, as shown in the shaded area; leave a ¾-inch allowance below the hemline of the garment and a ½-inch allowance below the hemline of the facing; this will result in a staggered seam.

step 3 Trim out the corner of the seam below the hemline as shown.

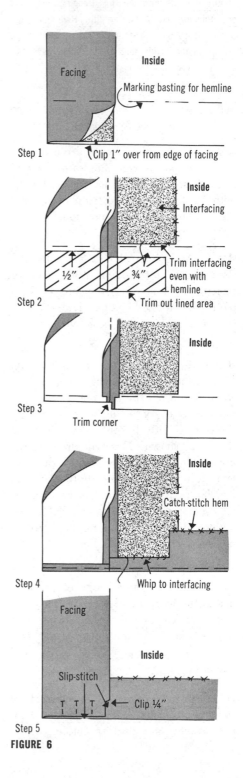

Step 1 — Facing / Inside / Marking basting for hemline / Clip 1″ over from edge of facing

Step 2 — Inside / Interfacing / Trim interfacing even with hemline / ½″ / ¾″ / Trim out lined area

Step 3 — Inside / Trim corner

Step 4 — Inside / Catch-stitch hem / Whip to interfacing

Step 5 — Facing / Inside / Slip-stitch / Clip ¼″

FIGURE 6

step 4 Turn up the hem allowance on the hemline and baste the entire hem in place with stitches ⅛ inch from the lower edge. Press the front corner area. Whip the lower edge to the interfacing. The hem can be catchstitched at this time.

step 5 Fold the facing to the inside and pin in place. The lining will not reach the lower edge of the garment, so something must be done to finish the raw edge of the facing for a short distance in all but heavy fabrics that do not ravel. Make a ¼-inch clip into the inner edge of the facing at a point about 1 inch above the hemline. Turn under the raw edge below the clip and pin. Sew the lower edge with secure blind stitches.

HEM TREATMENT FOR A PLEAT SEAM

Very often a seam will fall at the inner fold of a pleat, as shown in the upper sketch of Figure 7. This seam is not pressed open because it must lie flat as it is pictured. However, when the hem is turned up, a seam turned to one side is very bulky. The bulk in this seam, as the reader knows, eventually causes a distortion of the pleat. This construction method decreases bulk and at the same time ensures a pleat that will stay in position for the lifetime of the garment.

step 1 Press this seam open for about 5 or 6 inches from the lower edge. Trim both edges of the seam allowance down to ⅜ inch in the area below the measured hemline.

step 2 Return to the hem directions and finish the hem, treating this seam exactly as any pressed-open seam is treated. Clip

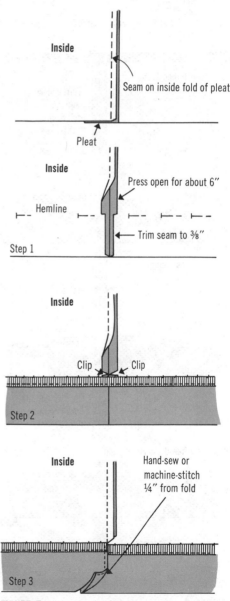

FIGURE 7

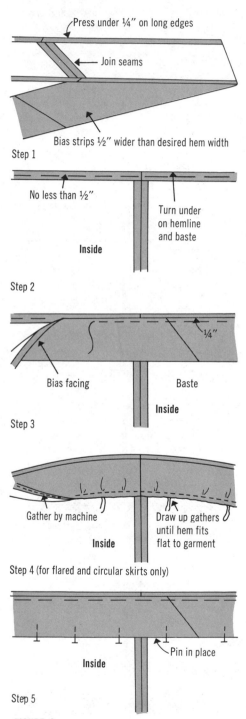

Press under ¼″ on long edges

Join seams

Bias strips ½″ wider than desired hem width

Step 1

No less than ½″

Turn under
on hemline
and baste

Inside

Step 2

¼″

Bias facing

Baste

Inside

Step 3

Gather by machine

Draw up gathers
until hem fits
flat to garment

Inside

Step 4 (for flared and circular skirts only)

Pin in place

Inside

Step 5

FIGURE 8

into the seam directly above the finished hem as shown.

CAUTION When the hem is finished, return to these directions for an additional step of construction.

step 3   Fold the pleat into position. This seam is still bulky, but it has been greatly improved by the preceding steps. As an aid to holding these very thick edges flat and secure during wear and washing or dry cleaning, sew by hand or by machine about ¼ inch from the finished folded edge. Hand stitches will be easier to remove if the hem length is changed; machine stitches hold the edge flatter and are recommended for very heavy fabrics.

THE FACED HEM

NOTE Study the entire section entitled General Notes on Hems on page 289, paying special attention to Preparation for Hanging the Hem and Hanging or Measuring the Hem on page 291. If there is a pleat in the skirt with a seam falling on the inside fold of the pleat, see page 299 for directions for handling this seam.

The faced hem is usually a "make-do" solution to the problem of a skirt cut too short or of a skirt that must be lengthened because of a change in fashion. On rare occasions the faced hem is used as a design feature to create a contrasting band of color; an example is the circular skating skirt with a hem faced in deliberate contrast to create interest as the skirt flares. Unless the faced hem is intentional for design purposes, one tries to avoid it whenever possible. The hem acts slightly differently from the usual fold-edge hem and also looks slightly different simply because a seam is involved near the lower edge and the seam and its extra thickness tend to stiffen this edge.

If the faced hem must be used, as in the case of pegged skirts, the secret to success is to avoid extra stiffness in every possible way. The directions given below result in a hem amazingly like the limp fold-edge hem because stiffness has been avoided in three ways: by cutting the facing strips on the bias, which molds and bends easily; by using a limper fabric for the facing than that of the garment; and by doing all sewing with hand stitches, which are more flexible than machine stitches.

The fabric used for the facing should be subordinate to the fabric of the garment. Reread Selection of Lining Fabrics on page 41; a lining fabric in a matching color is an ideal choice for a hem facing. Hem-facing strips are available on the market, cut on the bias and prepared ready for application. Certainly the purchased facing is a convenience and a timesaver, but it is not recommended except for heavier fabrics because it is made of a fairly stiff cotton or a relatively heavy and stiff rayon. The very limp lining fabrics are preferred.

See Figure 8.

step 1   Cut bias strips of facing fabric ½ inch wider than the desired hem width. Join the strips to obtain sufficient length for the sweep of the skirt. Press under ¼ inch on both long edges.

step 2   Turn up the lower edge of the

skirt on the measured pin line and baste in place. A turnup of at least ½ inch in width is required.

step 3   Place the facing strip along the lower edge, having one long edge ¼ inch from the fold edge of the skirt. Pin and baste in place.

step 4   *For flared or circular skirts only.* Machine-stitch ⅛ inch from the remaining fold edge of the facing with stitches about size 8 to 10 per inch. Put a pin through one of the bobbin stitches every few inches and draw up the edge by pulling out loops of bobbin thread as shown. This will draw in the upper edge of the facing; adjust the ease and pull up the thread until the upper edge of the facing fits flat to the skirt. As the hem is hand-hemmed, the loops can be tucked underneath.

step 5   Pin the upper edge of the facing flat to the garment. Both long edges of the facing must be hand-sewn in place. Hand hemming stitches are discussed and shown in actual size in The Most Essential Hand Hemming Stitches on page 137. Use small and secure blind stitches for the edge near the lower edge of the skirt; use the usual hemming-stitch length for the upper edge.

27

LINING JACKETS AND COATS; COUTURIER LINING FOR DRESSES AND SKIRTS

TO MAKE LINING PATTERNS FOR JACKETS AND COATS

Vogue patterns include lining pieces for those pieces that need special lining patterns; most of the other companies use *cutoff lines* on the pattern pieces in order to convert the pattern piece for the garment into a lining pattern. Some lining pieces are cut exactly like the pattern for the garment piece—sleeves, for example. In the main, it is the front section of the jacket or coat (narrower because of a facing) and the back section (wider because of a pleat extension) which require special pattern pieces or cutoff lines.

Directions for making these lining patterns are included for those few jackets that might not have directions for linings; most jackets and coats do, but occasionally a very simple little design may be offered without linings. Figure 1 shows the front and back pattern pieces for a jacket; all other pieces, sleeve or an underarm section, would be cut exactly like the original pattern piece.

The back lining pattern should have a center-back pleat not included in the jacket. Place a strip of paper along the center-back line and extend the pattern 1 inch. Put a few markings along the center-back line for use in tailor tacking that line in the fabric. If there is a back neck facing in the pattern, place it under the back pattern, cut edges even. Notice that the sketch shows a broken line to indicate the inner edge of a back facing. Construct a cutoff line for the lining 1¼ inches above the inner edge of the facing as shown; this 1¼ inches will allow for a ⅝-inch turn-under on the neck edge of the lining and a ⅝-inch lap-over on the facing when the lining is inserted.

The front lining pattern is considerably narrower than the garment because of a wide front facing. Place the facing pattern under the front pattern, cut edges even. Notice the broken line in the sketch, which indicates the inner edge of the facing. Construct a cutoff line for the lining 1¼ inches over from the inner edge of the facing as shown; this 1¼ inches will allow for a ⅝-inch turn-under

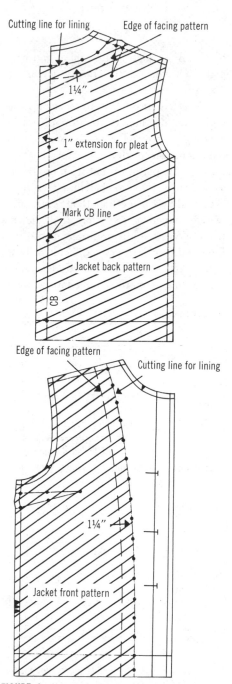

Cutting line for lining   Edge of facing pattern

1¼"

1" extension for pleat

Mark CB line

Jacket back pattern

CB

Edge of facing pattern

Cutting line for lining

1¼"

Jacket front pattern

FIGURE 1 How to make lining patterns for jacket front and back

on the front edge of the lining and a ⅝-inch lap-over on the facing when the lining is inserted.

See Figure 2. Pattern companies which do not include pattern pieces for a lining and which use this same cutoff technique make allowance for the back pleat as the pattern is cut from the fabric, as shown in the two sketches. The upper sketch shows a method that results in a wedge-shaped or dart-shaped pleat; this pleat serves the purpose for which it was intended, but it is more difficult to baste and press, and this method does force the grain line of the lining into a differ-

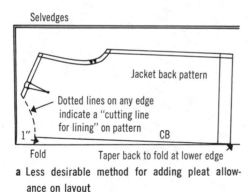

Selvedges

Jacket back pattern

Dotted lines on any edge indicate a "cutting line for lining" on pattern

1"

CB

Fold   Taper back to fold at lower edge

a Less desirable method for adding pleat allowance on layout

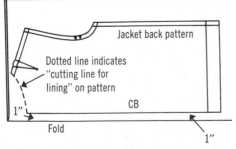

Selvedges

Jacket back pattern

Dotted line indicates "cutting line for lining" on pattern

1"

CB

Fold

1"

b Preferred method for adding pleat allowance on layout

FIGURE 2

ent position from that of the garment. The lower sketch shows a method which results in a parallel pleat and which is the much wiser choice.

LINING
THE JACKET
OR
COAT

PREPARATION OF LINING
See Figure 3.

step 1 All seams, darts, and tucks will eventually be machine-stitched, with one exception: the sleeve is not set in by machine. The back lining is shown in this step. Note the row of markings which denote the pleat line at the center back. Baste along this pleat line to hold the pleat in place, unless your fabric is satin. This basting thread will permanently mark the satin, and the pleat should be pressed in rather than basted.

Turn the pleat in one direction (it does not matter which one) and press. The pleat must be permanently held in place so that it will remain in good condition when the basting stitches are eventually removed. Bar tacks are used for this purpose. The sketch shows the placement of bar tacks. One is placed at the waistline and another at a point 3 inches down from the raw neck edge. They are placed about ⅜ inch in from the fold edge of the pleat, as shown.

step 2 The sketch pictures an enlarged view of the bar tack. It should be about ¼ inch long and ¹⁄₁₆ inch wide. The thread should match the lining fabric. Take several horizontal stitches ¼ inch long, catching through all thicknesses of the pleat. Then take vertical stitches ¹⁄₁₆ inch long, making sure to encase the horizontal stitches.

step 3 Turn under ⅝ inch on the long front edges and baste. Turn under ⅝ inch on the back neck edge, clipping the curve to allow the edge to lie flat, and baste. Stitch seams.

NOTE It is probable that the back shoulder edge extends beyond the front, as shown.

Press the body of the lining thoroughly, for this is the last opportunity to do a really good job; press the shoulder seams toward the back.

step 4 Note that the armhole edges of the lining were left raw. This means that the armhole edge of the sleeve will lap over these raw edges. To prepare the sleeve, stitch the vertical seams and press open. Then turn under the seam allowance at the armhole edge of the sleeve and baste; clips are required in the underarm region to make the seam lie flat.

TO INSERT THE LINING
See Figure 4. The lining illustrations require some explanation. A glance through the next pages will reveal that all illustrations show the coat turned wrong side

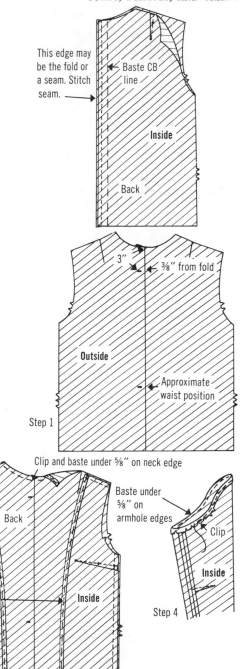

SKETCH IN ACTUAL SIZE

Step 2—How to make bar tacks

FIGURE 3

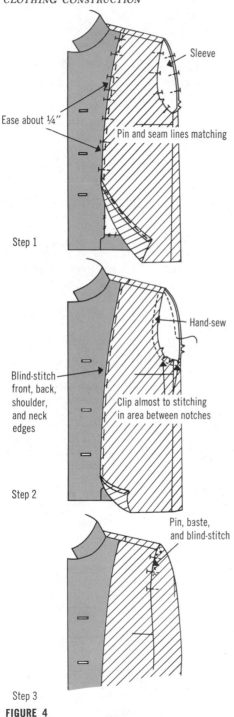

Sleeve

Ease about ¼"

Pin and seam lines matching

Step 1

Hand-sew

Blind-stitch
front, back,
shoulder,
and neck
edges

Clip almost to stitching
in area between notches

Step 2

Pin, baste,
and blind-stitch

Step 3

FIGURE 4

out, which is the only way it is possible to show the construction techniques. As work is done on the actual fabric, this construction can be done without turning the whole garment wrong side out; work is done inside the garment, and although it may be a bit tedious in spots, it can be done.

IMPORTANT NOTE The seamlines of the lining must match the seamlines in the jacket or coat. The fold edge of the front lining, for example, is the seamline and must be lapped ⅝ inch over the corresponding raw edges in the jacket or coat. Remember that a ⅝-inch turn-under and a ⅝-inch lap-over result in matching seamlines.

step 1 Slip the lining into the coat, matching seamlines. Lap the turned-under shoulder and neck edges ⅝ inch over the raw edges of the coat and pin in place in this area. Now notice that the illustration shows about ¼ inch of ease (extra length) in the lining between the shoulder line and a level about 3 inches below the bustline. The best way to obtain the correct result is to hold the coat on a curve over your left hand with the lining taking the outside curve; this way the lining will be slightly longer than the corresponding length of the coat. Pin this portion in place.

Place the coat flat on the table and pin the remaining front edge in place, lapping it ⅝ inch over the raw edge of the front facing. Be sure that the front edge of the lining makes a smooth, attractive line against the facing; notice that the line curves toward the front edge to about the bust level and then is ruler-straight to the lower edge.

Pin the armhole edges of the lining to the armhole edges of the sleeve, but in so doing remember that the sleeve seam has been trimmed to a ⅜-inch width, whereas the lining has the full ⅝-inch seam allowance; therefore, as these edges are pinned, the lining should extend ¼ inch beyond the raw edges of the garment in order to make seamlines match.

step 2   Baste the lining to the garment, taking the following precautions: Leave the lining free from the garment for about 6 inches at the lower front edge; basting stitches at the front and neck edges should catch into the facing only and not go through to the outside of the garment.

Slip-stitch the front and neck edges with small, ⅛-inch stitches, being sure that stitches catch in the facing only and do not go through to the right side of the garment.

The raw armhole edge must be permanently hand-sewn to the garment. Use a matching thread and small, firm basting stitches. These stitches should be just ⅛ inch outside the seamline of the lining —in the seam allowance, not in the body of the lining. These stitches must be very close to the seamline because the underarm area (between the notches) must be clipped almost to the seamline, as shown. These clips will eventually allow the sleeve lining to hang in the proper position.

step 3   With the garment sleeve turned wrong side out, slip the lining sleeve over it; check to see that the corresponding notches in the armhole match. Lap the turned-under edge of the sleeve ⅝ inch over the raw edges of the armhole and pin in place, taking the following precautions: Be sure that the notches match; match the marking on the top of the sleeve cap to the shoulder line of the garment; and match the underarm of the sleeve to the underarm of the garment. Now notice that there is fullness in the sleeve that must be eased into the armhole—ease in the fullness as the sleeve is pinned in place.

The sleeve must be sewn permanently in place with invisible slip stitches ⅛ inch long. This is difficult to do because of the fullness in the sleeve, and it will not look as smooth and attractive as the other slipstitched edges of the lining. The armhole will get great strain as the garment is worn, so make these stitches very firm and reinforce them often. It is better to allow a few slip stitches to show and have a stronger seam than to keep all stitches hidden if, by so doing, the seam will be insecure.

HANGING THE HEM IN THE LINING

See Figure 5. Try on the jacket or coat and let the lining fall in a natural position—as it "wants" to fall. Have an assistant put a row of pins about 5 inches up from the lower edge, pinning the lining to the garment as shown. Take off the jacket or coat and then put it back on again to see that the pins are correct. It

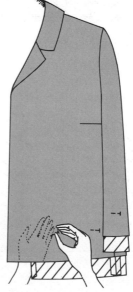

FIGURE 5

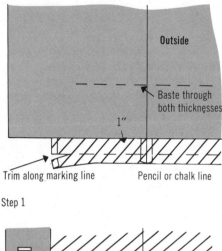

Step 1

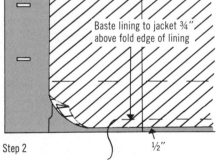

Step 2

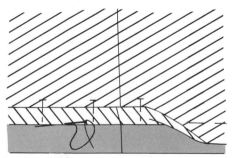

Step 3

FIGURE 6

is a good idea to remove the garment and put it back on again several times to be sure the lining hangs properly under all conditions. Sleeve hems are hung in an identical manner.

FINISHING LINING HEMS
See Figure 6.

step 1 Baste along the row of pins and remove pins. Smooth the lining down to the lower edge of the garment; place the garment flat on a table as shown. The lining should be 1 inch longer than the jacket or coat; it is probably longer than that—if so, trim the lining 1 inch below the garment hemline.

step 2 Turn under the raw edge of the lining to a point about ½ inch up from the hemline of the garment. Pin the lining in place, being very careful that the lower edge of the lining is parallel to, and ½ inch above, the lower edge of the garment. Baste the lining in place with stitches ¾ inch up from the fold edge of the lining. Do not press at this time.

step 3 The sketch shows the technique used at the lower edge. The hand sewing at the lower edge is done in such a way that there is a certain amount of extra length in the lining to allow for some shifting of the lining as the jacket or coat is worn. This is done by flipping up the folded edge of the lining and pinning it in place. Slip-stitch along this new fold line, catching the stitches into only one thickness of lining fabric. The stitches should be firm (fastened securely every so often) but rather loose so that the hem will not look overconstructed and obvious. When the basting stitches are removed, the hem will lie flat, but it will also shift in length, if necessary, as the garment is worn. Slip-stitch the remaining front edge flat. Press the lower edge of the lining and remove the basting.

TO CUT
LININGS
FOR SKIRTS
AND DRESSES

As a broad, general rule, the lining for skirts and dresses is cut exactly like the structural pieces of the garment, using the same pattern pieces. Figure 7 pictures pattern pieces to illustrate two exceptions to that general rule. In order to reduce unnecessary bulk in the pleat area, only a seam allowance is allowed beyond the pleat line; the illustration shows the most common design with a pleat at the center back. Notice that the skirt lining is cut as long as the garment; this means that there will be a hem allowance in the lining as well as in the garment and that the skirt and the lining could be lengthened, if desired.

Another exception to the general rule is illustrated by the bodice pattern in Figure 7. If a garment buttons at the front or back and therefore has a wide facing to finish the buttoned edge, the lining must be cut narrower than the garment piece. Place the facing pattern under the garment pattern, cut edges even. Notice that the sketch shows a broken line to indicate the inner edge of the facing. Construct a cutoff line for the lining 1¼ inches over from the inner edge of the facing as shown; this 1¼ inches will allow for a ⅝-inch turn-under on the edge of the lining and for a ⅝-inch lap-over on the facing when the lining is inserted. A design with a front facing of this kind would undoubtedly have a facing to finish off the back neck edge; if so, the back pattern should be altered in the same manner in preparation for cutting the lining.

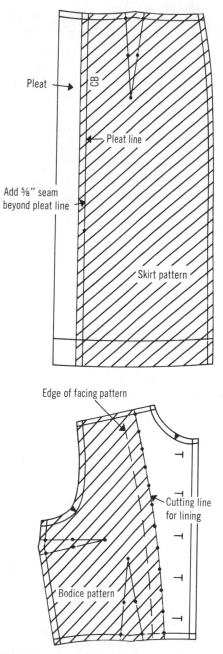

FIGURE 7

Whenever there is a facing to finish off a raw edge, the lining can be cut using the same principle of a cutoff line; for example, the lining for the sleeveless, collarless garment could be cut in this same manner. I think it is easier and more attractive, however, to cut the lining for sleeveless or collarless garments exactly like the pattern piece. Look ahead to Figure 13, which pictures this kind of garment. Cutoff lines were not used—the lining was cut exactly like the outside. This means that the edge of the lining can be turned under closer to the finished edge of the garment, so that just ½ inch of fabric shows. Had cutoff lines been used, about 1 inch of fabric would

have extended beyond the lining of the finished garment. The narrower band looks more delicate, and if the lining is being used as a protection against skin irritation (as it is when a person is allergic to wool, for example), then the narrower band would be preferred. However, either method of cutting is acceptable.

Because only the structural pieces (skirt pieces, bodice pieces, sleeves) of the pattern are cut for the lining and because collars, pocket flaps, and facings are not cut, less fabric will be required for the lining than for the garment itself; to obtain accurate yardage requirements, see To Figure Special Yardage Requirements on page 96.

LINING
A SKIRT
BY THE COUTURIER
METHOD

The skirt lining should be basted exactly like the garment; it should be fitted at the same time as the garment, and fitting changes should be the same for the lining and the garment. One cannot assume that the lining need not be fitted if it is cut and basted exactly like the outside garment because the garment might be made of fabric that will stretch (wool, knit, crepe, etc.), whereas the lining will not stretch. If a choice must be made, it is better to allow the lining to be slightly larger, rather than slightly smaller, than the garment because if the lining is made of the limp fabric recommended, it can be eased into the waistband of the skirt with no difficulty.

See Figure 8. If there is a pleat, baste and stitch the seam in the lining to exactly the same point where the stitching for the pleat ends; there should be a pattern marking at that point, but if

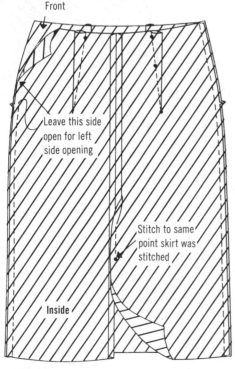

Front

Leave this side open for left side opening

Stitch to same point skirt was stitched

Inside

FIGURE 8

there is not or if you have changed the pleat length in the garment, check now and be sure that this seam ends exactly where the garment stitching ends.

Be sure that the opening for the zipper is exactly the same length it was in the garment; again, it will be if you have worked accurately, but it is well to check at this time. If there is a side-opening zipper, the opening must be reversed—in other words, in the garment the left side was left open for the zipper, and now in the lining, the right side must be left open for the zipper. When the lining is inserted into the garment, wrong sides together, the opening in the lining will be over the zipper side of the garment.

See Figure 9. If there are loose pleats or gathers in the skirt, the lining must be inserted into the garment and the zipper edge finished before the gathers or pleats are laid in because the loose pleats and gathers must be handled in such a way that the skirt and lining act as one.

TO FINISH THE REGULATION ZIPPER CLOSING

NOTE The sketches are labeled "back" and "front" for the traditional side-opening zipper; underneath these captions the words "right back" and "left back" indicate the situation for a back-opening zipper.

See Figure 10. The lining is inserted into the skirt, cut edges even and seam-lines matching. This is easy enough to do at all points except the zipper edges; at those edges, there are two different seamline positions. Keep in mind always the words "seamlines matching."

step 1   This sketch pictures a skirt before the lining is inserted. Notice that the seam allowance on the back opening edge is approximately in the position of the stitching line of the zipper; on the

front edge of the skirt the seamline is on the fold edge. Keep this in mind as the lining is inserted. If you pull up the zipper, you will see that in the regulation zipper construction, the metal part of the zipper lies under the front of the skirt, not halfway between the front and the back as you might have thought. This means that an opening for the zipper must be made in the front of the skirt lining.

step 2   Pin the skirt lining in place, seamlines matching and waistline edges even; baste in place. Turn under the seam allowance on the back edge of the lining, lap it to the stitching line of the zipper, and pin in place as shown. Now turn under the seam allowance plus ⅜ inch on the front edge of the lining and place the lining ⅜ inch over from the fold edge of the garment at the waistline edge and pin in place (this is the same as matching seamlines). In order to turn under the seam allowance plus ⅜ inch, a clip is required at the lower end of the opening. Make a diagonal clip to a point ⅜ inch over from the end of the stitching

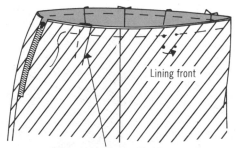

Lining front

Put loose pleats or gathers in skirt and lining in one operation

FIGURE 9

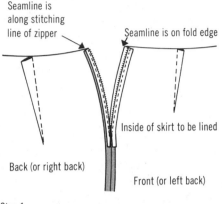

Seamline is along stitching line of zipper

Seamline is on fold edge

Inside of skirt to be lined

Back (or right back)

Front (or left back)

Step 1

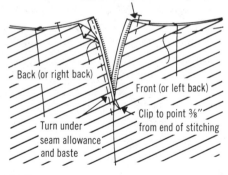

Turn under seam allowance plus ⅜″

Back (or right back)

Front (or left back)

Clip to point ⅜″ from end of stitching

Turn under seam allowance and baste

Step 2

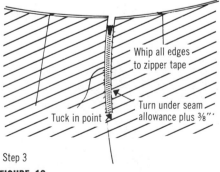

Whip all edges to zipper tape

Turn under seam allowance plus ⅜″

Tuck in point

Step 3

FIGURE 10

at the side seam, as shown. Now the entire front edge can be turned under the width of the seam allowance plus ⅝ inch.

step 3 Baste the edges in place to the zipper, turning in the little triangular piece at the end. Try on the skirt to see that the garment fits as it did before. Then whip these edges to the zipper tape with small whipping stitches; be sure to keep these stitches small so that the thread will not be caught in the teeth as the zipper is used.

TO FINISH SLOT–SEAM ZIPPER CLOSING
See Figure 11.

step 1 The lining is inserted into the skirt, seamlines matching and waistline edges even. The zipper edges create certain problems. The sketch pictures a skirt before the lining is inserted. The seam allowance on both opening edges is on the fold line. If you pull up the zipper, you will be reminded that in the slot-seam zipper construction, the metal part of the zipper lies over the seam, half of it under one part of the skirt and half under the other. This means that an equal opening for the zipper must be made on either side of the seamline of the lining.

step 2 Pin the skirt lining in place, seamlines matching and waistline edges even; baste. Turn under the seam allowance plus ¼ inch on the opening edges of the lining at the waistline and pin as shown. Make a ¼-inch clip on either side of the seamline to points on a level with the end of the side-seam stitching as shown.

step 3 Turn under the seam allowance plus ¼ inch on both opening edges and

pin to the zipper tape and baste, turning
in the little triangular point at the end
as shown. Try on the skirt to be sure that
it fits as it did before. Then whip these
edges to the zipper tape with small
whipping stitches; be sure to keep these
stitches small so that the thread will
not catch in the teeth as the zipper is
used.

TO FINISH THE LINING AROUND A PLEAT

See Figure 12. If you look ahead to the
sketch in step 5, you will see how the
finished skirt will look on the inside.
Hems are done by the catchstitch
method because they will not be exposed,
but notice that the hem in the pleat area
is exposed.

step 1   Because the hem in the pleat
area will be exposed, it is well to finish
that area of the hem by the seam-binding
method, even though the remainder of
the hem is catchstitched. Lay the pleat
in place as shown in the sketch and use
seam binding on the pleat area, allowing
about 1 inch to extend beyond the pleat
area, as shown. If the fabric ravels seriously, it would be well to bind the pleat
seam from the hemline to a point about
1 inch above the end of the stitching, as
indicated by the arrows in the sketch.

step 2   To hang the lining, try on the
skirt and allow the skirt and the lining
to fall in a natural position. Have an
assistant put a row of pins about 5 inches
up from the lower edge, pinning the
lining to the garment as shown; at the
same time, place pins outlining a rectangular area around the pleat as shown.

NOTE The sketch shows the usual knife pleat,
and in order to release the pleat for action, a cut
must be made as shown; if this were a box pleat,
a cut would have to be made on both sides of the
seam.

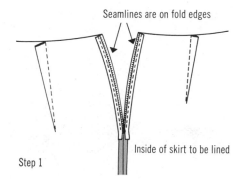

Seamlines are on fold edges

Inside of skirt to be lined

Step 1

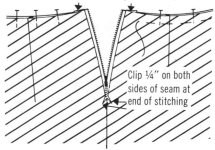

Turn under seam allowance plus ¼"

Clip ¼" on both
sides of seam at
end of stitching

Step 2

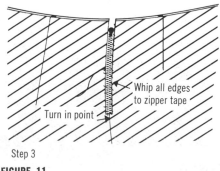

Whip all edges
to zipper tape

Turn in point

Step 3

FIGURE 11

In a skirt with a knife pleat, one edge of the lining (pictured on the left-hand side of the sketches) will fall in place with no complications. Turn under the seam allowance and baste to the skirt as shown.

In the sketch a dot is placed in the seamline at the end of the stitching as an aid to clarifying the sketch. Mark a dot on a level with the end of the stitching to a point just outside the inner edge of the pleat; stick a pin down at this point and flip the lining back to see that the pin is in the right position. Now make a diagonal slash in the lining to that point as shown.

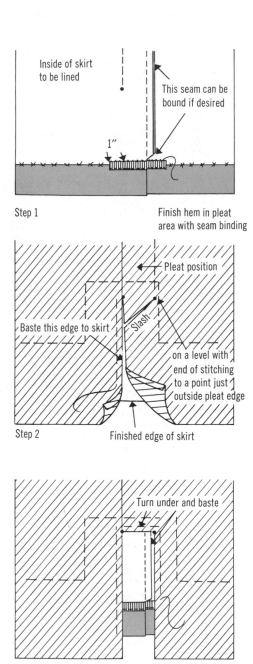

Inside of skirt to be lined

This seam can be bound if desired

1″

Step 1

Finish hem in pleat area with seam binding

Pleat position

Baste this edge to skirt

Slash

on a level with end of stitching to a point just outside pleat edge

Step 2

Finished edge of skirt

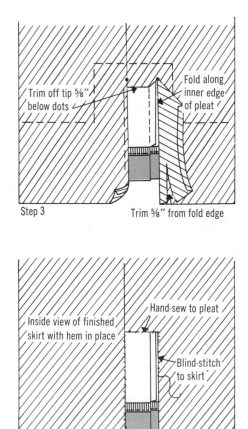

Trim off tip ⅝″ below dots

Fold along inner edge of pleat

Step 3

Trim ⅝″ from fold edge

Turn under and baste

Step 4

Inside view of finished skirt with hem in place

Hand-sew to pleat

Blind-stitch to skirt

Step 5

FIGURE 12

step 3 Fold back the lining, beginning at the point and folding on a line parallel to the edge of the pleat. Trim off the excess lining ⅝ inch from this fold edge as shown. Trim off the point to a level ⅝ inch below the dots as shown.

step 4 Turn under ⅝ inch on the remaining raw edges and pin and baste to the skirt. These edges are basted to the body of the skirt, and even a slight mistake will be conspicuous. To test the perfection of your work, remove the basting stitches which originally held that whole area in place and see that the skirt hangs as it should.

step 5 Finish the lining hem according to directions given on page 308 in the section entitled Finishing Lining Hems. In addition, blind-stitch the edges around the pleat, but remember that those stitches are placed in the body of the garment in a position that will show when the garment is worn. It must not look "sewn," and to avoid this, make very small stitches into the garment and do not pull them too tight. The short edge of the lining at the upper edge of the pleat exposure can be sewn more securely because those stitches need not go through to the outside of the garment.

LINING
A DRESS
BY THE COUTURIER
METHOD

Lining the dress can involve an infinite number of problems which require experience and the ability to figure out order of construction. The dress entirely fitted by darts is quite easy, but gathers, loose pleats, and other design complications make the problem much more difficult. The novice should not use this method unless she is working under the direction of a teacher. So many different problems can arise, and a book can do no more than give general principles. This section includes directions for certain special problems, and many of the details are done as in construction of the jacket and skirt. Refer back to other parts of this chapter for the directions for doing the following details:

1 If the garment has a buttoned front or back opening and therefore a cutoff line has been used in cutting the lining, the lining would be done like a jacket lining; refer to page 304.
2 If there is a set-in sleeve, refer to steps 1, 2, and 3 on page 307.
3 To finish the lining around a zipper, see page 311 for the regulation zipper and page 312 for the slot-seam zipper; bodice edges at the zipper edge are handled in exactly the same manner as the skirt edges pictured.
4 If there is a pleat in the skirt, see page 313 for finishing the lining around the pleat area.
5 Hems in skirts and sleeves are done exactly like jacket hems—see page 308, except that the skirt lining should have a wider hem. In step 1 on page 313, trim 2 inches from the lower edge instead of the 1 inch pictured.

LINING THE SLEEVELESS OR
COLLARLESS GARMENT
The lining for the sleeveless or collarless garment can be cut rather like the jacket with cutoff lines, in which case it would be lined like the jacket with a ⅝-inch turn-under on the lining and a ⅝-inch lapover over the facing edge. However, as

was suggested in the paragraph on cutting, the lining can be cut exactly as the garment was cut and handled as shown in Figure 13.

step 1 Insert the lining in the garment, seamlines matching, but remember that the seam allowance of the garment has been sewn and turned under and so the lining will extend the width of the seam allowance beyond the garment, as shown. Pin the lining in the proper position.

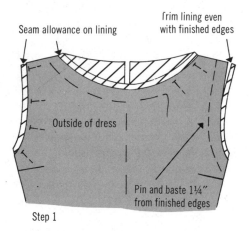

Seam allowance on lining

Trim lining even with finished edges

Outside of dress

Pin and baste 1¼" from finished edges

Step 1

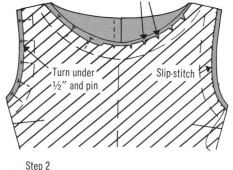

Make ⅜" clips into all curved edges

Turn under ½" and pin

Slip-stitch

Step 2

FIGURE 13

Baste the lining to the garment with rows of basting stitches placed about 1¼ inches in from the finished edge of the garment. Now trim the seam allowance of the lining, thus trimming the lining even with the finished edge of the garment.

step 2 Make clips ⅜-inch long into all curved edges as shown. Turn under ½ inch on the raw edges of the lining and pin to the facing. Baste and slip-stitch the edges, being sure that the stitches go through the facing only and do not catch through to the outside of the garment.

TREATMENT OF THE WAISTLINE SEAM FOR A DARTED GARMENT
See Figure 14.

step 1 The dress should be entirely finished—the waistline seam stitched, the zipper put in, the hem hung. The skirt lining should be done in exactly the same manner as the lining for a skirt, described in detail on page 310. The only additional step is that the skirt lining should be hand-sewn with firm stitches to the seam allowance at the waistline of the dress as shown; these stitches should go through only the seam allowance.

step 2 Insert the bodice lining and attach it to the garment at neck and armhole or sleeve edges. The zipper edge will be finished in the same manner as the zipper edge in a skirt. Turn under the the seam allowance at the lower edge of the bodice and lap it to the seamline of the skirt, encasing the raw waistline edges. Baste. Try on the dress to be sure that the lining is the proper length and then slip-stitch or whip the bodice edge to the skirt, catching the stitches into the seam allowance only and being very careful that the stitches do not go through to the outside of the dress.

TREATMENT OF THE WAISTLINE SEAM FOR A GARMENT WITH LOOSE PLEATS OR GATHERS

NOTE The sketches picture gathers in a skirt. The construction is the same if there are loose pleats instead. In both cases the skirt lining is inserted first. And it is essentially the same for the garment with gathers or loose pleats in the bodice; the only difference is that in that case, the bodice lining would be inserted first and the skirt lining done later.

See Figure 15. This is one of the most difficult problems encountered in this method of lining. The problem is that the lining and the garment must act as one when gathers or loose pleats are used, and therefore the lining must be inserted into the skirt before the gathers or pleats are done and before the waistline seam of the garment is stitched. But the lining must be left free near the zipper edge; the zipper must be inserted first and then the lining finished over it.

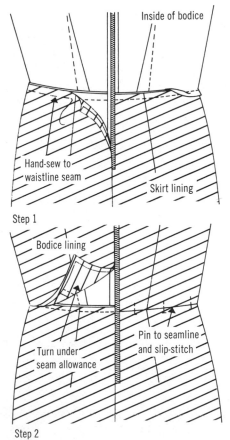

FIGURE 14

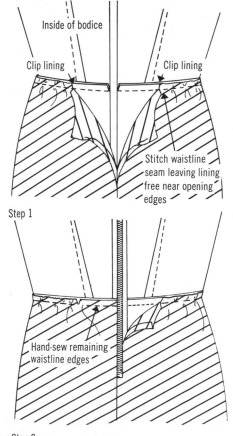

FIGURE 15

step 1 Before putting in loose pleats or gathers and before stitching the waistline seam of the garment, baste the lining to the skirt in the area of the loose pleats or gathers. Make a clip into the waistline edge of the lining at a point where the gathers or loose pleats end, thereby making it possible to baste and stitch the waistline seam of the garment near the opening edges without catching in the lining. Construction of the zipper is made easier if the lining is left free for a greater area, so make the clips as far away from the opening edges as the position of loose pleats or gathers will allow.

Now the zipper must be inserted in the usual manner, but care must be taken to work through the opening in the lining to avoid catching the lining in the stitching of the zipper.

step 2 After the zipper is inserted into the garment, finish the lining around the zipper edge (page 311) and hand-sew the remaining free edge of the lining to the waistline seam as shown. The bodice lining would be inserted like the jacket lining (page 304) or like the lining for the sleeveless or collarless garment described on page 315.

THE FINISHING
TOUCHES

SEWING ON
HOOKS
AND
EYES

See Figure 1. Hooks and eyes are available in various sizes and weights to serve every purpose. They are either black or silver. You will notice that two types of eyes are included on each card. The round eye is used to fasten edges that meet each other; the straight eye, called a peat, is used to fasten edges that lap over each other (such as a skirt waistband). The hook is placed on the right front for front openings, on the left back for back openings, and on the front for side openings.

Mark position and sew hooks on first. Set the hook back at least ⅛ inch from the finished edge so that it will not be pulled into a position where it will show. Take several small overhand stitches over the rings, being sure that the stitches do not show on the right side of the garment. Secure the hook end with overhand stitches around the looped end.

When the round eye is used for edges

which will meet each other, the end should extend ⅛ inch beyond the finished edge. Sew with small overhand stitches along the rings.

The straight eye, for edges that lap over, may be placed at various distances from the finished edge, depending on the amount of overlap. Remember that the eye will pull to the end of the hook;

1/8″

a How to sew on hooks

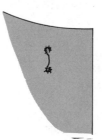

b How to sew on peats for edges that have an overlap

c How to sew on eyes for edges that do not overlap

FIGURE 1

therefore, to mark the eye position, lap the edge with the hooks in proper position, mark the end of the hook with a pin, and use this as the position for the eye. The eye has a curve in it; be sure that the hook will pull with, rather than against, the curve. Sew in place with several small overhand stitches over the rings.

SEWING ON SNAPS

See Figure 2. Snap fasteners are available in various sizes and weights to serve every purpose. They are either black or silver. Snap fasteners may be used to hold edges that will not have a great amount of strain when the garment is worn. Snap the two sections of the fastener together and notice that one surface of the snap is flat, while the other has a small bump. Place the flat surface on the edge of the garment that will be uppermost when finished. Mark the position of the snaps; if a row of them is required, space them evenly.

Use a single or double thread of matching color. Take several small overhand stitches through one hole, slip the needle under the snap, and bring it out alongside the next hole. Take small overhand stitches through that hole and continue; do not allow the stitches to show on the right side of the garment. Fasten the threads.

If snaps must be used in a position where they will be conspicuous when the garment is worn (such as at the front of a buttoned jacket), the snap can be covered with matching fabric or a lighter-weight fabric of matching color. Cut little circles of fabric that will extend ⅛ inch beyond the edge of the snap. Hold this little circle over the snap and tuck in the raw edges, holding them in place with the hand stitches as the snap is sewn in position. If raw edges tend to slip out of place (not likely), a few blind stitches taken into the snap covering and only one thickness of fabric underneath will solve the problem. As the snap is fastened, it will make the necessary center holes in the fabric; this little hole is not finished in any way. If the covering frays with extended use, the snap can be covered again.

FABRIC BELT CARRIERS

See Figure 3. Fabric carriers are used on tailored and functional garments because they are stronger than thread belt carriers. Cut a strip of matching fabric 1 inch wide and about 1¼ inches longer than the width of the belt. Turn under ¼ inch on all edges. Baste or press. Fold the strip in half lengthwise, encasing the raw edges, and stitch all edges. To attach the carrier, fold under ¼ inch and hand-sew the ends of the carrier over the side seam. Notice that the carrier does not lie flat on the garment, for there must be enough room for the belt to pass through.

THREAD BELT CARRIERS

NOTE For those who can crochet, a simple chain stitch can be used for this purpose.

See Figure 4. Thread belt carriers are more delicate and less conspicuous than those made with fabric. Most directions suggest using a buttonhole stitch over several strands of thread, but that is a slow and tedious task. The method

shown here looks complicated, but with practice it can be done very quickly—in less than a minute—so quickly that it is used even by the clock-watching manufacturers. Actually it is a chain stitch done by hand—somewhat like hand crocheting—and as in the case of knitting and crocheting, the resulting product is made more beautiful by giving an even pull to all stitches.

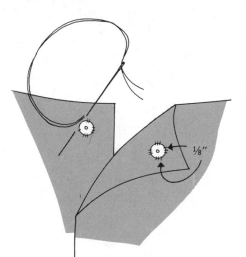

FIGURE 2

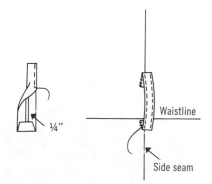

FIGURE 3 How to make fabric belt carriers

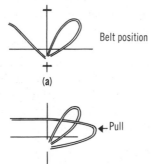

Belt position

(a)

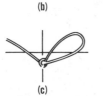

←Pull

(b)

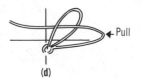

(c)

←Pull

(d)

(e)

FIGURE 4

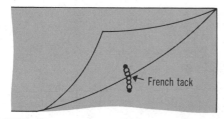

← French tack

FIGURE 5

1 Use a double thread about 20 inches long with a knot. Bring the needle up through the side seam to the right side of the garment at one of the markings for the carrier. Take a tiny stitch to secure the knot. Take another stitch leaving a loop about 4 inches high.

2 Transfer the needle to your left hand (if you are right-handed) and use that hand to hold the needle and to hold the garment firmly to the table or to your lap. Reach through the loop with your right hand and catch the long end of the thread, pulling it through the first loop and forming another loop.

3 Pull the thread until the first loop becomes tight as a link in a tiny chain.

4 Again reach through the loop with your fingers and catch the long end of thread, pulling it through to form another loop.

5 Continue until the carrier is long enough to reach between the markings, with enough excess length to allow the belt to pass through. Then bring the needle through the last loop and pull it tight; this will lock the stitch. Put the needle down through the side seam at the remaining belt marking and fasten the thread securely by taking several small stitches in the seam.

NOTE Thread loops for buttons and French, or swing, tacks are made using this same technique.

THE FRENCH,
OR
SWING,
TACK

See Figure 5. The French, or swing, tack is used to hold two pieces loosely together. For example, the hem of the lining is sometimes French-tacked to the hem of the coat to keep the two hems approximately together but to allow freedom of movement. If a cuff stands out from the sleeve but is so heavy that it cannot support itself, a French tack will hold it in place without spoiling the stand-out effect or making it look sewn. The French tack is done with the chain stitch as described above, with one end of the thread tacked to one piece and the other end fastened to the other piece. The chain can be as long or as short as necessary.

MITERED CORNERS

Miter means to join fabric in a seam at a corner by taking out a wedge-shaped area. One example of a miter is the corner made when a straight piece of fabric for a facing is shaped to a square or V-shaped neck edge, as shown in Figure 6.

Pin the facing in place so that the longer edge (the inner one) lies flat on the garment. Then pinch in a fold of fabric at the corner in such a way that cut edges meet each other in an angle at the corner. Stitch the diagonal seam as shown, ending the stitching at the seamline at the raw edge, and backstitch. Then trim off the excess to within ¼ inch of the stitching line and press open. The seam at the neck edge is stitched as shown.

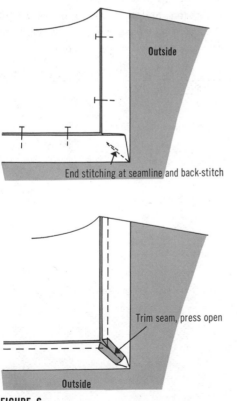

Outside

End stitching at seamline and back-stitch

Trim seam, press open

Outside

FIGURE 6

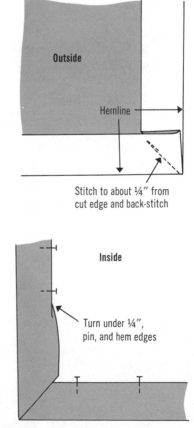

Outside

Hemline

Stitch to about ¼" from cut edge and back-stitch

Inside

Turn under ¼", pin, and hem edges

FIGURE 7

To miter hem edges (for tablecloths, napkins, draperies, or curtains) see Figure 7. Fold hems to the outside, the right side, along the hemlines. Pinch in a fold of fabric in such a way that cut edges meet each other in an angle at the corner. Stitch the diagonal seam, ending the stitching about ¼ inch from the cut edge as shown. Trim the excess, as in the miter described above, and press the seam open. Turn hems to the inside and

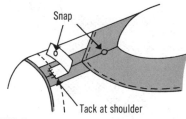

Snap

Tack at shoulder

FIGURE 8

turn under ¼ inch on the raw edges; pin and hem by hand or machine as desired.

SHOULDER–STRAP STAYS

See Figure 8. Good grooming requires that shoulder straps be forever hidden from sight. This is quite a problem with wide-scooped necklines, when the shoulder seam may be no longer than 1½ inches. To solve this grooming problem, cut a piece of seam binding about 3 inches long and double it over, encasing the raw edges. Tack one end to the end of the shoulder seam nearest the armhole. Snap the free end to the shoulder seam. Shoulder straps will stay out of sight, and the dress will not tend to slide off the shoulders, as wide-necked garments so often do. These tapes can be attached to the underside of shoulder pads, too, and they are a necessity for the person whose straps always slide down because of sloping shoulders.

NOTE Snaps can be attached with a thread chain if desired.

INDEX